The
CHILD
with
SPECIAL
NEEDS

ALSO BY STANLEY GREENSPAN

The Growth of the Mind
WITH BERYL LIEFF BENDERLY

Developmentally Based Psychotherapy

The Challenging Child
WITH JACQUELINE SALMON

Playground Politics
WITH JACQUELINE SALMON

First Feelings
WITH NANCY THORNDIKE GREENSPAN

The Essential Partnership
WITH NANCY THORNDIKE GREENSPAN

Infancy and Early Childhood

The Development of the Ego

The Clinical Interview of the Child
WITH NANCY THORNDIKE GREENSPAN

Psychopathology and Adaptation in Infancy and Early Childhood

Intelligence and Adaptation

*A Consideration of Some Learning Variables in the
Context of Psychoanalytic Theory*

The Course of Life
COEDITOR

Infants in Multi-Risk Families
COEDITOR

The
CHILD
with
SPECIAL
NEEDS

*Encouraging Intellectual and
Emotional Growth*

Stanley I. Greenspan, M.D.
Serena Wieder, Ph.D.
with Robin Simons

A MERLOYD LAWRENCE BOOK
LIFELONG BOOKS • DA CAPO PRESS
A Member of the Perseus Books Group

Many of the designations used by manufacturers and sellers to distinguish their products are claimed as trademarks. Where those designations appear in this book and Da Capo Press was aware of a trademark claim, the designations have been printed in initial capital letters.

A CIP record of this book is available from the Library of Congress.

ISBN 0-201-40726-4

Da Capo Press is a member of the Perseus Books Group.

Jacket design by Suzanne Heiser
Text design by Karen Savary
Set in 11-point Minion by Carlisle Communications

25 26 - 06 05

Find us on the World Wide Web at
http://www.dacapopress.com

*Dedicated to the many wonderful children and families
who have allowed us to work with them
and taught us so much*

*Dedicated to our families, Nancy, Elizabeth, Jake, and Sarah,
and Jonathan Blank, Nathaniel, Rachel, and Chany,
whose love and support made this work possible*

Contents

Acknowledgments

We wish to express our special appreciation to the late Reginald Lourie, who gave us the vision to develop ways to help the most challenging children, and to Steven Porges, Diane Lewis, Valerie Dejean, and Georgia DeGangi for the many years of collaboration through clinical work, research, and theory-building. Our thanks to Jan Tunney for her very helpful assistance with the manuscript and the reference preparation and to Sarah Miller for her sensitive support of the office and the families we have worked with. We also wish to express our gratitude to Merloyd Lawrence for her unusual sensitivity and insight in organizing and clarifying this work.

The
CHILD
with
SPECIAL
NEEDS

Introduction

In our recent clinical work with children with developmental challenges, many children with special needs (including such limiting syndromes as autism and mental retardation) have made gains far greater than previously thought possible. At the same time, a number of studies have documented that interactive experiences can actually change the physical structure of the brain. Extra auditory experiences early in life, for example, increase the neuronal connections used for processing sounds and words. Although an individual's potential is not unlimited, most children have a broad range of possible capacities. How they grow, however, depends a great deal on the types of experiences in which they have engaged.

We have identified six fundamental types of experiences that are most critical for healthy development. The challenge is to help a child who has significant differences in nervous system functioning and in relating and communicating to participate fully in these vital interactive experiences.

During the past 20 years, in our work with a large number of children and families, we have studied ways to enable each child to move up the developmental ladder. We have created a developmental approach that engages a child at her current level of functioning, works with the unique features of her nervous system, and utilizes intensive interactive experiences to enable her to master new capacities. This approach, presented in the chapters that follow, enables parents, educators, and therapists to construct a comprehensive program to mobilize each child's intellectual and emotional growth.

Traditionally, we have looked at children with special needs in terms of syndromes. We have used the global labels "autistic," "autistic spectrum," "pervasive developmental disorder (PDD)," "mental retardation," "Down syndrome," and so on. We have offered prognoses along with these labels. Children labeled autistic, for example, have been expected to lead rather limited lives. They have not been expected to go to college and live independently. Mental retardation has been classified according to levels, each carrying a prediction of the mental age children at that level are expected to reach.

Most labels reflect chronic, lifelong disabilities, and the descriptions and prognoses attending these labels have guided professionals' advice to parents as well as parents' expectations.

Underlying these assumptions is the belief that children classified under each syndrome are very similar to each other—more similar than they are different. But in recent years, as we have looked at the development of infants and very young children, the focus has shifted from older children who have lived with these syndromes for years to children one to three years old who are just beginning to show problems. And we've formed a different picture of the nature of these challenges. We've found that children who have been traditionally grouped in the same categories are quite different from each other. In some cases the differences are greater than the similarities. We've found that each child has a unique nervous system and a uniquely developing mind; each child is a class of one. For this reason we have developed a new way of observing and treating children with special needs.

This approach relies on the ability of parents and professionals to work with the features of each child's nervous system, to construct a therapeutic approach based on the child's uniqueness rather than follow a standard program designed for all children with the same diagnosis. To do this, parents and professionals must understand the unique patterns of the child. These patterns include not only the child's biology, but also how the child relates to the world and the people around him. Understanding these patterns makes it possible to tailor a treatment approach to the individual child's needs.

This approach has had a noticeable effect on children's prognoses and progress. Many children diagnosed as having autistic spectrum disorders have become warmly related and joyful—characteristics thought to run counter to the very definition of autism. Many children diagnosed as mentally retarded have developed the abilities to communicate, reason, and solve problems.

THE DEVELOPMENTAL APPROACH TO INTERVENTION

As we have worked with many different types of children, from the time they were babies until they were eight, nine, or ten years old, we have evolved a developmental model for working with children.

This approach focuses on helping each child climb the developmental ladder; specifically, it works to help each child master the six fundamental developmental skills that underlie all our intelligence and interactions with the world. The achievement of each of these skills represents a new level, or milestone, of development.

The Six Fundamental Developmental Skills

Six basic developmental skills—we call them the six functional milestones— lay a foundation for all our learning and development. Children without special needs often master these skills relatively easily. Children with challenges often don't, not necessarily because they can't, but because their biological challenges make mastery more difficult. By understanding these skills and the factors that influence them and by working directly on them, caregivers, educators, and therapists often can help even those children with what are thought to be chronic disorders master many of them.

1. *The dual ability to take an interest in the sights, sounds, and sensations of the world and to calm oneself down.* Infants try to process what they see, hear, and feel, and instinctively turn toward a pleasing face or a soothing voice. They learn to enjoy, understand, and use those pleasant sensations to calm themselves. This ability to self-regulate enables us to take in and respond to the world around us.

2. *The ability to engage in relationships with other people.* In our earliest experiences with our parents we learn to fall in love. We recognize our parents as something nurturing and joyful, we reach out for them, we trust them. This ability to be intimate allows us to form warm and trusting relationships with people that grow throughout our lives.

3. *The ability to engage in two-way communication.* Mommy smiles at me, I smile back. Daddy rolls me the ball, I eagerly roll it back. These early efforts at two-way communication teach us about our own intentions, provide our first sense of causality, of making things happen, and begin to establish our sense of self. As these early interactions become more complex, we learn to communicate with our gestures and understand the intentions and communications of others. We build the foundation for participating in much more sophisticated conversation later on.

4. *The ability to create complex gestures, to string together a series of actions into an elaborate and deliberate problem-solving sequence.* The toddler runs to greet Daddy at the door, holds up her arms for a hug,

then teasingly runs away, saying through her behavior, "Daddy, I'm glad you're home. Hug me, now chase me!"

5. *The ability to create ideas.* Simple play, such as stacking blocks, transforms into complex fantasy play—the blocks become a fort where good guys and bad guys engage in battle. The child uses these scenes to experiment with the wide range of feelings and ideas he discovers as his world grows bigger. He also uses words to indicate wishes and interests: "I want juice!"

6. *The ability to build bridges between ideas to make them reality-based and logical.* The child begins to express her ideas in play and in words, to describe her feelings instead of acting them out, and to string ideas together into logical, original thoughts: "I am mad because you took my toy!"

These basic skills are not the traditional cognitive skills of identifying shapes, naming letters, and counting. They are not the traditional social skills of taking turns and sitting still. They are more fundamental. We call them *functional emotional skills* because they are based on early emotional interactions and they provide the basis for our intellect and sense of self as well as the basis for such familiar skills as counting and taking turns. These fundamental skills underlie all advanced thinking, problem solving, and coping.

Three aspects of the child's world come together to influence how well he masters these functional emotional milestones. The first is the child's biology, the neurological potential or challenges that enhance or impede his functioning. The second is the child's own interactive patterns with his parents, teachers, grandparents, and others. The third is the patterns of the family, the culture, and the larger environment.

Biological Challenges

Children with special needs have a variety of biological challenges that impede their ability to function in the world. Although there are many ways to describe these biological challenges, for the purpose of considering how they influence development it is useful to divide them into three types.

1. *Difficulty with sensory reactivity.* The child may have difficulty with modulating information received from the world through his senses of vision, hearing, touch, smell, taste, and body awareness (i.e., the child may be under- or overreactive).

2. *Processing difficulty.* The child may have difficulty making sense of the sensory data she receives.

3. *Difficulty creating and sequencing or planning responses.* The child may have trouble making his body move the way he wants.

Each type of challenge makes it difficult for the child to relate to and communicate with his parents and caregivers and thus impedes his ability to learn, to respond, and to grow. Therefore, to help a child progress, we must understand how he functions in each of these areas. Once we have pinpointed his specific challenges, we can begin to design treatment programs to ameliorate them. Even more important, we can help parents and caregivers learn how to work around these challenges to help the child learn, relate, and grow. (See also Chapter 15 in regard to special-needs syndromes.)

The Child's Interaction Patterns

A child's biological challenges influence his interactions with others. A child who is underreactive to sound is unlikely to turn toward his mother's wooing voice. A child who is overreactive to touch may shrink, or even shriek, when her father tries to hug her. It's easy to understand how these reactions can influence a child's development. If a child continually withdraws from his mother, the mother may understandably decrease the degree to which she tries to woo the child into loving interaction. She may feel confused and believe he prefers to be left alone. On the other hand, special understanding of a child's underreactivity may enable a parent to work around the biological challenge to pull him into a relationship and begin interactions and communication. Very different trajectories are therefore possible.

Family and Social Patterns

All parents bring certain tendencies with them to parenting. Some of us are naturally demonstrative and "touchy"; others are more reserved. Some of us are born talkers; others are naturally quiet. These tendencies—some innate, others acquired through our families and cultural milieu—influence how we relate to our children. They can make it easier or harder for our children to master the emotional milestones.

A very soothing, cautious family may be ideal for a sensitive, overreactive baby. But imagine, for instance, a baby with low muscle tone who is also underreactive to touch and sound, and imagine that this baby's parents are low-key and reserved. It is likely that neither baby nor parents will naturally offer the kinds of interactions necessary to pull the other in. The baby may look quietly at her parents; the parents may look back and smile. But the kind of active wooing this baby needs in order to be pulled into intimacy—tickling, laughing, animated gesturing—will probably not occur.

Fortunately, by becoming aware of their own interactive tendencies, parents can alter their styles to work with their child's unique nervous system, and to promote the development of the milestones. Even though the challenge is biological in nature, the caregiver's interactive style can help the child master his own physical tendencies. We often have an opportunity to share with parents an important principle: although their behavior had nothing to do with their child's challenges, it can be an important part of the solution.

All these elements—the child's biological challenges, the way he relates to his caregivers, and the way his caregivers relate to him—influence how well he masters the developmental skills. In the developmental approach to intervention we work in all three areas to help children grow. We assess each child's unique biological profile; we observe the ways in which his profile influences his interactions with caregivers; we examine the ways in which his caregivers' patterns influence his developmental progress. Finally, we develop a therapy program to strengthen all three areas. This book explains each of these areas in detail and will help readers develop individual-based treatment plans for their own children.

THE DEVELOPMENTAL APPROACH TO COMMON SPECIAL-NEEDS SYNDROMES

If we look for developmental capabilities and individual differences within the most common special-needs syndromes we find that we can think about children with these labels in different ways. Instead of seeing them as similar, requiring similar programs of treatment, we see them as unique and can tailor treatment programs to their individual developmental needs. Let's look at the implications of this approach for a few of the more common syndromes. (See also Chapter 15.)

Autism, Autistic Spectrum, and Pervasive Developmental Disorders

For reasons not yet entirely clear (but that may go beyond improved early-identification services), programs that serve infants and young children and their families report an increasing number of children with severe relationship and communication problems. Very often these children seemed to be normal until 18 or 24 months of age. Parents recall that their child enjoyed hugging and cuddling and began purposeful gesturing on time, and family videos often document these observations. But between the ages of 12 and 15 months, the preverbal, gestural system of communication began to stop developing. The toddler did not, for example, grab her father's hand, lead him to the kitchen, and vocalize or gesture for a certain food. At the same time the child began showing (or intensifying existing) oversensitivity, or became less reactive, to certain sounds or kinds of touch. The child no longer seemed to understand even simple words or gestures, and language stopped developing. Gradually parents noticed that the child was increasingly withdrawn and aimless and was more often engaging in repetitive behavior.

Many of these behaviors fit the original description of autism, coined by Leo Kanner, a child psychiatrist, in 1943. According to Kanner, the autistic child's "outstanding fundamental disorder" is the "inability to relate . . . from the beginning of life . . . an extreme aloneness that . . . disregards, ignores, shuts out anything . . . from the outside."[1] These behaviors are systematized in the American Psychiatric Association's *Diagnostic and Statistical Manual* (*DSM-IV*) in the category of pervasive developmental disorder (PDD). PDD has a number of subtypes, including autistic disorder (the more classic and severe form) and pervasive developmental disorder not otherwise specified (PDDNOS; a more general type diagnosed when there is a basic impairment in relating and communicating but when all the formal criteria for autistic disorder are not met).

As more children are diagnosed with PDD at younger ages, we see clinical features that challenge the existing conceptual framework. Children's patterns of relating, communicating, and expressing emotions seem to fall along a continuum rather than into one distinct type. Because of the lack of more appropriate diagnostic categories, clinicians use the diagnosis of PDDNOS for many children who have various combinations of social, language, and cognitive dysfunctions, even when they show varying degrees of social relatedness. Most parents, however, are aware that autism and PDDNOS are part of the same broad PDD category.

For the majority of children, the relationship problem is not clearly in evidence in the first year of life, as thought by Kanner, but appears in the second and third years, in connection with difficulties with processing sensations. In contrast to other studies, we have found that the majority of children first develop clear symptoms in the second and third years of life (see Appendix C). Furthermore, each child has her own unique profile for processing sensations. These profiles vary in sensory reactivity (e.g., tactile, auditory, visual), sensory processing (e.g., auditory-verbal, visual-spatial), and muscle tone and motor planning or sequencing. Also, the assumption that children with PDD tend to remain relatively unrelated to others, rigid, mechanical, and idiosyncratic (as stated in *DSM-IV*) is not supported by our recent clinical experience. With early diagnosis and a comprehensive, integrated, and developmental relationship-based treatment approach, many children originally diagnosed with PDD are learning to relate to others with warmth, empathy, and emotional flexibility. We have worked with a number of children diagnosed with autism or PDDNOS between the ages of 18 and 30 months, who, now older, are fully communicative (using complex sentences adaptively), creative, warm, loving, and joyful. They attend regular schools, are mastering early academic tasks, enjoy friendships, and are especially adept at imaginative play. We have introduced the term *multisystem neurological disorder* to characterize children who have communication problems and are perseverative but can relate or have the potential for relating with joy and warmth (see Appendix C for further discussion of the study outcome and diagnostic issues). The capacity to become comfortable with intimacy and dependency and to experience joy often appears to be attainable early in the treatment program. In addition, cognitive potential cannot be explored until interactive experiences are routine.

The traditional pessimistic prognosis for PDD is based on experience with children whose treatment programs tend to be mechanical and structured rather than based on individual differences, relationships, affect, and emotional cuing. Approaches that do not pull the child into *spontaneous,* joyful relationship patterns may intensify rather than remediate the difficulty. We have observed even with older children with PDD-type patterns that as more spontaneous affect based on emotionally robust gestural or verbal interactions get going, perseveration and idiosyncratic behavior decrease and relatedness increases.

The existence of many types of relationship and communication problems, of significant individual differences among children, and of greater potential for intellectual and emotional growth than formerly thought forces us to reconsider our long-held assumptions about PDD. It is especially important that we reconsider the notion of a fixed biological deficit that prevents relating to others and experiencing joy, happiness, and eventually empathy. Evidence is suggesting that biologic processing deficits can be dealt with by the child in different ways, and that certain types of intervention can enhance adaptive outcomes, including joy and creativity.

Mental Retardation and Cognitive Deficits

Mental retardation is usually diagnosed when a child has a cognitive delay or deficit that is more than two standard deviations off the expected average, or, in other words, a score on the standard IQ test of 75 or below. Traditionally, children with mental retardation were thought to have across-the-board lags, that is, to lag equally in language, cognition, motor abilities, auditory processing, and visual-spatial processing. We assessed many children diagnosed with mental retardation; their individual profiles included both strengths and weaknesses in auditory processing, visual-spatial processing, muscle tone, and motor planning.

We also found that one deficit often kept other areas from developing properly. Sometimes severe motor impairments mask stronger abilities in other areas. For instance, a child who could move only her tongue was believed to have very severe cognitive delays and no communication ability at all. Once we taught her to use movements of her tongue to indicate yes and no, we revealed greater potential for deliberate, two-way communication. In a fairly short time she was using her tongue to indicate her wishes and intentions, abilities that clinicians had previously assumed were beyond her capability. Even subtle motor sequencing or planning problems may undermine a child's ability to communicate (for example, to put together a sequence of gestures) and therefore may lead to a decrease in the types of interactions likely to foster intellectual or emotional growth.

Children with low muscle tone or severe motor planning challenges often cannot participate well in formal testing, which can result in an inaccurate picture of their cognitive potential. Their abilities may look more uniformly low when in fact they are uneven.

All this does not mean that all children diagnosed with mental retardation have enormous potential, but it does mean that some do, and many have a good degree of undeveloped potential. Our challenge is to look at each child's unique strengths and weaknesses, for as long as we believe that a child's skills are uniform, we deny her the chance to maximize growth.

Cerebral Palsy

With cerebral palsy, as with mental retardation, one deficit can mask abilities in other areas. For instance, a child with severe cerebral palsy, who has severe motor impairments, may not have had a chance to develop language, thinking, or problem-solving skills because he has been unable to participate in activities that promote those skills.

We do know, however, that numerous children with cerebral palsy who have also been diagnosed with mental retardation have made tremendous gains once they have been helped to develop their assertiveness and their ability to communicate interactively. As we will see in subsequent chapters, interactions are necessary for learning. Without the opportunity to change one's environment or elicit a reaction from others, it is difficult to piece together the patterns that constitute learning. We have observed a number of children significantly increase their intelligence. The only way to help each child reach his potential is to look at his individual differences and work with an individualized, developmental treatment program.

Regulatory Disorders

In addition to the autistic spectrum and multisystem developmental disorder problems and the cognitive deficits associated with mental retardation, another broad area of difficulty falls into the category of regulatory disorders. Regulatory disorders involve differences in responsiveness to sensations, in processing sensations, and in motor planning.[2] Many children with learning disorders; behavior problems; attentional, focusing, and organizing problems; and sleep and eating problems have underlying difficulties in how they react to sensations, comprehend language or visual-spatial patterns, or plan motor actions. When these underlying issues are present, we call the symptoms regulatory problems. Regulatory disorders differ from autistic spectrum disorders in that children with regulatory disorders relate warmly to others. Regulatory disorders differ from mental retardation in that children with regulatory disorders do not have significant cognitive or language deficits even though they often have challenges in these areas. The problems of regulatory disorders have to do with how children share or cooperate or throw tantrums or become aggressive, as well as how they process information and learn, rather than with the basic ability to form a relationship, communicate, or think. We have identified five types of regulatory disorders:

> sensitive/fearful
> defiant
> self-absorbed
> active/craving
> inattentive

Attention Deficit Disorders

Although listed in the *Diagnostic and Statistical Manual* of the American Psychiatric Association (APA) as a disorder in its own right, attention deficit disorder (ADD) can also be thought of as a type of regulatory disorder involving problems with motor planning and sequencing. Sometimes it involves sensory modulation or processing difficulties as well. As with autism and mental retardation, attentional disorders are best viewed in terms of individual differences so that each child's unique patterns become the basis for an intervention program. Many different underlying individual patterns have attentional problems as a common symptom. For example, underreactivity and craving sensation can make some children active and distractible. Poor motor planning can make children appear lost and disorganized. Auditory or visual-spatial processing problems can lead to fragmented behavior and difficulty following instructions or rules. Oversensitivity to sound, sights, or touch can easily make children reactive, distractible, and overloaded and overwhelmed. Many children with severe regulatory and attentional problems are included in special education and are viewed as having special needs.

Other Special-Needs Conditions

Other disorders, including fragile X syndrome, Down syndrome, and other genetic syndromes, fetal alcohol syndrome, mother's substance abuse during pregnancy, and various types of cognitive or perceptual deficits, evidence a variety of attentional and regulatory problems. Although many of these syndromes involve cognitive, motor, and processing problems, they also are best viewed in terms of individual differences (i.e., how they are manifested in specific difficulties).

Many excellent programs are available to help children with deficits in hearing or vision deal with their specific challenges. But these children also share challenges with children who have regulatory difficulties, and they require intervention to emphasize their stronger senses as a basis for relating, communicating, and thinking. Later we describe some interactive experiences that can be added to traditional programs for children with visual or auditory deficits to foster their overall adaptation.

The Individual Profile

In this book we explain how to create a profile that pinpoints a child's individual differences in terms of (1) how the child reacts to sensations, processes information, plans actions, and sequences behavior and thoughts; (2) the level of functional emotional, social, and intellectual capacities; (3) typical and necessary interaction patterns; and (4) family patterns. This profile will enable parents and professionals to construct an intervention plan geared to each child's individual characteristics.

The syndromes listed here, as well as others, are expressed through the child's developmental level and functional abilities and skills, such as response to touch and sound, auditory processing, motor planning, and perceptual motor abilities. Children who share a syndrome or part of different syndromes may be more similar or different depending on the individual profile. *The individual profile, rather than the syndrome,* determines the appropriate intervention program. The exception is when a specific biological deficit underlying a syndrome can be corrected through medication or a medical procedure. Most developmental problems, however, require a comprehensive intervention program, which also may include a specific medication or procedure.

In the second part of this book, we demonstrate how to create an intensive intervention program based on a child's profile involving an approach that we have developed over many years and call "floor time." Although the case discussions illustrate some of the unique intervention features of a few of the more common syndromes, our goal is to show how to work with many of the developmental disorders by discussing how to construct a child's unique profile, which includes his functional abilities. Criteria for labeling and in-depth discussion of diagnoses of syndromes can be found in *DSM-IV* and other specialized texts; we instead focus on identifying a child's developmental level and unique processing capacities and on the means to strengthen the functional skills needed to make progress. We use relatively more examples of children with pervasive developmental disorder (autistic spectrum disorders) and multisystem developmental disorder because these disorders involve both challenges at several developmental levels and most of the processing deficits that accompany all kinds of special needs.

ASSESSMENT

An assessment should begin with a review of a child's current functioning, history, and observation of the child with caregivers for over half an hour on a few occasions. Standardized testing should not serve as a cornerstone of the assessment. Rather, it should be used, if needed, after the child is observed interacting and playing with his caregivers. In a review of over 200 cases (see Appendix C), many from leading diagnostic centers, more than 90 percent did not directly observe parent-child interactions. Yet this interaction reveals the child's capacity for relating and interacting and is the venue in which the child is most likely to perform at his highest level. Tests tend to emphasize how the child relates to the person administering the test and to highly structured tasks that may require motor-planning (attentional) skills the child does not have. This relationship and the tasks are foreign, perhaps even frightening, and thus the child is apt to function at a lower level. As a result, the assessment often supports a more global picture of the child, rather than a picture that builds on how the child relates to, and uses his unique abilities with, his most treasured caregivers. Under these circumstances it is not surprising that many children are inaccurately diagnosed with autistic spectrum disorder. Because they fail to relate warmly and spontaneously to the test giver, they are assumed to have similar interactive deficits at home.

And, since the parent-child interaction is the key interaction for promoting the development of the six emotional milestones, the results of standardized tests can be a particularly poor predictor of a child's progress.

We recommend using an assessment approach that identifies individual differences in each child's strengths and weaknesses. This means examining the child's sensory processing and motor profile; her patterns of interaction with her caregivers; and her caregivers' patterns of interaction with her; as well as her language and cognitive capacities and overall health. This information helps us understand the child's functional abilities and challenges and design a treatment program that will ameliorate and work around these challenges and build on the child's strengths.

The best assessments take place over a period of time rather than in the space of a single day. In fact, assessment should be an integral part of treatment. As we work with children on their individual differences, we are continually assessing their abilities and their caregivers' abilities and we typically see improvements in all areas. For example, in the first three or four months of treatment of children diagnosed as severely cognitively delayed in all areas, as the children learned to take more initiative (that is, to communicate more intentionally with their parents by negotiating for their needs), we observed strengths in visual understanding and problem solving that were not apparent on the initial test or observation. These children were capable of much more than was initially thought. Assessing and then working with these children's individual differences—rather than with a standardized treatment program—was the key.

By focusing on individual differences we've found that two things happen:

1. Children make better progress.

2. Children's individual differences change continually, for each leap in development means the profile has changed.

Thus assessment must be ongoing and the treatment program must be modified accordingly. Unlike traditional assessment, which occurs all at once, effective assessment of children with special needs should be sequential and treatment should be constantly adjusted.

THE IMPORTANCE OF EMOTIONS

In working with children's individual differences and developmental levels, we have observed that a critical component of their progress resides in our ability to help them use their own emotions, desires, or intentions to guide first their behavior, and later their thoughts. This means harnessing their natural desires to give purpose to their gestures and meaning to their words—holding a cookie we know the child wants and challenging her to grasp it and later challenging her to use the words "eat cookie" to get a goodie for herself or, during pretend play, for her favorite doll. From the simplest gestures—smiling, frowning, or turning away—to more complex behaviors—imitating a sound, taking a parent by the hand to recruit help in finding a toy, using words and concepts—the child's behavior is driven by his emotions, wishes, and desires—by his interests. The more we can help a child connect his emotions to his behavior and his thoughts, the more we can help him become a person with purpose, meaning, and the capacity for understanding his world.

Many children with special needs have things done for them, rather than initiate activities on their own in response to inner wishes. Because a child's own desires and interests are a critical part of who she is, caregivers and therapists seem to do best when they can entice a child to use her own initiative and desires to practice some of the necessary skills. When we challenge a child to take initiative, she develops a little more understanding of who she is, what she wants, and what she is capable of doing. When parents and therapists work this way with children, the children often surprise them with unsuspected new skills.

ABOUT THIS BOOK

This book explains in detail the individual-difference, relationship-based, developmental approach to intervention. In Part 1 we explore the child's individual differences, beginning with biological challenges. We look at the interaction patterns of which the child is capable at each developmental stage and at the interaction patterns of the caregivers with the child. Observation charts enable readers to observe both their child and themselves in order to assess their child's individual profile. (Parenting tendencies are discussed more fully in Part 3, Chapters 16 and 17.)

In Part 2 we show the developmental approach in action. In floor time, the key mode of intervention, parents (and therapists) interact on the floor literally and figuratively with the child in ways that promote the development of the six emotional milestones. We describe how floor time is used to create experiences for the child at each level of development that optimize his unique strengths and work around and improve his areas of challenge.

In Part 3 we describe how the individual-difference model can be used to organize the efforts of the child's intervention team, as well as of the child's school, and we discuss challenges to the family that commonly surface when a child has special needs.

Who Should Read This Book?

This book is for parents of children with developmental challenges, including, but not limited to,

autism
autistic spectrum disorders
pervasive developmental disorder (PDD)
pervasive developmental disorder not otherwise specified (PDDNOS)
multisystem developmental disorders
mental retardation
cerebral palsy
Down syndrome
cognitive delays and/or deficits
language delays and/or deficits
low muscle tone (hypotonia)
sensory integration disorder
attentional disorders (including ADD and ADHD)
chromosomal, metabolic, and other disorders where the challenge to the child's central nervous system and mental functioning is not progressive in nature but does interfere with a child's ability to relate, to communicate, and to learn

Although this book does not discuss the specific needs of children with hearing loss or visual impairment, most of the treatment approaches can be adapted for these children.

The book is also intended to be of use to professionals who work with children diagnosed with these disorders. Speech therapists, physical therapists, occupational therapists, clinical social workers, child psychologists, child psychiatrists, developmental and behavioral pediatricians, nurses, educators, workers in special education, counselors, play therapists, movement, dance, and art therapists, and family life and recreational therapists will find the principles described in this book helpful in their work with children.

NOTES

1. Leo Kanner, "Autistic Disturbances of Affective Contact," *Nervous Child* 2 (1943): 217–250.

2. Diagnostic Classification Task Force, Stanley Greenspan, M.D., chair, *Diagnostic Classification: 0–3: Diagnostic Classification of Mental Health and Developmental*

Disorders of Infancy and Early Childhood (Arlington, Va.: ZERO TO THREE/National Center for Clinical Infant Programs, 1994); Stanley Greenspan, *Infancy and Early Childhood: The Practice of Clinical Assessment and Intervention with Emotional and Developmental Challenges* (Madison, Conn.: International Universities Press, 1992); and S. I. Greenspan and J. Salmon, *The Challenging Child: Understanding, Raising, and Enjoying the Five "Difficult" Types of Children* (Reading, Mass.: Addison-Wesley, 1995).

PART ONE

Discovering Each Child's Unique Strengths, Developmental Capacities, and Challenges

1

Moving beyond the Label

Two-year-old Ben had just received the diagnosis of pervasive developmental disorder (PDD) and his parents, Sarah and Mark, were understandably upset. They had brought Ben in for further evaluation. At first he sat in his mother's lap, his back to the therapist, clinging to her tightly. But over the course of 15 minutes he gradually turned around. Furtively he watched the therapist, turning away quickly whenever the therapist looked at him. As his looks grew longer the therapist began to talk softly to him, calling his name and making funny faces. After about 5 minutes he smiled tentatively back. A few minutes later Ben giggled at the therapist's funny face and then shyly turned to Sarah and gave her a hug and one of the most joyful smiles a two-year-old could give. Mark and Sarah and Ben's therapist talked for a few more minutes, during which Ben looked curiously around the office. About a half hour into the session he climbed off his mother's lap, took her hand, and pulled. As she followed him, he toddled unsteadily toward the door (his sense of balance seemed uncertain), banged insistently on it, and made emphatic guttural noises. He was ready to leave! Patiently, Sarah explained that they had to stay a little longer. At this Ben threw himself on the floor and banged repetitively with his fists. When Mark tried to pick him up he threw a full-scale tantrum, kicking and screaming in frustration. Ten minutes of firm holding and soothing by his mom and dad helped him quiet down. Ben spent the rest of the session cuddled on his mother's lap, refusing to look anyone in the eye.

Ben had many features often described as autistic: he seemed to have a language delay and possible cognitive challenges; his motor system seemed underdeveloped; and he engaged in repetitive motor behavior. But he lacked the central feature of autism, unrelatedness. According to the classic definition of autism, autistic children are permanently unable to relate to others. They have no investment in the human world—they find a person no different from a chair. Although the definition of autism has changed over the years to include *relative* deficits in relatedness, a deficit in the capacity for intimacy and joy remains a central feature. Certainly this part of the definition did not apply to Ben. He was warm and cuddly and joyful with his mother, he turned to her for reassurance, he smiled and giggled at his therapist. Ben was quite capable of relating—although in a more limited way than most children his age. During the next few observation sessions, Ben vacillated between giving his mom joyful hugs, negotiating with gestures for a cookie and a quick exit out the door, and repetitively lining up toys and touching the windowsill in a self-absorbed state.

The therapist told Ben's parents that he didn't believe their son was autistic. Rather, he appeared to have a variety of sensory, processing, and motor problems, which interfered with how he took in, processed, and responded to information from the world. His problems were treatable, and an intensive program would help him with his processing challenges and would help him learn to relate and communicate more fully.

On receiving the PDD diagnosis, Ben's parents had rushed out and bought many books on that disorder, all of which had painted a dismal picture of the future. They had rebelled: "Not our son! He'll do better than that!" But despite their love, despite their anger, despite their determination not to let the diagnosis affect the way they cared for their little boy, subtle changes crept into their relationship with him. They no longer expected him to look at them every time they called his name; they no longer expected him to smile when they picked him up. A voice inside them said, "He won't respond. Don't expect him to respond; he has PDD." Little by little, even though they were fighting the diagnosis, they were coming to accept the limitations it implied.

Now that devastating label had been lifted. Their son wasn't limited to what was expected for a child diagnosed with PDD. He had a variety of sensory, motor, and processing challenges that might gradually improve. Although they understood that a long road lay ahead, their expectations rose. Most important, they began looking for more emotional responses. They became more animated and responsive themselves. Ben's therapist helped them establish an intensive program of therapy, which included occupational and speech therapists who worked on Ben's biological challenges and a therapist who helped Mark and Sarah work on tailoring their interactions with Ben to his needs. Within the first six months of treatment Ben began to make significant improvements. He could engage joyfully with the important people in his life for several minutes at a time; he sought his parents out for closeness more often and was less repetitive and self-absorbed. He initiated more facial expressions and gestures and responded to his parents' simple questions with appropriate gestures; and he had developed a speaking vocabulary of four or five words and was imitating new sounds more readily. He was beginning to climb the developmental ladder.

Ben is not alone. Many children today are given labels that are misleading. Instead of pinpointing a child's unique strengths and challenges, they obscure them and unwittingly demoralize and create negative expectations on the part of parents, therapists, and teachers.

THE PROBLEM WITH LABELS

Current diagnostic categories generally summarize a child's *symptoms,* but often don't tell us enough about the processes underlying a child's challenges— how the child takes in, processes, and responds to information from the world. These three aspects of biology lie at the heart of the child's ability to think, feel, and interact. Children with the same label may be more different than they are alike and children with different labels may be more similar than they are different in terms of their underlying profiles.

A child may be diagnosed with autism, for example, because he has difficulty relating to others, when his underlying problems are actually more specific and involve difficulty processing auditory information and a severe overreactivity to sound. As a result of these challenges the speech of the people around him is confusing and assaulting, making him physically and emotionally uncomfortable. To protect himself, the child withdraws and becomes aimless, earning the diagnosis of autism. Another child with similar biological challenges may earn a different label. If her auditory reactivity and processing problems are somewhat less severe, it may be difficult for her to take in speech and decode it, but the sound of speech itself is not overwhelming. This child may relate warmly to others but react slowly to or be confused by instructions. Thus she may remain close to others but avoid interactions that foster cognitive growth. If this child also has some motor planning or movement problems, she may receive the labels "cognitive delay" or "mild mental retardation."

Similarly, children diagnosed with mental retardation may do a little better with verbal challenges, others with visual ones. Some children diagnosed with PDD are especially strong in visual processing—they are good at knowing where things are and are able to put together complex puzzles; others have severe impairments in visual processing—they often seem lost, unable, for example, to figure out where the closet door is or to recognize pictures of familiar animals.

By grouping children into diagnostic categories that are too general, we may obscure the underlying biological processing differences related to their problems and gain no clues about how to treat them. If, however, we look at how each child takes in, processes, and responds to information from the world, we can pinpoint underlying aspects of the child's problems and develop a treatment plan to address them.

Another problem with very general labels is that they often don't let us know where a child is developmentally. Some children diagnosed as autistic, for example, avoid all human contact, whereas others, like Ben, are warm, cuddly, and responsive and communicate with gestures. Some children diagnosed with mental retardation are able to do pretend play, expressing abstract ideas; others play concretely, hugging dolls but never orchestrating dramas; and others are just learning to gesture intentionally with a smile or a sound. As most therapists and educators will attest, in order to work with a child to foster her development it is important to know where the child is on the developmental ladder of emotional, social, and functional cognitive skills, which milestones she has mastered and which are still to be mastered. We have developed a unique way of figuring out where a child is on their overall functional developmental ladder that will be presented in Chapters 4 and 5.

Although most parents and professionals are aware of the limits of labels and use their understanding of the child's developmental capacities to guide their efforts, several very important functional milestones, having to do with relating, preverbal communication, and creative reasoning, are often missed.

IDENTIFYING INDIVIDUAL DIFFERENCES

We advocate an individual-difference approach to assessment and intervention. This means looking at each child's unique profile—his particular biological challenges, his family patterns, and where he stands on the developmental ladder—and then using this information to design an intervention plan, which involves parents, therapists, and educators.

Later in Part 1 we present new ways of observing your child in order to discover his unique profile, and in Part 2 we explain how to use this knowledge to foster your child's development.

Most children with special needs have problems in more than one area. The label "language delayed," for instance, implies problems processing language and forming words, but many children given this label have subtle problems with other aspects of sensory processing. Children diagnosed with cognitive deficits and mild forms of mental retardation often have problems with their sensory processing and motor planning. We need to categorize in ways that clue us in to all these underlying challenges, so that children will receive comprehensive treatment.

Perhaps if we change the *way* in which we assess children with special needs we can minimize the incidence of incorrect assumptions. Today most assessments use standardized tests rather than observations of children's interactions with their caregivers to determine children's capabilities in communication and reasoning. But a child's behavior during a test may differ from her behavior at home. Observing interactions between the child and his parents and between the child and the clinician over a long period of time should, together with a review of current functioning and a detailed history, be the first step in the assessment process. (As we discuss later, standardized tests may have a selective role further on in the assessment process.) Had the clinician who diagnosed Ben spent sufficient time watching Ben relate to his parents he would have seen a child who was warm and emotionally available, who was able to communicate his feelings and intentions through a gestural vocabulary that included smiles and frowns, smirks and laughter, and who showed creativity in engaging his mother in play. Had the clinician spent more time engaging with Ben himself, he would have found that Ben could also be warm and flirtatious with him. In short, he would have found a child with sensory, motor, and cognitive delays, but not a child with autism.

A developmental pediatrician described a boy he had seen for a diagnosis. This boy was fairly warm and related with his parents, although he avoided strangers. His gestural and verbal abilities were a year or so behind age expectations. "Twenty years ago," the pediatrician said, "we would have called this boy 'difficult and shy, a slow learner with language delays.' But today things have 'improved.' Now," he said with a sigh, "we call him 'autistic spectrum.'" As indicated earlier, in a recent study we found that over 90 percent of children diagnosed with autistic spectrum disorders were not observed in spontaneous interaction with their parents.

Moving beyond the labels to an individual-difference approach opens the door to new possibilities for children. It is too early to make predictions about how much children can accomplish. Are *most* children capable of significant gains? What factors determine the degree of a child's improvement? We don't yet know all the answers, but we are tremendously encouraged by what we have seen, for it seems clear that with an optimal intervention program tailored to a child's individual differences, the possibilities are far greater than we had thought.

The following story illustrates how the developmental approach brought a family beyond an initial, immobilizing label.

AUSTIN

Paula Zuger was six months pregnant when she gave birth to her third child, Austin. For three devastating weeks he lay in an incubator, tubes and wires cementing his fragile hold on life. Finally, after further weeks of being gradually weaned from the machines, swaddled in three blankets, his tiny head swimming in his newborn's hat, he came home. His parents and siblings carefully inspected Austin's minute pink fingers and toes, his dimpled legs, his dark, shiny hair, and pronounced him perfect.

When he was four months old, however, Paula and her husband, Kurt, sensed something wrong. Austin didn't seem as interested in them as their other babies had been. He never reached for them with his arms or turned toward the sound of their voices, and he didn't seem to have any desire to roll over. So the Zugers took Austin to a child-development specialist, who assured them that premature babies develop slowly, not to worry.

But by the time Austin was nine months old, his parents *were* worried. Austin could now roll over with a great deal of effort, but he was unable to sit up by himself and he showed no inclination to crawl. Of greater concern, his unresponsiveness seemed to be increasing. "He acts depressed," Paula said. "If I touch his face he'll look at me, but he doesn't respond to our voices. He doesn't seem to care if we're there or not." Frightened by his strange behavior, she and Kurt took him to the Children's Hospital, where he underwent a lengthy evaluation. When it was over, the doctor invited them into her office and gazing at them across her desk, asked them matter-of-factly, "How long have you known he has cerebral palsy?"

Paula and Kurt were devastated. They pictured an unreachable child, confined to a wheelchair, cut off from siblings and friends. Driving home, they were silent, too numb to cry. Only Austin, fussing in his car seat, seemed able to express the family's pain.

Over the next several months Paula and Kurt began what seemed like an endless odyssey of doctor's visits and therapies, each designed to correct some aspect of Austin's cerebral palsy. Before each new round they thought, "Now everything will be normal." After each, when normalcy failed to materialize, they grew despondent.

Adding to their sadness was Austin's aloofness. Paula, with remarkable gentleness and patience, was able to elicit tiny smiles from her infant with a great deal of stroking and wooing. But Kurt could forge no connection with his son at all. He tickled the baby and tossed him in the air—games his other children had loved. But Austin only cried when the other children had laughed; he turned away when the others had clamored for more. When Austin was 15 months old, the Zugers took him for another evaluation. This one concluded that Austin was mentally retarded with significant autistic features. With a developmental quotient of 40 to 50, the doctor said, he might be capable of living in a group home. Once again, the Zugers went home devastated. The term *mentally retarded* seemed like a death sentence.

In the months since the initial evaluation, Austin had participated in an early intervention program run by the public schools, which provided physical, occupational, and speech therapy, but he had made little progress. When the program ended for the summer, the physical therapist suggested that the Zugers bring Austin in for an evaluation. Careful observation of Austin revealed that in addition to having significant problems with his motor system and cognitive abilities, he was very underreactive to many sensations, including most types of sound and touch. However, he was overly sensitive to low-pitched sounds, such as those of an engine motor or a very deep voice, and he became more self-absorbed when he encountered such noxious sensations. He was also extremely self-absorbed, rarely smiling, reaching, or in any way gesturing to or showing interest in his caregivers. He was aimless. Observations revealed that his low muscle tone and inability to execute even the simplest actions contributed significantly to his challenges. Equally important, though, were his self-absorption and his parents' growing despair.

The first goal of the comprehensive intervention program, which involved physical, occupational, and speech therapy, was to improve Austin's ability to engage, his ability to make consistent, loving, emotional contact. While observing Austin's seemingly aimless behavior, we noted that he occasionally looked at certain toys and sort of swiped at them with his left hand. We used this fleeting interest to capture his attention. Paula would wave the toy in front of his face until it caught his eye, then slowly move it. Moments later she did this again. Austin grew more interested in the moving toy and began following it with his eyes. Then Paula would hold it in front of her face, luring Austin's gaze to her own. When she could catch his eye for four or five seconds, she gave him something new to look at by changing her expression. Bit by bit his interest in eye contact grew, and soon he could watch her face for up to a minute at a time.

Paula found it embarrassing to be helped by a therapist to work with her child. With her older children she had considered herself a good mother, but Austin's aloofness had made her question her ability. Performing in front of a therapist only made her more unsure.

"You are a wonderful and gifted mother," the therapist reassured her, "but some children with disabilities don't respond the way their parents expect. Ordinary stimuli—lights, sounds, touch—can sometimes fail to get their attention or be upsetting to them. It's often hard to figure out what he likes and doesn't and what kinds of play will help him grow."

Indeed, Paula did learn tricks from the therapist that helped her capture Austin's attention, and gradually she grew both more confident with her son and more comfortable at the sessions.

Initially Kurt's efforts were directed toward modulating his voice. A successful lawyer, Kurt had a powerful, take-charge manner and a forceful, deep speaking voice. The occupational therapist pointed out that Austin disliked loud, low noises and crawled away when Kurt spoke forcefully. So Kurt practiced speaking to Austin in softer, higher-pitched tones. This wasn't easy, but with the help of frequent hand signals from Paula, he gradually learned. His effort paid off. Austin responded better to higher-pitched sounds and didn't look away as much from his father's new voice. After a few weeks father and son were able to look at each other more often.

Kurt was thrilled. His son's looking at him and occasionally moving his arms in Kurt's direction unleashed a wave of love in Kurt—a feeling that he'd been too scared to acknowledge earlier. Now, instead of relating to Austin primarily with his voice, Kurt clasped the boy in giant bear hugs and initiated efforts at playful wrestling. Unfortunately, these big, rapid movements were too much for Austin, whose physical insecurity and sensitivity to movement made him easily overwhelmed. So, again, each time his father tried to play, Austin would become self-absorbed. Kurt swallowed his rejection, but having opened himself up to his son the pain was hard, and after several weeks Kurt, too, began slowly to pull away. The therapist tried to help Kurt find gentler ways to interact.

"Try to join what he's already doing instead of introducing an idea of your own," she said.

"But he isn't doing anything," Kurt replied.

"He's always doing something," she rejoined. "If he is looking at a toy car on the floor, you look at it and move it closer. See if he will move his arms toward it."

Kurt tried following the therapist's advice, but playing with a child whom he felt rejected every overture was daunting. When Kurt rolled a car near Austin's, Austin often turned his back. After two months of therapy, Kurt was demoralized. Interacting with his son appeared impossible.

Then, one day, three months into therapy, the impossible happened. Austin was repetitively turning the wheel of a chair in the therapist's office. For Austin, this type of intentional action was a new, promising development. Looking for a way to follow his lead, Kurt gently turned the wheel the other way. Austin immediately turned the wheel back. Kurt's hand froze in midair; Austin had purposely responded. Quickly, Kurt turned the wheel again, but Austin was already looking toward something else. As Kurt watched him look away, he nonetheless felt a rush of love for his son. As simple as it was, with turning the wheel back and forth they had just had their first nonverbal conversation.

That conversation led to many more, and in another three months Austin was able to make two deliberate, intentional responses in a row. As he became more intentional, his repetitive motions, which we call *perseveration*, began to take on greater purpose. In addition, his progress in physical and occupational therapy accelerated and his ability to sit up without falling over and to make some crawling movements improved.

Austin still rolled toy cars back and forth endlessly and opened and closed doors obsessively. Kurt and Paula were disturbed by this behavior because it was so odd, but, like many parents in this situation, they were reluctant to challenge it because it seemed to make their son so happy. He used this obsessive repetition the way their older children had used pacifiers. But the therapist explained that although perseveration was soothing, it could also be used to engage him in interaction.

"When Austin rolls a car back and forth across the floor," she said, "put your hand in its way. Make him interact with you. If you're playful, you can turn his perseverations into two-person games."

So they did. Kurt began blocking Austin's cars with his hand, and each time he did Austin struggled to push the hand away. Paula began getting stuck behind the door or pushing back when Austin tried to open and close a door. Every perseveration became an occasion for interaction, and soon Austin was making three deliberate responses in a row. True, the responses were hardly warm and joyful, but they were there. "Even though he was angry, it was so much better than no response at all," said Paula. For the first time the Zugers felt they were actually communicating with their son.

Over time, with more interaction and purposefulness and a greater degree of engagement and expressiveness of motion, Austin made increasing progress in all areas of his development. Just before his third birthday he had a tremendous growth spurt. His greater purposefulness and relatedness helped even his physical therapy as he learned to use a walker. In turn his new freedom of movement and intentionality seemed to trigger a further surge of learning. He became more and more aware of his parents. "It was as if he woke up and realized we were there," said Paula. He began looking at them warmly, coming to them for hugs, initiating interactions. At the same time he began imitating their words. With the same exuberance that nondisabled children display when they discover that words hold meaning, he began labeling his world—his body parts, his parents, his dog, his favorite foods. After a while he could name letters, numbers, and colors.

A pivotal event for Paula occurred around this time. Austin hit her on the nose, and she scolded, "Don't hit me, Austin!" Immediately he touched her again, gently this time, saying "nose" as if practicing naming body parts. Paula was stunned. "Austin covered up his action by disguising it as practice," she thought. He had created a strategy to avoid her anger. That night Paula sobbed uncontrollably. For the first time she knew her child would be a thinking human being, not just a parrot who repeated words.

To encourage his thinking and to strengthen his communication, Austin's therapists urged Kurt and Paula to "playfully negotiate" with him. "Don't give him what he wants too quickly," they said. "Enjoy his arguing for his needs. But do it playfully." It wasn't easy. He'd had such a hard time, how could they deny him his wishes now that he had finally learned to express them? And why would they want to encourage his wrath? But they tried. When Austin wanted juice, instead of pouring it right away, they stalled him with questions: What kind? How much? Which glass? When he wanted them to bring him a particular toy, they played dumb, repeatedly bringing him the wrong one until he had communicated in numerous ways which one he wanted. When he shrieked his displeasure, they pretended not to understand, helping him use words or gestures to tell them what was wrong. Over the next several months Austin's verbal proficiency improved dramatically. The motivation to get what he wanted had taught him a powerful lesson: words are not merely labels, but tools for communication.

While this was going on, Austin was also introduced to the world of pretend play and visualization. When he wanted juice, the teddy bear was thirsty, too, and Mom, talking for Teddy, would say, "I need juice." Austin initially copied her; then, on his own, he began to feed Teddy. Later on he fed his other stuffed animals as well. Pretend play became an important part of his daily activities, and with it, his imagination grew and his capacity for creating new ideas gradually flowered.

Now that Austin was learning to communicate with his family it was time to give him real-world practice with his peers. Kurt and Paula worried that it would be hard to find children to play with their seriously delayed child; it was far easier to play with Austin themselves. But the therapists insisted, so one by one, the Zugers invited families to play. Invariably Austin sat in the corner while the other child played with his toys.

Reluctantly they arranged one, then two, then finally three and four play sessions a week. And in time, Austin did improve. After six months of regular dates, he would willingly play with another child, provided that his mom or dad sat between them as an intermediary.

When Austin was four, the Zugers felt he was ready for a small group of children in a private nursery school. With the help of an aide, he was able to keep up with the many classroom routines, although his play was initially more parallel than interactive. But the stimulating environment seemed to trigger another spurt of learning, and throughout that year his language skills grew. Toward the end of the year he began speaking in complex sentences with two ideas per sentence ("I like Mrs. Sheffield; she gave me a star"). During the next year he began following strings of commands ("Go get your cowboy hat and put it on"). And he began answering questions that required sophisticated, abstract thinking ("Why can't we take the car?" "Because the car is broken." "What do we need to do?" "Get it fixed."). As his thinking was becoming more logical and abstract, he and Paula had a remarkable exchange while playing with toy cars. Austin had given her a white car, taking the coveted Jeep for himself, and Paula had protested.

"No," said Austin, shaking his head and pointing to the white car, "this is your car."

"But you always get the Jeep."

"You have to have the white car," Austin replied firmly.

"I never get a chance to drive a Jeep and I want a Jeep now," Paula argued.

"Maybe you can have a Jeep later," Austin replied.

Kurt, from the next room, shouted, "He wants the Jeep. Give him the Jeep." But Paula dug in her heels.

Finally, after ten minutes of wrangling, Paula relented, but only after extracting a promise that she could have the Jeep next time. Austin placed his doll in the vehicle and flashed his mom a self-satisfied smile. Paula smiled too. Few four-year-olds could have argued it better.

When Austin was six and began kindergarten, life was more difficult. The class was larger and more chaotic; the work, such as identifying numbers and letters, was harder. And although Austin's social skills were improving, it seemed harder to make friends, in part because the other children were further along in their development and were able to hold long, logical, and almost adultlike conversations. Austin occasionally invited someone over, but no one invited him back.

"The parents were afraid," said Kurt. "They see a kid with CP and they think: Can he climb our stairs? Can he go to the bathroom? What if something happens?" For the first time the family was forced to confront the fact that where they saw a valiant and resourceful little boy, others saw a handicap.

Some of the depression they had felt during Austin's first year returned. Tension grew between Kurt and Paula. At times they felt they couldn't make it. But Austin's progress—physical, social, emotional, and academic—continued, and ultimately that carried them through. Often, even when a child is making excellent progress, as other children grow from being hard-to-understand preschoolers to logical, school-age kids the discrepancy between children who have special needs and those who do not seems to grow. One group has hit a new milestone, which the other group is still negotiating.

Fortunately, the second half of kindergarten was much easier. Early in the year Austin became best friends with a boy named Jesse, and for the rest of the year they were inseparable, spending virtually every weekend together. Toward spring he became equally close with a little girl. During this part of the year he also began to demonstrate great empathy. When a new child came into his class, he was the first to invite the child home. When his mother fell and hurt her leg, he commiserated, "I know how that feels." Paula and Kurt felt that his earlier ostracism had given him a greater appreciation for others' feelings. The therapists saw it as a tremendous sign of progress. Children who are as inward as Austin had been have a hard time learning to appreciate other people's feelings. Austin's sensitivity showed that he had turned a significant corner.

Austin's awareness of others' emotions led his therapists to believe that he was ready to broaden his own. Like many children with disabilities, Austin was comfortable with positive feelings such as love and nurturance, but was scared by such negative feelings as anger and aggression. To protect himself, he avoided those feelings by changing the subject when they occurred. The therapists showed the Zugers how they could use Austin's imaginary play to help him experiment with those scary emotions.

"Each time he makes up a story with his toys," they said, "he's expressing his emotions. Have your character ask him [i.e., his character] open-ended questions to help him talk about how his characters are feeling."

One day Austin began a drama by putting a baby in a crib. "You be the mommy and daddy," he instructed his parents. "Tell the baby to stay in the crib." Paula and Kurt did as they were told. Austin then made the baby climb out of the crib.

"Tell the baby to get back in," he directed, and again they obliged, but once more Austin made the baby climb out.

"Austin, how does the baby feel about having to stay in his crib?" Paula asked.

"Very mad," said Austin.

"Is that how you feel when we tell you to stay in your bed?" Austin looked away. "The baby has to go on a trip," he announced, and put the baby in a car.

Paula and Kurt exchanged glances at Austin's attempt to change the subject, but knowing how scared he was of anger, they played along for a little while. They realized that it might be easier for Austin to play out his feelings than to talk about them directly.

Austin then brusquely put another doll in the crib and blurted, "Put Mommy in crib!"

Paula and Kurt laughed to themselves. Austin was not only expressing anger, he was getting even, doing to Mommy what she did to him. Paula, speaking to the mommy doll, said, "I hate being in the crib. Let me out!"

Austin smiled with satisfaction and pushed the mommy doll down. "You have to." For the first time he had flexed his aggressive muscles and seemed to enjoy it.

Over the next year Kurt and Paula continued to use pretend play to help Austin experiment with anger and aggression, and also to promote his assertiveness. Like many children with motor problems, Austin was shy about asserting his will, as if afraid that his body wouldn't support his standing up for himself.

"Make sure he's directing the dramas," the therapists said. "But your characters can sometimes disobey his orders. That will challenge him to express anger and assert his will."

So when Austin told Kurt's army to fight a certain way, Kurt sometimes developed a battle plan of his own. When Austin told Paula to put the pirates in the ship, she sometimes put them in the castle. Initially Austin responded to these infractions by flying off the handle or by leaving the game. But as time went on, and his parents coaxed him gently back in, he became increasingly verbal about his wishes.

"No, no, no!" he yelled one day at Kurt who had "misunderstood" Austin's direction to put the black army on top of the hill. "Put it there; I said put it there!"

"Hey, you seem pretty angry at me," said Kurt, "I guess it's important to you to have the army where you want it."

"Yes it is," asserted Austin. "And I *am* angry at you because you never listen to my orders!"

Kurt tried to hide his smile as he dutifully moved his army to the top of the hill. In Austin's confident admission of anger, he recognized another major achievement.

By the time Austin entered first grade he had a stable group of three friends, his age or a year younger, with whom he interacted in largely age-appropriate ways. He was also becoming stronger academically. By the middle of the year he was tackling the second-grade workbook in reading. Math was more difficult for him, but he was keeping up with the class. Fine-motor activities, such as writing, were more difficult because of his poor motor control, and he was still mastering walking with braces, making sports something for the future. Delighted with his progress, the Zugers decided to have Austin tested again. This time his verbal IQ registered 110—a far cry from the 40–50 he had registered years before.

The increased rigor of the academic work raised another issue, however. Physical and occupational therapy, which Austin still did twice a week each, had greatly improved his motor control, but many deficits remained, including the difficulty with handwriting, which interfered with his schoolwork. Austin's teacher suggested that he use a computer; she also enlarged his math papers on the copy machine to give him more room to write the answers. But Austin, with a self-awareness new to him, resisted these adaptations. He didn't want to be different from his peers.

At the same time, Austin became self-conscious about his leg braces. When children asked about them, he took their questions as teasing rather than as curiosity.

"I keep telling him that nobody cares about his braces," said Paula. "If anything, it's his eating habits that will turn people off!"

Austin is now eight and a half years old and enjoying second grade. He is a warm, engaging, creative, and logical child who loves long conversations about almost anything. His work is at or above grade level in every subject; his verbal IQ is in the superior range. He is able to walk steadily with his braces, go down one or two steps at a time without a handrail, and run, albeit slowly, with his friends on the playground. (He falls frequently, but always gets right back up.) His handwriting is still poor, and that is the primary focus of his occupational therapy.

What do his parents think about his tremendous progress and about the future?

"Austin is going to a new school next year, and I worry about that," says Paula. "I know he'll do fine; he makes friends easily now, and he won't have trouble with the work. But he's always shy in new situations. And I worry that as he gets older, things will get harder for him socially. Puberty, especially, should be a real fun time! But we know he'll go to college; we know he'll get a good job. We're much more optimistic than we were when he was two. I think there are going to be some tough times ahead—but in the end it's going to be fine."

The program that helped Austin make progress was based on understanding the three processes that contributed to his intellectual and emotional growth: (1) his unique biological or physical profile, (2) his patterns of interaction during different developmental stages, and (3) the patterns of his caregivers and family.

Austin brought his physical differences, including how he reacted to and comprehended sights and sounds, into his interaction patterns. His caregivers brought their own personalities and the larger family and cultural and community patterns into the interactions. But it is the interactions between a child and his caregivers that determine how the child behaves and functions. In Austin's case, his physical differences made it hard for him to interact with others and his caregivers were understandably frustrated and stymied. Once we were able to help his caregivers find ways to inspire Austin to interact and become engaged and intentional, we saw that his physical differences, although significant, were not as limiting as originally perceived.

Children's physical or family patterns may be more or less limiting. Only when we begin the interactive journey up the developmental ladder can we know where a child's potential may lie. The interactive journey determines its own destination. In order to help children on their journey we need to understand all three of the contributing processes. The next chapters explore them one by one.

2

Biological Challenges

Frequently, children who are born prematurely, with low birth weight, who don't get enough oxygen during birth, or who have injuries to their nervous systems may have biological differences that can compromise development. An infant's or child's differences may have specific or nonspecific causes. These physical differences may be described in many different ways. We have found it useful to categorize these differences in terms of how they express themselves in daily functioning. These functional categories involve three broad areas of functioning of the central nervous system, which determine how we sense, understand, and react to our world.

1. *Sensory reactivity:* the way we take in information through the senses.

2. *Sensory processing:* how we make sense of the information we take in.

3. *Muscle tone, motor planning,* and *sequencing:* the way we use our bodies and, later, our thoughts to plan and execute a response to the information we have taken in.

When these three systems are working smoothly, they create a continuous feedback loop where we take in sensations such as sights and sounds, react to them with our emotions, and attempt to process and comprehend them and then organize thoughts and behaviors as well as feelings to interact smoothly with the world. But when one or more parts of these systems goes awry, we are less able to function well. A number of causes can account for these difficulties, including genetic anomalies such as fragile X syndrome, injury during childbirth, prematurity, or unspecified constitutional difficulties. Treatment means putting the feedback loop into working order by finding the parts of the system that are challenged and working to improve them. Because these three areas are so important, we address them one at a time.

THE SENSORY SYSTEM

We rarely stop to think about how vitally important the five senses are in terms of giving us information about the world. Without the ability to see, hear, touch, smell, and taste we would live in total isolation, unable not only to sense, but also to *think*, for we would lack any experience with which to develop ideas. In addition to these five common senses, there are the body senses: the vestibular system, which is sensitive to gravity and movement and influences muscle tone, balance, and arousal; and the proprioceptive system, which provides awareness of movement and the position of the body in space and influences motor control and body schema. These systems govern our ability to feel sure of our own body in space, to sense where "I" stops and the world begins. These systems enable us to feel balanced and safe as we move, sit, and stand, to let other people get close, and to protect ourselves if we feel endangered. In addition, our affects or emotions also function as a way to sense what is going on around us. A stimulus may be hard and scary at the same time. We will discuss the special role of emotions later.

Within each of these senses, people can be under- or overreactive depending on their sensory threshold (the point at which the combined sensory input activates the central nervous system and we see a response). People who are underreactive don't respond to small or even moderate amounts of stimulation in the area of their sensitivity; people who are overreactive find small or moderate amounts of stimulation overloading or irritating. People who are underresponsive to sound, for instance, may fail to respond to ordinary speech. They need loud, often highly rhythmic sounds to capture their attention. People who are extremely underreactive to sound fail to respond to noise at all. People who are overreactive, on the other hand, may find speech or television every bit as irritating as fingernails on a chalkboard. Vacuum cleaners and kitchen utensils may be especially bothersome. To these people, only the quietest, gentlest sounds are tolerable.

People who are underreactive to touch may barely perceive common tactile stimuli, such as a hug or the pressure of a chair beneath one's legs. They may be insensitive to pain. People who are overreactive to tactile stimulation, may feel pained at the slightest touch. A gentle pat or the feel of certain fabrics against their skin may register as severe irritation. Children who are sensitive to visual stimuli may overreact to lights and color or may be so overloaded by color, shape, and detail that they fail to see the big picture. Other children may miss the details and see only the forest but not the trees. Misperceiving the world in any of these ways affects all a child's interactions.

Children will often compensate for their under- or overreactivity. A child who is overreactive to certain stimuli may try to avoid those sensations, whereas a child who is underreactive may seek them out. A child who is hypersensitive to sound may retreat to a quiet place so as not to be overwhelmed. A child who is underreactive to touch, or whose kinesthetic or proprioceptive senses are underreactive and who therefore does not register where he is in space, may need to run or bounce or swing endlessly to get the sensory input to inform him. Alternatively, if an underreactive child also has low muscle tone, she may become self-absorbed and more and more impervious to the world around her.

What makes under- and overreactivity even more problematic is that sensory input is not discrete. Information comes to us from many sources at a time—from our eyes *and* our ears *and* from where our bodies are in space. It accumulates with time; at any moment it is being combined with the sensory data we took in seconds before. Thus a child's ability to process such data is context-dependent. For example, a child might respond pleasurably to a song sung by a parent in a quiet room while being held, but might not respond at all to the same song sung in a noisy, active classroom.

To make the sensory puzzle even more challenging, children with severe impairments are usually under- or overreactive in several areas. A child may be overreactive to sound and to touch, but underreactive to movement. This child may shy away from noises and physical contact, but crave the motion of spinning and swinging. Another child may be overreactive to sight but underreactive to sound. This child may be frightened of oncoming traffic, but fail to respond when his parent calls out a warning. To add further complexity, a child's reactivity may change from one moment to the next. Stress, fatigue, or high emotion can cause a child's reactivity pattern to change.

Sometimes reactivity varies within a sensory area. For example, a child may be oversensitive to sounds in a certain frequency range (e.g., vacuum cleaners and motor sounds) and underreactive to those in another (e.g., an ordinary human voice). Typically, though, children evidence a pattern, for example, of oversensitivity.

It's easy to see how people with sensory impairments can miss out on a lot of information from the world. For instance, we depend on hearing not only for big pieces of information, such as a person's words or the sound of a car hurtling past, but also for details, such as nuances in a person's voice that can mean the difference between genuine concern and sarcasm or between patience and impatience. The ability to distinguish all the gradations of sound enables us fully to take in and understand the world. The same is true for each of the other senses. Vision not only helps us discern one individual from another, but also helps us detect the nuances of facial expression that indicate when a person is genuinely interested or merely tolerant, or when a smile is warm and loving versus mechanical. Vision enables us to determine when objects in our space are arranged in one configuration or another. The sense of touch enables us to discern pain from pleasure, and the difference between a playful pat and an accidental bump of equal pressure. Most important, it provides a part of our boundary with the outside world.

Children whose senses function fully read and interpret billions of tiny sensory cues as they master the skills of human interaction. But children with sensory impairments may miss or misperceive these critical bits of information as they learn to interact with the world. Learning to pay attention, learning to engage with others, and learning to communicate may all be affected.

THE PROCESSING SYSTEM

Our senses enable us to "take in" information from the world, but it is our processing system that enables us to make sense of what we receive. Without processing we have a collection of raw, but meaningless, data. During processing, that data is interpreted. Bits of light are translated into colors, pictures, faces, and other understandable images. Sound waves are translated into words, music, sirens, and other meaningful sounds. Stimulation of the nerve endings in our skin is translated into gentle caresses, bear hugs, and other meaningful types of contact. The compression of our joints, the feel of the floor beneath our feet, and the sensation of air against our skin translate into an awareness of where our body is in space. In all these ways our processing system, millions of neurological pathways in the brain, interprets the millions of cumulative bits of sensory information it takes in every second.

Sensory processing is the earliest form of processing that takes place in the brain. Newborns live in a primarily sensory world; their biggest task and challenge is coping with all the sensory data they receive. But almost immediately a second kind of processing begins: *cognitive processing*—the ability to see patterns and create connections between things. The infant starts to associate a certain warm smile and soft voice with the bliss of being picked up and cradled; she starts to anticipate that feeling when she hears the voice approach; she develops an attachment to that face and voice and touch. Well before she can use the word, she links these pleasing sensations into a rudimentary pattern, the pattern of mother. This ability to form patterns is a result of cognitive processing.

As children grow, their cognitive-processing skills become much more elaborate. Ideas form, and by the age of four or five most children are able to manipulate abstract ideas, that is, they are able to think about things that are not right in front of them. They can remember the past and imagine the future; they can link two or more abstract ideas together; they can use language to put their ideas into words.

Sensory processing and cognitive processing are what most people think of when they think about a person's processing abilities. But there is a third, equally important, type of processing. *Affective*, or *emotional*, *processing* refers to our ability to interpret the emotional signals we receive from others—the ability to know, when we see a smile, that a person is friendly or to determine, when we hear a loud cry, whether it is a cry of warning or of distress. For many people the ability to differentiate among even subtle shades of emotional meaning is second nature. But for individuals with developmental challenges this ability can be impaired or nonexistent.

One reason children with disabilities have trouble with cognitive and emotional processing is that both types of processing rely on sensory input, and in children with disabilities the sensory input may be especially confusing. On the way in, the sensory signal may go unheeded, may be overwhelming, or may be without form or a recognizable pattern.

Cognitive processing, or thinking, involves manipulating the sensory data we take in. We combine numerous bits of data into patterns about which we can make judgments. Because most of us are stronger in one sense than we are in others, we tend to rely a bit more on the information we take in through that sense.

Some bird-watchers identify a shape flashing past, others identify a song. The predominance of certain types of sensory information occurs in even the highest-level thinking. Albert Einstein was a self-proclaimed visual thinker. When he conceptualized mathematical theories he imagined them not in numbers or in words, but in pictures, which he manipulated in his mind. Only after he worked out his theorems pictorially did he translate the results into mathematical symbols.

Despite favoring one sense over the others, however, we generally rely on sensory teamwork as we think. Information taken in through one sense is translated into other senses as it's processed. This step enables us to understand something fully, to get our minds around it, to consider it from multiple points of view. A baby examining a toy touches it, tastes it, and smells it. She may also lean on it or press it against her. She examines the toy with all her senses, obtaining the fullest awareness of the object. An adult reading a book takes the information in visually, absorbing the symbols on the page. He also processes that information auditorily as he imbues the words with the sounds of speech. As he thinks about what he is reading, the meanings of the words may call on experiences from other senses: he may visualize the people about whom he is reading; he may imagine the feel of cold air against his skin; he may hear the wind whistling through the trees as the characters traverse a forest in a storm. All his senses come into play to enable him to experience what he is reading. The senses overlap in this way to permit a person to engage in higher-level thinking, or cognition.

Children who have difficulty processing sensory information can't manage the sensory teamwork that is required for higher-level cognition. They may misread signals, mistaking a smile for a grimace or a gentle pat for an aggressive swat. Or they may have difficulty combining the many signals they take in into a useful pattern. They may be able, for example, to picture what Mom does, but have a hard time figuring out what she says or interpreting her tone of voice. As a result, the picture of Mom may be limited or confused. Their weaker senses keep them from working out the whole situation—Mom holding out a coat, announcing impatiently that it is time to go.

Emotional information is also taken in through the senses, through myriad visual, auditory, tactile, and other sensory cues. Thus children who have difficulty processing this information have problems with emotional processing as well. Imagine meeting a couple for the first time. You notice right away that the woman *seems* friendly. There is something in her smile, her voice, perhaps the way she holds out her hand that gives you that impression. Her partner, in contrast, immediately strikes you as aloof. It may be his lack of eye contact, stiff posture, or grudging nod instead of a warm hello, but, for whatever reason, sensory data have created that emotional impression. Your sensory system has acted as sensitive antennae, permitting you to pick up emotional signals.

As with cognitive processing, we rely most on our strongest sense when we take in emotional data, and we consider input from that sense first when we process emotional information. For example, two people angry at their spouses might think about their grievances in two different ways. The person who is stronger auditorily is likely to think about the spouse's harsh voice and unkind words when mentally rehearsing their argument. The person who is stronger visually may not remember the verbal argument at all. This person is likely to visualize the spouse's scowl, body language, and gestures as if replaying a movie. Yet although one sense is strongest, we rely on sensory teamwork to fully interpret what we see. Auditory cues, movements, and touch are juxtaposed as we process and respond to them emotionally.

Children with sensory-processing difficulties are unable to integrate incoming emotional data and interpret it from multiple points of view. Emotional processing can be greatly skewed by over- or underreactivity. A child who is oversensitive to sound, for example, may have such a strong reaction to the sound of a vacuum cleaner that it overpowers his other senses. Visual input and processing, which might tell him that the cause of the noise is only a vacuum cleaner, are blotted out by his enormous reaction to the sound. He hears a fearsome thing that could eat him alive, and before he lets vision or touch or any other sense contradict that impression he is howling in fear or trying to escape. Sensory reactivity or processing difficulties can cause a child to misinterpret emotional information from those around him, resulting in inappropriate—sometimes extreme—emotional reactions.

THE MOTOR SYSTEM

The sensory system enables us to take in information from the world; the processing aspect of that system enables us to interpret that information. The motor system is what enables us to respond. When a baby snuggles easily, when we laugh at a joke, when we run to catch a ball that's flying toward us, and when we answer a question that has been posed we are using our motor system to form our response. The use of the trunk to cuddle, of the mouth and tongue to form words, of arms and legs to run and catch, of muscles in the face to smile or frown or look away—all these are motor activities that permit us to respond to the world.

In children with developmental delays we often observe problems of muscle tone or motor planning. *Muscle tone* refers to the ability of our muscles to support our bodies without effort. Children with low tone, whose muscles are very loose, have to put great effort into holding their heads up and walking. Muscle tone in part influences the ability of individual muscle groups to respond the way we want them to. *Motor planning* refers to the ability of a person to plan and execute a *series* of muscle movements. Sound muscle tone enables a person to flex and contract muscles on command;

poor muscle tone means that those muscles will be too tight or too loose, resistant to the person's efforts to control them. Sound motor planning means a person will be able to figure out what action is needed and then execute it; he will be able to put one foot in front of the other and shift his weight from left to right while counterbalancing with his arms in order to walk across a room. Poor motor planning means a person may be unable to figure out which foot to start with, which one to move next, and which way to lean to keep her balance.

Problems with motor planning can make even the simplest tasks difficult. Acknowledging Daddy when he leans over the crib means turning to face him, making eye contact, and responding with gestures or a smile—sequencing numerous motions together. Many unimpaired infants can do that on automatic pilot, but a child with motor-planning difficulties has to work through each step. It's easy to see how he might get distracted along the way! Any activity that requires sequencing actions or behaviors presents similar challenges. Hence eating, exploring toys, playing games, and interacting socially are made more difficult for children with motor-planning or sequencing challenges. Later in life, complex social sequences—greeting new people, engaging in give-and-take behaviors such as two-way conversations, sports—require skills in motor planning and sequencing. Even our ability to sequence ideas into a logical flow may be related in part to this ability.

Sensory reactivity, processing, and motor planning and sequencing affect how a child functions in the world—how well he relates to the people around him; how well he communicates his wishes and ideas; how well he thinks and navigates the often bumpy world of emotions. When we look at a child's individual differences, these are among the abilities we examine. When a child is considered to have special needs, often one or more of these abilities are not developing or functioning optimally.

HOW DIFFICULTIES IN THESE SYSTEMS CREATE DEVELOPMENTAL CHALLENGES

Imagine an infant who has problems "taking in" auditory information. Ordinary speech simply passes her by. But because the problem is not readily apparent, her parents don't realize it exists. Instead, when their baby fails to respond to their eager calls they come to feel rejected. Bit by bit they stop trying so hard to woo her, and the child is left more and more to her inner world. If the child's problem is not detected, her ability to form warm and loving relationships and to communicate may be compromised.

Now imagine a child who has mild problems processing auditory information. He is unable to organize auditory signals into meaningful patterns. This child hears his mother call his name, followed by a long string of commands, but he is unable to decipher her meaning. When after several repetitions he fails to do as she directed, his mother grows annoyed. Unaware of her son's problem, she misinterprets his behavior as defiance and responds to him with anger. The child's problem in one area creates a problem with interaction that complicates his relationship with his parents.

A child with a severe auditory-processing problem, who doesn't understand *most* of what is said to him, may experience even greater problems with interaction. To him the world may be a hostile place, filled with sounds that make demands on him but to which he can't respond. He may come to feel shut out from the world of people, or, worse, people may seem frightening, always yelling because he is so often angering and disappointing them. Gradually he may draw more and more into himself and into the world of silent, inanimate objects. Here at least he can feel safe and secure. When this child is brought to a clinician he may be uncommunicative and unrelated. Even if he feels secure, a child with severe auditory-processing problems may find it hard to comprehend other people's words and may therefore not progress to two-way symbolic communication and the ability to form abstract ideas.

A child with a visual processing problem may exhibit a very different type of behavior. Because visual information helps us form mental images of things it is an important component of a child's ability to organize behavior and see the big picture. Without this ability a child may be easily distracted or get lost in details. Her capacity for problem solving and abstract thinking may be affected. The ability to visualize may also help children calm themselves. In times of stress a child can picture Mommy in her mind and use that mental image to soothe herself. But a child who can't process visual information can't easily form mental images. For her, once Mommy is gone from the room, Mommy may cease to exist. As a result, this child may suffer from extreme separation anxiety and sleep problems, may be excessively demanding, and later in life may become depressed when confronting strong feelings and conflict because she loses the inner image associated with being loved and can't easily reconstruct it.

It is also possible to have trouble processing at more cognitive levels. Children with cognitive-processing impairments may have difficulty in the realm of ideas. They may have trouble forming abstract ideas (visualizing things that are not right in front of them) or making connections between ideas (understanding when two or more abstract ideas are related). They may have difficulty learning language because language requires abstract thinking, using words to stand for things. Children with cognitive-processing problems may be labeled *mentally retarded, cognitively delayed,* or *language delayed.*

The area of processing that is most overlooked is affective, or emotional, processing. The child who has affective-processing difficulties faces challenges reading other people's emotional signals. He might cower in the classroom when the teacher talks loudly, believing that the teacher is angry and about to punish him. Or he might misread another child's helpful offer to push the swing as a hostile gesture and rebuff the other child or start to cry. Or he may interpret another child's cry as a warning of attack and attack the other child first. The world may be a frightening place. From hugs to back pats, smiles to frowns, laughs to cries, the child may feel besieged by sensations that he doesn't understand. And when he responds, often in unexpected ways, his response unleashes more confusing input as the person with whom he's interacting responds to him. Trapped in this escalating dialogue, the child can easily feel out of control and may react with tantrums, inappropriate body movements, or flight.

Problems in the motor system can also create challenges to interaction and communication. Imagine an infant who, because of poor control of the muscles in her neck, is slow to turn her head when her parents approach. Unaware of the problem, her parents view this "indifference" as a sign of rejection. Gradually, without really meaning to, they stop trying so hard to win her attention. Yet without her parents' encouragement she will have difficulty learning to form close and loving relationships.

Sometimes the problems are more subtle. Imagine a child with poor muscle tone who can walk, but not well, who can use his arms, but not easily. Place this child in preschool, where children naturally run and push, hug and hit, and what will happen to his sense of self? Unable to keep up with the other children or defend himself from their assaults, he may become passive, avoidant, and self-absorbed; alternatively, he may become overly assertive and aggressive. The signals he sends out may tell the other children to stay away from him, further disrupting his peer interactions.

Sometimes even a child's positive responses can cause social problems. A child with poor motor control who is excited about her coming turn on the slide may flap her arms or rock her head. To other children these gestures of excitement may look strange, or even scary, and they may back off or grow defensive, again disrupting the development of peer relationships.

GENERAL SEQUENCING CHALLENGES

Difficulties with motor planning are often related to general sequencing difficulties. If a child is unable to sequence her behavior in response to other people, interaction problems may result. For instance, when the teacher signals that it is time to sit and be quiet, the child must not only be able to understand the message, she must also be able to respond physically. She must make her body stop what it is doing, go to a chair, and sit down. And she must control her movements once she is sitting. Motor-planning problems can make such a basic sequence difficult.

Complex social interactions among children involve even more subtle types of sequencing of behavior. Figuring out how to be close to someone without being too close, how to be assertive without being aggressive, how to fool around without appearing belligerent or dangerous—these and other social behaviors involve complex patterns of sequencing.

Creating logical connections between words, ideas, or concepts also involves sequencing capacities. Frequently, what appear to be attentional or organizing difficulties relate to underlying challenges with sequencing.

Rarely do these problems occur singly. Almost all children with special needs have problems in two or more systems, and, not surprisingly, the problems compound each other. Consider a child who is overreactive to touch, has a poor kinesthetic sense, and has motor-planning problems. When in his effort to cross the playground he accidentally bumps into another child, his reaction is likely to be, "Stop hurting me! Watch where you're going!" He doesn't mean to be passing the blame; he's just confused about where his body stops and the other child's begins and about who caused the accident to happen. In addition, the moderate bump feels severely bruising. As a result, he sends out this unexpected signal to the other child, who may avoid him in the future. Thus his opportunities to make friends may be gradually undermined.

Once you understand your child's biological challenges you can begin to design a treatment program to ameliorate them. You can also begin to tailor your interactions with your child in ways that will play to her strengths and minimize demands on her weaker areas until they are more fully developed. The following case illustrates how parents were helped to understand their child's individual differences.

DYLAN

Dylan was a difficult baby. He was fussy and a poor sleeper; he nursed poorly; and he fought the switch to solid food with raging tantrums. But he was bright and alert, an early crawler, and eager to walk and talk. Best of all, he was warm and affectionate with his parents. His favorite game as an infant was "walking" on their tummies.

At 17 months Dylan began to jabber. At 19 months, he said his first word, "duck." Then, with all the exhilaration of discovery, he ran excitedly from his mother to his father, 10, 15, 20 times, shouting, "Duck! duck! duck!" Vicky and Bruce were thrilled.

But by 22 months they were beginning to wonder if something was wrong. Dylan was picking up new words quickly—numbers, letters, colors—each time running from mother to father as many as 20 times, calling out his discovery. But it wasn't as though he wanted to communicate. It was as if the repetition were only for his own private amusement.

A similar repetitiveness was coloring all his behavior. He now demanded the same books and videos time after time and threw a first-class tantrum if his parents suggested new ones. He played endlessly with his toy fire truck and ranted if they offered a different one. He wanted all his books lined up on his shelf and raged if one was out of order. He ate only baby food and threw anything else he was given. When his parents tried to dress him he refused to cooperate and went rigid. In hundreds of small ways he had begun ordering his parents around; he whined to be carried or brought a toy, and if his parents refused he threw a tantrum. Gradually, they had stopped refusing.

"He was tyrannical," said Vicky. "Everything had to be his way or he would have a fit."

It was equally impossible to take him out in public. Every loud noise frightened him, and a sea of cars and faces sent him into panic. Every trip ended in a tantrum. The only safe place to take him was the zoo, where as other children oohed and aahed about the animals, Dylan walked up and down the chain-link fence, eyes glued to a single row of links. Up and back, up and back he would pace for 20, 30 minutes at a time, while Bruce and Vicky sat, embarrassed, on a bench and watched. They knew their son was acting strangely, knew they should discourage his fixation, but they also knew the penalty of trying. For that half hour, at least, he wasn't crying.

A similar unresponsiveness was occurring at home. When Vicky or Bruce tried to join him in play, he ignored them, rolling his truck as if they weren't there. When they called him, he refused to answer. When Bruce rolled a ball, Dylan would throw it in the corner, and no number of entreaties could convince him to roll it back.

When Vicky and Bruce discussed their concerns with the pediatrician and Dylan's nursery-school teachers, they were assured that nothing was wrong. "Dylan's so bright!" everyone said. But as time went on and Dylan grew more difficult and withdrawn, they became anxious. Dylan spent more and more time saying letters and numbers over and over, and it became harder and harder to get him to look at another person.

"I began to think there were some pieces missing inside," said Vicky. So they took Dylan to a child psychologist, who conducted an intensive three-part evaluation. She determined that Dylan had autistic spectrum disorder and referred the family to us.

Vicky and Bruce were devastated by the word *autistic* and came to us with grim fears of a permanently disturbed and limited future for Dylan. We began with our own comprehensive evaluation, involving history taking and observations, including observing Dylan's responses to various attempts to interact with him. We found a number of important differences in how Dylan reacted to and processed sensations, planned actions, and discovered interaction patterns that helped and hindered, and we developed a comprehensive treatment plan to help Dylan's parents work with and around his specific biological challenges. The program included occupational and speech therapy twice a week; interactive developmental therapy once a week, with a wonderful, gentle therapist named Regina; and an intensive home program of interactive work.

The first thing Regina did was to help Vicky and Bruce understand why Dylan behaved the way he did. She explained that based on the assessment, he had low motor tone, poor motor-planning skills, and a poor sense of where his body was in space. As a result, he was insecure; he was literally unsure how to make his body do what he wanted. His ritualized movements, repeated over and over, were his way of making himself feel safe. He also had difficulty processing auditory information. He was very sensitive to certain sounds, and although he heard what was being said, he didn't always understand the meaning. This combination of deficits made Dylan anxious, understandably nervous about his ability to cope with the world. To reassure himself, he wanted everything in its place, everything familiar, everything under control. And because he had less of a problem expressing himself than taking in information, he tried to garner the control he needed by repeating familiar words and giving orders.

As Dylan's auditory-processing problems and anxiety made him unsure of what he was hearing, it was often easier for him to tune out the outside world and retreat to his own inner world where he controlled everything. There, he could play the repetitive games that were comforting, rolling his fire truck, lining up cars, repeating familiar words and patterns.

The first therapeutic goal was to help Dylan engage with his parents and become more intentional, shifting from self-absorption and repetition to engagement and purposeful interaction. Part of this process included opening and closing circles of communication, that is, responding when his parents or therapists responded to something he did. His repetitive, tuned-out behavior was obviously calming to him, and Vicky and Bruce had been reluctant to interrupt it. But, Regina explained, "Dylan needs to learn to interact, and you need to get involved and help him interact with you."

Dylan was generally overreactive to sensory stimuli, preferring the safety of his overfocused activities, so sounds and visual images had to be soothing yet compelling in order to register. Regina showed Vicky and Bruce how to use soothing voices and gestures to engage Dylan.

"Be calm but silly when responding to his play," she said. " 'Tease' his lined-up cars and trucks. Get marbles and magic wands and other colorful toys and bring them into his play. Use your wand to make his car disappear.

"Also, don't be so compliant. When he ignores you, be playfully obstructive. Get in the path of the truck he's rolling, but do it slow motion so that he can object even before you get there. The key is to be soothing, interesting, and—in a slow-motion way—challenging.

"Play this way for 20 to 30 minutes at a time, many times a day, to give him practice interacting."

This was entirely different from how they were used to behaving with their son. Both parents had a quiet manner. Both were more comfortable with words than with gestures. Gamely, they tried this new approach. With a little practice, Bruce got very good at it. He adopted a silly but soothing voice and talked to Dylan, running around the room, following Dylan to see if Dylan wanted to dance or chase him or go for a horsey ride, always trying to build on what Dylan was doing. Sometimes Dylan got caught up in the movement patterns and chased his dad and jumped on his dad's back for horsey rides.

It was harder to force Dylan to interact by getting in his way. Often when they got in the way of the truck Dylan would wail in anger.

"Do it playfully and more slowly," said Regina. "Make him see you're playing a game and that he can be in charge."

So Bruce would smile as he slowly reached for the truck. He would teasingly drop it in his pocket and then hold his pocket open for Dylan to reach in. After a few days, Dylan began to giggle as he reached in. A few days later he began to make more eye contact. Fairly quickly, Bruce's playful obstruction was evolving into a mutually enjoyable game of keep-away.

Rolling a ball down the stairs became another favorite game. Dylan liked to move the ball. Although he wouldn't roll a ball back on level ground, he found the motion of the ball on the stairs amusing. So Bruce began tossing the ball upstairs to Dylan, who then rolled it back down. In the first months of therapy they often spent 30 minutes repeating this cycle. It wasn't high-level communication, but it was the most sustained contact the two had had for some time.

Meanwhile, Dylan's speech therapist was using playful obstruction to help Dylan talk. She would patiently tantalize him with a toy and play dumb so that he would use words to tell her what he wanted. His whining and crying gradually gave way to speech.

Early on, Vicky and Bruce had said, "We had actually been making him worse. He would point at things and grunt and we would get them for him.

He had no use for language." Dylan's difficulties with processing and sequencing sounds made communication difficult, and he needed higher levels of motivation than would another child.

The occupational therapist tackled Dylan's low motor tone and insecurity in space by involving him in gross-motor activities, such as swinging, jumping, and rolling. Dylan was generally terrified of such activities. Outside therapy he refused to jump an inch off the ground, wouldn't go near a playground, and refused to play with other children because they often shoved. In therapy it often took a long time just to get him on the swing. "We're paying this much for him to swing for a few minutes?" Bruce would complain. But he did see gradual progress in Dylan's ability to cope with sensation and movement.

The first few months of therapy were difficult. It was hard to manage the amount of time advised by the therapists, especially for Bruce, who came home from work at seven, when both he and Dylan were tired. Regina told him he needed to come home earlier, but he had just started a new job and felt unable to comply. The play was also extremely demanding. "It's not like regular playing," said Vicky. "You're always working, always staying one step ahead, always thinking, 'How can I get his attention now? How can I keep it?' If you relax for a minute, you've lost him."

But by the third month of therapy, Dylan was making good progress. He could sustain eye contact with his parents and therapists, and he responded to all their gestures. His vocabulary was expanding rapidly; he was falling in love with words. With a passion he began labeling and categorizing everything he saw. "Backhoe, cement mixer, garbage truck," he would incant as they passed these vehicles on the road. "Screwdriver, pliers, monkey wrench," as his dad puttered in the toolbox. With great precision, Dylan recited long lists of his favorite things. But there was a peculiar private quality to his speech, as if Dylan still spoke to amuse himself rather than to communicate. He dissolved in a tantrum if contradicted or interrupted. He didn't answer questions posed to him, and although he frequently kept up a steady patter while he played, his words often bore no relation to his activity.

"It was so disheartening," said Vicky. "Here he was, finally talking, and it was the rantings of a madman."

The speech therapist explained that Dylan was using words as he had formerly lined up cars. He knew what he wanted to say, but he didn't always comprehend others. The classifications and repetitions were soothing, a way of exercising control over a confusing world as well as a way of shutting out that world. Also, because he had difficulty sequencing behavior and words it was far easier for him to repeat a single sequence than to work out a new series of verbal sequences. To progress, Dylan needed to learn to use words more interactively.

Now that Dylan was more related and intentional, the next therapeutic goal was to help him close verbal circles of communication, to connect his ideas to those of other people who spoke to him.

It took incredible persistence to wring answers from Dylan. "Where is the fire truck going?" Vicky would ask, once, then twice, then a third and fourth time. "Is it going to the house or to the fire station?" she would try again, simplifying the question by making it multiple choice.

"Fire truck red . . . apples red . . . popsicles red . . ." Dylan might respond in a listlike free association.

"Dylan, do the firefighters want red popsicles?" Vicky might ask, trying to forge a logical link between his thoughts.

"Firefighters popsicles," Dylan might reply.

"Do the firefighters want popsicles?" Vicky would ask.

"Firefighters want popsicles," Dylan might finally say. Slowly, he learned to select from a meaningful list of choices a word or phrase that would close a verbal circle.

Each of these conversations was exhausting, "like pulling teeth," said Vicky. Two circles could take 15 minutes; at the end of 30 minutes Vicky would be ready to collapse. But there was no question that Dylan was improving. After three months of intensive work he was closing verbal circles, building bridges between his words and other people's about half the time. When he was motivated, he could answer simple what or where questions most of the time.

To further encourage logic and to stretch the number of circles Dylan could close, the therapists suggested continuing playful obstruction. "When he wants the fire truck to go one way, drive it a different way. Help him argue for what he wants, and keep up the negotiation for as long as possible." So, reluctantly, Bruce and Vicky again became less cooperative play partners.

"I want that one!" they would say, taking Dylan's favorite fire truck.

"No! That one!" he would yell, pointing to a smaller one.

"No, this one," they would insist.

"No! No! That mine!"

"You take that small one."

"Big one mine!"

"Okay," they would relent, "but if I can't have that one, I'll take this one!" and they would select another toy sure to draw a protest.

Although such challenges incurred Dylan's wrath, the number of circles he could close was steadily growing. His parents made sure that there were also plenty of playful interactions that involved cooperation and joy rather than heated debates. For example, Dylan loved to tell his mom which spot to rub on his back.

Around this time Bruce and Vicky placed Dylan in a regular nursery school. His first week went smoothly, but when it came time to return for the second week he didn't want to go. The third week the teachers complained that Dylan was poking other children. Regina visited him at school and quickly discovered the problem. The structured program included large amounts of circle time, when the children were expected to sit still. They often sang songs involving finger play. Because of his low motor tone and postural insecurity, Dylan frequently leaned onto his neighbor's mat, disturbing the other child. Dylan's poor motor planning meant that he was unable to move his hands as the other children did when they sang "The Wheels on the Bus." Inadvertently, he poked his neighbors. The noise level often upset him, and he would try to walk away. Since the school was unable to offer more support, Vicky and Bruce transferred Dylan to a school with more staff and flexibility, and Dylan quickly began to thrive. He was still nervous about interacting physically with other children and became defensive if touched unexpectedly, but he was roughly on a par with them verbally and so could hold his own. Dylan's therapists also urged Bruce and Vicky to schedule play dates for him to encourage further interaction—no easy task, since Dylan would roar when someone took his toys without permission!

After about 12 months in therapy Dylan had made rapid progress in every area except motor skills. For some time Vicky and Bruce had questioned the efficacy of his occupational therapist. A patient, apparently highly skilled therapist, she seemed to have no feel for Dylan. She persisted at activities that Vicky and Bruce intuitively knew wouldn't work, and she often spent half the session reading to Dylan to calm him down—well past the point when he was already calm. Vicky said, "With all our other therapists I had the sense that they were better than I was, that I could learn from them. But with this one, I realized her instincts were worse than mine." After months of questioning their judgment they finally decided to switch therapists. The new therapist sensed when to push Dylan to try something new and when to hold back and had an intuitive ability to lure him onto the equipment he feared. Within weeks of the change, Dylan's tolerance for physical activity had grown noticeably. Two months later he was laughing as he played.

The new therapist also gave Vicky and Bruce hints for doing occupational therapy at home. "Take him to playgrounds," she said. "Get him to roll down hills. Play follow the leader and make him jump and hop. All these activities will build his motor skills." They did, and soon he began asking to go to the playground. For a boy who a year earlier wouldn't go near a swing, this was a tremendous improvement.

The next challenge was to help Dylan become more imaginative. Most three-year-old children are masters of pretend play, weaving intricate stories with their dolls and dinosaurs. Dylan's play was limited to four or five scenarios, which he played out time and time again: a doll would take a nap, wake up, then take another nap; a doll would get hurt falling off a slide, get a Band-Aid, then climb back up and do it again; a fire truck would race to a fire, a person would jump out the window, the fire truck would race away. This repetition was comforting for Dylan, but problematic. A new version of his old rigidity, it prevented him from thinking spontaneously or experimenting with new ideas.

To lure him out of repetition the therapists showed Vicky and Bruce how to thicken the plot.

"When the doll gets hurt, become the doctor," they suggested. "When the fire truck races away, notice that part of the fire is still burning. Do whatever you can to stay within his story, but to take the drama in a new direction."

Bruce and Vicky tried, but, again, it wasn't easy. Dylan screamed when they changed his scenarios. He turned his back and continued playing by himself. Bruce and Vicky racked their brains for ways to lure him into something new. Bruce found that using his high squeaky voice, which he had largely abandoned once Dylan became good at closing circles, was helpful. Better yet was to put on the Ernie puppet. When Ernie suggested twists in the drama, most of the time Dylan went along.

For Vicky, the easiest way to play with Dylan was to think of herself as another three-year-old. Asking herself what a preschooler would do in a given situation helped her be more gestural and interactive and less cooperative. "As a grown-up I made things too easy for him. I let him play the way he wanted. Other children force him to play differently."

When she got really frustrated in her efforts to get Dylan to try new things, Vicky would break down and buy new toys.

"I'd come home and see three new toys on the floor and know Vicky had had a bad day," joked Bruce.

"And I'd say," rejoined Vicky, " 'We're spending so much on therapy, what's $30 for some new toys?' "

Bit by bit Dylan's play expanded. Naps and fires gave way to animals in the jungle and soldiers marching. But his play still had a flat quality to it. People and animals went through their paces mechanically, with no emotion. They woke up, ate meals, went to school or work, went home. They never fought, never got frightened. There were no good guys and bad guys, no scary monsters, none of the fantasy elements that so often populate children's play, through which they work out their feelings and develop reality testing. It was as if Dylan were exercising tight control over his own emotions by not letting them surface in play. He exercised similar control in life. He rarely asserted himself. If another child took his toy he would run to his parents rather than confront the offender. If he was mad, he would cry or lose control rather than express his anger.

To loosen this control, Regina suggested that Vicky and Bruce encourage emotional play. "When he seems to be feeling a strong emotion, explore it with him. Have your character acknowledge it or express that emotion too. Show him it's okay to have strong feelings."

For Vicky and Bruce this task was difficult. "Neither of us is terribly confrontational," Vicky admitted. "It's easier for us to smooth over hurt feelings and anger than to play it out. Whenever there's a bad character around, I want him to go away."

But they worked at it. Pillow fights became popular as a game as well as a way to experiment with anger. Vicky bought some foam-rubber swords, and she and Dylan staged tentative mock fights. Bruce tried to introduce aggressive themes into Dylan's dramas, not always with positive results. Dylan grew scared when Bruce's elephant charged his knights; he threw the elephant deep into a closet. "He'll never come out!" he screamed, battering Bruce with his fists. Regina explained that Dylan couldn't yet differentiate between reality and fantasy. For him, the attack had been frighteningly real. "But with practice," she said, "he'll learn the difference."

Two or three months went by without any noticeable improvement. Then, at play therapy, Dylan ventured toward the basket of "scary toys." He had always avoided this collection of snarling tigers and sword-bearing action figures, but this day, unprompted, he pulled out a shark and waved it in the air. Moments later he put it back and didn't touch it again for weeks. Regina, smiling, said he was turning a corner. A month later he returned to the basket and staged a drama in which a truck entered the jungle and saw an alligator. The truck quickly turned around, but its metaphorical visit to the jungle marked the beginning of Dylan's venture into the world of scary feelings.

About 15 months into therapy Dylan backslid, or so it seemed to Bruce and Vicky. He became whiny and demanding, refused to do anything for himself, and began having inconsolable tantrums, as he had before treatment. Things he had learned to tolerate again reduced him to tears. Vicky and Bruce were frightened. Vicky once more had visions of Dylan in an institution. "It's growth," Regina reassured them. "He's letting more emotions in and that makes him anxious. So he wants to control everything to make the world seem safe. Each time he can't control something, he gets scared."

Upset by Dylan's tantrums, Bruce and Vicky nervously sheltered him and tried to please him each time a tantrum threatened.

"Help him stretch his ability to cope with frustration. Be soothing and playful about it," Regina advised. "When he insists on being carried down the stairs, say, 'Yes, Captain! Just as you say, Captain! Anything else, Captain?' Joke about it and at the same time delay and inspire him to help. 'Can you please climb on my back, Captain?' and after a few steps, 'Okay, I need a rest.' Then, 'Could you give me a push, please?' "

Dubious, Bruce and Vicky followed Regina's advice. Dylan responded badly at first, throwing the expected tantrum. After a few days, though, he began to waver, as if considering their words, and over the next two weeks, both the severity and the number of tantrums declined. Dylan seemed to enjoy a new type of play in which he was more assertive and more on his own.

Regina took this opportunity to encourage Dylan's parents to help him with problem solving. His reduced muscle tone and motor-planning problems made it difficult for Dylan to visualize the steps required to solve a problem. Hence when a toy fell under a table or his mitten fell off his hand, he became hysterical, feeling unable to correct the situation.

"Instead of getting the item for him," said Regina, "talk him through the process. Show him he can do it himself."

But Vicky and Bruce felt too guilty and sad when Dylan cried, "But *why* won't you get it for me? I *need* you to get it for me!" Regina helped them explore their feelings. Once again they needed to work through their guilt, their protective feelings, their fears, and their associations with earlier challenges. They had to address how Dylan affected their relationship, how it had been altered by their continuously tending to his needs.

With this support, Vicky and Bruce began coaching Dylan to find his missing toys and clothes. At first he was frantic each time they refused to find things for him, and Bruce and Vicky had to fight the urge to give in. But slowly Dylan's rages subsided. Three months later he was still asking them to find and reach things for him, but he no longer protested when they offered verbal coaching instead. Dylan even began to feel a sense of pride and security in what he could do himself.

By this time, 18 months into therapy, Dylan's speech had become responsive and more logical; he closed almost all his verbal circles. Yet his speech still had a peculiar formal quality, as if, Bruce said, he had learned English as a second language. If asked where his ball was, instead of saying,

"Over there," he was likely to say, "The yellow ball is behind the red dump truck." If asked to describe his teacher, instead of saying, "Miss Leows is nice," or "Miss Leows reads to me," he would catalog every event from his day at school. Regina explained that Dylan was not yet able to abstract a specific answer. Recording and reporting every detail was related to his difficulties with sequencing ideas. To abstract only the relevant information he would have to form new sequences quickly. That he easily became overloaded and anxious also contributed to this formal quality. Regina urged Bruce and Vicky not to worry, because as Dylan grew emotionally flexible, confident, and better at abstracting information from his environment, his speech would naturally relax.

Dylan is now almost four and a half and has been in therapy for two years. He is warm and engaging, with an infectious smile and eager manner. People meeting him for the first time are as taken by his charm as they are by his precise speech and large vocabulary. He now loves playgrounds and gross-motor games and enjoys playing with other children. He sees his occupational therapist once a week instead of twice, and they continue to refine his fine-motor sequencing skills.

Dylan's speech is still precise, but he is capable of logic, intuition, and subtle emotional interaction. Now when his parents refuse to do something for him, instead of breaking down and crying, he often looks at them plaintively and asks, "But *why* won't you do it for me? You're my parents; you *should* do this." Far more than most children his age, he is able to pinpoint the heart of the issue, verbalize his inner feelings, and argue like a lawyer.

Bruce and Vicky have come a long way, too. They are far better now at supporting imaginative play, engaging in lengthy dialogue, empathizing, and setting limits and tolerating Dylan's upset when they do. They are also better at encouraging his independence.

Dylan is improving at problem solving. Recently, in therapy, a container of toys he wanted fell behind a table and Dylan burst into tears. The therapist said nothing, and after a few minutes Dylan began to look for the container himself. For the first time, Dylan had initiated a problem-solving activity.

Also, in a significant demonstration of self-confidence, Dylan spent the night at a friend's house. This occasion marked another first—the first time Dylan had willingly separated from his parents.

Looking back over the past two years, Bruce and Vicky are tremendously relieved by their son's progress. "We're past the really scary part," said Vicky. "Now we know he'll be okay." But they acknowledge that the road wasn't always smooth and still has its share of bumps. "It's been a roller coaster," said Bruce. "The progress is forward and back, forward and back. After a lot of progress you suddenly hit a slowdown and you feel devastated.

"At one point we took him for a language test. He'd made so much progress, we were sure the test would show him at age level or close. It didn't. And we were just blown away."

"There were so many times when we were eager for him to learn something—to talk, to play with more than just the fire truck . . . we'd think, 'He'll do that and then he'll be just like any other kid.' But it never worked out that way. There was always some twist that made it not quite what I had been hoping and praying to see."

When Vicky and Bruce feel dejected, Regina reminds them to look at where Dylan has been as well as where he needs to go. She helps them recognize his accomplishments. In a short period of time he has made tremendous progress. He is an active, creative, and sensitive member of his class, and a sought-after friend. There's no reason to believe his growth rate won't remain the same or even improve.

Regina is fully confident that Dylan will complete his education, have his choice of careers, and enjoy close and meaningful relationships. He may have to work harder than other people to modulate his intensity and need for control; he may face more challenges with drawing and writing; but his history of developmental challenges should not prevent him from leading a full and satisfying life.

By understanding his individual differences in reacting to and comprehending sensations and planning responses, Dylan's parents and therapists were able to help him master the steps on his developmental ladder. Initially, his processing difficulties led to withdrawal and repetition. By working around and with them, his parents and therapists were able to help Dylan renegotiate his early stages of development, become engaged and purposeful, and master the subsequent stages, learning to be imaginative, verbal, logical, and more flexible in his interactions with family and friends.

3

Observing Each Child:
Biological Challenges and Strengths

As you interact with your child daily, you may feel only too aware of the areas in which she has problems. In the face of those challenges, it's easy to overlook the fact that she also has strengths. This chapter will help you take note of both. It will help you pinpoint the biological challenges that trouble your child's interactions with the world as well as appreciate the areas in which she functions smoothly, so that you can call on those as you and your child work together to help her grow.

Some of your child's biological challenges may already be apparent to you, but others may be hidden. Sensitivity to smell, for instance, is rarely noticed, but it can have a great impact on a child's tolerance for certain people, places, and foods. Many differences in processing are difficult to spot but can have a major impact on a child's behavior.

Assessing your child's strengths and weaknesses involves observing her during play, while she is engaged in activities with you and around the house, and when she is outside. By watching your child carefully, making many observations over a period of time, you'll get much of the information you need. Remember that each sensory modality does not operate in isolation, but in the context of the environment. What triggers a strong reaction in one setting may trigger a smaller reaction, or no reaction, in another. In addition, all the senses and the motor system work together.

When you think you have a good sense of your child's strengths and weaknesses you may want to jot them down. As you work with your child in floor time you can refer to your notations to remind you where you're going as well as what tools you can use to get there.

EVALUATING YOUR CHILD'S CAPACITY
TO REGULATE ROUTINE SENSATIONS

1. Sensitivity to sound. Most children can tolerate a wide variety of sounds, from high-pitched whines to low, throaty roars, from the motorized sounds of vacuum cleaners to the piercing sounds of whistles, from sudden loud explosions to quiet whispers. But many children with special needs are over- or undersensitive to sound. If your child has a strong averse reaction to loud or high-pitched noises, you're probably already aware of it. However, you are less likely to be aware of a moderate aversion or undersensitivity to sound.

When you talk to your child in a very soft voice, how does he respond? Does he seem to like that voice? What happens when you increase your volume to normal speaking level? Does his response change? What happens when you raise your voice to a loud, but not shouting (you don't want to frighten him unnecessarily), level? If he responds positively to the soft voice but shies away from the two louder voices, your child may be oversensitive to sound. Conversely, if he ignores the two softer voices but perks up at the louder one, he may be underreactive; he may not even register the softer sounds. Try this experiment again with other types of sounds, using whistles, musical instruments, or pots and pans, for example. Also try changing the speed and pitch of your speech.

Next, experiment with music. Play classical, rock, and other types of music and see what your child prefers. Try each type of music at low, middle, and high volumes. Does your child like soft, melodic tunes or louder, driving beats? Does he like songs with words or instrumentals? Does he like fast or slow rhythms? Complex or simple rhythms? New sounds or repetitive ones? Observe his reaction to environmental sounds. How does he respond to sirens, alarms, school bells? How does he react when you turn the vacuum cleaner on? When you start up an electric mixer? When you clang pots and pans? Does he enjoy certain vibrating sounds or ask to sit on the washing machine or dryer?

As you observe, remember that sounds do not occur in isolation and may have a cumulative effect. What is comfortable for a minute may be irritating if prolonged. The noise of a busy classroom, for instance, may make a child more sensitive to other sounds.

After you've cataloged the types of sounds that elicit favorable responses from your child, use these sounds in your play. If your child is undersensitive, use vibrant sounds to draw her out. Talk animatedly, varying the cadence of your voice. You could use drums, horns, and noisy windup toys. *You* may not appreciate the sound level, but it may please your child and help you get her attention.

2. Sensitivity to touch. Some children dislike being touched; they may dislike especially a light, feathery touch. The feel of a gentle touch, even from a loving parent, makes them anxious. The feel of certain fabrics makes them want to crawl right out of their clothes—they'd remain undressed if they could. The feel of water on their hands makes them cry out as if in pain. Other children crave the sense of touch. They need to be held and stroked. They are constantly leaning on or rubbing against things. They refuse to wear anything but long-sleeved shirts and pants. They feel lost without the sensation of touch and pressure on their bodies.

You probably already know how your child reacts to touch, but you may be unaware of certain subtleties that can help you interact. For instance, few children who are overreactive are sensitive to *all* types of touch. Most can tolerate, or even enjoy, certain tactile sensations. Many children sensitive to light touches enjoy firm pressure, such as that of a gentle bear hug. Learning what sensations your child enjoys can make the difference in your ability to develop a warm physical relationship with her.

Few children who are underreactive crave all types of touch equally. Most have strong preferences for certain types. Again, knowing those preferences can enable you to use touch to get your child to pay attention to you. A number of systematic experiments can help you determine exactly what types of touches your child likes and where and how she likes touch delivered.

First, think about how your child responds to being cuddled and stroked; to taking a bath and having his hair brushed; to having his clothes changed. Does he seem to take pleasure in touching? Does he use touch and holding to achieve closeness? To help himself relax? To explore the world? Think about how he explores the world. Does he like to touch things with his hands? Some children prefer to use their feet.

Experiment with different types of touch and with different parts of the body. Even children who are overreactive to touch can tolerate certain types of touch on certain areas. Try light touch (by running your fingertips over your child's body); then try medium touch; then try applying firm pressure.

See how your child responds to touch on his arms and legs, on his feet and hands, on his back, on his chest and stomach.

Next, experiment with rhythms. Some children like deep, steady massage; others prefer short, staccato movements; some prefer heavy pressure with no movement at all. Make it a game to try out as many different types of touching as you can, and then record the ones your child likes best. Through therapy you can help him broaden his tolerance for the others.

It's frustrating when your child dislikes touch because as her parent, you naturally want to hug and cuddle with her. But instead of coming forward to your embrace, your child may need to stand behind a protective barrier, such as a couch or table, to watch and listen to you. Or he may need to squeeze into a tight space between the couch and wall to glean the sensory information that tells him where his body is in space, and from there he can attend to your looks and words more comfortably.

If your child is overreactive to touch, don't despair. Reach out with your voice. Use your voice to tell your child how much you love her, to cajole her into playing with you, to woo her into a close relationship. Use your eyes also—looks can speak volumes. Use eye contact instead of light touch to tell your child of your warm feelings. Use facial gestures and body language to communicate, too. By pointing, opening your eyes wide, crouching over something interesting, you can encourage your child without touch. Join your child in a protected area to convey your understanding of his needs as well as your desire for closeness. As your child becomes intimate with you, gradually incorporate more touch into your play, using firm pressure and letting your child control the action. Many children tolerate touch better when they are in charge.

3. Sensitivity to visual stimuli. Most children are receptive to a wide variety of visual stimuli. They can tolerate bright lights and soft lights, bold colors and pastels, moving images and still ones, busy pictures and quiet ones. Children with special needs, however, are often oversensitive or undersensitive to visual input. A flickering TV can be so discomforting to an oversensitive child that she might need to hide, yet an undersensitive child might not notice it at all. The glare of kitchen lights might make an overreactive child agitated and frenetic, yet the same lights might help an underreactive child tune in to his mother's conversation. An unusual-looking, brightly colored toy may frighten one child, yet excite another.

To determine your child's visual sensitivity, expose him to a variety of sights and observe his response to each. Start by comparing how he reacts in a brightly lit room with how he reacts in a room with subdued lighting. A child who is overreactive to visual stimuli is often uncomfortable in a brightly lit room. He may become agitated, seem hyper, or appear distracted as he seeks a way to overcome his discomfort. An underreactive child may be positively stimulated by the bright light. She may become more alert and better able to pay attention to you.

Observe your child's reaction to different colors and moving images. When you are dancing with him, does he enjoy watching you or does he avert his eyes? If he's oversensitive, your movements may make him uncomfortable; if he's undersensitive, the movement may be pleasantly stimulating.

Does your child avoid eye contact? If so, stand in front of her and push her in a swing. Or, play a game on the floor of roughhousing and tickling while looking her in the eye. Movement may make eye contact easier because movement helps a child feel more organized (freeing her to look). The swing or the floor provides compression against her body, eliminating her need to work to support her body. As a result, she is free to look at you and interact.

Your child may not show an extreme reaction to any of these visual stimuli; he may be neither over- nor underreactive to visual input. If this is the case, you may be able to use visual information (gestures, pictures, photographs) to help him compensate for other, weaker senses. Visual information can help get communication going when auditory processing is delayed.

4. Sensitivity to movement. Some children simply need to be in motion, often because they are underreactive to movement and as a result crave certain motions. To satisfy that craving they're forever running, jumping, fidgeting, or swinging from one piece of furniture to the next. Some children are daring and seek novelty, while others repeat the same motions again and again.

Other children are overreactive to motion. The gentlest movement— being picked up out of a crib, being rocked too fast or without the support of their mother's arms—startles them, makes them feel insecure, makes them cry or whimper in discomfort. These children sometimes have low muscle tone. With little sense of their own bodies, they may be loath to move and prefer the safety of sitting or lying almost still. They compensate for their sensitivity to movement by avoiding it.

To gauge how your child responds to movement think about her movement patterns. Does she tend to initiate movement? Does she sit still and wait for you? Do you think of her as an active child or is she quiet and sedentary? When she goes to the playground does she make a beeline for the merry-go-round and swings or does she sit and play quietly in the sand? Does she like to be held and carried? Is she happier lying on the floor?

Think about what types of movement your child enjoys. Does he prefer the circular movement of a carousel ride, the straight-ahead motion of a walk in the stroller, the up-and-down movement of a pogo stick or baby bouncer, or the back-and-forth motion of a swing?

Most children who are underreactive love swinging for long periods, beyond the point at which you would expect them to feel dizzy or to have had enough. Notice how long your child enjoys swinging. Also notice what type of swinging your child likes best: fast or slow, high or low, or round and round. The more you can tune in to your child's preferences, the better you can use them to help her. Swinging may start out as an end in itself, but it can become a means of helping your child feel more organized; it can enable her to play in more complex ways. Swinging can help her process sensory information through eye contact, songs, and communication about her desires ("Go fast!" "Go slow!" "Higher!" "Stop!"). The vestibular input can improve her muscle tone, balance, attention, and emotional responsiveness.

Watch your child as he moves. Does he seem sure of his body in space? Able to go easily from couch to chair? From sitting to standing? Or does he waver, seem nervous, as if he's not sure his body will make it?

Pinpointing your child's sensitivity to movement will help you use it to his advantage. If your child craves movement, don't fight it; join it. Let him hop and run, swing and jump, while you supply "Ready, set, go!" or "Stop." Meet your child at his destination or hold hands and jump together to a song. The motion will help him become organized and thus help him pay attention, by providing feedback about where his body is in space.

Meeting your child's movement needs will free up his energy for other tasks. (Most schools, unfortunately, try to force movement-hungry children to sit still, rather than allowing the movement that would help them organize and get ready to learn. Some children use so much energy trying to sit that they have little left for attending and learning. If allowed to move around, many children would learn more and be less disruptive in class.) Modulating exercises—running at a fast, medium, then slow pace or tapping hands at a fast, medium, then slow rate—and doing things in slow motion can teach a child to regulate movement and eventually to exercise greater control. The key is not to inhibit movement, but to regulate it.

If your child dislikes movement—if she startles, loses her balance, or seems confused as to what movement to make next—focus on activities that involve being still, perhaps using only hands, such as doing a puzzle or building with blocks. Gradually, incorporate gentle motions into your play. For instance, introduce a seesaw or rocking motion while singing. If you start with almost imperceptible movements and tie them to a favorite activity, you may slowly build your child's tolerance for interactive motion.

5 and 6. Sensitivities to smell and taste. Sensitivities to smell and taste often go hand in hand because the physiology of these two senses is so entwined. Smell can affect the way a child responds to people and places, and smell and taste together determine a great deal about how a child responds to food.

It is easy to check for overreactivity to smells. Catalog any strong odors in your house—perfumes, shaving lotions, household cleansers, and other chemicals. Then note whether your child reacts negatively when those odors are present—withdrawing or becoming hyperexcitable or irritable. Be sure that your child is not reacting to breathing the fumes into his body as opposed to merely smelling them.

Undersensitivity is harder to recognize. It is most noticeable in relation to food, so try serving foods with different tastes and odors to see how your child responds. Some children who are underreactive to tastes or smells may prefer certain foods.

Even though you live with your child every day, it's not always easy to figure out your child's sensitivities. Occupational and physical therapists trained in sensory integration can assist in making these observations and planning appropriate interventions.

Understanding your child's sensory reactivity can help you decode some of her behavior, as behavior is often an attempt to cope or adapt to difficulties. A child who is sensitive to loud noise, for example, may run to the far side of the room, shut down, or become confused if someone comes in and greets her loudly. She's not being antisocial; she's merely responding the only way she can to an uncomfortable physical sensation. A child who is underreactive to sound may appear tuned out or willful if quietly asked a question. It's not that he doesn't want to answer; it's that his sensory system didn't process the invitation—he literally doesn't know he's been asked. A child who craves jumping or being squeezed is seeking input to locate his body in space.

Once you know your child's sensory profile, you can use that knowledge to improve all your interactions. Children pay attention better, communicate better, learn better, and are happier when their sensory needs are being met. If you know your child craves touch, particularly oral stimulation, don't expect him to keep his fingers out of his mouth. Letting him suck on them (or on an alternative such as a rubber-tube necklace or chewing gum) will improve his ability to attend and relate. If you know your child is sensitive to touch, don't force her to put her clothes back on each time she takes them off. The feel of the fabric against her skin is enough to thwart any effort at positive interaction. Instead, search for fabrics she can tolerate and begin a program to desensitize her to various kinds of touch. Your efforts to accommodate your child's sensory needs and help her master her challenge will make a difference in her ability to enjoy your company and learn.

EVALUATING YOUR CHILD'S PROCESSING OF SENSATIONS

Careful observations of your child will provide the clues you need to understand how he takes in and processes information through his senses. You will see how he learns and what information he cannot interpret or act on. You may wish to discuss these observations with professionals who can help you plan a program to support and improve your child's processing.

Auditory Processing

Auditory processing refers to the ability to interpret auditory information.

David could hear the full human spectrum of sound. He listened avidly to musical tapes his mother had given him, and he loved to play toy instruments. When words were embedded in music and always the same, as in songs, he came to recognize the patterns. He enjoyed the familiarity, the more so since he could not comprehend the numerous spoken sounds he heard all day long. His parents could comfort him with nursery rhymes and songs, but he never seemed responsive to human speech. For a long time his parents thought he was merely independent. They admired his ability to do many things on his own. But when David was slow to learn to talk, they became concerned. After numerous evaluations, they learned that David had difficulty processing auditory information. His hearing was fine; he just couldn't make sense of the information he was taking in. He heard his parents' sounds, but he couldn't sequence those sounds into words and imbue them with meaning. It was not surprising that he could not express himself either.

To observe a baby's ability to do auditory processing, sing simple patterns, such as dum, dum, DUM ... dum, dum, DUM ... dum, dum, DUM. After you've sung the pattern several times, does she seem to anticipate the last DUM? If you stop short of that DUM, does she look at you differently?

See what happens when you vary the pattern. Begin the original pattern, but instead of emphasizing the third dum, which your child now expects, throw in a third unemphasized dum and put the emphasis on the fourth beat. Does she react in any way to this change, indicating that she is recognizing a complex auditory pattern?

If your child reacts to the changes in your patterns she is processing them well. Now try a slightly more complex pattern by adding a few more syllables: dum, dum, de-DUM, dum ... dum, dum, de-DUM, dum ... Does she still react to changes? Does she seem as interested in this pattern as in the simpler one? Children who have trouble processing auditory information will tune out when the pattern gets too complex. You could also use a xylophone or piano to see whether your child imitates or completes a pattern. The different pitch and tone, as well as visual cues, may help her process the sounds more easily.

You can gauge a young child's ability to process auditory information by thinking about how he responds to sounds in daily life. Does he understand most of what you say to him, or does he respond only to familiar, often-repeated phrases that are related to his desires, phrases such as "Let's go outside," "Snack time," "Bath time," or "Time to watch TV"? Does he often need visual cues to get your meaning? For instance, when you ask him if he wants juice, does he know from the word what you mean, or does he have to see the juice? Can he follow oral directions, or do words alone fail to produce the action you want? Can he follow commands that contain two ideas in them—"Get your hat and bring it here"—or is one idea his limit? Since we often accompany what we say with gestures, actions, and affective cues, you may not readily notice that your child is not responding to the words.

Observe how responsive your child is to changes in your tone of voice. If you escalate your voice on a scale of one to ten in order to warn her off something, does she respond differently to the level 5 voice than to the level 10 voice? Or does she seem oblivious to the gradations? Does she stay away when your voice is angry and approach when you are enticing and playful?

If your child is a little older (age three or four), is she able to understand abstract questions, such as "What do you want to do?" "Where do you want to go?" "When should we do that?" "Why do you want to go outside?"

Cognitive and Emotional Processing

Cognitive and emotional processing are really more sophisticated forms of sensory processing in that they are based on information received through the senses and taken to a more abstract level. You can assume that visual and auditory processing problems will create problems in these two areas. Later, as you work to strengthen your child's visual- and auditory-processing skills, you will also be strengthening his ability to process cognitive and emotional information. Watch how your child processes emotional cues. Can he read your facial expressions? Can he pick up the cues in your voice? Does he know when you are expressing anger, sadness, or joy? Observe how he solves cognitive problems. Can he find hidden objects? Can he solve problems when his block building falls down or when a toy breaks? Can he substitute objects when pretending or use a gesture to represent an object he needs for his idea? Is he beginning to understand concepts of quantity (more or less), numbers, and time? Is he becoming more abstract in answering why questions, giving two or three answers instead of just one?

Visual and Spatial Processing

Visual processing refers to the ability to discriminate and decode visual information. Observe your child as she faces challenges that require her to use visual information. Notice whether she's interested in how things go together. If she takes a toy apart can she put it back together? When it's time to put the toys away, does she know which things belong in which baskets and which baskets go on which shelves? Can she find the room you are in when in a new house?

Look for clues to how she responds to visual information in her actions, such as inserting a triangle form into a shape sorter, selecting a picture of the object she wants, or understanding where she will be going next when shown a picture of the place or person she is going to see.

Be aware of problems with motor actions that may interfere with success. A child with visual-processing difficulties may have trouble scanning all the pieces of a puzzle to see which she needs, may not use visual-spatial cues to match one piece of the puzzle to another, or may have difficulty remembering what the object looked like when whole. A child with motor difficulties, in contrast, may process the visual information well but be unable to coordinate his movements to push the pieces together, insert one into another, or build.

Using shape-sorter toys requires both visual and motor processing; so does solving a jigsaw puzzle. Be sure to observe your child with a new puzzle, because some children memorize familiar puzzles and put them together by rote. Some children decipher a puzzle's design or use flexible trial-and-error strategies to put a puzzle together. Also, observe his use of blocks or Legos to create complex structures, such as a house with several rooms or a farm with pathways, corrals, and buildings. His ability to conceptualize and create from scratch may differ from his ability to imitate what someone else has built.

The use of visual information affects how your child navigates in the world. Does she have a good sense of direction? Does she intuitively know which direction is home and which is a friend's house? Some children are attentive to these visual details and become anxious if you drive a different route home or change the location of a favorite toy. They depend on keeping things the same to feel secure and know what is going on by what they see. Some children rely on visual processing because their auditory processing is inconsistent or compromised. If their visual-spatial processing is also compromised they are more likely to become rigid and repetitive.

Visual processing includes object constancy, being able to remember an object even when it is out of sight. If you hide an object in your hand, can your child find it? Try him at a version of three-card monte in which you hide a small object beneath one of three napkins. If you move it from napkin to napkin, can he find it or does he quickly become confused? Does he seem to forget what was there?

Think about how your child responds to the visual information in her environment. Does she seem to pick up on visual cues or do they seem to pass her by? Does she prefer to play with the same objects again and again, or does she explore new toys eagerly? Does she notice when things are out of place but not get upset because she can create a picture of where they are in their new place? In other words, does she see the big picture?

EVALUATING YOUR CHILD'S MOTOR SYSTEM

Muscle Tone

If your child has a severe problem with muscle tone, such as very low muscle tone, you are most likely well aware of it and have already sought a medical and physiological evaluation. But you may not be aware of subtle muscle-tone problems.

What happens when your child embraces you? Does his body feel firm, yet relaxed? Is he floppy? Tight and stiff? When he sits in your lap and you move his arms and legs, do they move easily with just the slightest sense of resistance? Do they move too easily, as if they were made of jelly? Or do they move too stiffly, as if the muscles don't want to follow your motion? Looseness may be an indication of low muscle tone; stiffness may indicate high tone.

If you stand facing your child, holding her hands, can she imitate you in a series of knee bends? Can she raise and lower her body using the muscles in her legs? Can she support her weight in a crouched position? Does she seem fluid and relaxed during this game, or is she unsteady and unsure of herself? Often a child's ability to push herself up by her legs is a good indicator of her overall muscle tone. If your child lies on the floor a lot while playing, for example, pushing cars or trains, she may be seeking the support of the ground to use her arms and to keep her head erect. Some children have difficulty keeping their heads up and lean on an arm while they play. If your child can't keep his arm in the air long enough to point to an object, he may have low muscle tone. When he points to what he wants, can he point precisely? How well can he control the muscles in his arms?

Fine-Motor Abilities

Good muscle tone is also needed for fine-motor skills. If your child is at least 18 months old, see if he can fist a crayon or pencil to make it make marks. If he's two, can he use the crayon both to scribble and to make a single stroke? If he's two and a half, can he use it to draw a straight line? By two and a half he should also be able to turn a knob, remove a cap, and make a tower of eight or more blocks. At age three or four he is expected to be able to hold a crayon or pencil with three fingers and to copy circles, Xs, and squares.

Motor Planning

In addition to certain fine and gross motor abilities, perceptual and cognitive processes are necessary for goal-directed behaviors as well. Doing something involves first having an idea, then planning the sequence of steps required to implement it, and finally executing the plan. The ability to plan the movements needed to fulfill a goal is crucial for learning.

To evaluate your child's ability to sequence her movements, observe her. Can she put together two or three movements in a row to accomplish a task? If she wants a toy that is several feet away will she walk or crawl toward it, reach out for it, and pick it up? Will she carry out some action with it or just drop it? Can she bat at a balloon and touch it? Can she walk up and down stairs or do you have to tell her where to put each leg? If she's over two, can she catch a large ball using her arms and hands? Can she imitate the gestures to nursery rhymes such as patty-cake and "Teensy Weensy Spider"? Can she follow a series of actions in a preschool movement class? Can she copy a series of shapes—figure out in which direction to move the pencil and then change directions at the right point?

Children who tend to wander aimlessly even in a room full of toys may not know how to plan the actions needed to select and explore the toys. Sometimes a child picks up a toy and then drops it on the floor, because he cannot sequence the two or more steps needed to use the toy or put it back on the shelf. A child with motor-planning difficulties may nonetheless be able to undo what you do, because undoing is an easier problem to solve. Can your child dump the toys out of a basket that you have just filled? Can he take the rubber band off two toys that you have just banded together? A child with less severe motor-planning difficulties is able to carry out single cause-and-effect actions, such as pushing a button to make a toy pop up or striking a key on a toy piano.

If you notice you are taking your child's hand to help him perform an action you are probably compensating for his motor-planning difficulties.

With practice he may learn to do things by himself. Sometimes it is initiating the action that is difficult, and the child can sequence subsequent actions himself. Hand your child an object to see whether he takes it and uses it.

Pretend play also requires motor-planning ability. If your child merely pushes a car or train back and forth without having it go anywhere, it may be that she cannot sequence the next action. She may not be able to use a doll to drive the car, because doing so is a two-step process (it also requires a higher level of abstract thinking).

More complex pretend play requires even greater motor-planning ability. Can your child set up a tea party, serve you, and put away the dishes? Can he drive his car to the pretend swimming pool, go swimming, dry off, and go home? Expressing these ideas requires longer sequences of actions. The idea drives the actions. Some children who have the ideas may be clumsy executing the actions and may prefer talking about the ideas; others may prefer to watch passively, not attempting to carry out the actions. A child with motor-planning difficulties may avoid activities that require motor planning. For example, some children may favor reading because the only action required is turning pages. Practicing actions can help children master them, but some children must learn each action sequence separately, as learning one set of actions does not automatically make similar actions easier.

Motor-planning capacities progress from aimless motions and single repetitive actions (often seen in children who have difficulties with motor planning) to problem-solving motor actions involving two or three sequences. Longer problem-solving sequences, such as taking a chair to climb on to get a toy down from a shelf, lead to complex imitations and pretend play and to more complex problem solving that involves spatial relations as well, such as using blocks to build a six-room house. Motor planning is also related to more general sequencing abilities.

OTHER IMPORTANT ABILITIES

The ability to sequence social behavior, such as taking turns, playing cooperatively, negotiating the activities of a playground, or, as an adult, working the party, also relates to our fundamental capacity to create sequences. Even our ability to put words into sentences and sentences into coherent paragraphs to build a logical sequence of ideas relates to this core capacity for sequencing our actions, behaviors, and thoughts. We discuss this critical ability further in later chapters.

Another important processing capacity involves connecting our desires, emotions, and intentions to our other processing capacities in order to give them purpose, direction, and meaning. Chapter 7 is devoted to this important capacity.

CONSULTING SPECIALISTS

You can begin to answer all the questions presented here through your own observations, but you may wish to discuss them with your child's therapists and specialists. As part of this evaluation your child should have a complete diagnostic work-up if one has not already been done. Professional evaluations may include a pediatric evaluation to rule out physical illness and investigation of any suspected metabolic or genetic disorders. A pediatric neurologist should examine your child for suspected neurological disorders. For problems with language, a speech therapist should be consulted, and for questions about motor or sensory functioning, a physical or occupational therapist should be seen. For questions about your child's cognitive abilities, you may want to consult a psychologist or special educator; for questions about emotional or psychological concerns, a child psychiatrist or child psychologist. Mental health professionals, such as psychiatrists, psychologists, and social workers, can help address the stresses on parents and between spouses that are common in families of children with special needs. Some evaluations involve a team assessment; the team then meets with you to discuss its findings as a group. Understanding the nature of your child's biological challenges puts you in a better position to evaluate the treatment your child is receiving and to support his therapists by following up with your child in day-to-day life.

4

The Six Milestones

In the last chapter we talked about how identifying your child's biological challenges can help you draw her into interactions. In this chapter we describe the six types of emotional interactions that constitute six early phases of development. Appropriate emotional experiences during each of these phases help develop critical cognitive, social, emotional, language, and motor skills, as well as a sense of self.

In the earliest days of a child's life, she knows herself primarily through her response to her physical world: gas, bubbles, movements, sights and sounds, textures, and other sensations. Soon she responds particularly to her parents, their voices, smiles, and special smells. Patterns of movement create states of shared joy. By 4 to 8 months she begins to take a rattle and may even give it back, or throw it back in frustration. She smiles and makes sounds, expecting to get a smile, a frown, or a sound in return. For the first time, she knows herself in part as distinct from others, as a person of volition, as someone who can initiate an action and have an impact on the world. As the year progresses, emotional gestures grow in complexity. By 12 to 16 months she doesn't merely reach when Daddy offers a toy, but she can take Daddy to the shelf to get the toy she really wants. She knows herself as someone who can string together a series of actions to communicate her intentions to another person. Months pass, and her actions grow more complex again. By 18 to 20 months she feeds her dolls instead of merely cuddling them and explains her actions, saying, "Dolly eat." Now she knows herself in terms of ideas. She can picture herself and others in her mind. She can generate ideas and tell the world about them with her words. More months pass, and she grows more complex again. By 36 months she can tell you, "Let's ride bikes!" Pausing at the door to see whether it's cold out, she might then say, "Better put our coats on first." Now she is a logical, cohesive, thinking person.

Through all these stages the child's emotional, social, and cognitive skills grow and her sense of self grows increasingly complex. This sense of self will continue to expand as the child grows older and as new experiences stir her interests and capabilities in new directions. But her *functional* sense of self, that core emotional sense that forms the foundation for further learning, is in place. It was nurtured through millions of daily interactions, primarily with her parents, as every glance, every smile, every tickle, every question built her sense of who she was. Thanks to these interactions, she can layer on additional cognitive, intellectual, and social skills to serve her throughout her life. She is prepared for the further challenges of her own development, and for the world.

These six basic steps form a developmental ladder; each layers new abilities onto those of the prior stage. We call these steps the six milestones because each one marks a major turning point in the life of a child.

Children who receive warm nurturing and do not have developmental challenges often master these milestones automatically by the age of four or five. But children with challenges need help from parents and therapists and often take longer to achieve mastery. Instead of reaching out to be picked up at 8 or 9 months, a child with motor challenges may do so at 14 or 15 months. Instead of imitating his mother's vocal tone and babbling reciprocally at 10 months, a baby with auditory-processing challenges may do so at 17 or 18 months. Instead of linking abstract ideas at the age of 3, a child with multiple challenges may do so at age 5, 6, or 7. That's fine. When your child is 45, it may not matter whether he learned to babble reciprocally at 8 or at 17 months or learned to write at age 6 or at age 10. It matters less at what age a particular skill is learned than how well it is learned and whether progress continues. As these basic skills are learned early in life, extra time is usually available to master them. These basic capacities are vital because they are the foundation for all future learning and development in your child's life. They are like the foundation of an 80-story building: to hold the building up, they must be very solid.

In the following sections we outline each milestone and describe how parents have helped their children work around challenges to climb the developmental ladder. In Part 2 of this book, we explain how you can help your child master these milestones; as you do so, you will be helping your child develop his emotional, cognitive, motor, speech, and social skills.

MILESTONE 1: SELF-REGULATION AND INTEREST
IN THE WORLD

After nine months in darkness, a baby is born. Suddenly he is plunged into a world of light and sound, movement and touch, taste and smell. A sensory extravaganza! All this information is exciting and stimulating to the baby, but at the same time he has to learn not to be overwhelmed. His very first challenge is to take in this sensory panorama while regulating his response and remaining calm.

Gradually he finds things that focus his interests and at the same time can be used to calm himself—Mother's face, Father's voice, the soft texture of a blanket next to his skin. Little by little the infant learns to balance growing awareness of sensations with the ability to remain calm. This pair of skills is the most basic building block of emotional, social, and intellectual health. Without it we can't learn, we can't develop relationships with others, we can't survive in our highly stimulating world. How an infant modulates and processes sensations is an important contributor to this first milestone.

From his earliest days, Peter was an irritable baby. He slept little and cried constantly, and nothing seemed to console him. When his parents sang him songs or rocked him in his cradle, he flailed his arms and legs unhappily. When they picked him up and held him he arched his back and screamed. His parents were despondent. Their baby was miserable and hard to live with, and all their efforts to help him only made him worse. Gradually, feeling frustrated, exhausted, and saddened, they simply stopped trying so hard. They left Peter alone for longer and longer periods of time, and after a while he would cry himself to sleep. By six months of age, he was sleeping or looking self-absorbed much of the time. He had already failed to master the first emotional milestone. The next step, intimacy, would not be possible until he mastered this step.

Peter's parents sought help from their pediatrician. A thorough evaluation determined that Peter was hypersensitive to touch, sound, and movement. This information enabled his parents to make Peter's world a more comfortable place. They stopped rocking him so briskly and tickling him. Instead, they held him gently but tightly and substituted a very gentle rocking rhythm. They softened their voices and facial gestures when they talked to him and spoke very slowly. Soon Peter could look at them for several moments at a time. They used their soft voices to attract his attention and to keep him calm. With a little experimentation they found that lower tones were particularly soothing. They could then begin some simple movement-pattern exercises to enhance Peter's pleasure in moving. They placed Peter on the floor and slowly moved his arms and legs. They massaged his arms and legs with deep pressure. Gradually, his tolerance for movement and touch increased, and Peter allowed his parents to carry him. Bit by bit, with patient help from his parents, Peter found the world a more hospitable place. And bit by bit, he learned to calm himself down without going to sleep. By the time he was a year old, by working with and around Peter's individual sensitivities, his parents had helped him master this first emotional milestone.

Unlike Peter, Angie appeared to be a lazy baby. No matter how much her parents talked to her or smiled at her, she seemed uninterested. She rarely made eye contact, didn't brighten when they looked at her, and didn't turn toward them when they approached. She was equally uninterested in their gestures. When they picked her up or tickled her, she flopped in their arms. Since her parents couldn't grasp her attention and she seemed happy, or at least quiet, on her own, they began to leave her alone for longer and longer periods. Angie had no trouble calming herself down. Her problem was the reverse: she had no interest in the world. Nothing drew her out of her own quiet shell. She, too, had failed to master the first emotional milestone.

Angie's grandparents recognized that something was wrong and convinced her parents to seek treatment. An assessment revealed that Angie was underreactive to sensations, especially to sound, touch, and movement. In consultation with a therapist, Angie's parents found other ways to attract their daughter's attention. She turned out to be responsive to visual stimuli, so her parents grabbed her attention by using animated expressions. They also raised their voices and used brisk movements. Angie liked their silly faces and soon began laughing when they talked to her using higher-pitched voices. She also responded to brightly colored objects and pictures held in front of her, and as her parents waved objects back and forth, Angie would break into a smile. They found that she liked being moved quickly in the air and swung briskly in their secure arms. She would kick her feet and tense her muscles, counteracting her normally weak muscle control. Gradually, by using visual stimuli and vigorous movement, and lots of finger and toe games to compensate for her underreactivity, Angie's parents were able to get her to show an interest in the world.

They also began experimenting with noises. They tried quick and slow rhythms to see what would cause Angie to react. They found that very energetic vocal tones in the middle range helped her tune back in to auditory information. Processing sound continued to be challenging, but by the time Angie was six months old, she seemed to find the world a delightful, stimulating place. With patient help from her parents, she had mastered the first emotional milestone and was ready to master the following ones.

MILESTONE 2: INTIMACY

Along with interest in the world comes a special love for the world of human relationships. But not just any relationships! The infant wants her primary caregivers or parents. She has singled them out as the most important aspect of her world, and she lets them know they're special. When they enter her field of vision she brightens, she looks them in the eye, she smiles. And in those moments of shared smiles and joy, parents and baby continue to fall in love. Together they discover and deepen their intimacy.

The ability to be intimate forms the basis of all future relationships. It teaches a baby that warmth and love are possible, that relationships with people can be joyful. A child who has learned this with her parents has built a foundation for continuing to learn about loving relationships throughout her life.

Mastery of this milestone also cements motor, cognitive, and language skills. The infant learns to use her body to seek out the face and touch of the parent, whether through eye contact or snuggling. She learns to scan her world for familiar objects and faces and to pay attention to them for 30 seconds or more. She learns to recognize the sound and source of speech, especially the speech of her parents. All these skills provide a foundation for her later capacity to move, think, and talk.

From birth, Jenny was oversensitive to sound and touch. (Doctors later found out that she also had a severe auditory-processing problem.) A ringing phone, a barking dog, her brother's cry would set her off. Even her mother's soothing voice irritated her. When her parents picked her up, stroked her, or sang to her, hoping to calm her down, the combination of auditory and tactile stimulation would cause Jenny to become more confused or to lose control completely. Jenny's parents didn't know what to do. Their first child had been so easy; he'd cooed and laughed and smiled with little prodding from them. What was wrong with this baby? What was wrong with them? Feeling terribly rejected, they gradually began spending more time with their older child and less with "angry Jenny." They didn't mean to ignore their daughter; they just didn't know what else to do. More than anything they wanted her to look at them and smile, but that was the one thing she seemed incapable of doing. At seven months, well past the point when most babies fall in love with their parents, Jenny still wouldn't easily smile or be joyful.

Jenny's grandmother lived close by, a remarkably patient woman who was willing to spend long hours with the fussy baby. She would put Jenny in an infant seat, set her on a table, and play little "I see you" games in which she would come into Jenny's world from the left or right, from below, from behind a napkin. She showed Jenny toys or picture books while humming softly. She sometimes put the infant seat on the floor and rocked it gently with her foot as she sat on the couch and knitted. While doing so, she'd gaze down at Jenny with loving eyes and make happy, silly faces at her. Jenny responded to these gestures. She was calmed by the gentle motion of the infant seat; she liked her grandmother's silly faces and brightly colored pictures. Her grandmother intuitively used simple vocal rhythms, repeating simple sounds, such as "bababa," rather than the more complex sounds of songs. As time went by, Jenny began to look her grandmother in the eye for longer and longer periods, and soon she began to smile. By stimulating Jenny's stronger senses and avoiding her hypersensitive ones, her grandmother wooed Jenny into intimacy. She had instinctively found ways to work around Jenny's sensory difficulties to help her master the second emotional milestone. Watching Jenny respond encouraged her parents to persist in similar efforts, modeling their approach after that of Jenny's grandmother.

It is not only babies who have to learn intimacy. Many older children fail to master this skill because processing difficulties have made loving contact with their caregivers confusing, scary, or painful. Regardless of a child's age, patient work by caregivers can help woo a child into closeness.

At age two and a half, Jay seemed to love playing with trucks—as long as he could play alone and repetitively. He wasn't talking yet, and his parents were understandably worried. Whenever Jay's father tried to join him, Jay grabbed the trucks from his father's hand and defiantly turned his back. Jay's dad, understandably upset, reacted by forcing his way into the game. He'd build bridges and tunnels for Jay's trucks to negotiate, or he'd issue directions such as "Drive it here!" from the sidelines. Jay rebuffed his father's advances. The harder his father tried, the more Jay closed him out. Eventually Jay began avoiding his father altogether. At an initial evaluation, he was diagnosed as having pervasive developmental disorder.

Part of the evaluation included trying to figure out why Jay was so avoidant and defensive. Careful observation revealed that Jay was extremely sensitive to touch and had motor-planning difficulties and mild auditory-processing difficulties. He was trying desperately to remain organized and to keep himself from being overwhelmed by controlling and avoiding interactions. Various interventions were suggested to help Jay and his dad begin relating.

Rather than force an interaction, Jay's dad needed to make it safe for Jay to approach him. First, Jay's dad had to learn to watch quietly on the sidelines while Jay played with his trucks. He could make an enthusiastic comment or two and gesture with his own car, but he was not to issue directives or take over. He was to woo and entice. Jay's father learned that it was best to help Jay do what he wanted to do by anticipating what objects Jay would need and handing them to him. After a few weeks, Jay began facing his dad some of the time while he played. Then his dad used a truck to encourage interaction. He played with it himself, imitated Jay's movements, or made nonintrusive comments such as "Can my car go along with yours?" Jay looked over at him from time to time but continued to play mostly by himself. Slowly, however, Jay moved his car nearer his dad's or let his father's car follow his own. Then one day Jay sat near his father as he played. Toward the middle of the play session he leaned on his father for a few moments. Jay's father was thrilled, but instead of reaching out and touching Jay, which would have caused him to retreat, he merely smiled and said, "Hi." Over the next few weeks Jay continued to lean on his dad sometimes, and he occasionally showed his dad where to move his trucks. Then one day Jay suddenly took his own truck and banged it into his father's. An invitation! His father took his truck and banged it into Jay's. Jay laughed. Then his father did something unexpected. He rolled his truck toward Jay's, but at the last minute pulled it back. Jay laughed again. He liked that surprise. After a few months of playing this way many times each day, Jay tried to surprise his father; he rolled his truck and stopped it, hid it behind his back, then pulled it out. Several months later, Jay's father held a truck out to Jay and to his surprise, instead of taking the truck from his hand, Jay climbed into his lap to look at the truck. As they sat together examining the toy they experienced their first real moment of intimacy. By being patient (painfully so at times!) and by following Jay's lead, his father had made it safe for Jay to come to him. By working around the boy's reluctance, he had helped his son experience the second emotional milestone.

Jay had other challenges. He required speech therapy to help him with his language difficulties and occupational therapy to help him with his motor planning. Helping him become more regulated was a critical first step in mastering his developmental challenges and sensory-modulation challenges.

MILESTONE 3: TWO-WAY COMMUNICATION

When a baby falls in love with his parents, an interesting thing happens. He realizes he can have an impact on them. When he smiles at Mommy, she smiles back. When he reaches out to Daddy, Daddy reaches back. The baby expresses a feeling or an intention, and his caregiver responds. This is the beginning of communication; the baby and his grown-ups are having a dialogue.

We like to think of these dialogues as opening and closing circles of communication. When a child reaches out—with a look, for example—he opens the circle. When the parent responds—by looking back—he builds on the child's action. When the child in turn responds to the parent—by smiling, vocalizing, reaching, or even turning away—he is closing the circle. When the parent responds to the child's response—by holding out a toy, by saying, "Don't you want to play?", by echoing the child's vocalization—and the child responds with another gesture (a look, smile, or hand movement) they have opened and closed another circle.

Fairly quickly the baby extrapolates from this experience; not only can he cause Mommy and Daddy to react, but he can cause other reactions, too. He bangs a toy, and the toy makes a sound! He drops a block; it falls to the floor. He has an impact on the world, and for the first time the baby becomes a person of volition, someone who can actively choose to do things, knowing that his actions will cause a result. He is learning fundamental emotional, cognitive, and motor lessons.

Two-way communication is essential for all human interaction. It also allows children to learn about themselves and about the world. The older child hugs a teacher and the teacher hugs her back; she learns that she is appreciated. She pushes another child, and that child begins to cry; she learns that her actions can move someone to tears. Without these essential experiences in two-way communication, children can't form a basic sense of intentionality, which means they can't begin to form a true sense of who they are or see that the world is logical.

From his very difficult birth Scott seemed hard to engage. Many of his senses were underreactive, his muscle tone was low, and his motor development delayed. His left side was weaker than his right. At eight months of age his parents were told that he had cerebral palsy and would need physical and occupational therapy to learn to coordinate and build strength in his arms and legs. Even with therapy he showed little interest in the world and initiated few activities. When his mother smiled and cooed at him and tried to get him to smile back, he turned away, closed his eyes, or stared past her.

After working on gaining his interest and building intimacy (using the approaches described earlier), his mother began to help Scott master the third critical skill, two-way communication. It was no longer enough to get Scott to pay attention to Mom and Dad; he now needed to be challenged to respond to their gestures with gestures of his own.

Scott's parents began showing him the power of his gestures. Whenever Scott made the slightest noise or movement, his parents oohed and aahed, or responded in an exaggerated way. They were careful to build on motor gestures that Scott could do easily, such as looking or moving his tongue or head. Soon he caught on that his gesture produced a reaction in them. He had an impact on his world! Gradually Scott's parents turned these gestures into dialogues. Each time Scott moved his arms, however slightly or seemingly unintentionally, Daddy waved his arms; then Scott would move his arms again. He had closed a circle of communication.

As Scott came to appreciate his power to make things happen, he began to take initiative. He would knock a toy off his high chair. Plunk! Now his parents could use toys to lure him into further communication. They would get down on the floor with him, face to face, and hold a toy he was looking at to see if Scott would reach for it. Or they would put a toy he was touching just outside his reach and challenge him to slither toward it. When he succeeded, they congratulated him heartily: he had closed a circle of communication. In this way, by using Scott's natural interests and existing motor capacities, they restarted the developmental progression. They helped him begin to master the third functional emotional milestone. With their work at home, his physical and occupational therapists also reported more progress.

MILESTONE 4: COMPLEX COMMUNICATION

Once a child has mastered the basics of two-way communication, the number of circles she can open and close grows rapidly. And with their number, so grows their complexity. When earlier she responded to things with a single gesture, now she can link gestures into complicated responses. When she sees her mother after an absence, she can run to her, put up her arms, and squeal with delight, a series of gestures that were impossible at an earlier stage.

For the first time the child has a vocabulary for expressing her wishes. It is a vocabulary of gestures, not of words, but by linking them together she can communicate fairly complicated thoughts. For instance, when she is hungry, she no longer needs to wait for Daddy to offer food; she can take him by the hand, lead him to the refrigerator, and point to what she wants. When she is angry at her brother for stealing her toy, she can hit and kick and try to grab the toy instead of merely crying. She can also go look for it in his room and bring it back to her own play area. When she is happy with her parents, she can run over, flirt with them, and hug and kiss them, rather than simply smile. When she is disappointed, she can give them longing looks and then punish them with a period of unforgiving coldness.

Her growing gestural vocabulary offers her more complex ways to express herself, and along with this expressiveness she becomes creative. She no longer has to do things exactly the way her parents do; she can now add her own elements to a game of chase or mimic her mother's gesture while adding a flourish of her own. Her new gestural and communication skills provide a myriad of ways for her to express her individuality. The child's personality emerges. At the same time, her sense of self is becoming far more complex. She now understands that 20 or 30 behaviors—a *pattern* of behaviors—are involved in being close to, or angry at, someone. She has a wide range of feelings and a varied behavioral vocabulary with which to express them.

As she uses her growing gestural vocabulary to express her many feelings and intentions, and as she responds to the growing complexity of her parents' gestures, she and her parents engage in lengthy gestural conversations. Twenty, thirty, forty circles are closed, and each circle builds the child's sense of self. She understands that "I" is built of patterns of intentional behavior, not simply of isolated responses.

Meanwhile, the child begins to comprehend the patterns of others. She can figure out from her parents' gestures whether she is safe or in danger, approved of or disapproved of, accepted or rejected, respected or humiliated. Before she uses words to any degree, she and her parents hold dialogues on life's major themes. She forms character patterns, expectations of others, and a sense of self. Patterns of helplessness or assertiveness and expectations for love and respect or harm or insult also emerge.

These growing dialogues are the prelude to speech. Through her extensive experience with communication the child builds the foundation for speech. During this stage, the child may begin to imitate the sounds of her parents' words. Communication difficulties are often first revealed by a child's difficulty in mastering this stage, long before the more obvious lack of speech is evident. If between 12 and 20 months of age your child is not making complex gestures, such as taking your hand and leading you to the door in order to play outside or pulling you along to help her find a toy, a full evaluation is probably indicated. Often when a child is not using words, parents and professionals are caught up trying to decide whether to wait and see or to implement a full evaluation. Even if a child is not talking, if she shows complex problem solving, such as taking you to the door or toy corner often, you can wait and see. If she does not engage in such preverbal patterns, however, waiting is unwise.

The ability to express herself through complex gestural conversations builds a child's motor and motor-planning skills. To convey her wishes and intentions she must first organize her behavior into logical sequences and she must learn to read the sequenced behavior of others. As her ability to use and enjoy the world grows, so grows her ability to grasp the world cognitively. Now she knows that when Daddy is hiding behind the curtain, Daddy hasn't disappeared. Now she can pull the curtain aside and find him.

At three years old, Andrew was an aimless child. He would pick up a toy then drop it, go over to another, look at it, then run to the window and clamor to go outside. If his mother refused to let him go outside, he would dissolve in bitter, unconsolable tears. This kind of random, piecemeal activity characterized his behavior. But most disturbing to his parents was Andrew's seeming lack of sustained interest in them. He would come over to them for a fleeting hug, but wouldn't stay for more than a few seconds. In that time he would close two or three circles of communication—perhaps meeting his father's eye, or responding to his mother's gestures by putting his head in her lap to be stroked, or taking a proffered toy—but before they could do more Andrew would run off and resume his aimless wandering. Three minutes later he might return, but only for several seconds. Andrew's parents were also troubled because his vocabulary was limited and he seemed clumsy to them—poorly coordinated and physically insecure.

An evaluation revealed that Andrew had fragile X syndrome. He had auditory-processing difficulties that made it hard for him to interpret sounds. His parents' words were lost on him, and even their enthusiastic hurrays, their soothing murmurs, their sounds of warning were difficult for him to comprehend. He also had motor-planning problems, which made it hard for him to negotiate sequences. Not only did Andrew face challenges coordinating sequences of movement, but interpreting sequences of sound or movement was equally challenging for him. When his parents used a series of gestures accompanied by sounds he couldn't understand to tell him to come downstairs for dinner or to put away his toys, Andrew literally did not understand them. Their communication was confusing intrusion. He loved his parents and craved their affection, hence his advances to them. Yet no sooner did he advance, than they began making these confusing (and slightly overwhelming) sounds and gestures, and he felt the need to retreat.

After his evaluation, one of Andrew's therapists showed his parents how to work around his challenges to help him gradually extend the length of contact. The therapist instructed them to keep their gestures going, but not to overload Andrew. When he came over for a hug, they should smile warmly and hug him back. When he broke away, they should keep smiling and say, simply, "More hug," then offer another or go over to Andrew and gently use hands, sounds, and facial expressions to offer an embrace.

Andrew's parents practiced these instructions, and during the next few months Andrew began coming for a hug, running away, then coming quickly back. "More hug" had become a game, one that Andrew could control and clearly enjoyed. By giving his parents a cocky little smile he could get them to open their arms and say, "More hug"; then he would run into their arms.

The therapist then suggested extending the game. "Try to go from three circles of communication to ten. After Andrew hugs you, say, 'Leg hug,' and point to your leg. See if he will want to give your leg a hug. When he's comfortable with that, perhaps your arm will want a hug. See how long you can keep the communication going. Perhaps he will point to his leg for a hug, or smile and say, 'No!' Either way, circles are being opened and closed."

Over the next few months Andrew and his parents extended the "more hug" game to arms and legs, knees and feet. They were closing eight, nine, ten circles at a time. All the while, Andrew's parents were working to keep their vocalizations and gestures energetic and clear. Instead of saying, "Andrew, come downstairs for dinner, please," they said, "Andrew, let's eat!" Instead of saying, "Do you want cheese on your sandwich?" they pointed to the cheese and said, "Oh boy, look, cheese!" They also tried to keep the backup to their words—facial expressions and gestures—as animated as possible.

Andrew responded readily to his parents' new vocabulary. Over the next six months he initiated more contact with them, sat in their laps for quiet hugging games, and responded to their simple gestures with gestures of his own. He was routinely closing 10 or 12 circles in a row with a deeper engagement, more pleasure, and longer chains of gestures. He also began to imitate more of his parents' sounds, using more variety. Not only was Andrew moving toward complex gestural communication, but he was also developing the skills that would lead toward richer speech.

Lucy, at three, was a far more difficult child than was Andrew. Willful and energetic, she was hard for her parents to control. She, too, ran aimlessly from object to object, but instead of quietly examining things, she tore into them with a frenzy, often leaving a trail of broken items. Lacking speech, she made loud sounds as she ran, ignoring her parents' entreaties to come and cuddle. Lucy could engage in limited communication with her parents. She would take objects from their hand; she would point to things she wanted; she would pound the door or television set or refrigerator to indicate her desires. But once she had what she wanted she would be off again, a whirlwind of agitated movement.

Lucy was diagnosed as having attention deficit disorder and a language disorder. An occupational therapist who focused on Lucy's individual differences explained to Lucy's parents that their daughter's continual movement in part stemmed from an underreactivity to sensory input. Because her body craved stimulation, she was on a continual mission to find it. Running, touching, squeezing, and fondling were all ways of satisfying her body's need for tactile and proprioceptive stimulation. The therapist suggested that Lucy's parents build these kinds of sensations into their interactions by playing games that involved jumping, running, touching, wrestling, and moving in space. This approach would help Lucy experience appropriate levels of sensation.

The therapist also encouraged Lucy's parents to try to lengthen Lucy's contacts with them. "When she bangs on the door to go outside, don't just open the door," said the therapist, "pretend you don't understand so that she has to show you more of what she wants. Try to stretch the communication from three circles to ten."

So each time Lucy banged on the door to go outside, her parents played dumb. They looked at her as if to say, "Huh? What do you want?" She would bang the door again, and they would push on the door as if that was what she wanted. She would bang even harder. Still her parents feigned ignorance. Finally, Lucy would take their hands and place them on the doorknob. "Oh," her parents would say, "you want me to open the door?" Lucy would jump up and down, but still her parents would delay her, perhaps fiddling with the latch until once more Lucy would move their hands to the knob and try to turn them in the right direction.

At first these exercises were intensely frustrating for everyone. Lucy seemed ready to lose control, and her parents hated making her so uncomfortable. But they could see that the strategy was working; each time they did it Lucy closed eight or ten circles in a row. They began applying the strategy to other encounters. When Lucy wanted a particular toy or a particular cookie, they pretended not to understand, offering her the wrong one or pretending not to know how to open the box, until Lucy had closed seven, or eight, or nine circles in communicating her desire. Her parents were always warm and supportive and had a gleam in their eye while negotiating with her. And they made their communications very animated. They communicated their love for Lucy while pushing her to work a little harder.

Several months later, Lucy was routinely communicating with her parents in these lengthier conversations. At the same time, her parents were continually chatting with her about the activity at hand. "You want a cookie? Okay. Oh, not that cookie? Which cookie? Oh, the chocolate chip cookie . . ." Occasionally Lucy imitated the sounds she heard her parents making. "Ooh-ooh," she might say, replicating the sound of "cookie." By giving Lucy so much interreactive emotional experience with communication, her parents were laying the groundwork for speech. Their persistence in stretching the circles of communication was helping her master the fourth milestone and also become more focused and attentive.

MILESTONE 5: EMOTIONAL IDEAS

The child's ability to form ideas develops first in play. The child uses toys to weave stories, and through these stories he experiments with the range of intentions and wishes that he feels. Baby dolls are fed by Mommy dolls.

People inside a house are threatened by giant bears. Cars crash into other cars.

Along with this idea-laden play comes expanded use of words. At first the child merely labels the important elements of his world—the people on whom he depends, his favorite foods and toys—or commands imperiously, "That!" to indicate a desired object. In time, he adds dialogues to his play. Later, with help from his parents, he puts names to his range of intentions, wishes, and feelings.

Through idea-laden play and expanding use of words the child is learning that symbols stand for things. The empty box in which he bathes his doll is a symbol for a bathtub. The word *bath* is a symbol for his activity in the tub. The word *mad* is a symbol for that bursting feeling he has inside. Each symbol is an idea, an abstraction of the concrete thing, activity, or emotion with which the child is concerned. As he experiments more and more with pretend play and words, he becomes increasingly fluent in the world of ideas.

Eventually he is able to manipulate ideas, to use them in ways that meet his needs. For instance, he can see, hear, and feel Mommy when Mommy isn't there. Now when he wakes at night, instead of simply crying, he can call for her. Sometimes just picturing and thinking about his mother is enough to comfort him. When he is thirsty, he can think about juice and say, "Mommy, juice," instead of hoping she will know what he wants. With this new ability to manipulate a world of symbols, he has made the leap to a much higher level of communication and awareness.

Ryan had had numerous medical problems and surgeries as an infant, and although he was healthy at age two and a half, he had difficult, disruptive behaviors. He never slept for more than three hours at a time; he rejected most food and was significantly underweight; and he was active and irritable.

The preliminary evaluation showed that Ryan had mastered the earliest milestone. He evinced an eager interest in the toys in the office and was able to keep himself calm. But his skills at intimacy and two-way communication were intermittent. He often tuned his parents out, refusing to interact and ignoring their words and gestures, but when motivated, he could string numerous gestures together to express his wishes. For instance, he pointed avidly at a dollhouse on a shelf until it was placed on the floor and then he methodically opened and closed all its doors and windows; but he showed little inclination to use the house to play out any ideas. When offered some dolls, he mechanically put them inside, but he didn't create a story. His use of words was limited also. He used some single words, such as *door,* but didn't use words to interact with others, other than occasionally to say "no" or "out." It seemed that Ryan had not fully mastered the earlier milestones, and hence his ability to tackle milestone 5 was impaired.

Observations of Ryan at play brought to light something else about him: his range of emotions appeared constricted. When things went wrong, he didn't get angry; when they went smoothly, he didn't smile. He was interested in the toys in the office but exhibited little curiosity. And when his parents tried to hug or encourage him, he showed no evidence of warmth or pleasure. His mother had described him as "always negative," and it was easy to see how this sullen little boy could seem so.

As part of the evaluation an occupational therapist discovered that Ryan was tactilely oversensitive in and around the mouth, which accounted for some of his pickiness about food. He was also posturally insecure, that is, not comfortable with how his body felt as it moved through space. A foot's moving off the ground made him feel uncertain and unbalanced.

Observations of Ryan and his parents playing together revealed that Ryan's sensory difficulties were only partly responsible for his problems. The way his parents played with him contributed also. In their efforts to engage Ryan, his parents were a little too quick to offer ideas; as a result, they hampered Ryan's ability to develop his own ideas. For instance, Ryan's mother handed him a doll. "What's this?" she asked. When he didn't answer immediately she said, "That's the boy doll. What's this?" Again he didn't answer immediately. "That's the girl doll," she filled in. "What do they want to do together?" Once more she supplied the answer. Ryan responded by turning away. His mother then put a puppet on her hand and said, "What are you going to say to the puppet?" When he didn't respond she said, "Say hi to the puppet. Say hi." Ryan turned away, then he took a block, put it on another block, and toppled them over. Ryan's father behaved similarly with his son. If anything, he was more directive, and Ryan's gestures and responses were even more limited.

Ryan's parents gave him so little room to move that turning away and making negative gestures had become his only way to assert himself! This emotional tendency was enhanced by his sensory patterns. His postural insecurity made him inclined to be passively negative—to turn away rather than to hit or kick—and his sensitivity around the mouth predisposed him to be negative when it came to food. Perhaps his inability to sleep was just one more way to assert himself with his parents. By tuning his parents out he gained some space for himself, but in the process he limited his chance to develop his own ideas.

The treatment program, in addition to working on Ryan's oral over-sensitivity and muscular control, worked with both parents on their interac-

tions with their son. They had to learn to give Ryan time to respond before offering a response of their own. They had to give him room to initiate play. Gradually both parents learned to be very engaged but less intrusive when they played. As they did so, Ryan became more engaged with them. He also began to show some leadership. In one session several months later, he put a whale puppet on his hand and held its mouth open. Instead of directing the action as she would have in the past, his mother put a puppet on her hand and had her puppet say, "What do you want, Mr. Whale?" Then she waited patiently for Ryan's answer. Ryan said the whale was hungry. Instead of feeding the whale herself, his mother asked, "What does he want to eat?" Ryan, taking a great deal of verbal initiative, generated a list of foods the whale wanted. As simple as this little interaction was, it was a major improvement in the family dynamic. Rather than telling Ryan what to do at each juncture, his mother had let him direct the play and inspired his initiative by joining him in his drama. She became a player in the drama; but he was the director.

Some weeks later, Mom and Ryan played with the whale puppet again. This time, the whale spit out its food. "How does the whale feel when it spits out his food?" Ryan's mother asked. Ryan didn't answer. "What does the whale want to do?" she asked. Ryan then had the whale bite everything in the room. When the whale was finished biting, he knocked down some toys. Ryan's mother watched. When he was through she said, "Is the whale mad or happy?" "Mad," said Ryan. Then he smiled. This was the first time Ryan had expressed anger in the form of ideas.

Ryan's father made similar strides. Around the same time, in a session with his father, Ryan noticed a flashlight. "What's this?" he asked. Instead of grabbing it, his father responded, "Let's see if we can figure it out." He pointed to the switch. Ryan began pressing the switch, and after a couple of times the flashlight turned on. Ryan giggled. Then he shone it at his father, and his father made funny faces. Then they switched—Ryan's dad shone the light at Ryan, and Ryan made funny faces. Through this little exchange both Ryan and his father laughed. Their exchange was warm and intimate, and for the first time, clearly pleasurable for Ryan.

Suddenly Ryan got an idea. He said to his father, "Me," pointing to the flashlight. When his father shone the light on him, Ryan stood in the spotlight and pretended to be onstage. With everyone watching, Ryan pranced and preened. When his audience applauded, he performed some more. This was an enormous step. For the first time, Ryan had initiated a complex drama in which his parents and therapist were importantly involved. With help from his parents he was opening up to the world of emotional ideas, strengthening his skills at intimacy and communication. He

was cementing his hold on the earlier milestones, and he was making good progress on milestone 5.

MILESTONE 6: EMOTIONAL THINKING

In the previous stage, the child's expressions of emotion are like little unconnected islands. Play moves from a happy, nurturing tea party to an angry crashing of cars to a monster threatening to tear down a house all within a few minutes, as the child uses whatever caught her eye to play out emotional themes. In this sixth stage, the child builds bridges between those islands. Ideas are linked together into logical sequences and play, and imagination is also more logically connected. Whereas in stage 5 a child might dress up a doll, then, seeing a crayon, scribble, then, seeing a drum, pretend to be a drummer, a child at the stage of emotional thinking connects the pieces together. For example, she might have the drummer play for the dressed-up little girl and use the crayon to make invitations for the performance; or, the doll might have a tea party, call friends to invite them, prepare refreshments, set the table, and determine the seating pattern.

At this stage the child is able to express a wide range of emotions in her play, and through experimentation she begins to recognize more and more what makes "me." She can even predict some of her feelings—if Mommy leaves I will be scared—and she begins to see that her feelings and behavior have an impact on others: if I get angry and hit, Daddy will get mad.

She also begins to understand emerging concepts of space and time in a personal, emotional way: Mommy is in another city, which is different from another room; if I hit Tommy today, he may hit me back tomorrow. The ability to conceptualize space and time and to link actions and feelings enables the child to develop a sense of self that has logical bridges between different perceptions, ideas, and emotions. She is also able to connect ideas in terms of spatial and verbal problem solving; instead of seeing separate block towers as isolated structures, she can link them together to make a big house. She can answer what, when, and why questions, enjoy debates, logically articulate an opinion, and begin the long journey to higher and higher levels of abstract thinking. Both verbal and spatial problem-solving abilities rest on emotional problem-solving skills. As with the earlier stages, emotional interactions create the thinking strategies that are then applied to the more impersonal world.

During this stage the child becomes more fully verbal. She still resorts to gestures to express her feelings—especially negative feelings such as anger and aggression—but she is now comfortable in the realm of words and understands that ideas and feelings can be communicated verbally.

At first we see children master islands of emotional thinking. Over time these islands coalesce into continents and the child's view becomes more cohesive, integrating more experiences into a sense of self and problem-solving ability. Higher levels of thinking build on this foundation.

When Robbie was one year old, he was diagnosed as having cerebral palsy with low muscle tone and right-side weakness. He made good progress, however. At four and a half he was an engaging little boy, with the jagged walk and unintentional arm movements of a child with motor difficulties. But he had a warm smile and he made good eye contact—intermittently. His mother described him as "mysterious" because he was not always easy to understand, or "realistic." His speech was immature for his age; he understood simple words but not concepts or abstract phrases, and he often gave silly, illogical answers to questions. Asked what he had for lunch he was apt to say, "The moon is green" or mutter illogical phrases to himself. But sometimes, such as when asked for a toy, he would be logical and connected to reality. His parents were worried because he didn't play with his peers and he so often seemed "lost in make-believe."

Robbie had achieved most of the early emotional milestones, although none appeared fully mastered. They fell apart when he felt stressed. For instance, he was eager to play with the toys and objects in the therapist's office and remained calm while he examined them, but when his mother tried to pry a toy away from him, he screamed in rage for 15 minutes. Sometimes he turned inward, babbling to himself as if only his inner thoughts could comfort him. Much of the time he was connected to his parents. He would look them in the eye and answer their questions, although he rarely smiled. Then suddenly, with no apparent provocation, he would turn away and willfully ignore them. He was clearly capable of two-way communication, both with gestures and with words. His word comprehension and use of ideas was sometimes quite sophisticated. But again, with no apparent provocation, he would suddenly stop closing circles and instead respond with silly, illogical phrases. His play was mechanical; he enjoyed putting dolls down the slide of the dollhouse rather than acting out a drama, and when he did begin a little drama what emerged were bits of unconnected action rather than a unified story. His range of emotion was narrow. In general, Robbie seemed unable to sustain an idea, a conversation, or a feeling for more than a few seconds. After that he needed to retreat to the comfort of his inner world. His incomplete mastery of the earlier milestones had undermined his ability to work on level 6.

Further evaluations revealed a number of factors contributing to Robbie's problems. He had an auditory-processing and word-retrieval problem, which meant that he often couldn't understand what was said to him and couldn't think of the word he wanted. It was easy to see how this might discourage him from closing circles. He had made great strides in his physical therapy, but he still had significant gross- and fine-motor deficits. His posture and balance was insecure, and it was hard for him to plan and execute his movements. This difficulty accounted for his jagged walk, unintentional arm movements, and general lack of coordination. To tackle these impairments, his treatment program included speech and occupational therapy along with his physical therapy.

Equally important to treatment was the program developed for Robbie's parents. It was clear from observing them play with Robbie that they could help him become more layered and integrated. His mother, rather than steer his conversations back to reality, often got lost with him in his self-absorbed elaborations of ideas. She called his fragmented ideas "his poems," but she didn't try to understand them. "Only he needs to know," she explained. Robbie's father was relatively uninvolved with him and avoided family activities. Untethered to reality, Robbie was moving further and further into his own world. In time, if the situation didn't change, he would relate less and less well to others.

As part of the treatment program, Robbie's parents were to play on the floor with him, encouraging him to close his circles of communication. Their goal was to prevent Robbie from withdrawing into himself and tuning them out. Each time he made a silly comment, they were to link that comment to reality by joining him in his play. By helping him close verbal circles, they would help him share his world with them *and* they would help him share *their* world rather than continue to live in his own. For instance, when Robbie slid a doll down the slide of the dollhouse and announced, "The doll is jumping out of the moon," his parents might say, "Where is the moon?" If he didn't answer they might say, "Is the slide the moon?" as a means of tying his idea to the reality of his action. If that elicited no response they might try, "How can we help him jump out of the moon?" or "How do we get to the moon?" as a means of joining his play. The slide might then turn into a spaceship and off they would go. Each time they joined him they tried to help him tie his ideas to their ideas so that there would be a logical bridge between what he created and what someone outside him created.

Robbie's parents also practiced reality-based conversations. They might ask what Robbie did at preschool that day. If he said something silly, such as "The chimney has water in it," they made a transition to something realistic. They might respond, "Did something happen with a chimney or with water?" and continue patiently until he was able to give them a logical reply. Robbie's teachers were similarly encouraged to help him close his verbal circles.

Robbie's parents were helped to set limits when Robbie had temper tantrums. In the past they had let him flail around or had given in to his demands. Now they held him tightly to help him calm down and then gradually helped him talk about the problem. After a few weeks they also used exercises from Robbie's occupational therapy to help him calm down.

Over time, Robbie made slow but steady progress. By a few months into therapy he was able to maintain two-way communication for a longer period of time and was having fewer tantrums at home. With a lot of cuing from his parents to compensate for his word-retrieval problem, he was doing a better job of describing his day at school.

A few months later, his pretend play took on a whole new emotional level. He began to develop elaborate dramas in which good guys were constantly being overwhelmed by bad guys and having to defend themselves. Occasionally he would blurt out while playing that he was mad at his sister or at a child at school because "they wreck my things." These comments began to provide a sense of Robbie's inner feelings. Apparently he often felt overwhelmed by other people, felt angry at them for hurting him, and fantasized about counterattacking. He had begun forming bridges between ideas, between the real world and his play.

A year and a half later, Robbie had made tremendous progress. He could hold a logical conversation for as long as his partner wanted. His tantrums had virtually disappeared, and he had become quite capable of regulating his moods. He was able to express a wide range of emotions— from happiness to sadness, dependency to aggressiveness—in play as well as in life. And when earlier he had tuned out and closeted himself in his inner world, he was now rooted in reality. In the past Robbie had used his creativity and cleverness to escape into fantasy, in part because processing other people's ideas and finding words was difficult and in part because of conflicts over certain feelings. Now he used his creativity to stay involved in two-way communication, to build logical bridges between ideas, and to work out his problems with auditory processing and word retrieval. He still has some of these problems, and his parents continue to work with him on that. But overall Robbie's progress has been excellent. He is now functioning at an age-appropriate level in all basic areas. With his parents' patient help he has mastered all six emotional and intellectual milestones.

Children achieve these milestones at different ages—there is wide variation even among children without challenges. What is important is not so much the age at which a child masters each skill, but that each one is mastered, for each skill forms a foundation for the next.

Once a child has mastered all six milestones, he has critical basic tools for communicating, thinking, and emotional coping. He has a positive sense of self. He is capable of warm and loving relationships. He is able to relate logically to the outside world. He can express in words a wide range of emotions (including love, happiness, anger, frustration, fear, anxiety, jealousy, and others) and is able to recover from strong emotions without losing control. He can use his imagination to create new ideas. He is flexible in his dealings with people and situations, able to tolerate changes and even some disappointments and bounce back. Obviously not all children do all these things equally well, but a child who has mastered the milestones will have important foundations for loving and learning.

5

Observing Each Child: The Six Milestones

Chapter 3 discussed how to observe your child's biological challenges so that you can pinpoint her strengths and difficulties and know how they affect your interactions. Once you've done that, you need to observe where your child stands on the developmental ladder: which milestones your child has already mastered, which need strengthening, and which still lie ahead. Together these two sets of observations will form your child's individual profile. You can then use this profile to tailor a therapeutic approach to her specific needs.

You can make these observations just as you did the others: watch your child play, watch her interact with you and others, and watch as she goes about her daily activities.

OBSERVATION CHART

Use the following chart to determine which milestones your child has mastered and which still need work. The abilities that signal mastery of each milestone are listed on the left. You can use the Rating Scale to rate your child in each one as she is now. If the skill is always present, record at what age it was mastered.

Rating Scale: N = ability never present
S = ability sometimes present
A = ability always present
L = child loses ability under stress (hunger, anger, fatigue, etc.)

Ability	Current Rating	Age Mastered

MILESTONE 1: SELF-REGULATION AND INTEREST IN THE WORLD

Ability	Current Rating	Age Mastered
1. Shows interest in different sensations for 3+ seconds	_____	_____
2. Remains calm and focused for 2+ minutes	_____	_____
3. Recovers from distress within 20 minutes with help from you	_____	_____
4. Shows interest in you (i.e., not only in inanimate objects)	_____	_____

MILESTONE 2: INTIMACY

Ability	Current Rating	Age Mastered
1. Responds to your overtures (with a smile, frown, reach, vocalization, or other intentional behavior)	_____	_____
2. Responds to your overtures with obvious pleasure	_____	_____
3. Responds to your overtures with curiosity and assertive interest (e.g., by studying your face)	_____	_____
4. Anticipates an object that was shown and then removed (e.g., smiles or babbles to show interest)	_____	_____
5. Becomes displeased when you are unresponsive during play for 30 seconds or more	_____	_____
6. Protests and grows angry when frustrated	_____	_____
7. Recovers from distress within 15 minutes with your help	_____	_____

MILESTONE 3: TWO-WAY COMMUNICATION

Ability	Current Rating	Age Mastered
1. Responds to your gestures with intentional gestures (e.g., reaches out in response to your outstretched arms, returns your vocalization or look)	_____	_____
2. Initiates interactions with you (e.g., reaches for your nose or hair or for a toy, raises arms to be picked up)	_____	_____

Ability	Current Rating	Age Mastered
3. Demonstrates the following emotions:		
• *closeness* (e.g., by hugging back when hugged, reaching out to be picked up)	_____	_____
• *pleasure and excitement* (e.g., by smiling joyfully while putting finger in your mouth or while taking a toy from your mouth and putting it in her own)	_____	_____
• *assertive curiosity* (e.g., by touching and exploring your hair)	_____	_____
• *protest or anger* (e.g., by pushing food off table or screaming when desired toy not brought)	_____	_____
• *fear* (e.g., by turning away, looking scared, or crying when a stranger approaches too quickly)	_____	_____
4. Recovers from distress within 10 minutes by being involved in social interactions	_____	_____

MILESTONE 4: COMPLEX COMMUNICATION

Ability	Current Rating	Age Mastered
1. Closes 10 or more circles of communication in a row (e.g., takes you by hand, walks you to refrigerator, points, vocalizes, responds to your question with more noises and gestures, and continues gestural exchange until you open door and get what he wants)	_____	_____
2. Imitates your behavior in an intentional way (e.g., puts on Daddy's hat, then parades around house waiting for admiration)	_____	_____
3. Closes 10 or more circles using		
• vocalizations or words	_____	_____
• facial expressions	_____	_____
• reciprocal touching or holding	_____	_____
• movement in space (e.g., roughhousing)	_____	_____

Ability	Current Rating	Age Mastered
• large motor activity (e.g., chase games, climbing games)	_____	_____
• communication across space (e.g., can close 10 circles with you from across the room)	_____	_____

4. Closes three or more circles in a row while feeling the following emotions:

• *closeness* (e.g., uses facial expressions, gestures, and vocalizations to reach out for a hug, kiss, or cuddle, or uses imitation, such as talking on toy phone while you are on real phone)	_____	_____
• *pleasure and excitement* (uses looks and vocalizations to invite another person to share excitement over something; shares "jokes" with other children or adults by laughing together at some provocation)	_____	_____
• *assertive curiosity* (explores independently; uses ability to communicate across space to feel close to you while exploring or playing on her own)	_____	_____
• *fear* (tells you how to be protective, e.g., says "No!" and runs behind you)	_____	_____
• *anger* (deliberately hits, pinches, yells, bangs, screams, or lies on floor to demonstrate anger; occasionally uses cold or angry looks instead)	_____	_____
• *limit setting* (understands and responds to your limits whether expressed through words—"No, stop that!"—or gestures—shaking finger, angry face)	_____	_____

5. Uses imitation to deal with and recover from distress (e.g., bangs on floor and yells after being yelled at)   _____   _____

Ability	Current Rating	Age Mastered

MILESTONE 5: EMOTIONAL IDEAS

1. Creates pretend dramas with two or more ideas (e.g., trucks crash then pick up rocks, dolls hug then have a tea party; ideas need not be related)

2. Uses words, pictures, gestures to convey two or more ideas at a time (e.g., "No sleep. Play."); ideas need not be related

3. Communicates wishes, intentions, and feelings using

   • words

   • multiple gestures in a row

   • touch (e.g., lots of hugging or rough-housing)

4. Plays simple motor games with rules (e.g., taking turns throwing ball)

5. Uses pretend play or words to communicate the following emotions while expressing two or more ideas:

   • *closeness* (e.g., has doll say, "Hug me," then child answers, "I give you kiss")

   • *pleasure and excitement* (e.g., makes funny words then laughs)

   • *assertive curiosity* (e.g., makes pretend airplane zoom around room, then says it's going to the moon)

   • *fear* (e.g., stages drama in which doll is afraid of loud noise then calls for mother)

   • *anger* (e.g., has soldiers shoot guns at one another then fall down)

   • limit setting (e.g., has dolls follow rules at tea party)

Ability	Current Rating	Age Mastered
6. Uses pretend play to recover from and deal with distress (e.g., plays out eating the cookie she couldn't really have)	_____	_____

MILESTONE 6: EMOTIONAL THINKING

Ability	Current Rating	Age Mastered
1. In pretend play, two or more ideas are logically tied together, even if the ideas themselves are unrealistic (e.g., the car is visiting the moon and gets there by flying fast)	_____	_____
2. Builds on adult's pretend play idea (e.g., child is cooking soup, adult asks what's in it, child answers, "Rocks and dirt")	_____	_____
3. In speech, connects ideas logically; ideas are grounded in reality (e.g., "No go sleep. Want to watch television.")	_____	_____
4. Closes two or more verbal circles of communication (e.g., "Want to go outside"; adult asks, "Why?" "To play.")	_____	_____
5. Communicates logically, connecting two or more ideas, about intentions, wishes, needs, or feelings, using		
• words	_____	_____
• multiple gestures in a row (e.g., pretending to be an angry dog)	_____	_____
• touch (e.g., lots of hugging as part of a pretend drama in which child is the daddy)	_____	_____
6. Plays spatial and motor games with rules (e.g., taking turns going down a slide)	_____	_____
7. Uses pretend play or words to communicate two or more logically connected ideas dealing with the following emotions:		
• *closeness* (e.g., doll gets hurt and Mommy fixes it)	_____	_____

Ability	Current Rating	Age Mastered
• *pleasure and excitement* (e.g., says bathroom words, such as "doody," and laughs)	_____	_____
• *assertive curiosity* (e.g., good soldiers search for missing princess)	_____	_____
• *fear* (e.g., monster scares baby doll)	_____	_____
• *anger* (e.g., good soldiers fight bad ones)	_____	_____
• *limit setting* (e.g., soldiers can hit only bad guys because of the rules)	_____	_____
8. Uses pretend play that has a logical sequence of ideas to recover from distress, often suggesting a way of coping with the distress (e.g., the child becomes the teacher, bossing the class)	_____	_____

6

Observing Yourselves

As we explained in the introduction, your child's development is like a braid. One strand is his biological makeup; the second is the way he interacts with you and others to master the six developmental milestones; the third is the feelings, values, expectations, behaviors, and family and cultural patterns you bring to those interactions. We all have ways of feeling and behaving that are automatic to us and that influence the way we relate to our children. We've learned these ways of being from our own families, as a result of circumstances in our lives, and from the culture in which we live. Most are so ingrained that they're invisible to us. But as we look for the best ways of raising our children, particularly children with special needs, as we look for ways to use each encounter to foster developmental growth, it makes sense to try to make the invisible visible, to examine these automatic ways of thinking, feeling, and responding so that we can make everything we do and say with our children as nurturing and developmentally facilitating as possible.

Parents may, for instance, have fears or fantasies about their children, or about themselves as parents, based on their own childhoods. A mother who fears being as controlling as her own mother may be wary of intruding too much with her child and therefore may be overly passive or aloof. A father who remembers being picked on as a child may feel uncomfortable with his child's quiet nature and may try to control him to make him more aggressive.

Parents also have emotional and behaviorial tendencies. Some parents are more extroverted and demonstrative, whereas others tend to be shy and reserved. All parents are more comfortable with certain emotions than with others, and their own discomforts may inadvertently lead them to make it more difficult for their children to express those feelings. A mother who is uncomfortable with anger may reflexively steer the conversation in another direction when she senses her son growing irate. A father who is uncomfortable with gentle nurturing may turn every encounter with his daughter into roughhousing. How they negotiated the different developmental milestones while they were growing up influences parents' approaches to their own children. A father who never mastered the stage of using emotional ideas with pretend play will understandably feel confused when his child starts to hug her doll. He may redirect her to roughhousing games, which are more familiar to him. A mother who has never experienced a deep sense of intimacy may have a hard time wooing her child into the full sense of engagement that characterizes the second milestone. With some self-reflection, and a helpful spouse or therapist, parents can grow with their children. They can negotiate the stages not yet mastered, and their children's growth and potential can provide the incentive and energy for this endeavor.

Parents reflect the values and expectations of the family and culture in which they grew up. A father who came from a milieu in which girls were expected to be docile and quiet may have difficulty encouraging assertiveness in his daughter. A mother whose family precluded the expression of anger may have difficulty encouraging the expression of anger in her children.

Parents' behavior may be influenced simply by having a child with special needs. Parents can be devastated when they find out that their child is challenged, and it often takes a family a long time to recuperate from the blow. In the early stages of that process the parents may be depressed and overwhelmed. They may feel unsupported, left to face the crisis on their own. Guilt and sadness, anger and exhaustion may spin them into paralysis. It may take all their energy just to meet the family's most basic needs, and they may have none left over to woo a loved but confusing child into engagement and two-way communication. Alternatively, they may be so worried that they mobilize into action, throwing themselves into a quest to obtain the best possible help from specialists, leaving little of themselves for daily nurturing. All these subtle, often invisible factors can influence how well a child is able to master the emotional milestones.

Major events in the household—even if they don't directly involve the child—can also affect a child's development. Illness, unemployment, or the birth of a sibling can change the family pattern, divert the parents' attention. Children with special needs are especially vulnerable to changes in routine, so household events that alter family patterns can easily take a toll on their development.

The questions that follow will help you examine feelings and habits that may have had an impact on your child's development. They are organized by milestone so that you can think about how your responses to your child at each step of the developmental ladder can promote or hamper his progress. We all parent the best way we know. The emotions that make us human also make us imperfect. Without these emotions we wouldn't be capable of intimacy or many types of interaction. The ideal we strive for is a process of continual learning. With hindsight, we may see how we could have done things better. Use this self-assessment to help learn for the future.

QUESTIONS TO HELP YOU OBSERVE YOURSELF

Milestone 1: Self-Regulation and Interest in the World

Think back to how you were feeling during your baby's first few months of life. Living with a new baby—especially one with challenges—is extremely difficult, and all families go through a period of transition. What was that time like for you? Depression, sadness, anger, and longing for the former life are common and expected feelings; they are often mixed in with warmer feelings for the baby. Adding a baby to a household often causes tension in a couple. How have you and your spouse dealt with the change in your family? If you have older children, they no doubt have added to your concerns. How have they handled the baby's arrival?

How a family handles this change makes a big difference in the environment in which a baby develops. Have you been able to focus on your child's unique individual differences, his response to sensations, his need for calm or stimulation? Or have you tended to want him to meet your expectations?

Understanding your feelings will help you nurture one another and create a sense of security in the entire family. This, in turn, will help you provide the soothing, but also responsive, home environment that any baby, particularly one with challenges, needs in order to develop.

Milestone 2: Intimacy

The mythology of parenting tells us that parents fall in love with their babies within the first few minutes or days. Many do, but many others don't. Any number of factors, including the sheer stress of having a new baby, can get in the way. Factors such as tension or illness in the household, competition and jealousy from siblings, or external stresses, such as moving or unemployment, can contribute to parents' ambivalence. The dashed expectations brought by the recognition that a child has special needs can make bonds between parents and infant slow to develop, although sometimes it may have the opposite impact. Think back to your own feelings during your child's first few months of life and since. Reflect on how you've responded to his looks and cries and his expressions of interest in you.

Milestone 3: Two-Way Communication

At this stage, a baby develops initiative. Have you been able to encourage your child in this direction? Parents and caregivers differ in their enjoyment of a child's initiative. Some want a more compliant child, others a more assertive one. What is your general attitude about assertive people? When you play, do you sometimes wait for your child to initiate play and follow along, rather than always initiating play yourself? When she tries to do new or difficult things—such as reaching for a distant toy or trying to feed herself—do you encourage her efforts, even if you know they may fail? When she explores her world—by crawling away from you or handling household objects—are you able to grant her a certain degree of freedom, rather than clamping down for fear she'll get into trouble? When she resists your initiatives—by throwing food or screaming when you move her from a favorite spot—can you sometimes let her be the boss, rather than insisting that she always do things your way? Do you withdraw when your child takes the initiative, thinking she can be on her own for a while, or do you get in there and challenge her to greater heights? It's not easy to foster initiative. Some parents get used to having a dependent baby, and when the child starts to assert initiative it requires a parental change of gears. But promoting initiative is important for the child's later growth.

Milestone 4: Complex Communication

As you look at your own behavior, consider how you respond to your child's growing independence and self-assertion. These new qualities are often difficult for parents, who miss the cuddly baby stage. When your child points to something he wants, or pulls you from your chair, do you encourage a dialogue? Do you ask what he wants or why, so that he can respond with ever more complex gestures? Or do you tend to want the task to get done and encourage quick closure, rather than a long dialogue?

A child's growing abilities sometimes cause stress in a marriage as parents respond differently. One parent may not like to be routed from chair and reading, while the other follows each lead. Or one parent may feel jealous if the other is constantly involved with a child's new demands and projects. These feelings can cause tension in a marriage, which can have an impact on the child. As you think about your child's development at this stage, also think about your own feelings. Think about your relationship with your spouse and talk about areas of agreement, as well as areas of disagreement or compromise. Think about how the whole family's needs are being met—for intimacy, for interaction, and for communication.

Milestone 5: Emotional Ideas

As children become more able to express their own ideas and feelings, such displays often trigger a backlash in their parents. Many parents, for instance, become uncomfortable when their child uses verbal expressions of anger, and respond by becoming angry or punitive themselves. Some parents have difficulty with their child's verbal requests for closeness and respond by pushing the child away. A child's growing delight in naming everything in her world and the new torrent of questions may delight or irritate a parent. Almost all parents are triggered by some new demands or feelings expressed by their child. Few are so emotionally balanced that they can tolerate all feelings or new pressures equally well. So examine your own behavior to see which of your child's demands or expressions of feeling you find comfortable and which cause you to "bite," or get defensive. Also think about how you and your spouse express feelings. Do you tend to be open? Do you tend to guard your feelings? People who keep their feelings to themselves usually prefer other people to do the same and so may be more uncomfortable when their children verbalize strong emotion. Ironically, even though we want our children to talk, sometimes it can challenge us if they talk about feelings or wishes that make us uncomfortable.

Your child also needs you to help her experiment with verbalizing feelings and expanding her grasp of the world through pretend play. Some parents find this kind of play boring. Others are uncomfortable when their child plays out certain themes, such as exploring dolls' bodies or having people fight. To eliminate their discomfort they withdraw, redirect the play, or end the game. How do you handle pretend play when your child plays out themes that make you uncomfortable? Can you stick with it or do you want to change the game?

Your child's challenge is to explore the world of feelings and ideas as fully as possible through a variety of outlets. If you can look objectively at how you deal with feelings—yours and your child's—you will go a long way toward helping her develop the skills to handle her feelings well.

Milestone 6: Emotional Thinking

Your child's challenge is to learn to build bridges between ideas and deal logically with the world. Are you helping him by bringing him back to reality each time he says something illogical or do you encourage illogical thinking by not correcting his statements? Can you enjoy, or at least tolerate, a debate over bedtime, or cookies, or cleaning up toys? Do you cut off debate quickly to make sure he learns obedience? Debates are the best practice for becoming logical. You can always set limits after the debate, but if you encourage debate first you will have a creative, logical, *and* well-disciplined child. Can you maintain logic in the face of strong feelings? Asking your child his opinion about food, colors, toys, play activities, or any other subject close to his heart will also improve his logical and abstract thinking. Do you prefer to give orders or have your child follow you most of the time or are you interested in exploring his ideas? Can you continue playing a make-believe game logically and calmly when his dolls are angry as well as when they're happy? Do you cut off an argument when your child becomes angry? The better able you are to remain cool and logical regardless of what your child expresses, the more you will help him understand his feelings and develop self-control.

Explore your own feelings to learn more about what your child is negotiating. Discover your own prior patterns. Use your insights to support your child's growth and to master the feelings and developmental milestones that may have been difficult for you while growing up.

PROMOTING DEVELOPMENT: GENERAL GUIDELINES FOR PARENTS

As you live and love and work with your child you can use a number of very basic steps to promote her development. You already do many of these without even thinking about them. You may want to pay more attention to others.

• *Comfort your child* (especially when he is upset) by using relaxed, gentle, firm holding; rhythmic vocal or visual contact; and other soothing behaviors. Your worry or tension can make your child more upset. Can you calm yourself or find support from others?

• *Offer the type of interaction that will help your child engage.* Do you use joyful facial expressions and sounds, other sounds, touch, and games and toys that appeal to her sensory profile? Playing in ways that are understimulating or overstimulating can make it harder for your child to participate.

• *Try a variety of approaches to engage your child in a relationship,* and explore which approach gives him most pleasure.

• *Read and respond to your child's signals in most emotional areas.* Can you respond as well to her desire for closeness as to her need to be assertive or independent?

• *Show pleasure, enthusiasm, and zest. Your* animation will captivate your child and woo him into interaction.

• *Read your child's signals.* If you watch closely, your child will tell you what she wants. Try to follow her cues, rather than proceed with your own agenda.

• *Encourage your child to move forward in development.* For example:

   • Encourage your child to take initiative and learn from his interactions with you instead of doing things for him most of the time.

   • Encourage from afar her efforts to solve problems in order to build her sense of engagement and interactive support.

   • Encourage pretend play and the use of language covering a range of emotions to help your child move from acting out behaviors to the use of symbols and language.

   • Help your child deal with reality and take responsibility for his behavior.

None of us are optimal parents all the time. Here are some styles and actions to try to minimize.

• *Overstimulating or understimulating your child.* Avoid revving up your child beyond what he needs in order to become engaged. Also try not to withdraw, be unavailable, or lack joy in him, or he may not feel drawn into a relationship with you.

• *Exercising too much control.* Follow your child's lead, rather than trying to direct the play.

• *Being overly concrete as your child moves to the symbolic level of play.* Follow the *ideas* in your child's play rather than the literal behaviors. If she serves you a dinner of rocks, don't feel insulted; try to imagine along with her.

• *Avoiding emotional areas that make you uncomfortable.* Try to stick with the theme your child has introduced—in play or in conversation—even if it makes you uncomfortable.

• *Withdrawing in the face of strong emotion.* Engage calmly with your child even when his emotions are very strong, even when they make you uncomfortable. If your child behaves aggressively, set limits, but do it calmly and firmly while soothing and regulating him. Help him learn to regulate himself with your soothing intervention.

7

Emotion and Interaction:
Keys to the Development of Intelligence,
Sense of Self, and Social Capacities

In Part 2 of this book we describe how to work with your child to help him develop emotionally, socially, and intellectually. As we do, two principles will come up over and over again: *following your child's lead* and *interacting*. Following your child's lead means appealing to his interests and motivation, using his *emotions* as the starting point for every interaction. Interacting means turning every encounter into a two-way exchange in which you and your child respond to each other, rather than engaging in parallel activities. These two principles are absolutely crucial to helping your child grow. So before we tell you *how* to implement them, we want to tell you *why*.

CONNECTING DESIRE AND EMOTION TO ACTION

Until recently the prevailing view of children's development focused on discrete skill areas—on social abilities such as cooperating, playing with peers, or reaching out for hugs; on cognitive skills such as searching under a blanket for a hidden toy; on language skills such as saying "baba" or "dada"; and on motor skills such as drawing a circle. We looked at the ages at which the skills occurred and judged a child's developmental progress based on whether she fit age expectations. As interest in infants and young children grew, the importance of social and emotional skills in development became apparent, and more of these skills were added to the list of skills charted. A baby's first smile, the first time he balks at being held by a stranger, his first turn taking—we now look for these skills, too, on a young child's path of development.

Until very recently, however, we had little systematic understanding of how all these pieces fit together into a larger whole. How does the child orchestrate her growing sensory, motor, cognitive, and social skills? What part of the emerging person makes the judgment to use this word rather than that one, to reach for the ball with the left hand rather than the right, to smile at Mommy rather than to run and hide? Clearly a child is more than the sum of her parts. There must be an orchestrating "I" or sense of self inside that makes these decisions. Charting the independent skills doesn't reveal how this sense develops, for it is larger than the individual skills. It's as if the cognitive, motor, sensory, and social skills are members of an orchestra and the sense of self is the conductor, coordinating all those separate sections. As the child develops, so does the sense of self. It becomes more sophisticated as the orchestra becomes more complex.

For children with special needs, however, there are special challenges in getting this orchestra conductor to work effectively. Children who are described as having autistic features, for example, often seem to lack a basic sense of purpose. They have a hard time acting in an organized, intentional way; their behaviors may be aimless, repetitive, or seemingly random. The ability to take a parent by the hand, walk him to the refrigerator, and point to the food they want is not evident with these children, as it is with others, by 16 to 20 months of age. Many parents report that this ability occurred at age two, three, or four or did not occur at all.

Older children who are already talking to some degree and who have been diagnosed as having autistic spectrum problems often use words rotely, simply repeating things they've heard on TV or on a recording. They do not speak in a purposeful way, but seem lost in a world of free-floating ideas, voicing one idea after another, each one unconnected to the next. A child may utter "butterfly," then bang a toy drum and make funny noises, then hold up a doll and giggle, then say a sentence from *Thomas the Tank Engine*. He can use words, and perhaps imitate the words of others, but cannot guide those words into purposeful, intentional communication. He lacks the ability to make his needs known, to respond to the ideas of others, and to hold a coherent, logical conversation. The basic sense of purpose that organizes the child's behavior is challenged.

The challenge of coordinating skills may be less difficult for children with severe motor problems (such as those that occur with cerebral palsy) or with expressive-language difficulty. With these children the sense of desire or purpose is operating and is connected to the motor and language systems; the challenge is to find ways to express this intent or purpose while remediating the motor or language system. For example, a child with motor problems may be helped to use her head (nodding yes or no), her tongue, or the limb over which she has the best control to communicate her intentions. A child with expressive-language problems might be helped to use motor gestures, signs, pictures, and as many sounds as he can make to communicate his intent.

For many children with severe developmental challenges (including autistic patterns, cognitive delays, expressive and receptive language problems, and severe motor-planning difficulties) the single biggest challenge—bigger than the cognitive, sensory, motor, or language problem—is this inability to organize purposeful communication, either with behavior or with words. In breaking down this missing skill we've discovered what seems to lie behind it: *Many children lack the ability to connect their underlying wishes, desires, or emotions to behavior or words that can communicate them.*

Although this deficit is most profound in children with autistic spectrum disorders or multisystem developmental disorders, it is challenging in children with motor, cognitive, or language disorders as well, but for a different reason. With these disorders, the child's sense of purpose is at least partially connected to behavior and words, though the connections are hard to strengthen and develop because deficits in the motor, language, or cognitive capacities don't permit the full expression of underlying intentions, wishes, or emotions. When we don't quickly find alternative routes for expression and therefore don't use these connections between intent and actions, words, or ideas, the connections are weakened, as with any capacity that is not exercised.

For most of us this ability to connect our feelings with our behavior and words is automatic. Underlying our choice of words, facial expressions, body postures, and other behavior are our desires, wishes, and inclinations. An adult who comes home from work doesn't simply list the day's events, but talks about what was good or bad about the day. She selects experiences to relate based on something that had emotional meaning—what was exciting or boring, challenging or frightening. At work, she is guided by these wishes and feelings. There is little we do or discuss that isn't cued by our emotions—our choice of friends or jobs, our political opinions, our choice of movies, books, and restaurants, our ideas about how we raise our children.

From idle chatter to crucial planning to romantic conversation, our acts and thoughts are cued and orchestrated by our emotional interests. Without these guiding emotional cues we would tend to lapse into more aimless and random activity.

COMMUNICATING DESIRE

The need for emotional cues, which has not been well recognized in the past, reveals a missing piece in our understanding of children with developmental challenges. Often their greatest difficulty is to create those links— links that other children make easily—between emerging emotions, or affects, and the complex behavior and verbal configurations that can express them. Development and thinking cannot easily progress when a child can't engage in purposeful, organized interactions at either a preverbal or a verbal level.

Ordinarily this ability to link feelings with communication emerges gradually during the first year of life and is readily apparent by the middle of the child's first year. A 6-month-old baby reaches for something, indicating her desire for it, her parents hand her the item, and she takes it; that's the beginning of purposeful interaction. By 10 months the baby and her parents are exchanging objects, playing peekaboo, and mimicking each other's gestures. By 18 months she is taking her parents' roles. They're also engaging in more complex imitations and sometimes even verbal exchanges as part of their purposeful interaction. The infant's ability to interact intentionally with her parents serves as a foundation for even more sophisticated emotional, social, and cognitive development later on. The 18-month-old can lead her mother to the shelf and point to cookies; when Mommy holds up a raisin cookie, the toddler can point to the chocolate one, adding yet another element to their interactive dialogue.

When a sense of purpose or interest is not present or can't be communicated and interaction remains random, however, the progression of thinking that depends on purposeful interactions cannot occur. The ability to talk in logical, complex sentences ("I don't want to go to sleep") builds on a simpler logic of pointing to the shelf and saying, "Cookie!" The still more complex ability to build logical connections between ideas ("I'm not tired now, but if you let me watch another movie then maybe I'll be tired") cannot occur without this earlier foundation. Without the ability to make a connection between our own feelings and our behavior or words, the more complex tasks of communication are impossible. Without the most basic ability to connect underlying feelings with behavior (or words), the child's sense of purpose, the key ingredient in the developmental progression, is missing.

Children with developmental challenges can be helped to make this connection and strengthen it. If every time you see an expression of interest in your child, which often conveys emotion, affect, or desire, you respond to it and interact with him around it, you can gradually help your child begin to communicate more intentionally. The more you create opportunities for your child to express his wishes or intentions, the more you can help him build that connection between emotions and communicative behavior.

Sometimes severe motor or auditory-processing problems make it hard to engage a child in interaction. The purposeful self may be lost in a swirl of aimless behavior or words, or the child's movements may be severely restricted. Yet even a child who can intentionally move only his neck and head can respond meaningfully. A single look with his eyes can be the opening for a dialogue. A parent can offer him two choices of food, one she knows he likes and one she knows he doesn't, and ask him to look at the one he wants. He'll have communicated a desire! Later on, when the child has mastered some intentional behaviors, his parents can deliberately act confused—hand him something he didn't look at, challenge him to use his eyes to clarify before they "understand," and then apologize for not getting what he wanted sooner.

Each time we pretend not to understand a child, each time we encourage a child to ask again, we build his ability to communicate intentionally. We strengthen his purposeful self, his sense that he can act on the world, and this sense of self provides the foundation for more complex cognitive, emotional, and social skills.

When we have not worked proactively to develop this sense of self along with other specific skills, we have seen children with special needs hit a developmental ceiling at an unnecessarily young age. But when we work with developing intent while working on strengthening many of the different motor, language, and cognitive capacities, we see greater progress. When we work simultaneously to develop the conductor *and* the members of the orchestra, children tend to progress far beyond the traditional expectations.

EMOTIONS AS THE BASIS OF LEARNING

The idea that feelings underlie cognitive learning is still a radical one. Throughout history we have believed that emotions were subservient to thought or reason. Freud likened the emotions to a wayward horse, controlled by the rational ego. But our recent clinical work with infants and young children, as well as an emerging body of observational and neuroscientific research, suggests this view is inaccurate. Rather than being separate and subservient to thought, emotions seem to be responsible for our thoughts. Because emotions give direction to our actions and meaning to our experiences, they enable us to control our behavior, store and organize our experiences, construct new experiences, solve problems, and think.

From the time we are newborns, all our experiences have both a physical and an emotional component. The physical component is the concrete part of the experience. The emotional component is the part that makes the experience meaningful. Think about one of the newborn's very earliest experiences: the experience of mother. A baby's sense of mother is a collection of physical sensations—a voice, a smile, a touch. These sensations become important because of how they make the baby *feel*. Each time this combination of physical sensations comes, it brings feelings of pleasure— warmth, security, happiness. Soon the baby *anticipates* those feelings whenever she hears her mother's voice. She automatically links those physical sensations with the pleasure she feels inside. Her emotions thus give rise to a most powerful idea: the idea of mother.

Later in life the concept of mother is expanded. Mother becomes someone who comforts the child when she is hurt, who gives food when she is hungry, who scolds when she misbehaves. Again, each experience is double-coded. The child registers the physical properties of the experience— the feel of her mother's sheltering hands, the taste of her food, the echo of her angry voice. Simultaneously the child registers the emotions generated by the encounter—the feelings of warmth and comfort or of anger and fear. These feelings give the experiences meaning and lasting resonance in the child's mind. They also organize the experiences by grouping them in a growing database called mother. By means of that database, the child learns to conceptualize mother broadly, to think of her in many different ways, to think about her abstractly. Emotion has made storing, organizing, and retrieving those experiences possible. More important, it allows the child to form abstract concepts by connecting an idea, such as mother, with many different types of affective, or emotional, experiences.

This emotional coding of experience guides all our learning. A child learns the concepts of hot and cold not by memorizing the words, but by experiencing the sensations against his skin. As his brain registers the physical sensation, it simultaneously records the *emotions* those sensations provoke. "Ow, that's hot!" or "Yikes, that's cold!" It is this emotional response that secures the learning in his mind.

The same is true for such concepts as time. When forced to wait for a surprise, 20 minutes feels like half a lifetime, yet at the playground it passes in the blink of an eye. Our early concepts of time and quantity, as well as space, are emotional, as the brain records not just the physical sensation of waiting or playing, but also the emotions generated by the activity—a lot to a two-and-a-half-year-old is more than he expects, a little is less than he wants. As we become older, we apply the rules of logic and measurement to systematize our experiences—ten is a lot; one is a little. But the subjective, *emotional* sense of time and quantity never leaves us and is what gives meaning to our more formal systematization.

Spatial concepts are equally emotional. The crawl across the bedroom may feel like half a mile to an infant just as a grocery-laden walk across a steamy parking lot may feel like a ten-mile hike to us. The child will learn, as the adult already knows, that the actual distance is far shorter, but for both, the concept of space is always first learned by the emotions generated in navigating through it. The emotional feel of space provides the basis for understanding more formal calculations. A child who doesn't have a feel for more or less, whether in terms of time, space, or number of cookies, will have a hard time later applying numbers to solve problems.

Just as our understanding of ideas is emotionally based, so is our ability to *think* and solve problems, for thinking is no more than the manipulation of ideas. Consider asking a person what he did on a trip. This question appears to require a rational, nonemotional response. He can simply rattle off a list of sights and events, as would a computer programmed to respond to this question. But human beings aren't computers. We aren't programmed, we *think,* so our answers are usually quite different from what a computer would answer. Instead of simply listing what he did, our traveler would reflect on his trip and select certain aspects to relate—those with emotional significance, the parts he especially liked or didn't like. His *feelings* become a sorting and retrieval tool that permits him to think about the trip.

This same process of emotional sorting and discrimination occurs in more complex thinking. When we asked several young boys what they thought about bossy people, one child answered, "Most of the time I don't like being bossed, especially when my parents get too bossy and try to tell me when I can watch TV and when I should sleep, and I'm big enough to decide that myself. If I hit my sister, I guess I need to be bossed, so it depends." The boy answered the question by reflecting on his experiences with bossy people and the emotions he'd felt. He put an emotional framework in place, based on his lived emotional experience. Then, in saying "It depends" (on circumstances), he applied rules of logic as he understood them ("I'm big enough to decide that myself"). The result was a thoughtful, creative argument.

A child with developmental delays and a very narrow range of emotions answered the question quite differently. "Well," he said, "parents are bosses and teachers are bosses and sometimes baby-sitters are bosses." Period. A much simpler answer, devoid of any creative thinking or reflection. Unlike his peer's, his answer lacked emotional content. It was simply a list of people who fit the category, a list such as what a computer might generate. Since the boy was unable to use lived emotional experience, his thinking was concrete and idiosyncratic, rather than creative, selective, and logical. We found that whether the questions involved bosses, the concept of justice, or any other abstract notion, responses that were intelligent and abstract involved two parts, lived emotional experience and reflection on that emotional experience. When the child did not generate ideas related to emotional experience, his answers tended to be concrete and rote. Thinking, therefore, appears to involve a generative, reflective aspect.

Because emotions enable us to organize, store, and retrieve memories, they also enable us to remember what we experienced in one situation and apply it to another. This is the essence of learning. Consider a child learning to smile and say hello. The child must learn to offer this greeting selectively; friends, relatives, and even certain strangers warrant it, but menacing strangers don't. How does she learn to discriminate? Not through a set of rules passed down by her parents. The child teaches herself by comparing her feelings in one situation with her feelings in another. Through countless emotional experiences she learns that a warm, friendly feeling rightly prompts a greeting, while a wary or frightened feeling prompts the desire to hide behind Mommy's leg. Her emotions are the sorting tool that transfers her learning from one experience to the next.

Abstracting from emotional experience makes cognitive learning possible. Cognitive skills fall into place once the emotional foundation has been laid. A child develops his earliest sense of causality by making his mother smile with his smile. Early experience with math is also acquired through personal emotional experience. A child feels that a lot is more than he needs; well before he has the words to count or add, he gains a sense of quantity. Later he learns the verbal shorthand and uses numbers for the quantities he already senses emotionally. Still later, he learns formulas for manipulating quantities quickly. If the child has had a lot of emotional experiences with quantity—more than/less than, bigger/smaller, sorting and classifying—he can make the transition to formal cognitive operations easily. What helps him learn to do math is not a lot of rote practice memorizing formulas, but a lot of hands-on experiences that cement the emotional meanings of basic concepts.

Contrary to the theories of Jean Piaget and his followers, as well as those of many modern cognitive theorists, a child first learns about how the world works, be it with regard to concepts or causality, quantity, or abstract logic, through emotional experiences. These emotional insights are then applied to understanding the physical world as well as to other intellectual challenges.

Speech also depends on early emotional development. Long before a child learns words, she learns to communicate. She uses sounds, gestures, and body language to tell her parents what she wants, and she learns to read the gestures they use to respond. Later, when the child substitutes the word *balloon* for her earlier babbling and pointing, she is merely using shorthand for what she already knew emotionally. The knowing comes from lived experience; the cognitive process of labeling comes later, and comes relatively easily, if the child has had a lot of wordless experience with signaling her intentions and desires and reading those of others.

This process applies equally to grown-up learning. Whenever we are in a new situation—whether interviewing for a job or encountering a new idea—we flash back to previous experiences and then abstract those emotional experiences; that is, we *think* about them. We turn them into ideas that we can manipulate in our mind. We apply rules of logic and test them against our experience. We synthesize our previous experience with the new data and formulate a plan of thought and action. All this happens automatically and instantaneously; the emotional coding of all experience makes instant retrieval, construction, and synthesis possible. This process enables us to think creatively, to think on our feet, to learn.

THE ROOTS OF INTELLIGENCE

This view of the role of emotion in learning has important implications for what we think of as intelligence—and for the learning of children with developmental challenges. We have traditionally measured intelligence in rather limited ways. The IQ test, our standard measure of intelligence, uses a compilation of cognitive, memory, motor, sensory, language, and spatial tasks. Many items on a traditional IQ test are influenced by children's processing abilities; they don't look behind auditory-processing or motor-planning problems to see latent reasoning and thinking skills. Even though a skillful examiner can sometimes discern the child's real potential, the test itself does not reveal enough about the child's ability to think creatively or to solve problems in real-world situations. Nor does it provide enough information about the skills that will be needed in relationships, family life, or in jobs that require dealing with people and feelings or coming up with innovative solutions. It is far more useful and accurate to define intelligence as the ability to generate ideas from lived emotional experiences and to reflect on and organize those ideas. Children with these two capacities will be able to think on their feet and create innovative, logical solutions to problems. These are the skills we want to instill in our children.

The ability to create ideas based on emotional experience and abstract from lived experience is a large part of what makes us human. A child with these skills is able to pursue goals, operate with a sense of purpose, develop a sense of morality, and know himself. A child with this kind of creative intelligence has had the experiences necessary for a strong sense of self.

Intelligence as defined here is within the grasp of many children with special needs. It is built gradually by mastering both emotional and cognitive skills. As you work with your child daily, as you engage in millions of little interactions, you strengthen his ability to think logically, creatively, and spontaneously. Each time you hand socks back and forth while dressing, each time you exchange soap in the bath, each time you take the toy he hands you, each time you negotiate with gestures about turning on the TV, another little piece is added to his sense of purpose, his sense of who he is, and his ability to be part of true, two-way communication. Through these daily interactions you help him build the social, emotional, motor, and cognitive skills that add up to intelligence, as well as develop his sense of self.

We have discussed the role of affect, or emotion, intent, and desire in the development of intelligence. Emotions are important for learning to focus, engage, be causal and intentional, solve problems nonverbally, create ideas, and use ideas to think. Emotions enable us to label experiences, discriminate among experiences, form patterns or groupings of experiences (i.e., classify experiences), use experiences to figure out how to behave in new situations, and solve problems. Emotions also enable us to give purpose to our behavior and meaning to our words and to form abstract ideas and concepts. They are essential for academic tasks, such as reading and doing math, because emotions enable us to understand what we read and to form base concepts of quantity, time, spatial relationships, and causality. Most important, emotional experience enables us to build a sense of self, separate reality from fantasy, control impulses, become involved with peers, and navigate the different stages of emotional, social, and intellectual development.[1]

EMOTIONS AND THE SPECIFIC CHALLENGES OF CHILDREN WITH SPECIAL NEEDS

Understanding how emotions enable us to be intelligent and to think helps us answer some of the most puzzling questions we've had about children with special needs. Why do they have a hard time learning to think creatively and abstractly? How can we best help them master their developmental challenges?

Think of the human brain and mind as having many component parts that must work together and be organized according to some purpose. Intent, affects (emotions), or desires (wishes) provide the critical sense of purpose that gives direction to and organizes the various components of our minds. With most children with special needs, the connection between affects and the component parts, including the ability to sequence behavior and words, is present but underused. It is underused for a reason. Children with special needs often have a problem with one or more component parts— with motor-planning or sequencing behavior, auditory processing (which also involves some sequencing of words in terms of understanding), expressive language, or visual-spatial processing. When the component part is not working well, it tends to be used less; it therefore is used less to express the sense of purpose or intent conveyed by the affects. Because the intent or emotional direction can't be easily expressed through language or motor patterns, the connection between affect or intent and the component parts tends not to develop as fully as it should. Thus an intervention program needs to focus on connecting intent to the component parts. In Part 2 we explain how we work on both the intent and the various biologically based abilities together.

Autism: A Special Case of a Deficit in the Connection between Affect and Sequencing Capacity

The autistic spectrum disorders, including the pervasive developmental disorders, appear to involve a deficit in this core capacity, that is, in the connection between intent or affect and the different component parts, especially the ability to sequence motor patterns (motor planning), behavior, words, and spatial configurations. Autistic spectrum disorder represents an extreme example of what happens when there is a deficit in the ability to connect intent or affect to the other capacities of the human brain and mind.

We studied 200 children who had been diagnosed with autistic spectrum disorder (see Appendix C). Although a variety of mechanisms have been suggested, there is no consensus about underlying psychological and biological patterns associated with autistic spectrum dysfunction. To reach a greater understanding of the role of these underlying processing difficulties, we looked at the processing challenges of both children who did very well and children who continued to have significant difficulties.

All the children in our study evidenced auditory-processing, motor-planning, and sensory-modulation difficulties. Many of the children also had visual-spatial processing challenges, but some children showed relative strength in this area. A number of researchers have postulated that these and other psychological and cognitive mechanisms, such as a difficulty in understanding another person's state of mind (e.g., to be able to empathize with another) underlie autistic symptoms.

We explored differences between groups of children who had good-to-outstanding outcomes and the group that continued to have severe difficulties. The group with poor outcomes and more severe difficulties had a preponderance of children with low muscle tone and motor-planning difficulties. Children in this group also generally had a greater degree of underreactivity to sensation, including both greater craving and greater self-absorption; were less hyperreactive to sensation; and generally showed less mixed degrees of reactivity to different sensation.

Children in the group that did very well tended to have more overreactivity and mixed reactivity, less severe motor-planning difficulties, and slightly higher muscle tone. However, there was significant individual variation. Some children with low tone and severe motor-planning problems made outstanding progress, and some who were oversensitive, with less severe motor-planning problems, continued to have great difficulties. Such patterns suggest that different degrees and types of processing difficulties contribute to autistic spectrum disorders. The nature of these difficulties and the resulting deficit may have some role in the presentation and severity of symptoms as well as in the outcomes. Of special interest was the observation that, regardless of the processing profile, the key turning point for the children who made good progress was the development of the capacity to connect "intent" or affect to motor-planning and sequencing capacities to provide purpose, direction, and meaning to behavior. Affect also needed to be connected to auditory and visual-spatial processing to give meaning to ideas.

This study confirmed, in detail, the core role of emotion in giving purpose to our actions and meaning to our words and in developing abstract thought. The lack of the capacity to connect affect or intent to our planning sequencing and processing capacities therefore may be the core psychological deficit in autistic problems and may provide important clues as to where to look for underlying biological mechanisms in these disorders. It is also a key capacity for promoting growth in most children with special needs.

NOTES

1. For a full discussion of the emotional basis of intelligence, morality, and sense of self, and the stages of intellectual and emotional growth, see Stanley Greenspan, *The Growth of the Mind and the Endangered Origins of Intelligence* (Reading, Mass.: Addison-Wesley, 1996).

PART TWO

*Encouraging Emotional and
Intellectual Growth*

8

The Floor-Time Approach

In the first part of this book we talked about the factors that contribute to a child's problems. In this part we talk about how to ameliorate those problems. Floor time, a systematic way of working with a child to help him climb the developmental ladder, is the heart of what we call the developmental approach to therapy. It takes a child back to the very first milestone he may have missed and begins the developmental progress anew. By working intensively with parents and therapists, the child can climb the ladder of milestones, one rung at a time, to begin to acquire the skills he is missing.

Most children with special needs are involved with therapists and educators who are helping them master developmental challenges. But to climb the developmental ladder, a child needs intensive, one-on-one work. Even daily speech or occupational therapy often does not provide enough practice. After all, a child may have 12 or more waking hours, during which she is learning something. The question is, what? Is she learning about TV (one-way communication)? Is he learning about staring out a window or repetitively opening and closing a door or lining up toys? Is she learning the pleasure of engaging with others and the satisfaction of taking initiative, making her wishes and needs known, and getting responses? Is he learning to have long dialogues, first without words and later with them, and eventually to imagine and think? Floor time creates opportunities for a child to learn these critical developmental lessons. It can be implemented, both as a procedure and as a philosophy, at home, in school, and as a part of a child's different therapies. First we describe floor times as an intensive, one-on-one experience; then we discuss the overall therapeutic team and educational approach.

The developmental approach to therapy consists of three parts.

1. *Parents do floor time with their child,* creating the kinds of experiences that promote mastery of the milestones.

2. *Speech, occupational, and physical therapists, educators, and/or psychotherapists work with the child* using specialized techniques informed by floor-time principles to deal with the child's specific challenges and facilitate development.

3. *Parents work on their own responses and styles of relating with regard to the different milestones* in order to maximize their interactions with their child and create a family pattern that supports emotional and intellectual growth in all family members.

While all three of these processes are important, floor time is the hub around which the other two revolve because it is primarily through floor time that your child will learn to interact in a way that fosters growth. As his specific needs are met with therapy he will bring his new abilities to floor-time interactions. As you learn how your own responses influence your child, you will put that learning to use in floor time. In the interactions and free play of floor time, you can help your child build interpersonal, emotional, and intellectual skills.

Floor time is precisely that: a 20-to-30-minute period when you get down on the floor with your child and interact and play. How can playful interactions help your child master the milestones? The answer has to do with the nature of the interactions. Certain types of interactions with other people promote a child's growth. In the chapters that follow, we describe these specific types. First, though, we want to explore the importance of human relationships.

Human relationships are critical to a child's development. Human beings seem to be created to learn and grow in the context of relating to other humans; the brain and mind simply don't develop without being nurtured by human relationships. Without relationships, self-esteem, initiative, and creativity do not grow either. Even the more intellectual functions of the brain—logic, judgment, abstract thought—don't develop without a constant source of relating.

Much of our best early learning happens through our relating to other people. An infant learns about cause and effect in part by dropping her spoon and watching it hit the floor. But she learns far more, and far earlier and more solidly, by smiling and getting a smile back. Later she learns by reaching out her arms and having Mommy pick her up. The pleasure that results from this learning is far more intense; the subtleties in Mommy's response far more varied. This kind of rich and intense response, which becomes deeply etched in the child's emotions, is possible only in human interactions. The child then applies this emotional lesson in causality ("I can make something happen") to the physical world. That the emotional lesson comes first and is the basis for the cognitive lesson is opposite to the traditional view of cognition and learning. This insight is essential for mobilizing intellectual and emotional growth in children with special needs.

Through interactions, you can mobilize your child's emotions in the service of his learning. As explained in the previous chapter, emotions make all learning possible. By interacting with your child in ways that capitalize on his emotions—by following his interests and motivations—you can help him climb the developmental ladder. You can help him *want* to learn how to attend to you; you can help him *want* to learn how to engage in a dialogue; you can inspire him to take initiative, to learn about causality and logic, to act to solve problems even before he speaks and move into the world of ideas. As together you open and close many circles of communication in a row you can help him connect his emotions and his intent with his behavior (such as pointing for a toy) and eventually with his words and ideas ("Give me that!"). In helping him link his emotions to his behavior and his words in a purposeful way, instead of learning by rote, you enable your child to begin to relate to you and the world more meaningfully, spontaneously, flexibly, and warmly. He gains a firmer foundation for advanced cognitive skills.

Children with special needs require a tremendous amount of practice in linking their intent or emotions to their behavior and then to their words. Like a right-handed person learning to throw a curve ball with her left hand, they need to practice the skill over and over to master it. Floor time is your child's practice time. Each time you get down on the floor and interact— spontaneously, joyfully, following your child's interests and motivations— you help him build that link between emotion and behavior, and eventually words, and in doing so move forward on his journey up the developmental ladder.

THE NUTS AND BOLTS OF FLOOR TIME

Floor time is like ordinary interaction and play in that it is spontaneous and fun. It is unlike ordinary play in that you have a developmental role. That role is to be your child's very active play partner. Your job is to *follow your child's lead and play at whatever captures her interest,* but to do it in a way that *encourages your child to interact with you.* That means if she wants to roll cars, you roll cars with her, offering her a faster car or a competitive race or, if necessary, crashing her car with yours—doing whatever it takes to create an interaction. If she wants to build with blocks, you build with her, adding blocks to her tower, even knocking a block off her tower with an "oops"— again, doing whatever it takes to create an interaction. Your role is to be a constructive helper and, when necessary, provocateur by doing whatever it takes to turn her activity into a two-person interaction.

Following a child's lead means building on the child's natural inclinations and interests. It does not necessarily mean going along with what a child wants to do. Many parents and professionals frequently follow a child's lead passively, without generating a lot of opening and closing of circles. Active following of the child's lead means building on what the child does in a way that literally compels the child to want to open and close more circles of communication. Sometimes the child will readily build on your attempts to expand his interactions. Other times you will need to be much more compelling, but always in the context of his areas of interest. For example, when the child is focused entirely on a toy horse and avoids your overture to have your horsey talk to his horsey and begins wandering toward the door, having you and your horsey block the door challenges the child to negotiate with gestures and/or words, and in so doing, open and close a number of circles. You are following his lead in an active and challenging way because you're dealing with his interest in horsies and his interest in going out the door. You are not going along with him, but you are building on what he's doing.

Initially this won't be easy. Some children with challenges fight tooth and nail to be left alone. You may have to be playfully obstructive—literally get in your child's way—to create an interaction. But with time, he may come to anticipate your initiatives and even to like them. Once that happens you can work on extending your interactions, prodding him through play to close multiple circles of communication. As his joy in engaging, emotional expressions, and gestural communication grows, you can introduce the world of ideas. By putting a puppet on your hand or a doll in the car he is rolling, you can woo your child into complex imitation and pretend play; by being a character in his dramas, you can continue to foster interaction while introducing words. As his dramas become more complex and his language ability grows, you can help him begin to verbalize his feelings rather than act them out. You can encourage him to close verbal circles, just as he closed gestural ones. In this way, you may gradually entice him into the world of ideas and logical thinking.

Four Goals

Earlier we described the emotional milestones as six discrete skills that a child must master in order to communicate, think, and form a sense of self. Your floor-time goals will not be pegged exactly to the six milestones, because several of these milestones naturally overlap as your child learns. You will work on four goals in floor time.

Goal 1: Encouraging attention and intimacy. As your child learns to remain calm while exploring her world, she will also be developing an interest in you because you are the most important person in her world. You both will work on maintaining mutual attention and engagement. Your goal is to help your child tune in to you and enjoy your presence. (This goal contributes to milestones 1 and 2.)

Goal 2: Two-way communication. Next you will help your child learn to open and close circles of communication, at first with subtle facial expressions and a gleam in the eye, a dialogue without words. By creating a gestural dialogue, you build interaction, logic, and problem solving. Your task is to encourage a dialogue, to help your child use his affects or emotions, hands, face, and body to communicate wishes, needs, and intentions. Over time, you try to help your child open and close many circles of communication in a complex, problem-solving dialogue. (This achievement correlates with milestones 3 and 4.)

Goal 3: Encouraging the expression and use of feelings and ideas. Your child can now begin learning to express her feelings or intentions in words and pretend play. Your goal is to encourage dramas and make-believe, through which your child can express her needs, wishes, and feelings, and gradually to help her express these in words. (This goal corresponds with milestone 5.)

Goal 4: Logical thought. Finally, you can help your child link his ideas and feelings to come to a logical understanding of the world. Your goal is to encourage him to connect his thoughts in logical ways. (This ability corresponds to milestone 6.)

Where to Begin?

The purpose of floor time is to help your child master the emotional milestones one by one, in sequential order, starting with the earliest one that he hasn't mastered. For many children with special needs, this means beginning with the ability to feel calm, focused, and intimate. It's hard to start working on so basic a skill when your child is two, three, or even older. It's tempting to work instead on language skills, color recognition, or some other age-appropriate behavior; but such an approach is not effective. Each milestone lays a foundation for the ones that follow. If your child has serious behavior problems—banging his head, throwing tantrums, repetitively opening and closing doors—it's equally tempting to begin work on those. You need to deal with such behavior to keep your child safe, but it is important to keep the primary goal in mind. Once the basic skills are in place, you will find it easier to work with problem behavior because you will be dealing with an interactive, communicating child. It's often possible to work on your child's most basic needs in the context of a more advanced skill, such as using imitation games to foster calm, joyful, focused relating.

A milestone is fully mastered when a child can exhibit that skill even at times of high emotion; she should be able to be *intimate* with her caregiver shortly after being angry, to sustain *two-way communication* even while upset, to *express feelings through words or play* shortly after frustration, and to *connect ideas logically* even when she is disappointed. Most children learn the milestones at times of emotional equilibrium; it takes a lot of practice to sustain them under stress. But when children can do so, all subsequent learning will be on a firmer foundation.

Children don't naturally master the milestones in neat sequential order. It's common for children to be somewhat verbal but still become avoidant when stressed, or to have episodes of pretend play but still be inconsistent at gestural communication. For that reason, you'll find yourself working on several milestones at once. But your primary job is to broaden and stabilize the earliest milestone your child has not fully mastered.

You may already have an intuitive sense of where you need to begin. To confirm your ideas, conduct the following simple exercise. Ask yourself these questions and consider how you would answer if your child were stressed and how you would answer if he were content.

- Can he calm himself down? Can he be warm and loving?

- Can she engage in two-way gestural communication, express a lot of subtle emotion, and open and close many circles in a row?

- Can he engage in pretend play and/or use words to convey intentions or wishes ("I want juice")?

- Can she connect her thoughts logically and hold a conversation for a sustained period of time?

Any observations you made of your child based on Chapter 3 should also help you determine in what areas he needs work and in what areas he is strong.

Floor-Time Guidelines

The next chapters address tailoring floor time to each of the goals, but certain guidelines apply regardless of the skills you are trying to build.

- *Pick a time when you know you can give your child an uninterrupted 20 to 30 minutes.* Your child needs your undivided attention. Even the busiest parents can find 20 to 30 minutes to give undiluted attention to their child. Many children will require many 20-to-30-minute sessions.

- *Try to stay patient and relaxed.* If you're feeling pressured, distracted, or nervous, you won't be able to help your child tune in and stay calm. Whether they are four months or four years old, children know when an adult has time and patience for them.

- *Empathize with your child's emotional tone.* If your child is troubled or tired, let him know you see and understand. To a verbal child you might say, "Gee, I see you're feeling tired today," using a warm and understanding voice. To a preverbal child you can gesture, perhaps by tilting your head or making a pillow of your hands while looking at him warmly. Doing this makes the child feel understood and helps build rapport between you. As you interact with your child, show him you understand his mood by the way you engage in floor time. For an overloaded, tired child, floor time might involve lying on the floor together and letting your child show you or tell you where he likes his back, arms, fingers, or toes rubbed. For an energetic runner, floor time may involve pretend play with lots of action. By empathizing, you can make floor time a pleasurable, meaningful, and developmentally facilitating experience regardless of your child's mood.

- *Be aware of your own feelings* because they will affect how you relate to your child. If you're on a different emotional wavelength, you'll have a harder time tuning in to hers. So before you begin floor time, take stock of how you're feeling. For instance, feeling irritable or angry may make you brusque and demanding. In particular, be aware of depression. Sometimes when parents are depressed, their interactions slow down to half speed; there are lengthy pauses between their sentences and between their child's actions and their own. They may speak and gesture without joy. It is very difficult to respond to this kind of behavior, especially for a child who needs to be drawn out. Occasional depression is common in parents of children with significant challenges. Choose a time for floor time when you are feeling more cheerful, or seek help yourself if the despondent mood does not lift.

• *Monitor your tone of voice and gestures.* You want to be and sound warm, enticing, and supportive—not impatient, angry, or demanding—even when your child is not responding as you would like. Remember that your child is doing his best. He's not thwarting you on purpose; he's doing what his abilities and stage of development permit. Your goal is to encourage him to play with you, and you'll only do that by sounding like someone he might *want* to play with. Would you want to play with someone who was stern, accusatory, or impatient?

• *Follow your child's lead and interact!* Look for ways to turn all your child's actions or seeming nonactions into interactions. Treat all her behavior as purposeful and as an opportunity to build two-way communication.

- If she is moving a car, move your car near hers. See if she will create an interaction; if not, offer a race or playfully block her car.

- If she wants to read, read together. Challenge her to point to the pictures; discuss what you see or read; turn reading into an interactive game. If your child is preverbal, hold the book upside down or turn the pages backward, challenging her to interact with you by fixing the problem. Simply reading *to* your child—without discussion, without letting your child finish the story or point to a favorite picture— although great for other times, is not appropriate for floor time because it doesn't involve enough interaction.

- If your child wants to build a block tower and wants you to assemble the blocks, make sure he directs the activity. If you respond to his directions, you're interacting. If you build the tower for him, you're not.

- If he wants to do nothing but look out the window, look out the window with him and comment on what you see; see if he will point or vocalize to show you something. Point excitedly to birds. Laugh at dogs trotting by. Imitate the sound of cars roaring past. Use gestures, noises, and facial expressions to turn looking into a joint activity in which your child can take some initiative rather than simply listen to or ignore you. If it is difficult to attend together to something outside, put family pictures or colorful stick-on pictures of Sesame Street or Disney characters on the windows to look at. If your child objects and takes them off, interactions begin.

- If your child runs to the other side of the room each time you come near, turn her dodging into a game by saying, "Ready, set, go!" and switching sides yourself. Keep up the game as long as your child does.

- If she turns away each time you come near, turn her avoidance into an interaction. Say playfully, "You can't get away from me!" or "I'll get to your spot first!" or "I'm the cat and I'm chasing you, the mouse!" Even if your child does not understand your words, your actions will help you keep up interactive dialogues. Try not to feel rejected, but instead to see her avoidance as an opportunity for interaction.

- *Tune in to your child's multiple developmental levels.* Foster attention, engagement, the exchange of gestures—including long sequences if possible—and, as your child becomes ready, the shared use of ideas in pretend play and discussions.

- *No hitting, breaking, or hurting.* For your child this is the only floor-time rule. Anything your child wants to play at is fine, as long as it respects this basic tenet. If he becomes overexcited, soothe and calm him. If he responds violently, you may have to hold him firmly, helping him organize himself while you are making clear this is not allowed.

How Often?

Children with special needs often need many sessions of floor time a day. Many family members, as well as friends, other caregivers, or students, can be a part of your floor-time team. Because you need to remain calm, energetic, and joyful, it is unwise to go beyond your own capacity, but many parents do find that their capacity enlarges with practice. You should try to have floor-time sessions as often as possible, depending on your schedule, the number of people who can assist you, and the nature of your child's challenges. For many children, especially for those with severe challenges, in addition to a floor-time philosophy during all waking hours, six to ten 20-to-30-minute floor-time sessions a day is optimal. One to two sessions a day is often not enough.

Try to establish routine times for your sessions and then set up a schedule. Otherwise, other needs, phone calls, or sheer avoidance may take over. Floor time can occur before or after school or work, before or after meals, and before or after bath time.

At times, your whole family can do floor time together. Being involved in floor time will help your other children relate constructively and positively to their sibling with special needs and will help them feel that they're getting your attention as well. Each child might be the floor-time leader for 15 to 20 minutes with the other(s) in a support role. You take your cues from the leader, but all the children are drawn into the interaction.

Try to sit down or have a conference call weekly with all the people who are interacting with your child to discuss what went well and what was difficult, to share tricks and ideas, to discuss frustrations and concerns, and to reset goals. These team meetings will support everyone's efforts.

Most important, you can use the floor-time principles even when you're not engaged in a floor-time session. Interactions during dinner, while getting dressed, while driving in the car, while negotiating bedtime—all can be geared toward enhancing interactions that promote your child's development. Remember, the keys are to (1) harness your child's natural affect or intent, when necessary, creating circumstances to mobilize emotions, joyful interactions, and more purposeful, intentional behavior; (2) build on these intentional behaviors and open and close many circles in a row; and (3) move your child up the developmental ladder from attention, engagement, and two-way gestural and behavioral interaction to complex imitation, pretend play, and discussions that use ideas, logical dialogues, and patterns of thinking. The following four chapters describe how to mobilize your child's development through your interactions with her.

THE FLOOR-TIME APPROACH FOR
THERAPISTS AND EDUCATORS

Many therapists and educators are very innovative in the way they engage and motivate children. Many incorporate floor-time principles or their own similar techniques into their existing strategies. Tying occupational therapy, physical therapy, speech therapy, and education skills into the six milestones will strengthen the child's learning of those skills.

> • An occupational therapist, for example, while helping a child learn to point and reach, can also woo the child into relatedness by inviting him to take an object from the therapist's hand or mouth, rather than from a box. She can help the child practice

two-way communication by first offering a desired toy, then playfully whisking it away, then offering it again, then hiding it behind her back. Through this game of keep-away, the therapist and child can close many circles of communication.

• A speech therapist working with a child on particular sounds can incorporate those sounds into pretend play, encouraging the child's use of ideas as well as her use of language. She can create a play environment in which the desired sounds are present—a kitchen with food and forks and frying pans, for instance, when the child is working on "f."

• An educator teaching the concepts of big and little, more and less, and up and down, can incorporate them into pretend play or create situations in which the child will want to use the concept, for example, to get *more* stickers or cookies.

Connecting therapy and education skills to the milestones makes the child's learning richer and more solid because the skills become connected to affect and interaction and are incorporated into the child's growing sense of self. (See Chapter 18 for more discussion on an integrated approach.)

9

Floor Time I:
Attention, Engagement, and Intimacy

HELPING A CHILD BECOME
INTERESTED IN THE WORLD AND
CONNECT WITH PEOPLE

At 26 months, Max was flapping his arms excitedly as he joyously sang the
ABCs. He had just discovered a letter puzzle and sang his beloved letters over
and over again. His back was turned to his parents and he was clearly
oblivious as they called his name again and again. Anxious to interrupt him,
his mother picked him up from behind and twirled him around. He startled
for a moment but then shrieked with delight. When she put him down (he
was heavy!), he resumed his alphabet song, his back to her. She twirled him
again and he stopped singing, giving way to her abrupt but pleasant
movement. The moment she put him down, he resumed singing without
turning around even once.

A moment later, Max's mother moved in front of him and called out,
"Here comes the ABC mommy!" this time bending down to eye level and
reaching out her arms. Max stepped away and looked around her as he
continued to sing his ABCs. She moved in front of him again; he moved
away but stopped singing. She again asked if he would like to swing, reaching
out once more. Max sidestepped her and was about to walk away when she
handed him the puzzle. As soon as he saw her extend the puzzle toward him,

he glanced at her and resumed singing. This time, she sang with him as she held one end of the puzzle and he the other. They began to swing the puzzle back and forth as they sang, and Max's joyous voice rang out loudly as he started to look at his mother, swaying back and forth. If she paused, he pulled, reminding her to go on. After several rounds, she tried to sing the next phrase before he did, but to no avail. She went back to singing with him. She then asked if he would like to do the ABC dance and dropped her end of the puzzle in order to reach out to him. This time, Max let go of the puzzle too and lifted his arms to his mother. They started a rhythmic dance together; she moved and swung Max from side to side until he could sustain eye contact. As she slowed the pace, Max sang more slowly, matching her rhythm. Their intimate dance went on and on until Max slid from his mother's arms. He ran back to his ABC puzzle. His mother followed and repeated her earlier efforts. This time, Max reached for his ABC mommy sooner, and again they danced joyously.

As his mother became associated with, and as predictable as, Max's ABCs, they shared more joyous dancing together. Within a few weeks they could sing the song reciprocally. New meanings were established. Max's flapping had turned into reaching for his mom to lift him and dance. The alphabet song was now a shared experience. By following Max's lead without taking over, and enriching his movement with face-to-face dancing, Max's mother had helped him learn to enjoy intimacy.

At two and a half, John rarely made eye contact with his parents and turned away if they tried to play. Capturing his attention would not be easy. But Randy, John's dad, was game to try. As John rolled a truck back and forth on the floor, Randy put his hand on the truck. John immediately screamed and tightened his grasp. Undaunted, Randy got a second truck and tried crashing it into John's. John turned his back and continued playing by himself. These rather aggressive overtures were not going to work. Randy had to find a way to interact with John's repetitive motion without trying to dominate or change it. Randy thought for a moment, then put his hand, palm down, on the floor in the path of the truck.

John drove the truck up to his dad's hand, stopped for a moment as if deciding what to do, then drove the truck right over the hand. He didn't look at Randy as he did it, but by not avoiding the contact, he had tacitly interacted. Randy left his hand where it was, and on his return trip, John backed the truck over the hand. A second interaction. The two kept up this low-level interaction for five or six more trips, then Randy raised the stakes. He rested his hand sideways on the floor so that it formed a barrier the truck could not go over. This time John ran the truck right up to Randy's hand, bumped the hand with the truck, and laughed. Randy grinned. This was the first time during this session, and one of the few times all year, that John had acknowledged his father's presence. Over the next few weeks John and Randy developed other games with the truck. Randy found ways to interact with, instead of trying to change, John's actions, creating problems for John to solve. Their games were often accompanied by laughter and even a little eye contact. After several weeks John began bringing the truck over to his dad, inviting him to play. For the first time, Randy felt they were on their way to building a relationship.

FINDING MUTUAL PLEASURE

If your child is given to wandering aimlessly around a room, touching everything, holding on to one object until he finds another he likes better, then dropping that for another, it's easy to wonder how on earth you can entice, and hold, his attention. The way to do it is to *join him in the myriad little things that give him pleasure.* Offer or notice things he finds enticing. Gather the things he has dropped and put them in a basket. If you can share these little pleasures with him you will build a basis for interaction. Your first goal is not to force interaction; it is merely to connect, to share the pleasure of doing something together, to experience mutual joy. At first this sharing may last for only two seconds; gradually it may stretch to ten; in time, it will last much longer. But first, just try to establish a sense of mutual pleasure.

ADAPTING TO YOUR CHILD'S MOOD

Before you begin looking for ways to engage with your child, take note of her mood. If she is irritable or overexcited, sleepy or withdrawn, it may be very difficult to engage her. Your first goal should be to help her into a state of calm alertness. If she is excited or irritable, soothe her. Think about what sensations calm her. Does she particularly enjoy a certain type of touch or holding, a certain song, or a tone and rhythm in your voice? Does she like a certain type of movement—gentle swinging or rocking? Does she grow calmer when she's in semidarkness or in brighter light?

If he is sleepy or withdrawn, you'll want to rev him up a bit. Again, appeal to the senses that you know he likes and that tend to energize him. Does he perk up when you speak in a certain animated way? When you sing particular songs? When you move in quick or silly ways? When you make faces at him or put scarves or hats on your head? Do certain types of movements energize him—rocking, swinging, jumping, or rolling?

Think about your child's sensory-motor profile (Chapter 3) and about what activities he finds soothing or energizing, and use those to draw him into a state of calm alertness.

HOLDING YOUR CHILD'S ATTENTION THROUGH HIS SENSES

Once you've used your child's preferred sensations and movement to calm or stimulate him, continue using them to engage him. Although each sensory modality is described separately here, remember that information is taken in simultaneously so that your child may look, listen, and move all at the same time.

Sound

Offer your child the sounds she likes best.

- Is she more attentive to high-pitched noises than to low-pitched sounds? Talk to her in a high-pitched voice to grab her attention.

- Does he like low, guttural noises? Lower your voice as you woo him. Speak more slowly or describe his actions in sound.

- Does she respond positively to certain vibrating noises, such as the sound of the clothes dryer? Sit her on top of or next to the dryer as it runs. If the sound of the dryer calms her, her attention will be more available for you.

Use the items that make the sounds he likes to help engage him. Smile and call his name, or play ball, or wave a Slinky together. If he likes a particular music box, position yourself and the box so that as he looks at the music box he also looks at you. Wait for a signal that he would like to listen, then turn on the box so that when he enjoys the music box he will also be enjoying you. Look for other ways to bring his favorite noises into your interactions.

Finally, use vocal gestures as much as possible—phrases such as "uh-oh!" and "oh, no." The exaggerated effect will grab his attention and give him a chance to figure out what the problem is.

Touch

What kinds of textures does your child like to touch or be touched by? Use those textures to draw her attention to you.

- Does he like firm pressure against his skin? Lie next to him on the floor with your faces close together and press him firmly with your hands. Or squish next to him on the couch and wait for him to signal you to move.

• Does she like slimy, squooshy textures? Offer her Play-Doh or Silly Putty and help her stretch it to make spaghetti. Or fill a large pan with flour and water to knead and pull.

• Does he like to dig his hands in a basin of beans or rice? Meet his fingers "underground" or hide marbles for him to find. Outdoors, play in the sandbox and offer him sand and toys to play with.

Many children enjoy playing with their food—not to irritate their parents, but because the activity gives them tactile pleasure. Instead of viewing playing with food as making a mess, view it as a chance to engage your child. Put your hand in there too, and mush her food together. If she throws down pieces of food, have a bowl ready to catch them. Don't be surprised if she manages to avoid the bowl. When she's warm, related, and communicating there will be time enough to teach her to be neat. At this point you want to do anything you can to help her enjoy your presence.

Sight

What kind of visual experiences attract your child and give him pleasure?

• Does he like bright colors? When you see him gazing at something bright, put a brightly colored scarf on your head and stand between him and what he is looking at. Use his interest in color to attract his attention to you.

• Does she like animated objects, such as mobiles, electric trains, or pinwheels? Next time she's gazing at a mobile, play peekaboo, coming out from behind it and calling her name, then moving back behind it again. Or hold a pinwheel near your face and blow, calling her name as you do so. Use her interest in animation to call her attention to you.

• Get two flashlights and explore his room in the dark, or chase each other and track the light around objects.

Smell and Taste

If you know that your child particularly likes certain foods, enjoy those foods together. Eat from the same bowl. Use your hands. See if she tries to stop you or pulls the bowl toward her. Give her more just when she suspects this sharing may not be worthwhile. While she is eating, cue her with your voice and actions, holding her attention as long as possible. Coo, laugh, and make funny faces at her. Gently make yourself part of her taking pleasure in food.

Motor Experiences

Many children move in ways that don't seem purposeful, for instance, flapping, jumping, spinning, aimlessly wandering, or rubbing up against things. Although you may be concerned about this behavior, it's important to view it as another opportunity for engagement. If certain motions give your child pleasure, try to find ways to join him in those movements. Once you do, you are in a better position to go from repetition to interaction by giving these actions new meanings.

- If he's flapping his arms, flap your arms too and pretend to fly. If he doesn't notice, flap closer. Perhaps touch him gently as you do so. If necessary, get your arm caught under his. He may resent your intrusion and run away—or he may smile or giggle. Either way, he'll be interacting.

- If he's turning round and round, take his arms and sing "Ring-around-the-Rosy," changing speed until you both fall down. Your child will come to recognize the song and actions after a while and join in.

- If she's rocking back and forth, sit face-to-face with her and rock along with her. If she doesn't notice, rock closer. Let your knees touch. Rock in the opposite direction so that you create friction, or rock a little harder so that your movement pulls her slightly from side to side. Get stuck in the path of her rocking. See if she will let you rock her to different rhythms. Try gently to turn the rocking into a two-person game. You might sing "Row, Row, Row Your Boat" to establish a rhythm with push-and-pull actions.

- If she's lying stonelike on the floor, say, "You're tired. I'll be your blanket!" and lie down on top of her. She may push you off, or she may smile, enjoying the firm pressure. Or, turn off the lights and hand her a pillow and blanket while you sing a lullaby. She'll recognize this routine and wonder what's going on. If she gets up, say, "Good morning!" and turn the lights back on.

Here are other ways to take advantage of your child's favorite ways of moving to engage him and share his pleasure.

- Has he shown you that he wants to jump? Crouch down in front of him as he jumps so that with each pleasurable landing he sees your face. Smile and call his name, or use some other visual or aural signal that works to draw his attention to you.

• Has she shown you that she wants to swing by pointing at the swing in the park? Push her from in front, not from behind, so that you can make eye contact as she swings. Again call her name, clap your hands, sing a song, appeal to her visual and auditory preferences to make your contact even more pleasurable. Feign a push sometimes to see if she will react. Does she grin or blink with pleasure as you whisk her through the air? Do it again and again and again. See if she will look at you for more. Do it as many times as you can until she indicates she's ready for a break.

Use your child's pleasure in a movement to create a moment of joy with you. Never interrupt interactions your child wants to continue, but add to them to make them more complex. Doing so will challenge him to make more responses. If he enjoys sword fighting, move the sword to unexpected positions, hold it backward, or put it down. This may provoke him to communicate, "No! Stop! Do it the right way!" as he puts the sword back in your hand.

PLAYING TO YOUR CHILD'S STRENGTHS AND WORKING AROUND HER CHALLENGES

As you try to capture your child's attention remember her strengths and difficulties in processing information. Does she process visual information easily, but auditory information less so? Or do visual cues seem to slip right by her while words and sounds get a response? Tailor your wooing to her strengths. If she takes in visual signals well, use a lot of facial expressions and body gestures, perhaps make some simple signs with your hands, while keeping your words basic. If she listens well, use a variety of sounds and words to woo her, while keeping your facial and body movements uncomplicated.

If Your Child Has Auditory-Processing Problems

Auditory-processing problems can make it especially difficult for your child to tune in to you because he may miss, or misinterpret, some of your signals. He may not be comforted by your soothing voice, for example, or he may not respond when you call his name. You can work around this challenge by talking slowly, making your sounds distinct and energetic, and using lots of hand gestures and facial animation to give your child additional cues. If your child likes to be touched, you can use touch to get his attention and offer reassurance.

If you child is also overreactive to sensation, be careful to keep your voice and gestures soothing (but still energetic and distinct) so as not to overwhelm him. Change your tone quickly if he covers his ears. If he is underreactive, rev up your voice and gestures. Talk slowly to help him process the words, but talk with more animation and make your gestures bigger. Remember that there may be a delay before your child can organize a response to what he has heard. Be patient and wait for a few moments.

Children with auditory-processing difficulties learn to recognize words and patterns of sounds that are expressed with great emotion or that have special meanings, phrases such as "Ready, set, go!" for example, or "Oh, no! What went wrong?" Use these words and phrases whenever appropriate. Even if your child does not repeat the words, he will come to recognize them through your emotional tone. Also, label your child's actions with single words as he does them; say "run," "jump," or "climb" as he moves, and imitate his actions as you do so.

If Your Child Has Motor-Planning Difficulties

If your child has trouble with motor planning he will find it hard to organize a sequence of gestures. When you roll him a ball, instead of rolling it back he may stare at it, look at you, then look away. If he sees a puppet nearby, he may pick it up and begin fingering it, but not put it on his hand and move it. This apparent randomness may suggest to you that he is easily distracted and that it's hard to hold his attention. But the root of this randomness is not lack of interest; it is difficulty stringing together a series of movements. The seemingly simple movements required to reach toward a ball and push it back may be too difficult for a child with motor-planning problems.

You can help your child improve her motor planning by helping her master each movement of a series, one step at a time. You might roll a ball to her from nearby, just a foot or two away. When she starts looking away, get very close, animate your face and voice, and say playfully, "Ball! Ball! Give back! Give back!" It may take five minutes, but if you are patient and animated, she is likely to complete the action. You will have had her attention on you while laying the foundation for that sequence of actions. (If your child appears overwhelmed by your excitement, hold a basket in front of you or use a small basketball hoop to signal where to drop the ball. Hold the ball out for her to take again.)

The important thing is for your child to complete the action. If you take her hand and push the ball, she will not learn anything. But if you can use your voice to spark her interest, to compel her to want to roll you the ball, then she is interacting with you meaningfully as well as learning the motor pattern. The key is to mobilize her feelings, for feelings are what will give direction and purpose to her motor acts. The weaker her ability to sequence her movements, the stronger the motivation needs to be. (Some children need help just to get the motor pattern started. You can help them by putting the ball in their hands. This step will signal it is time to act.)

When your child has motor-planning challenges, it's all too easy to take his seeming aloofness and inattentiveness personally, to assume that he is deliberately turning away from you. As you live and work with your child, remind yourself that this isn't the case; his difficulty with motor planning may make it difficult for him to be more purposeful with you.

TAKING YOUR CUES FROM YOUR CHILD

With all these activities, the most important thing to remember is to follow your child's lead. Don't introduce an activity just because you know your child likes it. He may love to swing, but that doesn't mean he wants to swing *now*. Instead, join him at the thing he is already doing.

This can be hard. It's natural to want to take over, and you may introduce new elements into play or try to direct your child's attention without even meaning to. You need to remind yourself to fight this tendency. Your child will take the most pleasure in activities he chooses himself. If you want to become part of that pleasure, you have to go where he is leading. You can build on what he is doing or, as we explain soon, playfully obstruct it. But remember to begin with his interests. At the start, it doesn't matter what he is doing; it only matters that you join him, that you help him do what he wants to do and become interactive.

The cues your child gives you may be very subtle: a blink to tell you he enjoys something, a slow turning of his head to follow an object of visual interest, a sober staring that makes it seem as though he is doing nothing. As you tune in to your child's sensory preferences, recognizing those cues will get easier and your avenues of mutual pleasure will grow.

Even children who are very fragmented and tuned out take pleasure in certain behaviors. They may love touching a spot on the floor, rubbing a particular pillow, looking out the window, wandering aimlessly, jumping up and down, flapping their hands, or making funny sounds. You probably already know many activities that make your child seem comfortable and happy; if you watch her closely you will discover others.

Your first goal is to join your child as she begins any of these behaviors, to do them right along with her. Then, slowly and gradually, make yourself part of the behavior. In this way you will give this seemingly aimless behavior new, interactive meaning.

- If your child is jumping up and down, jump alongside her and sing, "We are jumping up and down, up and down . . ." to the tune of "The Wheels on the Bus." If she allows you, take her hands so that she can jump higher and higher or hold her so she can jump "to the sky."

- If he is flapping his arms, stand near him and flap your arms too. Usually flapping represents nervous excitement or motor overflow. Try to identify the emotional tone—happy, scared, or angry—with simple words.

- If she is rubbing a favorite stuffed animal, rub the animal too. If she allows you to do this, turn the animal over and see if she will restore it to its original position. Identify feelings related to rubbing the animal, for example, saying "Poor bunny," or "I love you."

- If your child is making funny sounds, hold an echo microphone in front of his mouth so he will hear his sounds amplified. Try imitating his sounds.

- If she is rubbing soft fabric, put your shirt next to the fabric and see if she'll rub your shirt. If she does, then see if she'll rub your skin or hair.

Don't initiate any of these activities. Wait for your child to start and then join him. If he has difficulty initiating purposeful actions, your taking over will deprive him of the chance to learn to initiate.

Join the Object of the Child's Attention

If your child is already busy with a toy or object, don't compete with the object by trying to draw her attention away from it and toward you. Join the object. Make it part of yourself so that as your child enjoys the object she'll also be enjoying you.

- If she is turning her head to look at a lamp or an overhead light, put a flashlight on your head and see if she'll look at that. Smile and talk to her while you are doing so to attract her attention to your face.

- If he is rolling on the floor, roll with him and occasionally bump into him or stop and let him roll into you. When he does, smile and talk soothingly to let him know you're playing a game.

• If she's playing with a ball, hold the ball in your mouth so she'll have to take it from you. Make a funny noise as she grabs it, then open your mouth and gesture for her to put it back. Make another funny noise when she puts it back in. Make "ball in, ball out" a funny, cooperative game.

• If he's rolling a toy car, have the car get caught under your leg, or under your head as if it were your pillow, so that to get it he has to deal with *you*. Laugh or tickle him or make a funny noise when he gets it to make the interaction pleasant. A moment later have the car get caught under you again. Your child can still play with his car, but now he has to play with you as well.

• If she is mushing food and putting it in her mouth, put some of the mushed food on your face. Smile and laugh and call her name, then encourage her to take the food from your face as well as from the table.

The goal of these activities is not to force your child to interact with you by withholding a desired object, but to show her that playing with you can be *fun*—maybe even more fun than playing with the toy alone.

Join Your Child's Games

• Is your child lining up cars? Turn his lineup into a game by handing him the next one in the sequence. When he protests, let him have his way—he interacted! Then keep on trying. Eventually (it may take days) he'll get used to your presence and take the car from your hand. Then *you* start putting the next car in line. Or look at him for permission. He may shake his head or look annoyed. That's fine—he's made contact.

• Is your child playing with marbles? Get your own bucket of marbles, sit as close as he'll let you, and play the way he does: pour them, run them through your hands, rub them between your palms. If after a little while he shows no interest, move a little closer, or roll a marble toward him, or put one of your marbles in his pile. If he protests, take it back to show you understand. Then put a different marble in his basket as if you made a mistake. Talk soothingly but also keep challenging. Eventually he will accept your overtures. When he does, add a new element to the game.

• Is your child picking up objects and dropping them or brushing objects off a shelf? Turn her random behavior into a two-person game by moving along behind her with a basket to catch the things she drops. She'll be startled by your action, possibly angry at your intrusion, or perhaps pleased by the thump of the objects against your basket. Whatever her response, she'll have attended and related. Don't be surprised if she dumps her next basket in a different direction, or furiously takes your basket and dumps it on the floor. If necessary, preempt her dumping by doing it first. Keep up the game and gradually she'll come to accept your presence. Within a few days or weeks she may be waiting for you to offer the basket before she drops each object.

Remember, don't try to change the game. Don't take over. Just follow your child's lead by gently joining, or playfully obstructing, the activity she's started.

Join a Favorite Activity

The more you harness your child's natural interests the easier it will be to engage him in play. He is letting you know what motivates him, and this is at least half the task! If he likes to draw, draw with him. Hand him new markers or pencils and sit alongside him. If he is controlling, you may need to draw on a separate piece of paper. Gradually move closer until he lets you draw on his paper. See if you can start a game in which you take turns working on the same drawing or copying each other's pictures. After a little while this shared activity will probably lead to smiles and eye contact.

Children with motor-planning difficulties often like to scribble because it is an easy motion to maintain and it has an immediate effect: you can see the design. As does playing with the telephone, this exercise suggests they are aware of and trying to imitate an important adult activity.

If your child likes to sing or play instruments, develop sharing games based on those activities. Sing one of her favorite songs and keep it up even if she turns away. If after a few minutes she shows no reaction, drop it, but pick it up again a little while later. Or use musical instruments that play different melodies and see which she chooses. If you persist over several play sessions, your child may begin to sing too, either with you or during your silence. Then try singing a duet. How long can you keep it up? Can you sing alternate verses? At fist she may only be able to fill in the missing word at the end of each line, but she will welcome hearing something familiar. Have a chart with pictures of her favorite songs and ask her to show which she wants to sing.

If your child does well at gross-motor activities—climbing, jumping, doing somersaults—turn those into two-person activities. Help him climb up your body as if he is climbing a ladder, or hold his hands to help him jump down from something high, or hold your arms out like a limbo pole when he somersaults so that he's forced to go over them. Look for ways to turn all your child's natural interests and talents into shared games.

If your child is older and is already counting or recognizing letters or words, you can use this interest to spark engagement. If she's counting, jump in and say the next few numbers; see if she'll continue. If she does, then say the wrong numbers and see if she'll correct you. Try repeating each number in a funny voice, hoping to trigger a giggle. If he's reciting letters, make a different funny face for each letter he says, so that *you* become an enjoyable part of the activity. If he's saying random words, after each word tickle him or hug him or give him some other sensory experience that you know he really likes so that he will want to continue that activity with *you.* Don't focus on the numbers or letters or words. At this stage they are unimportant. Your child can learn them—quickly—later, after he's mastered engagement and two-way communication. What's important now is that he enjoy his interaction with *you.*

Don't Entertain—Interact

As you insert yourself into your child's activities, remember that you are not trying to entertain your child, but to interact with her. You don't want her watching as you bounce her ball, roll her car, or mush her cereal. You want her in there with you, vying for her turn. Interaction creates engagement, and the more you follow her lead, the more you encourage her to respond to *you,* the longer you'll hold her attention.

Enjoy the Moment

As you find ways to turn all your child's activities into interactions, keep something else in mind: the goal is not to focus on the activity—the drawing, the swinging, the rolling of cars through the tunnel of your body—the goal is to do the activity *together.* The activity is merely a tool to encourage intimacy. To that end, take advantage of every smirk or smile. Each time something happens that makes your child laugh, make eye contact and laugh along with him. When something unexpected happens—the car rolls under the couch, the spoon drops to the floor, one of you burps—make eye contact and giggle together. When you're rolling on the floor or roughhousing and you bump heads or end up eye to eye, hold the position for a moment and grin. Don't rush right back to the game. Try to stretch those moments of intimacy. After all, that's what you're really working to achieve.

Above all, try to be patient. It may take weeks or even months to get your child to look you in the eye and smile, but if you are gently persistent in your efforts you can build a sense of togetherness, synchrony, and fun as you engage in these simple activities together.

ENGAGING THE HARD-TO-WOO CHILD

If your child is very avoidant and seems to find pleasure solely outside the world of people, you can still use the tactics described here to woo her into engagement. Examine her avoidant behavior closely; notice how it gives her sensory pleasure or helps her avoid uncomfortable stimuli. Then try to join her in this behavior so that *you* are providing those same sensory pleasures without overwhelming her if she's hypersensitive.

- If she's lying on the floor, don't assume it's because she wants to avoid you; assume it's because she enjoys the sensation of pressure under her body. The floor provides support for her low muscle tone and an awareness of her body in space, which compensates for gravitational insecurity and helps her feel more confident. In this sense, lying on the floor is pleasurable. Say, "I'll be your floor," and try to get underneath her so that you can provide that pleasant pressure.

- If he's under a blanket in the corner, don't assume he doesn't want to be with you; assume that he enjoys the feeling of protection and semidarkness and the sensation of pressure on top of his body. Say, "I'll be your blanket!" and drape yourself over him so that you can provide that sense of darkness and gentle pressure.

Work from the Bottom Up

Once again, return to the sensory and motor profile (Chapter 3) and think carefully about all the sensations you know your child likes. Examine his favorite behavior for *any* clues you may have overlooked that will tell you what sensory experiences he enjoys. Make almost every interaction with you one that offers those pleasures. Do not hesitate to go back to baby sensory-motor games. Join whatever activity he is doing by introducing the sounds, touches, movements, or visual stimulation he likes. Gradually your child will come to associate his interactions with you with those pleasurable feelings, and your opportunities for interaction will grow.

"But My Child Isn't Doing Anything!"

Often parents say, "But my child isn't doing anything; how can I join her activity?" The answer is, "Your child is always doing *something*. You need to find a way to join her in that something." Even avoiding you is doing something, usually something quite purposeful.

• If your child is staring into space, stand in front of her so that she sees *you* instead of what she was looking at. If she turns away, playfully run to where she's looking now and smile. If she turns away again, get down on your knees next to her and stare too, leaning against her with your body. Make staring a two-person game. She may be turning away because she does not comprehend what you want or because your unpredictable actions alarm her.

• If he's wandering aimlessly around the room, be his shadow and wander with him, pinned closely to his side. Or run to where he's going and get there first, then kneel down and greet him when he arrives. Treat what he is doing as purposeful and intentional. This may surprise him, but it will also reinforce his self-awareness.

Your child may find it difficult to initiate purposeful behaviors because of motor-planning problems; or she may avoid you by repeating the few actions she can easily do or by engaging in self-absorbing play. In all these instances, her avoidance is a response.

A good principle to follow when your child seems tuned out and unresponsive, when you can't for the life of you figure out how to insert yourself into his world, is simply to imitate him. Do what he is doing right along with him, then gradually and gently work your way into his attention. Or get a step ahead of him, arranging a collision so that he has to deal with you.

You Can't Force Closeness

Working with an avoidant child can be very frustrating. At times you may feel that your child will never look at you and smile. You may be tempted at such moments to hold his head and say, "Look at me!" just to get the kind of contact you crave. But that won't encourage the kind of behavior you really want—warm, loving eye contact and cuddles—because those behaviors have to well up from inside. They can't be forced.

So even in your most frustrated moments try to be patient. Remember that your goal is never to force your child to engage with you, but rather to *entice* him to do so by offering the sensory pleasures he most enjoys. If you keep appealing to his sensory pleasures, if you keep joining him at his own activities, gradually your moments of eye contact and connectedness will grow. Remember, it takes far more ingenuity to help a child *want* to relate than to create circumstances in which he *has* to relate. But the result is a child who will genuinely enjoy you and other people, rather than one who has mechanically learned the niceties of social interaction.

Be Playfully Obstructive

There will be times when even your most carefully designed sensory overtures won't work, when no matter how much you try, your child simply won't let you in. At such times, you can up the ante a bit by becoming playfully obstructive; you can playfully insert yourself into her activity in a way that makes it harder for her to ignore you.

- If she's wandering aimlessly around the room, and you've already tried shadowing her and getting to her next spot first, try being a doggy and getting between her legs. Bark playfully as you do it so she knows you're playing a game. The idea is not to frighten or annoy her, merely to create an interaction.

- If he's staring into space and you've already tried standing next to him and in front of him, try covering your eyes with his hands. Smile and talk to him softly; you don't want to scare him, you just want to interact.

- If she's flapping her arms and you've already tried flapping along with her, try getting your arms caught in hers. When she accidentally hits you, say playfully, "Whoops! You got me!" to let her know it's a game.

The challenge of playful obstruction is to engage in it playfully and joyfully so that your child isn't scared or overwhelmed. Be slow and gentle, talk softly and warn your child so he knows what to expect. Sudden or unpredictable actions may frighten him away.

- If he's rolling a car and won't let you join in, move in slowly, calling out your intention. "I'm coming," you can say gently, "I'm coming to get your car." Give him a chance to respond before you make your final approach so that he can look at you and motion "No!" Respect his wishes; you've succeeded in getting his attention.

Your child may resist your overtures. Despite your playful intent, he may feel frightened or overwhelmed and he may run away or push you away. That's okay; this is a *purposeful* response. He is answering your question, telling you to stay away, purposefully acknowledging your presence. Even though the response is not shared pleasure, you have generated an interaction. Over time, if you are gentle and soothing, as your child gets used to your availability, his reactions will become more positive.

If your child does respond with displeasure, give him a moment to recoup, then try again. "Here I come again," you can sing. "I'm going to get your car again." Move in slowly, smiling. When he swipes at you, acknowledge his response. "Oh, you don't want me to? Okay. Uh-oh, my fingers seem to want that car. Here they come again." If you remain gentle and playful, you can probably engage him three or four times without making him lose control. Try to gauge when he's had enough and then move on to something else. The idea is not to annoy your child, but to make your presence fun.

As you do these playfully obstructive things, also keep in mind your child's individual differences. If she's overreactive to sound, keep your voice soft and soothing. If she's underreactive, talk more loudly and eagerly to help her pay attention. If he has trouble with auditory processing, keep your sequence of words uncomplicated; "Coming" is easier to grasp than "I'm coming now." If he's stronger at visual processing, stay in his line of vision and make sure he can see your fingers as they approach; he'll be relying on visual cues to gauge your intentions. If your child likes touch, touch her on the arm as you approach in a way that seems friendly rather than aggressive. As much as possible try to catch her rhythm. When your child is moving fast, move fast and talk fast to get her attention; when she slows down, you slow down too. The more in sync you are, the better able she'll be to respond.

The one thing to avoid is trying to control your child's body (unless you feel he is in danger). Don't push or grab him or try to make him move a certain way. You want him to take initiative and be in charge, and he needs control over his body to do that. He may not respond the way you hope, but any response, even running away, will be intentional, and that's a great beginning.

PERSEVERATION

Many children with severe developmental challenges perseverate: they repeat the same motion over and over as if trapped in an endless cycle. Children may engage in perseveration because it offers a sense of security. Constantly bombarded by things they can't control, children try to take control over the little things when they can. Whether it's opening and closing a door, lining up cars, or turning their heads back and forth repeatedly, they create tiny islands of reassuring repetition in an otherwise overwhelming world. Children may also perseverate because they don't know how to sequence the next step; therefore, they repeat the same single action again and again. A third reason children perseverate is that they find perseveration pleasurable and self-stimulating. Many children learn to use relationships and interactions for various types of sensory pleasure. Children who aren't able to engage fully with others or to communicate may rely more on their own bodies.

Although it may be comforting to children, perseveration is usually extremely troublesome to parents—for good reason. Perseveration is the kind of noninteractive behavior that should be discouraged. Rather than trying to stop your child's perseveration or to distract her from it (which rarely works well) though, look at perseveration as an opportunity—a gift from your child that tells you where her natural interest lies. You can then use that interest as a basis for interaction. Does you child repetitively pat her head? Great. Put *your* hand on her head before *her* hand can get there; help her interact. Does he repetitively open and close doors? Great. Get on the other side and exert pressure; help him interact. Some children immediately enjoy the interaction. One child, who repetitively rubbed her mouth and nose with her hand, lit up with a big smile when her mother reached in and rubbed her nose for her. When her mother stopped, the child grabbed her mother's hand and drew it to her face to keep the interaction going.

Other children resist the interaction. They see it as interference. Yet even your child's resistance is a form of interaction, for it is an acknowledgement of your presence. From that unhappy acknowledgment you have a chance to build a longer, more positive, interaction.

Ellen felt very estranged from her daughter, Krista, because Krista would not acknowledge her presence. Instead, Krista engaged in perseverative behaviors, such as scratching at the floor. After months of trying to force an interaction, Ellen decided to put her hand down in the very spot her daughter wanted to scratch. Now Krista had to contend with this annoying hand. She had a problem to solve. And she solved it; she pushed the hand away and grunted her annoyance. Ellen counted that a success. Her daughter had interacted with her hand, and had commented on it, too. As Ellen varied her interaction—sometimes putting her hand down, sometimes not, sometimes taking it away at the very last moment—Krista began to react to the interaction as a game. She began to grunt with pleasure and even to look up to see who was causing this funny disruption. Her perseveration had developed into an interactive game of cat and mouse. Once interactive, it was no longer perseverative.

Several months went by before Krista was comfortable making sustained eye contact with her mother, but once she was able to do so she also began showing pleasure in the encounters. She would giggle when her hand met her mother's, and she sometimes touched her mother's hand provocatively, as if inviting her to play.

Other children repeat a word, a phrase, a verse of a song, or a portion of a videotape script over and over. This is another form of perseveration, and you can treat it in exactly the same way. Get in the way of the sounds. If your child is saying a word or repeating a sound, you repeat them also, but with a different pitch or rhythm. If she's singing a song or reciting from a video, join in but change the words. When she turns away to avoid your intrusion, get in front of her, smilingly put your face in front of hers, and continue your vocal counterpoint. Turn reciting into a game in which her every utterance is matched by yours. She may protest, but she'll be attending and interacting. And eventually she'll accept your participation and let you turn her perseverative recitation into a shared activity. You may even notice that the scripts she selects are relevant to the situation at hand and may have communicative intent, usually representing feelings.

SELF-STIMULATION

Some children engage in what we call self-stimulatory behavior, which gives them sensory pleasure. This behavior is often an attempt to compensate for sensory underreactivity, to seek extra sensation in order to register input. A child may jump up and down, spin, stare at a light, or move his head in a certain way to control what he sees. Because such behavior is so consuming, it is often very hard to break into. Again, instead of seeing this self-stimulation as problematic, see it as a clue your child is giving you about what kinds of sensory pleasure he likes. Then join the behavior, providing those same sensory experiences yourself.

> • If your child rotates his head while he looks toward a light, try putting a small flashlight in your mouth and standing between him and the light. When he becomes interested in the flashlight, wobble it around, flick it off and on, take it out of your mouth and smile at him, then put it back in your mouth. Create games with the flashlight that will attract his attention to *you*.

Another approach is to create an interaction by getting between your child and her self-stimulatory behavior, just as we explained for perseveration.

> • If your child is staring fixedly at a light, stand between her and the light, blocking her view. If it's a ceiling light, use a dimmer to

change its intensity. Pretend the light is "Twinkle, twinkle, little star." When she moves her head to see it again, get in her way again. Smile and talk playfully while you do it, so she knows you're playing a game. Try moving back and forth, blocking her view then unblocking it, to see if that gets a giggle. Try blocking it with your hands, your feet, your leg, a pillow, perhaps making silly noises as you do so. If you are persistent and playful, you are likely to pull her attention to *you.*

INTIMACY THROUGH ALL THE EMOTIONS

If you are diligent about working daily with your child, your periods of intimacy should grow; the glimmers of eye contact will lengthen; the feelings between you will warm; your child will begin to seek you out. You will have given your child the most essential skill he needs: the ability to attend to and enjoy human relationships.

Human relationships are not always warm and intimate, however. Inevitably, anger, disappointment, frustration, jealously, sadness, and other feelings intrude. The challenge is to help your child experience those feelings while staying related to you.

Strong feelings are scary to children who may fear literally being swept away by the tide of emotion. What they need more than anything is the sense that you are there, a strong and stable anchor that will protect them. It's not always easy to be that anchor, since a child's feelings often trigger similar feelings in his parents. You will best help your child if you remain calm and supportive when he falls apart. Your goal is to help him return to intimacy.

Here are some suggestions for coaxing your child back to intimacy when he is experiencing strong emotions and for helping him learn that relationships and intimacy encompass many feelings.

1. Anger and aggression. Anger can make a baby turn away or bite; many older children with special needs withdraw or tune out when they feel it. You need to help your child stay in the relationship even when anger overwhelms him. You can do this by helping him feel safe. When you see him grow angry, acknowledge his anger. Talk soothingly—he'll read your gestures and tone of voice more than your words—but be firm as well. Set needed limits. Your strength will help him feel safe in the face of the strong emotion inside. If your calm voice does not get through at first, try to mimic the tone of his anger and then soften your voice. He may be able to recognize your empathic understanding through the more intense tone and be reassured when you then calm down. Above all, try to keep the situation calm. If he withdraws from you, or you from him, he won't learn to feel secure and close even when angry. With practice he should start to trust you and cease feeling the need to turn away.

Assertiveness and aggression are related to anger. Many children with special needs have a hard time with these feelings; they have trouble being assertive because they can't trust their body to carry out their orders. Understandably, most parents have mixed feelings about aggression, too. On the one hand, parents want their children to be assertive; on the other, they fear overly aggressive behavior. They don't want their children to be victims, but they fear for their safety. However, because children with special needs must learn to assert themselves in the world, it's important for you to support your child's constructive attempts at being assertive. When he rages, hold him firmly, so he can do no harm, and empathize with his feelings using words, facial expressions, and tone of voice. Calm him down by providing the kind of sensory experiences he likes. Don't go away until he's recovered. Show him that you can be part of his recovery.

If he seems inconsolable, join this aggressive motor behavior by channeling it into an area that's not destructive. Perhaps you have a big, soft doll you can both jump on, or a pillow you can pummel. Don't give him a time-out away from your presence—that would only reinforce his tendency to withdraw. Instead, have him sit on your lap and be still, and prohibit him from doing the destructive activity. The goal is to show him that he can be angry and engaged with you at the same time.

Later, when he grows more comfortable with abstract symbols, you can help him translate his feelings into words and pretend play, but right now you just need to let him know that you recognize his feelings, that you can help him cope, and that anger is part of the human drama. (Be aware that his aggression may sometimes be a defensive action when he is alarmed by someone's unpredictable or misunderstood behavior. Try to reassure him with your words by telling the provocateur to stop or go away.)

2. Dependency. Some children have an easy time expressing aggression but are unable to express dependency. Babies may look away when they feel too needy; older children may play out scenes of war but never scenes of closeness. They may never cuddle or ask for help. If you child is uncomfortable with dependency you need to let her know slowly and patiently that you're available. Sit next to her when she's frustrated. When she plays out scenes of feeding animals or putting dolls to bed, help her elaborate with warmth and acceptance. Show her gently but repeatedly that helping is okay. Gradually, as she becomes more comfortable with relating, her palette of emotions will grow, and with it her ability to ask for help.

Some children seem too dependent. Babies may cling; older children may cling, whine, or be reluctant to try things on their own. This behavior can be tiresome for parents who wish their children were more independent. It's easy to forget just how overwhelming the world is to them and to perceive their neediness as manipulation. If your child seems too dependent, remind yourself that she is doing her best, she is doing what her abilities and her developmental stage allow, and your patient encouragement will help her grow beyond this stage into a stage of greater confidence. Instead of resenting her neediness, become more available. Anticipate situations that may frighten your child, such as the transition to a new school or a new baby-sitter. Be prepared to take extra time to comfort her when those transitions occur. Provide additional support by showing her pictures of who is coming or where she is going if words don't suffice.

Schools and sitters often hurry parents to leave, thinking the child will cope better on her own. For a child who is related this may be true, but for a child who is only intermittently engaged this is poor advice. Your goal with an unrelated child is to show her that she can depend on you, that you will be there for her at times of stress, and she doesn't have to cope with things on her own. Periods when your child is clingy provide the best opportunities to reinforce that message. So rather than feeling rushed into a premature departure, use events that inspire clinginess as chances to engage your child. There will be plenty of other times to teach her independence, for instance, by supporting her when she is assertive. If you provide both security and support for her initiative, you will encourage both behaviors.

You can also help your child begin very gradually to modulate her needy behavior by not always conceding to it immediately. Sometimes you can say, "Just a second," when she demands something. After a great deal of practice, she'll find that she can tolerate her needs for longer periods of time, that she doesn't have to have them all met immediately.

3. Sadness and jealousy. Because children often find these negative feelings scary, they often find ways to make them go away. They may bury them so deeply that they seem to disappear, or they may convert the scary feelings into other feelings that seem more acceptable. Sadness may masquerade as anger, or jealousy as depression. If you sense that your child rarely expresses one of these feelings, look for times when you think he's experiencing it. Talk to him. Use your voice to empathize since he may not understand your words. Gradually he may find the feelings less scary and may be more willing to experience them with you.

4. Excitement. Children often have a hard time controlling their excitement. They become wild or begin to seem aggressive. A normally withdrawn child may suddenly jump into her parent's lap. These periods of overexcitement sometimes frighten parents. If your child becomes overexcited, try not to pull back. Rather than stop the excitement, try to modulate it, to slow it down. Soothe your child while showing moderate excitement yourself, then work at slowing down her behavior. "I'm going to touch you s-l-o-w-l-y," you can say, reaching out very slowly with your hand. "I'm going to talk to you s-l-o-w-l-y," you can say, smiling and slowing your voice to a crawl. Playfully slow the whole pace of your interaction so that you share your child's excitement while helping her get it under control. Try to understand why your child is so excited. Is she scared? Happy? Is she anticipating pleasure or stress? Is she using symbolic ideas, such as pretending to be a lion or a ghost, in order to give form to her excitement and to permit herself to be wild? If so, join her pretend scenario and help modulate it.

5. Shutting down. You may find that after a period of pleasant engagement while playing with your child, he suddenly shuts down. Chances are that something in the interaction has overwhelmed him. To help him reengage, switch to a more soothing version of the same activity. If you were rolling a ball, roll the ball more slowly, perhaps adding a cooing song that he particularly likes. If you were rolling around on the floor bumping into each other, lie next to him and roll very gently, giving him the kind of tactile pressure he likes. If you combine his sensory pleasures with a gentler version of the activity he will probably reengage. Even simply handing him back the toy you were playing with will help him resume interacting with you.

Learning to accept—and express—one's feelings is a long process. Many adults never accomplish it. So don't expect your child to do it quickly. She'll continue to work on her feelings through all the developmental stages. A child is never wrong for feeling what she feels. There may be better ways to express feelings (in Chapter 11 we address verbalizing feelings and finding appropriate ways to express them). But regardless of your child's behavior, the most important thing you can do is to accept her feelings when she has them. In that way she will learn to accept her own emotions, which in turn will help her build a trusting relationship with you.

TAILORING FLOOR TIME TO YOUR CHILD'S NEEDS

Your child's sensory profile has a decisive impact on how he perceives the world and how he behaves. Although no child is exactly like another, many children fall into one of four sensory/emotional/behavioral groups. Knowing your child's pattern can help you tailor floor time to his needs.

1. Children who are *overreactive* to most sensation and have *distractible*, fragmented behavior.

2. Children who are *overreactive* to sensation and *avoid* people and sensation.

3. Children who are *underreactive* to sensation and are *withdrawn.*

4. Children who are *underreactive* to sensation and who crave input and are *distractible.*

If Your Child Is Overreactive and Distractible

At three, Max had dark, curly hair and brooding dark eyes that rarely smiled. They darted feverishly from thing to thing as if looking for the object that would bring him solace. His movements, too, were disjointed. He would wander from object to object, touching everything briefly. Nothing held his attention for more than a few seconds or seemed to bring him joy.

His parents were particularly confused by his relationship with them. At times he would seek them out, look curiously at what they were doing, take a toy from an outstretched hand, smile at them fleetingly, or lean heavily against them. But when they tried to hug him or pull him onto their laps he would shriek and pull away. Often he would crouch on the far side of the room or lie motionless on the floor, only to return a little while later to seek them out again in a classic pattern of approach/avoidance.

Max was hypersensitive to sensation, and as a result he was easily overwhelmed. His seemingly aimless wandering from thing to thing was in part a way of avoiding overload and calming himself down. Despite his tendency to become overloaded, however, he wanted contact with his parents. He sought them out, only to run away when the contact became too much. If he did not initiate the contact, he felt out of control. The challenge for his parents, therefore, was to find ways to make contact with them feel secure.

With a child such as Max it is helpful to be extremely soothing, to woo him so gently that it feels safe. This means talking in a very soft voice, keeping facial and body gestures related, and using firm rather than light pressure when you touch him. Rhythmic movements, such as swinging, and large-muscle activities, such as jumping, are also often comforting. When your child pulls away after approaching you, gently seduce him back. Don't grab him or the toy and raise your voice. Instead, say in a soothing whisper, "Here I come to take that toy. . . . Can I have it?" and very slowly reach for the toy with your hand. Give him plenty of time to move it out of your way before you touch it. Or try to trade toys, offering him another toy he likes, saying, "Here, you take this, let's trade." If you can keep your voice and movements quiet and soothing, you can reduce the sensations that might cause discomfort as well as prepare him for your actions. Gradually he will come to experience comfort in your interactions, and he won't need to be so guarded about unexpected or unpredictable moves.

If Your Child Is Overreactive and Avoidant

At four years old, Stuart was built like a prizefighter. He was stocky and muscular, with a stubborn set to his jaw and a determined look in his eye. He always clasped an action figure fiercely in his fist as if the figure were his link to power in the world. Stuart loved to run and jump and climb his backyard jungle gym. At the top he could sit for hours, repetitively imitating the karate chops of warriors on TV or flailing his arms and uttering angry guttural sounds as if warding off invading armies. His parents sensed that he had an active interior life—he seemed to be making up stories in his head, they said—but his stories were never shared with them. Instead, Stuart ran off when they approached, turning stonily and stubbornly away. Getting him dressed or bathed and getting him in the car were difficult, frustrating tasks, since Stuart used his considerable strength to resist. He had a vocabulary of three to four words—but mostly said, "No!"—was often negative, and rarely made eye contact with his parents.

Stuart was a negative, avoidant child. Like Max, he was overreactive to sensation and therefore prone to overload, but he had greater control of his body. He was therefore able to use his body to help himself avoid stimulation. Whereas Max wandered aimlessly from object to object, Stuart was able to run away, seeking solace in his backyard fort and in his negative and repetitive behaviors. Like Max, he found contact with his parents overloading, especially when they spoke quickly, agitated by his play actions and negativism. But unlike Max, who returned cautiously after he'd regrouped, Stuart avoided contact altogether. Although he could not adequately process what he heard or express himself, his visual-processing skills were good enough that he could see the big picture and anticipate situations that would overload him. As a result, instead of engaging in approach and avoidance, he merely stayed away. His avoidance was unyielding, as if he'd made up his mind that human contact was upsetting and to be avoided at all costs.

What complicates the picture for some avoidant children is that although they tend to be oversensitive to sensation, they may have islands of underreactivity. For instance, they may be oversensitive to sound but underreactive to touch. As a result, they crave tactile stimulation; they may want to touch and fidget with everything. As they become absorbed in the soothing world of inanimate objects, their tendency for avoidance is strengthened, and they shut out the more stimulating world of people.

With a child who is avoidant, be extra gentle and soothing, avoid power struggles, and try to find sensory experiences that are relaxing. Give her more of what she likes so that she lets you in. You may need to use playful obstruction to make it hard for her to avoid you, but do it gently and soothingly so as not to overload. Don't grab a toy or talk loudly, but gently get in her way so she has to deal with you to reach the toy she wants. Talk slowly, move slowly, smile playfully as you do it. Make your obstruction as soothing as possible.

Your child may use perseveration to avoid contact. All the techniques we mentioned earlier for dealing with perseveration—joining the activity and making it interactive—should help. Again, however, do them soothingly.

If Your Child Is Underreactive and Withdrawn

Jessica's parents called her their quiet princess because of her striking looks and silent demeanor. They would have given anything for their three-year-old daughter to laugh and smile, but no matter how they entreated she rarely did. She seemed not so much unhappy as self-absorbed, as if the world of human contact was uninteresting to her. She could spend long hours splayed across the floor watching her favorite videos or equally long times just staring out the window. When her parents called her name she rarely responded. The one thing that seemed to catch her interest was the game playing of her brother and sister. When they wrestled or chased each other, Jessica frequently tucked herself behind a chair and watched them cautiously, often stroking the chair repetitively. But if they encouraged her to join them she would turn away, hiding her head behind the chair.

Occasionally she would let her parents hold her. But even her cuddling seemed passive. She didn't snuggle or hug. Her body rested limply in their arms. "It's as if everything takes too much energy," her father said. "Hugging, playing, even smiling. She just likes to sit and watch the world go by."

Jessica was underreactive to sensory input, so it took a great deal of sensory information to get her attention. Ordinary speaking voices, her parents' gentle entreaties and gestures, and the quietness of the house when her older siblings were in school made little impression on her sensory system. Unstimulated by the external world, Jessica focused inward. However, like all children who are underreactive, she craved sensory experience. Loud noises, bright colors, animated movements, firm pressure, and strong textures made her feel more involved. So when her siblings played raucously, she tuned in, energized by the heightened sensory input.

Compounding Jessica's challenges was her low muscle tone. It took a great effort to mobilize her body, and she couldn't trust it to respond the way she wanted. As a result she was cautious, not daring to play with her siblings or try new motor tasks. Her perserverative movements, her repetitive stroking of the furniture, required minimum energy and motor control.

In working with Jessica it was important to provide lots of sensory experience. It took high energy to woo her into interaction. But when her parents energized themselves with animated facial expressions, lots of touching, movement, and vocalizations, and, as needed, playful obstruction, she gradually became more and more engaged. By going back to hands-on infant games, such as tickling, dancing, jumping, and peekaboo, they could expand her tolerance and pleasure in interaction.

If your child is underreactive, be aware he may not be underreactive in every area. You need to investigate each sensory area and then develop an interactive style accordingly. If he is overreactive to sound and underreactive to touch, for example, you need to keep your voice soothing while being physically vigorous.

To foster your child's initiative and assertiveness, as soon as you draw him into interaction, let him take over. Continue to interact, but be careful to follow his lead. The more room you give him to take initiative, the more confident and assertive he can become.

If Your Child Is Underreactive, Craving Sensation, and Distractible

Caley was a whirlwind. "She never sits still," lamented her mother. "You always know where she's been by how many things are on the floor or broken. I know she doesn't mean to be destructive. She just has so much energy. I just wish she'd pay attention to me the way she does to everything else in the house."

It's hard to imagine a better description of an underreactive, active, distractible child. Like Jessica, Caley craved sensory stimulation, but unlike Jessica, her normal to high motor tone permitted her to seek it out. As a result, she ran everywhere, touched everything, put everything in her mouth. The only thing that did not interest her was human contact.

To help a child such as Caley, use her interest in sensory stimulation to engage her. Energize your voice and movements. Build sensory experiences into your interactions by doing a lot of chasing, roughhousing, and the like, and make eye contact and purposefulness an integral part of the activity. For example, play a tickling game, but wait for your child to direct you to give more tickles. Or give horsey rides and make her pat you or vocalize to make you stop or go.

Look for ways to join in her activity to make it interactive. Notice what types of sensation she likes best, for she may have islands of overreactivity. She may crave bright colors and loud noises, for instance, but be uncomfortable with certain types of touch or textures. Experiment as you play, and then try to avoid the sensations she dislikes. She may also be able to organize her attention around cause-and-effect toys—toys that she can make move rather than move herself. Have such toys available. If she looks but is reluctant to touch and does not initiate playing with them, you play with them, enticing her with your excited reactions: "Wow! Look at this!" "Uh-oh!" "Get ready, jump!" Her curiosity will draw her closer, and you can play together, negotiating turns, experimenting, trading, and even expanding into pretend play.

10

Floor Time II: Two-Way Communication

HELPING A CHILD COMMUNICATE
WITH GESTURES AND EXPRESSIONS

Three-year-old Sam sat on the floor playing with a car. Paul, his father, tried to join in. "That's a nice car," Paul said. "Look how fast you're moving it. Look at it go. Oh, now you're moving it slowly. Now it's going to the right. Now it's going to the left." Since Sam was patently ignoring his father's running commentary, Paul tried to be more interactive. He switched to questions. "Can you move the car here?" he asked, cupping his hands into a garage. Sam continued to ignore him. "Look, here's a tunnel," Paul said, making a tunnel with his hands. "Can you drive the car through the tunnel?" Again Sam ignored him. Paul decided to be commanding. "Bring the car here," he ordered. Sam didn't. Finally, frustrated, Paul grabbed the car from his son and hid it behind his back. Sam, predictably, threw a tantrum; then he sulked and refused to touch the car again.

Why did this encounter fail? Paul was trying to interact above his son's developmental level. Because of receptive and expressive language delays, Sam couldn't understand or respond to his father's words (although he heard them) or sophisticated gestures. His father's sudden frustrated move to grab the car frightened Sam into a tantrum. Had Paul found a way to interact with

Sam through very simple gestures, the scene could have gone quite differently. Here's what happened the next time they tried.

As Sam rolled the car around the carpet, the therapist suggested that Paul play with Sam using gestures rather than with words. Paul looked confused. "Take out other cars and move them along with his. Use actions to go with his actions."

Paul pondered for a moment, then placed his cupped hands in front of Sam's car, hoping Sam would roll the car into them. But, as before, Sam ignored the gesture. One of two things was happening: either Sam was choosing to ignore his father, or Sam didn't understand the meaning of the gesture, or perhaps a little bit of both. How was he to know that cupped hands meant garage—a word and concept he didn't know—and that his father was *implying* that Sam should roll the car into them? Paul needed to think of something simpler.

When Sam began rolling the car back and forth again, Paul got a second car and rolled it toward his son's. Sam saw it coming and pulled his car out of the way, closing a circle of communication. Next, Paul turned and chased Sam's car. But this time Sam didn't pull his car away; he held it tight and let Paul crash it. Another circle closed. Over the next few minutes the game escalated as father and son chased each other with the cars, going first fast then slow, sometimes crashing and sometimes not. At the end of the game, Paul again cupped his hands in front of Sam's car—this time not as a garage, but as a barrier. With no hesitation Sam drove his car around his father's hands, understanding and responding to this more complex gesture. The game had become a full-fledged, nonverbal dialogue.

Over the next few weeks Sam's communication flourished. For the first time, he and his parents had a language in common! Three weeks later he was closing 20 to 30 circles of gestural communication in a row.

Once your child is comfortable with intimacy, you're ready to move to the second stage, two-way communication. Of course, in the process of building intimacy you've been communicating; intimacy is itself a form of communication. Now the focus needs to broaden. Earlier your goal was to establish rapport with your child, to acknowledge and enjoy each other's presence. Now you want to encourage *ongoing* interaction. In establishing rapport with your child you opened and closed at least one circle of communication; now you want to turn one circle into 2, then 3, then 20.

There are two levels to two-way communication, which, for practical purposes, occur together. One consists of simple circles of communication, such as reciprocal head nods, smiles, frowns, vocalizations, and the like. Animated face-to-face interaction gets this level of communication started. The second level involves complex nonverbal behavioral communication, such as leading a caregiver toward the VCR and pointing to some tapes or pointing to a favorite toy in the playroom. This level involves closing many circles, as many as 40 in a row. Let's take these two steps one at a time.

SIMPLE COMMUNICATION THROUGH ANIMATED, FACE-TO-FACE INTERACTION

The use of facial expressions is one of the most basic elements of communication, so basic that we often take it for granted. Imagine talking to someone who remained stone-faced, never widening her eyes, tilting her eyebrow, or releasing a glimmer of a smile to demonstrate interest, surprise, or disagreement. You'd probably be confused. The ordinary cues you rely on to know that your words are getting through would be missing. It would feel as though you were talking to a wall. Some children with developmental challenges are similarly unexpressive, adding to their difficulties with communication. However, even the most unexpressive children can learn to be expressive by interacting with their parents.

Until she began therapy at 15 months, Delaney had been a rather unresponsive child, preferring to spend her time in corners of rooms, in closets, or in a tiny space behind the couch. She seemed to have no need for human contact. Her occupational therapist soon discovered that she was overreactive to auditory input, finding even moderate noises such as her parents' and siblings' often loud, fast voices and the sound of the television unpleasant. She also had difficulty with auditory processing, making it doubly hard for her to use the information that flowed in through her ears. As her family lowered the noise level in their house and worked at wooing Delaney with calm, soothing voices, she slowly began to respond. Several weeks into therapy she was spending less time in her hiding spots and was responding more to her family's overtures.

She remained, however, very stiff. Even when she was engaging with her parents she showed few signs of warmth or pleasure or excitement. As it turned out, both her parents had very subdued facial expressions. In effect, they were modeling a straight-faced way of engaging, and Delaney was learning to respond in kind. The therapist explained to Delaney's parents how important it was for them to rev up their own expression in order to inspire their daughter to do the same, and reluctantly they tried. Animated facial gestures didn't come naturally to them. The mother said she felt like a mime. But fairly quickly, as her parents succeeded in exaggerating their gestures, Delaney became much more expressive herself. The change in their daughter was motivating for the parents, and over time they became more comfortable with the new style of relating. The more animated they became, the more animated Delaney became. Soon they were able to engage in long, face-to-face, wordless conversations—smiles, smirks, giggles, and head nods forming a rich vocabulary.

You can begin to create this same kind of wordless conversation with your child.

• Always play with your child face-to-face, enabling her to see your face and read your expressions. If your child still finds a way to keep her back to you by sitting in your lap or rotating to avoid face-to-face contact, position a large plastic mirror in front of you so that you see each other in the mirror. You can also help your child become more comfortable with eye contact by adding other sensory support. Put her in a swing and push from the front. Hold the swing and let it go only after eye contact is made. Or, entice your child through tickle games, holding out until eye contact occurs.

• Be as animated as possible—even exaggeratedly so—in order to promote animation in your child. Vary your voice and use vocal signals such as "uh-oh," "yay," and so on.

As you escalate your expressions, make sure to do so in a reciprocal, back-and-forth rhythm. You shouldn't be doing all the work. Your job is not to be a clown and entertain your child, but rather to interact with her. Your goal is to have a conversation in which her smile leads to your smile, which leads to her giggle which leads to your giggle, which leads to her laugh which leads to your laugh. Your expression should always be in response to something she has done—a smile, a sound, a nod; hers should then be in response to you.

At times it may seem as though your child is doing nothing and therefore there is nothing for you to respond *to*. But as we said in the last chapter, your child is always doing *something*. Your job is to find some little behavior, regardless of how tiny, to which you can respond. Maybe he's moving his arm in a way that doesn't seem purposeful. Good enough! Bump his arm with yours and make a funny face. Perhaps he's simply staring into space. Fine! Get right in front of him and wiggle your tongue or cover your face and play peekaboo. Then block his vision, open your hands, and say, "I see you!" Whatever he's doing has room in it for you to intrude playfully with an animated facial expression and supportive tone. That simple intrusion can be the beginning of an animated gestural conversation. Add simple words and varied tones so words connect to these simple gestures and become ritualized.

COMPLEX GESTURAL COMMUNICATION: INCREASING THE NUMBER OF CIRCLES YOUR CHILD CAN CLOSE

Once you have simple gestural communication going, the next challenge is to increase the length of those communications, to stretch the number of circles of communication. Here's how this can happen.

If your child is touching his hair he has opened a circle. If you say warmly, "Can I touch your hair?" you are building on his gesture. If he then responds—by looking at you, by smiling, or even by turning away—he has closed that circle; he has responded to your overture. But in closing that circle he has also opened a second circle, and it is up to you to build on his response. Suppose he turned away. You might jump to the other side of him so that he is facing you once more. If he turns away again, he has closed a second circle. You might then jump to where he is now looking, building on his response. This time, instead of turning away, he may giggle, closing a third circle. Next, if he looks at your hair, you might offer it for him to touch, saying warmly, "Want to touch my hair?" If he reaches out to it, he has closed a fourth circle. Now you build on that circle by offering your hair again, and again he may reach out and touch it, closing a fifth circle. If all of your child's responses are flat, lacking emotion, you might start making funny noises each time he touches your hair. If this action elicits some giggles, you are closing vocal and motor circles simultaneously. You are also encouraging your child to keep playing by making him feel that his action is causing a funny response from you. If you vary your sounds or make certain sounds in response to certain types of touch, you may keep him in the interaction even longer. In this way you may be able to stretch that very first circle into five or ten circles.

The guidelines for stretching circles are the same as those for helping your child tune in.

• Appeal to your child's sensory preferences.

• Join your child's activities rather than introduce new ones.

• Follow your child's lead.

• Be playfully obstructive if necessary to create interaction.

Build on Natural Interests and Intentions

Instead of introducing a new activity in order to interact with your child, join her at whatever she is already doing.

• Is your child hiding? Don't ask her to come out. Instead, throw a blanket or pillow on top of her to highlight her intentions. Call her: "Maria, where are you? Where are you?" She will throw the blanket off and you can enthusiastically greet her. Then you hide, too. Chances are she'll be so curious about what you're up to that she'll come out to see, closing a circle of communication. When she emerges, run to a new hiding place and let her look for you again. If she doesn't search, run from one hiding place to another or run out, do a little dance, then run back in. Tantalize her with your behavior until she can bear the suspense no longer and comes to see what you're doing. With practice you can stretch this interaction into a lengthy cat-and-mouse game.

• Is your child aimlessly rubbing a window? Try saying, "Are you tickling that window? If you're tickling that window then I'm going to tickle you! Here I come!" Then approach him, smiling, in slow motion, so he has plenty of time to avoid you if he wants to. If he puts his hand up to stop you, stop or let him push you away. He'll have closed a circle of communication. Then try again. "If you're going to tickle that window, I'm going to tickle you. Here I come!" Perhaps he'll push you away again, closing another circle. If so, insert yourself between him and the window, saying playfully, "If you're going to tickle that window, maybe you can tickle me!" If he responds by pushing your hand away, come at him slowly with the other hand, "Okay, here comes Mr. Lefty!" If he pushes that hand away, butt him playfully with your head. Each rejection is a response, both closing and opening a circle. Give him more opportunities to turn you down. Your goal is to keep the circles cooking, treating each response from your child as the opening of another circle. If you move slowly and give him a chance to show you what's acceptable, you can woo him into an ongoing interaction. He will soon be waiting to see your next move.

• Is your child playing with a favorite toy? Try luring her into a game of keep-away. Tell her you want to play too. Hold out the toy, but before she can take it whisk it behind your back. Then slowly take it out, give her a moment to study it, and whisk it away again. If after a few times your child doesn't respond, walk the toy slowly toward her. Bounce it over her knee or fly it through the air, singing a melodramatic "dum de-dum dum" as you do so. By lending drama to the offer you can probably encourage her to take the toy, closing a circle of communication. When she does take the toy, make aborted attempts to get it back—swipe at it with your hand, march your fingers toward it on the floor. These gestures should elicit some response, and your child will have closed another circle. You'll be on your way to a reciprocal game of keep-away.

It's helpful to play in an area with lots of toys so you can quickly bring in reinforcements to keep the interactions going. Stock up on small, appealing toys such as marbles, Slinkies, bells, maracas, magic wands, and windup toys; these are favorites and lend themselves readily to interaction. Multiples of toys are important. You can hand your child another one of something he showed interest in. You can start trading games, opening and closing many circles. Later, having multiples of toys will make it easier to encourage play with another child.

Building on your child's natural interests is critical, for if you continually introduce new toys or ideas, you'll soon run out of tricks and become demoralized. The toys are there for him to choose. In addition, by building on your child's interests you create a link between his behavior and his emotions; you enable his behavior to feel purposeful and to build his sense of self.

Certainly you want to have a number of tricks ready—favorite toys or favorite activities you can hold out. But as soon as your child shows interest in one toy, or in a facial expression you made, or in a sound your puppet made, or in an object on a shelf, you want to go with that interest. Respond to your child's interest by making the sound again, or picking up the object he liked, or putting the toy in your mouth in order to provoke another response. In this way your entire gestural conversation can be built on your child's interests.

Build on Your Child's Favorite Behavior

Don't overlook your child's seemingly random behavior as a basis for interaction. Treat whatever she does as intentional. Precisely because your child is attached to this behavior it holds a lot of potential.

One extremely uncommunicative little girl, Cleo, liked to make noises that sounded like growls at her parents. They had long ignored her eccentricity, but her therapist suggested trying to turn her growling into a game. Instead of ignoring her, why not pretend to be frightened? The first time her parents feigned fear, Cleo stared at them. Then she regained her composure and growled again. This time it was clear that her growl was intentional. Both parents jumped, and this time Cleo gave a faint little smile. Over the next several weeks this became a game. Then, gradually, the parents varied it. Occasionally, instead of feigning surprise, they growled back or made a different noise. After a while, their daughter began to imitate their noises; eventually, a whole dialogue of noises developed. Then the parents added physical gestures, flapping their wings while chirping like a bird or prancing around the room while neighing like a horse. By several months later Cleo's seemingly random behavior was not random at all, but the basis of a very deliberate and enjoyable interaction. She now responded to cues such as "Ready, set, go!" "louder," "softer," "fast," and "slow."

Lex, a rather avoidant boy liked to jump down the stairs. His parents were frustrated by this activity, since they regarded it as unsafe, and as a result, they were constantly trying to get him to stop. The stairs had become a focal point of tantrums and bad feeling. Lex's therapist suggested that instead of arguing about the stairs, the parents take advantage of his interest and turn stair jumping into a game. They agreed that if they were with him they could prevent a dangerous fall. By joining the activity and making it interactive, they could change its meaning.

So the next time the boy jumped down the stairs, his father jumped with him, stair for stair. Lex stopped jumping. When he jumped again and his father followed, Lex stopped jumping again. But by the time they'd covered three or four stairs, the boy began to anticipate his father's jumps and began waiting for his father to land beside him. After a few more steps, he smiled at his father as he waited for his father to jump. Over the next few days father and son played the game many, many times. Gradually the father introduced variations, such as bumping down the stairs on his rear end or hopping on each step before jumping down. Lex's father added singsong phrases to their movements, which his son came to recognize. Soon the pair were playing similar follow-the-leader games throughout the house. Lex's irritating behavior had become the jumping-off point for warm and intentional communication.

Both these sets of parents did a good job of turning existing behavior into interaction. But they didn't stop there. Once they got their children to respond, they upped the ante; they changed the game slightly to give their child something new to which to respond. Even a child with motor-planning difficulties can be encouraged to solve problems if they are set up for him. This is important. It helps the child handle increasing levels of complexity, and it helps him become spontaneous and flexible.

Some children with special needs want above all for their world to stay the same. Since they find so many things upsetting and they have so little sense of control, they maximize their sense of security by creating tiny islands of safety—familiar toys played with over and over, familiar routines enacted day in and day out, familiar motions repeated endlessly. When they cannot process auditory and verbal information very well, they depend on routine to know what will happen next. When it is difficult for them to sequence actions and play in more complex ways, they resort to doing the same thing again and again. When it is difficult to use toys, they rely on moving their own body parts. Any change from these patterns provokes protests, and understandably so; change challenges the safety nets on which they depend. But children must learn to cope with a changing world, and the only way they can do that is with help.

You must help your child tolerate change by introducing it very slowly and patiently within the safety of your relationship. This means, once you have an interaction going, look for ways to change it slightly. Introduce a new toy to the keep-away game or a new gesture to Simon says or a new route to the chase. If your child is participating actively, she's likely to adopt the new element with barely a notice. If she balks, go back to the old game once or twice, then try again. As long as you're inventive in your part of the game, you'll encourage your child to be flexible in hers.

Increase the Complexity of Behavior

As the number of circles your child can close increases, you want to begin adding to the complexity of those circles. If your child takes a spoon from you and puts it in her mouth, she is closing a circle. But if she first watches you turn the spoon upside down and put it in your mouth and then copies you, the circle is more complex. Handing a ball back and forth is good circle-closing behavior, but it is less complex than looking at both hands and guessing in which hand the ball is hidden. In the more complex examples, your child is combining motor, cognitive, and spatial-relations behavior while she is closing the circle. This kind of behavior is important because it leads to the kinds of complex imitative behavior that children use in pretend play—talking on a toy phone, feeding a doll, putting a doll in a car. By beginning to work on this behavior now, you will help your child pave the way to the next developmental stage, developing ideas through pretend play.

You can work on this step by making your own interactions with your child more complex. For instance, when you are playing with cars, instead of simply blocking her car with your hand, block it with another car, creating the most rudimentary element of pretend, but not necessarily talking about it or working it into a scenario. If your cars are racing, put a doll in your car and say, "Dolly race." Don't work it up into a racing scenario; adding the doll and those simple words is enough for now. Gradually your child may begin adding some complexity of her own.

Incorporate All Sensory and Processing Modalities

As you take advantage of your child's natural interests to open and close circles of communication, look for ways to bring in a variety of sights and sounds, movements and textures, and auditory- and visual-processing challenges. In this way you'll find things that give him pleasure *and* gradually stretch his abilities in weaker areas.

- Use auditory and visual cues in your games, such as different voices and noises and different facial expressions and body postures, to help your child process a variety of auditory and visual stimuli.

- Introduce shaving cream, Play-Doh, wet and dry sand, beans, rice, finger paint, and other textured items to give your child experience with a variety of textures.

- Play complicated chase games, games of opening boxes or screwing open jar lids to get desired objects, and imitation games such as Simon says or reciting nursery rhymes with hand gestures to help your child practice motor planning.

Use Times of High Motivation

One of the best times to stretch circles of communication is when your child really wants something. At those times she's highly motivated and therefore willing and able to close a lot of circles. Building on her interests also helps her connect her emotions with her behavior, giving meaning to her behavior and strengthening her sense of purpose and self.

Three-year-old Jocelyn is not yet verbal, but she is adamant about wanting juice.

JOCELYN: *hits the refrigerator door.*

MOTHER: (*knowing Jocelyn wants juice, but stretching the encounter in order to practice communication*) Are you thirsty?

JOCELYN: *looks at her mother and continues to hit the door.*

MOTHER: Do you want a drink? *(raises a pretend glass to her mouth)*

JOCELYN: *stamps the floor and continues to hit the door, now more frenetically; she has answered her mother's question in her own way, closing a circle of communication.*

MOTHER: Do you want milk?

JOCELYN: *screams, clearly a sign of anger and rejection, again answering her mother in her own way, closing a second circle.*

MOTHER: No milk?

JOCELYN: *clearly frustrated, pounds the refrigerator door again and begins to cry, closing another circle with her expression of displeasure.*

MOTHER: Can you show me what you want?

JOCELYN: *nods her head and grunts, closing a fourth circle.*

MOTHER: *(opens refrigerator door)* Show me what you want.

JOCELYN: *points to juice, closing a fifth circle.*

MOTHER: Oh, you want juice?

JOCELYN: *jumps up and down, indicating approval, closing a sixth circle.*

MOTHER: Okay. I'll give you juice. (*takes juice from fridge and shows it to Jocelyn*)

JOCEYLN: Wa-wa. *(indicating approval, closing a seventh circle)*

MOTHER: Juice. Juice for Jocelyn.

JOCELYN: Ju. *(eighth circle closed)*

The key is to try to stretch out the exchange for as long as possible. This isn't easy when you're facing an angry, demanding child, but if you can resist the temptation to solve the problem quickly, you can eke out some valuable communication practice. And this learning will stick. Although you may think that practice would be wasted with a child in such an emotional state, exactly the opposite is true. People learn best when highly motivated, and nothing is quite as motivating as wanting something. So the longer you can resist satisfying your child's demand, the more valuable time you will have to squeeze in learning that will last.

Use this kind of circle stretching any time your child wants—or doesn't want—something.

• Don't simply let him play with blocks; stall him. Ask him by shrugging and holding out your hands: "Why blocks?" Point to other options. How about his ball? He'll become frustrated. He may rant. But he'll also close 10 or 20 circles in the process of arguing for what he wants. Finally acknowledge what he wants and help him proceed: "Oh, we're going to play with blocks. Here's one. Do you want more?"

• When your child wants to leave the dinner table, don't let her go right away. Ask her with gestures, "More fruit? More milk?" After she has rejected everything, hold her chair in place and encourage her to tell you, "Get up" or "Down" with words. Demonstrate with gestures. Or tell her you're not finished: "Wait for Mommy." By negotiating for just three minutes around "more," "down," and "wait," you can close 10 or 20 circles.

• When your child takes your hand and puts it on the doorknob to show you he wants to leave the room, don't simply turn the knob and let him out. Turn it the wrong way. Or look at him, confused. Or pull the knob instead of turning it. Or knock on the door as if someone else will open it. Or hand your child some keys and indicate that keys are needed to open the door. Your child will be frustrated, but that's good. In his frustration he'll close 10, 15, or 20 circles trying to show you what he wants. He will also learn some symbolic solutions to the problem at hand.

• If your child wants a toy that is high on a shelf, don't hand it to her; become her step stool. Make her direct you to what she wants by playfully misunderstanding. "You want that book?" you might ask, lumbering with her toward a different shelf. When she directs you to the right shelf, don't lift her high enough; make her gesture to go higher. When she gets the toy she wants, "forget" to let her down; make her tell you what she wants.

• If your child wants a horsey ride, just trot him around the room, but make him show you where and how fast to go.

• If he wants to go outside, don't let him open the door; make your hand an extension of the knob and make him turn it to get out.

If you do these things playfully you not only open and close more circles of communication, you also broaden your child's relationship with you. The more you build on his own strongly felt needs while varying your role, the more he will learn to relate with you in different ways, not just as a nurturer or obstacle.

Getting dressed, brushing teeth, going to bed, getting ready to go out, and eating all lend themselves to this kind of negotiation. You can't always take the time to lengthen these activities by purposely arguing with your child. But if you can plan ahead to use one or two activities each day as educational opportunities, instead of rushing through them, you can provide valuable learning for your child.

What happens if your child loses it during the negotiation? That's okay. Sometimes you push a little too hard and that happens. Back off. Comfort her. Then later in the day try again over a different issue. The recurring battles won't scar your relationship, but they *will* strengthen your child's interactive skills. You want your child to be warm and spontaneous, flexible and creative. You want her to engage with others confidently. Most children with special needs are capable of that, but only if they can learn to close 30 or 40 circles in a row. That's why it's important to close 10 or 20 circles while negotiating about going outside, another 10 or 15 while negotiating about juice, 15 or 20 more during a game of catch. With all this practice your child will get the hang of it; slowly, incrementally, she'll master two-way communication.

It's difficult to stand between your child and his desire, to see him grow annoyed. However, his anger and disappointment will pass as soon as he gets what he wants, and if you follow your negotiations with soothing warmth he'll leave the encounter with the satisfaction of having his desire met, as well as with your love and support.

Be Animated!

Expressive, animated gestures are important in stretching out your child's communication. This takes practice.

Will, four years old, was bright and verbal and most of the time warmly related. But, like Delaney at the beginning of this chapter, he showed very little emotion as he played. His posture and facial expressions were wooden and his voice barely strayed from a monotone. His parents were warm and attentive, yet as they interacted with their son, they, too, were rather flat. Their voices were even, infrequently rising or falling to show excitement or disappointment, and they rarely gestured. There was no drama in their play. "Try to be more animated. Laugh, pout, jump up, sit down. The more animated you are, the more animated he will be," the therapist suggested. Since this behavior was unnatural for them, the parents tried using puppets. They each put a puppet on one hand. Then the mother used a squeaky, high-pitched voice and the father used a deep, growly voice as they talked to Will. The boy first looked at them in surprise, but quickly he became intrigued by the two new characters in the room. He talked excitedly to the two puppets, with more variation in his own voice. After a little while the parents got up off the floor, letting their puppets explore the room and talking in their puppets' voices about what they saw. Their son promptly followed them. As his parents made squeaky and growly noises about their discoveries, Will began to imitate their noises. Soon the whole family was parading around the room making funny noises. Over the next few weeks, the parents worked on animating their play at home. At first they used puppets with the same two voices. After a little while they tried out different voices. Gradually they felt comfortable using exaggerated voices even without the puppets on their hands. As his parents became more experimental, Will did too. Within several months his emotional range had broadened considerably.

Unfortunately, animated gestures are foreign to many adults. A staid lot we become by the time we're old enough to be parents! We find it hard to make BIG gestures without feeling foolish. But making big gestures is essential, because if you are timid in your communication, you give your child less to respond to. That doesn't mean you should be grandiose and phony. On the contrary, your gestures should be natural and spontaneous because you're acting as a role model for your child. But you need to make an effort to boost your level of animation beyond what might come naturally. Here are a few guidelines.

> • *Don't limit your gestures to your arms and hands.* Use your face, your eyes, your voice, and your emotions. Grin with pride when your child rolls a ball; sigh in sympathy when his block tower falls; open your eyes wide as you search for a spot to tickle. Facial gestures show him you're involved and encourage him to make faces back.

> • *Use your voice,* regardless of whether your child understands speech. Certainly use words to comment on the action, but also use *sounds* to draw your child in: "woo-oo-woo-oo" to imitate cars and trains; "dum de-dum dum" to create suspense; chortles, squeals, and growls to lend drama to your game. Think of sounds as teasers for hooking your child. Also, if you use certain emotional phrases again and again, your child will come to recognize them, just as she recognizes songs.

• *Use your whole body.* Run, jump, wriggle like a snake, hop like a bunny, draw and scribble, dance and sing. Follow your child's lead when he engages in these activities to turn them into two-person interactions.

• *Play chase and hide-and-seek games.* Children who are avoidant can often be wooed into interaction through these types of games and often come to love them. Not only do they draw your child in through large-motor activity, they also strengthen her visual and spatial-relations abilities.

• *Don't be embarrassed to exaggerate your gestures slightly.* What feels awkward and flagrant to you probably appears quite moderate on the outside. (It's like getting Novocain at the dentist—no one else notices what feels like a grapefruit in your jaws.) The slight exaggeration will seem lively and inviting to your child.

Keeping your play at the gestural level may not come easily. We are accustomed to talking and unaccustomed to using our bodies when we interact. But let your child guide you. If you truly follow her lead she will keep you at the gestural level. With a little practice, it will grow comfortable, and as your child begins to respond, your nonverbal dialogues will become pleasurable and rewarding.

THE RESISTANT, UNCOMMUNICATIVE CHILD

Some children seem particularly reluctant to engage in two-way communication or to keep the circles of communication going. If your child is like that, several principles can help you.

Playful Obstruction

It's natural to want to play nicely with your child—to hand him the toys he wants, to roll your car peacefully next to his, to comply with the rules he lays down. But such behavior may not always help him close circles of communication. Your goal as your child's play partner is constantly to challenge him to respond to you. That may mean

• purposely misunderstanding his rules in order to keep the interaction going;

• getting between him and the thing he wants;

• creating playful situations in which he has to deal with you to get what he wants.

The following strategies work with even the most avoidant children.

• *Beat him to the spot.* You can enter obtrusively into your child's play so that he can't entirely avoid you. Suppose your child is playing with a toy truck. You say warmly, "Can I see your truck?" He turns away, closing a circle. You then jump around him so that he is facing you again; he turns away again, closing another circle. You jump around him again; he walks away. And so on. After several repetitions of this game, your child may begin to smile or giggle. Now you can add some emotion to it. Each time you beat him to the spot, make a funny noise or say, "Gotcha!" or make an airplane noise while you run. When you "land" right next to him, tickle him and grin, or say, "Airplane landing!" Before long he may join your game of make-believe.

• *Gently block her escape routes.* If your child is avoiding you by turning or running away, use your movements to back her gradually into a corner of the room. When you are close enough, reach out with both arms and touch the two walls, enclosing her in a little cave. Now she has to crawl beneath your arms or legs or push your arm in order get out. As long as you remain gentle and playful, with a big smile on your face and a twinkle in your eye as you say the magic words, "I'm going to get you!" your child may find this game compelling. Even the most avoidant children often respond by giggling, smirking, and pushing their way out. Of course, after your child wriggles or pushes several times, let her push you over; moan, "You win! You win!" so she feels that she has overpowered this silly grown-up.

• *Blanket.* As we saw in Chapter 9, even lying down can become an interaction. If your child is lying face down on the floor avoiding you, become his blanket. Say playfully, "You're napping? I'll be your blanket!" then lie down on top of him (don't put all your weight on him, of course). Keep talking playfully as you do this. "Are you warm now? Ready for a nap? Are you comfy?" Your child will wriggle out or push you off, at which point you can invite him to become your blanket. Or turn down the lights, give him a blanket, and sing a lullaby. He will probably get up quickly, afraid you are putting him to bed. It is important not to rationalize that he is tired or has especially low muscle tone that day. Treat his behavior as purposeful.

• *The veil or scarf.* This is a great way to interact with even the most avoidant child. Take a large, colorful scarf or veil and cover the window your child is staring through; or cover your own smiling face, or cover the toy your child is looking at. Make visual designs with the scarf as you run it by your child's eyes or across her face. Smooth it or float it over her skin to create different types of touch. Use the scarf as an all-purpose attention getter to entice your child into interaction.

• *The tub.* If your child is especially avoidant and moving away from you, suggest a trip to the pool. Put on a swimsuit if that is what you usually do when going to a real pool. The warm water and bubbles in the tub will provide lots of sensory support and pleasure. Your child will not need to move away. Get the bath toys and negotiate with him for who gets what, then splash, pour, and play interactively for as long as possible.

As you entice your child into two-way communication and slowly stretch the number of circles he can open and close, you will also be teaching him the social convention of give-and-take or turn taking. This reciprocity in communication is fundamental to all human interactions; it has to become second nature. But instead of teaching it in a rote, mechanical way, by using these techniques you will be doing it in a dynamic, emotionally driven way.

The "Undoing" Approach

Some children have such severe motor-planning difficulties that they are unable to initiate actions. They tend to wander aimlessly, lie passively, or seek constant sensory-motor stimulation, running, jumping, and dumping everything in their path. Even if your child finds it difficult to initiate purposeful actions, however, she can respond to your actions; in fact, she will be eager to undo what you have done if your action is not what she expects or if it upsets her. The need to undo is a powerful motivation to seize back control, even if only to resume a state of passive avoidance. As is the case with a toddler, "No!" is not necessarily final, and, it can mean yes in the sense that your child will keep going, protesting many moves you make and thus interacting.

Children who have severe motor planning difficulties in addition to auditory-processing difficulties benefit from this approach. In a sense, avoidance is an undoing response in that your child moves away from and undoes your action. It is her step two to your step one!

In many cases, if you use playful obstruction your child will undo your move to get something you are blocking or to put things back where they were.

Sammy was lying on the floor rolling his car back and forth. His mother began to move her car behind Sammy's and say, "Keep moving, please!" pushing his car forward beyond his reach. He usually got up to retrieve it and resumed rolling it away from her. After she had kept this up for a while, she got some annoyed looks, if not growls, at which point she backed up. Rolling cars soon became an interactive game.

Susie was lying on the couch, and her father decided to give her some covers, throwing the blanket on her to cover her head. When she threw it off, he did it again, covering her upper body but not her legs and feet. She threw it off and looked at him while he pondered out loud, "Uh-oh, I didn't do it right again." Next time, he put it under her legs, asking, "Is this okay?" When she did not respond, he made his move again and found another mistake to make. Sure enough, Susie began to watch him and was ready to undo what he did. A few minutes later, Susie decided to sit up, and her father sat right down, asking her to move over a bit and pushing her to the edge of the couch. Susie was puzzled, but rather liked being squished. Her dad insisted he still didn't have enough room and nudged her some more. This time, Susie started to push back. When that back-and-forth interaction started to end, Susie's father "realized" that the big doll probably wanted to sit where Susie was sitting. Susie did not like being displaced and threw the doll off the couch. It took a while before everyone found the right place to sit!

Danny loved the "I'm going to get you" pursuit. He also loved being tickled and having Koosh balls stuffed in his pockets, socks, under his shirt, and so on. But how many times could his dad do this? Instead of pursuing Danny, his father set up gates, stretching his body across Danny's path. In order to run forward, Danny had to stop and open the gate. This led to a lot of interaction and joyous roughhousing. Danny's father was trying to think of a variation for the gate game when he noticed a Slinky on the floor. Danny had shown some interest in the Slinky before, so his dad decided the Slinky would become the new gate. He wound it between some chairs and furniture legs while Danny resumed running. When Danny came back through, he faced a whole new set of obstacles. How would he get by? First, he tried stamping the Slinky down with his feet and legs (legs are easier to use than hands and get much more practice). When one side of the Slinky unwound, it "somehow" got wrapped around Danny's leg. Danny's father expressed concern, "Oh *no*! How will you get out, Danny?" Danny had a problem to solve. It became necessary to use his hands and feet. Every time he turned, he seemed to get wrapped up some more. Of course, his dad was being very "helpful" and encouraging. Undoing the Slinky and getting through the rest of the obstacle course took some doing—and lots of interaction.

Your child has not only developed many types of ritualized behavior and preferences, but has probably ritualized you so that you may be doing the same thing over and over again without even realizing it. At first, the ritual made things more predictable and was helpful. Now these rituals can be used to create problems for your child to solve. For example, if your child is used to searching in your bag for a container of crackers, but you put in pretend ones, he might taste the pretend ones before protesting. Similarly, you might simply move the container to a paper bag and encourage your child to search and explore. Consider putting something unexpected in the bag so that it sometimes holds surprises and looking pays off in more ways than one.

Think of other things you always do in a certain way and consider alternatives. What if you started to put your child's socks on her hands when she was getting dressed? What if you started to read his favorite book upside down or backward? What if the trains were not in the blue basket, but in the pink one? What if the two boxes she likes to bang together were tied up? What if the cars were dispersed all around the room and you had to start a search because it was crucial they all be together? What if the shoe box containing marbles suddenly had six rubber bands around it?

Most likely, your child will not only quickly try to solve these dilemmas by undoing what you did, but will start watching you, waiting, and eventually enjoying being more active and interactive. These problems require more attention, more use of two hands, more involvement with objects, and more communication. They present a different kind of puzzle for your child to solve, rather than presenting the same obstacles again and again. In these examples, the ritual is the lead that opens the circle of communication, the problem you create is your first response, and your child's reaction closes the circle. In other words, the ritual you change is step one and your child's response is step two, whether he solves the problem independently or turns to you for help. The emotion aroused, whether positive or negative, will fuel more interaction and will get your child to explore, experiment, feel, and think. If your child does not notice or does not respond, have no shame—try something else. What may not work one day might work the next time. Although you may feel rejected or inadequate, consider it a problem to solve. There is no one right or wrong answer. Focus on setting up the tone and momentum that will help you and your child interact more and enjoy it. Later, the problem solving will become more symbolic as you create dramas and go on to solve real and imagined problems.

COMMUNICATING THE WHOLE RANGE OF EMOTIONS

As your child gets better at gestural communication, he should begin using gestures to communicate the whole range of emotions.

• He may express a desire for closeness by reaching out to be picked up.

• He may knock food off his tray or throw toys to express assertiveness and anger.

• He may smile, laugh, and wave his arms or legs to express pleasure.

• He may push away the doll you are feeding to express jealousy.

• He may push you away and make forays across the room to express independence.

Look for these signs. If you sense that certain emotions are missing, encourage them.

• To encourage playfulness, tickle him, put your head on his tummy, make silly faces and movements. Then laugh together to share the funny, playful moment.

• To encourage exploratory behavior, hide toys in places where you think he can find them, then crawl around together searching for them.

• To encourage the expression of anger and frustration, don't give in right away to her demands. Stall her. Act confused. Prompt her to open and close extra circles of communication while feeling frustrated and annoyed.

• To encourage the expression of sadness, sit quietly with her when she is sad. Don't be in a hurry to banish her tears or cheer her up. Soothe her, but don't rush to fix the source of the sadness.

GESTURES AS THE FOUNDATION FOR COMMUNICATION AND SPEECH

If your child is already talking you may understandably question the need to work on gestural communication. Yet gestural communication is extremely important. Gestures are an expression of your child's desire. She wants something; she points and grunts. She wants Mommy: she holds up her arms and cries. Her gestures translate her wishes, desires, and feelings into communication. Words do the same thing, but in a more abstract way. Instead of communicating the desire directly, they represent the wish or feeling as a symbol. Unless your child is fluent at communicating with gestures, she won't be ready to communicate in the more difficult abstract language of symbols.

Your child uses gestures and behavior to figure out who she is and what she wants and feels and to let you know those same things. Words do the same in shorthand. Almost all verbal exchange communicates something of emotional meaning: "I like this," "I don't like that," "This part of the day was good," "That part was bad," "The movie was great," "I wish he wouldn't do that." Children who are not able to use gestures to communicate this kind of emotional content in a continuous, two-way flow will have the same problem with words. They will tend to use words in a fragmented, isolated way. To help them, we have to build their skills at ongoing, gestural, two-way communication. Generally children are ready to move toward speech when they can regularly close 30 or 40 gestural circles in a row.

While working on gestural communication, you should also be talking to your child. It is natural for you and will keep your own spirits and interest up. Be careful not to become silent just because your child does not talk back. Labeling your gestures will help her begin to associate words with their meanings and will speed the transition when she is ready. As you pour her juice, talk about what you're doing. As you help her get dressed, ask her, "Which foot first?" or, "Head first or arms?" As you bump your car into hers, say, "Bump car! Are you going to bump me?"

Keep your words directly related to the activity at hand. Once gestural communication is mastered, you and your child are ready for the transition to speech.

THE IMPORTANCE OF PLAYING WITH FRIENDS

Floor-time interactions are the most effective way to lure your child into the world of human warmth, spontaneity, and interaction, but they are not enough. Your child also needs to interact with peers, both because he will need to engage with peers throughout his life and because children who are the same age or at the same developmental level will provide a lot of practice in social skills. Children are naturally very interactive. They intuitively make good floor-time partners who can bolster your own efforts.

For many children with special needs, playing with other children is initially difficult. For the child who is still new to warmth and intimacy any new relationship seems scary. And for parents, who intuitively sense how difficult it may be to mediate a relationship between their child and a peer, the idea of arranging play dates is equally intimidating. But play dates are essential. Without play dates children will not learn how to use their new abilities in the company of their peers.

As soon as your child can easily open and close ten or more circles of communication, you need to introduce playtime with peers. Start by arranging one play date a week, at home, with a child of the same age or a little younger who is very interactive. Expect the first few sessions to be awkward. The visiting child is likely to rummage through toys, eliciting howls of protest or sullen withdrawal from your child. But if you persist, your child will get used to the visitor's presence. You can help the process by acting as mediator. Use all the strategies you've learned in working with your child to draw her into play. Appeal to her strongest senses to get her attention. When she's engaged with you, draw her into two-way gestural communication. Then slowly bring the visiting child into your two-person game. If either child backs off, wait a moment, then try again. You can also give the visiting child tips on how to engage your child as well as on what to avoid. But don't worry about coaching the playmate too much. Most children intuitively know how to engage a withdrawn peer. In fact, if you watch closely, you may pick up a tip or two!

Encourage attention between the children. Such phrases as, "Oh, look!" "Wow!" "What are you doing?" "Come see this!" will help your child become more aware of the other child. The visiting child will also respond quickly to such gestures.

With a withdrawn child, you might show the visitor how to be playfully obstructive, how to notice what your child is doing and then playfully interfere. Children are naturals at this; they spontaneously find playful ways to draw shy children into their games.

If your child is underreactive to sensory experiences and withdrawn, he will respond well to the other child's energetic initiatives. A game in which everybody runs around trying to get in everyone else's way could be interesting for all. Games with a lot of motion and contact and outdoor play are good ways to begin. Remember, there are no right or wrong moves; just keep it going in a lively and enjoyable way. Balls, bubbles, and balloons can be very enticing; so can a tug-of-war with a Slinky and water or sand play.

If your child is overreactive to sensory experience (if he doesn't like loud noises, for example), suggest that the children play in whispers. If your child doesn't like to be touched, remind them of the "bet you can't not touch" game. Help them create interactions that everyone will enjoy.

Once your child is comfortable playing with one other child, bring in a second child so he can practice playing with two friends. When he's comfortable with two, increase the group to three or even four. Each time the group size increases, your child will need your support. Adding one more child may not seem like a big difference, but to a child who is not terribly flexible it can feel like a significant change. Be prepared for regression, and be available to help your child reclimb the developmental ladder. With months of practice he will grow more comfortable interacting with groups of peers.

When your child can engage in pretend play with toys, you will want to go back to mediating such play between just two children. Once your child can share and negotiate verbal ideas you can add another child.

It may not be easy to get the same child to come back repeatedly, since children are apt to resent the planned and structured visits, so try to create a group of children you can recruit for regular dates. Turn to friends, neighbors, and relatives who will be supportive. As your child's comfort level grows, up the number of weekly sessions. Five a week is not too many—at least for your child—but as they can be cumbersome to arrange and supervise, that many may not be feasible. If you can get in four sessions a week you'll be doing very well. The key is practice, practice, practice. Every play date will help your child learn to be joyful and spontaneous with peers. (See Chapter 19 for a more detailed discussion of peers.)

TAILORING FLOOR TIME TO YOUR CHILD'S NEEDS

As you work with your child to help her master two-way communication, you will need to keep her biological challenges in mind.

If Your Child Has Auditory-Processing Difficulties

Children with auditory-processing difficulties have problems at this stage because sounds play a significant role in gestural communication. Imagine a toddler who holds his arms in the air for his mother to pick him up. As she reaches for him, his mother murmurs soothing sounds. For the toddler these sounds are as much a part of his mother's response as is her holding, and he comes to rely on them for reassurance. Soon even at a distance, the sound of his mother's voice can soothe him. Or imagine a toddler who reaches toward an electrical outlet. Even before he leaps from his chair, Daddy's voice rings out, "Don't touch!" The toddler doesn't understand the words, but the tone of voice is clear. She pauses and looks at Daddy before reaching for the plug. The voice communicates every bit as much as the gestures the child sees.

The sounds your child hears (aural information) give him important information about the world and about himself. Fortunately, there are ways to compensate for auditory-processing problems. Instead of relying on your voice, you can make an effort to talk to your child through motor gestures—touch, body language, facial expressions. Think of a sixteen-month-old with auditory-processing difficulties who is starting to explore the far side of a room. Since she can't rely on her mother's voice to make her feel safe, she needs to return to her mother's leg every few minutes to be reassured. Her auditory challenge impairs her ability to take initiative and explore the world. But if her parents smile and clap or wave whenever she looks at them from across the room, they can *visually* communicate their support. The same is true for the child who reaches for the plug. If crying "Don't touch!" won't stop him, getting between him and the plug with a stern face and a wagging finger probably will. Before physically restraining the child, his parents can show him through gestures that he can see that he needs to stay away. Gradually, as these gestures are combined with simpler sounds, such as "uh-oh" and words, the child's understanding of vocal gestures will grow.

The same principle holds true for older children. Suppose you're asking your child to clean up. Auditory-processing challenges may make it hard for her to understand your instructions. So compensate by making your instructions visual as well. Sing a cleanup song to alert her to what will happen next. Point to the toys and where they are supposed to go. Use facial expressions and hand gestures to show her what you want. Take one toy and put it back, then hand her one to put back. Back up your gestures with slow, clear speech. Say or sing good-bye to each toy as you name each one. Don't assume that your child's recalcitrance is negativism. Give her the benefit of the doubt and a lot of visual and emotional support. There may be a response lag just because it takes her longer to process what you say.

You may want to use photographs to help communicate with your child, especially to refer to places, people, or things not on hand. For example, to let your child know where you are going next, show him a photograph of the place or person. On busy days, use a picture schedule to help your child understand the sequence of events; this will make transitions easier.

You can also use photographs to help your child make choices and express desires. Shoot a roll of 36 distinct pictures of the significant aspects of your child's life: people, places, toys, foods, books, clothes, rooms. Order a double set, and laminate each set. Put one set on a key ring that you can carry with you. Put Velcro tabs on the backs of the other set and make cardboard holders for them with reciprocal Velcro tabs, then put them around the house in the rooms where you are most likely to need them. Use them to help your child indicate his needs and wants. After he gestures, if his gestures are unclear, have him pick out or point to the object, place, or person he wants.

As you concentrate on communicating visually with your child, continue to use words. Only by doing so will you build his auditory-processing skills. But use those words simply and strategically, as backup for your gestures. As you encourage your child at a distance, back up your smiles and claps with the words "Good boy, good boy!" As you frown and shake your head to warn your toddler away from danger, say, "No, no, no," in a firm, but not angry, voice. Through repetition your child will learn these verbal phrases, and in time you may be able to use the words without the visual gestures.

Another device that will help your child communicate is the limited use of sign language. Just a handful of gestures for everyday actions can go a long way toward helping you understand one another and develop two-way communication. Useful signs are those meaning want, more, help, all done, stop, go, and play. Even if your child does not have the motor-planning abilities to imitate these simple actions, he can see you doing them and will learn what they mean if you use them consistently. In this case the signs enhance your verbal communication with visual cues until the auditory connection is made. Later, when your child is speaking, the signs can serve as prompts to help retrieve the words. If he can also imitate the signs he will have an interim language with which to communicate. Using signs in this way will not delay verbal expression.

As you work with your child to develop his communication and initiative, keep these guidelines in mind:

• *Read your child's intentions.* Because your child's signals may not be clear, look for subtle signs—smiles, gestures, facial expressions—that may indicate what he really means.

• *Take every opportunity to encourage initiative.* Follow your child's lead; encourage him to explore; let him do things for himself.

• *Talk to your child through gestures, not just through words.* When you want her to come, call her with a hand sign. When you want to encourage exploration, smile broadly, clap your hands, and use other big gestures that your child can read from across the room.

• *Think of words as a backup to your gestures.* Use words as an accompaniment to your gestures and gradually your child may learn to recognize the words without the clarifying gestures.

• *Build a gestural vocabulary with your child.* Help him develop a vocabulary of gestures that he can use to express his needs so that he can communicate accurately despite his language delay.

• *Use photographs and signs as a means of communication.* These tools can help both you and your child communicate your intentions.

• *Use touch as a means of communication.* Vary your touch; it can be just as varied as your tone of voice.

• *Emphasize the warmth of your feedback.* We often communicate warmth with our tone of voice. If your child is missing that feedback, compensate by putting extra warmth into your gestures, your facial expressions, and your touch.

• *Open and close thousands of circles of communication.* Above all, your child needs practice communicating. The more circles you open and close, the better she will get at making language and gestures work for her.

If Your Child Has Visual-Spatial Processing Challenges

Children with visual-spatial challenges may have problems with gestural communication because they lack a clear picture of the world. Their spatial sense may be fragmented. They have a hard time forming an integrated picture of their environment. To understand what it is like to have a visual-spatial challenge imagine yourself exploring a maze. You have lost your way and can't see where you are going. You feel alone, isolated, and anxious. What would reassure you in that scenario? Probably the sound of someone's voice. While that voice might not tell you exactly where you are, it would provide a handhold, a connection to security and comfort.

A child who has a hard time understanding what she sees and how the parts fit into the whole may misread your facial expressions, body posture, or hand gestures. She may cling and feel worried about where you are even if you are nearby. You can help her compensate for her visual-spatial difficulty by working with your voice. As you play, give her a continuous flow of auditory information; talk constantly and animatedly so that she can always rely on your voice to stay in touch. Also provide her with clear visual information by using simple, explicit gestures. Don't be impatient with her anxiety over separation, since she may not feel certain of her road map.

You can help your child become more comfortable being away from you by practicing that skill. Once you are warmly engaged, gradually move away, always maintaining voice contact. Move slowly; if she loses you and tunes out or if she grows anxious, come back into her visual field, then try again slowly. Have someone else help her find you, using your voice as a cue. Over a period of weeks or months try to increase the distance that you can comfortably put between you. With time and practice you should be able to talk to your child from another room and have her feel comfortable. This exercise will also help her develop her internal map. Gradually she will learn the contours of your house *and* realize that you remain in her life even when out of sight.

If Your Child Has Both Auditory- and Visual-Processing Challenges

With a child who has auditory- and visual-processing challenges you need to work patiently and clearly with both your voice and your gestures to sustain contact. A child with this double challenge is likely to appear very self-absorbed—not because he wants to avoid contact, but because he is aware only of what is within his immediate visual and auditory field.

To help your child maintain ongoing communication, don't take his tuning out personally. Realize that you need to help him stay in touch by deliberately controlling your speech and gestures. Talk and move slowly but animatedly. Slowing down makes it easier for him to process the messages you are sending. Animation gives him more to look at and listen to and makes it easier for him to track you and take you in.

The same visual-spatial problems that make it difficult for your child to find you in a group of people may make it difficult for her to select a toy from a crowded shelf, enjoy a jigsaw puzzle, or build a block structure. To help her notice toys, set them up on tabletops, inverted boxes, or open areas on the floor so they stand out. Even creating a square on the floor with masking tape or colored paper will make an object more noticeable. Your child will soon begin to look for what's there. Toys with moving parts will help her learn to discriminate because she will be more able to track the movements. You can interact around a roller coaster of beads or shapes that move on wires twisting up and down and around through space. Children with motor-planning difficulties especially like these toys because they can make things move on the wires with minimal movement of their own.

Other activities that encourage visual-spatial processing include rolling a large ball toward your child and encouraging him to first push and then jump out of the way, and batting or catching a soft toy that is suspended from a string. You can also use flashlights to shine on different objects in a darkened room. Give your child a flashlight too, so that he can see what he can find. Next try using the flashlight to track the frame of the windows, the edge of the ceiling, the outline of the furniture, and so forth. If your child has difficulty focusing on a book, darken the room and use a flashlight to focus on the pictures. Add excitement by saying, "Look! There's Cookie Monster!" Give your child a small flashlight to shine on the pictures too. Place stick-on notes on top of specific parts of the pictures. Your child will enjoy discovering what's underneath as he pulls them off.

Even if your child cannot construct a building of blocks, she will be able to knock one down or pull one apart. Start by setting up tall structures with large cardboard blocks in the middle of the room. Sooner or later your child will notice the structure, and she'll probably knock it down. When she looks at it again, rebuild it, and again she'll knock it down. Once she's interested, you can hand her a block. When she puts it down, add one to it, then hand her another. When she puts that one down, add to that one too. Soon you'll be building together. Once she is visually attentive, put some of her favorite figures in the "house" or on the "roof," on the "road," or the "bed." Naming the structure adds a symbolic, pretend-play element to your interaction.

All these activities involve more than visual-spatial processing, since you are using your voice, touch, and movement simultaneously. In this way you are appealing to your child's stronger abilities while supporting the development of the lagging processes. When you set up the colorful blocks for your child to push down you are meeting her halfway, and the pleasure she gets will bring her back for more. Using the flashlight provides instant fun with minimal frustration, while developing your child's use of his eyes. Even children who have visual-spatial processing strengths will enjoy these activities, all of which can be made more challenging.

If Your Child Has Motor Challenges

Motor challenges can compound a child's difficulty in forming an internal map of the world. To form such a map, a child must coordinate motor movements with visual perceptions. To form a picture of his bedroom, for instance, he watches his mother as she moves from spot to spot, following her with his eyes and remembering how she and the room looked as she moved about. After several repetitions, the three-dimensional image of his room is locked in his mind. But if a child can't turn his head or focus his eyes to follow his mother's movements, his ability to form that image is hampered. Not only will he not remember what he saw; he'll be unable even to collect the data to construct the image.

To understand what it feels like to have a motor problem, imagine wearing a suit that controls your movement. Each time you try to move in one direction, the suit moves you randomly in another. You try as hard as you can to reach your mother, but you can't make yourself get close. Or, by the time you organize your movement, get your muscle tone up to support your moves, and decide which way to go, your mother has already moved in another direction.

If your child has these compound challenges, work with him at close range using very simple movements that he can repeat again and again. Work with him in the positions in which you know he feels comfortable. If he likes to lie on the floor or lean against the couch for support, let him. Prop him against the couch facing you. If he's touching his nose, put your face right next to his so he can see it and say animatedly, "My nose! Touch my nose!" When he does, keep your face right there and make a funny beeping sound, so that he can connect the sound and the image and his touching movement. Your sound may compel him to touch your nose again; when he does he'll have closed another circle. If you repeat this sequence four, five, or more times, your child will have sustained communication over a minute and will have built a map of that interaction. If he touches your lips, blow raspberries. The more of these intimate encounters you have, the better your child will get at sustained communication and the more maps he will build. Bit by bit he will develop an internal image of his world.

Children with motor-planning challenges also have problems with gestural communication. They often have a hard time learning that they can signal intentionally to get what they want because they have difficulty forming the gestures and their gestures are often misunderstood. If a child can't raise his arms to tell his parents he wants to be picked up, he must wait for them to decide to hold him. As a result, instead of learning that he can signal his need for closeness, he learns that closeness is randomly determined by someone else. If a child accidentally hits her father's nose when she means to caress it, her father may misinterpret the gesture as an act of aggression. He's likely to respond by getting angry, inadvertently teaching his child to curb her actions and feelings.

To prevent these inadvertent thwartings of initiative and emotion, you face a dual task. You must work extra hard to read the *intention* behind your child's gestures, and you must create opportunities to build your child's initiative. Here are some ways to accomplish these tasks.

> • *Build a gestural vocabulary.* Since your child may not be able to form the complex motor gestures she needs to tell you what she wants, help her develop alternative means of expressing herself. Take note of any spontaneous movement she makes when you show her something or do something she enjoys. Treat that movement as intentional by imitating it and highlighting it, even moving her hands or feet the next time to intensify the meaning of her actions. Then repeat the behavior she desired and enjoyed. But wait until she makes a clear gesture indicating "more." She may blink her eyes, stick out her tongue, make a sound, or wrinkle her nose when you point to the options. If she can't raise her arms to be picked up, help her learn to kick against her chair to convey the same intention. If she can't crawl or walk to reach her toys, teach her to wave her arms toward the things she wants so you can get them. Use the universal sign for "more" each time you give her more of what she wants. (Hold your hands up,

moving your fingertips together, then apart.) If she does not imitate the gesture spontaneously after a while, take her hands in yours and show her how to do it. Most children can approximate this action. In these ways she can use two-way communication to express her needs and feel a sense of power over her world.

• *Give your child choices.* Once you've built a vocabulary for communicating intentions, create opportunities for your child to use it. Don't simply offer him cereal; show him several foods and let him pick. Don't assume he wants your help when he gets stuck; let him ask for help when he becomes frustrated. Don't hand him a toy the minute it rolls beyond his reach; let him tell you if he wants it. In these ways you can encourage your child to take initiative rather than be passive. Try using pictures or empty cartons of what he wants. Even if he cannot yet point, he will be able to pick up the carton or picture to hand you.

• *Respond to your child's gestures promptly.* The best way to build your child's sense of power and initiative is to show her that her communications get results. As soon as she tells you she wants to be picked up, pick her up. As soon as she demonstrates a desire for closeness, say, "I love you, too," and give her a hug. As soon as she shows she wants a particular item, say, "Do you want that spoon?" You don't need to give it to her, but you do need to show her you understand her request. By doing so, you give her a sense of her power in the world. You can challenge or play dumb once the gesture is well established.

• *Be especially sensitive to your child's emotional state.* Since your child may not be able to gesture his emotional needs, you'll need to look for subtle signs. Perhaps he seems unusually exerted or withdrawn. With time you'll come to recognize his signs. Then, before you act, ask him what he wants. Use the vocabulary you've established to let him tell you what he needs.

• *Consider your child's intention.* Guard against misinterpreting your child's behavior by considering the context in which it occurs. If you're playing warmly and she boxes your nose, it's probably safe to assume the blow was unintended. If you're engaged in a bedtime power struggle and the same thing happens, your child may be expressing some aggression! The challenge is to control your reaction until you've gauged your child's intent. Then react to her intention, not just to her behavior.

11

Floor Time III:
Feelings and Ideas

HELPING A CHILD DEVELOP AND
EXPRESS FEELINGS AND IDEAS

Tammy was a beautiful child. With her red curls and bright blue eyes she might have been on the cover of a magazine. She was diagnosed with autistic spectrum disorder. When her parents first took her for an evaluation at 24 months old, she made little eye contact with them or with the therapist and sat quietly in a world of her own, twirling a piece of ribbon through her chubby fingers. She occasionally looked and reacted with a few gestures, but she was unable to engage continuously in a flow of interactions. Over the next year Tammy made considerable progress. Thanks to intensive efforts by her parents (along with speech and occupational therapists, a psychologist who coached her parents, and students they hired to play interactively with her), Tammy began to relate warmly to her family and could interact gesturally, opening and closing 20 or 30 circles of communication in a row.

In many ways, though, her behavior remained quite rigid. She did the same activities over and over, resisting any attempts at change, and her speech, which consisted of about 15 words, was equally rote. She often repeated the last word she heard or said the same phrase over and over as if finding comfort in its sound. But Tammy's significant progress in the areas of intimacy and communication made her able to tackle the next stage, the flexible and creative expression of feelings and ideas.

190

The challenge was to draw Tammy into make-believe, a difficult prospect since Tammy's play was so mechanical. The key to success involved Tammy's favorite coping behavior. Whenever she felt overloaded, Tammy ran to the far side of the room and threw herself on the floor. She lay there for 3 to 30 minutes until some interior signal told her it was time to move, then she wandered aimlessly until her mother was able to reengage her. The plan was to use this behavior to start some pretend play. Each time Tammy lay on the floor, everyone was to pretend she was napping. By giving a meaning to her behavior, she might be lured into make-believe.

After playing for a few minutes in the therapist's office, Tammy pulled away, ran across the room, and threw herself on the floor. Instead of cajoling her, her mother said, "Tammy's napping. Everybody quiet." Her father put Tammy's teddy bear next to her. The minute the bear touched her, Tammy ran farther across the room and lay down again. Clearly her parents' gestures had been intrusions. They were alarmed, but tried again. Bravely, Tammy's mother said, "It looks like Tammy still wants to nap." She brought the bear closer to her daughter and said, "My bear sleep, too." This time Tammy threw the bear at her mom. Her mother tried once more. "Maybe I can nap with you," she said cautiously. She picked up a toy lion and lay down three feet from her daughter. Tammy eyed her suspiciously as if to say, "You'd better not get too close!" but her mother held her ground, merely watching Tammy warmly. After a minute, Tammy got up, cautiously approached her mother, grabbed the lion, and put it back with the other dolls. Seeing an opportunity her mother said, "Can I be a lion?" and got on all fours. Tammy looked at her for a minute, then climbed up on her back and went for a ride on the mommy lion.

Over the next several days, each time Tammy threw herself on the floor her parents picked up a toy animal and lay down near her, attempting to join her in her activity. Each time, they exchanged glances and then offered her a ride on their backs. One day two weeks later, Tammy ran to get her bear, looked at her mom and said, "Sleep." She had decided to join the make-believe.

Delighted, Tammy's parents slowly began adding elements to the game. First they offered her a blanket; then they turned off the lights and sang a goodnight song; when she got up they said, "Tammy woke up! Good morning!" and turned the lights back on. Each of these additions sparked a protest, but after several repetitions Tammy accepted them.

Soon Tammy's mother introduced another element. After Tammy put a doll to sleep her mother got another doll, covered it with a blanket, and said softly, "Sh, dolly napping." To her surprise Tammy adopted this scenario immediately. She seemed to identify with the doll and began adding her own ideas; she gave the doll her bear and eagerly woke the doll saying, "Wake up!"

Gradually her parents thickened the plot. They'd have the doll set the table or ask to serve breakfast to Tammy, and after a little while Tammy began augmenting these scenes with ideas of her own.

Through these activities, which she knew so well from real life, Tammy began to experiment with pretend play. Little by little her play expanded, and as it grew, so did her ability to negotiate the world of ideas.

THE IMPORTANCE OF PRETEND PLAY

The transition to pretend play is one of the most important leaps your child will make. By pretending that the box is a stove or the closet is a store she will loosen her reliance on the concrete world and begin to imagine the objects in her mind while using a substitute for them. Next, she may use a gesture to signal putting the pot on the stove, as in mime. In doing this, she is beginning to think abstractly. This is tremendously empowering. Abstract thinking is key to most of what we do in the world. It enables us to experiment with ideas in our mind without actually having to carry out the acts. Thanks to abstract thinking we are able to imagine, to understand others, to conceptualize things that aren't right in front of us; we are able to calculate time, space, speed, and rate of change; we are able to see the consequences of our actions. Without the ability to think abstractly we are limited to the here and now; we cannot plan, we can only react.

For most children, the move into make-believe is automatic. They need no prodding from parents, only engagement by parents and others to weave elaborate fantasies around the experiences of intimacy and two-way communication and the most ordinary objects. But for many children with special needs this transition must be practiced. It's easier for them to play concretely, to see things as they are, not as they could be.

Pretend play involves the use of symbols, and using symbols is difficult for many children with special needs. When a child pretends that a bucket of rocks is a bowl of candy, he is using the rocks to symbolize the candy in his mind. He is calling on his previous experience with candy—how it looks, how it tastes, how it smells, how it feels in his hand and in his mouth—to create a multisensory mental picture, *the idea* of candy in his mind. A child who has had a huge number of experiences is able to create multisensory ideas about candy and millions of other things and is able to use them fluently as he plays.

But a child who has difficulties with sensory reactivity and processing or who has motor problems has not had the millions of unencumbered experiences that give rise to this palette of ideas. Her experience will have been limited by her difficulties. She may lack information from certain senses; information from other senses may be distorted or fragmented; motor problems may have physically limited her experience with many things. If she has visual-processing problems she may be unable to hold the image of an object that is no longer right in front of her. As a result, she may have difficulty creating the mental pictures of her world that she needs to pretend. She may be able to play with the rocks in front of her, but have difficulty pretending the rocks are candy, for she may have trouble holding the idea of candy in her mind.

If a child has auditory-processing difficulties he may have trouble holding sounds and words in his mind; it may be hard for him to connect the word for a thing to its visual image and the tactile experience and motor exploration that goes with it. Our ideas grow from our experience with all our senses as well as our motor system; we integrate all that input when we form the idea. Children with processing problems have a hard time interpreting each of the experiential elements with which they come in contact. Children with only partial hearing or sight but who can process those experiences can nonetheless integrate them into a larger whole.

Another factor that makes pretend play difficult is that it requires the child to picture his own wish or desire, to link his desire to actions and symbols. As we explained in Chapter 10, because of processing problems many children with challenges have difficulty forming a link between emotion and behavior and ultimately between emotion and symbols. The basic unit of communication—the connection between emotion, behavior, and symbol—is missing.

To help a child with special needs form this critical link, it's important to connect all her learning to her wishes and intentions. If each time she reaches for a doll you say, "Dolly. Want dolly," she will come to associate the idea of "want doll" and the words "want doll" with what she is feeling inside. That bit of learning will have deep-seated emotional meaning. It will define a little bit of herself, the part of her that wants that doll. If each time your child pounds on your leg because you denied her a cookie, you say, "You're angry. No cookie. Want cookie," she will come to associate the ideas of angry and want cookie and the words for those ideas with the feelings that press her from inside. Again, that learning will define yet another meaningful piece of herself.

Therefore, the guiding rule as you work to help your child learn to use ideas and words is always, *always,* to connect your words and ideas with your child's wishes and intents. As long as you work with him on the things in which he is interested and about which he has feelings, you will help him move into the world of ideas. You can work on this skill in two areas— through pretend play and through your daily conversations, whether gestural or verbal. In the pages that follow we explain how you can do that.

HELPING YOUR CHILD LEARN TO PRETEND

When your child is closing many circles in a row you're ready to introduce pretend play. The best way to do this is to add an element of make-believe to his favorite activities.

- When your child initiates tickling, tickle him with the "tickle bug" instead of with your fingers.

- If your child is playing with a doll, get another doll and have your doll talk to your child or put a puppet on your hand and talk in the puppet's voice.

- When your child is mechanically rolling a car across the floor, ask for the driver or put a doll in the car and say, "I want a ride!" Use Silly Putty to connect a small figure to the top of the car if you cannot put it inside.

- When your child climbs the slide, call it a mountain. When you swing your child, hold the swing high, do a countdown (5, 4, 3, 2, 1) and let the spaceship blast off to the moon, or row your boat over the stormy sea.

- When your child gets hungry or thirsty while playing, first offer pretend food and drinks (have a tea set and toy food). Take a drink and comment—"Yum!"—then offer your child some.

- Add a role to your child's name when you call him: Captain Juan, Astronaut Sarah, Chef Darryl, Doctor Selina. This will encourage him to imagine he is someone else.

Begin to treat all your play actions in an imaginative way. Try to remember yourself as a child playing imaginatively, going on adventures, and pretend again with your child.

Become a Character in the Drama

The most effective way to engage your child is to get involved in the action yourself. You must become a character in the drama.

• When your child is playing with her doll, talk for her doll or another doll you hold. Say, "I'm hungry! I want food! Now I want applesauce! Now I want milk!" Don't watch from the sidelines commenting on what your child is doing. Make yourself a character in her drama. Also, talk to her doll directly. Instead of asking your child about the doll, ask the doll: "Do you want milk? Or apple juice?"

• When your child is rolling a car across the floor and you put a doll inside, talk for the doll. Say, "I want to go to the zoo! Can we go to the zoo? Can we go home?" If he balks at your intrusion, put a building in front of the car and say, "Here's the house. Now your car is home." If he balks at that, get a second car and say, "Let's race. I'm faster!" Keep trying different scenarios—all built around his car theme—until you engage his interest. Once you do, stay in the drama yourself, as the character you have created.

• When he is banging pots together, bang with him, saying, "I'm in the band, too!" Introduce new instruments and see if he'll take them from you. Turn his concrete banging into pretend by making yourself a key player in the drama. Start to march so that you give the banging some purpose. Even add an echo microphone; demonstrate, and then hand him the mike or put it to his mouth.

Until your child expands his range of pretend ideas, he may want to drive the car, push the shopping cart, or eat the food himself. When he can use figures or dolls to represent himself—when he stops rejecting figures in the car he is driving—you will know he has taken one more step up the symbolic ladder.

Ideas For Pretend Play Are Everywhere

As you introduce pretend into your child's play, you will be following his lead. Rather than introduce new activities, you'll add imaginary elements to the activities he is already doing. This will be easier if you have a lot of props available. Cooking utensils, pots and pans, empty food containers, and other everyday items can contribute to the drama, as can toy cars and trucks, garages and houses, blocks and trains, animals and puppets. These open-ended toys will allow your child to develop dramas as he wishes. They represent aspects of real life that your child will recognize, leading him to recreate real-life scenes.

When your child is playing with her favorite dolls and stuffed animals, look for opportunities to simulate everyday activities. Dolls can cook and set the table; stuffed animals can be put to bed; dolls can go to the store for groceries. These activities, so familiar and important to your child, are usually the earliest material of make-believe.

Because children build pretend play from their real experiences, make sure your child has a broad base of experiences. Go to the airport, the fire station, the zoo; go on the bus, on a carousel, on a train; then bring these experiences home through play. Relive the carousel by running around in circles, and bobbing up and down or by galloping toy horses in a circle. When you see an airplane in the sky, make believe you're flying far away. Use these experiences to help your child practice using his imagination.

Don't be afraid to enlist your child's coping behavior in pretend play. Just as Tammy's parents turned running away into napping, you can give meaning to your child's particular behaviors. For instance, if your child often flaps his arms, see if being airplanes is fun. If she perseveratively opens and closes doors, make a point of looking for someone on the other side, have her bear get stuck in the door, or give her keys to use to lock and unlock the door. Children with motor-planning challenges may do very simple actions repetitively. Giving such actions symbolic intent will change their meanings and help the child go beyond them.

Thicken the Plot to Keep the Drama Going

One of the most common complaints parents voice is, "My child is so repetitive! He plays out the same scenes over and over." It's true. Left to their own preferences, most children with special needs *will* play out the same scenes over and over; familiarity is comforting. Children with multiple developmental delays rely on familiarity for a sense of safety. Your challenge is to stretch the drama in new directions, to stay within your child's theme, but to introduce elements he might not have thought of.

> • If your child is repeatedly using her fire truck to put out a fire, become a cat that's stuck in a tree and needs a rescue or put a cat toy in the tree and speak for it. Then call 911 for the fire truck.

> • If your child makes repeated trips to the store and buys the same items every time, be the storekeeper who says, "No more milk. All sold. Bread instead?" Or close the store just as your child arrives.

> • If your child plays at napping over and over, be a child who refuses to nap or refuses to get up.

If your child repeatedly acts out familiar scripts—a verse from a song or lines from a book or video—use pretend play to build on these scripts.

Gradually introduce new elements; play the scene a slightly different way or use a new prop in place of an old one. Bit by bit, embroider the familiar script or the familiar cartoon character into a new one. The more script-oriented your child is, the more creative you have to be, using actions and words to inspire him to move in new directions. Don't be shy about physically interfering with his preferred activity. If Thomas the train goes only in circles, block the track with another train and say, "Track closed," or put a doll across the track who says, "I want to get on!" By becoming a character and taking the drama in a slightly new direction you can slowly expand your child's repertoire. If you're not repetitive, he won't be able to be either. See his repetitions as a challenge to you to become more creative. If you are patient and persistent you can build your child's flexibility while you help him move into the world of ideas.

Don't limit your child's ideas because of physical disabilities. Children with motor difficulties especially need pretend play to practice actions they cannot yet perform. This practice encourages them to think of themselves as someone who can and will be able to do what other children do. Do not underestimate your child's ideas even if his motor development is delayed. He can have his doll climb the ladder to go down the slide, make his puppy jump in the pool, or pretend he is riding horseback, even though he still needs support just to sit on his bench. (Use rubber bands, putty, or tape to secure figures so your child can move them easily.)

Introduce Conflict or Challenge

Instead of merely going along with whatever your child has initiated, become a character with a will of his own. Protest your child's decisions and offer alternatives.

- Have your puppy puppet refuse to open its mouth and moan, "Uh, uh, uh!"

- When your child's doll tells your doll to eat her corn, don't comply. Say, "No!" or, "I want ice cream! Give me ice cream!"

- When your child's car speeds down the road, don't just race your car next to it. Talk for your car and protest: "That's my road! Move over!"

- When your child puts her character into the spaceship, have your character say, "My turn! *I'm* going to the moon!" If your child pushes your character aside, say, "You can't push me away, I've got my laser gun!" Use your child's negative response as an invitation to insert another thickening element.

By creating problems for your child to solve rather than labeling or mirroring what he did, you spur him onto the next step or idea. To encourage him to go on whisper, "Uh-oh, what are you going to do? He's so mean!" Or if he's stuck, whisper two suggestions from which he can choose.

After you introduce a new element give your child a chance to respond. Given time, she may take your new idea and run with it or solve the problem you posed, adding more of her own. If she doesn't respond, try again with the same idea or with a new one. Eventually she'll become more flexible.

How often should you do this? Introduce novelty as often as necessary to keep spontaneous action flowing—whenever your child bogs down, when his play becomes rote, when he tunes you out of the drama. You don't need to do it every few seconds, and certainly not so much that you feel that you're taking over the drama. The goal is to spur your child in a new direction and then follow along. Even exaggerating his controlling or inflexible ideas will help him realize what he is doing and help him step back. You might tell his figures not to move because the boss said so—and he means it!

Don't be concerned at this point that this contrariness seems negative or sets a bad example for your child. You'll have opportunities later to work on good manners, taking turns, and other rules of etiquette. Right now what's most important is helping your child develop the richest dramas possible, and each time you get contrary and introduce a conflict, you challenge your child to become creative and to develop and express new ideas.

Involve Your Child's Senses and Motor and Processing Abilities

As you look for ways to thicken the plot try to bring in the sensory experiences and motor and processing skills that are difficult for your child. If she doesn't like touching and is averse to many textures, try bringing different textures into your play. Dolls can cook with Play-Doh, or sand, or cornstarch mixed with water. They can swim in water, Styrofoam peanuts, or shaving cream. Cars can race over sandpaper or aluminum foil, through the sandbox, and down hills of cardboard.

Also introduce sounds into your play. Trains and cars can have all different kinds of horns and whistles. Dolls can play musical instruments and dance to all different kinds of music (not only children's tapes). Use a simple echo microphone and tap on a drum (a stick and tray will do). Dramatize these actions with "Ladies and Gentlemen, introducing the Great Jacob and his marching band!"

If your child has difficulty maintaining his posture and often lies down in order to gain support from the floor or couch, he may be reluctant to undertake unpredictable movements through space. You need to find ways to make him *want* to move. If his train moves in short, straight lines back and forth, suggest racing your trains over the mountain of a living-room chair. Zoom your train forward ("Oh no! the train speeded up!"). He will get up to retrieve it or follow it, welcoming whatever comes next. If his doll plays in a small area, become the doll's little dog who runs away from home and needs to be rescued several feet away. Often difficulty with sequencing keeps a child stuck doing the same thing over and over. Your moves will suggest the next step to take.

If your child has auditory-processing challenges, keep most of your dramatic dialogue short and simple. Use familiar cues. But as you play gradually introduce longer, more complex phrases, always closely tied to your child's actions, slowly stretching his abilities to comprehend.

Make all these introductions gently. Each one may cause discomfort for your child and may engender resistance. Don't force it. If she doesn't want to cook with play clay today or tomorrow or the next day, maybe she will next week or next month. By making these new experiences available in a nonthreatening way, in the context of pretend, you may slowly decrease her discomfort with them. She will remember what you did and may be willing to try another time when she initiates the move. But she may also welcome the novelty. Expect a delay until she can organize a response before you move on.

Use Words While You Play

Even if your child is not yet verbal, be sure to talk to him while you play—not with long soliloquies, but with single words and short phrases that relate directly to what he is doing or feeling. By connecting your words with his underlying emotions, you will help him move into speech.

Sam and his father, Paul, were rolling trucks around the room. Each time Paul moved his truck fast, Sam's eyes lit up. When Paul slowed it down, Sam seemed less entranced. To add words to the action Paul began to say "fast" each time he rolled his truck fast and "slow" each time he moved it slowly. After a few minutes he looked at Sam and asked, "Fast or slow?" Sam didn't answer, so Paul rolled the trucks, saying the words again, then repeated the question. After several attempts, Sam waved his hand fast in answer, but Paul just looked confused. "Fast or slow?" he asked again. Sam waved his hand, but again Paul looked confused. After he had repeated the question for the fourth time, Sam said, "Slow." Paul moved the truck slowly. "Fast, fast, fast!" shouted Sam, saying what he had meant to say the first time. When Paul raced the truck across the carpet Sam got a huge smile across his face. The game had lasted half an hour, and he had made his first verbal communication.

Paul later commented that he was surprised Sam had learned the word so quickly. Words *can* be learned quickly if they're related to the child's gestures, motivation, and strong feelings.

When a child is absorbed in something—whether a toy, his mother's face, or even the raging desire to go outside *now*—the child is motivated to learn. His interest in the activity means the learning will be real. Not only will he say the word, but he will understand the concept and remember the word in the future.

Such learning is very different from what occurs when children memorize. You've probably witnessed what happens. A child memorizes the days of the week or other simple words and spews them out articulately when asked. But put the child in a new situation and suddenly the learning is gone. With all the prodding in the world, she can't remember what she was supposed to say. She didn't absorb the full meaning of the words—she merely memorized their sounds—because the words were taught in isolation.

You can help your child learn the meanings of words by always, *always*, introducing new words in the context of an absorbing activity. If the context is full of feelings, the words will get tied to those feelings and to their underlying sense of purpose.

• As your child gets ready to run, jump, or go down the slide, call, "Ready, set, go!" Say, "Go!" just as he starts to move. He will soon begin to fill in the blanks. You can also do a countdown: "1, 2, 3, go!" or "5, 4, 3, 2, 1, blastoff!"

• As you give your child a horsey ride and he gestures for you to go left and right, name the direction he has chosen.

• As she races her car and her face lights up with glee, say, "Car went fast."

• As he pets the dog next door, say, "Pet dog."

• As you try to take some of your child's marbles, say, "Mine." He may pull the basket away and repeat, "Mine!" even more loudly.

If new words are always connected to your child's feelings and gestures, his vocabulary should steadily grow in a meaningful, not rote, manner. Keep your voice full of enthusiasm and vary your tone when you speak. Heighten your affect and match the situation at hand with various feelings.

Surprisingly, some children who are slow to begin speaking use words that carry strong emotions, such as "Oh, no! What happened?" "It's stuck! Fix it!" These words relate to something that went wrong and reflect the child's strong feelings of disappointment, surprise, anger, or despair. Because the child hears others express these words with strong emotions, the words get through and are echoed. They also make an impression because they usually lead to problem solving and empathy.

HELPING YOUR CHILD USE IDEAS IN DAILY CONVERSATION

As you begin naming your child's feelings and gestures during play, you can do the same thing in daily life.

- When your child points to the popsicles in the freezer, say, "Popsicle. Want popsicle?"

- When he fusses because he dropped his spoon, say, "Uh-oh!" to tune in to his emotion, then, "Want spoon?" to offer a solution. Do not hesitate to repeat the words to hold the emotion and stretch the moment. "Oh no, Sarah's hurt. You hurt your knee. Does it hurt? Hurt a lot?"

- When your child cries as you carry her up the stairs to bed, say, "Sad? Angry? No bed?"

By connecting your words with the feelings she carries inside, you will help your child link the meaning of the words with her self. Gradually she'll be able to use the words too.

If you can, hold out whenever your child wants something until you get some response—a look, a reaching out, a vocalization, a word. Seize these moments and hold out just until you think your child will break down or give up.

Increase the Number of Verbal Circles

Just as you worked with your child to increase the number of gestural circles he could close, you now want to work on increasing the number of verbal circles he can close—his ability to engage in an ongoing verbal dialogue. Again, you can do this by stalling or negotiating his demands.

- When he puts his hand on the doorknob and says, "Outside!" don't let him out, stall him. Say, "Too cold," or, "Need boots." He's likely to complain, "Now! Outside now!" "No," you can shake your head, "too cold." "No too cold!" you're likely to get back. "Too cold," you can repeat, "and need boots." "No need boots!" he may wail. At this point you can relent and let him go. He'll have closed multiple verbal circles instead of just one.

If he comprehends the sequence of events that lead to going outside, it may be better not to say no immediately; doing so may trigger so much frustration and anger that your child may be unable to continue the dialogue. Instead, pursue his desire to go out and try to expand on it. "Oh, you want to go outside." When he goes to the closed door, ask if he has the key. This may surprise him, but he will probably recognize the need for the key. You can look for the key (have an old set available for this purpose), try it out, have it not work, knock on the door, find a different key, and so on, to keep the interaction going. Your child will not only close many circles, but he may become engrossed in playing with the keys. This interaction can expand to a discussion of what to take, where to go, what to get, who should come along, and so forth.

You can also play dumb.

• When your child says, "Juice!" pretend not to understand. "Milk?" you can ask. "No, juice!" he'll cry. "Water?" you can try again. "No water! Juice!" he'll respond. If he asks for water, "Want bath?" you can ask confusedly. "No bath! Drink water!" he may shriek. He'll be frustrated, but he'll have turned a simple, single circle into a multicircle conversation.

• When your child wants a certain toy, give her a different one but say, "Here it is, sweetheart," using a positive rather than a teasing tone. Or if she wants a drink, offer a play cup or cookie rather than a real one. She may play along or insist again on the real thing.

The Importance of Negotiating

Once your child is more verbal, it is time to begin a second kind of negotiation—not merely stalling, but questioning his intent. *Why* does he want to go outside so badly? What does he want to do outside? Why must he go outside *now*? This kind of negotiating is tremendously important. Not only does it increase the number of verbal circles your child can close, but it also helps him make the leap into abstract thinking.

When your child pounds on the door and demands to go outside, his reality is wholly concrete. It is focused on the door that stands between him and his desire. When you stall him, asking, "What do you want to do outside?" you help him picture what he wants in his mind. In that moment—when he visualizes the bike he wants to ride, for instance—he makes the leap into abstract, or symbolic, thinking.

By asking your child about his desire you also help him begin to think about what he is doing. This shift from *reacting* to a situation to *thinking* about it is critical to your child's development. It is what enables him to talk about his feelings rather than simply to act them out. Your general attitude in this process is as important as what you say. Simply looking at your child with a "What's the hurry?" expression as he bangs on the door encourages delay and thinking, rather than merely acting. This is the key to symbolizing, or representing, wishes or actions; it's the key to helping your child shift from doing to *thinking*.

You will benefit considerably from this shift as well, since this kind of interaction momentarily diverts attention from the power struggle over who will get her way. Your child may not be distracted for long, but even a short break is often enough to let you consider her demand, to suggest a compromise, or to think of other questions that will extend the negotiation.

Although important for all children, this kind of negotiation is especially important for children with special needs. Most children make the transition from pure reactivity to thinking at around two years of age. Children with special needs, especially those with multisystem and cognitive delays, have a particularly hard time with this change and are often assumed to be unable to make the leap. Without prodding by their parents, teachers, and therapists, they often continue to learn new intellectual skills but fail to develop the emotional capacity to think before they act. The result is children with the interests and vocabulary of four-year-olds, but who act out like 16-month-olds, unable to control their behavior.

For many children with special needs, learning to think before they act requires concentrated effort by caregivers. You may be reluctant to negotiate with your child at first, for fear of provoking arguments. And you will provoke them! But in the short term these arguments will promote your child's communication skills, and in the long term they'll help her become a more flexible, reflective person.

- When your child says, "No bed!" don't grab her and carry her upstairs. Negotiate. Ask, "Why no bed? Why not now?" Drag the negotiation out. Set the limits *after* your negotiations, when you understand how she feels and what she wishes. Then you can empathize. Suggest another time for what she wanted to do and be firm about bedtime.

- When your child demands to wear the Batman costume again for the fourth day in a row, say, "Why do you like Batman so much? Can't you wear the pirate costume? What's so great about Batman?" Don't be afraid to talk about his desire. It will help him with his longings (for power, for winning, for whatever) and make it easier to accept limitations once he is understood. Later, explain why he can't have his wish: "It's in the wash, sweetheart," or "You can wear it after school."

• When he refuses to eat his broccoli, ask, "Why no broccoli? What's so terrible about broccoli? What do you like better? It's not broccoli, it's a tree! Do you want a small tree or a big tree?"

Make these sessions last five minutes, seven minutes, even longer if you can. Don't be afraid to make your child angry. The more circles he closes the more he'll learn to think about his feelings and behavior.

Your child does not need to be verbal to engage in this kind of negotiation. You can question her every bit as well with gestures as you can with words. When she bangs on the door to tell you she wants to go outside, don't just open the door. Raise your arms and shoulders and look confused, as if to say, "Why?" Go to the window and point, as if to ask which objects out there she wants to play with. Try not to let her out until she has answered your question by pointing to the thing she wants. You can also have photos of things she does outside on the door. She can point or give you the photo of what she wants to do. The more you question her about her feelings and behavior, the more she will have to identify for herself what she wants to do, and the more of an abstract thinker she will become.

The Three Phases of Speech

As your child learns to speak you may see her move through three discrete phases. Phase one is the *random* use of words, the babbling or labeling of common items such as milk or juice, not to meet a need but for the sheer pleasure of making the sounds. The second phase is the *intentional* use of words—"juice now!"—to tell you what she wants. Although far ahead of the earlier phase (she now understands that words have meanings), this phase is still one-sided; she doesn't respond when you talk to her. The third phase is the ability to use words *intentionally in collaboration* with you, the ability to carry on a conversation.

These three stages overlap. Your child may still babble at times while he also uses words intentionally. He may say "juice" when he wants juice, but mutter "car" and "cheese" in a meaningless way or because of some association. Or he may engage in reciprocal conversation at some times and at others ignore you while muttering to himself. This behavior is a natural part of learning to talk. As long as his trend is toward increasing intentionality, your child is on the right track.

You can help the process along by linking all your child's words to his behavior. As soon as he starts babbling, give him the object he's naming. As he babbles "milk," give him a glass of milk or point to the milk in the fridge. As he babbles "Josh," take him to his brother or show him a picture if Josh is not there. The more you connect your child's growing speech with the objects it represents, the more meaningful his language will become.

Some children's vocabularies grow while their speech remains random and idiosyncratic. Your child may talk a lot, but make little sense and seem not to be communicating with you. If so, examine his behavior. Are his gestures intentional? Can he take you by the hand and lead you to the fridge? Can he point to the door to say he wants to go outside? If he's mastered the gestural building blocks of speech, be sure you're using words as you interact with him: "Can I have the ball?" as you hold out your hand for him to hand it to you; "Do you want the bread?" as you offer it to him. As you do more of this, he'll probably begin to connect his words with purposeful behavior. You may first hear word approximations, or subliminal speech, which become clearer as intentionality increases.

If your child's behavior is as aimless as her speech, help her master the basic give-and-take of interaction. Open and close lots of gestural circles (see Chapter 10). Use words as part of these interactions. Don't simplify, try to teach words, label objects, or have your child repeat phrases. Interact and talk. Don't give up working on words—you can still teach your child the names of objects tied to her actions—but don't expect intentional speech until she's mastered intentional gestures.

Correcting Your Child's Speech

Often as children learn to talk, they seem to latch on to certain mistakes. "He" is substituted for "she," or "I" for "you," or the child repeatedly misuses a word. Sometimes these mistakes persist for long periods of time until parents grow anxious that their child will never learn to speak correctly. It's natural to want to correct those errors, but try not to. Far more important than these details are your child's ideas. Chances are, your child will correct himself as his fluency and thought processes grow. If you feel you must tackle his mistakes, don't do it by correcting him. That approach leads to a controlling, nonspontaneous discussion in which you are telling your child what to do. A far better method is to lead your child into an open-ended discussion that furthers his ideas. When he refers to himself as "you," say, "Wait a minute. I'm confused. Do you mean you or me?" Persist playfully until he corrects himself. In this way you can help him see his error while still interacting spontaneously.

HELPING YOUR CHILD EXPRESS FEELINGS

As your child becomes more verbal and her pretend play more elaborate, she will use both skills to express her feelings. As a result, you will have a variety of ways to help her deal with feelings that are confusing or uncomfortable and to help her expand her range of emotions.

At first glance it may not look as though your child's play is about emotions. It may look as though she's playing house or store or school—and of course, on the surface, she is. But underneath, in the impulses that lead her to play one way rather than another, her play is an expression of her feelings. You can learn to see through the surface details of the play—which doll wears the blue dress and which the white—to the emotional content underneath.

Jason and his father, George, were playing with a toy car. "Look at my car!" Jason called to his dad. "I see it," George answered. "It goes fast. Zoom!" Jason said, racing the car down the carpet. "I can see that," nodded George. Then he added, "It looks exciting that it's going so fast." Jason gave a big smile. "Watch," Jason said, "I can make it go like a rocket ship," and he raised the car high in the air. "Wow. That's a powerful rocket," George admired. "Here it comes," Jason hollered, beaming with pride, and he flew the car high in the air above his father's head.

George could have talked about the color of Jason's car or about the fact that cars don't fly. He could have asked all kinds of questions. But instead, he recognized that Jason's drama was really about power. He helped Jason express that feeling by acknowledging it himself ("It looks exciting that it's going so fast") and by giving a name to it ("That's a powerful rocket"). Jason's pride when George expressed what he was feeling was proof that George had hit the nail on the head. He did not get distracted by asking lots of questions that were not relevant to the feeling.

You may wonder how you can possibly see through the surface details to get at the hidden drama underneath. It's actually not as hard as it sounds, because the number of emotional themes that underlie children's play is fairly small. Certain themes tend to come up over and over again. With a little practice, you can become adept at recognizing them in your child's dramas. These themes usually derive from real-life experiences or from ideas children have identified with in familiar videos or books. Here are a few of the more common themes.

Theme 1: Nurturance and dependency. Children are preoccupied with nurturance and dependency because they are so dependent on their parents, so it's not surprising to see these feelings surface in their play. What do these feelings look like? Just what you would expect: dolls hugging; taking care of babies; baby animals clinging to mommy animals or asking them for food. All of these are ways your child plays out his awareness that he depends on you.

Theme 2: Pleasure and excitement. You know when your child is excited: she laughs and jumps; she may flail her arms or kick her feet; she may even have trouble controlling her movements. Now start watching for those signs in play. Dolls jumping excitedly, dancing, or running wild may be signs of pleasure and excitement.

Theme 3: Curiosity. Most children are inherently curious, and children with special needs are no exception. As your child tunes in more and more to the outside world, you will find him playing games that involve looking for things, searching for hidden treasures, exploring new spaces. He'll use his imagination to create games that show he is curious about things and places beyond those he can touch and see.

Theme 4: Power and assertiveness. All children feel powerless in the world; children with special needs even more so. There are so many things they cannot do! To combat this sense of powerlessness, and to maximize what feelings of power they do have, children with special needs over time and with support may learn to play out themes of power and assertiveness. This play takes a number of forms. It can involve making a toy unusually powerful, as Jason did when he turned his car into a rocket. It can involve pretending to *be* something powerful, such as a giant who squooshes everything underfoot. It can involve playing out a drama in which one dinosaur is much more powerful than the others and pushes them around. Or it can involve construction cranes and diesel trucks, objects that are every bit as powerful as the child would like to be. As your child becomes more aware of the culture around her, she may become interested in the power figures of the day. She may want to dress up as a Power Ranger or as Superman or to play with toy figures of these characters. At first your child will enjoy the image and gestures of these figures but will not be able to express a story or tell you why they are so powerful (good) or always win. Later, motives will emerge in play; your child will begin to differentiate good guys and bad guys—"Capture the pirates; they're bad because they steal silver and gold." Eventually, your child will be able to tell you why one side is right or wrong, even though they both may be fighting the same way.

Theme 5: Anger and aggression. Most parents think they see this theme all too often! It is easy to recognize. Your child has soldiers battling or animals fighting or dolls killing each other or cars crashing. The variations are endless, but the underlying theme is the same. Your child is using play to express aggression. Remember, this is a safe, and the only acceptable, way to express this impulse.

Theme 6: Limit setting. Limit-setting play is about containing feelings— aggressive feelings, excited feelings, deep, yearning feelings. Strong feelings are scary, so children control their feelings by setting limits.

They put bad guys in jail. They make dolls go to bed early. They refuse to let a favorite doll have dessert because she was naughty. When you see your child clamping down on characters in his play, chances are he's practicing clamping down on some of his own wishes or feelings. He is also identifying with the limits you place on him, and placing limits on others makes him feel less helpless.

Theme 7: Fears and anxieties. Fear of separation ("My parents will leave me"); fear of injury ("I'll hurt my body and never recover"); fear of catastrophe ("A hurricane will hit our house and blow it down")—these are some of the common anxieties that children feel. Even children who have the verbal skills to do so are usually too afraid to express them openly, but these frightening feelings almost always surface in play. Mommy animals leave their babies. Big bears sit on houses and squash them. Dolls get in car wrecks and lose their limbs. The scenarios are not all that subtle, and once you start looking, you'll find it fairly easy to recognize them. You'll also encounter these themes when your child wants to read certain stories again and again, such as "The Three Little Pigs" or "The Billy Goats Gruff."

Theme 8: Love, empathy, and concern for others. As your child begins to feel comfortable relating to others, her capacity to feel love and empathy will grow. You'll see this reflected in her play. Dolls will start helping each other. Animals will feed each other. Dolls will fall in love and get married. Your child will also express these themes through role-playing, such as playing house. She may act like the parent and make you the child. Don't be surprised to find your child the bossy—yes, bossy—mom or dad!

Theme 9: Control. "I'm the boss!" Whether your child says it, whines it, cries it, or throws a tantrum because of it, you've experienced his demand to be in control. Precisely because he controls so few things in his life, this is a major issue. What your child can't control in real life he sometimes makes up for in play—being the sheriff who gives orders to the posse, having the little dog tell the big dog what to do, making sure that every item at the tea party is set exactly right. He may enjoy making you the child and barking orders!

Feelings Expressed in Play and Feelings Expressed Directly

What your child acts out in his play may not match the emotional theme he is acting out with you at that moment. For instance, he may be engrossed in a drama about a happy family in which the mommy, daddy, and baby bears all hug and kiss before sitting down to a great big meal. "That's easy," you think, "a drama about love and dependency." But the minute you make a move to help with the action, he may push you aside, asserting his need to do it all himself. Nothing very dependent about that! Don't be surprised. Children are complex and so are their emotions. They rarely feel one emotion at a time. Your child is aware of his dependence on you, and is glad you're there to support him. But he's also eager to grow up and become more dependent on himself. Both sets of feelings show up in his play: one in the content of the drama, the other in how he treats you. The content is about closeness and dependency; the way he deals with you has to do with who's the boss.

Here's another example. A child and his father are building a giant tower out of blocks. As the boy directs, the father carefully places block on top of block. Then, when the tower is as tall as it can be, the boy directs his father to place a soldier on top. There, from his lofty perch, the soldier looks down fearlessly on the world below. You probably think that this is a drama about power and control. And that's absolutely right; the boy is making himself feel bigger, and more powerful, by empathizing with the tower and the soldier. But suddenly, instead of exercising his power by telling his father what to do next, he grows timid. He loses interest in the blocks and crawls into his father's lap. What happened? A second, competing, emotional theme has surfaced. Like most children, the boy craves power. But power is also scary. Perhaps he feels that if he has too much power he may lose his daddy. To protect himself, he becomes dependent and crawls to his father for reassurance.

A similar emotional conflict could play out a different way. Instead of snuggling with Dad when he gets anxious, a child with more fragmented behavior might knock the block tower over, then throw the blocks around the room. Rather than get angry at the child because he's ruined the play, it's important to empathize with his underlying conflict. If he's verbal his father might say, "Oh, the man and the blocks got too high; you had to knock them down." If he's not yet verbal, the father might indicate something big with his hands, say, simply, "It was too big," and mimic knocking it down. The father can be like a big teddy bear who can help his son slow down if he's starting to get wild, holding him if necessary until he can calm down. By seeing through the surface action to the emotional drama underneath, it is possible to give the child the security and reassurance he is seeking.

What should you do when you see these feelings surface in your child's play? Acknowledge them. You don't need to answer them, fix them, or even discuss them. Just say—with words and gestures—what you see your child expressing and try to extend the dialogue. If the theme is power, offer to race your rocket ships and discuss which is more powerful. If the theme is dependency and your child wants a hug, ask, "How big a hug?" Join the theme. A verbal child will hear your words; a nonverbal child will read your gestures.

It's useful to talk to the figures with which your child is playing, putting their gestures into words. Use exaggerated tones of voice that will get through even when specific words do not. You can initiate interaction with words or gestures and then extend the drama.

• If dolls are hugging, smile warmly and empathetically at your child and mimic hugging to show her you see what she is saying. You might say, "Oh, Susie loves you so much!" and blow her a kiss.

• If dolls are fighting, mimic the hitting gesture and frown to show your child you get his emotional drift. You might say, "Uh-oh, David is angry! You'd better stop!" or, "Go away!" depending on the gestures his doll is making.

• If a monster knocks a house down, say, "Oh no! A big monster broke the house. It's scary. Go away, monster! Go away!" Or "I'll get you! You can't hurt my Sarah." Mimic knocking down the house and look alarmed so your child knows *you* know how she feels.

• If, like Jason, your child is flying a car like a rocket, pick up a second car and fly it fast. Say, "Wow! Look at it go! Zoom! Zoom!" to indicate its power. Even without words he will know you've caught his emotional tone.

Name the feelings your child expresses toward *you* as well.

• When your child insists on doing things her way, recognize her need for control by saying, "I see. You're the boss," and make a show of letting her direct the action.

• When he seems clingy and dependent, snuggle with him. Ask what type of hug he wants until he's ready to rejoin the play.

• When she pushes you away and doesn't let you join her play, let her know you understand by saying, "I see you want to do things for yourself." Move back physically a tiny bit so your body language tells her you're giving her more room.

Your job is not to change your child's feelings; it's to let her know that you see them, you're comfortable with them, and together you can communicate about them.

Helping a Nonverbal Child Explore Feelings through Pretend Play

Three-year-old Jeremy loved to race the toy train around its track, filling it with animals and people who often had angry territorial disputes. The scenario seemed a fitting outlet for his feelings. His parents' challenge was to help him use the scenario to understand and expand those feelings. For Mary, Jeremy's mother, meeting this challenge was sometimes difficult; instead of playing *with* her son, she tended to talk about what he was doing.

One day, Jeremy's people pushed the animals off the train. "Oh, mean people," Mary said. "They pushed those animals off the train."

Ignoring her, Jeremy brought in animal reinforcements who roared at the people. "Wow," said Mary. "They sure are making a lot of noise." Again Jeremy ignored her.

Mary needed to get into the drama herself. She thought for a minute, then picked up a giraffe and marched it over to the conductor. "Bad person!" she scolded in an angry voice. "You won't let me on the train. I must get to the zoo."

Jeremy stopped the train and watched.

"You can't ever drive our train again!" she continued. Then she picked up the conductor and speaking for him, said plaintively to the giraffe, "I'm sorry I pushed you off the train. Please can I drive again?" She moved the man closer to the giraffe as if asking forgiveness. She was doing a good job of modulating her voice and using exaggerated gestures to express her intentions, rather than relying on words that she knew Jeremy wouldn't understand.

Jeremy watched this drama quite intently. Wanting to keep him involved, Mary decided to address the question to him. So she marched her man over to Jeremy and said with the same plaintive tone, "Please can I drive the train?"

Jeremy stared at the man for a moment. "No!" he said with the assurance of a little dictator.

Mary started to cry. "Boo hoo," she said. "I want to drive the train. I promise I'll be nice."

But Jeremy was decisive. "No," he said again, and pushed the man away.

As they continued to play, Jeremy seemed to relish the reverse roles he and his mother had adopted—she asking him for a favor, he adamantly refusing. By joining in his play, Mary was helping him express ideas, and the intentions behind them, in a warm, nonthreatening way.

DEEPENING AND BROADENING THE EXPRESSION OF FEELINGS

As you watch your child play you may notice that she feels more comfortable with some feelings than with others. You may sense that certain feelings scare her, that she expresses them only timidly. If so, she needs your help in experimenting with those feelings. By gently introducing them into your play you can increase her level of comfort with a wide range of feelings.

Even before your child has a lot of language you can deepen and broaden the feelings in pretend play by the way you join in the drama. For example, if your child's dolls only hug, you can have your doll ask for a bigger hug, for a kiss, or for milk. These requests amplify the drama, but stick to the theme of nurturance your child has established.

To deepen the drama you can also give the plot more of a story line, perhaps even using single words. For instance, a doll saying "No!" or "More!" can create conflict and deepen a drama about control or assertiveness. You can introduce new themes or emotions by bringing in real-life experiences. Suppose after you and your child hug, he plays out anger by having dolls fight. When one is knocked down, see if the doll is hurt and offer a Band-Aid. Or, when the fight is over, your "soldier" can say, "Now I want to eat, be strong." In this way you are adhering to your child's theme of aggression while bringing in nurturing themes as a twist.

The challenge of deepening and broadening the drama is still more important as your child becomes more verbal. Even as her language is taking off and she is talking and imagining all the time, her overreactivity to sensation and her motor-planning difficulties may constrain the range and depth of her dramas.

Jill was acting out a drama while her mother watched. As the drama unfolded, a bear and a monkey were eating happily at a table when suddenly the bear swiped a cookie from the monkey's plate. The monkey got angry and threw the bear's plate to the floor. For a second, Jill looked delighted with her show of force; then suddenly she grew timid. She stared at the plate on the floor as if someone else had put it there and quickly arranged a make-up scene between the animals. Clearly her own display of anger had frightened her.

Jill's mother picked up the monkey and, making an angry face, said, "I want my cookie!" Then she made as if to grab the cookie back.

Jill watched but didn't say anything.

Seeing that Jill was not upset by her intervention, her mother continued. She reached over to the cookie on the floor and gave it to the monkey. "Yum! I want this cookie!" said the monkey defiantly. "I'm angry you took it away."

Jill continued to watch in silence.

Jill's mother chomped noisily to imitate the monkey eating the cookie, then she said, "Give me more cookies!"

Jill didn't move.

"I want more cookies!"

Still Jill didn't move.

Now her mother made the monkey get really angry. She made the monkey jump up and down and say angrily, "More cookies, more cookies!" When Jill still didn't move she made the monkey push all the plates off the table. They landed on the floor with a clatter.

Jill laughed.

Mother and the monkey pouted. "I'm mad. I want more cookies!"

"No!" said Jill defiantly, smiling. She was enjoying the monkey's anger as well as her own power.

The monkey knocked his chair over.

For a second Jill looked frightened, then she laughed again. "No more!" she said.

The monkey knocked over another chair.

"Stop!" Jill shouted, gleeful. It seemed that the angrier the monkey got, the giddier Jill became.

Seeing that Jill had comfortably rejoined the drama, her mother knew she could move on. "I'm sad you won't give me more cookies," she said mournfully, with an exaggerated pout. "Please?"

Jill thought for a moment, then said, "Okay," and handed the monkey a cookie.

"Goodie!" said the monkey, jumping up and down. Jill's mother's face wore a big smile. "Do you want half my cookie?"

Jill nodded. Then she fed the cookie to the bear.

Over the next several weeks Jill's mother made a point of looking for openings to deal with anger during Jill's play. Sometimes Jill gave her a cue, as she had with the monkey and bear. Sometimes Jill's mother made her own character get angry in response to something frustrating or in response to a limit Jill had imposed. At first Jill's mother did most of the expressing of anger, but gradually Jill experimented with anger, too. As the weeks went by she was able to stick with the anger theme for longer and longer periods of time. Dolls would fight, hit each other, and then make up. Animals would bite each other or steal each other's food, make up, and then get angry again. By the second month of practice, Jill was able to move comfortably in and out of angry confrontations as if she'd been doing it all her life.

Todd was uncomfortable with anger and tiptoed gingerly around it. One day in a therapy session he put a whale puppet on his finger and began biting his father's finger with it. After a few seconds, however, he threw the puppet down and began jumping around the room. His father was confused.

"Stay with him," the therapist suggested. "He got anxious about displaying anger, so he's temporarily lost his engagement with you. Try to bring him back the way you did when you were working on engagement."

Todd's dad thought for a moment, then got up and began jumping with his son. As he did he talked in a soothing voice, saying, "Hi, Todd. Daddy jumping too. Daddy jumping with Todd."

After a few minutes Todd was making eye contact with his father and giggling a bit.

"Now try to bring him back to the puppet play," the therapist suggested.

Todd's dad put the whale puppet on one hand and a bear puppet on the other. "Look, Todd," he called, "whale and bear are jumping too."

Todd watched his dad but didn't reach for the puppets or say anything.

"Bear is going to bite your finger," said the father gently, waving the bear puppet toward his son's hand.

Todd withdrew his hand but laughed.

"Bear going to bite your finger," repeated the father playfully, reaching again toward Todd's hand.

This time Todd didn't move his hand, but let the puppet bite it.

"Yum yum yum," said Todd's father, speaking for the bear. "But I'm still hungry. I'm going to eat this whale." And Todd's father turned the bear puppet toward the whale on his other hand.

"Can you draw Todd into the drama?" the therapist asked.

Todd's dad thought for a moment, then put the whale puppet on the floor. "Uh-oh," he said, "Bear is going to eat this whale," and he moved the bear puppet slowly toward the whale. "Help! Todd! Whale needs help! Can you help whale!"

Todd sized up the situation, then just as the bear puppet was about to reach the whale, Todd reached forward, grabbed the whale, and put it back on his hand. Giggling, he moved it out of the bear's reach.

"Oh! You took my dinner!" said the bear.

Todd chortled.

"I want my dinner!"

"Whale go!" Todd shouted, and moved the whale behind his back.

Todd's father put on a scowling face. "I'm mad you took my dinner away," he said, his voice gentle but firm.

Todd laughed. "Whale go away!" he said assertively.

"No!" said his father sternly. "I want my dinner! I want it now!"

"No!" shouted Todd, grinning. He was enjoying his own assertiveness and his ability to turn the tables on his dad by denying him something he wanted.

The play continued for several more minutes as Todd's father repeatedly demanded the bear's dinner and Todd continued to refuse. By the time play ended, Todd had been successfully brought back into it and had begun to experiment a bit more with anger. Giving the biting a purpose—to eat because he was hungry—helped Todd become more comfortable. There was now a cause and effect to which he could relate.

"But when we help Todd explore anger," asked his mother, "aren't we making him too aggressive?"

"No," Todd's therapist answered. "Aggression is a natural human impulse. Todd will feel it whether you want him to or not. Your goal is to help him elevate it to the level of ideas and express it through words and pretend play instead of just acting-out behavior."

Todd's mother nodded, but she was still uncertain.

"Todd has to be able to use ideas and feel comfortable with all the emotions," the therapist went on. "You saw what happened today. He experienced a little bit of anger and immediately went from high-level, organized play to aimless jumping."

Todd's mother nodded again.

"You're not introducing anger as a theme. You're just seeing it as part of his repertoire and helping him express it at a higher level."

Over the next few weeks Todd's parents looked for signs of anger or aggression in their son's play. They began to notice when he angrily threw naughty animals or action figures to the other side of the room and when he had one figure hit another. Instead of letting those incidents pass, they tried to draw them into the play. Sometimes they picked up a discarded figure and said, "Don't throw me away!" giving Todd a chance to continue the drama. Sometimes they spoke for a figure who had been hit, saying, "You can't hit me. I'll hit you back!" Each time, they kept their voices firm, but not loud or scary, and accompanied their words with angry facial gestures.

At first Todd ran from these encounters, becoming aimless as he had in his therapist's office. Then he began to hit one doll with another. His parents were encouraged to thicken the plot, to go from simple hitting and fighting, even if pretend, to a drama with greater depth, dialogue, and a story with reasons and consequences. As they worked on this over several months, Todd became better able to play out angry scenes. Eventually he was able to stay in the drama, modulating his activity and remaining engaged with his parents as he did so. He learned he could make happen whatever he wanted to happen and that he could remain safe.

EXPANDING THE RANGE OF THEMES AND EMOTIONS

In addition to expanding the depth of your child's feelings, you need to help him broaden the range of his feelings. Many children are comfortable with only a narrow band of feelings. They may play out only themes of compliant niceness, or only themes of anger and aggression, or only themes of dependence. Your challenge is to help your child become comfortable with the full spectrum of feelings by slowly and gently helping him introduce all the emotions into his pretend play.

Chris's favorite activity was to build elaborate villages out of Lego blocks and then attack the villages with dinosaurs. He laughed gleefully as they attacked. As his parents and therapist watched him play this scene over and over again, they applauded his expressions of power and assertiveness. But the one thing they didn't see was any sign of nurturance. No villagers helped the others. No mommies comforted frightened children. This lack of closeness was apparent in Chris's life, too. He hugged his parents only when they pressed him to and rarely sought them out for comfort. He seemed more interested in them as mechanical play partners than as warm, loving human beings. His parents wanted to introduce closeness and dependency into Chris's play.

So, they looked for openings in his village-disaster scenes. Just as the dinosaur was about to stomp a house, Chris's mother grabbed one of the people inside and called, "Help me, Mommy!" Then she pulled out a second person. "I'll help you," she said, and clasping the two figures together, she had them hop out of the house.

Chris watched for a moment, then turned his dinosaur toward another house.

His mother tried again. She reached into that house, grabbed two more dolls, and said in a high-pitched baby voice, "Mommy, Mommy, the dinosaur is coming! Help me!" The mother doll replied soothingly, "Don't worry, Baby. I'll take care of you." Then Chris's mother cuddled the two dolls together and helped them out of the house. As soon as they were out, Chris stomped the dinosaur through the roof.

Next Chris moved his dinosaur to another house. This time, his mother tried a different tack. Reaching into the house she pulled out two dolls and said defiantly to the dinosaur, "You can't hurt my baby because I'm the mommy and I won't let you!" For the first time Chris paid attention. He stopped the dinosaur in midstride and stared at the two dolls. His mom continued, this time speaking as the baby. "You're big and strong but you can't hurt me because my mommy will protect me." Chris pondered this for a moment. He was clearly perplexed. His dinosaur had never met with resistance before, and he wasn't sure what to do.

Suddenly Chris's mom got an idea. Speaking for the baby she said to the dinosaur, "Do you have a mommy?"

Chris said nothing for a moment, then raised the dinosaur and continued the attack.

While playing out these pretend themes his mother looked for opportunities outside the play to be extra nurturing—prolonging a hug, soothing Chris during a tantrum, giving him extra cuddles at night. Then, at another play time, she found another way to introduce dependency into Chris's drama. She picked up a second, smaller dinosaur, and just when the destructive action was at its height, she turned to Chris's dinosaur and said plaintively, "I'm scared. Can you help me?"

Again Chris was taken aback by this sudden turn of events. He had always controlled the dinosaurs, and they were always objects of power, not of need. His mother repeated her request. "I'm scared," she said again. "Can you help me?"

"No!" said Chris forcefully, and rammed his dinosaur into the house.

Chris's parents began to worry whether they would ever balance the various emotions in their son's pretend play. The therapist told them they needed to be patient. Chris would learn about nurture and empathy not only from his parents' real-life warmth, but also from their empathy with his aggressive pretend play. They should continue to empathize with the power of the attacker as well as with the fears of the victims and let Chris shift gradually to new themes on his own.

After two months, Chris's dinosaur play showed some remarkable changes. He gradually alternated his attention between the dinosaur action outside the houses and the human dramas inside. Occasionally Chris protected a doll or fixed a "broken" animal after an attack. In real life, he began cautiously to approach his parents and ask to sit on their laps. Closeness was beginning to have a place in his life.

Caitlin had a hard time expressing nurturing feelings. At three she had very limited language and was just beginning pretend play. One day in a therapy session she picked up a doll and pretended to feed it, but then suddenly began banging the doll on the floor.

"No, Caitlin," said her mother sternly. "Don't bang the dollie." Frustrated, she turned to the therapist. "She always does that," she sighed. "It makes me not want to play with her."

The therapist reminded Caitlin's mother that a child learns through her relationship with her parents. "So if you get mad at her, or pull away, that won't help her learn to be warm and empathetic. But if you can stay with her and empathize with her banging, she'll gradually learn to be empathetic too. If you can say, 'Wow! Your dollie is a good banger. What a good banger. What else can she do?' in a warm and playful voice, you'll be accepting her play and her feelings. Each time she bangs she'll feel your warmth and empathy, not your criticism, and over time, she'll become comfortable with those feelings.

"After a while you can introduce a new theme. You can say, 'Oh, dolly hurt.' But don't tell her to be a doctor. In time she'll experiment with other emotional themes, especially as she gets more verbal and as her play sequences develop further. The key thing is to bring in the nurturing theme just by being nurturing yourself."

For children like Chris and Caitlin who are quite repetitive in their play, floor time can be used gently to introduce new elements. Don't try to make a major change all at once. Introduce a twist on the existing drama. If your child only likes to fly planes, try being a passenger in the cockpit. If she only has monsters fighting, try being a doctor who can heal the monsters that get hurt. If he only pretends to be a doggie in your lap, try being a second doggie who wants to play a game.

MOVING FROM ACTING OUT FEELINGS TO EXPRESSING THEM IN WORDS

Your child's transition from acting out her feelings to putting them into words is dramatic. Although she enters this stage crying every time she is frustrated and pummeling you when she is angry, she leaves this stage able to stop herself before she takes those actions and instead tell you how she feels. This transition is significant for your child and for you—it is a major leap into the world of ideas.

Until your child can express her feelings in words, she doesn't really picture her feelings as you do. This idea is difficult for adults to grasp since we are so familiar with feelings, but until your child has negotiated this stage she lives in an action- and body-oriented state. She experiences her feelings as impulses in her body—a sudden urge to strike out, for example, or a tightening in her chest that causes her to fall on the floor in tears. The sensation is concrete, as is the rest of her experience. Until she grows into the world of ideas, she doesn't have the capacity to understand the very abstract idea of feelings.

Through pretend play and labeling her experience with words, your child gets ready to understand her body's sensations in a more abstract way. When she shows feelings you can help her make that transition by asking how she feels, introducing a dialogue about feelings into the pretend play, or asking multiple-choice–type questions ("Are you happy or sad?") to help her label what she feels. She may ignore your questions and comments, especially if she is in a rage, but be persistent; your question is not merely a question, but a moment's pause between your child and her bodily sensation. During that pause she is forced to step back from the physical sensation and reflect. She will come to understand that the sensation is a feeling that can be recognized and tolerated and does not require immediate action.

Imagine a person who is habitually involved in barroom brawls. A fellow patron eyes him derisively, and before he thinks about what he is doing, the brawler raises his fist and slugs the other customer. Questioned later about his feelings, the brawler might say, "Nah, I wasn't angry. He looked at me, so I hit him." Like a presymbolic child, he felt the urge to act without recognizing his feeling. He describes his behavior, not his feeling state. But suppose that just as he raised his fist you grabbed it and said, "Wait a minute. What are you feeling?" With his impulse waylaid, he has a moment to look inside himself, and in that moment he can say, "My arms want to swing, my muscles are tense, I feel ready to explode." Eventually, as he describes his state first in terms of physical sensations, he will get to the point of being able to describe a feeling: "I'm mad!" He then has an opportunity to decide what to do about his feeling.

So it is with your child. The moment you stop her and say, "What are you feeling?" you give her the distance to step back from the impulse to hit or kick or cry and translate that physical impulse into an idea. As difficult as this will be for her at first, if you are patient and persistent she will gradually come to expect your questions and will slowly begin to answer. Multiple-choice questions can help get this process going. Introducing feelings into pretend play will also help.

As an actor in your child's drama you can verbalize your character's feelings and also ask about your child's feelings. If your doll frequently says, "I'm happy" or "I'm mad," following some event, eventually you may hear your child's doll verbalize a feeling, too. If your doll frequently asks your child's doll, "Are you happy or sad?" when she does or does not get more cookies, little by little your child may be able to verbalize an answer. Be patient. Move from concrete reasons for the feelings to more abstract ones, such as being sad because you miss your mommy or happy because your daddy will be home soon. It often takes years for a child to become fluent at recognizing her feelings and expressing them in words.

Here are some other things to try.

• When your child's doll grabs your doll's cake, rant and rave and say, "No! No! No! Angry, angry, angry!" Make it clear you're comfortable with anger so your child can be, too.

• When your child's dolls exclude your dolls from the action, let him know you're sad. Don't be afraid to ham it up; sob and shed some tears and say over and over how sad you are. Make it clear that you're comfortable with sadness, so he can be, too.

Sometimes you can verbalize his character's feelings. "He sure looks mad," you can say when your race-car driver cuts off your child's driver during a race. Or "I guess he's pretty scared," when a big flood destroys his character's house. Whispering your question or comment about your child's character will quickly get his attention. Then get back into your role.

MONITORING YOUR OWN FEELINGS

Dealing so directly with your child's feelings may not be easy. Being around strong emotion is often uncomfortable, especially when the emotion is directed at you. When your child says, "I hate you!" or "Go away!" the temptation is not to empathize, but to lash out, withdraw, or change the subject. However, your child is using play to experiment with his feelings, and he needs you to provide a safe haven. Here are a few suggestions.

• *Recognize your own feelings.* It's easy to know when your child makes you hurt or angry. At those times you have to control your reflex to strike back, withdraw, or be bossy, and instead remain supportive. It is not so easy to recognize subtler responses to your child. He may be experimenting with sexual feelings, for example, or playing out themes of aggression, and these may make you uncomfortable, rather than hurt or angry. In that case you may have a more subtle reaction, perhaps a desire to end the play, to change the subject, or to steer your child toward something else. Even boredom or lack of interest can be a sign that you're anxious about his ideas. Every adult has an Achilles' heel, which may show up in unexpected ways. So when you find yourself feeling bored or antsy, irritable or uncomfortable, ask yourself if there's something in your child's play that makes you feel that way. As much as possible, you need to put your own discomfort aside to give him room to express himself.

• *Don't try to "fix" your child's feelings.* When your child's feelings make you uncomfortable, you may tend to try to fix them by giving in to your child's demands, cajoling him into a different mood, or trying somehow to change his feelings into feelings that are more acceptable to you. Doing this suggests to your child that his feelings are wrong. You need to honor his feelings of the moment, no matter what they are, by listening to him and supporting him in whatever way he will allow—with hugs, firm pressure, or a soothing voice from across the room.

• *Don't merely tolerate feelings; encourage them.* Don't simply let your child rant or cry; help her elaborate on her feelings by offering an accepting look, a pretend dialogue, or, if she is very verbal, a question.

• *Separate feelings from behavior.* Your child's behavior may be abysmal, but the feelings behind it should be accepted and supported. That doesn't mean you have to tolerate misbehavior (we'll discuss in Chapter 14 how to help your child change his behavior). But it does mean that when your child misbehaves, you need to help him talk about the feelings that provoked him. You can empathize with those feelings even as you teach him that there are better ways to deal with them.

• *Remember the risk of communicating strong (and scary) feelings directly with words.* There are reasons for your child's feelings. Your job is to hear her out. Ask her to tell you all the reasons she hates you, all the ways you've been unfair, all the reasons she wishes someone else were her mom. If you can support her even then, you'll have built a tremendous bond of trust and closeness.

• *Remember that feelings are transitory.* Feelings don't last very long, especially when they are given free expression. So when your child rants and raves with anger, cries in sadness or frustration, or clings and whines at the prospect of separation, listen to him. Empathize with him. But don't take those feelings too seriously, because later today he'll be in a different mood. The negative passion of the moment will have passed, replaced by other feelings from his palette of emotions. The more comfortable you can be (or at least act) with every emotional outpouring, the broader and healthier that palette will be.

• *Stick with the pretend play.* If your child touches on a sensitive spot during pretend play, remember that it's only play. Stay with the game and respond as your character would—supportively. If you treat her character's aggression or fears as real, you remove the safety of the play and send the message that expressing feelings in play is as dangerous as acting them out in reality.

Here's how this looks in practice.

Two-and-a-half-year-old Darryl and his mother were talking on a toy phone when Darryl suddenly got mad and yelled and screeched at his mom. Feeling rejected, she blurted, "I don't want to talk to you either!" and threw down her end of the phone. Darryl looked at his mother in confusion and then began to cry.

This upsetting encounter could have been avoided had Darryl's mom realized that anger was just one of Darryl's feelings—soon he would love and trust her again—and that he was using the game to practice expressing it. Instead of ending the game and rejecting him, she, too, could have used the game to explore his angry feelings.

DARRYL: *screeches.*

MOM: (*makes sad face, points to phone, and shakes her head*) Are you yelling?

DARRYL: *looks angry.*

MOM: (*makes exaggerated pout*) You look very angry. Are you angry at me?

DARRYL: *reaches out to slap her.*

MOM: (*in a quiet, firm, but not punishing voice*) No hitting! It hurts when you hit me. I can see you're very angry. (*Looks intently but supportively at him. She is not intimidated by his action.*)

DARRYL: *looks at her but doesn't move.*

MOM: (*looks concerned and sympathetic. Uses soothing tone*) I must have done something to make you so angry.

DARRYL: *seeing he is understood, nods and goes back to talking to her in a babble.*

Played out this way, Darryl has learned that feeling and expressing anger in pretend is okay. His mother, rather than punish Darryl for his feelings, has accepted and supported him. With her glance and posture she has also set useful limits.

APPROACHES TO AVOID IN PRETEND PLAY

As you coach your child away from mechanical, reactive behavior and toward spontaneous, creative use of ideas, there are a few things to keep in mind.

• *Don't overdirect; follow your child's lead.* As much as you want to thicken the plot by adding new elements, you need to be careful to add elements that are closely related to your child's theme. Your twists should open a new direction in the existing plot; they shouldn't introduce a new plot.

• If your child is cooking dinner for the two of you and starts to lose interest or cooks the same meal over and over, don't suddenly say, "Let's go feed the gerbil!" Feeding the gerbil, although it involves food, is not related to the drama your child had going. Instead try "Want some new food!" and pout.

• If your child is building a castle with blocks and tunes you out, don't start attacking her castle with an army. You might create an interaction, but you won't be following your child's lead; you won't be joining her in her current area of interest. Instead, become a fellow architect and try adding new elements to the castle. "What if we put this piece here?" you might say as you add the beginnings of a bridge. Maybe she'll see it's a bridge and then the two of you can build the bridge together. If not, try again. "Look, this can be a bridge!" you might say as you add another piece. "The castle can have a bridge to another castle!" If after several attempts your child seems uninterested in the bridge, try another idea, perhaps a moat or a prison within the castle's walls. Any of these ideas will enable you to stay within the existing theme. You'll still be following your child's lead.

• *Don't slip into parallel play or running commentary; become a character in the drama.* Sometimes, because you are not used to doing pretend play, you slip out of it all too easily. You start with the best of intentions, talking for a doll, but before you know it, you've slipped to the sidelines, watching your child play and commenting on his actions. Your child needs your interaction, he needs to bump up against your responses and to create counter-responses of his own. This will happen only if you are a character inside the drama.

- If your child is feeding a doll, don't merely comment on what the doll is eating. Become the doll. Speak for her. Say, "More peas! More peas!" or "No more peas! No more peas!" or "Not hungry! Want to sleep now!" By speaking for the doll you help your child interact with you.

- If your child is feeding a doll, don't simply feed the doll too. Often parents take turns with their children: first the child feeds the doll, then the parent feeds the doll. This has the illusion of interaction because they are feeding the doll together, but the child isn't interacting with the parent. You should talk for the doll so that your child's gestures and words are a response to yours.

• *Don't feel embarrassed or stymied.* Some parents have a hard time with pretend play because they feel silly or unimaginative. Understanding the importance of pretend play will help you see that it's not silly. As for imagination—leave that to your child. All you need to do is play along and look for occasional openings when you can suggest something new. If you feel you're no good at it, practice! Not being good at pretend play is not an excuse to avoid it or to let someone else do it. Your child needs this help from you to expand her skills, to experiment with her feelings, and to express her view of the world. It's also, as you'll see later in this chapter, the best way for you to learn who she is inside.

• *Avoid repetition.* Children with developmental problems often like nothing better than to do the same thing over and over. A limited amount of repetition is fine, but if there is too much repetition throw a curve ball to take the familiar routine in a new direction. If your child likes to play out stories from books or videotapes, do the same thing; stick to the characters but deviate from the familiar story line to inspire your child to play in new ways.

• *Don't talk mechanically or too slowly.* It's tempting to talk slowly to children with severe disorders because slow speech seems easier to understand. But it is actually harder to understand speech that is slow and mechanical than it is to comprehend words spoken with a normal rhythm and inflection. Talking mechanically encourages your child to talk that way too. Your real goal is to help your child listen and speak spontaneously and with feeling; the way to do that is to speak that way to him. You can talk in simple terms and in short sentences without talking slowly or mechanically.

• *Don't encourage rote learning.* Some children with developmental problems develop a tremendous capacity for memorization shortly after they begin to talk. They can rattle off alphabets, numbers, subway stops, car names, and reams of other listlike information. Parents often encourage these displays of knowledge. But because the learning is rote—sheer memorization—it reinforces the child's tendency toward mechanical repetition. If encouraged, list making can overwhelm the child's fragile new ability to engage in spontaneous speech and interaction. So resist the temptation to support your child's list making. If your child is holding numbers or letters and saying their names repetitively, ask her to give you one. Have a puppet say, "I like M. Which letter do you like?" Try to turn the recitation into a two-way conversation.

Similarly, avoid quizzing your child on academic skills, even though she may take pleasure in it. You may be proud of her ability to count or read. But don't dwell on these skills. Acknowledge her accomplishment and then move her into a more interactive conversation. The goal is to encourage spontaneous dialogue, not mechanical recitation.

TAILORING FLOOR TIME TO YOUR CHILD'S INDIVIDUAL DIFFERENCES

As with the two milestones discussed earlier, it is important to take into account your child's sensory reactivity, his way of processing sensation, and his motor patterns as you help him express emotions and ideas.

If Your Child Has Auditory-Processing Difficulties

A child with auditory-processing difficulties needs words that are clear and a lot of visual support. Pretend-play characters should be extremely animated. Instead of sitting and talking, they have to act out their intentions. Have your doll say, "Hug! Hug!" then reach out toward your child's doll with her arms. Or ask, "Are you hungry?" and put her doll's hand to her mouth. A response in gestures will speak louder than her words. Lengthy monologues will be lost on your child.

Your child may repeat or echo what you say. This is her way of showing that she registers what you say even though she does not elaborate on it. Try not to echo her in return, but rather make your next comment.

Sometimes your child will make a spontaneous comment about her toy ("Train fast!") but will be unable to answer your question about it ("Where is the train going so fast?"). She may be at a stage in which she is better at expressing certain words or scripts than she is at understanding open-ended comments or questions. Responding to such questions may be especially difficult without the aid of visual cues. Go back to what she was doing so that your language is again linked to her actions. Zoom your train fast and say, "My train is faster. You can't catch me! You can't catch me!"

Children with auditory-processing difficulties often memorize fragments of videos or books that they use with and without communicative intent. Typically, they see a toy or figure that reminds them of the video or book and they associate it with some part of the script. If you recognize the script, try to join in and talk about it, because your child is likely to understand it. Knowing the figures from the stories she enjoys will help you elaborate on the script—define who will be which figure and use the figures to make changes in the story.

If Your Child Has Visual-Spatial Processing Difficulties

If your child has trouble with visual-spatial processing, he may go from one play theme to the next in a fragmented manner as objects literally disappear from sight and mind. Your job is to help him integrate his visual and thematic spheres by reintroducing the forgotten objects into the play.

 • If your child is playing with a stuffed lion and suddenly switches his focus to a pig, bring the lion back over to the pig and say, "Hi! Can I play too?" You'll remind your child about the lion and about the things he saw and thought about moments earlier. If he does not respond, ask if he's all done with the lion or if he wants the lion to go home. Saying "bye-bye" may prompt a response.

If your child has visual-spatial processing difficulties he may not discriminate well among the objects before him. If his shelves or baskets are cluttered, he may not explore or seek out objects. It can help to set things out on platforms (boxes) or colored sheets of paper. Each box or paper can be a symbolic set—the house, the zoo, the train station, the supermarket—with the relevant toys on it. By making the sets and the toys more visually obvious to your child, you will make it easier for him to initiate ideas with them and even to link one idea to another.

The more your child is helped to integrate different aspects of his visual field, the stronger his visual processing will become. Masking tape can create tracks and roads on the floor over which trains and cars can go places and come back again. Tracking games—shining flashlights, rolling balls, tapping suspended toys—can help your child look out and find his way. Any activity that requires using vision in combination with motor activities—coordinating animals at a tea party, kicking a ball, having a sword fight, identifying hidden objects in a bag by touch, even playing pin the tail on the donkey (a game in which a visual image must be retained while blindfolded)—will train your child's visual-processing system. The more training it gets, the better it will operate.

If Your Child Has Motor-Planning Difficulties

If your child has motor-planning problems, she will have trouble sequencing ideas as well as movements. You can help her practice this skill in pretend play. First, give her choices about what to do next. "Are you going to the zoo or to the garage?" When she decides, build physical challenges into her play by creating problems she needs to solve through a sequence of actions.

• If her car crashes, cry out, "Oh no! It's broken! What should we do?" Get a tow truck or a tool kit and ask her to fix it. Pick up the hammer and hand it to her. Get the screwdriver and start to use it. Check the repairs, return the tools, and go on.

• If his doll falls, ask if the doll is hurt and whether he needs to go to the doctor. Hand your child a doctor's kit so he can go through the steps of examining and treating the baby. Have masking tape ready to use for Band-Aids and casts. Once the doll is better, the original play can continue.

• If she starts to play a musical instrument or sing a song, get an echo microphone and introduce her with "Boys and girls, introducing the Great Sarah! Her first song will be . . ." Expand on the performance, clap, take bows, put on props or costumes. Your child will enjoy this sequence because of performances she has watched.

• If your child is racing a rocket to the moon, become the moon by holding your hands in a circle, then gradually move farther and farther away.

• If her animal is exploring the jungle, use your body, books, chairs, or other objects to create obstacles in the jungle that she and her animals have to negotiate.

• If his toy figures are shopping at the store, write down all the things he wants to buy, then put the milk, cereal, and bread in different aisles and difficult-to-reach places, requiring him to search and stretch a bit in order to reach them.

Once your child expresses symbolic ideas, you can build more elaborate motor sequences right into the play as the ideas get more complex. She will remember these sequences as ideas and use them again and again, giving you more opportunities to expand on them.

Respecting Your Child's Sensory Preferences

As always, when you interact with your child take her sensory preferences into account. Try not to overwhelm her by subjecting her to visual, auditory, tactile, kinesthetic, or olfactory experiences that will be overloading, and try to provide lots of sensory experiences that you know she likes. When she gets frustrated or anxious during play, use her preferences to help her calm down.

You can also use play to help expand your child's sensory tolerances.

• If your child dislikes sticky textures, don't have a lot of sticky stuff around. But you might have one sticky thing—say, double-stick tape or a little ball of Silly Putty—that your child can voluntarily explore when she is ready. If she sees you use it several times perhaps she will be curious to try it. If so, let her explore it slowly, at her own pace. You can work the Silly Putty into your play by using it to stick a mustache on the daddy figure. After a while, perhaps your child will want to make a mustache too.

• If your child is sensitive to loud noises, let her control the volume on your voice while you play. Ask, "Should I talk louder or softer?" and then follow her instructions in a Simon says kind of game. If you very gradually (over several weeks) increase the volume, you can help her build her tolerance for louder sounds.

If Your Child Is Underreactive and Withdrawn

If your child is underreactive and withdrawn, you need to really ham it up to draw him into play. Use all the theatricality you can muster to energize the interaction.

• If he is putting a doll into the dollhouse, crouch down on all fours, breathe down his neck, and say in a robust and playful voice, "I'm the big bad wolf! I'm going to blow your house down!" If he ignores you, say it again, louder. If he still ignores you, tap him on the shoulder. Bare your teeth. Growl in his ear. Huff and puff noisily. Use your voice and body gestures to make him notice you. You can also use puppets. Then you can whisper support to your child by asking, "What are you going to tell the wolf?"

If Your Child Is Underreactive, Craving Sensation, and Distractible

If your child is underreactive and fragmented, she craves sensory input and is constantly on the move trying to find it. Your pretend play may be best accomplished in a large space where she can do a lot of vigorous motor activity as part of the floor-time drama. Before floor-time sessions, bounce on a therapy ball, work on a trampoline, or swing, run, climb, and jump in order to meet her needs most efficiently. This activity will help your child become more organized and centered, and she will not have to spend as much energy being physical during the play. Then move into floor time.

You can graft pretend play onto your child's existing gross-motor activities.

- If she's sliding down a slide, put a stuffed bunny on the slide and say, "Bunny wants to slide too." If she seems uninterested, have the bunny bump into her or get in her way. If she protests, say sadly, "Bunny is sad. She wants to play with you."

- If you're playing chase, bring an animal into the chase. "Lion's going to get you! Lion's going to get you!"

- If your child is rolling in the grass or in the snow, roll with her and say, "I'm a whale rolling in the ocean!" or "Let's be cars and bump into each other!" Add an element of pretend to the activity she's already doing.

- Play hide-and-seek with dolls, so that when your doll hides, her doll has to find it.

When your child uses more complex ideas, you can expand the pretend play.

- Put on a circus show or gymnastics Olympics. Have all the people figures take their seats or be judges at the events.

- Be a horse and give her rides, but ask her to direct you which way to go. Have her direct you around obstacles, over mountains, through rivers, and into other pretend environments. Develop a mission, such as getting back the money the robbers stole and bringing them back to jail.

- Get a big doll, one she can identify as another child, that your child can lie on, sit on, dance with, hit, or sleep with, and then add bits of pretend to the actions she does. Say, "I'm going to hit you back!" when she hits the doll, or "I love you," when she gives the doll a hug. Use the doll to imitate or join her when you can't do so yourself. Give the doll a name so you can talk to both children. For instance, the doll might get to the slide (couch) before your child does, triggering competitive or jealous feelings; you can then help your child deal with those feelings.

The idea is to build motor activities into the drama so your child's cravings can be satisfied while she is expanding her use of ideas.

If Your Child Is Oversensitive and Avoidant

If your child is oversensitive and avoidant, you need to make your pretend characters playfully obstructive in order to draw him into interaction.

• Have your dolls block his dolls so they can't get into the house.

• Have your cars crash into his cars so that he can't ignore them.

• Have your horses beat his horses to the watering hole so that his horses have to push yours out of the way.

Keep giving him problems to solve. Be playful and smiling as you do so. Remember that he is defensive, you don't want to scare him. You just want to create opportunities for interaction. You might even tell him what you will do next. Use verbal cues ("Watch out! They're coming!") to put him on guard so that he turns to watch what you do next.

If Your Child Is Oversensitive and Easily Overloaded

A child who is oversensitive and easily overloaded needs a soothing voice and almost slow-motion actions. Don't frighten her. Your voice needs to be both calming and compelling in order to engage her in interaction.

• If she is holding a doll, approach her slowly with another doll, singing softly, "Here I co-ome." Give her plenty of time to avoid you as you approach.

• If she is playing with a dollhouse, walk a doll across the floor whispering, "Can I play too-oo?" Slowly walk your doll into the house.

• If she is cradling a stuffed animal, hold out a cup and ask soothingly, "Does your kitty want a drink?"

Always approach slowly. Make sure your child can see you. If she turns or runs away, give her a minute, then try again. With time her tolerance will build.

12

Floor Time IV: Logical Thinking

HELPING A CHILD CONNECT IDEAS
AND DEVELOP A LOGICAL UNDERSTANDING
OF THE WORLD

Four-year-old Lindy had grouped several dolls around a table and was organizing a tea party. Two minutes into the activity, Lindy suddenly pointed toward a closet at the other end of the room. "What there?" she demanded, and took off for the closet. Like most children with multiple developmental challenges who have mastered a number of the presymbolic and early symbolic milestones, Lindy operated with little islands of ideas. She moved quickly from one idea to another with no logical connection between them. Her mother's challenge was to help her form logical bridges between her ideas.

"What about the tea party?" her mother asked, trying to bring Lindy back to her former idea. Lindy ignored her. "But I'm hungry," continued her mom, pretending to be one of the dolls. "I want tea and cookies." Lindy, however, had apparently forgotten the tea party and was now focused on the closet. Her mother at this point did something quite clever. Instead of relying on words to lure Lindy back to the tea party, she also used gestures. Following her daughter to the closet she opened an imaginary door and exclaimed, "Look! Cookies!" and with her hands she lifted an imaginary box of cookies. Lindy immediately got excited about her mother's find. Her mom lifted the hungry doll and said, "I'm still hungry!" "Here, eat," said Lindy. Then the two of them went back and forth several times, bringing cookies from the closet to the hungry dolls at the tea party.

Once a child begins to express her feelings and ideas, she may do so with a vengeance. Hold on tight, because she may be so excited about her new abilities that she will practice them nonstop. You may hear her walking around the house, carrying on a running conversation with herself as ideas pop into her head. As you listen to the conversation, however, instead of logical ideas moving sequentially from one to the next, you may hear random, unconnected thoughts. She may look out the window and comment on the leaves, then demand juice, then, without waiting for a response, begin playing out a scene with her animals—all within 90 seconds.

At first you might be discouraged to hear such disjointed ramblings. But don't be; they're signs of progress. They're the myriad thoughts and feelings that earlier your child was unable to express. Now your task is to respect her new excitement and spontaneity while challenging her to become more logical. Your goal is to increase the number of verbal circles she can close from just 1 or 2 to 40, 50, or more and to enable her to carry on a logical, 20-minute conversation—about pretend play, school, friends, or what to have for dinner—with flexibility and spontaneity. Even pretend play with astronauts traveling to the moon should have a plot, and the drama, however creative and fantastic, can be made up of elements that are logically connected. ("The spaceship went to the moon and landed and they saw gigantic monsters" versus "They went to the moon and there is a green crayon cars go zoom!")

CLOSING SYMBOLIC CIRCLES

When your child closes a symbolic circle—by building on your idea in pretend play or by responding logically to your words with words of his own—he makes a bridge between his ideas and yours, between his internal world and yours. Through millions of bridges, millions of closings of symbolic circles, he learns to differentiate what is inside him from what is outside, to understand himself and his world better.

In the last stage you wanted to help your child develop as rich a drama with as many feelings and ideas as possible. When you put a doll in your child's car and said, "I want a ride," you were happy if he elaborated on that theme with his own ideas for the next five minutes. In this stage you want every action and idea in that drama to be hooked to one of yours. Twenty seconds shouldn't pass without an interaction.

In the last stage when your child crashed his cars and you said, "Crash," you were happy if he repeated the word himself, using it appropriately each time he crashed a car; he was learning to express his ideas in words. In this stage you want to get a running dialogue going.

The dialogue can address the motives or consequences of his actions. Now when the car crashes you might comment, "Uh-oh, is someone hurt? I'll call the ambulance!" Or you might make the sound of a siren and have the police officer arrive to see who was driving recklessly ("Don't you even know how to drive, Mister? You need driving lessons!"). Depending on the intensity of the crash, you can respond to the underlying emotional tone, which may be deliberate and energetic (out to get someone) or more anxious and sensory (to hear the noise or knock over a building). If the latter, note it: "Wow, that was loud!" Your child will probably repeat the crashes several times. Then deal with the consequences of his actions: "Will that car ever work again?" By examining the consequences you help your child expand his logical thinking.

In the last stage you inserted yourself in the play in order to spark your child's ideas. In this stage you want every idea of his to interact with one of yours. You want him to close at least 80 percent of his symbolic circles by elaborating in a more logical way and taking into account what you just did.

The way to accomplish this goal is to be even more interactive, to engage in, talk about, question, and challenge what your child says and does. Look for ways to make everything he does a collaboration, but in each situation, let your child take the initiative.

- If your child is rolling dolls in a car, bring over another doll and say, "Can I come too?" Keep asking until he answers. If after three tries he doesn't answer, ask him, with genuine curiosity, not anger, "How come you won't answer?" Keep playfully engaging him until he closes the symbolic circle.

- If your child is arranging animals in the corral, perhaps one of your cows can jump over the fence and say, "I'm running away!" If she doesn't respond, try, "Why won't you answer me?" Keep playfully engaging her until she closes the symbolic circle. When she protests, ask if you took the wrong cow (play dumb), or tell her why you are running away. Maybe she can solve your problem.

• If he is building a castle, say, "Can I help you build?" If he replies, "See my big sword?" say, "Yes, but first tell me if I can help you build." If he then talks more about his sword go with the flow. Ask if he wants to see your sword or a different sword; ask if his sword is sharp. Try to get the circle closed. Sometimes you'll succeed in closing the original circle; sometimes you'll succeed with the next opportunity.

Respond to the emotion that underlies your child's comments. Your response will heighten the meaning of the words and symbols and encourage your child to continue. Asking, "Is it sharp?" "Does it cut or kill?" may help put him in touch with his underlying feelings—a desire for power, a fear of injury, or the need to protect himself. You can then explore these feelings through play.

Stretch Dialogues during Day-to-Day Interactions

Each time your child closes a circle, open another one by saying something else, because the real goal is not to have islands of conversation, but to have an ongoing dialogue. To converse, your child needs to practice opening and closing 10, 20, 50 symbolic circles in a row.

Don't limit your circle closing to pretend play. Do it all the time. Use everything your child does as an opportunity for conversation.

• When she asks for candy, say, "What kind of candy?" "How many?" Keep the conversation going, making sure she closes each circle before you move to the next.

• When he's looking at a book say, "Can I read with you?" After he answers try, "Tell me about this book. Which picture do you like best?" Keep the conversation going for as long as possible.

• When she wants to go outside ask, "What do you want to do? Where? First or second?" The magic words are "What else?" "What else do you want to eat? Where else should we go? Who else should come?"

• When you're driving in the car, make chitchat along the way: "What a beautiful day!" If he says nothing, try again: "Don't you think it's a beautiful day?" If he says, "We're driving fast," say, "Yes, but what do you think about this day?" Keep pestering him until he closes the symbolic circle.

• When you're brushing teeth say, "Should we brush fast or slow?"

• When he says, "I want juice!" say, "What kind?" If after several repetitions he still hasn't answered, simplify the question to multiple choice: "Orange or grapefruit?" Keep at it until your child closes the symbolic circle.

Every day has a million opportunities for closing symbolic circles, and the more of them you use, the better your child will get at logical conversation. The more you insist on logical answers, in a fun way, the more bridges your child will learn to make.

Ask Open-Ended Questions

When you're talking with your child—as a character in a drama or as yourself—it's helpful to ask open-ended questions. If you keep your questions broad and open-ended your child is free to supply her own answers. If you ask questions that can be answered yes or no, you're limiting her response. For example, if you say, "That horse has nice curls in its hair; do you want to comb it?" your child can only answer yes or no. If you say, "Where did the horse get his curls?" she can go in many different directions. Another useful technique is to summarize what's already happened, to say things like, "Let's see, the horse has done A, B, and C. I wonder what will happen next." That kind of comment lets your child know she's been understood and encourages her to continue the conversation.

Combine Action and Words

Once your child becomes comfortable opening and closing verbal circles, you may find yourselves having many conversations that are not linked to your play or your actions—conversations about what to have for dinner, what to do later in the day, which TV programs he likes. If your child is having trouble with this kind of dialogue, if he has difficulty sustaining a conversation and loses interest after one or two circles, go back to building your conversations around your actions. If you link your words directly to the action and, therefore, the emotion at hand, he'll have a much easier time sustaining the verbal interaction.

• If you're talking about what to have for dinner and your child isn't responding, go to the refrigerator and start taking out food. Hold up things you know he doesn't like and say, "I guess we'll have this." Chances are, you'll get a rise out of him—at least a "No!"—on which you can then begin to build. "No? How about this?" showing him something else. "How about walruses for dinner?" "What do you want? Show me." Poring through the fridge and cabinets together will probably generate a conversation about food.

• If you're playing with cars and your child stops talking or answers monosyllabically, move your car to race hers or block hers while talking directly to her character: "I'll beat you in the race!" Your action will draw your child in and give her a context for the words.

Avoid Parallel Conversations

The main thing to watch out for as you help your child close symbolic circles is parallel conversation. Although it may have the appearance of real engagement, in parallel conversation the child is actually talking to himself while the parent tailors his words to the child's.

William was busy fitting a car into the garage of the dollhouse. "Car in house, car in house," he muttered several times. "Yes," said his mother, "you're putting the car in the garage." After several attempts, William was unable to squeeze the car into the narrow space, and he dropped the car in frustration. "Car doesn't fit?" asked his mother. "Table in house!" announced William happily, picking up a toy table instead. "Oh, now you're going to put the table in the house," said his mom, and she watched as William maneuvered the table through the door. He bent down and peered through the door as if admiring his handiwork, then looked for something else to put in. "Man in house," he declared, and began slipping a little figure through the door. "William's putting the man in the house," said his mother, and at that moment William dropped the man with a satisfying thud onto the dollhouse floor. He grinned broadly at his mom. "Good work," she clapped. "You got the man into the house."

Throughout this exchange William's mother was wonderfully empathetic and supportive and had the illusion that she was conversing with her son; his words and gestures seemed to respond to hers. But as she went over what had happened she realized that William had not closed a single circle. He had done and said whatever had come into his mind. She had followed his actions with her words, but had not challenged him to connect his ideas to hers.

As William continued to play she continued to follow his lead but at the same time tried to inspire him to deal with her ideas and words as well as his own.

"William, are you putting the car in the garage?" she asked, as William once again tried to fit the oversized car into the garage.

The boy didn't answer.

"William, car in garage?" she repeated.

Since he continued to ignore her she got closer to the drama.

"William, putting car in garage?" she said again, touching the car and then putting her hand in the garage as if to translate her words into gestures.

This time William looked at her briefly as if to see who was intruding. "Yes!" he said. He had closed the circle. Now his mother tried for another.

"Car too big?" she asked empathetically.

"Car big," said William. He had closed a second circle.

"Car too big?" asked William's mom. "No fit?"

"Car big," said William again, closing circle number three.

"Maybe this fit," suggested his mother, handing him a smaller car.

William took the car from her hand and rammed it into the garage.

"That car fit?" asked his mom.

William was busy moving the little car back and forth in the garage.

"That car fit?" asked his mother again.

Still William ignored her in favor of the car.

"William, little car fit?" she asked again, putting her hand into the garage.

William looked at her as if he'd forgotten she was there.

"Little car fit in garage?" she asked a fourth time, still patient.

"Little car," said William.

"Little car fit in garage?"

"Little car in garage," agreed William.

Although William repeated some of his mother's phrases, he was nonetheless connecting with her ideas, which were an extension of his in the first place.

Through her patient repetition and her use of gestures to grab William's attention and help convey her meaning, William's mother had encouraged him to close four circles in a row.

How many times should you go back and try to get the same circle closed? Keep trying until you feel you've really lost your child's interest. William was still playing with the car in the garage, so his mother was right to keep asking him about its fit. Had he dropped the car and moved on to something else, she would have been better off trying to get him to close a circle about his next area of interest. When you start working on closing symbolic circles have as your goal closing 30 percent of the circles. When your child achieves that goal, bump it to 50 percent, and then to 80 percent. At 80 percent, your child will be logical most of the time.

Use Conflict and Challenge to Promote Logical Circle Closing

Another way to help your child build logical bridges in her play is to introduce conflict and challenge. There's nothing like conflict to bring out a child's feelings, and feelings can fuel more abstract, logical dialogue and play.

At four years old, Crystal was verbal and expressive, but her play had a fragmented quality. She rarely stayed with a theme for more than 30 seconds. Her mother, Sylvia, was trying to lengthen each theme into minutes. During one session Sylvia helped her daughter prepare two dolls for a bath.

"Clothes off," said Crystal.

"Are they ready for their bath?" asked Sylvia.

Before Crystal answered, her gaze caught a nearby truck. "Truck going to store!" she announced with delight, dropping her doll.

Thinking quickly, Sylvia placed her doll in the truck. "*My* truck!" she said defiantly.

"No, *my* truck!" Crystal yelled in anger.

"No, my truck," Sylvia repeated, speaking for her doll, "I'm going to drive it home so I can take a bath," and she pushed the truck along the floor.

"You can't! My truck! It taking me to school!" yelled Crystal furiously.

"You can drive it to school, but first I'm going to drive it home so I can take a bath," said Sylvia's doll.

"I don't want you to drive it home," shouted Crystal, reaching for the truck.

"Zoom! Zoom!" called Sylvia, scooting the truck quickly a few feet away.

Crystal looked after her for a few seconds, then turned her gaze in the other direction.

Sylvia realized she was about to lose her daughter's attention. "Do you want to drive my truck?" she asked compliantly, taking out her doll and pushing the truck toward Crystal.

Crystal stared neutrally at the truck.

"Do you want to drive my truck?" Sylvia asked again. "It goes really fast."

"No!" Crystal pouted.

"Well, I guess I'll drive the truck again then," said Sylvia and put her own doll back in.

"No! My turn!" yelled Crystal, unseating her mother's doll and fiercely putting in her own.

Over the next several minutes mother and daughter continued to play with the truck and dolls, with Sylvia appealing to her daughter's emotions each time she grew distracted. Finally Sylvia eased into a more cooperative, less challenging mode. "I guess you are the boss," she said, and Crystal smiled and relaxed. By that time the truck theme had lasted close to four minutes and Crystal had been clear and logical throughout.

By deftly drawing her daughter's feelings into the play, Sylvia coaxed out many extra minutes of coherent dialogue. Why did this happen? Because emotion motivates us. It gives meaning to our activities. It drives a connection between what we think, what we say, and what we do. You can think of attention as the persistence of a wish or an emotion; the more persistent your emotion, the more attentive you are. So when your child is inattentive, engaging her emotion may guide her words and actions and help maintain her focus.

Also, in confronting conflict, your child is pushed to go to a higher level of thinking to work out a solution. Trying to resolve two competing needs fuels more abstract thinking.

Use Your Child's Natural Motivation

To induce emotion, it's not always necessary to introduce conflict, however. Equally effective is working with the emotions that are already there.

A father was reading *Pinocchio* with his six-year-old son, asking the boy questions as they went along. To the father's annoyance, the boy insisted on clowning around. Instead of sitting quietly and answering the questions, he would jump out of his chair to act out parts of the story. The father grew exasperated, and eventually decided to reevaluate the activity. Since the point was to start some logical interaction—not to test the boy's knowledge of *Pinocchio*—he might be better off following his son's natural motivation, which in this case appeared to be in performing in front of an audience. The father began to talk to his son about the scenes the boy was enacting. This soon led to a conversation about which scenes the boy liked best, which parts he should do and which his dad should do, and the fun of acting. Fifteen minutes later, this distractible boy was still engaged in a rich, coherent interaction with his dad.

By capitalizing on the emotions the boy brought to the encounter, this father was able to engage him logically for a protracted period of time. The trick, of course, is to recognize those emotions. They're not always in a child's words; they are more often in the child's behavior. You need to look past what your child is saying to what she is doing to find where her real interest and motivation lie.

The same principle applies to real-life conversations. The more you can talk to your child about subjects that genuinely interest her, the more involved and logical she will be.

• If she loves basketball, talk about her favorite teams and players.

• If he loves horses, ask about his favorites, where he would keep a horse if he could have one, what he would name it, and where he would ride it.

• If she loves ice cream, ask what her favorite flavor is, what is the most she's ever eaten at one sitting, and what she'd do if she owned an ice cream store.

• If there's a bully at his school, talk about what makes the bully so scary, how he can avoid the bully, and what he can do if the bully attacks him.

Parents often worry that their child's interests will be perseverative, or too rote. One dad complained that his son "just wants to tell me baseball statistics." The key is to use your child's interests but broaden them. For example, if your child says that Cal Ripkin hit .305, say that another ballplayer is better. Use your child's interest as a starting point to get a dialogue going.

As we've suggested before, you can also engage your child's natural motivation by stalling him and negotiating his demands.

• When he demands five cookies *right now,* don't say yes or no; ask, "Why five?" "Why right now?" "Why not four cookies? Or six?" "Why not in five minutes?"

• When you know you're going to give her something she wants, don't just give it to her; make her negotiate. "Do you think I should give you a Popsicle? Why? What color? Do you think I should let you eat it all now or save some for later? Why?"

The more you enlist your child's natural motivation, the more he has to argue for his desire and the more logical circles he will close.

FORMING BRIDGES BETWEEN IDEAS

As your child becomes more verbal and better at closing symbolic circles, she may still jump abruptly from idea to idea. She may start telling you about something that happened in school, only to switch suddenly to a game of pretend. Or in the middle of a drama about a tiger she may suddenly ask for her favorite cookies. All of us often make abrupt transitions as new thoughts come into our minds, but if we don't have communication difficulties, we recognize the transition and close the first thought before opening the next. "Oh, I just thought of something," we might say, or "I have to change the subject." With these phrases we alert the listener to the fact that a new idea is coming and we build a logical bridge between the new idea and the old.

Children with communication difficulties often don't recognize when their minds have sped from one idea to the next because the bridge between ideas is missing. No inner voice warns them, "Wait, you've changed the subject." No inner logic says, "Wait, these ideas don't make sense together." If your child has communication difficulties, you need to help him see when these abrupt transitions occur. You need to point out the leap his thoughts have taken and then bring him back to the first thought, at least long enough to bridge it to the second.

- If your child is talking about something that happened at school and then suddenly tries to draw you into pretend play, say, "Wait a minute, I'm confused." He may clarify and say, "School done; now play," in which case you can respond, "Oh, now I understand." You'll have helped him make a logical transition. Alternatively, he may ignore you. Then you might say, "A minute ago you were talking about school and now you're being a lion. What are we doing, talking about school or being lions?" If he says, "Being lions," ask, "How come? What happened to school?" If he says, "Don't want to talk about school," he'll have made a logical bridge. You want him to see that he switched subjects, and you want him to close the circle, close the school conversation, before moving on to lions. At a later point, when he is a little better at closing circles, you may want to say, "I know you don't, but tell me just a little more about school and then we'll play lions."

- If your child is playing out a drama about a tiger and then suddenly demands her cookies, say, "Wait, I just got lost. You were being a tiger and now suddenly you want cookies. What happened?" If she doesn't answer, say, "What happened to the tiger?" or "Does the tiger want cookies?" Help her see that she switched subjects and help her make a bridge from one to the next.

- If you're in the middle of a game of catch and your child suddenly drops the ball and runs to the swing, say, "What happened? I thought we were playing catch!" If he doesn't answer or says, "Want to swing," say, "But I was having fun playing catch.

Don't you want to play anymore?" Help him see that he switched ideas and help him close the first idea before moving on to the second.

Your goal is not to keep your child talking about the first subject, but to help him follow his own thoughts in a logical way.

You want to build bridges in pretend play as well as in reality-based conversations. Even though pretend play is imaginary, you want your child to make logical connections between imaginary ideas.

• When your child offers you tea, then abruptly starts playing with her horses, demand your tea. Say, "Wait! I want my tea!" Keep after her until she either brings you tea or closes the circle by saying, "No tea now. Horses first."

• When your child's dolls have been fighting but suddenly start kissing, ask, "Wait, they were fighting but now they're kissing. What happened?"

• When his boat is a pirate ship looking for treasure, then suddenly becomes a spaceship headed for the moon say, "Wait, I just got lost. We were on a pirate ship but now we're on a spaceship?"

The specifics of the transition are not important. What's important is that the play move from episode to episode through a series of logical connections, rather than changing abruptly each time a new idea enters your child's mind. As your child closes more symbolic circles, it will be easier to help him make bridges between ideas. Expect him to think in islands of ideas at first, and then gradually to connect the islands into continents.

Create Multifaceted Characters in Play

Another way to help your child build bridges between ideas is to create pretend characters who are complex rather than simply black or white. If your child tells you to play a bad guy, your character need not be all bad. He can be good in selective areas. For instance, after shooting the good guys and robbing the bank he can suddenly say, "Oh, the dog hurt his paw. I have to help him," and bend solicitously over the dog. At first this may confuse your child, but gradually, after a lot of experience interacting with a complex character like that, she will learn to bridge the multiple aspects of his personality. Eventually she, too, may start creating more complex characters.

It is equally helpful to create characters with quirks: a character who is always hungry; a character who is never satisfied; a character who is always losing her shoes. As your child interacts with these characters he will learn to build bridges between those predictable aspects of their personalities and other traits.

You can help your child understand complexity by using two voices, one for the pretend character and one for yourself. Speaking as yourself you can observe the pretend character and discuss his actions with your child. ("David, the lion said he's going to eat you!") This approach is especially useful when your child is not responding to or elaborating on your comments. You can continue to elevate the action as the pretend character ("Roar! I'm coming and I'm hungry!") while also helping your child find a solution to the problem ("David," in a whisper, "he's getting closer! What are you going to do?") Be sure to make your two voices distinct so your child can differentiate between them. Also, when you play the pretend character, be sure to respond to your child's action. If he crashed a car into the character's car, say, "I'm hurt. Help!" or have the character get out and say, "Hey, what are you doing? You almost killed me!" Your response should depend on your child's emotional tone and the context of his idea. If his car crashed into the robbers' car because they were running away, you can cheer him on and applaud his bravery.

By responding to the feelings expressed in your child's actions, you can help your child expand his ideas. Even a simple crash can represent being strong and powerful or vulnerable and afraid. It can be exciting or anxiety inducing. Tuning in to the feeling and even exaggerating it will help your child identify his own experience and label the feelings he is having.

Do not rush into solving the feeling by fixing, comforting, or reassuring too quickly. Sustain the feeling as long as possible to help your child feel it more clearly, see that it's possible to tolerate strong feelings, and realize that his strong feelings are accepted and understood. "Wow! He's angry!" "Oh, that must hurt so much." "He really likes crashing with that strong truck." These are useful comments for highlighting your child's feelings. Once he's safely expressed his feelings for a while, he will be able to find a solution to the challenge at hand.

COMMON ESCAPES

Silliness or fantasy: It's common for children to try to avoid a difficult subject by escaping into silly play or nonsense. In the middle of a tough conversation about school, for instance, your child may suddenly pick up two dolls and begin banging them together. Deal with this behavior by acknowledging what she's doing in a supportive, playful way. "Hey, we were just talking about school and now you're banging your dolls. How come?" She's likely to ignore you, in which case, persist. "Don't you like talking about school? Why not?"

"What's hard about talking about school?" After a few of these questions you may get, "I don't want to talk about school." "Would you rather play?" you can ask. "How come? Why is playing more fun?" After she answers, try, "Is there anything fun about school?" See if you can get a conversation going about why playing is more fun. Once you've closed about 30 circles, join your child in the play.

Fragmentation: It's also common for a child to race from idea to idea so fast that you can't follow along. What you hear may sound like a jumble of unconnected ideas swirling around in his mind. When you encounter this fragmentation you have two choices. You can say, in a supportive, soothing voice, "I don't understand. Can you slow down and tell me again?" Try to get your child to elaborate on one idea at a time, asking him to stop each time he races on to a new one. Repeat each idea as he says it to show him you understand and to help him see the boundaries of his ideas. Don't assume there's a hidden meaning in his seeming nonsense. There may be, but if so, you can talk about that later. At the moment you're working on helping him organize his thoughts.

Your second choice is to try to pick up the emotional tone of his fragmented chatter—excitement, fear, anger, the desire to show off, whatever. Then empathize, through your tone and your words.

> • If behind the chatter you sense a desire to show off, for example, respond to your child with a look and a tone that suggest you're impressed. "Boy, you're using so many wonderful words! But I still need you to slow down a little. Can you explain that again so that even a dummy like me can understand your great ideas?"

If your child continues to be fragmented, try to repeat a few of the ideas you hear him saying. "It seems like you're talking about good guys and bad guys, and about the circus, and about rocket ships. I'm confused." See if he can either pick one idea to talk about or explain to you how these ideas are related. If he still wanders from thought to thought, give him a multiple-choice question: "Well, which one do you want to talk about—good guys and bad guys, the circus, or rocket ships?" Push him to pick one and then help him elaborate on that theme. The goal is not for you to guess and figure out which idea he wants to talk about, but for him to begin linking his ideas together rather than rushing from one island of thought to another.

If you can't sustain your child's attention, add visual support. Write down his ideas on a series of small cards, one idea per card, using just a few simple words or line drawings. Then ask him to look at the cards and choose which idea he wants to talk about or decide in what order he wants to talk about them. He can also group the cards together to show which ideas go together.

HIGHER-LEVEL ABSTRACT THINKING

Most of us take abstract thinking for granted. We do it constantly, automatically, without thinking about what it involves or about the underlying skills it requires. But if you dissect your thought processes on any given day, you'll find that certain abilities are required over and over again:

- The ability to answer what, where, when, how, and why questions.

- The ability to compare and contrast ideas and group them into categories.

- The ability to understand causal relationships: if I do A, then B will happen; be*cause* of A, I feel B.

- The ability to understand details as well as broad themes, to see the forest as well as the trees.

- The ability to manipulate concepts of quantity, time, and space, and to understand gradations such as more than/less than and bigger/smaller.

- The ability to understand and talk about feelings.

Whereas children without communication difficulties often develop these abilities without special help from their parents, children with developmental challenges typically need a lot of deliberate practice. Once your child is closing 80 percent of her symbolic circles and is starting to build bridges between ideas, you may want to begin helping her practice these additional skills.

You can help simply by talking to her as she plays and interacts with you. Practice isn't a formal thing; it will happen naturally in the course of your conversations if you keep these skills in mind and bring them into your dialogues.

What, When, Where, How, and Why Questions

Ironically, as children get better at opening and closing symbolic circles, their parents often get frustrated. On the one hand the child is becoming a better conversationalist; on the other, so many seemingly simple questions still trigger that old tuned-out behavior. "What did you do in school today?" or "Why do you want to go outside?" are often all it takes to trigger turning away, ignoring, or tuning out. Why?

These seemingly simple questions are hard to answer. Questions that begin with "what," "when," "where," "how," and "why" are abstract; before a child can answer them he must be able to manipulate numerous ideas in his mind. To answer "What did you do in school today?" for instance, he must be able to visualize himself in another place and time. To answer "Where is your hat?" he must be able to visualize his hat as well as the places it might be. Answering "When do you want your juice?" requires visualizing a time in the future and linking that time to a desire. Answering "How will you get the juice?" means visualizing his own actions in the future. Why questions are the most complex of all because they require causal thinking about his own wishes, desires, or feelings. For example, to answer the question "Why do you want to go outside?" with "Because I want to play," the child must have a sense of "I," a sense of inner desire or "want," and an idea for an action that will satisfy that desire, "to play." For a child who is new to abstract thinking, these are difficult and sophisticated tasks.

Children usually learn to answer what and where questions first because these questions typically refer to actual objects or places and children get more practice with these questions as they are offered choices. Children often learn how questions next because they relate to functions children experience, for example, "How should we get there?" "How should we fix it?" "How does it go?" "How does it work?" Answering when questions requires some sense of time and can be encouraged through choices ("Now or later?" "At 1:00 or 3:00?"). Since why questions are the most difficult to answer, work on the easier questions first.

You can help your child master what, when, where, how, and why questions by working them into the context of your play and your daily chitchat. Ask your child's opinions about everything. The more emotional the context (short of extreme emotions), the more likely your child is to use her thinking abilities. Children require lots and lots of practice at abstract thinking.

• When his doll demands that your doll give up the Jeep, challenge him with "What are you going to do with it?" or "When can I have it back?"

• When your horses are galloping across the plains, ask, "Where are we going?" "What's in the other direction?"

• When you're driving to Grandma's house in the car, ask, "What do you want to do when we get there?"

Why questions are the most difficult to answer because they require the greatest degree of abstract thinking. Children ease their way into why answers gradually. Their earliest answers are simple and concrete: "Why do you want to go outside?" "Because." Or "Because I want to." Or "Because I said so."

When your child answers this way she is not being stubborn. She is answering the question the best way she can. Over time, her answers will become more sophisticated. "Because it's fun," she may answer when she gets a little better at abstraction, or, "Because my doll is there."

When your child is able to give three reasons for why she wants to go outside—"Because it's a nice day and I've been inside all morning and I feel like running around"—she'll not only have achieved true fluency with why questions, but she'll also be able to teach you about causal thinking.

To help your child master these abstract questions, rephrase the questions in an easier form. You can simplify why questions by changing them to what questions.

- Instead of "Why do you want to go outside?" try "What do you want to do outside? When do you want to go out?"

- If your child has trouble with the what question, change it to multiple choice. "Do you want to swing or ride your bike?" This type of question is more concrete and therefore easier to answer.

- If your child has trouble with the multiple-choice question, make one of the alternatives ridiculous. "Do you want to swing or do you want to find gorillas?"

- When he answers, rephrase his answer as a why answer: "Oh, to swing, *that's* why you want to go outside!" That will help him answer why questions in the future.

You can also help your child by giving him cues about the answer. What, where, when, how, and why questions can be especially difficult when they concern the reality of his day. If you sense that your child knows what he wants to say but is having trouble thinking of the words, give him cues. For instance, if you ask how school was and your child grows sullen but can't articulate the problem, ask, "Did that red-haired girl steal your toy again?" That may be all you need to get him talking.

After a while, giving your child multiple choices or cues may make finding the answer too easy. Suppose you ask what he did in school and he doesn't answer. You then try, "Did you play with the red-haired girl or with the blue-eyed boy?" He may answer simply, "With the red-haired girl." But you want more information, so you try again: "Tell me more about what you did today." Your child doesn't answer. Instead of supplying another choice, try, "Don't you want to talk about it?" You're likely to get "No." Stay with it. Rephrase your question: "Oh, come on, can't you tell me anything about school?" "No." At that point you can offer a silly choice: "Well, did you play with the elephant today?" Chances are, he'll laugh and answer, "No! Bobby made funny faces at me." "Oh! So that's something that happened at school!" When you ask a completely open-ended question, such as "What happened at school?" your child has too many choices from which to pick—it can be very hard to answer. When you throw out a silly incident, you narrow the field; you make it easier for him to think of one or two things that happened that he can relate. Don't take no for an answer. Even rejecting your question may help your child retrieve another answer. It is not usually a problem with memory, but a problem with retrieval or meaning that makes responding difficult.

Emotion-Based Questions

Many of us fall into the trap of quizzing our children with rote memory questions. "What did you do after lunch?" "What color are your blocks?" "Who did you play with?" But children with developmental challenges often already favor rote ways of thinking, and this approach only compounds the problem. In addition, higher-level thinking tends to be cued by emotions, as we discussed in Chapter 11. Most conversation among adults, for example, isn't "What did you do after lunch?" but rather, "What's new?" or "Anything exciting today?" These questions reference the emotion of the person being asked, which helps her access the most relevant memories of the day. If you can do this with your child, you will help her develop truly abstract thinking that's relevant to the context.

- Instead of asking, "What did you do at school?" ask, "What was *fun* at school?" "Anyone make you *mad* today?"

- In pretend play go after emotion also. Have your character talk about how happy she is, or how angry. Have her ask your child's character how she feels.

Using Emotion to Categorize Ideas

Emotion also helps us group ideas into categories—things that are similar and different, things that are related and unrelated, things that are good and bad. This kind of grouping is another important abstract-thinking skill. It enables us to find patterns and meaning in the world, to make sense of our environment. You can help your child develop this skill by appealing to her emotions in daily conversation and in pretend play.

- If your dolls are trying on clothes, your doll can ask your child's doll, "Which are your favorite clothes?" encouraging your child to group the clothes into favorites and nonfavorites. "Why are those your favorites?" your doll can wonder, encouraging your child to explain the reasons behind his choice. "I think these are nicer," your doll can protest, adding an element of debate to encourage your child to expand or justify his thinking.

• If you're fighting a battle with plastic swords, you can challenge your child with "My sword's better than your sword!" When she counters that her sword is better than yours, ask, "What makes your sword better?" encouraging her to list the qualities that make her sword superior. Bet her she can't find other weapons that are better than yours; when she does, ask what makes those weapons so good. Each time your child rises to your challenge she'll be categorizing ideas in an abstract way.

• If your child is playing out a scene of good guys fighting bad guys, ask, "What makes your guys good?" To answer, he'll have to think through his idea of goodness and delineate the qualities that his good guys share. The more qualities he can list, the more adept he'll become at handling abstract ideas. Then try asking, "What's bad about my guys?"

• Let your child pick the dimension in which ojects are compared. For instance, instead of asking, "The red one or the blue one?" you might say, "Tell me which one," and let your child choose the dimension (big, round, scratchy, etc.).

One little boy was fascinated with the labels on his toys. He called all toys by their manufacturer's name ("the Fisher Price house") instead of their descriptive names ("the yellow house"). His parents used this fixation to help him move into the world of the abstract. They engaged him in conversations about which toys he liked better, the Fisher Price toys or the Mattel toys, and why. They remembered that it was emotion—"What do you like best?"—that would help him move from rote, or concrete, thinking to abstract thinking.

Don't worry about the specifics of your child's answers. As long as they make sense, any answers will do. What's important is that your child be able to use his emotions logically to compare and contrast a variety of ideas and see how they fit together into larger groups. As we discuss later, higher-level abstraction, such as concepts of love and justice, emerges from experiencing a word in multiple emotional contexts. I understand the concept of love when I understand emotionally that it means hugging, giving, recovering from anger, putting the other person first, and numerous other elements that I have actually experienced.

Seeing the Forest as well as the Trees

Another important component of high-level abstract thinking is the ability to understand broad themes as well as details, for these two aspects work together to describe a situation fully. Suppose you went to the doctor and complained that you didn't feel well, but when the doctor asked what was wrong you were unable to pinpoint the symptoms. Or imagine the reverse: when a friend asks you about your day you rattle off a list of 20 things you did—all details, no summation. Was it a good day? A bad day? Who knows? Without the ability to draw your details into a theme, both you and your friend are at a loss to understand your situation fully. Any kind of argument— from a demand to stay home from school to a college thesis—requires forest-trees thinking. "I want to stay home" is the broad theme, the reasons for staying are the details; the decline of civilization is the broad theme, the reasons for the decline are the details.

You can help your child develop this skill by using play and everyday opportunities to challenge his thinking.

> • When you're chasing each other around the house, stop and look confused. Ask, "Why are we chasing each other, anyway?" He'll have to explain the broad theme of the action, the reason behind your chase. Perhaps he'll say, "I'm chasing you because you're the bad guy!" Great! Then you can go for the details: "What did I do that was bad? What will you do when you catch me?"

> • When the animals are jumping out of the corral, stop and say, "Wait! Why are you running away?" Your child will have to tell you the broad theme of the action. Perhaps she'll say, "We hate the farmer, and we don't want to live here anymore." Great! Now you can ask for details: "Why do you hate the farmer? What did he do to make you mad? What can he do to make up to you?"

> • When your child demands to stay up late, to have more candy, or to wear a certain pair of shoes, ask him why he wants to do that. Push him for as many reasons as he can supply. Each one will be a detail that supports his broad theme.

Broad themes and details also show up in your child's pretend dramas. Who rides which horse and which army wins the battle are the details of the story. The underlying emotions—competition, aggression, loss, and so on—are the broad themes. As you talk with your child about what she's doing you want to shift your discussion back and forth between these levels. For example, if your child is playing with horses and is intently describing their features—blue eyes, yellow hair, big teeth, and so on—you may sense that all those details are ways of expressing that one horse is special. At that point you might empathize, "That's a great horse," or "Why do you like that horse so much?" By asking about the details you let your child know you're interested in her story. By verbalizing the emotional theme you help her recognize the feeling that underlies her actions.

Not all children are equally comfortable talking at both levels. Your child may focus only on the emotion of the drama, ignoring all the details. Then question her about the circumstances of the emotion: "Why is the horse sad? What happened?" If your child is focused exclusively on the details, help her address the emotions underneath. "How did the horse feel when her friend ran away?"

The more you encourage your child to reflect on both details and broad themes, the more flexible his thinking will become. Of course, you do not want to question or challenge your child too much, or you may undermine the joy of your play or dialogue. Just slip in these clarifying questions once in a while. And remember that many of your child's broad themes will derive from his emotions and emotional judgments.

Cause and Effect

Although we don't stop to think about it, a great deal of our process of thought has to do with cause and effect. "The alarm went off, so I woke up." "I'm hungry, so I'll stop for lunch." Be*cause* you're hungry, you decide to take an action. "This hamburger is too well done; I don't like it." Be*cause* the burger is too well done, you don't want to eat it.

To be a fully fluent thinker, your child has to learn the logic of cause and effect. You can help by giving him lots of practice. Opportunities for practice are built into almost every situation. Every time you ask why your child wants to do something, why he likes or dislikes something, or why he did something a certain way, he has to use cause-and-effect thinking.

- When your child says he wants to go outside and you ask, "Why?" he has to answer with a causal statement: "Be*cause* it's nice out," "Be*cause* I want to ride my bike," "Be*cause* I want to run around."

- When your child says she didn't put her toys away and you ask, "Why?" she has to answer with a causal statement: "Be*cause* I didn't want to," "Be*cause* it was too hard," "Be*cause* I was too tired."

Anytime you negotiate with your child around his needs (bedtime, more candy, not eating his dinner) he will automatically use causal thinking.

Concepts of Relationship

Concepts of relationship—bigger/smaller, more than/less than, sooner/later, closer/farther, and so on—are so automatic that we don't think about them, but children have to learn them through practice. Again, pretend play and everyday situations provide thousands of opportunities for you to help your child master these concepts.

• When dolls are brushing each other's hair, you can talk about whose hair is longer, prettier, or darker.

• When cars are racing each other across the room, you can talk about which one is faster or more powerful or can go farther.

• When the mommy bear goes hunting and leaves the baby bear alone, you can talk about whether she's gone far away or only a little bit away and whether she'll come back soon, not so soon, or much later.

• When you're pretending to be frogs jumping around the room, you can decide whether you should jump a lot or only a little, or whether you should jump very high or only a little bit high.

Preacademic Skills

Perhaps your child is beginning to recognize letters and numbers or to work on concepts of quantity. As you work with him in these areas, always work with real objects in everyday situations (rather than in contrived, "educational" situations), because doing so will make the learning emotion-based. Even if he knows how to read letters, numbers, and logos because of his good visual skills, the numbers may not represent quantities to him and the letters may not connect to sounds. You can help those understandings along in everyday situations.

• When you give your child cookies, ask if he wants two or three. Count each cookie as you give it to him. What happens if you take one away? Will he want one more? Are two cookies more than one cookie or less? Don't try to pack all these lessons into one session, but use moments when your child is eating, playing with, or coveting something to introduce these simple mathematical concepts. Focus on quantities rather than on rote counting. Even if your child is not verbal, if you put two cookies in one hand and three in another, he will know which is more!

• If your child is learning letters, as soon as he can recognize C, A, and T, have him read the word *cat*, then get a picture of a cat, or better yet let him pat a real cat. Tying his learning to a real, emotionally charged experience will give it a solid conceptual base.

We discuss more about teaching academic skills in Chapter 19.

Opportunities to Practice Abstract-Thinking Skills Are Everywhere

We've given you a long list of abstract-thinking skills to work on with your child. The list would be totally overwhelming if you had to work actively on every item. But you don't. As long as you play dynamically with your child, as long as you get inside the drama instead of sitting on the sidelines, you will automatically be building these skills. Look at how they come up in even the simplest drama.

> Dustin was building a house of blocks.
>
> "I'm the wolf!" hissed his dad, coming up behind him on all fours. "I'm going to blow your house down!"
>
> Dustin wheeled around fiercely. "You can't blow my house down because I'm going to shoot you first!" he cried in a demonstration of causal thinking. (He was expressing a time relationship as well: "I'll shoot you *before* you blow the house down.")
>
> "You can't shoot me. I'm going to eat you first!" threatened his dad.
>
> "I'm going to eat *you* first!" yelled Dustin. "I'm going to eat your head."
>
> "You can't eat my head. Your teeth aren't big enough!"
>
> "My teeth are bigger than your teeth," replied Dustin, handling a size-relationship question.
>
> "How do you know your teeth are bigger than my teeth?"
>
> "My teeth are the biggest in the world!" exclaimed Dustin, answering the how question without a pause. "They can chew you into lots of pieces!"
>
> "Yeah? How many pieces?"
>
> "Five pieces!"
>
> "Well, my teeth can chew you into ten pieces!"
>
> "My teeth can chew you into a hundred pieces!" crowed Dustin, practicing concepts of quantity.

By getting inside the drama (as the wolf), Dustin's dad automatically challenged and questioned his son. He didn't have to think about introducing how questions or causal thinking; they flowed naturally out of the action. And his son asserted himself naturally, driven by his desire to be more powerful. As a result, his responses just flowed.

This is equally true in everyday life.

> "I want another piece of candy!" demanded Elizabeth.
>
> "Why?" asked her mom.
>
> "Because," Elizabeth fielded the why question, "I do."
>
> "But you've already had two."
>
> "No, I only had one," Elizabeth argued, practicing concepts of quantity.

"I thought I saw you eat two."

"I want another one."

"It's too close to dinner."

"I'll still eat dinner. It won't fill me up, I promise." Elizabeth intuitively supplied a detail to support the broad theme of her argument that she'll still eat dinner.

"What happened the last time you ate candy before dinner?"

"I ate dinner anyway," said Elizabeth, answering a what question.

"But how much dinner did you eat?" reminded her mom, smiling.

Elizabeth stuck out her bottom lip. "A lot," she said petulantly, answering a question of quantity. A second later she brightened. "But if I eat candy now I'll eat even more dinner tonight!" She envisioned her actions in the future and created a cause-and-effect argument to support her desire.

Resist your temptation to invoke rules at these highly motivated moments. Instead, use your child's strong interest to discuss with her what is right or wrong and when the ordinary rules might not apply. As these two vignettes show, as long as you *negotiate your child's demands* and *play dynamically,* abstract thinking can automatically become part of your dialogues.

This is equally true with children who are less advanced verbally and who are just learning causal thinking.

Amanda was demanding that her mother give her candy.

"Can't you wait until after dinner for candy?" asked her mom.

"No!" pouted Amanda. "Candy now!"

"Why no wait?" asked her mom.

Amanda pointed at her tummy. "Tummy want candy now."

"It's yucky!"

"No, good."

"Do you want one or two pieces?"

Expand the dialogue as much as possible in these highly motivated opportunities.

EXPRESSING FEELINGS

Now that your child is able to identify and verbalize her feelings, you want to help her *think* about her feelings—to understand what makes her feel the way she does, to recognize gradations in feeling, to compare one feeling with another. This is one of the most advanced forms of abstract thinking, but it is achieved in the same manner as the other abstract-thinking skills—through lots and lots of practice. And, as with the other skills, this practice occurs in the course of your daily experiences as you talk with your child about what she is doing. Simply by empathizing with your child's feelings—using words, tone of voice, and body language—and asking what's going on, you can help her learn to reflect on the feelings she expresses. Gradually, she will develop this skill.

• When your child is crying, kneel down in front of him, take him in your arms, and ask warmly and supportively, "What's wrong, honey? What's making you cry?" When he answers, continue to empathize: "She said that? Did that make you feel bad? What did you say?" Through patient questions, encourage him to elaborate on the scenario that upset him. You might refer to a recent incident that provoked similar feelings to show him the consistency in his response. You might tell him a short story in which the same thing happened to you. Don't prolong the encounter to the point of irritation, but continue to discuss the situation for as long as your child seems emotionally involved. The more he talks about it, the more he will come to understand his own emotions as well as what triggers them.

• Do the same thing whenever your child expresses strong emotion—whether it's anger, or jealousy, or frustration. These feelings may be more difficult to stay with since they may inspire strong emotion in you. But if you can be patient, if you can empathize with the feeling, help your child describe it, and talk about what triggered it, you can help your child deal with her feelings in a more reflective way. You do not have to fix the feelings; just show her that she can safely have strong emotions and that she can reflect on them. The more reflective she is, the less need she will have to act out those feelings.

• If necessary, help your child label his feelings by giving him multiple choices. If a situation has provoked tears and stomping, bend down and ask gently, "You seem to have very strong feelings right now. Are you feeling mad? Sad? Frustrated?" Do the same in pretend play when his characters show strong emotion.

• Ask your child to compare her feelings and to reflect on their intensity. "Are you sad or mad? Are you a little more mad or a little more sad?" When you ask, use tones of voice that reflect the feelings of sad and mad. Your vocal change will help her process your words. This sounds contrived, but when delivered with real warmth and empathy along with a back rub, it isn't. It actually helps your child differentiate one feeling from another. Children with special needs have trouble processing their own emotional signals. Asking these sorting-type questions helps them make sense of what they feel but may not understand.

• Question the absence of feelings. You might ask how your child feels when you know something has disappointed him. If he says, "Nothing," try again: "Not even a teeny, tiny bit sad?" If he still denies having feelings, try a different approach: "I think that might make me sad. It might even make me cry." You could also bring out a doll and ask Mr. Dolly how he feels. Don't push too hard, however. If your child maintains his reluctance even with all your empathy, switch gears and empathize with his reluctance. "I can tell maybe you feel it's best not to have feelings," you might say. Or "Sometimes it's hard to know how you feel." Or "Sometimes it's hard to talk about stuff."

• Introduce feelings into many conversations. When your child talks about friends or school ask, "Did you like that?" "How did it make you feel?" "Did it make you happy or sad?" Connecting feelings to events makes them easier to talk about and helps your child practice verbalizing her feelings.

Expressing Feelings through Play

Your child's play offers numerous opportunities to raise the subject of feelings. Whenever characters are showing strong emotion through actions such as hugging or fighting, try to get feelings into the dialogue. Your doll might say, "I love you," "I'm so happy," or "That makes me mad!" Then see what your child says. If she doesn't respond your doll can ask, "How do you feel?" You can also comment on what you don't see. If her bears are always nice, for example, never displaying anger, you can try creating an opportunity for anger to arise. "Accidentally" drop a plate as the bears are setting the table and apologize for your clumsiness: "Uh-oh, I broke a plate. Will your bear get angry at me?" Over time, your child may start providing answers, especially if you do not discourage her from expressing her angry feelings as they occur in other situations.

If you see what you think is a connection between two themes, you may be tempted to ask about it. For instance, if the bears are attacked by wolves while reading quietly by a campfire, you may be tempted to say, "Why do the wolves want to attack the nice bears? Is it because every time people are warm and close something dangerous happens?" That's a good guess—but don't say it. Even if you're right your suggestion may not be helpful. When your child is ready, she'll talk about it herself. Until then, she's likely to reject your interpretation.

However, you could make a simple statement and see how your child reacts. For instance, you might say, "The wolves attacked the bears just when they were so happy," and then let your child elaborate. That way she can acknowledge the connection if she's ready to do so, or disregard it if that's more comfortable for her. As long as you make it safe for your child to express her emotions as she feels them, she may eventually make the connection on her own. If you see your child pondering the question, provide support by asking, "Will he do it again?" Don't be afraid of having your child pretend to be aggressive in play. By symbolizing aggression she is safe; she can then go on to explore the motives behind her impulses.

Stages in Expressing Feelings

As your child learns to translate his feelings into words, he goes through several predictable stages. First, of course, is acting the feeling out. Your child is angry and he hits; he feels loving and he hugs. He doesn't recognize the feeling as an emotion; it wells up inside as an impulse to behave a certain way. Next, he may begin to express his feelings through the action of his dolls or animals; they hit or hug each other as different feelings come up in play. Then, he may begin to describe his feelings as bodily actions; instead of delivering the punch he may say, "My arm wants to hit!" When he feels sad he may say, "I cry." This is an important step on the road to learning to translate feelings into words, although it is not yet full symbolic representation. Your child may next describe how his body feels inside. When moved to anger he may say, "I want to push," "My head hurts," or "I feel jumpy." This recognition of how his body feels is another important step toward symbolic representation. When he makes the leap to describing emotional, rather than physical, feelings, he is apt to do so in the most general terms: "I feel good" or "I feel bad" may be as specific as he can get. The final stage is when he can describe his emotions in more specific terms: "I'm angry," "I'm sad," "I'm excited."

Your child may not be at the same stage in relation to every feeling. He may be able to verbalize feelings of love and nurturance but still act out feelings of aggression and anger, or describe them as bodily states rather than as emotions. Learning to verbalize feelings is a slow and gradual process. The goal is to help your child move up the hierarchy in each emotion—from the action and action-language stages, through the physical-description stage, to naming the global feeling, to being able to express the specific feeling in words.

*Negativism, Negotiation, and Power: Aggression as
a Sign of Developmental Progress*

As your child becomes more logical, you are likely to see more feelings of aggression and power. Some children with special needs are cautious or sometimes passive because they have difficulty controlling their bodies as well as understanding what they hear and see. Some are very controlling and grow furious if you make a move without their consent. Some children are impulsive or disorganized. But as their abilities grow, so does their confidence. They begin risking more organized assertive behavior; they may even be deliberately aggressive. These assertive and aggressive tendencies and feelings often come out in play. So don't be surprised if GI Joe threatens to blow up everybody in his path or the wild stallion tramples his mean owner, or if these actions are accompanied by a spate of angry words. In an organized form, these are natural, healthy expressions, and their emergence through symbolic play means they are not coming out through behavior. Remember, feelings can be acted out or expressed through pretend play and words. The latter is a higher level of expression that supports reasoning.

In the earliest stages children often hit, push, and bite when they are angry, frightened, or want to defend themselves. If another child takes a toy, gets too close, or alarms them with an unexpected move, they are liable to strike out in response. They use their bodies because they are otherwise unable to express how they feel. When they see how other people react to their aggressive behavior, they sometimes continue in it, enjoying the effect they are able to cause (not because they truly wish to harm someone). Gradually they learn that such aggressive actions are not acceptable; they learn to restrain their intentions and not act on their feelings, to wait, to share, to say "please," and to take turns.

As children develop, their aggression becomes more organized, more intentional, and more gratifying, for it becomes linked to power. They see that they are able to control others and even to make others afraid of them. Finally the tables are turned! They can do to others what was done to them. This behavior is acceptable only in symbolic pretend play, usually when they are playing the good guy.

You will know that your child is moving toward this stage of development when he becomes fearful of ghosts, monsters, aliens, and other such creatures. This fear reflects an awareness of danger and aggression in a more abstract form, since these creatures are not real. (Earlier signs of awareness were embedded in animal figures, such as the big bad wolf.) Children solve these fears for themselves by creating fantasies of power figures who are even bigger, stronger, and faster than the creatures they most fear. They pretend to be Superman, Peter Pan, or a Power Ranger and imagine that they really have power. Their play may get so intense that they don't realize it is pretend.

Children with challenges may reach this stage later than children without challenges; they may stay in it longer; and they may have to work harder to differentiate between what is real and what is not. Their sensory and motor processing may not be able fully to support the development of reality testing and becoming logical, and it may be harder for them to develop the self-confidence to exercise their power and aggression safely. They may experience considerable anxiety in dealing with their imagined fears or with the symbolic play of other children and may resort to attacking others (as they did when younger), or they may avoid aggressive play themes altogether or constrict the range of play.

Many children experience some anxiety when making this transition to reality testing and expressing their own aggression. This anxiety is exhibited through heightened aggressive impulses and preoccupation, overreaction when others play aggressively, avoidance or withdrawal, or sticking with safe, familiar (often obsessive) themes.

When your child realizes he is only a child—that he can only *pretend* to have power, rather than exercise real power in the world, and that he can be aggressive only symbolically, or else the world will come down on him—he has moved on to the next stage of logical and representational thinking. At that point he will have the flexibility to play good guy/bad guy and be either one. During this transition, your child will probably begin to test again to clarify the boundaries of power and logic. You're likely to see increased negativism. "No, I won't go to bed!" "No, I won't get dressed!" "No, the bears won't follow their mommy to the park!" These reactions are part of the same phenomenon. Your child has waited a long time for a sense of his own power; now he's eager to exercise it. So try to restrain your irritation when he seems especially uncooperative and instead use it to generate conversation, debate, and the exercise of logical thinking. Remember, there must be a reason that your child is saying "No!" and needs to be the boss.

Take advantage of your child's motivation to negotiate. When he says he won't eat his vegetables, ask, "Why not? Why don't you like them?" "Are there any vegetables you do like?" "Will you eat two forkfuls of carrots?" Whether he wins or you win, whether he eats his carrots or doesn't, is secondary to improving his conversational skills. You can get 30 or 40 verbal circles closed as your child puts forth a logical argument.

It's important to talk with your child about his negativity for another reason. Sometimes a display of anger or aggression is triggered by a good, and avoidable, cause.

A five-year-old boy with severe cerebral palsy had recently begun hitting his teacher each time she took him to the bathroom. When his parents gently and patiently questioned him, he explained that he was embarrassed about having a woman teacher take him into the boy's bathroom; he wanted a male teacher instead. With a little more questioning he revealed another reason for his hostility: the teacher was taking him when she wanted to go, rather than when he needed to. After this discussion the school arranged for a male teacher to take the boy (on a prearranged schedule that was explained to him), and immediately the hitting stopped.

If your child is compromised in his ability to articulate his needs or to be physically independent, he will need extra help in meeting these challenges, especially in areas such as eating and going to the bathroom. You can provide that help by

- patiently exploring negative behavior to see if there is a fixable cause;

- anticipating areas that may provoke resentment and discussing them ahead of time;

- encouraging your child to express his needs verbally as much as possible.

Your discussions will strengthen your child's ability to be assertive in a constructive way. They will also help him grow more comfortable in the world of abstract thinking.

STAGES OF ABSTRACT THINKING

Some children with multiple developmental challenges get to the point of carrying on short, logical conversations about everyday matters or following simple directions, but never progress much beyond that. They lack the ability to see nuances of meaning, to weigh contradictory viewpoints, or to read between the lines. They have difficulty talking about deep feelings, such as anger and sadness, and don't grasp complex abstract concepts, such as love or justice. They may become competent readers, able to decipher long words on a page, but by the time they get to third or fourth grade, they have limited comprehension of what they read because they can't grasp the abstract concepts or motives behind the story.

Many therapists and educators have been at a loss as to how to promote abstract thinking and comprehension in children with special needs. They have successfully taught children to speak and read, but not how to understand and use abstract concepts. Recently, however, through careful observation, we have recognized four predictable stages in learning to think abstractly and have developed theory and principles to help children with developmental delays progress through these stages.

The first stage in abstract thinking is the building of causal bridges between two ideas: "You were mean, so I'm mad." At this stage your child is still caught up in the immediacy of his feelings (even though he is using words to describe them). You're mean, he's mad, and he needs satisfaction *now* because he literally cannot imagine a later resolution.

At the next stage your child can step back a little from the immediacy of his feeling. Now he can begin to imagine a later satisfaction. "You're mean, I'm mad, and I'm going to tell Daddy." His ability to think abstractly now allows him to imagine himself in the future and to imagine a solution that involves people or objects that are not right in front of him.

Until this time your child's thinking is wholly black and white: I'm good, you're bad, and there is no in-between. In the next stage, however, he begins to comprehend gradations, gray areas, multiple possibilities. "You're mean—but only a little mean; and I'm mad—but only a little mad," he may say, and while he's acknowledging his anger he may indicate that he has other feelings also. No longer is he caught up in a concrete, all-or-nothing view of things, nor is his view limited to his immediate feelings and situation. He can step back and consider (alone or with help) whether something is a big deal or a little deal.

As your child continues to mature, he grows into a stage in which he is able to differentiate even further between what is true right now and what exists at other times. He becomes able to understand two realities within himself: one that feels a certain way right now ("You're mean! I'm mad at you!") and another that can reflect on those feelings in relation to a more stable sense of himself and of you. ("You were mean and I'm mad, but I'm a nice person so I'm not going to get even, and most of the time you're nice to me so I guess I can forgive you.") At this stage true self-reflection becomes possible because for the first time your child has an ongoing sense of self from which he can fashion opinions, values, and ideals, and on which he can draw to approve or disapprove of his own behavior. He can curb his impulses not because he fears punishment or because he desires to please, but because he is developing an inner morality that is connected to this new stable sense of self. Children without special needs generally reach this stage between the ages of 11 and 13. Many children with special needs get locked into preceding stages, caught up in the immediacy of the here and now and reacting to experiences of the moment in the absence of this overarching sense of self. Many of these children can move into this stage, however, if given a wide range of emotional experiences to help strengthen their abstract-thinking skills. Sometimes children with special needs can become more abstract than their peers as they have grown through many challenges.

A more advanced stage of abstract thinking occurs as your child moves through adolescence into adulthood. Both of his realities—his day-to-day experiences and his stable sense of self—expand further as his range of experience continues to broaden and as biological, neurological, and cognitive growth occurs. New activities, new relationships, new responsibilities, sexual maturation, and the further development of the nervous system all help your child define his sense of self. He is now able to form a more complex, more abstract picture of himself and the world. As he separates from you, goes away to college or gets a job, develops intimate relationships with others, has a family of his own, and contends with his own aging, his ability to comprehend and manipulate abstract images of himself and his world continues to grow. He can not only imagine himself in the future, but he can manipulate those images, contemplate various hypothetical futures, and make judgments about how to behave. An individual who is capable of hypothetical thinking can consider the various consequences of different kinds of sexual behavior, for example, and reach a mature judgment about what kind of practices are both safe and satisfying.

If an adolescent's experiences become complex too quickly, however, they may overload the more stable sense of self that has to process and comprehend them, and the child may become disorganized rather than abstract. On the other hand, if she is not helped to engage in ever more challenging experiences, the opportunity for intellectual and emotional growth may be unnecessarily limited. Many people assume that children with special needs can't reasonably be expected to engage in many of the experiences that promote more abstract thinking. But another possibility, more consistent with our experiences with younger children with special needs, is that they simply may need more time to master new experiences. It is important not to confuse response lag—which results because a child needs a longer time to retrieve words and organize her response or has difficulties with sequencing movements—with a child's ability to think abstractly. Each child's potential is different. The only way to gauge and help children reach that potential is to assist them in participating in the types of experiences that will support the progression described here.

To help your child participate in these experiences, you need to offer time and support. Make sure your child has consolidated her experiences before introducing additional ones. For example, until your child is able to hold on to one set of values in a stable way as a basis for a self-image and use it to evaluate changing day-to-day experiences, she will not be able to participate fully in hypothetical thinking or intellectual debates that require hypothetical thinking. Your child must demonstrate the ability to create two inner worlds—one that includes herself in reality and an imagined world in which she feels, anticipates, abstracts, chooses, and problem solves.

BROADENING EXPERIENCE TO ENCOURAGE ABSTRACT THINKING

As we've studied how children learn to think abstractly, we've realized that the understanding of abstract concepts comes not from facts or didactic instruction, but from a tremendous amount of rich, emotional experience. The more experiences your child has—the more her emotions are brought into play in daily life—the better she will become at handling abstract concepts. All abstract ideas are based on experience; it is a person's multiple emotional experiences with a concept or word that gives that word or concept its abstract meaning.

Take, for instance, the abstract concept love. A two-year-old understands the concept of love in a narrow, concrete way; love is when his mommy hugs and kisses and nurtures him. The bad mommy who yells at him or refuses his request is not incorporated into his concept of loving mommy. As the child grows older, his understanding of loving mommy grows. By five, he knows he loves his mommy and she loves him even though they sometimes get angry at each other. His concept of love now includes occasional moments of anger. For the twelve-year-old, the concept is broader still. He knows that his mom's devotion and reliability are part of her love, and he understands that he can feel angry, annoyed, and hurt while continuing to love her. His abstract sense of love is complex and includes seemingly contradictory notions. Furthermore, he knows that the kind of love he feels for his siblings is different from the love he feels for his parents, although it has certain shared features. By the time the twelve-year-old becomes an adult and experiences one or more loving relationships with peers, his notion of love will be broader still. All his lived experiences with love contribute to his broad, abstract understanding of what love means.

The same is true for any abstract concept, from seemingly simple notions such as near and far to more complicated ideas such as empathy, competition, and justice. The more experience we have with these concepts, the better we understand them, both intellectually and emotionally.

The implications of this principle for children with special needs is profound. It suggests that part of what stands between them and fluency with abstraction is a lack of experience. Children with special needs have difficulty with abstraction, in part, because they often lack the rich experiences that would help them understand abstract concepts. We may unwittingly deny children with special needs those important experiences because we believe they can't handle them, because we're unaware of their significance, or because we believe these children need to focus on more structured tasks in order to learn specific practical skills. Whatever the reason, many children do not get the chance to participate in the rich range of emotional experiences that would help them learn to abstract and reason.

Recent clinical experience suggests that when some children with developmental difficulties are given a rich menu of experiences, they can become capable abstract thinkers. Leah, a nine-year-old girl diagnosed as autistic, has made tremendous progress in the last seven years. She is grappling with the idea that her family may move. When asked if she thought she would probably move, instead of answering with a simple, concrete yes or no, she said, "Yes, Dad got a job. When the house gets sold, Dad will go and Mom and I will come afterward." She added that she would feel sad to leave her current home, "but not as sad as when my chickens were taken away." These were sophisticated, abstract answers. They entailed an understanding of the future, of contingencies, and of planning, and they required Leah not only to recognize and talk about her feelings but to compare feelings over time. Leah's parents did not merely tell her the logistics of the move, but they discussed the move with her: its pros and cons, the factors that would determine when and where they would move, their own feelings about moving. They have provided a rich emotional life for their daughter, which involves travel, outings, social occasions, and conversation, as well as responsibilities, including responsibility for pets, about which Leah has strong feelings.

In contrast, consider the case of two young adults, both diagnosed with pervasive developmental disorder, who lived in a group home. Both had good command of concrete skills; they were able to carry on simple conversations, follow simple directions, hold simple, mechanical jobs. Soon after they met in the group home, they fell in love and asked to live together. They were delighted to be granted permission, and shared a room for two months. When they began cohabiting, however, they began arriving late for work. Apparently one of them was slow to get ready, and the other, out of a sense of devotion, was waiting so they could leave together. The group home found an easy solution: the two were sent back to individual rooms. Although this solution was expedient—the angry, unhappy teenagers began getting to work on time—it taught the couple nothing. Worse, it denied them a chance to solve the problem themselves. If these two youngsters had enough intelligence and sense to care for themselves, to hold down jobs, to fall in love and manage a relationship, wouldn't they have had the ability to figure out how to get to work on time? Suppose, instead of separating them, someone in the group home had said, "You need to figure out how to get to work on time. We can help you discuss it if you'd like. If you can't get to work on time we'll have to separate you." They may have solved the problem themselves, and in so doing would have had a challenging experience that would have promoted their abstract thinking. But partly out of concern for their welfare (the home didn't want them to lose their jobs), and partly out of habit (the habit of limiting the opportunities of people with special needs to think and problem solve, inadvertently encouraging them to do things in a rote manner), the home denied them this valuable experience.

You can help your child learn abstract thinking and problem solving.

• *Don't simply tell him what to do, discuss things with him.* Tell him *why* you want him to do something. Help him anticipate the repercussions of his actions, for himself and for others. Discuss the pros and cons. Talk about the ramifications of doing or not doing it. Give him plenty of time to argue his viewpoint, and make sure it's a 50-50 conversation. Give him a chance to practice complex, abstract reasoning.

• *Explore feelings behind viewpoints.* Discuss why certain points of view feel right or are important. Be patient. Use multiple-choice suggestions when necessary, such as, "Do you want to do this for this reason or that reason?"

• *Don't stick to questions to which you know the answer.* You want your child to express an opinion, not just a learned, rote answer. You want to encourage original thinking.

• *Don't solve problems for your child; let her solve them herself, with your help as a coach or brainstorming partner as needed.* If she's bothered by a child at school, ask her for ideas about how to handle the situation. Give her practice with ideas by discussing and comparing alternative solutions. Give examples of your own.

• *Help your child learn about people, places, and ideas.* Don't overload him, but don't limit his experience either. Give him responsibility for pets. Have people over for dinner who include him in the conversation. Make his life rich with experiences, because every one will strengthen his ability to do abstract thinking.

• *Provide experiences suitable to your child's highest developmental level.* Don't talk down to her or simplify her experiences because she sometimes regresses below that level. As she develops, shift your expectations upward.

• *Expose your child to a rich range of activities and encourage his natural interests and abilities.* Provide experiences with music, sports, drama, and art. Watch for his excitement and help him follow it.

HELPING YOUR CHILD BECOME SELF-AWARE

You can also promote abstract thinking in your child by encouraging her self-awareness. By questioning her about her feelings and her behavior, you can help her observe herself, and in the process build a stable, ongoing sense of self.

• When your child says something mean to her brother say, "It looks like you want to be mean! How come?"

• When he wants to play the same game, read the same book, or watch the same video over and over again, comment, "You really like that. What's so great about it?" Your comment will help him pay attention to his own behavior and the feelings that prompt it. If your child becomes defensive and continues to perseverate, ask, "How many times would you like to see this?" This will give him a chance to think about limits. Many children with a realistic sense of numbers will choose something reasonable and stick to it. Others will say something like "a million," in which case you can make each time count for a hundred thousand!

Each time we stop to reflect on our behavior and understand our motives, we learn something about ourselves. The same is true for your child. Each time she notices "I like chocolate ice cream" or "I like watching this videotape because I like to feel scared and then not scared anymore," she learns more about who she is. She forms one more piece of an ongoing stable sense of self.

This approach can also be used to help a child deal with certain behavior or fantasies.

After seeing the movie *Aladdin,* six-year-old Jackie adopted Princess Jasmine as her alter ego. She spent large portions of every day playing Jasmine, answering only to that name, and refusing to do any of the things that Jackie was supposed to do. When her parents asked her to stop, or said, "Jasmine is just pretend," Jackie became more entrenched in the character, ignoring her parents altogether.

"Instead of arguing with her about it," suggested the therapist, "ask her about what she's doing. See if you can find out why she likes Jasmine so much."

"Honey, why do you like being Jasmine so much?" asked Lorraine, Jackie's mother.

Jackie, who was busy being Jasmine, looked at her disdainfully and turned away.

"Jasmine," said her mom, realizing that she'd have to get inside the game in order to reach her daughter, "Jasmine, why are you so special?"

Jackie immediately turned toward her mom. "I'm special because I'm beautiful and I can fly."

"Wow," said her mom, "that must be fun. I'd like to fly."

"Yeah, and I can fly really high and look down and see everybody on the ground." Jackie ran around the room and flapped her arms, showing her mother how she could fly.

"Now you know why she likes it," said the therapist. "See if you can get playful with it. Tease her a little in a playful way."

"I wish I could fly," said Lorraine. "Can Jasmine teach me to fly?"

"No," said Jackie, "only Jasmine can fly. You have to stay on the ground."

"Well, maybe I can be Jasmine, then," suggested her mom.

"No!" barked Jackie quickly. "Only me. Only me can be Jasmine."

"Can't you be Aladdin for a while and let me be Jasmine?"

"No!" Jackie screamed. "I'm Jasmine. You be Aladdin."

"Maybe *I* can be Jasmine," interjected the therapist, smiling mischievously.

Jackie looked at him in surprise. When she saw his smile she began to grin. "No," she said, giggling. "You can't be Jasmine. You're a man."

"Well then why can't your mom be Jasmine? She's a woman."

Jackie looked at her mom, troubled for a moment by this bit of logic. "She too old," she said authoritatively.

Mother and therapist both laughed.

"Okay, I'll be Aladdin for a little while," said Lorraine, "but then let's switch. Don't you think that's fair?"

"No. I get to decide who we are," said Jackie. "And I'm going to be Jasmine and you be Aladdin, and he can be Aladdin, too!" She paused for a moment looking at the two adults, making sure they understood their roles. When they nodded she added, "And if you're good, maybe later you can be Jasmine."

By interacting with Jackie about her preoccupation, her mother and her therapist were able to help her see it with a little more clarity. They helped her articulate why she liked it so much—she liked being able to fly. By the end of the interaction Jackie could acknowledge it was pretend and even negotiate which role each person would play. Rote obsession became creative interaction, which she hadn't been able to do at the beginning. Over the next few days her parents continued to question and kid her about Jasmine—always respectfully, never impatiently—and by a week later her obsession with the character had waned. She still played Jasmine, but came out of the pretend easily and even let other people take the role.

You can use this type of approach to deal with much of your child's repetitive behavior. If he flaps his arms or makes funny noises, for example, join him. Interact by making a game out of it, and if you can, find out why he enjoys doing it. What about it gives him pleasure? Are there other movements that give him equal pleasure? When does he do it? In certain situations or at certain times of day? Ask patiently, not critically. These questions won't be easy to answer and can be explored over many days or weeks, a little bit at a time. When your child is stumped or frustrated, let it go until another occasion. Just talking about the behavior won't eliminate it, but it will help your child become more aware of what he is doing and why he likes to do it. That self-awareness is part of abstract thinking and is the first step toward channeling an activity into more socially acceptable behavior. We talk more about curbing idiosyncratic behavior in Chapter 14.

HELPING YOUR CHILD BECOME AWARE OF, AND COPE WITH, HIS OWN CHALLENGES

At age two Doug had been diagnosed with autistic spectrum disorder. By age eight and a half, after six years of intensive therapy, he had become a thoroughly engaged and engaging little boy. He was bright and talkative, had many friends, and functioned at grade level in a regular school. Although he had completed occupational therapy for motor delays and sensory-reactivity challenges, he still had motor-planning difficulties. His interactive therapist was working to broaden his limited emotional range. His parents finally began to feel that they had come through the wars victorious.

Then, a seemingly new problem emerged. Doug became very emotional. In the space of a day he would go from intense joy to despair, and from rebellious acting out to sullen, uncooperative withdrawal. At school he had begun to throw tantrums, sometimes running from the room when upset. The warm and relatively stable child his parents had come to expect seemed to have vanished.

Along with this volatile behavior, Doug began verbalizing a fantasy. He was an alien from outer space, he announced, and other aliens had put things in his brain that made him behave in funny ways. Because of these implants he was forced to do and say things he didn't intend. Doug's parents tried alternately to ignore and to tease him about the fantasy, but the more they tried the more Doug stood his ground. "No!" he would shout. "It's not a fantasy! It's real!" and then he would run away in anger or dissolve on the floor in tears. His behavior felt to his parents like a frightening regression.

Although Doug claimed to believe his fantasy, he didn't act on it, except for having emotional outbursts. He continued to do his homework, do his chores, play with his friends. His personality was still organized around being realistic and logical; only one piece was caught up in the unrealistic thinking.

Doug's therapist was consoling. "It's not regression," she explained. "It's partially progress. Doug is much more aware now of what he's feeling, and that includes feelings about his body. In a way he's newly aware of how his 'equipment' makes things difficult for him, and that generates a lot of feelings. Think how you would feel. He's angry and frustrated, and embarrassed and sad. At times he hates his body and doesn't trust it. He's felt some level of those feelings in the past, but he's never had the skills before to express them. He hasn't had the range of emotions, and he hasn't had the ideas. It's his new command of feelings and ideas that enables him to be so self-aware, and then to express the range of all he's feeling."

She went on. "Think about his fantasy. It's a perfect metaphor for how he's feeling. He must indeed feel alien, as if some foreign implant was forcing him to behave the way he does. For the first time he's had the intellectual and emotional skills to put that feeling into words."

Doug's parents were relieved to hear that their son was progressing rather than regressing, but they were pained at the cause. Doug had suffered enough because of his "equipment," yet now self-awareness was adding insult to injury.

"Yes, it's difficult," agreed the therapist. "And it can't be avoided. But there's a silver lining in this cloud. If you help Doug work through his sad and angry feelings, he can discover that the body that has given him so much grief is also a source of pride. For he has faced challenges far greater than other children face, and he has overcome many of them."

Doug's parents were partially comforted, and over the next two years they made a diligent effort to help Doug explore and cope with his feelings. They helped Doug elaborate on his feelings instead of getting anxious, annoyed, or avoidant. They helped him verbalize when the alien made him feel alone, sad, angry, or confused. They tried not to become scared or angry when he was withdrawn or irascible, but to remain patient and engage with him. When Doug did something special, his parents reminded him of all the ways he had grown and all the skills he had mastered. They made extra time for floor time so that Doug would have more play-based opportunities to express his fantasies and range of feelings.

When Doug was ten, he built an elaborate space colony in his room using a combination of Legos and other elements he had made himself. One night as he was explaining the operation of the colony to his dad, he introduced the colony's head, the space commander. "You know, Dad," he said, after outlining the commander's numerous responsibilities, "he used to be just a little guy who could hardly do anything."

It seemed like another perfect metaphor.

Doug is typical of some children with special needs who come through these developmental stages. Along with their ability to express feelings and ideas comes self-awareness—a sense of what they can do well and also of what they find difficult. And along with that awareness comes a host of unpleasant feelings. Embarrassment, humiliation, rage, frustration, sadness, disappointment, the desire for power all crowd in on these children, often seemingly in the space of a day. Because their equipment is still somewhat unpredictable, still a little unsteady, their ability to cope with these feelings is uneven. Sometimes they may be able to verbalize their feelings maturely; at other times they may revert to acting them out. Sometimes these feelings are so strong that they cloud a piece of the child's sense of reality, as did Doug's feelings, when he insisted his fantasy was real.

More than anything else, your child needs patience and understanding at this time. Your ability to remain calm and to empathize with what she is feeling will be her greatest tool in learning to handle her feelings herself. Eventually, with your help, she should come to love herself despite her challenges. She will even take pride in those challenges because they have given her a chance to prove herself, to shine, to achieve a very special kind of success. Most important, as she comes to accept all the parts of herself, she can shore up her sense of reality, she can separate what's make-believe from what's real.

Here are some things to keep in mind as your child begins to express these difficult feelings.

• *Listen and empathize.* The feelings may be difficult to hear, and their accompanying behavior may be unpleasant, but your child needs you to be patient and understanding. Don't try to fix the feelings. Don't try to interpret them. Just give your child room to talk.

• *Honor fantasies.* As we saw with Doug, children with developmental disorders often develop fantasies about their lives that seem very real to them. Use your child's fantasy to help him understand and express his feelings. Don't argue over what's real and what's not. If you can discuss your child's fantasies calmly, you will gradually help him put them in perspective. As happens when you talk about a dream, the unreal aspects will gradually become apparent. By listening, empathizing, and asking questions you can help him realize it's a fantasy without ever saying so in words.

• *Let your child deal with her core personality conflicts through pretend play.* Allow disappointment and frustration to emerge in play. Let her play out the different sides of her self.

• *Learn about your child as you help him talk about his feelings.* As you talk with your child about his feelings and his fantasies you will glean valuable insights about his concerns. Later those insights may be helpful. For example, suppose your child tells you that he is afraid he might hurt someone as an alien. Days later, when he is angry at his sister, you notice that he is upset. You might ask, "Do you sometimes worry that you'll get *too* mad at her? Do you worry that it's hard to control yourself?"

• *Consider involving a therapist to help your child cope with her feelings.* If you feel that your child's feelings or fantasies are frightening to her, or if they seem unduly troubling to you, consider taking her to a child therapist. She may benefit from talking about and understanding her feelings. A good empathetic therapist can help her explore those feelings and can help you understand your child. (The senior author's earlier books *Playground Politics* and *The Challenging Child* may also be helpful.)

HELPING YOUR CHILD OPERATE AT
THE TOP OF HER ABILITIES

As children move up the ladder of abstraction they tend to fluctuate. One moment they may be highly abstract, able to hypothesize about a future event, the next moment they may seem wholly concrete, unable to discuss anything but the toy right in front of them. This fluctuation is expected—it's a natural part of learning—but you can help your child move beyond it to the higher levels of abstraction by regularly challenging her to operate at her highest level.

Leah, the nine-year-old girl mentioned earlier, had made tremendous strides since her early diagnosis as autistic. She was warm and related and when challenged was able to use and respond to words logically. However, her ability to talk about her feelings and to form bridges between her ideas still needed work. Unchallenged, she often spoke as if free-associating, spouting ideas without connecting them to each other, and she often answered abstract questions concretely. A teacher or observer might have thought Leah was capable of operating at only a six- or seven-year-old level, although her parents and therapist knew she was able to think and talk as an eight- to ten-year-old. The challenge was to help Leah operate more often at age level.

One day her therapist asked Leah what made her happy.

"My animals," she answered, and then began free-associating about her pets, of which she had many. "My bunnies like cereal," she said, "I feed them Cream of Wheat."

"But why do they make you happy?"

"Cotton is my favorite bunny."

"Does he make you happy?"

"I like to let him out of his cage. Once he hopped in the bathtub."

She was still saying only what came into her mind, without connecting her ideas to those of her therapist. She wasn't reflecting on the question.

"But are you going to tell me how Cotton makes you happy?" the therapist asked, with a twinkle in his eye and an overtly enthusiastic demeanor to try to get her full attention.

This time Leah gave him a sophisticated, abstract answer. "Being able to care for him makes me happy," she said, rising to the challenge with an age-appropriate, or even precocious, response.

Later in the session she said, out of the blue, with a note of alarm in her voice, "Dad didn't lock the car!"

"Why is that important?" the therapist asked.

"One of our geese disappeared," she answered.

"What does that have to do with the car?"

"In Tennessee something got stolen."

The therapist looked confused and wondered, "What does that have to do with the car?"

"Things got stolen from our car in Tennessee."

"Are you worried here?"

"Well, I guess it won't happen here, but if you lived in a bigger city, I guess you'd have to lock your door."

Leah's sophisticated answer suddenly made her earlier statements more sensible. She had been worried about things getting stolen—her goose, things from the car in Tennessee, things from the car here—but she had failed to bridge those ideas either in her mind or in her speech. Unchallenged, her speech had seemed like the free-associative ramblings of a younger child. When challenged, however, she had tied her statements together into a clear, abstract response.

As the conversation continued, Leah talked about Wobbly, her cat, and how Wobbly had disappeared four weeks after giving birth. "I don't know where she is now," she said, "but I'm in charge of the babies. Wobbly left them to me."

"How do you know Wobbly left the babies to you?"

"Well, she knows I'm gentle and would take good care of them." This response sounded logical, although it was not a direct answer to the question. Leah was more answering the question *why* Wobbly left her in charge of the babies. Many children with processing challenges answer questions somewhat indirectly. The therapist decided to try for a more precise reflection on the question.

"How did you *know* Wobbly wanted you to take care of them?" he asked again very gently.

"She knew she wouldn't be a good mother," Leah replied. Again her answer was related, but not a direct answer to the question.

"But how do you actually know Wobbly thought you would be a good mother?" the therapist tried again.

"She knew I was gentle," Leah answered, still not closing the circle.

The therapist then asked the question a different way. "How did you find out that Wobbly thought you would be a good mother? Did you decide that on your own?"

"No, my mom said that I would be good at taking care of the babies."

"Oh," he said, "your mom let you know that Wobbly thought you would be good."

"Yes," Leah said assertively, nodding her head, "Mom told me about Wobbly and how good I would be."

Unchallenged, Leah was unable to completely close the symbolic circle; but when challenged and when the question was rephrased, she was able to provide a more precise comment.

"Leah is capable of operating at this level all the time," the therapist told her parents. "And once she can do that, she can move up to an even higher level. But you need to challenge her to do it. Make sure you always understand her. Don't nod your heads yes and then walk away only partially knowing what she's talking about. Stay with her, and gently and patiently help her make her thinking clear and related to your ideas. It may take 15 minutes for her to answer a question, but each time she does, she'll get a little better at higher-level thinking."

As discussed before, many children require additional practice to gain a skill. If you believe your child can't do something that he can do, you may not give him the practice he needs. If you nod and say "okay," rather than challenge his response, you keep him at that level. On the other hand, if with warmth and a twinkle in your eye, you challenge him a bit more, you provide the needed practice. Many children with special needs remain at more concrete and fragmented levels of thinking although they have the capacity for more organized and abstract work.

MAINTAINING DEVELOPMENTAL PROGRESS

Learning to think logically and abstractly, like most learning, is often a process of two steps forward and one step back. One day your child may be closing 80 percent of her circles and building bridges between ideas while remaining warmly related to you, and then later that same day, she might avoid eye contact, hide under the table, tune out your comments, and throw a tantrum if you try to challenge her. It's easy to be perplexed by such changes in behavior, but it's also important to realize that this broad range of behavior is to be expected when a child has developmental challenges. It may help to think of your child's abilities as a range. Sometimes she operates at the top of her abilities, the top of the range; at other times she operates in the middle or toward the bottom of the range. The goal is not to push her to operate only at her highest level, but rather to move the entire range by degree up the developmental ladder. You want the bottom of the range to rise at the same pace as the top, so that over time both her highest and her lowest abilities are improving.

Even when your child is operating in the middle or toward the bottom of her range, you will encounter important opportunities to help her grow. Each time her abilities slide, you can help her reclimb the developmental ladder, and climbing that ladder will help her become more stable at her most advanced level.

Six-year-old Amy and her father, Jim, were building a Lego castle. Amy was directing Jim to hand her specific pieces and was putting them in place with great care and precision. She was proud of her creation. As she built, she and Jim chatted warmly and logically about the castle and the prince and princess who would live there. Suddenly, as she pressed a Lego piece in place, one whole wall of the castle toppled. Frustrated and angry, Amy grabbed handfuls of Legos and began throwing them across the room, sobbing as she did so.

"Amy, Amy, we can fix it," said Jim, trying to lure her back to the project. But Amy was screaming and throwing Legos in a disorganized way. She had regressed to the level of behavioral discharge—presymbolic, prepretend play, pre–two-way communication.

"Can you find a way to reengage with her?" asked the therapist. "Try using the techniques you used at level one, inserting yourself in her activity in order to get her attention."

Jim watched his daughter for a moment as she hurled a Lego across the room. Then, just as she hurled the next one, he shot out his hand and caught it.

Amy looked at him, startled.

"I got it," he said, smiling, and held up his hand for her to throw another.

She did, and he caught that one, then motioned for her to throw another. She did, and for the next minute or two they engaged in a game of catch during which Amy smiled and giggled.

"Now that she is engaged and interactive, see if you can take her up to the next level," suggested the therapist. "Can you make it more complex?"

Jim looked around the room for a clue. "I know," he said, "I bet we can play basketball with these Legos. Can you throw the basketball into the basket?" and he made a basket with his arms.

Immediately Amy tossed a Lego in.

"Whoa!" he cried. "You're better than Michael Jordan! I'd better move back!" and he backed up several paces.

Amy fired off another shot and missed.

"One point for my team!" sang Jim. "Try again."

He leaned forward as Amy tossed, encircling the Lego with his arms.

Amy grinned.

"One point for Amy!" called Jim. "Try again."

For the next several seconds they played Lego basketball, Amy racking up points with each throw. After her fifth or sixth throw, she walked up to her dad, looked him mischievously in the eye, and dropped the Lego into the basket. "I win," she said, and flashed him a knowing smile.

"Ooh," he said, "you're too smart for me," and he gave her a squeeze.

"That was great," commented the therapist. "Let's see if the stuffed rabbit wants to shoot a basket."

So Jim held the rabbit up, and almost immediately Amy said, "Let's have rabbit jump into the basket." She brought in a more creative level of pretend.

"Now see if you can get some dialogue going," said the therapist.

Jim nodded and thought for a moment. "So, who's your favorite basketball player?" he said. Jim was a big basketball fan and he and Amy often watched games on TV together.

"Shaquille O'Neal," she answered without hesitation.

"Shaquille O'Neal!" cried Jim, making a disdainful face. "He can't even dunk!"

"Yes he can," said Amy assertively. "He's bigger than you."

Jim and the therapist laughed. Amy was back up to her logical level. "Now," the therapist said, "see if she's interested in building with the Legos again, or if she wants to continue with the basketball theme."

Jim opened his eyes wide. "Hey, Shaquille," he said, motioning to Amy, "now that we've thrown these basketballs all over the gym, do you want to build something with them?"

Amy followed his glance around the room and giggled at the sight of Legos everywhere.

"I was thinking maybe we could build a special kind of basket out of Legos."

"That's silly, Daddy," Amy said, laughing. "I want to make a castle."

And together she and Jim rounded up the Legos and began to build a new castle.

By engaging his daughter at the level to which she'd regressed and then slowly helping her move from one level to the next, Jim was able to coax Amy back up the developmental ladder to logical thinking.

Amy regressed because of frustration. Children also regress when they encounter emotions that are uncomfortable. They don't always regress all the way down the ladder, however. They may drop back just one level, temporarily losing the ability to carry on a logical dialogue while they are engaging in rich imaginative play. Or they may drop two levels, to two-way communication, losing the ability to do pretend while remaining gesturally connected to you. They may drop three levels, losing the ability to close gestural circles while still staying warmly engaged with you. Regardless of how many levels your child regresses, your approach should be the same: work where he is. If he's engaged but not closing gestural circles, get involved in whatever he is doing to help him interact with you. If he's closing circles but not doing any make-believe, interact and then try to get some fantasy ideas going. If he's making up dramas but not closing symbolic circles, join the drama and then try to close symbolic circles. Once he's back on track, work him slowly up the ladder until he's where he was before he regressed. This whole process may take half an hour or it may take only minutes. The more often you do this, the better your child will be at reclimbing the developmental ladder. Each time he regresses and works his way back up, he gets better—and faster—at climbing the ladder.

As you help your child maintain developmental progress, remember the guiding principle: emotions drive behavior, and emotions and behavior drive language. If you can build on your child's emotion—by joining her activity or by discussing a favorite topic—you make it far easier for your child to respond. Whenever your child is distracted or unresponsive, whenever you are at a loss as to what to do, follow this principle. *Build on his emotions and join his activity to open a door to interaction.*

It's easy to feel demoralized or even depressed when your child regresses, to think you've done something wrong or that he's lost his top level of functioning. Remember that children can usually retrieve the skills they have lost, and the very process of retrieving skills strengthens them. Each time you help your child reclimb the developmental ladder, you make his skills more stable.

Don't view regression as something to fear. It is actually a blessing in disguise. It gives your child an opportunity to regain his balance when temporarily thrown, a skill he'll need throughout his life.

STRENGTHENING EARLIER STAGES

Throughout this book we've described the different developmental levels sequentially, as if children master each one in order. But life is rarely so neat. Children often move on to higher levels before they fully master lower levels. Much of the time that's okay. A child who is operating at a certain level 50 to 80 percent of the time is usually ready to move to the next level, for his work on the new level will strengthen his earlier abilities. A child who is learning two-way communication, for example, must be able to engage with his parents. By helping him close gestural circles his parents reinforce the work they did on engagement; they are following his lead and using their voices, facial expressions, and body language to get and hold his attention and engagement. Similarly, a child who is learning to develop and express ideas must be able to engage with her parents and do two-way nonverbal communication. In helping her move into the world of make-believe, her parents are reinforcing her engagement with them and also using her gestures to spark ideas and generate further communication. While the parents' focus is on the new stage, they are automatically working on all the earlier stages at the same time. Hence the child has many opportunities to refine the lower skills.

Occasionally, however, despite this ongoing work, children may not fully master a lower stage. They continue to move up the ladder, working on each of the higher stages, while constrictions exist at an earlier level. When that happens, the unmastered levels form weak links in the chain of development. The levels above seem largely in place, but fall apart under stress as if the foundation were too weak to withstand an assault, or the missing skills may leave holes in the child's abilities.

Like many children, five-year-old Beau had a weak link at the first level, the stage of emotional engagement and intimacy. Although he was very verbal and could carry on long and logical conversations, he was somewhat aloof. He rarely looked anyone in the eye and often seemed indifferent to the presence of others. His parents rarely got a sense of warmth from him.

Because Beau had been diagnosed with pervasive developmental disorder and had come a tremendous way in two and a half years of floor time and therapy, it was easy to overlook this slight aloofness. But it had a subtle hampering effect on his abilities. Whereas he could discuss school, dinosaurs, or construction equipment at length, he could not talk or pretend with real creativity. He tended to describe facts. In addition, he couldn't talk about himself or his feelings. When under stress he would break down into tears or tantrums rather than talk about what was troubling him. Even pleasant feelings were difficult for him. In a subtle way Beau was unconnected to his inner core. He lacked a link with important aspects of himself.

To help him deal with this constriction, his parents and therapists actively worked at strengthening their rapport with him. Every activity became an opportunity to engage emotionally with Beau. When he and his dad played catch, Mike would throw the ball right to him so Beau could experience the pleasure of an easy catch. At other times he would try to trick Beau, throwing the ball high, then low, then high, then low and then suddenly changing the pattern. After a few of these sequences Beau would try to trick his dad as well. Soon the two would be laughing and making eye contact, engaged emotionally as well as physically.

When they played knights and soldiers on the carpet, Mike began trying to insert more emotion into the play. Until then their soldier play had always been fairly mechanical, focused on the logistics of the battles rather than on their emotional highs and lows. First Mike tried to increase the pleasure by not only letting his son win the battle, but also being more emotional in acknowledging the victory: "You really got me!" Later on, Mike upped the emotional ante in other ways as well. Instead of letting Beau arrange and rearrange his soldiers into neat columns as they prepared for war, Mike made sneak attacks, charging Beau's battalions before they were ready. Instead of allowing Beau to decide the pace of the action and the outcome of the war, he began savaging Beau's forces, or sacrificing all of his, or bringing in reinforcements at the last minute to turn a battle around. All these techniques were designed to spark Beau's emotions. They did.

Sometimes Beau ranted and raved at his father's actions. Sometimes he threw his soldiers and regressed to lower levels. As Mike helped bring him back to the level of logic, he tried to talk to Beau about his feelings. Often Beau would grow stony and silent and refuse to answer his father's questions, instead fingering his soldiers and trying to restart the play. But additional soothing and warmth always helped. Mike *gradually* introduced more conflict into their play, and over the next several months Beau grew better able to withstand his father's new battle strategies. After a while Beau began to adopt them too, surprising his father with sneak attacks and reinforcements that could wipe out an entire army in one fell swoop. As Beau became more comfortable with themes of assertion, aggression, and warmth, he became more flexible. Five months later the emotional tenor of the battles had broadened, and so had Beau's ability to experience, show, and talk a bit about his feelings.

Meanwhile, his mother made a point of bringing Beau's feelings into conversations. Instead of asking about what he did in kindergarten, she asked what happened during the day that made him happy, mad, or sad. She let him help her cook dinner so they could talk about which foods he liked and which he didn't like. When he complained about going to bed, she didn't just send him up, but helped him discuss his wishes and feelings even if he didn't get his way all the time. At first Beau resisted these conversations and tried to turn them away from feelings and toward more tangible elements. But as months passed he grew better at them. Six months later, Beau could not only talk about his feelings with greater ease, he could also relate much more warmly to the significant people in his life. By noticing a vulnerability and working on it, Beau's parents helped him fill in the missing skills. Their effort made the rest of Beau's development more solid.

HELPING YOUR CHILD TOLERATE FRUSTRATION

One of the greatest challenges to a child's developmental stability is frustration. The most logical child can suddenly become a whining, tantrum-throwing hellion when things don't go his way. Frustration is a very real part of living, and your child, like all children, has to learn to deal with it. He has to learn to wait his turn and to share, and he has to learn that other people's ideas sometimes take precedence over his. These lessons are difficult for every child! But once your child has become logical in his thinking, he is ready to move in this direction. You can help with a three-step process.

1. *Help your child take in and process other people's ideas.* You want your child to get used to hearing and responding to other people's ideas, and

the best way to do this is to provide a lot of practice. Instead of commenting and questioning, provide practice in pretend play by becoming a player with your own ideas and desires. Whenever you play, introduce new ideas within the context of your child's drama. Each time you do so—each time your elephant wanders into his circus, each time your doll asks for soda at the tea party—you're asking your child to take in and process your idea. Each time you foster dialogue instead of simply listening to your child, you are helping him take in and process your ideas. Awareness that other people have desires and goals is one of the first steps in learning to tolerate frustration.

2. *Help your child grapple with your ideas.* It's not enough for your child to hear your ideas; she also has to pay attention and respond to them. You can help her through gentle but persistent prompting. "Wait a minute! You didn't answer my question!" "Waiter! I said I wanted milk with my lunch!" "Look! Mr. Elephant came to join the circus. He wants to know what to do!" By staying inside the game and reminding your child that you need an answer, you can help her get used to responding to someone else's needs.

3. *Help your child accept your ideas as well as his own.* After having had his own way for a long time, it may be hard for your child to learn to compromise, but compromise is an important skill. Remind your child frequently that other people's ideas count too. In pretend play, when he's directing the lions, have your lion get stubborn. "I don't want to go through the hoop; I want to jump on the trampoline!" Stay within the drama, but be obstinate. Ask why things always have to go your child's way. Pretend you're another child and act suitably uncompromising. Little by little your child will loosen the controls.

You can also foster this skill in your daily interactions. If your child always wants to put on his left shoe first, say, "Come on, can't you put on the right shoe first?" When he wants a drink, try, "Why do you always have to have the big glass? Can't you have the small glass today?" Do it playfully, with a big smile on your face, so he knows you're not being mean. He may resist anyway. He may even throw a tantrum—and if he does you'll soothe him and help him calm down. But the more you negotiate these little encounters, the more flexible he'll become. Do you have to negotiate all the time? Yes. Because your child needs to learn that he can't rule every encounter, and this is the stage at which he's ready to learn that.

While you are working on these steps with your child, you also want to give her practice with her peers. Be involved in her play dates. If you hear wrangling over who will go first, who will hold the fire truck, or how the tower will be built, and your child insists that things go her way, step in and remind her that that isn't always possible. "You're not being fair to John," you can say. "How about sharing that fire truck? How about taking turns?" Your child is likely to resist; you may have to soothe her before she can continue playing; but you're teaching her a valuable life skill, which she needs to function in the world.

To make this learning tolerable, step in infrequently at first, then gradually increase the number of times you become involved. Rehearse with your child before her friend comes over: "John is coming over and he may not always want to play the way you do. How do you think you'll feel when that happens?" Help her anticipate how she'll feel and how she normally responds. Then talk through other responses that might work better. Plan strategies she can use for negotiating a conflict, such as first . . . next, now . . . later, and if . . . then: "We'll do your game first, my game next"; "We'll go outside now and play inside later"; "If we do what you want now, then we should do what I want later." Practice doing "eeny meeny miney moe" and flipping a coin as means to make decisions. These sessions will also help her prepare for the eventuality of losing. You can even play out the scenario ahead of time. One parent can play the guest, the other can be your child's coach, and together you can rehearse some positive ways to handle the situation. Then, when the friend actually comes over, have one parent there to help your child handle any difficulties that arise.

Once you've started helping your child tolerate frustration with his peers, you can begin helping him handle difficult tasks. Tying his shoes, reading, throwing a ball—whatever tasks your child finds challenging can be approached in the same way. Talk about the task ahead of time, help him anticipate how he'll feel and how he normally responds, then talk through alternative responses that might be more productive. As much as possible try to make the difficult task fun. Chances are, if your child doesn't like doing something it's because it doesn't feel good—just as throwing a ball with your nondominant hand feels awkward and frustrating to you so that you want to stop fairly quickly; to make you want to keep throwing you need an external stimulus that makes the throwing fun, a target to aim at or a kiss each time you throw. Similarly, you can motivate your child to pursue a difficult task by thinking of some way to make the activity fun.

The more you help your child handle difficulties and frustrations, the more flexible she will become. This is a gradual process—it happens over a period of years—and through it you have to be flexible yourself. You have to be extra soothing and nurturing as your child bumps up against frequent frustration. As you expect more of her, you want to increase both your patience and your floor time.

USING PRACTICE TO HELP YOUR CHILD
MASTER NEW ABILITIES

Over the course of your child's development, particularly as he masters the early stages—and really as a result of this mastery—you will face new challenges. As your child improves, he graduates to higher rungs of the developmental ladder. To the degree that sequencing or processing problems remain, however, he will need extra practice in some of these newer, more advanced skills. As he may not be able to practice them completely on his own, you may need to create opportunities for this extra practice to occur. Your guiding principle is to create opportunities for extra practice of the basic skill, rather than a specific task.

For example, imagine your child wants her own way all the time when she plays with her peers and is demanding and impulsive when she doesn't get it. The specific task at hand is to teach her to share with her peers. So, when she is with her peers you might insist that she take turns. This approach will undoubtedly help somewhat. But it would be more helpful to build a more fundamental skill that goes beyond just sharing with peers. It would be more helpful to teach her not to be so self-centered and think only of herself in a variety of situations, but to take other people's needs into account. This is the broader category of which sharing with peers is a part. Each day brings hundreds of such opportunities for practicing this skill. At home it may be as simple as passing the bread during dinner, sharing a cookie, or letting somebody else go first to the bathroom. You can probably identify 10 or 15 situations each day in which you are teaching your child to consider the needs of another person as well as her own and to balance the two.

Here is another example. A parent is on the phone, and her child wants to speak to her right away. A year earlier, when the child was still improving his language, his parents would have dropped everything—the phone call—to hear those wonderful words coming from his mouth. Now, though, the child is a chatterbox, he has not only mastered a lot of words, but he uses them all the time. Learning language is no longer an issue. The issues now are fine-tuning the use of language and, more important, becoming more understanding of other people. The child's mother might say deliberately, "You have to wait. I'm talking to Grandma. Don't you think Grandma wants to finish the conversation?" "Mommy, I need you to get that cookie now," he'll reply.

"Sh, sweetheart, wait."

"Mommy, now."

"Wait. How does Grandmother feel if I don't finish my conversation with her?"

"I don't care about Grandmother."

"Maybe you should talk to her and see whether she wants to give permission for me to help you with the cookies or whether she needs to finish telling me something."

"I don't want to talk to Grandma. Get me the cookie now."

"Sweetheart, you have to wait a little bit more and I'll get that cookie for you. I have to finish with Grandma because she has something very important to tell me."

And so on. Although this exchange has indeed interrupted the mother's conversation, by not giving in to the child's desire to have a cookie right away and by emphasizing that he has to be patient and wait because his grandmother has needs that may be more important than his at the moment, the mother is teaching her child a valuable lesson. He's getting frustrated, he may be getting angry, but he is mastering a fundamental ability—he is learning to wait when his needs are not met immediately. Even though he has distracted his mother from what she was doing, she did not give in to him quickly and, instead, substituted dialogue and debate for meeting his immediate needs.

During the course of a day you will encounter many such opportunities to teach your child to be considerate. You will pay the price of being distracted from what you are doing, but it will be worth it.

Some children with special needs don't respect the needs of others for personal space and may climb on top of them or speak while they are speaking. Children who have problems with auditory or visual-spatial processing or with motor planning have difficulty judging spatial relationships, such as distance, and modulating, regulating, or controlling their own needs. Particularly as language comes in and their cleverness begins to emerge, they tend to be more demanding and seem to lack good social judgment. In this situation, again, it is important not just to teach the task at hand—"Stand three feet rather than six inches away from a person"—but rather to teach the broader category of reading social nuances. And there is only one way to master this broader challenge: children need lots of interactive experiences with a variety of people, especially with peers, and they need a lot of feedback. Children can begin to notice people moving away when they get too close, gesturing to them to distance themselves, raising their voices to push away the child who is talking too loudly. Children who have trouble modulating their behavior and activity and who are intrusive can benefit from doing structured modulation exercises: deliberately talking in a loud, then soft, then in-between voice; running fast and slowly; playing high-five games with hard, medium, soft, and very soft touches. In this way children can learn to modulate their emotions, voice, and behavior rather than take an all-or-nothing approach.

It is all too common to become discouraged when, with the help of your heroic efforts, your child has learned to speak and relate warmly to others, is engaged, warm, often sweet, and intimate as well as highly creative, bright, and verbal and in that sense seems just like any other child, but still has problems modulating his voice or behavior, or remains self-centered, or has some other continuing issues. At this point it is easy to lose sight of the tremendous pride you should take in your role in helping your promising and creative child come so far, and instead to picture a glass that's half empty, focusing on the relatively insignificant challenges remaining. Rather than become discouraged, you can make use of the same principles that helped you help your child in the first place, that is, create practice opportunities for learning new skills.

Another issue is illustrated by an interchange between a therapist and the mother of a child with special needs. The child had done extremely well and was creative, highly intelligent, and warm, but had problems such as those we've been discussing, which his mother found frustrating and annoying. To put these problems in perspective, the therapist asked the mother to compare her child with herself and her husband in terms of respecting other people's needs, being demanding, reading subtle social signals, and so forth. Although the mother did not acknowledge that she had any challenges in these areas, she readily confessed, "Well, he's not as bad as my husband," and was able to start laughing and appreciate things from a different angle. She still wanted to help her child fine-tune his abilities, but the recognition that her child's behavior was no worse than her husband's helped her feel less frustrated; she realized that sometimes it can be hard to teach a child subtle skills when some of these skills are not in evidence in the family. It is not unusual for a parent to focus on a distressing aspect of his child's behavior when the parent has a similar difficulty but does not fully acknowledge it.

A variety of the challenges that arise in many families are actually a testament to the child's successful mastery of earlier levels. The developmental ladder goes right through adolescence, into adulthood, middle age, and old age. If and when it stops—which means the challenges stop—at the latter stages of the aging process, you will want your child to be able to look back on a full and rich life. Therefore, you should welcome the challenges of helping him climb the developmental ladder. These challenges are a part of normal growth; and if your child needs extra practice in certain areas, that, too, is a part of the lifelong process of learning.

ENCOURAGING LOGICAL THINKING

As you help your child increase his logical understanding of the world, keep in mind the following suggestions:

• *Don't ask long strings of questions.* As your child begins to talk logically it's tempting to pose long strings of questions: "What color is the car?" "Where is it going?" "How fast can it go?" There is nothing wrong with these questions—each one can open up a dialogue—but when asked relentlessly, followed by one- or two-word answers, the conversation takes on a mechanical, singsong quality that does little to help your child build bridges between ideas. Try to pick a theme that has emotional meaning for your child (such as likes and dislikes or favorite things) and follow it, extending each line of discussion as far as you can. This activity gives your child practice thinking rather than merely responding.

• *Don't overscript your child's dialogue.* When your child has trouble with abstract questions, you may be tempted to simplify her task by subtly scripting her answers—asking yes-or-no questions, leaving only one or two words to fill in, creating familiar routines that always elicit the same response. A good rule of thumb is that if your child's answers don't frequently surprise you or if you have a correct answer in mind, you are probably overscripting. Open up your dialogue. Introduce new subjects. Only that way will she truly learn to *think*.

• *Don't overstructure your interactions.* You want to encourage spontaneity and creativity in your child, and you'll only do that if you give him room to react in open-ended ways. Avoid playing structured games (games that are played the same way over and over again). If your child insists on playing Candyland, change the rules or have your game piece forget where it was going and ask his to remind you. Use the context of the game to create spontaneous interaction.

TAILORING FLOOR TIME TO YOUR CHILD'S INDIVIDUAL DIFFERENCES

As you work with your child to help him become a more logical and abstract thinker, take into account his sensory reactivity, his way of processing sensation, and his motor patterns.

If Your Child Has Auditory-Processing Difficulties

If your child has trouble with auditory processing, your biggest challenge will be getting her to close symbolic circles. Since she now has a rich inner world of ideas, she may tune you out in favor of that world. You can take steps to counter this tendency.

• *Back up your words with a lot of animation and gestures.* Your lively manner will help get and hold her attention.

• *Avoid the trap of parallel conversation.* Don't simply empathize with her words and actions; interact in a way that inspires response.

• *Insist on getting 80 percent of circles closed.* If your child doesn't answer your question the first time, try again. If she still doesn't answer, simplify it, make it multiple choice. Be patiently persistent until she gets the circle closed.

• *Offer rich experiences in visual processing.*

Jimmy always greeted people by saying, "Say, 'Hi, Jimmy,' " telling the other person what to say to him. He would go on to tell them how to answer his questions, too. Jimmy understood a lot, but when presented with information auditorily, he depended on scripts or visual support to be sure he comprehended the words. He had learned to express social scripts, and to be sure he understood what was said back to him, he ordered others to follow the same scripts. This behavior made Jimmy's abilities appear limited, and he was offered fewer and more structured experiences from which to learn.

His response to a nonverbal, abstract-thinking task in which he had to copy a block design was therefore surprising. Jimmy looked at the design for a while, analyzed the different parts, then took a set of blocks and put it together quickly and deliberately. He was given more designs and continued to demonstrate strong analytic and synthesizing abilities when he could use his visual-spatial strengths to express them. The discovery of Jimmy's abilities had important implications for his educational program.

The more you challenge your child to close circles of communication, the more accustomed he will become to having two-way symbolic dialogues and the more his auditory processing will improve. And the more experience you can give your child in visualizing information, in picturing problems, the less difficulty his auditory challenges will cause. A system called Lindamood-Bell, developed by Pat Lindamood and Nancy Bell, has been used by many parents to help enhance their child's visualization skills.[1]

If Your Child Has Visual-Spatial Processing Difficulties

If your child has challenges with visual-spatial processing, his world, and therefore his ideas, may be fragmented, because visual-spatial abilities help children see the big picture and put the pieces of their world together. He may be more likely than other children to jump abruptly from one idea to the next without forming logical bridges between them. Your job is to help him see where he changed ideas and inspire him to form the bridge. "We were talking about the car, and now you're talking about the sky. Which do you want to talk about?" You need to help him link his thoughts.

Children with visual-spatial processing challenges also have a hard time with visual problem solving. Doing puzzles, finding lost or hidden objects, locating the bathroom in an unfamiliar house can all be daunting tasks. You can help your child with these challenges by giving him lots of practice. Look for the red sock in the drawer together, or the blue book on the shelf, or the fire truck in the toy box. When visiting a friend's house make a point of hunting together for different rooms. Play hide-and-seek or hide the bunny and have your dolls hide from his doll in pretend. As you do all these things together, talk about them. Ask, "Are we going forward or backward? Left or right? Up or down?" "Do you think we'll find the bathroom soon? I hope so!" "When did we have the fire truck last? Do you remember?" Use all your visual searches as conversation starters so that you can keep up a two-way symbolic dialogue while you practice visual-spatial skills.

If Your Child Has Motor-Planning Difficulties

If your child has trouble with motor-planning challenges she may have trouble sequencing her behavior. As a result, many of her actions, in play and in real life, may be fragmented. She may jump abruptly from putting a figure in the dollhouse to feeding milk to her doll, because she had difficulty completing the earlier motor action. Your job is to bring her back to the first action and creatively, within the drama, help her complete it.

If your child has motor-planning or visual-spatial processing problems she may have trouble with games because games require sequencing. Games that involve the body (such as musical chairs), that require taking turns, and that have three or four steps are particularly difficult. Precisely because they are challenging, though, these games are beneficial; they give your child a lot of practice in weak areas. You can help her by using words and gestures to talk her through them. Play slowly, verbally describing everything she's supposed to do and using hand signals and body language to illustrate the required movements.

Do the same in pretend-play situations in which your child may have trouble with sequencing. If her doll is looking for your doll, for example, she may have trouble coordinating the movements required to search, especially if she has to search in more than one place. Give her lots of practice by introducing mazes, hide-and-seek, and follow-the-leader activities into your pretend play.

Difficulty with sequencing sometimes hinders a child's ability to perform social functions and deal smoothly with complex social situations. Simply greeting a person involves making eye contact, holding out a hand, smiling, and saying "hello"—a complex string of actions. Working a crowd at an adult party is especially challenging as it involves so many quick, automatic social sequences. Give your child lots of practice with social skills, moving gradually from simple to more complex.

If Your Child Is Underreactive and Withdrawn

If your child is underreactive and withdrawn, you'll need to put a lot of energy into getting a dialogue going. Lots of sensory input and physical movement will help him tune in and close symbolic circles. Build lots of movement into your play. Roughhousing, chase games, follow the leader, building forts and mountains—all these activities will provide plenty of opportunities for dialogue and will keep his attention focused. When he doesn't respond to something you say, prod him energetically. "You didn't answer my question!" Raise your voice (playfully, not meanly), wave your arms, run over and put your face near his. Use your whole body as well as your voice to grab his attention to get those circles closed.

At the same time, remember that your child may have some areas of oversensitivity. Perhaps light touch, bright colors, or certain sounds make him uncomfortable, especially if they are unexpected. Try to avoid sensations that make him uncomfortable and warn him that you'll be coming toward him by giving him cues or signals ahead of time.

Keep these principles in mind:

- Use a lot of animation in your voice and gestures.

- Use a lot of physical action and sensory input in your play.

- Make your questions and comments very clear.

- Prepare your child for what you will do next.

If Your Child Is Underreactive and Distractible

If your child is underreactive, active, and distractible, she will crave sensory experience. If you use a lot of sensory input in your play you'll keep her attention and help her close symbolic circles. But because she craves stimulation she is apt to overdo it and to lose control. You can teach your child self-control by building modulation into your games. When you're playing chase, say, "I'm chasing you fast. Now I'm going to chase you slowly," so that she learns to move at different speeds. When you wrestle, say, "First let's wrestle hard. Now let's wrestle soft," so she learns that she can move her body in different ways. When you have jumping contests, say, "First let's jump high, then let's jump low," so she learns she can control the way her body jumps. When you sing together, say, "Let's sing this song loudly, but let's sing the next song in a whisper," so she learns she can modulate the sound of her voice. Modulate in more and more gradual ways over time.

As your child grows more comfortable with symbols, make up symbols that will remind her to slow down, or speak more softly, or stop running—perhaps hand signs, facial gestures, or vocal sounds. Incorporate these symbols into your play.

As you play these games, talk about what you're doing. Keep up a running dialogue about your activities. Which does she like better, wrestling hard or wrestling soft? Whose doll jumps higher? Whose jumps lower? Which song is her favorite? Which does she like least? When her needs for sensory experience are being met she is best able to close symbolic circles, so use any gross-motor play as an opportunity for conversation.

If Your Child Is Overreactive and Avoidant

If your child is overreactive and avoidant he easily becomes overloaded, and when overloaded will assertively avoid you. Your challenge is to engage him and keep him engaged. Earlier you wanted to lure him into two-way gestural communication and pretend play. Now your emphasis is on sustaining logical conversations. Your main tool is still playful obstruction, inserting yourself between your child and his interest in order to engage him. But now, once he's engaged, you want to be verbally obstructive; you want to insert yourself verbally to get him to close as many symbolic circles as possible.

> • When your child turns away and starts playing with his car, put your car in front of his and say, "Road closed!" When he protests, ask, "Why should I open the road?" "Because you want me to? But I don't want to!" "You still want me to? Well, what will you give me if I open it?" Keep challenging his answers to keep the circles going. Don't frustrate him for too long; after a few circles go ahead and open the road, but then look for another avenue to verbally challenge him. "Hey, your car's going too fast for this road!" Or, "This road doesn't go to Grandma's house. You're on the wrong road." Then turn each of his answers into an opportunity to open and close more circles.

As long as you stick with your child's interest, you should be able to lure him into dialogue.

If Your Child Is Overreactive and Distractible

If your child is overreactive and distractible, she, too, gets overloaded easily; she protects herself by moving quickly from one thing—whether it's an idea or a behavior—to the next. Your challenge is double: you want to help her stick with her ideas by closing as many circles as possible before moving to a new one, and you want to help her build logical bridges between her ideas. Be calm and comforting, talking soothingly about whatever interests her.

• Keep the conversation going.

• Ask your child to clarify things she's said so that you know exactly what she meant.

• When your child jumps to a new idea, bring her back: "Wait, I'm confused, we were talking about A, but now we're talking about B."

• Be soothing when you challenge your child.

• Help your child recognize her excitement as well as what she does when she's excited.

Be careful to avoid sensations that might overload your child: loud noises, very animated facial gestures, quick movements, light touch. Appeal to her sensory preferences to help her stay organized.

Because your child is sensitive to sensory input, she is likely to be cautious, avoiding experiences because she fears they'll overload her. You can help her become less cautious and more assertive by encouraging her use of ideas. Be sure to pick up on the themes she suggests rather than suggesting your own. Give her lots of room to experiment—with new ideas as well as new behaviors—and support her efforts to branch out. If you keep your voice and behavior warm and supportive, she will grow increasingly confident about her ability to try new things. Take special pride in her assertiveness and create opportunities in which she can be the assertive leader.

RULES OF THUMB FOR DOING FLOOR TIME THROUGH THE DEVELOPMENTAL STAGES

• Tune in to your child's current developmental level and gradually help him work up to his highest level.

• Identify your child's individual differences and tailor your interaction to them.

• Follow your child's lead; look for ways to interact with her around the activity she's already doing. Let her take the initiative often.

• Work to increase the number and complexity of your circles of communication.

• Work to increase the depth and range of your child's emotions.

• Use your child's natural interests and motivation as tools to help you close circles.

• When necessary, be playfully obstructive to create interaction.

STAGES IN PROGRESS: A SUMMARY

No one can accurately predict the course of a child's progress, for each child is unique. But one pattern occurs repeatedly in some children whose treatment takes the developmental approach. Although this pattern is most frequently seen in children diagnosed with autistic spectrum disorders, it is seen with many other developmental problems as well.

Often the child starts out withdrawn, avoidant, and aimless. But as parents, caregivers, educators, and therapists draw him into engagement, focus, and concentration, he begins to use minimal gestures. Bit by bit, simple circles of communication get opened and closed. Initially, the circles are opened and closed in a reactive way; the child reacts to a gesture of the adult rather than initiating an interaction on his own. Gradually the child's initiative takes over, particularly if his parents are careful to follow his lead, and simple gestures give way to more complex ones.

As interactive gestures become more routine, the child may begin to develop more detail and subtlety in his facial expressions. For the first time he may use the expressions of his parents! This is a significant step in the development of his sense of self.

As the child moves from complex gestures to symbolization, he begins to use ideas and perhaps even words to stand for concrete objects. Instead of pointing to the food he may be able to rub his tummy and say, "Eat." Instead of banging the puppet on the floor, he may put it on his hand. This capacity to use symbols is at first fragmented—it may be there one day but not the next—as the child's comfort with symbols slowly grows.

Gradually the ability to symbolize becomes more routine, and then comes a stage that is sometimes surprising. The child seems to be so excited by his new abilities that he begins to talk nonstop. He may become needy or clingy, as if he's discovered that the human world is a great place and he doesn't want to lose it. He may chitchat endlessly—only the chitchat is illogical; it consists of little islands of disconnected thoughts rather than of complete and organized thoughts. Bridges—between the child's own thoughts, and between his thoughts and yours—are missing.

After the child goes through this driven stage, the intensity often evens out. His gestures and emotions, as well as his use of words, become calmer and more adaptive, and gradually he becomes more capable of organized thought. Even now, however, the child's thinking may tend to be based on his own imagination; he still has more difficulty receiving information from others than listening to his own ideas. During this phase it is important for parents, caregivers, educators, and therapists to help the child open and close symbolic circles so that he can build on other people's information instead of developing more and more idiosyncratic thinking. The more he is helped to respond to the ideas and feelings of others, the more flexible he becomes.

If your child has reached only some of these early stages, is engaged warmly, and is gesturally interactive but is having difficulty becoming symbolic, you can use other methods to help him go further. These are discussed in Chapter 18.

NOTE

1. For further information on the Lindamood-Bell learning processes, call 1-800-233-1819.

13

Strengthening Biologically Based Processing Abilities

We have described ways to use interactions to strengthen attention and regulation, engagement, and nonverbal communication and the use of ideas, as well as the capacity for emotional thinking. In this chapter, we present additional exercises to strengthen self-regulation, auditory processing, visual-spatial processing, and motor planning and sequencing. These capacities allow children to take in, process, and comprehend information and to plan and execute actions as well as thought processes. They provide important building blocks that, together with the types of interactions we have been describing, enable a child to move up the developmental ladder and attempt to master the six milestones.

Speech therapists, occupational therapists, physical therapists, special educators, and others also work on these important aspects of the child's nervous system.

SELF-REGULATION

To strengthen your child's ability to modulate sensory input, achieve states of calm, and focus attention, offer him several chances throughout the day to have 15 or 20 minutes of jumping; running or changing directions; swinging and spinning; deep tactile pressure, such as deep massage; and perceptual motor exercises, which involve looking and reaching or listening and reaching, when possible reaching past the midline of his body. A mattress, a small trampoline a few inches above the floor, and indoor and outdoor swings are useful pieces of equipment for such exercises. You can also take your child by the hands and help him swing around.

Perceptual motor games can be fun for your child if they involve an object, such as a special ball, doll, or action figure, in which she is especially interested. Have her reach first right, then left, and then across the midline to get what she wants. You can also tie a ball to a string and move it back and forth while your child tries to grab it on the left, on the right, and then in the middle. If your child's motor abilities are more advanced, have her catch when the ball is thrown to the left, right, and middle, or have her try to bat the ball with a tennis racket or a bat. If your child is hard to motivate, give her a Nerf bat and see if she can hit your hand before you move it away, or bang the bat to the right, left, and middle.

Physical activity of almost any kind that causes your child to deal with sensory experience and plan motor actions will support the development of her nervous system. Try to integrate these workouts with the developmental level at which your child is operating. If your child is already using imagination and words, create make-believe dramas in which you're flying on an airplane, you're underwater explorers, you're jumping higher than Michael Jordan, you're astronauts discovering new worlds, or you're sailors defeating evil pirates. If your child is not yet imaginative or using words but is just learning to be intentional and purposeful, help him communicate nonverbally with gestures to indicate whether he wants to go faster or slower or stop or go. Challenge your child to direct the activity and action. Most children love spinning and being held high and are willing to gesture and even use some sounds to get their favorite movement patterns.

You can also help your child regulate her sensory and motor patterns by playing games that focus on modulating activity and experience. For example, have your child jump as fast as she can, then jump at a medium pace, and then jump very, very slowly, almost in slow motion, or ask her to run from fast to slow. Play a high-five game in which she slaps as quickly as she can, then medium slowly, and then super slowly. Your child can direct you to spin her at fast, slow, or medium speeds, or you can play an airplane game and she can tell you how fast to fly.

As your child moves his motor and sensory systems through different levels of activity, he learns to be in charge of his own sensory and motor experiences; he also learns self-regulation. If he can make his legs go fast or slowly, he is learning how to master his body as well as experiencing different levels of activity. The two together will enable him to slow down, focus, and concentrate as well as speed up and get excited. These exercises will help your child self-regulate and shift to a medium or even slow speed when he becomes overexcited. These experiences are especially important for active or distractible children, as they help regulate attention and activity.

Many of us take these capacities for granted because our nervous systems function so effortlessly. But many adults and children need extra practice in self-regulation and modulation. Many people feel anxious when they feel out of control, and their anxiety stirs even greater levels of activity or sometimes greater levels of passivity and tuning out, neither of which contributes to the state of calm, focused attention that comes with an optimal level of self-regulation.

Children have a great deal of difficulty coping with their own tendencies to be over- or undersensitive to sensations in each modality. As we've discussed, if your child is underreactive, you have to generate a great deal of affect through the different sensory modalities to pull your child into interacting, then help your child focus and attend. If your child is oversensitive, you need to combine soothing activities with gradual exposure to a reasonable range of sensory input. You begin by making your child relaxed and comfortable (e.g., talking in slow, low tones rather than in high, fast tones). As you help your child learn to be a self-soother through lots of soothing activities, including rocking, deep tactile pressure, and your child's own ability to coordinate her motor system more effectively, you can begin very slowly and gradually to expose her to a larger range of auditory or visual input, always with soothing activities available to help her reorganize and master the experiences at hand. It's beneficial for your child to be the regulator of these experiences, turning the radio to be loud, soft, or medium, for example. You can make a game in which your child can regulate the intensity of light by using a dimmer switch or make sounds louder or softer or emphasize the bass or the treble. You may need to help your child initially, especially if he overshoots the mark and frightens himself with a too-loud sound. Put your hands and his on the dial so that he can gradually be exposed to greater challenges as he learns better tactics to stay soothed and organized.

As your child's self-regulation capacity and sense of mastery over his body become stronger, the degree and ease to which he experiences out-of-control anxiety often diminishes.

AUDITORY AND VISUAL PROCESSING

A variety of games, both simple and complex, focus on processing and comprehending visual and auditory information and connecting the information with the ability to plan and sequence actions. For example, using an animated and expectant tone of voice when you're speaking, to hold your child's attention for four seconds, then for six seconds, improves his ability to take in sound. The rhythm of your voice in terms of its degree of animation and expectation may strengthen your child's attention, particularly if tailored to your child's preferences (louder, softer, slower, or faster rhythms, for example). Build expectation into the rhythm so that your child's attention is focused, much as a good speaker keeps his audience awake.

In much the same way, visual animation can increase the amount of visual focus and attention your child is able to mobilize. Again, tailor the stimuli to your child's nervous system in terms of lights, colors, rapid changes versus slow changes, and so on. You want to find the types of visual experiences that will mobilize and maintain your child's visual attention.

Both auditory and visual attention can be practiced most readily when connected with actions or motor patterns that give your child what he enjoys or wants. For example, when your child is able to get his favorite toy or cookie from a box, after he listens to some noises that tell him where it is, or by following visual cues, his interest may increase. You can start by having a cookie in a simple music box. A visual cue could be a flashlight flashing in the direction of the box or a visual design that is a giveaway or a picture of a cookie on the box (which is among other boxes with no pictures or with other pictures).

In these games, both the auditory and the visual cues can gradually become more complex, as in the old hot-cold game, when you say to the child, "You're getting hotter, hotter, hotter," if your child is approaching the hidden object and "Colder, colder, colder," if he's moving farther away. If your child is preverbal, but motivated to try to find an object he desires, you can use natural sounds that might have words associated with them. Your child might not understand at first, but eventually he will pick up the rhythm of your voice. You might utter an excited, "You're getting closer, closer, closer," conveying with the rhythm of your voice that your child is on the right track. A "no-o-o-o, no-o-o-o, uh, uh," in a slower rhythm, conveys that he is going in the wrong direction. After a few times associating faster sound sequences with getting closer to the object and slower ones with getting farther away, your child might abstract the general principle and begin using your voice as a kind of guidance system, which helps focus on the auditory processing. If your child is verbal, you can give him verbal cues, starting with simple ones and slowly offering more complicated cues, making a treasure-hunt game.

For visual cues, you could provide your child with two or three pictures arranged out of sequence. When pieced together in a sequence that makes sense the pictures would tell your child where to find the hidden object.

As your child becomes more capable, you can provide verbal directions involving two or three steps; following such directions to find hidden objects will help your child's motor planning and sequencing. Similarly, you could develop two- or three-step visual sequences, using pictures or other visual cues as well as, eventually, words for early readers. For all these activities, from the simplest to the most complicated, the key to making them work is to have a highly motivating payoff.

In addition to games that work on auditory or visual-spatial processing, you want to offer activities that involve these systems together as both provide cues to actions that will bring your child a special reward. These search games can be expanded to include both auditory and visual cues, which your child needs to integrate in order to locate the box; for example, an auditory instruction and a visual instruction (pictures) added together will tell your child where the box is. At a simpler level, the hidden box may make some sounds and may be brightly colored or have flashing lights to help your child find it.

MOTOR PLANNING AND SEQUENCING

Even more challenging than working on sensory modulation and sensory processing is helping children with their motor planning and sequencing. As discussed earlier, many children have a hard time learning to plan their actions and, later on, to sequence their ideas. For a child who cannot sequence even simple actions, getting his hand to his mouth for comfort is a significant challenge; figuring out how to go to the door to open it is an even more significant challenge. When a child has a hard time executing even a one- or two-step action pattern, getting his basic needs met (for affection, food, or safety) is not at all an easy matter. Difficulty with motor planning accounts for a good deal of the repetitive and aimless patterns we see in some children with special needs.

Some activities you can do at home to bolster this ability involve strengthening muscle tone if your child has low muscle tone by playing games that entail your child's using extensor muscles. For example, running and changing directions requires your child to push off and use her extensor rather than her flexor muscles (which are used when she is in the fetal position, for example). Or you could play airplane; your child wraps her legs around your waist and faces the floor, putting her hands out, while you hold her at the waist and turn her around like an airplane. To hold her body out and erect your child is using lots of extensor tone. She could lie on the floor on her tummy with her back arched and rock like a boat, or you could hold her up in the air with your hands on her tummy while she arches her back, or you could try wheelbarrow walking; all these activities support extensor tone.

Next, try very simple one- and two-step motor patterns, in which your child has to solve a problem. Here again, the key is motivation. For example, take an object your child wants and place it at the other end of an obstacle course. At first, the obstacle course may be as uninvolved as opening a door. This one-step motor planning may be well within your child's capacity but still require practice. In the next step, your child may have to crawl over a barrier made from the cushions of a couch and then open a door to get her desired object. Eventually, the obstacle course can include four or five steps that involve crawling through, around, and over things, opening or closing doors, and reaching high or low. Sometimes the sequencing challenge is at a very basic level. Consider the following example of helping a child go from solving a motor-planning problem that consists of one step to solving a problem involving two steps.

Susan could search under the rug for her M&M bottle, but as soon as her mother hid the M&M bottle in a little house and put the house under the rug, Susan got confused and looked elsewhere. Her mom kept showing her that the bottle was in the house and rehiding the house and finally Susan solved a two-step problem. Later on, as Susan was practicing using her words to ask for a car, her mother said, "Oh, car going into garage and then garage hiding under rug." Soon Susan was asking for "car," and searching for the car in the garage under the rug.

You can help your child advance from one-step to two-step and three-step problem solving by

• increasing her affect or desire by, for example, hiding a favorite cookie, candy, a toy, or her passion of the moment; and

• setting up motor and spatial challenges that she can solve, gradually adding a more difficult task (e.g., hide an object in your hand, then under the rug, and keep showing it to your child until she goes after it).

Throughout this book we have emphasized the importance of affect or desire in giving direction to actions and meaning to words and concepts. This basic principle is never more important than when your child is practicing motor planning and sequencing. By its very nature, motor planning is not a repetitive action, but an action that is created to enable a child to meet a need or desire, to adapt to something in his environment.

Children who aren't able to do this because they can't connect the affect or intent to their sequencing ability tend to engage in repetitive patterns, action sequences with no goal or purpose. As you practice action sequences with your child, therefore, it is critical to have a purpose or goal loom large. Even when your child is copying an action there is a goal; your child derives pleasure from copying.

As we look at improving sequencing abilities, it is important to include both gross-motor activities (crawling, running, jumping, walking, reaching, opening, etc.) and fine-motor activities (copying circles, squares, and Xs and eventually sequencing letters into words, etc.). It is also important in motor planning and sequencing to involve and integrate all the senses—touch, smell, movement in space, and so on—with the motor pattern. Games in which three or four senses—for example, smell, touch, sound, and sight—provide cues together are useful tools to help your child practice integrating motor patterns and senses.

A great deal of emerging evidence indicates that rhythmic activity, especially music, dance, or sports, is helpful for motor planning and integrating the senses with sequencing ability. Simply playing classical music in the background has been reported to facilitate language development in children. Children appear to benefit from playing different drumbeats to music and exploring the piano, keyboard, or xylophone, as well as from participating in rhythmic movements as long as they don't become part of rote routines and separated from a sense of goal or purpose. For example, dancing around the room with Daddy or jumping up and down with Mommy to get to the door or just to have fun and giggle may be beneficial, but jumping and making funny faces and sounds alone in the child's own room may not be.

Once again, to facilitate the connection between intent or affect and motor planning and sequencing, as well as connections between the affect system and sensory processing in general and the sequencing systems, games in which your child uses sensory and motor activities that cross the midline of her body appear helpful. Young children can play looking-reaching and listening-reaching games, and older children who are already using words and concepts can identify sounds and sights or different textures presented on different sides of their body.

As your child progresses and her auditory processing improves, her motor-planning and sequencing ability may remain a significant challenge. And a method for improving her sequencing ability may not be easily discernible. Many of the games described for improving auditory or visual processing can be used for improving motor planning if the emphasis is placed on gradually making the motor task more complex. Let's say your child has a favorite big doll that she loves to squish. Play a hide-and-go-seek game with the doll. Provide your now somewhat verbal child with some clues to the doll's location, perhaps telling her that the doll is in a big box and the big box is in a red place. She'll have to sequence a series of behaviors and create a road map in her mind. Start with a simple problem, then make it more complicated, and eventually initiate a real treasure hunt.

Whenever there is something your child really wants, make use of that desire. For example, there is no reason you have to take a cookie and hand it to your child. If your child asks for a cookie, you say, "Oh, these are wonderful cookies and you are going to love them. I just baked them, but you are going to have to help me get them." Your child will likely be only too delighted to help you get them. If you say, "Well, I think the cookie jar is up on the shelf," your child might take a chair, climb up on it, and reach up on the shelf; this activity might require four or five motor actions. Alternatively, you might say, "Oh, I made some cookies, but I forgot where I put them. If you can tell me where they are and how to get them, I'll get them for you." If the cookies are in an obvious place, say, "I'm pretty sure they are here in the kitchen, somewhere out in the open, but I just don't see them." Your child may spot them quickly and say, "There they are, Mommy." You can reply, "Okay, I'll get them for you, sweetheart. But how do I get there? What should I do?"

"Walk there, Mommy."

"Okay, but I can't reach."

"Mommy, step on the chair. Reach up high, Mommy, get them."

"Which hand should I use?"

"Your left one."

"Okay, here they are." Your child will have sequenced ideas in an organized and logical way to tell you how to get his cookie. In either scenario your child is practicing sequencing, with motor acts themselves or with ideas, telling you what to do.

Many parents complain that their children don't follow directions. Many of these children have sequencing difficulties. The best way to teach children to follow directions and improve their sequencing is to use just such occasions for practice.

Remember that in practicing sequencing skills, your child needs to progress through the developmental stages of attention: engagement, to simple, one-step, gestural problem solving, to multiple-step, spatial, motor, gestural problem solving. Multiple-step problem solving, which involves complex sequencing, is hard for some children, but practicing it is important because it is the foundation for imitation and using ideas in speech and pretend play.

Many therapists systematically work in the areas we have been discussing, and parents often come up with very exciting and original ways to provide extra practice for their children. While the spirit of this chapter is to encourage creative initiative on the part of parents, educators, and therapists, we want to make note of a few important principles as well.

1. Create challenges with strong motivation (strong intent or affect tied to some goal or reward). Doing so ties your child's sensory processing and motor planning to his affect or intent system; this area is challenging for many children with special needs, especially for children with autistic spectrum problems.

2. Begin simply and work toward more complex patterns in each sensory pathway and in motor planning and sequencing.

3. Create games and exercises that allow your child increasingly to take more initiative and to experience a great deal of pleasure and joy in solving a problem. Your child will want to do more, similar kinds of exercises, and at the same time will be gaining a sense of mastery over and confidence in his body.

4. As much as possible make the experience your child is having part of relationships and interactions. If an experience initially involves little interacting, take the essence of the experience and recreate it in a more interactive context. For example, after practicing drawing a circle, your child could play a game with you that involves both of you drawing funny faces together, using circles for eyes and noses as well as the overall contour of the face.

5. As you carry out these different exercises, mobilize as many of your child's basic developmental capacities as you can. In other words, mobilize attention and focus, engagement, nonverbal gestural interactions, use of symbols and words, and back-and-forth dialogues, including fantasies and imaginative scenarios.

14

Going to Sleep, Toilet Training, and Other Difficult Challenges

Learning to fall asleep by oneself, learning to use the toilet, learning to control the impulse to bite or hit—all these are difficult challenges for any child. For children with special needs the difficulty is compounded by their limited control over their bodies, problems with communication and self-regulation, and discomfort with strong emotion. Nonetheless, most children with special needs can learn to master these challenges with extra patience, time, practice, and support. In this chapter we present a six-step process that you can use to help your child tackle these and other difficult behaviors. The six steps are (1) small steps, (2) floor time, (3) solving the problem symbolically, (4) empathizing, (5) creating expectations and limits, and (6) the golden rule.

First we briefly explain each step. Then we show how to put these steps to work in challenging situations.

STEP 1: SMALL STEPS

All challenges are more manageable when they are broken into steps, and this approach is especially important with a child with special needs. The very notion of trying something new—whether it is a new food or a new bedtime routine—is distressing, but you can make that new behavior doable if you break it into steps so small that each new step is barely distinguishable from the one preceding it. If you're asking your child to try a new food, give him a portion he can barely see, sprinkled on top of a food he already likes. When he tolerates that tiny dose, make his next portion just a tiny bit bigger. Slowly, very slowly, build up to a regular-size portion. It may take a month to get him to eat a quarter of a cup of potatoes, but what's the rush? It doesn't matter if he eats potatoes this month or next, or this year or next. What matters is that he will learn to tolerate new foods because they have been introduced in an agreeable way.

Slow and steady are the bywords for introducing any new behavior. The learning curve will be long, but the slower the learning, the more solid it is apt to be. Try to resist the impulse to rush it. Instead of focusing on the big victory of fully mastering the challenge, celebrate the hundred little victories as your child masters a hundred tiny steps along the way.

You can facilitate mastering challenges by using your child's love for the predictable. As much as possible ritualize your new demands so that your child will come to expect them. If you're working on toilet training, *always* ask him to go to the bathroom before you leave the house. If you're working on sleeping alone, *always* tell him he has to stay in bed by himself but you'll be back in a few minutes to check on him. Make the new behavior you're encouraging as predictable as possible to build his sense of comfort.

Build predictability into your transitions too. If you're working on going to bed, ease the transition by telling your child ahead of time, "Bedtime in five minutes," before "Bedtime now." If you're working on eating new foods, remind her before dinner, "Tonight you'll need to eat three spoonfuls of peas," rather than putting them on her plate with no warning. The more you prepare your child in this way for new challenges, the easier it will be for her to accept them.

Lastly, whenever you add more challenges to your child's life, also add more support and rewards. Give your child even more hugs and kisses and more praise; don't be shy about recognizing her accomplishments with small rewards.

STEP 2: FLOOR TIME

When you ask your child to use the toilet, to fall asleep by himself, or to control his impulse to kick or bite, you are asking him to eliminate behavior that is familiar and comfortable and replace it with behavior that is new and strange. Even people who do not have disabilities dislike sacrificing the familiar for the strange; it generates strong feelings of discomfort. For children with severe disorders, who cherish the familiar above all else, such changes are even more disturbing. Giving up comfortable behavior rocks their entire world. Adopting new behavior prompts strong, uncomfortable feelings. To cope successfully with this level of stress, your child needs to feel especially secure and engaged and he needs room to vent the feelings stirred up by this stress. Floor time can help.

When you are working with your child on a particular challenge, give her more than the usual amount of floor time, following the ordinary floor-time rules. Don't try to direct the play toward the challenge at hand. Let your child direct the play. If she needs to, she will direct play toward the challenge. By giving her additional time to express her feelings, she will feel increasingly secure and will find a way to tell you what she needs you to know.

What types of feelings are you likely to see expressed? You may see feelings of sadness and anger because your child is no longer permitted to do the old, familiar things (such as urinating in a diaper or sleeping in your bed). You may see feelings of rage and frustration because his body doesn't cooperate as he tries to master the new behavior (curbing the urge to bite or to indulge an idiosyncratic motor behavior, for instance). You may see feelings of fear or insecurity because he is not sure whether he *can* master the new behavior (he may fear that he will fall into the toilet or that monsters lurk under his bed). These feelings may surface in pretend-play sequences that relate directly to the challenge at hand (his doll may play at using the toilet), but they are more likely to surface in other contexts. If your child is fearful about using the toilet, the small animals he carries with him may suddenly encounter an extraordinary number of hungry bears or his rocket ship may blow up every time it takes off for the moon. As these feelings emerge, don't try to relate them to the challenge, simply respond support-ively within the context of the drama: "Boy, your rocket is having a scary time!" Your child needs to know that you empathize with his feelings; he doesn't need you to fix them.

In the process of trying to meet her new challenge, your child is likely to become angry and anxious with you. You are the one forcing this new behavior on her; if it weren't for you, she could continue with her old, familiar routine. It's natural for her to feel some hostility toward you. She's also likely to feel anxious. What if she can't please you? What if she can't master the behavior you've requested? Additional floor-time sessions give her extra security and at the same time allow her to express these anxious and negative feelings. Again, the feelings are unlikely to surface in the true context. Her doll won't say, "I'm afraid my mommy won't love me if I can't learn to sleep alone." But her doll may beat up your doll, or steal her food, or commit other aggressive acts. Or one animal may refuse to fight another as if uncertain about his ability to win. Or your child may refuse to cooperate with you in play, in a last-ditch effort to maintain a sense of control. As before, don't feel the need to comment on her behavior; don't try to relate it to the challenge at hand. Simply have your character respond sympathetically within the context of the drama.

Even if your child is preverbal or unable to create pretend dramas, floor time provides the extra security and trust that a new challenge demands. The feelings stirred up by the challenge are uncomfortable—and will remain so until the challenge is mastered—and can become overwhelming if they do not find an outlet. Expressing them through floor time keeps them manageable. Plenty of supportive floor time will make it easier for your child to cope.

STEP 3: SOLVING THE PROBLEM SYMBOLICALLY

When adults face a challenge—whether it's giving up cigarettes or making a presentation at an important meeting—they prepare themselves ahead of time. They may prepare physically—by carrying gum to chew when they crave a smoke—or mentally—rehearsing the meeting in their head. This advance preparation makes meeting the actual challenge easier and improves the chances of success. Children with severe disorders need this same kind of advance preparation when they face difficult challenges. They can gain this preparation in symbolic ways through pretend play and conversation.

In daily sessions of semistructured play you can use dolls or animals to play out the challenge your child is facing. For instance, a doll's mommy may have told the doll he has to stop biting, but the doll may find himself in a situation that makes him want to bite. "What can the dolly do?" your doll can ask, and you and your child can play out various options. Perhaps the doll can run away; perhaps he can hug his own doll; perhaps he will bite anyway! Play out several scenarios to help your child consider a range of options. When you agree on the best one, play it out several times to help your child rehearse it.

If your child is verbal you can talk through these scenarios with or without the help of dolls.

- Ask her to imagine herself in the challenging situation: "Imagine that Min-Yee has just grabbed your doll."

- Ask her to imagine how she will feel: "How will you feel inside when Min-Yee grabs your doll?"

- Ask her to imagine how she usually responds: "What do you usually do when Min-Yee grabs your doll?"

• Ask her to picture alternatives: "What else can you do—besides bite Min-Yee—when she grabs your doll?"

• Or you can rehearse the situation with you pretending to be the friend.

Such problem-solving discussions and rehearsals, lasting 20 to 30 minutes, will help your child anticipate challenges before they arise and prepare better responses than those he usually makes.

STEP 4: EMPATHIZING

As we mentioned earlier, meeting a challenge—trying a difficult new behavior—unleashes a host of emotions, from anger and frustration to fear and insecurity. Above all, your child needs to know that you understand her feelings and that you empathize with her. The knowledge that she is understood will go a long way to increasing her sense of security. Go out of your way to be empathetic. When you see your child shrink from tasting a new food, acknowledge her distress: "I know you don't like new foods, that's why I gave you just a tiny, tiny bit." When you sense him growing anxious about going into the bathroom, acknowledge his unease: "You look a little worried. What can I do to help?" When you feel her tense as you start to put on her shirt, verbalize your perception: "Is it uncomfortable to put on clothes? How can we make it easier?" Verbalizing your child's feeling won't make it go away, but it will take some of the sting out of it. And it will build trust between you and your child because your child will know that you understand.

Empathizing with your child's feelings is also helpful to you. All too often, efforts to get your child to try a new behavior will deteriorate into a power struggle. When your child, frightened, angry, and insecure, becomes belligerent, his recalcitrance can trigger anger in you. Acknowledging his feelings can defuse this struggle. Simply hearing his feelings expressed may help your child back down, and hearing yourself express them will remind you that your child isn't a tyrant, but a small child overcome by powerful emotions. Even if your child is not yet verbal, he will respond to your patient and encouraging tone of voice.

STEP 5: CREATING EXPECTATIONS AND LIMITS

As you work with your child to meet a challenge, you'll be *expecting* him to behave differently than he has in the past. You will be asking him to eat a tiny bit of new food instead of throwing it on the floor or to go to sleep alone, after a back rub, instead of with you. In order for your child to meet these expectations, you have to make them very clear.

The first step is to establish realistic expectations. Break the challenge into many small steps; each step is a new expectation you have of your child. The second step is to communicate your expectations clearly. One way to do this is through problem-solving play. A doll can face the same tiny step your child is facing. Then you can talk with your child about the real-life situation and help him comprehend his new challenge and opportunity.

Sometimes after you've made your expectations clear and re-hearsed them, your child nonetheless has trouble meeting them. When this happens the problem is likely to be with the expectations, rather than with your child. Your expectations are probably too high. Break the challenge into even smaller steps—an even smaller portion of food to eat—and try again. Children generally want to please. Your child would rather meet your expectations than not; your challenge is to help him find a way to do that.

Sometimes you have to use limits. If your child has difficulty with impulsive behavior, for example, set the limit firmly, then back it up with immediate sanctions: holding him, if necessary, or if he can understand delayed repercussions, restricting TV.

STEP 6: THE GOLDEN RULE

The golden rule is simple, but inviolable: *Whenever you increase expectations or limits on your child, also increase floor time.*

Increasing floor time is important for all the reasons we've discussed. Eliminating old behavior and engaging in new behavior is difficult and frustrating, frightening and angering, and, when your child succeeds, thrilling. She needs room to express this barrage of feelings. She also needs a chance to reaffirm her connection to you, for one of her concerns as she faces a difficult challenge is that she will disappoint you by failing to live up to your expectations. Floor time is your chance to show her you're there, supportive and loving, regardless of how she performs. If you need to set limits, increasing floor time keeps life from deteriorating into a power struggle. You expect more *and* you give more.

Let's look at how this six-step process can be used to help your child master some of the common problems faced by children with special needs.

SLEEP PROBLEMS

All sorts of things can make it difficult for your child to fall asleep or go back to sleep by himself. Overreactivity to sensation may mean that noises in his environment are disturbing; problems with self-regulation may hinder him from relaxing into sleep; motor problems may make it hard for him to find a comfortable position. If he is just learning to use ideas, he may imagine scary creatures in his room or have scary dreams; if he has a new sibling he may conjure frightening, aggressive images at night. He may be in the habit of sleeping with you. It's common for children to have trouble falling asleep at bedtime or to end up in their parents' bed in the middle of the night. Taking your child into bed with you may be wonderful and compassionate, but it doesn't do much for *your* sleep and doesn't teach your child how to go back to sleep on his own. You can help him build this skill by using the six-step process.

Step 1: Small Steps

If your child needs a lot of help from you to fall asleep—if he needs you to lie with him, to read many, many stories, or to cuddle for an extremely long time—your big goal will be to reduce the amount of help to something you feel is reasonable, say, two or three stories followed by a short period of cuddling in a chair. But you can't do this all at once. You need to break that big goal into tiny, tiny steps.

• Start by reducing the number of stories by one or two at a time.

• When your child is comfortable with only two or three stories, gradually reduce the amount of time you spend with him by cutting back five minutes at a time.

• At the same time try to replace lying down with him with a back rub or with some other gesture that he finds soothing.

• When your child is comfortable having you rub his back instead of lying next to him, gradually replace the back rub with firm, motionless pressure. Then gradually decrease the duration of the pressure. All the while talk to your child in a soothing voice.

• When he's comfortable with a short period of firm pressure and your soothing voice, eliminate the pressure and use only your voice.

• If you have been sitting on the bed, begin sitting on the floor, then in a chair a few feet away, then close to the door, and finally just outside the door. At that point you'll have reduced the bedtime routine to two or three stories and a short period of talking softly.

• Before you leave, tell your child you will come back to check on him; then do so in 20 seconds. Next time return in 40 seconds, then in a minute. Keep stretching the time until he falls asleep.

If your child wakes up in the middle of the night and can't go back to sleep without coming into your bed, you can use a similar small-step program to help her.

• Start by taking her back to her bed and going through your normal bedtime routine. Stay with her in her room as you did earlier.

• If she insists on coming into your room, let her have her own mattress on the floor. Make it comfy, with its own little pillow and blanket; bring in stuffed animals if she wants them. Then go through your bedtime routine to help her fall asleep on the mattress.

• When she is falling asleep by herself on the mattress, take her back to her own room. She may be able to transfer the skill of falling asleep by herself to her own bed. If not, use your bedtime routine again to help her.

These steps may take months to accomplish for an anxious child, but done gradually, they will give him a valuable portfolio of skills. He will learn not only to put himself to sleep, but also to believe in his ability to calm himself down, to trust his body to do as he asks, and to overcome fears and difficulties on his own.

Step 2: Floor Time

Make sure that your child has ample opportunity to feel secure and express her feelings through your daily floor-time sessions. As you begin to tackle the sleeping problem, things that are scary to her at night will probably emerge in her play. If she airs them in the light of day they will have less power over her at night.

Step 3: Solving the Problem Symbolically

You can work with your child on sleep issues both at bedtime and in semistructured play. At bedtime, use rituals to help your child learn to sleep on his own. First make sure he has eaten and drunk as much as he needs. Then have a floor-time session, letting him be the leader—this will make him more receptive to your demands. Play calmly, addressing issues about which he may have concerns. If your child is young, roll a ball back and forth, play hide-and-seek, explore the room with two flashlights, or sing and play musical instruments. With an older child, hunt for wild beasts or chase monsters out of the room. Next, give him a bath if it is calming for him. Then read stories and sing lullabies. Ritualized stories such as *Goodnight Moon* work well.

Encourage your child to use a teddy bear or other transitional object and share your ritual with it. Talk to the object as if it were your child's friend and ally. Have your child hold it while you read. Then tuck the doll or animal in if your child will let you and say good night to all the toys, dolls, family photos, and other beloved objects nearby. This activity lets your child be the one who helps others go to bed. Finally, say good night to your child and assure him that you will check on him. Try to preempt his getting up by checking on him frequently. Gradually lengthen the periods between your visits.

Consider having your child share a room with a sibling for a while or, if your child is older, having a friend sleep over.

You can use your floor-time tools to create semistructured play situations in which you help your child anticipate the problem and look for ways to solve it. For instance, if you are playing with dolls, you might have a doll wake up in the middle of the night. When the mommy doll tries to put her back to sleep, the doll can say, "I'm scared. I want Mommy's bed." The dolls can then play out various scenarios: the mommy doll comforts the child doll for a few minutes, then puts her back in bed; the mommy doll lets the child doll sleep on a mattress on the floor of the mommy's room; the mommy doll comes in and gives the child doll a back rub, then the child doll decides she can stay in her bed by herself; the mommy doll leaves a picture of herself near the child doll's bed so the child doll can see her mommy as she falls asleep. Invite your child to get involved in these scenarios. Ask her what she thinks the mommy doll should do and how the child doll will react. If your child is not verbal, she can gesture or nod to show approval or to add elements of her own.

Don't be surprised if your child rejects this play at first. She'll know what you're up to! It may be more comfortable for her to use animal figures or characters from stories, which will provide distance and make it easier for her to problem solve.

Step 4: Empathizing

As you engage in problem-solving negotiations with your child, empathize with how scary it is to be in bed by yourself. Use facial expressions, tone of voice, and body language, as well as words. Empathize again when your child faces the real challenge in the dark of night. The more he feels understood, the easier meeting the challenge will be.

Step 5: Creating Expectations and Limits

If necessary, create limits—such as not coming into your bed—and reinforce them with sanctions and rewards to establish structure and motivation. Remind your child of her successes, highlight them with a star chart or token rewards. After a few weeks the need for reinforcement will fade.

If going to sleep becomes a problem all of a sudden, be reassuring and use floor-time play and talking to address whatever concern may have arisen—perhaps someone in the household has taken a new job, or you've moved, or there's a new baby. Any change can upset the sleeping routine. But if you are reassuring and firm about restoring the previous patterns, your child will regain her ability to fall sleep alone.

Step 6: The Golden Rule

Each time you introduce a new step or new limit, give your child more floor time. By making yourself more accessible during the day, you'll ease his fears at night.

EATING PROBLEMS

Children with special needs may be fussy eaters for a number of reasons. Hypersensitivity to texture, taste, and smell makes food sensations especially intense, so that foods that seem unexceptional to others may be extremely unpleasant to children with this hypersensitivity. Undersensitivity to texture, taste, and smell eliminates some of the pleasurable aspects of eating. Motor problems and reduced muscle tone may make chewing and swallowing difficult. Taking these individual differences into account can help you plan an eating program for your child. (If your child begins to reject foods that he formerly ate and to limit the food he will eat, perhaps to three to four processed foods, it is important to consult with your pediatrician and with a nutritionist who is familiar with such patterns. These professionals can suggest changes to his diet as well as dietary supplements.)

If your child is a poor eater, the first thing you should do is review her eating habits and analyze the problems. Does she snack all the time? Does she want to eat at unpredictable times? Do you—or does someone else, perhaps a sitter—carry food with you, using it to placate your child or shoveling it in whenever you have a chance? Does your child eat all over the house? At meals does she bypass the main course and then get dessert anyway? Making adjustments in these behaviors may go a long way toward fixing the eating problem.

- Establish regular mealtimes, at the table, taking into account times of day when your child may be hungry.

- Set up snack times, also at the table.

- If your child leaves the table, remove his food; if he wants more, make him sit down again.

- Don't let your child eat in front of the TV or while involved with other distractions.

- Keep your child engaged through conversation or by showing him pictures of foods.

- Give him small amounts to start with, so that he finishes and asks for more.

- Talk with him about food. If he is verbal, discuss the issue (it may be a problem only for you). If he is preverbal, use signs, gestures, and pictures or use pretend food and dolls and animals to help him talk about and categorize foods. Food is usually motivating, so insist on a response.

- Let him choose foods he likes, then blend in a little bit of the food you feel he needs. If he eats only pureed baby food, add small pieces of other foods, such as apples, banana, or peas.

- If he has food sensitivities, consider a rotation diet with predictable offerings each day.

Step 1: Small Steps

Introduce new foods gradually, always taking into account your child's sensory and motor preferences. If she has difficulty chewing and prefers pureed food, puree the new item. If she is overreactive and prefers bland food, prepare her portion before you season everyone else's. If she is underreactive and prefers strong flavors, add extra seasoning to her portion. Then introduce the new food by adding it to a food she's already comfortable eating.

- If you're introducing broccoli, chop up a fingernail's worth until it's very, very fine and sprinkle it over mashed potatoes.

- If that goes down without a protest, add a little more each night until your child is eating a normal portion.

• If he protests, make the portion smaller. If he objects to the slightest fleck of green in his potatoes, try introducing a different vegetable.

• Use the same strategy to expand the temperatures and textures your child tolerates. For instance, if she doesn't like cold food, warm it, but warm it less each time. If you introduce changes very slowly and view each small step as a victory, you'll gradually broaden her menu.

Your child's occupational therapist and speech pathologist can suggest ways to work with and around his sensory and motor problems, and a nutritionist can help you decide what foods to introduce and how to rotate your child's diet.

Step 2: Floor Time

While you are implementing these strategies, continue working with your child in floor time. As you tackle the eating challenge, make sure you give her ample room to feel engaged and secure and to express her feelings through play. Let her be the boss now. Later, you can ask her to try some new food.

Step 3: Solving the Problem Symbolically

Once your child is doing symbolic play, you can use semistructured play to expand his eating behavior. Eating often crops up in children's play, whether it's feeding babies or denying food to hungry bad guys—even pirates and lions have to eat sometime. So it should be relatively easy to create scenarios in which the characters eat.

Play a game in which you and your child shop and cook for dolls and feed them. What happens when the doll gets so tired chewing he wants to leave the table? Can you fix that problem by cutting the food up into smaller pieces or by having the doll eat smaller amounts at one time? What happens when some foods taste too strong for the doll and he wants to throw them off the tray? Can you fix that problem by choosing different foods or by eating less of the strong food? What happens when the doll doesn't want to taste a new food? Can your child help him change his mind? If your child is verbal, help him picture himself at the dinner table as you introduce a new food. How will he feel? How will he want to behave? Can he figure out alternatives?

Your child may want to use pretend play to play out getting exactly what she wants, say, a great feast of junk food. Indulge her wishes and enjoy it together: "Wouldn't it be great if this was all we had to eat?" You may be surprised by how much your child elaborates with pretend food even though she refuses real food. Play along, and every so often reject the food she offers just to see how she deals with your challenge.

Step 4: Empathizing

As you conduct your problem-solving negotiations, empathize with how the doll and your child are feeling. Let your child know he's understood. When he works at meeting the challenge each night at dinner, empathize with how difficult it is to try something new. Feeling understood will strengthen his desire to meet the challenge.

Step 5: Creating Expectations and Limits

Make each expectation and success clear. Try to avoid power struggles, and use limits only for behavior such as throwing food.

Step 6: The Golden Rule

As you increase your expectations of your child, give her more time during the day to express her feelings. Doing so will build her desire to cooperate and decrease her need to express her negative feelings when confronting the challenge itself.

DISCIPLINE

Children learn about discipline through nonverbal communication. Between the ages of 12 and 24 months your child learns what it means when you raise your voice, when you make a stern face, when you wag your finger in a reprimand. He learns this through the opening and closing of hundreds of gestural circles as you repeatedly warn him away from electrical outlets, reprimand him for biting, and otherwise convey limits. Eventually, after closing hundreds of gestural circles, it takes only a single look to stop your child from misbehaving. After hundreds more, he sees your face and hand gestures or hears your voice in his mind and curtails the behavior even without your presence. Through his practice with gestural negotiation, he internalizes a sense of limits.

Children with special needs often don't have this gestural foundation. Processing and motor-planning problems may have kept them from opening and closing these hundreds of circles, and without this practice they may have difficulty internalizing limits. To help your child, you need to work with her on gestural negotiation; you need to open and close as many circles as possible around every disciplinary infraction. If your child is verbal, you can back up your gestures with words, but the real learning will come from the nonverbal dialogue you establish.

You also want to help your child use ideas to reason about his behavior. A parent's first response when his child misbehaves is often to punish, the idea being that if the child is punished for this behavior he will learn not to do it again. However, this logic often backfires, especially with children with special needs. Your child won't learn to control his misbehavior until he has internalized a sense of limits, a picture of what is permissible and what is not. To have this picture he must be comfortable in the world of ideas; he must be able to hold and manipulate ideas in his head. When you punish a child you are reacting to his behavior with behavior of your own. In effect, you are encouraging him to remain at the behavioral level. More effective in the long run is to talk with your child first about his transgressions. By involving him in a discussion you elevate him to the level of ideas; you help him reflect on his behavior. Gradually you move him toward the point of being able to discipline himself in his mind. He may still misbehave, and you may have to punish him later on, but by talking—firmly and supportively— you both build his ability to correct himself *and* help him graduate to the level of ideas.

Step 1: Small Steps

You need to begin by creating manageable steps for changing your child's behavior. If she's biting other people, provide her with a substitute to bite—a teething ring, a rubber doll, or a pretend hot dog. When she's old enough, she can chew gum (first work on trading objects so she'll trade you for a new piece). Don't confuse your child by sometimes allowing her to bite you playfully. Even in play, offer a substitute. (Not all biting relates to anger. Some children bite because they crave oral stimulation. You may want to establish some oral-motor routines, such as brushing her teeth and massaging her face and lips, to help increase your child's muscle tone and activate her mouth. These activities will also help her eating and talking.)

If your child won't pick up his room after playing, do it together. Negotiate who puts what away, slowly increasing his share. Say "good-bye" to the toys to help him separate and create homes for them to go to. If he flatly refuses to clean up his room, set the goal of cleaning up once a week. When that goal is met, make it twice a week, then gradually work up to every day.

Step 2: Floor Time

As your child gets older she faces more and more limits—and feels more anger and frustration as a result—so floor time is especially important. Floor time gives her a chance to express those feelings and to compensate by playing the boss, throwing things, making a mess. As long as she's not hurting or breaking things, give her a wide berth. Let her be the ruler and tyrant. What she expresses safely in floor time won't need to come out in other situations.

Step 3: Solving the Problem Symbolically

Create situations with dolls that mimic the disciplinary situations your child is facing. What happens when the mommy doll tells the child doll he can't bite? How does the doll feel? What does it do? What can the doll do instead? What happens when the child doll bites anyway? What should the mommy doll do? What can the mommy doll do so the child doll doesn't want to bite? Play out a variety of scenarios for each problem and talk as you do so about your child's own feelings. If your child is not yet verbal, keep your conversations mostly gestural. Use tone of voice and facial expressions to empathize with his feelings.

If your child is verbal, help her anticipate situations in which she'll be tempted to misbehave. What will happen tomorrow at school when Alex takes your toy? How will you feel? What will you want to do? Can you do something else instead? With a great deal of practice, your child can learn to anticipate her feelings in difficult situations and plan her actions accordingly.

Step 4: Empathizing

Let your child know that you know how hard it is to control his behavior and that you know how angry and frustrated he feels inside.

Step 5: Creating Expectations and Limits

Try to keep your big goals broad, so they encompass whole groups of behavior. If you make the goal no hitting, your child is liable to switch to kicking. You're better off making the goal no hurting people, which is really what you want him to learn. When he's comfortable with these behavioral goals you can gradually work up to attitudinal goals. The broadest goal is to respect other people, which includes no hurting, no taking things from them, no sitting in their chairs without permission, and so on. As your child learns to respect and empathize with other people, he will have less need for goal setting and he will internalize his own sense of discipline.

Be clear with your child about your expectations, and be prepared to mete out sanctions if needed, but only as a last resort after a long period of verbal or gestural negotiation.

Suppose that after many long discussions your child throws a toy at her brother. At that point it's time to go over and restrain her. Hold her until she calms down; remain firm, but gentle. If you lose your temper she will get scared and her behavior will become worse. You want to give her the message that she *can* calm down and that you can help her through your own calm behavior. Think of yourself as a giant teddy bear, enfolding your child in your warmth and security.

Once your child is calm you may feel that, through your negotiation and restraint, she's gotten the message that her action was intolerable. Or, you may want to reinforce that message with a traditional sanction—asking her to reflect on her behavior, taking away TV time or dessert, or forgoing the game you were about to play. (It is probably best not to isolate her from others, because all children, but especially children with special needs, need social interaction, and will learn more from being around you than by sitting alone in a room.) All these traditional sanctions are fine, but only after 50 or 60 circles of gestural negotiation. With punishment alone your child may learn in a frightened, nondiscriminating way not to do something, but she won't be able to reason for herself about when a behavior is acceptable and when it isn't. Gestural and verbal negotiation will help her internalize the concept of limits.

Be sure to use sanctions that are appropriate for your child's developmental level. Taking away TV may not mean much to a child who is developmentally 18 months old even if chronologically he's 4. He can't make the connection between behavior now and sanction later. Use an immediate sanction instead, perhaps asking him to sit still for three minutes instead of playing with his toys. If your child is preverbal, the gestural negotiation is probably enough to get your message across. Loud voices and angry body language are aversive to a child; capping them with sanctions is unnecessary. Use positive as well as negative sanctions if necessary.

Step 6: The Golden Rule

With challenges involving discipline it is especially important to increase floor time. Your child is facing more and more limits, which are coupled with angry feelings toward you. Giving him extra time to vent those feelings in play will minimize the extent to which they spill out into other situations. Extra floor time will also strengthen the bond of trust between you, which is particularly important now that you are expecting more from him.

TOILET TRAINING

If your child has motor-control problems, he may have difficulty sitting on the toilet and controlling the sphincter. If he is underreactive to sensation, he may not even notice that he is urinating. If he is overreactive to sensation or has a poor kinesthetic sense, the feeling of something leaving his body may be overly frightening or intense. Or, he may not like the open feeling of sitting on the toilet after being accustomed to having the closeness and warmth of the diaper to push against. Because learning to use the toilet can be especially challenging for a child with special needs; your approach to toilet training should be very, very slow.

A child is usually ready to begin toilet training when she is developmentally about age three, which, for a child with special needs, may be chronologically age four or five. (In some cultures toilet training is done with very young children at ritualized times—when they usually go, or right after meals when the likelihood of going is greater.) If your child is very willful or fearful or has poor sensory registration and control issues, have patience. If she doesn't notice when she is wet, she probably isn't ready for toilet training. However, if she seems interested—if she sees siblings or schoolmates using the toilet and seems eager to try herself, for instance—go ahead and start. Proceed very gently, and don't push her if she loses interest. Toilet training should be at the bottom of your list of priorities. You have much bigger, more important challenges to master—intimacy and gestural communication— and once your child is comfortable with these challenges, she'll be ready to take on the toilet.

Step 1: Small Steps

Some children learn quickly in one step; they have a bowel movement on the first or second try. If your child is taking longer, consider smaller steps.

• Start by making the bathroom the only place where you'll change his diaper. This will help him associate elimination with the bathroom.

• If he goes off to hide every time he poops, encourage him to hide in the bathroom. Reassure him that he'll have privacy. He may even be willing to sit on the toilet (with his clothes on).

• Take him into the bathroom after meals. If he's hesitant, don't ask him to sit on the toilet, you simply want him to get used to visiting the bathroom after eating. Establishing a schedule is an important part of toilet training and a useful first step.

• Once your child expects to visit the bathroom after each meal, encourage him to poop in his diaper there. If he can regularly poop in his diaper in the bathroom, he'll have mastered a major step.

• If he can't poop readily after eating, help him relax by using sensations he finds soothing—the sound of running water, of his favorite music, of your soothing voice, or of the voice of a puppet he likes. Some children like to hold a favorite toy while on the toilet; others like to play games in which they tighten and relax their muscles or drop bombs from airplanes. Experiment until you find the right combination of sensations.

• Once your child can poop on schedule, try shifting him to the toilet. Put a box or stool under his feet because feeling his feet on the ground will make him feel more secure and help him regulate his body. If he's nervous about sitting over a black hole, put the diaper back on him. Then gradually loosen it. Then put it under him, but not around him. Give him whatever physical support he needs to feel secure. If he seems very uncomfortable, make the small steps even smaller. Make the goal to sit on the toilet for five minutes, then gradually increase the time. He's already got the elimination part down; once he's comfortable on the toilet he'll have mastered the entire procedure.

• If he doesn't seem to notice when he's peeing, give him lots to drink, then play outside at a small plastic pool (with a potty nearby) or inside in the bath. Soon he'll need to pee and you can help him quickly to the potty or toilet. If he pees or poops in the tub, just end the bath calmly. He will have noticed.

Step 2: Floor Time
Use floor time to create a sense of engagement. The success of toilet training depends in part on your child's wish to please you, and the more you build closeness during floor time, the stronger this wish will be.

Step 3: Solving the Problem Symbolically
Books and videos on toilet training can be helpful in reinforcing what you are working on with your child. They give your child a chance to look, point, ask questions, and cheer. You can also work toilet training into your play. Keep a potty-chair in the playroom (not to use), and when playing with dolls, include this life function. Interrupt the scene from time to time because your doll has to go potty. Use gestures and tissues and tape to change her diaper or take her to the toilet. Your child may be intrigued by this digression and may want to copy you, she may be completely uninterested, or she may grow furious and reactive.

Let your child help as you walk through the various steps. Make the doll express what you sense are your child's concerns, taking into account her individual differences. If your child is verbal, walk through the procedure verbally. Have her picture herself sitting on the potty (or doing whatever small step you're working on). Have her picture how she'll feel and what she'll want to do and if there's anything you can do to make her challenge easier. Then ask her to picture herself accomplishing the goal.

Step 4: Empathizing

As the doll expresses your child's concerns, empathize with the doll's feelings and also with your child's. Later, when your child is sitting on the toilet, let her know that *you* know that what she's doing is hard. Remind her how proud she'll be to wear big-girl underwear.

Step 5: Creating Expectations and Limits

The sense of routine and expectation is a big part of toilet training. Sanctions are not appropriate because your child may simply be unable to comply. When he meets each small step, reward his effort with a sticker or an extra story before bedtime. The long-term goal of being in big-boy underwear is also a positive incentive.

Step 6: The Golden Rule

Give your child extra floor time as she is mastering each small step in training. If she senses that toilet training is very important to you, she may fear disappointing you. Since she probably shares your desire to do this grown-up behavior, she may also fear disappointing herself. Give her room to express these and other feelings and to reaffirm her closeness to you in extra floor-time sessions.

STUBBORNNESS AND NEGATIVITY

You probably don't view your child's stubbornness and negativity as positive, but for a child with developmental delays it actually is, because it is organized, intentional behavior. A child with developmental challenges spends a long time learning to be intentional, so his fierce "No!" and "I won't!" and his defiant turning away are signs of progress. He now has a more organized sense of who he is as a separate person and is trying to define himself. You want to use that defiance to draw him into conversation and interaction. To do so, make your approach soothing and gradual.

Your child's negativity can provide excellent opportunities to open and close circles of communication. If you can resist the tendency to shorten the argument by immediately saying yes or no, you can give him a great deal of practice at communicating his desires and expressing himself logically. And because he will be negotiating in a state of high emotion, the learning will be real.

There are tens of opportunities for this practice during the day. Sometimes use humor and absurdity. If your child doesn't want to put on her shoe, negotiate by pointing to her hand and suggesting she put it there. When she says no, suggest she put it on her head. When she rejects that idea, suggest she hang it on her ear. Each time she responds she'll have closed a circle of communication, and after a few such silly suggestions she may even give you a little smile. She may still not put the shoe on her foot, but you'll have eked out valuable practice at communication and encouraged her expression of emotion. When your child refuses to eat a certain food, play dumb. Make him explain repeatedly that he wants something else by handing him the first food several times, by looking confused, by encouraging him to point to what he wants. After you've opened and closed four or five circles of communication you can suddenly get the message, rewarding his effort with the food he prefers. If your child is verbal, instead of commanding her to do something turn your request into a conversation. "Oh, you don't want to hang up your coat? Why not? What if the coat rack could reach out and take your coat from your hands?" Turning the situation into a conversation strengthens her communication skills *and* diverts her attention from the conflict.

Of course you won't always have the time or the patience for stretching out these negotiations; sometimes you really need flexibility from your child. At those times be especially soothing and gradually try to make the action you're imposing as positive as possible. If your child is resisting getting in the car, suggest he bring his favorite toy, try to lure him with play, give him a snack to eat on the way, or try soothing him with hugs. If he's still screaming and kicking, pick him up and put him in the car, but be soothing as you do so. Hold him firmly but gently—like that big, firm teddy bear—and tell you know he doesn't want to go but sometimes we have to do things we don't like. Above all, try not to lose control because if you do, you're likely to scare your child. He may be oversensitive to sound or to exaggerated gestures and what may seem like mild anger to you may seem overwhelming to him. If you couple this firm-teddy-bear strategy with plenty of playful negotiations, you can gradually help your child become more flexible.

Remember that children are rarely negative because they want to be mean. They are often oversensitive to sensation and try to control things to keep from being overloaded. When your child rejects your ideas she's not trying to thwart you; she's merely trying to assert herself, to find out who she is, to develop a sense of self. That's why, as much as possible, you need to respect her efforts. You don't have to agree with her ideas; you can try to negotiate her to a different position. But by negotiating rather than simply imposing your will, you respect her feelings and strengthen her sense of self.

Step 1: Small Steps

The key is to tackle one problem area at a time. If your child is negative about food *and* dressing *and* going to school, don't tackle all three issues simultaneously. Start with the issue that is most important to you and work on the others later. You won't overwhelm your child by forcing too much learning at once, and you'll allow him to remain the boss in several areas, which is important to his sense of self. Gradually you can whittle down the problem areas until you have a largely cooperative child.

Step 2: Floor Time

Floor time is the time the child can safely say no to everything. She can refuse to let you put the doll in the car; she can insist the cars get lined up just so; she can make you the slave while she plays the autocratic master. As long as she's not hurting or breaking anything, she can be the boss. Being the pretend boss won't make her spoiled; it will eventually help her tolerate not being the boss in reality.

Step 3: Solving the Problem Symbolically

With problem solving you help your child practice doing things he doesn't like. If he always resists getting in the car, play out scenes in which dolls have to ride in the car. Can he make the doll want to ride? If he always resists getting dressed, play out scenes in which dolls protest while they're getting dressed. Can your child make the dolls more comfortable? When he's solved the problem with doll play, move your practice to the real world; play chase games in which you both get in and out of the car. Play dressing games in which you take turns putting clothes on your heads and having the other person pull them off. Tell him while you play how proud you are that he is learning to do these difficult things.

Your child may resist getting dressed because she is sensitive to textures and the feel of clothing on her body is extremely unpleasant. Test her reactions to different fabrics and choose clothes that are the least offensive. Cut labels out and turn socks inside out if they seem to bother her. Play games with new clothes for a while before asking your child to wear them. And play lots of dress-up games, putting on different costumes to build your child's tolerance for dressing. Speak to your occupational therapist about massage and brushing your child before dressing her to make her more comfortable.)

Step 4: Empathizing

Whenever your child faces a difficult task, let him know you understand his discomfort.

Step 5: Creating Expectations and Limits

When limits are needed, be that big, firm teddy bear. Empathize soothingly with her feelings, but remind her that in this area she has to be flexible.

Step 6: The Golden Rule

As you tackle each problem area, increase the amount of floor time. You're asking your child to change a behavior that is important to him. Give him room to express the strong feelings that engenders.

UNUSUAL FEARS

Most children develop fears as they become aware of who they are and what can happen to them. At around age two, for example, when toddlers fall they get very frightened. They realize their bodies can get hurt, but they cannot yet judge which falls are serious. At this stage kisses and Band-Aids help their boo-boos. By age four these solutions are less needed; children have gained confidence in their bodies and know when they really need help. Their growing sense of reality may also allow them to anticipate fears. They may worry about new experiences and separations because they realize ahead of time that they may feel afraid. At this stage children may worry about going off to school or they may be shy at a family reunion.

As your child gets older and better able to express herself through words and pretend play, she is likely to go through a stage of being fearful. She is now able to use her imagination, but her imagination can scare her. She can picture you giving her a hug, but she can also picture a witch under the bed. All children go through this phase when they come to understand that there are things in the world that can hurt them. Fears indicate that your child is beginning to differentiate fantasy and reality. Previously, magical thinking and a less-developed sense of self offered protection and power; now your child is beginning to understand that she is just a small child, and she must adapt to this new reality. This happens over a period of time during which she'll learn the limits of her real power and use pretend and imagined power to cope with imagined fears and reality.

Children with special needs are especially susceptible to fears because of their individual differences. If your child is oversensitive to noise he may be overwhelmed by the vacuum cleaner and turn that vacuum cleaner into an angry elephant in his closet. If your child is sensitive to touch, she may be upset by a stranger shaking her hand and later conceptualize that sensation as a hairy gorilla eager to squash her in her bed. The unsettling experiences of the day are often transformed into irrational fears.

Your child's own feelings may also scare her and therefore become transformed in her imagination. Her knowledge that she is dependent on you—and vulnerable to your loss—may be represented by a fear that a calamitous event will cause your separation. Strong feelings of anger or aggression may be embodied in fear of fire, invading armies, or other forces of destruction. If your child has motor problems she is even more likely to fear aggression. Unable fully to control her body, she may fear that she is unable to control her anger, too. And if she can't control her anger, how well can others control theirs? To a child with motor challenges the world may seem full of creatures ready to attack. The knowledge that she can't trust her own body to protect her—or even to take her to her mother's arms—heightens her discomfort.

All these influences conspire to make children with special needs go through a stage in which they have irrational fears. Fortunately, the stage is temporary. As your child develops a logical understanding of the world and an improved ability to express her feelings in words, her irrational fears can decline. In the meantime, it may help to remember that the fears themselves are a sign of progress; they are a healthy step on the way to more logical thinking and feeling.

Step 1: Small Steps

Pick one fear to work on at a time and help your child master it in tiny doses. For instance, if he's afraid of going to school, go with him to the school before he's scheduled to begin. Visit his classroom, meet his teacher, watch the children play. Find something about the class for him to look forward to. When he starts school, go with him the first few days. Go early, so that other children join your child; then gradually reduce the length of time you stay. Or stand outside the door where your child can see you, again, gradually reducing the length of time you stay. If necessary, take your child home with you the first day, but ask him to stay a little bit longer each subsequent day. Alternatively, arrive early to pick him up so that he is reassured that you will always return for him.

If your child is afraid of monsters under the bed, check her room and help her find ways to try to combat the monsters before she calls you—she might keep a flashlight under her pillow to shine at them or a horn to blow to frighten them away. Ask her to use her new defense a little bit longer each night before calling you. Then amply reward her bravery.

Your child will accept magical solutions until he is developmentally about four years of age. When he is more realistic, he will quickly reject such solutions ("Really, Mommy!"). Then, read books and discuss other children's solutions or ask what he would do if his friend or sibling were scared.

Step 2: Floor Time

If your child is experiencing fears she will probably play them out in floor time. Children often become the very thing that frightens them, so your child may become the monster that attacks the baby or the angry lion that eats the zookeeper. She will find ways to capture and defeat the robbers and grizzly bears. Playing out these scenes is beneficial. By becoming what she fears she is able to change and control her fear; she can be its master. She'll also learn what it feels like to be in power and will gain experience with negative emotions. If she plays these fears out in the light of day, she'll have less need to feel and express them at night.

Playing out fears also opens the door to aggressive energies, which your child may find safe only in play. Don't be afraid to encourage her assertiveness in play. Go along with her fantasies. If you treat them realistically, she may become more frightened.

Some children are especially anxious about aggression. They may take longer to learn to differentiate fantasy from reality. They may react to aggressive ideas in play as if they were real, succumbing momentarily to panic because they are afraid they will be hurt. You can help your child gain comfort with aggression by encouraging the use of play figures with whom he can stage confrontations and battles. He will probably feel safe only if he always wins, so let him win! Don't rush this stage. During floor time let your child win as long as he needs to win. If he feels unsafe being the bad guy, you can both be good guys looking for the enemy. Fight the enemy together, imagining what the bad guys are doing. Gradually, your child will begin to experiment at being the bad guy, but he will need to stay in control. And chances are, he'll still need to win! That's fine. Over time, his range will expand and he will become more flexible.

Step 3: Solving the Problem Symbolically

You can use problem-solving sessions to help your child anticipate things that may be scary. Whether it's going to bed at night or going to a friend's house for the first time, you can use dolls to play out the situation ahead of time. How will the dolls feel in the new situation? A little afraid? Medium afraid? Very afraid? What will be scary? What can the dolls or Mommy do to make it less scary? Perhaps they could take their favorite animal or a picture of the family or set up a time to speak with their parents on the phone. Play out various scenarios until your child seems comfortable with the situation.

Step 4: Empathizing

You know your child's fears are irrational, but they are very real to her. So even though you've checked the closet umpteen times and twice raked the broom under the bed looking for monsters, continue to empathize with her feelings. She needs your warm support; it's the only defense she has.

Once your child is more realistic, do not join her fears, but empathize. Tell her about times when you were frightened as a child. She'll want to hear your stories again and again.

Step 5: Creating Expectations and Limits

Children with irrational fears benefit from having firm limits in other aspects of their lives. Underlying many of his irrational fears is your child's fear of his own aggression; knowing that you will stop him from doing something very destructive reduces some of that fear. So provide your child with a clear sense of boundaries.

It is especially useful to encourage the use of play figures so that your child can be safe in his battles. But remind him that he can hurt people if he oversteps the bounds.

When you do set limits, don't be harsh about enforcing them. Your big-teddy-bear strategy of soothing firmness will be more productive and persuasive. But be consistent. Your child needs to know exactly how far he can go because that knowledge will keep *his* worst fears at bay.

Step 6: The Golden Rule

You're asking your child to tackle her fears head-on, and that isn't easy, so support her in the process by giving her extra floor time. Your nurturance as she plays will be her greatest tool in combating her internal monsters. Extra floor time will also help her understand social rules.

IRREGULAR MOTOR AND SELF-STIMULATORY BEHAVIOR

Many children with special needs have irregular motor behavior—they flap their arms, spin, open and close doors over and over again, or engage in some form of involuntary, repetitive movement. This behavior is not a sign of autism, brain damage, or mental retardation. (Such motor behaviors are sometimes included on a long list used to diagnose these disorders because they occur frequently in children who have the disorders, but they do not themselves indicate autism, retardation, or brain damage.) These movements are caused by problems in the motor system—high or low tone, motor-planning problems, or difficulties regulating motor flow—that result in the child's having incomplete control. When the child is stressed, tired, or excited or craves stimulation, his muscular control is affected, and he may respond with involuntary actions. (Think back to when your child was a baby and waved his arms or legs when he was excited by pleasure or anticipation.) Contrary to popular misconception, children who are extremely warm and loving or unusually gifted and bright can evidence these motor overflows when stressed or excited.

Consider a common example of facial muscles operating involuntarily—a twitch around a person's eye. When the person is stressed or tired, the twitch becomes more pronounced. If you call the person's attention to the twitch, it will become even more pronounced. But if you draw the person into smiling interaction, the twitch will go away; now the person has voluntary control over those muscles. You can use a similar strategy if your child has motor irregularities. You want to try to draw your child into a soothing interaction that will call on the same muscles that cause his irregular movements. If your child is flapping, you might shake hands, hold his hands and dance, or hand him something he likes to hold and then offer to make an exchange. As he makes the effort to join your game, voluntary control will override his involuntary motor movements. If your child is spinning, try singing "Ring-around-the-Rosy," taking his hands to turn around and "all fall down." If your child is perseveratively opening and closing a door, get stuck behind the door, turning his action into an interactive game. He now has to *choose* to push or pull the door, and his automatic movement becomes voluntary. Or give him a reason to open and close the door by having an army of his stuffed animals arrive one by one. You might knock on the door, offer your child the keys, and treat the episode symbolically.

By drawing your child's motor behavior into interaction you are also making it purposeful rather than self-stimulatory. Your child is now using his muscles to *act* or *communicate intentionally,* rather than to generate sensory stimulation. You further strengthen his sense of purpose by tying his behavior to an emotion—by offering him something he wants, or by getting in his way. In this way you are helping your child gain even more control over the movements of his muscles.

Equally helpful in minimizing irregular movements is work with an occupational therapist and developmental optometrist to strengthen your child's motor and visual-motor systems. As your child develops greater muscular control, her need for these movements will lessen and her ability to control them will grow. This process takes time, however, and many children never completely eliminate such movements; rather, they learn to control them most of the time, but continue to experience them during times of stress. This behavior need not interfere with the quality of life, though. People with irregular motor behavior can get married, raise children, hold challenging and meaningful jobs, and live happy and fulfilling lives. Compared with the much more serious problems some children face—including problems with interaction and communication—irregular motor behavior pales.

Nevertheless, irregular movements can be embarrassing, both to your child (if he is teased or feels rejected) and to you, as you endure stares and questions in public. You may be reminded of your own childhood embarrassments and feel all over again the pain of being different. You can take several steps to minimize these irregular movements and give your child some control.

Step 1: Small Steps

Since the irregular movements comfort your child, they are hard to control not only for motor reasons, but for emotional reasons as well. Respect your child's need and help her control her movements in very tiny steps, starting with the one area in which the behavior is most problematic. Use problem-solving play and discussions to practice different strategies for that particular situation. In all other situations, let your child do what she likes. This first step will show her that control is possible. Gradually she will come to prefer interacting with you *without* her irregular behavior to being alone *with* that behavior.

Step 2: Floor Time

If your child begins an involuntary behavior during floor time, turn it into a purposeful game. If he spins, put on music, hold his hands, and turn his spinning into a dance. If he sucks his hand, put *your* hand in his mouth first and force him to deal with you before he can satisfy his craving. If he rocks back and forth, put a doll in his arms and sing "Rock-a-bye Baby," turning his rocking into cradling a baby.

Your child may seek visual stimulation by rotating an object close to her eyes, as if inspecting it closely from different angles. She may engage in this behavior to avoid you or the world around you, which may be overwhelming, to eliminate other visual input, to focus on something familiar if her auditory comprehension is poor, or because she enjoys the cause and effect of blinking her eyes and the varied visual sensations it creates. As with other perseverative behavior, you want to try to make these efforts interactive. Join your child as if she is looking at something interesting. If she won't let you look, offer her additional objects to look at. Add a flashlight, magnifying glass, or sunglasses to create different visual effects. Turn her behavior into an interactive experiment.

If your child engages in visual perseveration, he will also benefit from games that develop his visual processing and visual-motor coordination.

• Start with two flashlights and play tag or "I'm going to get you" in a darkened room before bedtime.

• Then try tracing the outlines of the windows or furniture with your lights.

• Practice language as you name different objects and spotlight them.

• Buy a small projector flashlight with changeable plastic caps that have cutouts of planets, spaceships, and stars. Move the flashlight in and out so the images get larger or smaller.

• Hang up mobiles so your child can track their movements.

• Suspend a stuffed animal on a string thumbtacked to the ceiling and push it back and forth like a swing. Challenge your child to bat it back to you. Change directions every once in a while so your child will have to track it to push it back.

• Have sword fights, moving your sword slowly in different directions (up and down, side to side) so that your child has to find it in order to tap it.

• Make a game of offering your child toys while he is on a swing; he'll have to track them in order to get them.

• Play dodgeball just by rolling the ball along the floor.

These activities will help your child's visual system develop. (Even if he has good vision, his visual processing may be immature.) If his vision and visual processing are weak, these games will provide new uses for his eyes. If your child is older and understands numbers, ask him how many times he wants to play each game; this will give him a way to control, but limit, the activity.

You may worry that paying attention to your child's irregular movements will only exacerbate them, that your attention will reinforce the behavior. This concern is understandable, but it doesn't work that way, because as soon as you pay attention to the behavior you change it, you turn it into interaction. So, instead of repeating her involuntary behavior, your child is practicing interaction. Reinforcement of the behavior comes when you don't pay attention to it, because then your child repeats the behavior over and over and never turns it into interaction.

The same principle is true for all out-of-control behavior—even aggressive behavior. Kicking, yelling, biting, and punching can often be brought under control by interaction. If your child is kicking or punching at you, hold up a pillow and give him a target. Turn the kicking into a game. If he is yelling, cover your ears and make a funny face each time he yells, or make a funny sound back. Or get your echo microphone and see how loud and soft he can be. You may even be able to turn his screaming into a game. The more you interact with his behavior, the more he'll be able to bring it under control.

Another way to help your child gain control over involuntary behavior is to work with her to modulate it. Join her in the behavior and then say, "Now let's do this r-e-a-l-l-y s-l-o-w-l-y. Now let's do it really fast! Now let's do it really hard. Now let's do it really gently." Executing the behavior in different ways will help her bring it under control. Modulation games are also helpful for very active children.

In tackling your child's involuntary behavior, remember the universal principle: *the more challenging something is to your child, the more practice he needs.* More work in that area, not less, is the key to resolving the problem.

Step 3: Solving the Problem Symbolically

If your child is older and verbal, talk about the problem and how to handle it. If he is getting teased at school, help him think about when it happens. What triggers it? Certain times of day? Certain people? How does he feel just before it happens? How does he feel while he's doing it? How does he feel when he gets teased? Can he think of a way to change the behavior to make it more socially acceptable? Perhaps he can stretch or scratch his head instead of spinning or flapping his arms.

If your child is always touching things or tapping, give her a few small Koosh balls to keep in her pocket to squeeze. If she needs to mouth things, encourage her to chew gum. If she is young, give her a Theratube necklace she can put in her mouth.

One of the goals of these problem-solving sessions is to help your child become more self-aware. Discussing his involuntary behavior is a good way to promote self-awareness. The better your child knows himself the more confident he will be. Eventually, even if he can't completely eradicate the behavior, he will find ways to minimize and live with it.

Some parents try to squelch their child's behavior, hoping to spare her the pain of being different. This effort, although well intentioned, rarely succeeds in suppressing the behavior, and it doesn't provide practice at self-observation. Thus, the child never has a chance to think about why her behavior is satisfying or to find appropriate substitutions for it. Children whose behavior is squelched often end up feeling even more different because they haven't learned how to cope with their behavior in social situations.

Step 4: Empathizing

Empathize with your child's feelings while you talk about the problem. If he's being teased or rejected by others, he especially needs understanding at home.

Step 5: Creating Expectations and Limits

Although it is critical for your child to control aggressive impulses and channel them into words, it is not terribly important for her to control her irregular motor behavior. This behavior is a comforting and fundamental part of her and she needs to know that you will love and respect her despite it. She must never feel that she will be punished for her involuntary movements or even that she will be rewarded for eliminating them. The rewards—which should be frequent, each time she meets a tiny goal—should be for *exercising self-control*, for learning to interact or find other ways to comfort herself, for meeting the challenge of a tremendously difficult task.

Step 6: The Golden Rule

Give your child additional floor time as he works through these challenges.

Following these steps may help minimize your child's behavior in a few key situations, but his overall therapy program—including work on the emotional milestones and occupational therapy—should reduce them significantly over time.

SILLY AND ANXIOUS BEHAVIOR

It's worth saying a few words about silly behavior—making raspberries or other funny noises, giggling loudly, making silly faces or postures, and so on. Many children seem to love doing these things, especially in public when they are most embarrassing to their parents! There's probably not a parent in the world who hasn't lost her temper when her child has refused to stop. The best way to deal with this behavior, however, is not to tell your child to stop, because that almost always leads to confrontation, but to try to figure out why the behavior is so pleasurable to your child. What pleasing sensory experience is being created? If your child is making raspberries, for instance, the real pleasure may be in feeling air pass through his lips. If he is rolling on the ground, he may crave pressure next to his skin. Then, instead of criticizing the behavior, try to satisfy his sensory need in a socially acceptable way. "Boy, you really like the feeling of air across your lips, don't you? Let's see how many ways we can do that!" Then engage him in a game of whistling and whispering that will provide the desirable sensation.

This kind of behavior may also be an indication of anxiety or stress in a child who usually behaves on a higher level and cannot meet the social expectations of the moment. If you think this is the case with your child, reduce the momentary stress by joining her at something you know she enjoys, such as a favorite game or conversation. Later you may be able to explore how your child was feeling when she began the silly or anxious behavior. Was something scaring her? Worrying her? Use problem-solving techniques to help her develop alternative solutions. Perhaps she could ask the other child to play something else. Perhaps she could say, "It's too crowded!" or "It's too noisy!" or indicate that she doesn't feel like talking. If the behavior occurs during floor time, try to understand what might be frightening your child and take her side in the game. That way you can ward off the discomforting challenge and suggest symbolic solutions: "Let's capture the robbers and put them in jail." Or "Let's throw the wild animals into a pit." Help your child think about what the bad guys wanted to do and why. If she panics, speak calmly and remind her it is just make-believe. Try to reason later: "Did the wolf really eat the pigs?" "Did Captain Hook kill Peter Pan?" The more your child plays, the more she will realize that she controls her imagination and can make things as safe, exciting, or dangerous as she wants. And the more she controls her imagination, the less need she will have to control you.

Once you figure out what types of situations cause stress for your child, work those situations into your play so that he can assume the role of boss. He can be the teacher, the police officer, the doctor, the guard, or the bully and order others around. Give him as much support as he needs to feel secure, then slowly challenge him, encouraging logical, if not realistic, solutions.

REPEATING STORIES OR SCRIPTS

Some children engage in repetitive verbal behavior; they repeat the same question or the same story over and over again. They do this because it's comfortable; they understand it; they know what's coming next. They do not have to listen to someone else's words, which are unpredictable and hard to comprehend. Their language delays and motor planning and sequencing problems make it easier for them to do things that are rote and repetitive.

If your child has a favorite script, start by joining her and playing one of the roles. Once she accepts that, move on to conversations within the script, staying with the predictable story line but using your own words. Since your child already knows the story, she'll find it easier to understand your different language. Your child may talk a lot, depending on her role in the script, but may find it hard to listen. If you sense that she has a hard time listening to you or understanding your words, provide visual cues through gestures and use action figures and emotion to help her. Try, with your tone of voice, to mimic the emotional themes or tone of the script, since that was what helped her remember the script in the first place. You'll notice when your child moves from merely repeating her own script to taking in what you say.

If your child has memorized one script, he has probably memorized others as well. Use this knowledge to help him think more broadly and abstractly. Once he can engage in a dialogue about one script, bring in characters from other scripts wherever they fit the story. For instance, if you're playing out a scene from *The Rescuers Down Under* and the poacher is capturing Cody, suddenly bring in Jafar or Aladdin to help. If Pocahontas is in trouble, bring Jasmine to the rescue. Most children's movies and stories have good guy–bad guy themes; borrow characters back and forth to help your child generalize and abstract.

Perhaps you have noticed that your child uses only small speech fragments from a movie or book script, but likes to arrange figures or toys in a way that relates to that script. She may set up a scene as she remembers it and insist that none of the pieces be moved because in her mind, the scene she is creating is a static image. Rather than challenge her to change her scene, which would only meet with resistance, help her build the scene, while talking to the figures: "You stand here. Don't move. Where should the girl go?" Then hand her the figure. Take small steps and try to repeat and build on your child's comments until she is comfortable with your participation. Gradually offer suggestions about ways to change the scene. Perhaps the family would like some ice cream or some dinner. If a figure falls over, give it a masking-tape Band-Aid where it got hurt. Add in familiar experiences from daily life so as not to trigger anxiety and your child's avoidance. Respect her "no," but gently offer something else. Gradually she'll come to accept your suggested changes.

If your child is older and repeats questions, you can help him move out of that pattern and stretch his nervous system by teasing him away from his repeated vocalizations.

Five-year-old Haley had asked her therapist four times if all babies came from their mommies' tummies. The fifth time, instead of answering her, he said, "Gee, you're so interested in babies. What got you thinking about babies?"

Haley repeated the question.

Now the therapist answered, "I want to tell you about babies, but first tell me which *animal* baby is your favorite."

Haley ignored the question.

The therapist made his voice more animated. "Come on, Haley, please tell me which one you like best."

She told him she liked the cat. Now the discussion had moved away from her repetitive question.

"Why the cat?" he asked.

Again she avoided the question, so the therapist energized his voice. "Why the cat, Haley, why the cat?"

"Well, because I have a cat at home and I like to play with the cat."

The therapist sensed that they could take the conversation further. He asked, "Which animal baby do you *hate* the most?"

Haley ignored him, so he repeated the question more animatedly: "Which one do you hate, Haley, which one?"

"The mouse."

"Why?"

No answer.

"Why? Why? Why the mouse?"

"Because the mouse is bad," she answered.

When asked why the mouse was bad, Haley changed her mind, apparently not finding anything bad to report. When the therapist then asked her what was good about the mouse, she listed several qualities.

"Are you afraid the good cat might eat the mouse?"

Her eyes opened wide and she nodded slowly. She was clearly troubled. How could her nice cat also be so bad? Apparently Haley had been using repetition to avoid a conflict she could not resolve.

The therapist helped her think about what else her cat could eat so that it wouldn't want to eat the mouse, and finally Haley decided that only other cats ate mice. She seemed visibly relieved. They then returned to her original question and explored that.

By prodding Haley playfully, but with increasingly high levels of energy, her therapist was able to tease her beyond her initial repetitiveness into a rather lengthy and logical conversation.

Another way to deal with repetitive questions is to ask, "What else do you want to know?" or "How many times should I answer?" If your child can read, write down his questions and answers. Record them in a little book labeled "Juan's Questions." You can read the book together later, or he can show it to someone else and ask what he thinks. You will change the meaning of the behavior through this elaboration, and if you do it regularly with your child, you will strengthen his abilities to process and sequence language and ideas and make the things that are now difficult for him routine.

SWEARING AND SIMILAR INAPPROPRIATE BEHAVIOR

Charlie enjoyed experimenting with aggression through swearwords. When he tried them out, his affect and emotion were really involved and he seemed to come alive. In a therapy session, the therapist asked Mr. Whale (Charlie), "What's up?" Charlie answered for Mr. Whale, "Well, I'm becoming better."

"What's 'becoming better'?"

Charlie replied, "I'm not using cusswords anymore."

"Which words are you not using?" the therapist asked. At that point, Charlie really got into it. He laughed and smiled, and his whole body relaxed. As they talked about the swearwords—which were the best and which were the worst; what the therapist could say and what Charlie could say—Charlie's heart and soul came out in his spontaneity. His thinking became more creative and abstract and less fragmented. Although Charlie was not engaged in fantasy play per se, he was engaged in a rapid back-and-forth dialogue with his therapist about a subject that interested him greatly, laughing, kibitzing, and being imaginative and creative—the essence of floor time.

If your child swears at inappropriate places and times, do what the therapist did with Charlie—bring the swearing into the pretend play in floor time. During pretend play, swearwords are okay, in fact the more the better, because floor time provides the best opportunity for dealing with them. You can also bring swearwords into regular household discussions in a real way, talking about why they are fun, what makes them fun, and so on. In the privacy of your own home your child can use these words; in school or other more formal situations, however, they're not appropriate. By allowing your child to use these words in one setting and not in other settings, you are teaching him to discriminate, not to inhibit. There is a difference. Adults tell jokes and use "bathroom" words in the privacy of close friendship. They don't do it in church. They don't do it in schools. They don't do it at work. They discriminate. And this is what your child needs to learn to do. Inhibiting, on the other hand, can be harmful for your child. Thinking he's bad for using swearwords can make him even more anxious. He simply needs to learn that there are some places, such as at home with Mommy and Daddy, where it's okay to talk about swearing in a fun or curious way, and there are other places where it's not okay to use swearwords at all. You can remind your child in an accepting, not critical, way, "Yeah, those are great words, but you can't say them in school. Those are for home." You can have fun with him and let him enjoy the words at home. If there's still a problem, you can say, "If you really have to talk about it, pull me off to the side. You can tell me. I'll be your swearword person."

Charlie's mother was concerned about Charlie's desire to pull his pants down. Charlie's therapist suggested that the next time Charlie spoke of this desire at home, his mother should let him enjoy the fantasy: "Have him picture it, take the fantasy to the nth degree. What would be funny? Whom does he want to show his butt to? Let him really ham it up in the fantasy. Let him giggle and get it out. Then talk with him about what he really can do. Ask him if he knows in what situations he can act out the make-believe and in what situations it is not appropriate. After he's enjoyed his fantasy, help him discriminate."

When you discuss these issues with your child, let her challenge you and have a debate about it. Have a problem-solving discussion. If she behaves inappropriately in public, pull her aside and ask, "What's making you want to do that now?" Perhaps she's bored, anxious, or unsure of herself. Be very calm and reassuring. When you are at home again, bring the issue up in pretend play until your child understands the distinction between what is appropriate and what is not.

WHERE TO START

How do you decide which problem to work on first? Start with the one that is most important to you.

- If your child is keeping you up at night and also refusing to eat, start by helping him learn to go to sleep. As long as he's not getting sick, eating can wait, but *your* sleep is important.

- If she experiences terrifying fears at night and also refuses to go to school, work on going to school. Once she's comfortable there, the night fears may go away. If not, you can tackle them later.

Keep your goals. Don't overload your child with too many challenges. Pick one or two areas to work on at a time and make sure your child is comfortable with each new behavior before moving to the next. His success with each challenge will build his confidence for moving on.

CHALLENGES OF LATER CHILDHOOD

Moving into older childhood brings new challenges, such as the tendency to avoid reality and escape into fantasy, fragmented thinking, and the need to cope with anger and deal with conflicts, bossiness, and regression. These challenges are characteristic of children who have done extremely well, as they have become related, logical, abstract thinkers and have in a sense graduated to these problems. Think of it as being named CEO of a large company—you have been promoted, but you now have new problems. Because your child now has a rich fantasy life, he faces the tendency to escape into fantasy, because he has so many rich ideas, his thinking may be fragmented; because he has the wherewithal to know what he wants, he tends to be bossy. If he becomes overloaded and others don't do things his way, he may get impulsive and aggressive, or if he is distracted by many ideas or competing agendas, he may become inattentive.

The major processing challenge that goes along with these issues is the continuation of sequencing and sensory-modulation problems. To help your child through the stages of childhood involves a few core strategies. Most important is to keep up the nurturing side of floor time and to continue to help her abstract and organize thoughts by having reality-based discussions of her opinions and ideas. Help her work out her conflicts around aggression, grandiosity, power, and dependency. You often see little pieces of these issues—grandiosity when your child wants everything her way, dependency when she wants to be taken care of and protected, neediness when she becomes whiny, and anger when she becomes frustrated because she is not yet comfortable with being assertive and maturely aggressive when competing with peers. Create settings in which your child can work out these conflicts. Continue to do floor time so that she can play them out. She needs floor time with each parent.

Floor time at later ages does not have to involve pretend play. It can be a shared activity of your child's choosing, following his lead or his interest. Stay away from mechanical activities because they provide less opportunity for dialogue (it's hard to hold a discussion with someone who is playing a video game, for example). To deal with assertiveness, competition, aggression, and grandiosity, your child needs to do a lot of floor time with the parent or caregiver of the same sex. Games that have a competitive aspect, that can be won or lost, are beneficial as well (let your child win two-thirds of the time). To help with dependency, move away from overprotective patterns; switch the balance of relationships in the family. If your family is one in which the mother is more protective and the father is less available, have your child spend more time with the father.

Encourage peer relationships by arranging lots of play dates and helping your child make distinctions and deal with disappointment. She needs to move from "I'm the leader" to "Sometimes I'm the leader, but sometimes I'm not." She needs to learn what she is good at and what is hard for her. She needs to deal with competition and with the pecking order among peers.

As your child gets older, he needs to internalize a sense of who he is as a person. He lives in two realities. One is his peer group. He is up or down depending on how other children treat him. The other reality is his sense of self independent of the peer group—"I'm a good person" or "I'm a nice person because of all the things I do, independent of what happened to me today." As your child works through competition, rivalry, disappointment, and loss, he experiences a broader range of emotions, stays in reality for longer and longer periods of time, and copes with strong feelings. He stabilizes a stronger sense of self. This sense of self will make it possible for your child to move into the challenges of adolescence, when his sense of self will expand with biological changes, new interests, including sexual interests, new school activities, broader community interests, and new temptations. All these changes can be scary. With a stable sense of self, your child will get through them. In adulthood, his sense of self will expand even further as he faces marriage, children, and a career. The better your child can tolerate emotions, conflicts, aggression, competition, and dependency, the more stable his growing sense of self will be.

USE PROFESSIONAL HELP

As you work with your child on meeting challenges, take advantage of any professional expertise at your disposal. Your child's teacher, occupational therapist, physical therapist, and speech pathologist can help you tailor your small steps to your child's individual differences. They can also support your efforts in their own work. If your child is worried about monsters under her bed, her speech therapist can bring that into their discussions. If he is worried about falling into the toilet because of poor postural control, his occupational therapist can have him practice sitting on a toilet. Your child's teacher and interactive play therapist can introduce the themes that worry her into class and therapy sessions, where many children share those issues. These professionals are your partners in working with your child; let them help you.

15

Special-Needs Syndromes

We often look at special-needs challenges from the point of view of what causes them: Down syndrome and fragile X syndrome involve certain chromosomal patterns; fetal alcohol syndrome stems from alcohol use during pregnancy; developmental problems occur in many children exposed *in utero* to substances such as cocaine. We can also look at these problems from the point of view of the child's specific functional abilities. For the vast majority of developmental problems we have not identified causes, although we are likely to discover more about them in the future. The functional profile, however, often provides an important guide for our interventions because it pinpoints the areas that need to be improved, as well as the strengths.

It is helpful, as we have been discussing, to view special-needs syndromes in terms of the different processing problems that characterize them. Picture the mind as having a number of components, including motor planning and sequencing, auditory processing and verbal comprehension, speech, visual-spatial, and sensory and affective regulation. How do all these component skills work together? In a human being, and in many mammals, there is an intent or purpose to behavior. This intent comes from affect or emotion (desires). Emotion tells us what we want to do. An eight-month-old baby, seeing something interesting in his mother's mouth, feels curiosity, an anticipated sense of joy "if I can get that thing." There's an urge, a drive, a desire, an affect or emotion that initiates reaching for the object. Like an orchestra conductor, this intent organizes the components into action. Later on, this same intent or affect gives meaning to words and activities; a word or activity has no meaning if there is no purpose or goal to it, no emotion invested in it.

All children need to develop the various components of their minds, such as the ability to sequence actions or to form words. They also need an orchestra leader, a conductor, to provide organization, purpose, and goals. Emotions or intents, which derive from early interactive relationships, provide this sense of purpose and organization.

As we look at the different syndromes from a functional point of view, we identify the location of the problem. We see which component skills are affected and whether the emotional conductor, the guiding emotion, is underdeveloped or unconnected to the skills.

THE COMPONENT SKILLS

We can divide component skills into several functional areas. Motor planning and, more broadly, sequencing allow us to carry out what our intent or affect tells us. Without sequencing, we could have the strongest intent, the strongest desire or wish, but we wouldn't be able to translate it into an action plan. For example, if you wanted to go out the door to play outside, and the action plan (the motor planning or sequencing) weren't present to guide you, you might end up endlessly spinning around. If you had a fantastic idea for a story that would rival Shakespeare's dramas, but you couldn't sequence your words into sentences and your sentences into paragraphs to create a series of broader ideas and concepts, you might never be able to convey your inspiration to others or even fully to yourself. From going to the door and opening it, which requires two steps (walking, and putting a hand on the knob and turning it), to sequencing words into sentences and longer paragraphs, it is our sequencing capacity that enables us to communicate our intent.

Another component skill is the ability to process and comprehend what we hear, to decode sounds and words. Yet another involves decoding and comprehending what we see, understanding spatial relations. The latter skill enables an infant or young child to understand how the rooms of the house are connected and how to get from one room to another to locate his mother when he hears her voice. The child who can't solve this spatial problem may feel insecure and become clinging and demanding or may panic and withdraw. The child who can solve this problem knows where his mother is and can go to her when he wants her. This child feels more secure and stable; he can explore and be more adventuresome because he carries a map in his head that serves as his security blanket. Consider a busy preschool classroom. One child is overwhelmed by the various activities going on around him. Another child can create an integrated spatial map and knows exactly what's going on in every corner. She knows where the teacher is, where the other children are, which toys are near and which far away. She has an integrated sense of her world. The ability to understand spatial relations becomes important as we integrate the different pieces of who we are. Our sense of self relies on spatial and temporal maps of people, feelings, and things.

The ability to modulate sensation helps us negotiate with the world without feeling overwhelmed or underaroused and uninvolved. Some children are oversensitive or undersensitive to touch, sound, smell, or movement. As we have seen in earlier chapters, we can use other classifications or divide these component parts into more subparts, considering, for instance, musical ability, artistic ability, verbal ability, and athletic ability, among various other talents.

THE ORCHESTRA CONDUCTOR

The components evolve during the early months and years, as does the ability to develop intent and connect it to the components. In the first few months of life, the sense of intent is just beginning to form. We first see it clearly at about 3 to 8 months, when a baby starts reaching out for things or purposely looks or vocalizes at a smiling face. By 8 months, the baby evidences a lot of simple, purposeful, interactive behavior.

As the baby progresses to 18 months, she can take her parent by the hand, walk her to the door, bang on the door, and point as though to say, "Out." She can look for toys in the next room and get help from a parent to reach a toy on a high shelf. She can open and close 50 or 60 circles of communication in a row to carry out complex problem-solving behavior. Such complex problem-solving behavior suggests that one sequencing ability—the capacity to plan motor actions—is now under the direction of the conductor, the sense of intent. Now the child can feel the desire for a toy and sequence a complex action plan to get it. The child can also process sounds. If her parent looks confused and says, "Where?" or "Over there," the child can process the sound and perhaps even understand the word *where*. If instead of saying, "Want toy?" her parent says, "Want milk?" she will shake her head and point to the toy. She is also able to vocalize and read facial expressions and gestures. If her parent points to the wrong spot, she can use her visual-spatial processing to direct the parent to where she wants him to go.

The child is now using three component skills (sequencing ability, auditory processing, and visual-spatial processing), which are under the direction of intent, or emotion. The connection between intent and the component skills is developed in a fundamental way by 18 months of age.

We can understand the different special-needs challenges in terms of this model of needed component skills and emotional orchestra conductor. Which components are not developing in which syndromes? Which syndromes involve a lack of ability to connect intent or emotion to the component skills?

INDIVIDUAL SYNDROMES

A large group of developmental problems are types of *static encephalopathy* (*static,* meaning "nonprogressive," and *encephalopathy,* meaning "disorder of the nervous system"). These problems are static in that damage has been caused by trauma, infection, metabolic problems, chromosomal patterns, or unknown factors. These problems may be contrasted with progressive or neurodegenerative disorders, in which the condition worsens over time, even with an optimal intervention program. The static problems include Down syndrome, fragile X syndrome, fetal alcohol syndrome, low birth weight, maternal substance abuse, most types of cerebral palsy, most autistic spectrum disorders, many cognitive deficits, many forms of mental retardation, and many serious language disorders, subtle motor problems, and impairments of vision and hearing. Let's look at how considering underlying processing problems can lead to a plan for intervention for these problems.

Autistic spectrum disorders involve both component parts and the orchestra conductor. With these disorders as well as with *multisystem developmental disorders* we see a broad range of development in the component skills. Some children with autistic spectrum problems are also labeled *mentally retarded* because many of the component skills are severely affected. Other children are considered autistic but have unusual abilities. They may be able to memorize whole books or carry out certain mathematical operations, they may even be precocious in some areas, such as reading—but they can't connect intent or emotion to these component parts and thus give purpose and meaning to the way they function.

Consider a child who is babbling, reproduces some sounds, makes funny, self-stimulatory sounds, and occasionally comes up with a word or a random sentence. This child is showing us that the ability to process sounds, although it has problems, is more developed in him than in a child who can't repeat sounds at all or vocalize. There is some strength in this component part, even though it is not well developed. With autistic spectrum problems, while we are remediating the component parts, we must work on the bigger job of helping the child hook his intent, his desire, his emotions up to these component parts. Therefore, when the child is babbling or involved in a self-stimulatory pattern of sounds, we need to pull him into an interaction. We start this process by babbling back, perhaps trying to imitate the sound the child is making. This act often gets a look of recognition. When we have a rhythm of back-and-forth sound production, we are playing a babble game. Many effective ways of initiating this interaction are described in the chapters on floor time.

The key is to create a sense of intent around the component parts that are working. While speech and occupational therapists and special educators address the lagging skills, we try to give them intent and purpose. For children who have problems with both their conductor and their component skills, that is, children with autistic spectrum difficulties and mutlisystem developmental disorders, the goal is to pull them into a relationship so that their emotions become connected to another person. To achieve this goal, rely on the component skills that are working at their highest level. If the child is already making sounds and words, we incorporate that skill into the interaction and combine it with very simple gestures and a sense of relatedness. We woo the child into warm smiles, cuddles, and simple, interactive games that might involve reaching for an object. If the child is capable of some words, we ask, "Do you want the apple?" "Do you want the milk?" and so on. If the child's actions seem aimless or self-stimulatory, it's a sign of how poorly that conductor is working and how little emotion is connected to the actions.

With some of the other syndromes, such as cerebral palsy, cognitive deficits, or severe language disorders, the ability to connect emotion or intent to action is working fine, but there are severe deficits in the component skills. We face a double challenge with *cerebral palsy*. We have to remediate the motor problems and help the child learn to use her motor system *and* we have to get the child to use her motor system intentionally and purposefully. The child's emotion and intent are already connected to her motor capacities. She wants to babble and say the word *apple*, but her motor problem won't allow her to form the word; her arm won't reach for the apple in her parent's mouth because she can't control her arm movements. She is not reaching for that apple and not looking at her parent because she can't move her head or eyes in the direction of the apple. She has low muscle tone and very poor motor-planning abilities. When the component skills are so hard to use, the child stops using them in a purposeful way. The child can then lose the connection between affect or intent and sequencing ability or, more broadly, motor abilities, through disuse. If therapists and parents are not aware of the importance of intent—if, for example, they try to help the child learn to make motor movements in a passive way by manipulating her arms for her—the child's own intent will not become involved.

As with any function of the body, if we don't use it, we lose it. In many syndromes that involve a severe deficit in a certain ability, the connection between affect or intent and that ability can be lost through disuse. Therefore it is imperative to pay attention to the affect or intent, even in syndromes in which it is not the primary problem. Often we see a child with cerebral palsy or severe processing problems who is very self-absorbed; he doesn't have purpose and intent. Once we start working with the child, the intent comes in rather quickly. Initially, we can't be sure whether the child has an autistic spectrum problem plus cerebral palsy plus cognitive deficits, or only cognitive deficits or cerebral palsy. The problem may be misdiagnosed at first because the child is self-absorbed, repetitive, and self-stimulatory. Within a month of working to bring out his emotions, the child is very related, interactive, and more intentional. Even though he has a long way to go, the primary connection between intent and his various component skills is there.

A critical challenge with cerebral palsy is to identify movements that the child can make. Each successful movement connects his emotions or intent to his motor and sequencing abilities. While using approaches developed by physical and occupational therapists to help the the child with his motor patterns, we must always work on connecting these motor patterns to the child's desires. We start with the simplest motions that the child can make, such as tongue movements, trunk movements, head-turning movements, and eventually movements of the arms, legs, and hands, which are almost always more difficult. We help the child use any part of his body in an intentional way by creating challenges in which he wants to use that part and we help him practice a lot on his own. In this way we are hooking up the intent system and we are making sure the child's orchestra conductor is working. As healthy emotional experience is critical for the growth of future intelligence and problem-solving ability, even with nonautistic syndromes we need to pay very close attention to the emotional orchestra leader and how it's working. It will often improve more quickly when there isn't a primary processing deficit in the connection between intent and other capacities. Although in the nonautistic syndromes the deficit is in the component skill itself, the child may appear to lack intent and purposeful behavior because of disuse.

Cognitive and language deficits require a similar approach, with traditional speech therapy and special education carried out in the context of a floor-time model, as described in earlier chapters.

Low birth weight, fragile X syndrome, maternal substance abuse, fetal alcohol syndrome, and severe *attention deficit disorders* all involve, in varying degrees, challenges to sensory modulation (over- or underreactivity to touch, sound, sight, smell, and movement) as well as visual-spatial or auditory-processing problems and more or less severe motor-planning and sequencing problems. As every child is unique, it is important to diagnose each child's regulatory pattern. How undeveloped is the motor planning and sequencing and the motor tone? Is the child over- or undersensitive to sound or touch? How much of an auditory- and visual-spatial processing problem does he have? What functional developmental milestones has he mastered or not mastered? Is he engaged, intentional, a complex, nonverbal problem solver, using ideas creatively, thinking logically? An appropriate intervention plan is developed based on the child's profile, rather than on the diagnosis.

Children with *Down syndrome* almost always have low muscle tone and severe motor-planning challenges. They tend to be slower than others to register sound, and they usually have some auditory- and visual-spatial processing problems, although the extent of these problems varies enormously. The ease with which these children learn abstract, cognitive skills also varies enormously. We haven't tested the limits of the abilities of children with Down syndrome and many other syndromes, because we haven't involved them in an intervention program that addresses both intent or affect and the component skills. Each year we learn more about how to strengthen these component parts in innovative ways. Children with Down syndrome are often very warm and very engaged; their emotional system is usually working very well. We can build on this strength to encourage higher and higher levels of cognitive development. It is important to challenge them. For example, when we try to teach math to a child who has poor motor sequencing, we work with addition, subtraction, multiplication, and division using small numbers, perhaps zero to six. We work with simple sequences so that the child can master the concepts rather than get lost in the details of sequencing. With routine ways of teaching math, the child who has sequencing problems (which includes many children with Down syndrome), may become so confused that she will shut down. Yet some children can master simple division and multiplication and even fractions and decimals if we work with a pizza cut into sections. We describe this approach in Chapter 19.

Excellent programs are available in most communities for children with *visual deficits*, but we can add pieces to these programs based on our developmental approach. The child with severe visual deficits needs extra help practicing vocal gesturing as she attempts to master the stages of development—to engage, attend, have purposeful interactive gestures, solve complex preverbal problems and then complex verbal problems. The visual system is an important part of learning to gesture and of coming to know Mommy's facial expressions and Daddy's hand movements. Therefore, we need to work on *preverbal* skills—auditory gesturing, tone of voice, and subtlety of the emotions expressed in voices. The child can discover a great deal through subtle vocal gesturing, as well as touch, movement, and other senses, and needs additional practice in intonation and more rapid back-and-forth vocal gesturing.

The child with *visual deficits* also needs extra practice in perceptual coordination. For many children, the motor system depends on the visual system; they see an object and reach for it. The child with a severe visual deficit may depend on hearing something about the object, locating the sound in space, and then reaching for the object. Objects that have different sound qualities will help the child learn to judge distance and location. The motor world and the ability to solve motor problems, to have a sense of where things are, and to form spatial relationships, which is typically very dependent on the visual system, can be learned through the auditory system and the other senses, such as touch and smell. We need to devise more innovative ways of fostering these motor connections. Games that involve sound and reaching and, for toddlers, lots of problem solving—using cues from sounds to figure out where an object is hidden—can contribute to a sense of auditory space. In mathematics, big-picture thinking is often based on visual-spatial concepts. Mathematical principles are often easier to learn with visual-spatial patterns in part because most visual-spatial dimensions are continuous, as are many mathematical concepts. Children who don't have these visual-spatial concepts need to learn big-picture thinking through other sensory perceptions. Although words have distinct meanings, sound can be continuous. So, we can teach big-picture thinking through sounds, for example, moving from softness to loudness. It's important to work with dimensions of time and space as well. Is something big—"B-i-i-i-g!"—or little—"l-i-i-i-ttle"? Not only can we see big and little on a continuous dimension, but we can hear them and touch them on a continuous dimension also. We can convey the sense of bigness through sound as well as through touch.

Many children who have sight nonetheless have visual-spatial problems. For these children, more typical visual-spatial games can be helpful. For a baby, hide things in your hands; for a child, find things using clues; for an older child, do things that involve visual discrimination, visual categorizing, and perceptual problem solving.

For children with *auditory deficits,* many excellent programs are available. Again, we can add developmental ideas to these programs. For example, we rely on hearing to figure out subtle emotional expressions; tone of voice is an especially helpful clue. Most adults can figure out how someone they are talking to on the phone feels, even though they don't see a face. Our auditory system connects our perceptions to our motor system more rapidly than does our visual system. If we hear a dangerous sound, we may move more quickly than we would if we saw something dangerous. The auditory system is very adaptive; it picks up subtle emotional nuances and alerts us to danger or safety in the environment.

The child with a hearing deficit has to rely more on sight. To enhance visual perception and the other senses, we can play with the child not simply face-to-face, but with exceptional animation and subtlety. We also use other components, such as touch and movement patterns and rhythms. The child needs to use his other senses for perceiving emotion. If you hold the child's hand and squeeze a little bit or tickle it when you're happy, he is receiving the tactile as well as the visual sensation; he also senses the rhythm in which you are holding his hand. Rocking or other movement patterns can also convey feeling. There is a historic tendency, which still exists to some degree, to have parents of children with some auditory deficit stand behind their child and talk, so that the child has to rely on hearing and can't use visual or other cues. We have seen this practice result in children's developing severe relationship, communication, and thinking problems in addition to their auditory-processing problems. Children treated in this way also have more autistic features than do other hearing-impaired children. Finally, this practice does not help children to use the visual system for affect cuing, engaging, or problem solving.

The child with an auditory deficit needs extra practice to negotiate the different stages of development (attention, engagement, simple affect gestures, complex problem-solving gestures, using ideas, and then logical thinking). To help the child climb the developmental ladder, we have to provide practice in emotional and motor gesturing, because the child is trying to master the developmental steps without the benefit of full sound registration. We want to help the child use visual affective cuing and motor cuing; we want to challenge the child to use her initiative and develop visual motor patterns. We want the child to use whatever sound recognition she has for auditory-perceptual motor sequencing and for comprehending tone and gestures and, eventually, words. Cutting off sensory channels may undermine the experiences needed to negotiate the developmental milestones.

Because the auditory system tends to be faster than the visual system in transmitting information to the motor system, working on visual motor exercises, such as looking-and-reaching games, flashing light signals, movement games, and complex visual-motor problem-solving games as children become older, is valuable. If the child has sound recognition, it is important to work on sound-motor patterns and, to whatever degree possible, connect sound patterns to motor patterns to strengthen the ability for perceptual-motor coordination and integration. We also want to create exercises and games to help the child bring sound and sight together and coordinate them with different motor patterns. We might play games that provide visual cues and, to the degree possible, auditory cues to signal particular motor patterns. For example, older children can put the ball in box A, B, or C, depending on the visual and auditory information they receive. Information that comes through other senses—touch, smell, or movement, including rhythmic movement and music—will also help build a more solid foundation of perceptual-motor patterns. It is important to build the capacity to integrate even limited information from the different senses. Even when the child has stronger senses in terms of her ability to process information, it is still helpful to coordinate, as much as possible, information from the weaker senses.

Ordinarily, sound and comprehension of words is associated with verbal language. Verbal language is often involved with aspects of sequencing information. The ability to sequence words into a sentence, to sequence sentences into a paragraph, to sequence a series of ideas explained in a paragraph into a tight essay, all involve sequencing verbal information. Many parts of the nervous system are involved in sequencing: the motor and verbal systems as well as spatial relationships. When one sensory-processing system is not able to contribute as fully as possible to learning to sequence, we need to provide extra practice through the other senses and the motor system as well as emerging symbols.

The child using sign language should be challenged to sequence long dialogues and can use pictures and spatial designs to do so too. A child can tell a long story with pictures as well as with signs. The child can also practice sequencing with musical rhythms or sound sequences that might be within her auditory perception range if she has partial hearing. Sequencing is very important as a foundation for communication, thinking, and problem solving and therefore, should receive extra practice, especially when hearing is impaired.

The child with hearing challenges may need extra practice integrating details into a big picture, seeing both the forest and the trees. Big-picture thinking is typically facilitated through visual-spatial reasoning. Abstract categories, in a sense, are the houses for the details. But auditory processing is necessary to understand the details in our perceptual world. Because the auditory system contributes to our understanding of specific meanings, to our understanding of how each tree in the forest is unique and separate and distinct, lots of extra practice with using the different sensory pathways—vision, touch, smell, movement—for comprehending both the details and the big picture is very valuable. Exercises that focus on both visual discrimination and visual categorization can be an important part of the overall educational program for the child with a hearing deficit. Using signs or pictures to practice seeing how the parts fit into the whole and how the particular details of a subject can be organized in different ways is also helpful. Participation in classroom discussions that require defending big-picture conclusions with specific examples provides excellent support for this type of thinking. Describing a picture from the point of view of the whole and its parts is similarly useful.

In assisting children who have visual or auditory deficits we also need to help them deal with strong emotions or affects. Most of us are able to deal with strong emotions because we experience emotional interactions through the different senses—vision, hearing, smell, touch, movement. We synthesize these different sensory experiences and integrate them through the creation of abstract categories of experience. We experience anger as a tightness in the fists, tension in the stomach muscles, a hollow feeling in the chest, a series of potential action patterns (hitting, yelling, or screaming), a series of words ("I am mad"), a series of visual images that may convey action, as well as a particular smell or tactile sensation ("bristling" with anger). In development, these multiple aspects of anger are ordinarily synthesized and integrated into a concept that can be experienced at higher and higher levels of integration and synthesis. For example, "I am angry and I have good reason for being angry, but I'd better not do anything about it now because the situation isn't right. I'll just have to be patient and bide my time" might be a high-level synthesis of an angry feeling of the moment. To promote the ability to tolerate strong emotions without either acting them out through direct behavior or being inhibited or becoming avoidant of them, we need to be able to integrate and synthesize our experiences through the different senses and form abstract categories to reflect on these strong feelings.

To promote reflection in the child who has processing problems in a sensory pathway or deficits in perceiving information through a sensory pathway, it is useful to provide extra practice in coping with strong affects and synthesizing whatever experiences come in through the different senses. On a practical level, this means helping the child experience his emotional world in doses that he can tolerate and master. It means soothing a toddler before he becomes too angry or too upset or too scared or too needy. It also means helping the child experience his full range of affects and emotions through pretend play and real-life experiences. It means avoiding entering into overprotective patters than will undermine the child's ability to experience the wide range of affects that are part of life. For example, trying to remove frustrating experiences in the belief that the child shouldn't experience anger might be counterproductive; the experience of intense anger may help the child learn to cope effectively and synthesize emotions. Fostering the child's creativity, independence, and assertiveness, even though he has difficulty using one or another of his senses, can enable him to tolerate an ever wider range of emotions, to put emotions into symbolic form, visual or auditory, and to reflect on these emotions.

PART THREE

Family, Therapy, and School

16

Marital Challenges

Ann and George Lewis were overjoyed at the birth of their son. Michael was their first child, and they basked in his beauty: his tiny, well-formed hands, his dark eyes and long, thick lashes, his thick head of curly black hair. He bestowed his first broad smile on his parents at 3 months and rolled over at 4. At 8 months he was crawling and cooing and exploring his world. By a year and a half he had mastered several words. Friends and grandparents extolled his quickness to learn, and his parents reveled in his accomplishments. It was true that Michael was also a difficult baby—fussy about food (he had never nursed well), nervous around loud noises (the doorbell always set him off), and reluctant to sleep (he never slept through the night). But he was warm and affectionate and always available for a snuggle and a kiss.

When Michael turned 19 months the Lewises felt a subtle change. It was nothing concrete, nothing they could really put a finger on, but Michael seemed less responsive. He no longer answered when they called his name, and when they pointed to pictures in his books, instead of naming some as he always had, he now stared sullenly at the pages. Whereas just months before, he had been constantly demanding new books, now he insisted on the same three books all the time. The same thing happened with videos; he wanted his two favorite videos to be played over and over, and the mere suggestion of a different video sent him into tantrums.

When the Lewises mentioned their concerns to Michael's day-care provider, she said that she hadn't noticed anything; he still seemed "well behaved." Michael's grandparents agreed. "What are you worried about?"

they chided. "He's a two-year-old. It's a stage." Ann and George weren't reassured. These days, when they took him to the park, he no longer ran joyfully to the sandbox or the slide. He refused to leave the parking lot and slowly walked along the line of cars, staring intensely at their headlights as if examining them for defects. Or he walked along the chain-link fence, scouring one row of links as if his eyes were glued to it. To Ann and George it seemed that Michael's world was constricting. Each day he could take in less and less.

Finally, when Michael was two and a half, Ann Lewis mentioned her concerns to her pediatrician. He agreed with the day-care provider that nothing was wrong, but when Ann began to cry he relented and recommended a child psychologist. The child psychologist said that Michael had pervasive developmental disorder.

Ann and George were in shock. Why had this happened? Who was responsible? What did it mean for Michael? What did it mean for them?

They began a frantic search for what they needed to hear—that the diagnosis was a mistake. But a third specialist confirmed the evaluation. Ann began to read voraciously everything she could get her hands on about pervasive developmental disorder. Books, medical journals, magazine articles—the more she read, the more she nursed the secret hope that she would find the little-known piece of information that would say it wasn't true or that there was a cure. At the same time she blamed herself. "It was that time I didn't strap him into the car seat and he bumped his head." Her seething guilt made her redouble her readings, redouble her attentions over Michael.

George reacted differently. He didn't read. He didn't search for answers. He didn't even talk to Ann about the diagnosis. He withdrew. He spent more and more time at work—he even brought work home at night—to avoid facing his feelings about his son. He came home at eight or nine o'clock, knowing that Michael would be in bed, to find Ann sleeping on the sofa.

Michael's condition grew worse. He retreated entirely into an inner world from which no amount of coaxing could extract him. The bright and verbal boy who just months before could repeat numbers now spent all his time, pacifier in mouth, scrunched under a chair or table. Efforts to bring him out or to feed or dress him produced uncontrollable tantrums that lasted an hour or more.

Ann enrolled Michael in an early-intervention program, but his condition intensified. Ann felt angry, abandoned by George to the problems of caring for their son. Wasn't he as responsible as she? Wasn't Michael his son too? Why wasn't he helping her? Why wasn't he there when she needed him? Maybe Michael's problems stemmed from George, who had a history of depression. So as George withdrew from his wife and son, Ann withdrew from George. She stopped expecting anything from him, stopped talking to him, stopped feeling anything toward him except sorrowful, leaden anger.

George felt angry also. What had happened to his family? To the comfortable life he'd grown to love? To the wife who used to greet him warmly when he came home and listen to the tales of his day? This new wife seemed to have no time for him—only for that child, that child who had ruined their lives. George found himself wishing Michael hadn't been born. What was he thinking? He loved Michael! But the knowledge of his ambivalence, and the guilt it produced, were too much to bear. So George stayed away. At least at work he could feel normal.

Then one night, about a year after the diagnosis, the family went out to dinner at a family restaurant. It was their first outing in months, their first determined attempt to get on with their lives. Sitting in the booth, Michael began to bellow. Ann and George stared down at their uneaten food, all too aware of the stares they were receiving. A few moments later an elderly couple passed their table on their way toward the door. The man leaned over and said, "You should know better than to let your child behave that way in here!" Before he knew what he was doing George leaped from his seat, followed the man outside, and yelled, "This is the first time in a year I've taken my family out. I don't need your advice. For your information, my son has a serious mental illness." The man was abashed. He'd assumed Michael was merely uncontrolled. He couldn't apologize enough for his action. But George wasn't mollified, and for days he walked sullenly around the house, unable to speak or make eye contact with Ann.

Horrifying as that incident was, it was also a turning point. Somehow it galvanized the Lewises into action. They decided that they were no longer willing to stay at home, to give up their former lives. Ann stopped searching for a specialist who would tell her the disorder would go away and instead intensified the therapy program. George gradually stopped staying so late at work and arranged his schedule so that he could take Michael to some of his therapy appointments as well as work with him at home in the evenings. They also began seeing a marriage counselor to help them deal with their conflicted feelings about each other and their son.

Ann and George still felt tremendously pained and angry about Michael's disorder and the dramatic change it had created in their lives. They still mourned the son they no longer had. But for the first time in over a year, those feelings didn't prevent them from dealing honestly with the son they did have and with each other. Michael's birthday was tremendously hard for them; it reminded them of all the expectations they had had when he was born and all the ways those expectations might not be met. Christmas was almost as tough. But by Michael's next birthday they were able to anticipate and cope with their disappointment better. By that time Michael had made significant progress in therapy. He was no longer avoiding his parents. He had begun to look at them more, to seek them out, and to gesture to them, and he was beginning to use a few words. The Lewises, after a year in counseling, had learned how to trust each other with their feelings so that they no longer felt they had to handle Michael's problems alone.

REACTING TO A CHANGED LIFE

Although Ann and George each felt very alone in coping with their son's challenge, they are far from alone in the way it affected their family. The conflicted feelings, the anger and estrangement, the eagerness to blame themselves and each other are common in families who are coping with a child's developmental problems.

Many parents greet the news of a significant developmental problem with shock and denial. "This can't be true!" they think and seek avidly to confirm that they are right. They read extensively. They contact myriad specialists, hoping to find one who will tell them what they want to hear: that somehow life can go back to normal.

At the same time they often experience tremendous guilt and anger. Both parents blame themselves for causing the problem. They also blame each other: "He has a history of depression in his family." "If she hadn't smoked this never would have happened." They may become intensely angry with each other—for causing it to happen, for not preventing it, for reneging on the bargain they made when they got married. They may also be secretly angry with their child—for ending their life as they knew it.

But, they ask themselves, how can they be angry at their child? He didn't ask to have problems, and he's the one who has to live with them! So they may deny that anger and instead feel overwhelmed with guilt: guilt that they feel angry; guilt that they caused the disability; guilt that they can't make it go away.

Together, the guilt, the anger, and the underlying sorrow can become paralyzing. Some family members try to cope by becoming perfect, determined to find a perfect solution. Others become avoidant or depressed.

Sometime during this period the child begins therapy, and then comes a period of vacillation. At times parents believe that therapy will make all the difference—their child will totally recover, and they are perfect parents for making this possible. At other times they are in anguish—all the therapy in the world won't help their child; she is forever impaired, and they are awful parents for letting this happen. Life becomes an excruciating roller coaster. One parent may be up and able to cope, while the other sinks into despair.

Sometimes, although the family is able to meet its day-to-day crises, this alternating up and down reinforces the couple's different styles of coping with the stress and can magnify their problems. One parent may cope by aggressively catering to the child. The child becomes the focus of attention as the parent goes to therapy appointments, talks to doctors, meets with teachers, and ministers to the child's needs. The other parent, meanwhile, may go to work as usual. Work becomes a safety zone, a place where life is as it was before, a world the family's troubles don't invade. There the parent can find refuge from spouse and child. The parent feels needed at work, feels competent there, whereas at home the family is falling apart and the parent doesn't know what to do.

Before long, the parents have fallen into a mechanical pattern. They exchange few words, only a few bitter complaints: "You no longer care about me! You don't help me enough!" Inside, both parents are terrified—terrified of this new life, terrified that their marriage is falling apart, terrified of being alone. But both are too upset to share their painful feelings.

Further contributing to the family challenge is the intensification of a pattern that faces all families. Couples often gravitate to each other *because* of their differences. They complement each other. One provides the nurturing chicken soup, the other the competitive edge for business success. One is shy and avoidant, the other outgoing and wooing. Once a child comes along, however, the old pattern is forced to change. The parent who provided the chicken soup is now up all night with the baby and wants to be fed and cared for by the other. But the other parent feels betrayed and depleted, thinking, "I work hard; *I* need care!" A new emotional contract needs to be negotiated, but parents are often not enough aware of their patterns or are too locked into blaming each other to work it out. When the child has special needs, this pattern is intensified. Parents must reach inside to find the strength and emotional sustenance to give their child, but since they don't feel their own needs are being met, they have precious little to give their child. To solve this problem, they need to recognize what they originally gave each other and see how it's changed, and they need to arrange a new balance that can nourish both them and their child.

If parents learn to accept their conflicted feelings, they can work together as a team. Sometimes counseling can help. Gradually parents can grow realistic about their child's problems and begin working with their child toward improvement. Parents who are able to confront their own feelings honestly are usually able to emerge from the devastating period after the diagnosis stronger as a family. Marriages in which the parents continue to shy away from their feelings, however, may become more difficult, sometimes ending in separation and divorce.

Even for parents who do learn to share their feelings as well as the responsibilities of caring for their child, life is not easy. Birthdays and holidays rekindle old feelings of hope or despair, experienced again in milder form. Parents whose children were diagnosed in the first year of life, and who by year two have surfaced from the initial trauma, often find that they have a relapse when their child turns three or four. At that point the child enters preschool, and suddenly it is all too easy to compare him with other children. His difficulties become glaringly apparent as other children are becoming more verbal, more outgoing, and more competent, and parents often sink into a second depression in which the old sadness, guilt, and anger reemerge. A third bout of depression sometimes occurs when the child enters first grade. If their child has been doing well in therapy, parents often hope she will be mainstreamed. If she isn't, or when it becomes apparent that she still functions below grade level, those feelings play themselves out once more. As with holidays, these second and third depressions are shorter and milder than the first, and parents exit from them with renewed, but realistic, hope.

"The hardest thing for us now is not knowing where Michael will end up," says Ann Lewis. "And there's just no answer to that. But on a day-to-day basis we can cope with him and his problems."

RECOGNIZING COPING PATTERNS

Zachary Solomon was also diagnosed with PDD and like the Lewises, the Solomons were devastated by the news. But their means of coping with their distress was different. Melissa had always been strong and assertive; Rich, her husband, laid-back and flexible. In the early years of their marriage, their contrasting temperaments had meshed comfortably. But the birth of Zachary changed that. Melissa, who had felt competent mothering their first son, suddenly felt inept and insecure. Unable to "fix" or even console her son, she grew less willing to reach out and nurture and more needy of nurturing herself. Yet she was unwilling to cry or ask her husband for help because she was unwilling to expose her vulnerability. Instead, when he didn't respond to her unspoken need, she grew angry at him and attacked.

Rich, meanwhile, coped differently. He, too, felt insecure about fathering this difficult son, but rather than grow angry, he focused on his son and avoided his angry wife. The more he pulled back from her, the angrier Melissa got. And the angrier she got, the more he pulled away and gave all his attention to Zachary. So a vicious cycle began; each exacerbated the reaction of the other, and each faulted the other for reacting the way he or she did. Paradoxically, the very traits they had first enjoyed in each other became the loci of blame. Melissa blamed Rich for his passive acceptance of the situation; Rich criticized Melissa for her aggressiveness. By the time the Solomons went to a family therapist, they could see little in each other beside the qualities they had come to hate. Neither saw the frightened, hurting individual beneath the protective armor.

Over the next year their therapist helped them examine what had happened in their marriage. She helped them see that in reacting to the stress each had adopted a coping pattern learned as a child. Melissa had learned from her family to deny her vulnerability and mask it with aggression. Rich had learned to play it safe, to become passive and go with the flow, avoiding confrontation. This pattern had worked well in the early years of their marriage when stress was minimal. But the birth of Zachary had pushed these patterns to the limit.

Recognizing their styles of coping with stress was the first step. Harder was learning to change them. Both partners had to make themselves, through sheer force of will, reject their habitual responses and instead do what was better for the marriage. Melissa had to swallow her pride and tell Rich how scared and insecure she felt and how much she needed him. Rich had to force himself to pay attention to his wife and face her concerns.

The process was difficult, but it began to pay off. After several months in therapy their cold war began to thaw as each partner began to see the other more fully. By the end of the year they felt they were closer than they had been before. The experience had created an intimacy that had been lacking in their relationship.

In most marriages, the spouses react differently to the stress of having a child with special needs, and it is not uncommon for these differences to threaten the stability of the marriage, at least temporarily. To recreate a stable emotional partnership, both partners have to examine their own coping style and then work to change it.

Of course, it's hard to see your own patterns; they are set in childhood, and they're the way you're used to perceiving the world. Suppose, for instance, that each time your parents reached out to you, they also humiliated you. Your emotional reaction to closeness might be one of caution and anger. Rather than view closeness as a haven of safety, you might pull away, distrusting the person who is wooing. Obviously, that reaction would make it hard to establish a close and loving relationship.

To change these patterns, you need to be carefully self-observing, step back and see that your reaction to a situation may not be what is warranted. Since it is hard for us to see our own reactions with any objectivity, you may benefit from the help of a therapist, a spouse, or perhaps a trusted friend, who can serve as an outside observer.

Even with self-knowledge, it takes a lot of work to change, because change means countering your intuitive sense of how to behave. When you see a warm and smiling face you won't think, "I know that's a warm and smiling face but I feel threatened because my parents undermined me when they were warm," you'll think, "That's a *threatening* face," because that's how it will feel to you. It will take a great deal of maturity and discipline to step back from your initial reaction to say, "Aha! There I go again!"

However, it can be done. As you become familiar with your own ways of reacting, you can learn to take countervailing steps. It's a little like resisting a luscious piece of chocolate cake. Everything inside says, "Eat it!" but with a great effort of will you can put aside the momentary drive in exchange for the long-term good.

For any marriage to succeed, some ability to do this is necessary. For families with a child who has special needs, it is crucial. Without the ability to change, the partners are liable to drift further and further apart. With it, they can rebuild the trust and intimacy they knew before. Often they can build an even greater closeness.

ENCOURAGING FAMILY COMMUNICATION

• Set aside time to be together as spouses, rather than as parents. Get a baby-sitter and go out weekly, or set aside a long evening a week when you can be together after the children go to bed. Set aside time each evening to talk about feelings as well as events. Taking time together can help you see each other as people instead of as adversaries in the daily grind.

• Try to be honest with your feelings—both with yourself and with your spouse. Acknowledging difficult feelings is scary, but once you verbalize them, they lose a great deal of their power. Give each other time to talk without interruptions, intrusions, explanations, or reassurances. You will become less afraid of what your spouse has to say and will feel more reflective and empathetic. Talking about your feelings will bring you and your spouse closer.

• Talk to other families who share similar experiences. You won't feel so alone, and you will be able to share ideas and feelings.

• If necessary, seek help. It can be extremely difficult to deal with these strains alone. Counseling can often strengthen a marriage, and can make for stronger parents as well.

17

Family Challenges

Three-year-old Steven had a moderately severe form of cerebral palsy, and a child psychiatrist had suggested that he might be mentally retarded as well. Indeed, he was only minimally responsive to his mother's overtures; he rarely looked her in the eye and only occasionally indicated that he'd heard her voice. Despite these obstacles, however, Sally, Steven's mother, made Herculean efforts to reach him. She followed his eyes as they searched the room and brought him each object on which they settled. Patiently she held the objects out, encouraging Steven with her voice, but Steven refused to look at her hand. Undaunted by his rejection, she talked softly about the object, pointing something out, hoping to engender some interaction. But Steven ignored her. Often after Sally had pointed to the object, he looked away as if it were now tainted by her touch. Patiently, Sally followed his gaze again, and brought him the next thing that caught his fancy.

For the first five minutes or so of watching Steven and his mother the therapist marveled that Sally could marshal such patience and tenacity in the face of her son's rejection. Intuitively she seemed to know exactly what to do—how to follow his lead, how to persist gently in her efforts to engage him, how to refrain from being overly intrusive. She seemed to be doing everything right.

But as five minutes stretched into ten the therapist began to notice something else. Although Sally was doing everything "right," there was a mechanical quality to her efforts. There was no gleam in her eye as she looked at her son, no emotional range in her voice when she spoke to him.

It was as if she'd read the instruction book and knew what to do, but took no pleasure in doing it. In part, she'd lost touch with her own emotions and had limited vitality to bring to their relationship.

"You're working very hard to be a good partner for your child," the therapist commented. "You're doing a wonderful job. I bet you'd like to enjoy it more."

Sally looked at him for a second, then looked away, but not before tears formed in her eyes. Haltingly she began to talk. "At first when he wouldn't look at me or smile at me, I would get mad at him and want to shake him. Then I began wondering what I did wrong and what my husband did wrong. I found myself vacillating between trying very hard and then giving up and just feeding him and making sure he was comfortable. I couldn't bear looking into his eyes and not getting even a twinkle back. So I began doing what I'm doing now—just trying to get him to react, but not expecting much. It's too painful; I don't dare hope for much from him. I try not to get too excited or too happy when he does look at me because I'll only be disappointed next time."

Sally's response to her son was painful—and typical of some of the reactions parents of children with special needs have. Parents may react in different ways. Some become aware of their feelings and find extraordinary strength and capacities to cope. Some deny their sadness and disappointment, their frustration and their anger, and instead become overly controlling, as if by working extra hard to make their child perform the way they want they can reduce his disability. They don't mean to overcontrol; their guidance is offered with the best of intentions. But it is the only way they have to keep their own fears and sadness at bay.

Other parents are so saddened and disappointed by their child that they become hostile and rejecting. They withdraw physically as well as emotionally, keeping their interactions to a minimum. They don't mean to reject their child—they love her—but only by keeping her child at arm's length can they protect themselves.

Still other parents feel the impulse to escape, to pretend their child and his disability don't exist. But they are so uncomfortable with that feeling that they defend against it by adopting the opposite behavior; they becoming overprotecting and anxious. They fear letting their child out of their sight and letting him interact with others; they hold him back from trying things on his own. They don't mean to overprotect him, but only by keeping him so close can they protect against their own disturbing mix of feelings.

Often parents respond in several of these ways, vacillating from one way of coping to another. They may overcontrol for a period of time, insisting their child relate to them in a certain way. When that doesn't work, they may get frustrated and angry and cope with those feelings by withdrawing. "Fine," they think, "if you won't give me what I want, then I'll stop trying!" and they pull back into a shell. How else can they stay sane? How else can they bear the disappointment?

Often, many of these ways of behaving are not intentional; they're not the ways parents *mean* to relate to their child. They're the only ways parents *can* relate, given the extreme circumstances of their lives. It's hard to get their child to eat, to sleep, to go potty in the bathroom, to get dressed without a scene, to refrain from hitting, kicking, and biting, to smile—such a small thing, to smile. When parents can't control any of this behavior they begin to feel like bad parents, bad people who can't even help their own child. All the rational arguments in the world can't assuage their inner sense of failure. On top of that, the parents are tired, dog tired, from not sleeping through the night, from ministering to their child's demands, from fighting doctors and therapists and schools to get their child what she needs. They are also drained from fighting each other—for not helping enough, for not meeting each other's needs, for not being there when they're needed.

These coping behaviors don't surface suddenly in response to children with special needs, however. Usually they are learned in childhood. One mother always sulked when her child grew distant. When asked why, she thought for a few moments, then said, "What my mother did when she didn't get her way." Some of us adopt behaviors we used as children to protect ourselves from pain. One mother became aggressive whenever her daughter withdrew; she would poke her and tickle her and try to draw her out through almost hostile gestures. When asked where that tendency came from she replied, "My mother was unpredictable. Sometimes she'd be really warm and loving and then suddenly she'd withdraw. I'd get so angry at her for ignoring me that I would poke her and hit her to make her pay attention."

By the time we are parents ourselves this behavior is old and familiar. We carry it with us, the way a child lugs a teddy bear, into any stressful situation. Much as we depend on them, however, our coping behaviors are often invisible to us. We fall into them reflexively, and it's not until they prevent us from handling a situation in the present or clash with the needs of another person that we become aware of them. Often it is marriage that brings them to light, as the relationship's unavoidable stresses trigger defensive maneuvers in both partners.

Then, all too often, parents fall into an uncomfortable cycle. One partner gets frustrated and responds reflexively, by withdrawing or becoming hostile. That triggers an equally reflexive and unproductive behavior in the spouse. With each new response, anger builds. Soon talking stops, and neither partner knows how to quit the cycle.

Fortunately, when parents examine their patterns of coping—and the effect those patterns have on their child—they can change behavior that has lasted a lifetime. Doing so isn't easy. It doesn't happen overnight. But the motivation to help their child is so great that parents can often do it. Although most of us have some defensive coping patterns, in *many* families, parents learn to restrain unproductive behaviors; they learn to become more flexible in their reactions to frustration and disappointment.

A TENDENCY TO WITHDRAW

Sally coped with her disappointment in her son by withdrawing from him emotionally. It was easier to wall off her feelings than to live with the daily pain. As Sally talked about her sadness, she realized that she'd felt similar feelings toward her own parents, who were often unresponsive to her when she was a child. Busy career people, they had little time for their children, and tended to treat Sally and her brother mechanically. "They always did what they had to do," Sally said, "but somehow their gestures always felt empty. I never felt like they really enjoyed being with me." As she spoke those words a look of recognition crossed her face; she saw her own behavior in her parents.

This realization helped Sally determine to be different. As she worked with her son on opening and closing circles, she concentrated not just on the mechanics of interaction but also on listening to her emotions and expressing animation in her face. One day, as Steven accepted a block from her hand, he gave a little smile, and to Sally's amazement, she felt a flutter of joy. As time went on and Steven was able to close first one, then two circles of communication in a row, Sally slowly let her emotions thaw. As mother and son both opened up their range of communication, a chemistry evolved between them.

It isn't always possible to figure out where your coping behavior comes from. But you can do your family an equally valuable service by being honest with yourself and acknowledging the full range of your feelings toward your child. It's tremendously hard and frightening to admit to yourself that you are angry and disappointed in your child and that your fear and sadness feel overwhelming. But those feelings are natural and real. You would be less than human if you didn't feel them. Hiding them—from yourself as well as from others—won't help. Once you deal more fully with difficult feelings, your capacity to energize and support your child's development may become more flexible.

A TENDENCY TO OVERCONTROL

David's evaluation at age three and a half suggested that he had multisystem developmental delays. He was often tuned out, had very little speech, was not yet toilet trained, and had tantrums lasting an hour or more. He occasionally imitated a parent's gesture, but he couldn't close more than one circle at a time and he didn't engage in any pretend play. When David and his father, Frank, played together, a pattern became apparent. Rather than wait for David to express interest in something, Frank would try to start the interaction. He would hand items to David, quickly moving on to another if David didn't immediately take one, or he would tickle David or try to roughhouse with him in order to get a response. David would become passive or turn his back. When David did initiate an activity, by picking up a car and looking at it, for example, rather than wait to see what David would do so that he could play alongside, Frank would grab the car and do something with it himself. In every way, he tried to control the play. His actions left David little room to develop initiative or even a sense of himself. The only way David could stand up to his father was to turn his back or tune him out.

In discussing his feelings about David, Frank admitted that he was frustrated and angry with his son for having the problems he did. "I was a slow developer," he said, "but unlike David, I got it together." Frank felt let down by his son's "refusal" to do the same. By controlling the play he was trying to make David do what he wanted him to do. Inside, Frank hoped that if he tried hard enough, played aggressively enough, David would "come around" and be the son he wanted him to be.

Once Frank acknowledged these feelings, he was also able to get in touch with the tremendous love and empathy he felt for his son. All his life he had wanted to do things better than he could, and he suddenly empathized with the part of David that must feel that way too.

The therapist emphasized the importance of letting David take the lead and of Frank's restraining the impulse to take charge. When David ignored his father, instead of switching to a new activity, Frank was to stick patiently with the activity at hand until David had closed the circle. Frank was also to empathize verbally with whatever David was doing.

Two months later, they had made considerable progress. Frank was still impatient and had to fight his tendency to take the lead, but he was working on it. At their therapy session, Frank grabbed a gun and pretended to shoot. But when David reached out for it, Frank let him take it. David smiled slightly and in a soft voice said, "Boom, boom." Frank smiled too and repeated, "Boom, boom." They exchanged three or four gestures while making booming noises back and forth. This was the most connected David had ever been—closing five or six circles in a row and actually doing a bit of pretend play with the gun. Best of all, he was warmly related to his dad. Frank was enjoying the situation also; throughout the session he smiled at David proudly.

In the two years since, David has continued to improve. At five and a half, he is now engaged with people almost all the time. He has made friends at school and is working on putting his feelings into words, rather than acting them out. He is becoming increasingly logical in his thinking. David has benefited from an intensive program of speech, interactive, and occupational therapy. But it is likely that none of his progress would have been possible without the changed behavior of his father (and mother, whose story follows). As the most important people in David's life, their feedback was critical. Had Frank continued to overcontrol him, David probably would not have developed the ability to think and act for himself and take advantage of the therapy he was offered. Even more important, he might never have learned that relationships with others can be warm and supportive, well worth the risk of tuning in to.

A TENDENCY BOTH TO OVERSTIMULATE
AND TO WITHDRAW

David's mom, Lucinda, shared her husband's tendency to overcontrol their play. She initiated activities rather than letting David take the lead, and she hurried David from one activity to the next whenever he didn't immediately respond. Unlike Frank, however, Lucinda would abruptly shift gears. When her eager attempts to engage David failed, she would suddenly pull back. She would stop talking, stop handing him toys, and just watch him passively, as if she had disappeared into herself. Hurt by her son's rejection, she pulled away to spare herself further pain. The result was a frenetic, start-and-stop rhythm in which she and David never really connected.

David seemed confused by his mother's pattern. When she was being assertive he would become petulant and start to whine or cry. When she grew distant, he would become self-absorbed, as if her lack of energy had released him from the need to stay in touch.

When the therapist commented to Lucinda on what he saw, she nodded slowly, as if recognizing herself in his words. "You're right," she said. "That's what I do when I feel overwhelmed. First I get churned up and try to make things better; then I get depressed because my efforts aren't working. I did that in school. I do that with Frank. I guess I do it with David too."

Again, the therapist explained the importance of letting David take the lead and of working hard to close circles of communication. He let Lucinda know that she had to practice that skill and to fight her tendency to pull away.

Two months later mother and son were doing better. When David took out a doll, Lucinda waited to see what he would do with it. To her obvious delight, he held it out to her and said, "Dirty." "Yes, dirty," she agreed. Then David rubbed the doll with his hands while looking at his mother, a clear indication that he wanted her help in giving the doll a bath. During the next few minutes Lucinda and David exchanged four or five gestures as they pretended to bathe the doll. Both were warmly engaged through the entire sequence.

Over the next several months, as David and his parents improved their interactions, a pattern emerged. As Frank and Lucinda restrained their tendency to overcontrol his play, David grew better at taking the lead. And as he did, his parents felt less need to overdirect. The less directive they were, the more pleasure David took in their company. As he enjoyed their presence more, the less Lucinda needed to pull away. Their counterproductive old approach had given way to a highly constructive new one; as David's parents made it possible for him to grow, David made it equally possible for them to grow.

A TENDENCY TO OVERPROTECT

Rick was three and a half when his mother, Marsha, took him to see a therapist. He had severe motor delays and his speech was quite limited. It was hard to know how much language he understood since he tuned out quite a bit. He did a little bit of pretend play with puppets and horses, but he switched gears quickly, not sticking with anything for very long. Marsha was very warm and supportive, but made no attempt to engage her son. As he drifted from one toy to the next she merely gave a running commentary on his actions.

"You're very supportive in the way you engage Rick," the therapist said. "You make it so easy for him to play. But we also need to entice him into interactions. For example, instead of just commenting on his horse, you might put your horse in front of his, smile, and say, "Bet your horse can't get around mine!"

Marsha looked anxious. "I don't know," she said. "I don't want to make things hard for him."

"Too many challenges?" asked the therapist.

"Yes," she said, and as she continued to talk it became clear that she felt guilty about her son's disabilities. To make it up to him now she wanted to make his life as easy as possible.

Moments later Marsha revealed another reason for her protectiveness. "As long as I don't expect too much, I don't have to see him not be able to do something." As she said this she began to cry, and talked about how hard it was to see him struggle. By examining her complex feelings toward her son, she began to see how, inadvertently, she wasn't challenging him enough.

There was a marked improvement at their session four weeks later. When Rick put a puppet on his hand and waved it at his mom, instead of describing what he was doing, Marsha put a puppet on her own hand and waved back. Rick then started to take his puppet off, but Marsha said, "Wait! I want to ask you a question." Rick stopped and looked at her, surprised. "What's your name?" asked Marsha's puppet. Rick didn't answer. "What's your name?" Marsha repeated. Rick stared at her puppet but didn't answer. Marsha reached forward with her puppet and tickled Rick's puppet's nose. "Is your name Barney?" she asked. Rick giggled. "Is your name Ernie?" she asked. Rick giggled again. "Is your name Big Bird?" she asked. "Rick!" Rick yelled out. "Oh! Rick!" Marsha said, smiling broadly, and she made her puppet rub noses with Rick's.

A TENDENCY TO AVOID

Rick's father, Ed, coped with his discomfort with his son in a different way. He avoided him. Already busy, Ed became a bona fide workaholic. He left the house at six or six-thirty in the morning to prepare for his day's clients, and returned at seven-thirty at night with his briefcase full. When Marsha complained that she needed more help, he countered that his company was facing a merger and that if he didn't "make himself indispensable" he was likely to get cut.

Ed described himself as a details person, more comfortable with numbers than with creative ideas. For this reason, he said, he had trouble playing with Rick. When they sat together on the floor, he had no idea what to do. So, he took over the more mechanical details of Rick's life—feeding and bathing—and left playtime to Marsha.

The therapist explained to Ed that Rick needed *both* his parents to play with him and suggested strongly that he find a way to work 20 minutes of floor time into his daily schedule.

"Well, I'd like to, but I just don't know what to do."

"Don't do anything. Just see what Rick does and follow along."

Ed laughed nervously. The methodical planner in him was uncomfortable with so little structure. But he tried. He got down on the floor, and as

Rick placed people in the dollhouse Ed put people in too. When Rick switched to a new activity, Ed began to talk to the therapist. Until recently, he said, his world had felt secure; he had felt comfortably in charge. But Rick's birth had changed that. Suddenly he had a son (and a wife) with tremendous needs, and he had no idea how to meet them. The strategies he knew— rational dialogue and manipulating numbers—were no help at all in this world of emotion and unpredictability. To preserve his self-esteem he had to stay away, in the realm where he still felt omnipotent. Then suddenly that realm was shaken too. When his company announced plans to merge, Ed's only source of competence was threatened. In light of that threat, Rick's problems became even more frightening; Rick represented the loss of competence and power that Ed so feared at work. Now it was even more important to put in long hours on the job; not only did Ed need to feel indispensable, he needed to avoid the son who so threatened his self-esteem.

As Ed slowly expressed these feelings he realized that Rick's difficulties at home had no bearing on his performance at the office. By building a relationship with his son he would *gain* competence rather than lose it. He left that session more eager to do floor time.

When they returned a month later, their practicing showed. Rick put a puppet on his hand and Ed did the same. "Hello," said Ed's puppet. Rick didn't answer; instead he made his puppet push a car. So Ed's puppet got a second car and mimicked Rick. Rick giggled. Ed waited to see what Rick would do next. When, after a few moments, Rick hadn't moved, Ed pushed his car close to Rick's and bumped it gently. Rick made a noise of protest and started to push his car away. Ed followed him, going "vroom-vroom," and for the next minute or so Rick let his father chase his car around the room.

This was a tremendous improvement from Ed's almost complete uninvolvement the previous session. Not only was he actively playing with his son, he'd had the courage to stick with the game when Rick protested. Over the following months Rick and Ed became adept at playing with each other, especially as Rick became more verbal. Talking was more comfortable for Ed than doing gestural play, and he became good at helping Rick close circles verbally before moving on to another idea.

WHEN A CHILD'S FEELINGS MAKE PARENTS UNCOMFORTABLE

Children have a way of triggering strong emotional reactions in their parents—reactions that seem to take over before we can stop them. When that happens it's because something in our child's behavior has struck an emotional soft spot, an area of unresolved feelings. Feeling bruised ourselves, we tend to protect ourselves by adopting our characteristic coping behavior.

Four-year-old Molly was bright; her verbal and motor skills were advanced, and her parents were proud of her accomplishments. She was also aggressive, demanding, and resistant to control. Several times a day she threw uncontrollable tantrums during which she could cry and whine for hours.

Molly's mother was understandably unnerved by these episodes, but instead of trying to comfort Molly, she grew angry and defensive. The minute Molly began to fuss, Janet become enraged and yelled at her to stop. When Molly didn't stop, Janet would leave the room. This response only intensified Molly's outbursts. Feeling abandoned, she would kick the furniture, scream, and throw whatever was at hand. Seething in the other room, Janet ignored her. She knew her response was inappropriate, but she was so angered by her daughter's behavior, she felt she had no choice.

Over several sessions, Janet gradually explained why she reacted so strongly to Molly's outbursts. "Molly's always been so good at everything—so smart, so athletic—I wanted her to be my 'success story'—to be better than my brother, which I could never be. But every time she throws a tantrum, I feel like that won't happen. And I get so angry. I feel let down."

"How do you respond in other situations when you feel disappointed or angry?" the therapist asked. "For instance, when your husband lets you down?"

Janet smiled sheepishly. "The same way. I storm out. Then I go away and seethe."

Janet's emotional soft spot was the feeling of being inferior to her brother, and every time Molly threw a tantrum she touched her mom's Achilles' heel. Other parents have soft spots in other areas, but as with Janet, they often stem from childhood.

About a month later Janet reported an "amazing insight." "Molly and I were drawing," she said, "and for no apparent reason after we had been getting along nicely for fifteen minutes, she started yelling and screaming and breaking the crayons. Normally I'd be enraged that she'd interfere with our nice playtime together. But this time, instead of yelling back and leaving her, in which case she would probably have screamed for a good half hour or more, I counted to ten and thought to myself, there must be something here that's bothering her. I stayed there and let her cry for a minute or two, and then just talked in a calm voice, asking her to let me know what was so upsetting. To my surprise, she said, 'I messed up what I wanted to do.' 'Sweetheart, how did you mess up?' I asked. Then Molly showed me how she had drawn something that didn't look like what she wanted. This time I didn't yell back. I actually felt bad for her. She crept into my lap and cried for a minute or two. I hugged her and then she said, 'I feel okay now.' Then we went back to drawing and we were both fine for the rest of the time."

Over the next several months, Janet and Molly's relationship grew noticeably smoother.

One mother was very uncomfortable with the anger her daughter's dolls were expressing. "Oh, why don't they ever hold hands?" she finally blurted, after the dolls had pushed each other for the umpteenth time. When asked why she was so uncomfortable with the dolls' behavior she eventually elaborated that growing up, she was never permitted to be angry. "If we raised our voices at all we were sent to our rooms. I still don't get angry."

Another mother was quite loving of her son, but in a rather overprotective way. When the boy began doing pretend play, one of the first themes to emerge was the theme of separation. He often had dolls and animals "going away." His mother became visibly upset at these scenarios. "Doesn't the monkey want to go back home?" she would ask, or, "Can't the mommy doll come too?" Almost invariably the boy ignored his mother for a minute or two, then adopted her suggestion. But after another minute he would lose interest in the game, as if having changed the script to please his mom, his heart was no longer in it. When it was brought to her attention that she always wanted to keep the mommies and babies together, the mother grew reflective. "I always felt like my mother loved my sister more than me," she said. "I guess I'm trying to love him the way I wanted my mother to love me."

A father was uncomfortable when his son, who had motor delays, played with dolls. He admitted that as a child, he had always felt weaker than other boys, and that as an adult, he spent a great deal of time keeping himself in shape. He saw his son's motor impairments as a threat to his own fragile self-image. The boy's interest in dolls seemed to magnify his weakness.

We all have these emotional Achilles' heels. It helps to understand where your own feelings come from and to try to accept the fact that your child is a separate person. It's important to realize that the choice is not between feeling a certain emotion and not feeling it. (Your child will feel that emotion whether you want him to or not.) The choice is between expressing it appropriately and expressing it inappropriately. Remember, feeling a certain way does not mean behaving that way, and recognizing feelings often means better control over behavior. When you disapprove of your child's feelings you don't remove the feelings, you merely drive them underground. There they tend to magnify and surface in inappropriate ways. Aggression bottled up may come out in fisticuffs rather than through toy soldiers battling. Healthy feelings of dependency, expressed through requests for reassuring hugs and verbal support, if rebuffed, may turn into clinginess and fear of separation. Normal sexual curiosity, if reprimanded, may make a child uncomfortable with his own body. Help your child express his different feelings, but at the same time set firm limits on inappropriate behavior.

WHEN EXTERNAL EVENTS COLOR YOUR FEELINGS ABOUT YOUR CHILD

Three-year-old Elliot was making slow but steady progress when his maternal grandfather suddenly died. When the family returned from the funeral, Elliot's mother, Vivian, seemed surprisingly composed. She didn't talk about her father and rarely cried, and when Elliot's therapist asked about her feelings she claimed to have already mourned him. Several weeks after the death, however, she began a steady rain of complaints about Elliot's progress: "Why isn't he learning new words?" "Why isn't he closing more circles?" The therapist pointed out that he had learned several new words and was closing seven or eight circles, compared with three or four a month earlier. But she was determined only to see what Elliot *wasn't* doing, and not what he was. Because Vivian hadn't been this way prior to her father's death, her complaints seemed to be misplaced sadness; instead of examining her feelings about her dad, she was transferring her sadness to her son. When the therapist suggested as much, Vivian argued, "My father is gone, but my son is here now, and I'm worried that he won't ever improve." Over the next several sessions the therapist urged Vivian to talk about her dad, and finally she began her mourning. By a month later, Vivian's optimism had returned.

A child with special needs can become a magnet for other stresses and sadness in your life. Emotions are easily displaced. But if you talk openly about your feelings—with your spouse, with a therapist, or with a friend— you will be less likely to displace them.

WHAT ARE YOUR EMOTIONAL SOFT SPOTS AND COPING PATTERNS?

To identify your emotional soft spots and the behavior they typically trigger, answer the following questions.

1. How do I behave when someone

    rejects me or *withdraws* from me?
    is *angry* with me or *aggressive* toward me?
    expresses *sexual feelings* or curiosity?
    is clingy or *dependent* on me?

is *curious* and *exploratory* around me?

is *assertive* toward me, expressing his own opinion?

acts *powerful* or asserts her will around me?

2. If I tried a new response, what feelings might it stir up in me (e.g., if I tried to woo my child instead of running away each time she rejected me)?

COUNSELING FOR PARENTS

Observing yourself is never easy. If needed, don't hesitate to get professional counseling as part of your child's therapy. Without outside guidance it's sometimes hard to see and change lifelong patterns. Counseling should have as its focus the three following goals:

1. *Helping you deal with the inevitable tensions in your marriage.* Tension is always present, but with a child with challenges it's almost always more intense. A professional can help you acknowledge the feelings between you (both positive and negative), examine the often hidden, and sometimes unrealistic, assumptions you hold about your relationship, and learn ways to improve your communication.

2. *Helping you recognize and change the strategies you use for coping with stress, anger, and disappointment.* A professional can help you understand how your own histories influence the ways you relate to your child and can help you replace counterproductive coping strategies with constructive ones. The right coping strategies can smooth the relationship between you and your spouse as well as help you provide greater support to your child.

3. *Helping you broaden the range of feelings you are comfortable with so you can better support your child.* A professional can help you recognize your own emotional Achilles' heels. By examining these sensitive areas you can become more comfortable with those feelings, and better able to support your child when she expresses them.

Our own emotional conflicts necessarily present themselves when we interact with our children because no relationship is as intensely tied to our feelings about ourselves. It is impossible to parent our children without harking back, consciously or unconsciously, to how our own parents parented us. For these reasons, parenting presents us with an opportunity to grow. If we are ever to outgrow our emotional conflicts, if we are ever to enlarge the scope of our emotions, if we are ever to broaden the ways we relate to other people, parenting is one of the main arenas in which that will happen. Perhaps one of the blessings of having a child with challenges is that the stresses of parenting often push these issues to the surface more than they do in a family without them, so the opportunity to address, and resolve, these issues is even more potent. Pursuing them with a professional is the safest and most thorough way to do it. Professional guidance can help parents become more supportive and families become stronger, so that they can work through future stresses by themselves.

SIBLINGS: HELPING YOUR OTHER CHILDREN

"Craig takes up so much of our time and energy. I always feel like I'm shortchanging his brother and sister."

It's hard not to feel that way. A child with special needs does demand more time and energy than do her siblings and it's virtually impossible not to feel concerned and guilty at times. However, you can take steps to help your other children.

• *Make sure your other children get at least one floor time session a day.* Floor time is not just for children with special needs. That one-on-one playtime when the child is boss is important for all children. Knowing they can have you all to themselves compensates for your limited attention at other times. It provides an avenue for expressing thoughts and feelings that they may not be able to put into words.

• *Have problem-solving discussions.* If your children are verbal, engage them in problem-solving discussions about their sibling with special needs. Give them room to talk about how they feel about their brother or sister, being careful not to criticize or judge their negative feelings. Often children worry that what happened to their sibling will happen to them. They may resent their sibling for the amount of time and attention he demands. They may feel guilty that they have bad thoughts about him or that they are not disabled as well. Some of these feelings may come out in floor time. If so, you can gently ask about them during your problem-solving talks. Don't feel you have to fix the feelings. Just listen carefully. Your simple listening will make your children feel better.

• *Make it a family challenge.* When you talk with your children about their sibling's special needs, make it clear that this is a family challenge. The family members were not responsible for creating the problem, but together you can help the child with special needs grow and learn. Give your children without special needs roles to play in helping their sibling. Perhaps they can help her dress or eat. Perhaps they can read a story or sing a song at bedtime. Perhaps they can be paid to baby-sit. Don't mete out chores in a way that interferes with their lives and don't assign responsibilities without discussing them and gaining your children's agreement; but teaching them how to help can instill a sense of accomplishment and teamwork that strengthens them as individuals and you as a family.

• *Involve your other children in floor time with their sibling.* Often siblings feel a sense of loss. "I want a brother or sister who can talk or play," they may think. You can moderate this situation by showing them how to do floor time with their sibling; they can be built-in play dates. Once they get the hang of it (which they will much more quickly than grown-ups), they are likely to find that even nonverbal play is very satisfying and that they *can* have fun with their sibling. Sometimes let the child with special needs be the leader; sometimes let another child lead. In this way, all the children get to feel like the boss and they all get lots of interaction. Because whole-family playtimes are so rare, they will be special occasions for everyone. Having group floor time, in which each child is the leader for 15 or 20 minutes and the sibling is pulled in in a support role increases every one's floor time and often encourages the siblings to play more constructively on their own.

• *Don't be afraid of hostile feelings.* Sometimes it's hard to be the sibling of a child with special needs. One child gets an unfair share of time and attention and often puts a damper on family activities. As a result, siblings sometimes feel anger toward the child with special needs (just as their parents sometimes do). Don't be hurt or angry or afraid when your children express these feelings to you. They're only natural, and it's much better they get expressed to you than locked up inside or acted out toward their sibling. Also, don't take them *too* seriously. Just because children express anger toward their sibling doesn't mean they don't love him. Just because they express a wish to harm him doesn't mean they wouldn't defend him at any cost. Their feelings are often a fluctuating mix that varies with their mood, the day, and their sibling's behavior. Your role is not to judge, but to listen and to give your children room to express themselves. At the same time you need to set firm, gentle limits on any hitting or hurting among siblings. By doing both these things, you can strengthen each of your children's sense of self and your family interactions.

BASIC GUIDELINES FOR PARENTS

1. *Try to comfort your child when he is upset in a relaxed and gentle way.* Hold him firmly; make soft, rhythmic noises; make visual contact; or do whatever he will accept. *Try to avoid* making your child more tense by being overly worried, tense, or anxious yourself.

2. *Try to find appropriate levels of interaction.* Offer the level and type of stimulation your child responds to best—sights, sounds, touch, movement. Incorporate these things into your games. *Try to avoid* being overstimulating and intrusive (e.g., poking her to get her attention).

3. *Try actively to engage your child in a relationship* by looking at her, vocalizing to her, touching her gently, and so on. *Try to avoid* understimulating your child by being depressed, withdrawn, or preoccupied.

4. *Try to read and respond to your child's emotional signals.* Notice when he wants to be close and respond with a hug. Notice when he wants you to stay away, or when he wants to be assertive, and respond with verbal acknowledgment. *Try to avoid* responding the way you want rather than the way he needs. (Don't hover over him when he needs to be independent. Don't put him off when he needs a reassuring hug.)

5. *Try to encourage your child to move on to the next stage of development.* Encourage her to crawl, gesture, and express initiative by not doing things for her. Help her feel independent by staying in vocal and visual contact while she explores across the room. Help her move into pretend play by getting on the floor and taking a role in her drama. Help her deal with reality by negotiating her demands. *Try to avoid* stalling her development by doing what's comfortable, rather than what she needs.

18

An Integrated Approach to Therapy

There are many approaches to intervention and education for children with special needs. Yet many of these strategies fall short because they (1) deal with children in a group, rather than as individuals in the context of their individual differences; (2) concentrate on altering overt symptoms and behavior rather than addressing underlying processing difficulties and mechanisms; (3) work on selected areas of development, such as motor, language, or certain cognitive skills, rather than using a comprehensive approach that involves all areas of functioning; and (4) focus almost exclusively on the child, rather than working with the caregivers, family, and the child in an integrated manner.

Different approaches to helping children with special needs, whether based on relationships, behavior, education, or family, highlight various aspects of human complexity. Human beings are members of families, engage in behavior, experience inner feelings and emotions, and have various social, cognitive, and intellectual skills. Advocates of particular methods of intervention often believe or hope that a positive impact on one aspect of the child's or family's circumstances will create a positive spillover effect in other areas. For example, a therapist may assume that changing a child's behavior enough will favorably alter relationships in the family and the family structure as a whole, or that learning certain academic skills will spill over into a child's peer relationships and feelings about himself, or that changing the way the child feels and experiences relationships will cause the child to

377

want to talk more and eventually to participate in routine educational activities. Unfortunately, progress in one area often does not catalyze progress in related areas.

To be successful, an intervention program must address many aspects of both child and family, including their special needs and special strengths. Over the past 20 years we have had an opportunity to work with a variety of children and families with differing special needs.[1] This experience has suggested the value of an integrated framework tailored to each child's and family's unique developmental challenges and strengths.

INTEGRATED DEVELOPMENTAL INTERVENTION: A PYRAMID

The intervention model that we have found helpful in working with infants, children, and families with a variety of special needs can be conceptualized as a pyramid. At the base of the pyramid are the stable, nurturing, developmentally supportive, and tailored family patterns that all children require, but that are especially important for children with developmental challenges. This foundation includes physical protection and safety and an ongoing sense of security. Some families function very well in these areas, whereas others require a great deal of support or therapy to stabilize and organize these basic family patterns. Some families may be dealing with extreme poverty and chronic states of fearfulness; relationships within some families may be abusive, neglectful, or fragmented. In such cases, intervention programs need staff trained to assess family needs, develop alliances, problem-solve, advocate (including for social and economic support), and provide family counseling and family or personal therapy as indicated.

At the second level of the pyramid are the ongoing and consistent relationships that developing children require to have a chance for emotional and cognitive competency. As children with special needs often already have a compromised capacity to relate, they have a particular need for warm, consistent caregiving. Yet their caregivers often face challenges in sustaining intimate relationships because it is easy to misperceive the child's behavior or intentions. If caregivers can learn to understand the child's behavior as an attempt to cope with difficulties or as a result of being overwhelmed by difficulties, they can correct these misperceptions and move toward more creative and empathic ways of helping the child relate. For example, a child who is hypersensitive to touch may not be rejecting her parents' comfort and care when she turns away and cries. For such a child it may be important to avoid light touch and to use deep pressure to help her feel more comfortable. A child who is generally avoidant or self-absorbed and appears to prefer to

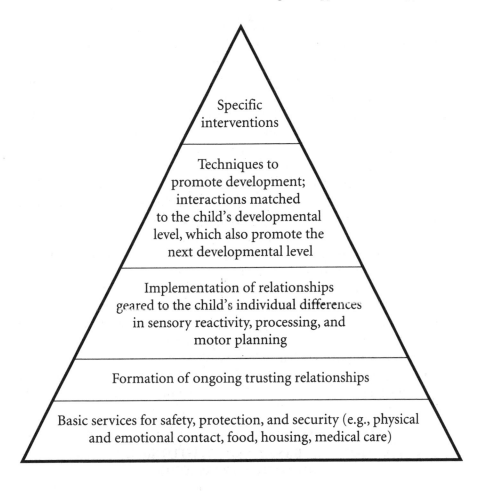

Specific
interventions

Techniques to
promote development;
interactions matched
to the child's developmental
level, which also promote the
next developmental level

Implementation of relationships
geared to the child's individual differences
in sensory reactivity, processing, and
motor planning

Formation of ongoing trusting relationships

Basic services for safety, protection, and security (e.g., physical
and emotional contact, food, housing, medical care)

play alone can be giving a signal; he may be underreactive to sensations, with low muscle tone, and need greater wooing to get beyond his self-absorption.

To support the child's ability to relate requires a lot of time, consistency, and understanding. Family difficulties or frequent turnover of child-care staff or teachers may impede the child's progress.

At the third level of the pyramid lie consistent relationships that have been adapted to the individual differences of each child. Caregivers need to learn a variety of strategies, such as wooing the low-tone, underreactive child, protecting and soothing the overreactive child, creating challenges to facilitate purposeful behavior and circles of interaction in the child who is aimless or fragmented, and making gestures and auditory communication more deliberate and visual-spatial communication clearer to the child with severe auditory-processing difficulties.

At the fourth level of the pyramid, relationships and the interactions that flow from them are matched to the developmental level of the child. Some children are still unrelated and unpurposeful and require work on engaging and intentional communication; others are purposeful but require extra help in using symbols; still others are using symbols or ideas in a fragmented way and need to learn how to be logical and more abstract. Special types of interactions can be used for each developmental level to enable the child to master that level and its related capacities.

At the apex of the pyramid are specific therapeutic or educational techniques that promote development in children facing particular challenges.[2] In this model, specific therapies must build on a foundation of developmentally based family, relationship, and interactive approaches. Biological interventions to improve attention, processing skills, and affect regulation can also be considered, as can the educational, auditory-processing, and nutritional approaches now being developed.

The integrated pyramidal model takes into account certain fundamental experiences that every child requires. These core experiences enable the child to become a warm, loving, communicative, intelligent, and creative individual. He does so by connecting his emerging abilities to an underlying sense of his own purpose—his affects, wishes, and desires. In this model, therefore, specific interventions must be included in or must build on interactions that make new skills a part of the growing child's sense of self.

INTEGRATING THE INDIVIDUAL-DIFFERENCE, RELATIONSHIP-BASED MODEL WITH BEHAVIORAL AND OTHER APPROACHES

A family- and relationship-based model provides a foundation for intervention, but many children require specific help to master challenges to communicating, relating, motor planning, or sensory processing. This help may involve intensive speech therapy, occupational therapy, physical therapy, special education, behavior therapy, relationship-based approaches, psychotherapy, biological treatments, and strategies now emerging that facilitate auditory processing. These intensive technical approaches should be made part of the relationship-based intervention pyramid.

Many early-intervention programs are designed to serve a group of children viewed as having a common problem (e.g., children diagnosed with autism). The program philosophy dictates the overall intervention approach, presumed to be useful for children with the same diagnosis. Intervention programs of this type less frequently profile each child's individual differences and unique developmental pattern. They often fail to take into account, for example, that one child diagnosed with autism may be underreactive to sound and touch, may tend to withdraw, and may be just beginning to engage others with gestures, while another child with the same diagnosis is overreactive to sensations, clings to his parents, and uses many words and gestures. Both children are perseverative, self-stimulatory, and self-absorbed—hence their common diagnosis. We have found that children with this diagnosis differ greatly in their capacity for relating and being warm and joyful with caregivers and suggest that children with the capacity for warm relating or with good potential for relating be described as having multisystem developmental disorder rather than autism.[3] In our intervention pyramid, each child's profile, *not* his diagnosis, determines how different therapies can be used together; that is, in this model, the child's characteristics determine the therapy program that fits him, rather than making the child fit into an existing program or curriculum.

Although we cannot discuss all useful approaches to helping young children with severe developmental challenges, we will illustrate the principle of integration by looking at two approaches that are often considered polar opposites: the intensive, developmentally based, interactive strategies described in this book and behavioral techniques.

The developmentally based interactive approach builds on the strength of relationships and family structure and uses relationships in a systematic way to deal with the child's individual differences, including processing and developmental challenges.[4] (See Part 2.) With floor time, parents are helped to follow their child's playful lead while sitting on the floor. They engage their child in warm relating, using ever more complex nonverbal communication patterns, including affect cuing (building on the child's emotional expressions with expressions or gestures of their own and inspiring the child to initiate another emotional expression in turn). Through opening and closing circles of communication and increasing the complexity of nonverbal interactions, they promote the emergence of presymbolic and symbolic capacities. Parents work around auditory-processing problems by appealing to visual cues in their interactions with their child. They simplify auditory cues until their child masters them. They respect their child's individual differences in order to maintain the engagement and interaction. They tailor stimulus input to their child's unique pattern of auditory, tactile, or visual-spatial sensitivities. Adjusting the approach used in relating to their child encourages him to remain engaged, to develop intentionality and increasingly complex affective and interaction capacities, and to move into symbolic reasoning, from which other skills can develop.

Floor time is part of a collaborative effort of occupational therapists, speech and language therapists, educators and special educators, and parents on behalf of young children with severe difficulties relating and communicating. Often parents or helping caregivers need to engage in eight or more

20-to-30-minute, special, uninterrupted floor-time sessions with the child in the course of a day. Each person caring for, teaching, or treating the child is engaged in an interactive relationship with that child. Floor-time principles can be incorporated into all these interactions, as well as into such routine activities as eating, bathing, and dressing. During free play in group-care settings, caregivers can be down on the floor following the child's lead as she explores and shows interest in different things, as well as mediating her interaction with other children.

Everyone interacting with a child provides another relationship in which the child can learn. Speech therapists can use play-based approaches during their sessions; occupational therapists can harness the child's natural initiative and put activities into a symbolic framework (e.g., a motor or sensory activity becomes "swinging over the ocean" or "blasting off to the moon"). Floor-time principles are integrated into daily life by giving children more choices and engaging in gestural conversations (exchanging looks, smiles, frowns, and toys) while dressing, eating, shopping, and playing in the tub.

Even with a floor-time approach, some children with severe difficulties in relating and communicating continue to show very fragmented behavior. Because their ability to sequence behavior is severely impaired, these children have difficulty problem solving, being purposeful, and imitating simple and complicated patterns. They are unable to move spontaneously from a state of engagement and intimacy, accomplished through improved relationships, to more complicated nonverbal communication and eventually symbolic communication, which require more complex sequences of actions, play, and language. In clinical work with a number of these children, we found it useful to combine behavioral and floor-time methods in the context of a broader relationship and family-support approach.[5] (See also Appendix C.)

This model is one that might be abstracted from teaching a skill such as tennis. A certain amount of structure and practice (a person hitting the ball a certain number of times with the backhand) is combined with matches and games (hitting the ball while moving). The more structured behavioral approach may be similar to practicing the backhand while standing still, whereas the relationship-based, dynamic-interaction approach might be similar to practicing under game conditions with more spontaneous action patterns. Some children appear to require both approaches to make progress.

Behavioral techniques are quite helpful in enabling children to sequence behavior and learn to imitate and use some words, but when the techniques are not integrated into a broader floor-time, relationship and family-support model, these behaviors tend to remain dependent on external prompts. For example, only questions asked in a certain way may be likely to elicit responses; "What do you want for dinner?" may produce an answer, whereas "Are you hungry?" may not. Skills that are initially learned in a behavioral manner can be brought into a dynamic-relationship context through floor-time activities such as pretend play and spontaneous interactions. For example, the child may learn to imitate the word *cup* and to use it to label a picture. Later, as cups are used in pretend play, Dad's doll may ask the child for the cup, and the child may respond, "No, *my* cup!" The word and concept are becoming the child's own, ready for spontaneous use. As behavior is organized under internal emotional cues rather than external prompts, the child's spontaneity and flexibility increase. We often recommend 30 to 45 minutes of structured work followed by 30 to 45 minutes of floor time that incorporates whatever was just practiced. This pattern is repeated many times each day. We also recommend that the goals of the integrated intervention be based on the key developmental foundations that need to be in place for healthy development, rather than on compliant behaviors or isolated academic skills. These goals often are joyful engagement and attention, a continuous flow of gestures (many circles of communication in a row), spontaneous and creative use of more complex, purposeful gestures, imitation, symbols (words and imaginative play), and nonverbal problem solving.

We have also observed in our clinical work that the capacity for abstract thinking develops when a child becomes able to connect different ideas and behaviors to underlying emotions. Behavior and thoughts are tied to desires and wishes, which carry from one situation to the next. Higher-level abstractions often become possible because of the connection of ideas to multiple contexts and, even more important, to multiple aspects of one emotion (the many variations of fear or love, for example). Children ordinarily learn when to wave, hug, argue, or use any other behavior, thought, or conceptual tool by connecting these behaviors to internal emotional prompts.

The hope that behavior controlled by external prompts will generalize is a hope that it will come under internal emotional control, because children take their emotions with them from place to place and use these emotions to determine what to do and say in different situations. Our experience is that children's behavior comes under control only through practice under game conditions. Consequently, many children with severe difficulties in relating and communicating who are in behavioral programs only, and whose parents are not working intuitively with emotions and interactions, are likely to be less flexible and abstract than they could be. We found that several children who had been in intense behavioral programs and could sometimes master rote academic skills and do well on IQ tests lacked the ability for spontaneous, creative interchanges with adults or peers and could not generalize or engage in abstract thinking (they might match words to pictures, for example, but be unable to explain why they wanted to go outside or debate the merits of staying up later). When we initiated a dynamic, problem-solving approach, these children began to acquire abstract-thinking skills.

Because such a range of outcomes is possible for children with severe disorders of relating and communicating, it is especially important to look at each child's unique individual characteristics and developmental capacities when planning intervention. It is also important to consider which type of program will offer which types of children and families the most opportunities for substantial gains. A child without severe processing difficulties may be able to generalize from rote-learning experiences to construct abstractions. A core difficulty of children with autistic spectrum problems (as well as of many other children with different types of special needs) may be their inability to make generalizations and construct patterns of abstract thinking. It is critical to involve children in dynamic, emotional-based, problem-solving interactions that are likely to foster abstract thinking and the ability to generalize. An integrated developmental model can help determine the most appropriate interventions.

THE PARENTS' ROLE

For therapy to be maximally effective, therapists need to work together as a team. That means talking to each other regularly to exchange notes on the child's progress and reinforcing each other's work as much as possible by working on the same milestones at the same time. This kind of teamwork doesn't usually happen naturally. It happens because parents push to make it happen by assertively taking on the role of team leader.

For many parents it may seem awkward at first to be the team's leader. After all, the therapists are the professionals. But no one is better qualified for this job than the parents who live with their child 24 hours a day. Parents see their child's reactions to therapy as well as to other experiences. They can provide feedback about their child's progress and well-being that is vital to the therapists' job. Parents and therapists are partners in helping the child. Therapists are experts in their individual fields of specialization; parents are the experts about their child.

In addition to being assertive about integrating the work of the therapists, parents must be assertive about how they and the therapists should work together. Parents should ask for the kind of feedback they want.

They need to tell therapists what is helpful and what isn't. Many therapists balance reports of progress with a note of "realism": "Johnny is doing very well; he's saying three words, *but* he still has a long way to go." Most parents would do just fine without the addendum. What parents need from therapists are strategies to master challenges. A sense of positive teamwork can make the march of therapy easier.

FINDING A TEAM COLEADER

In some communities parents have access to a professional who can put the pieces together, monitor progress, and suggest changes in the therapy program. Often a therapist or the professional who did the original workup, fulfills this extremely helpful role.

Finding the right therapists and creating this type of program takes effort. It may be necessary to convince therapists to work with the child in a way that differs from the therapists' usual approach or to put together a program that is more intensive and comprehensive than what is generally offered. Some needed services may fall outside the scope of what a community is legally required to provide; others may fall outside the scope of insurance coverage. Such problems limit the ability of some families to provide comprehensive treatment for their children. We hope that as new diagnostic codes are adopted—broadening the definitions of severe disorders—regulations will change and these services will be easier to obtain. Meanwhile, the heart of the intervention is within each family's reach—daily floor time with the child.

THE IMPORTANCE OF STARTING THERAPY EARLY

The therapeutic program must begin as early as possible—at the first sign that something is wrong—because the more quickly the child is engaged and interactive, the more quickly she'll start learning *and* the fewer maladaptive behaviors she'll develop to cope with her difficulties.

Despite parents' best efforts, it is often hard to get a child into therapy. Often a parent senses something wrong, only to be pooh-poohed by relatives and sometimes even by professionals: "All babies are different. Wait and see what happens." However, children with severe disorders can't afford to wait, because months or years lost waiting will be very difficult to regain.

It typically takes eight months from the time a parent seeks help until the time intensive therapy starts. This is too long. When a child exhibits difficulties in relating or communicating, the situation should be evaluated as soon as possible. Assessment should begin *within days,* and intensive therapy should begin *while the assessment is in progress.* Only in that way can the process of decline be halted and the child spared months of lost development.

The best way to catch problems early is to have pediatricians, educators, and parents act as an early warning system. Pediatricians are in an especially strategic position; they are close to families and have the training and perspective to catch problems that parents may miss. If at each well-baby checkup pediatricians routinely examined infants for age-appropriate developmental skills, including subtle emotional, cognitive, language, sensory, and motor patterns, potentially severe disorders could be caught before they derailed a child's development. For instance, by 18 months a child should be warmly engaged and capable of initiative and two-way communication. She should also be able to use complex gestures to communicate what she wants—taking her mother's hand and leading her to the door or toy chest, or pointing, for example. Without the use of words she should be communicating with her parents, clearly understanding much of what they say to her, and communicating many of her own wishes back. If by 18 months the child can do these things, her gestural communication is developing on track and the building blocks of symbolic expression and language are present. But if she is not communicating gesturally in an age-appropriate way, the assessment and, if needed, the intervention, should begin immediately. It does not make sense to wait until she is 24 months to see if language is delayed. The child who has a circumscribed language problem that will take care of itself will be mastering these preverbal gestural communication patterns. The child who is not using gestures and behaviors to communicate needs and wishes and solve problems often is showing the signs of significant challenges. (See also Appendix C.)

COMMITMENT TO THE PROGRAM

An integrated therapy program based on the floor-time model must be undertaken with full commitment. Approaching it halfheartedly or in bursts doesn't work as well; the child won't achieve the kinds of gains desired, and the gains won't be as sustained.

When Neil first went to therapy he behaved more like a one-and-a-half-year-old than like the four-year-old he was. He largely ignored his parents and resisted their overtures to play. His speech consisted of garbled sounds, and his muscle tone was low. However, after six months of intensive therapy (speech therapy three times a week, occupational therapy once a week, play therapy twice a week, plus daily floor time with his parents) Neil had made significant improvements. He was much more affectionately involved with his parents; a gleam in his eye replaced the vacant look he had worn before; and he was able to "converse" with his parents, closing four or five gestural circles in a row.

Everyone was quite surprised, therefore, when over the next six months Neil's progress leveled off. Instead of becoming more flexible and moving into pretend play and speech, he continued to play mechanically and to prefer familiar routines. His parents began to think that perhaps his early evaluation had been right, that Neil had mental retardation.

In talking with the family, however, the therapist discovered a possible source of the problem. Neil's father had changed jobs and was arriving home from work at eight or nine o'clock, too late to do floor time with his son. Neil's mother, now single-parenting Neil and his younger sister, was often too exhausted to do floor time daily. Without that rigorous daily interaction, Neil had ceased to forge ahead.

His parents had attributed his success to the professional therapists, and they'd assumed that a little time off while his father adjusted to the new job would make no difference. They weren't acknowledging the social and intellectual skills each of their own interactions with Neil was helping him practice. They didn't realize that many of the skills he built in speech and occupational therapy were being practiced and strengthened in floor time with them. When their piece of the program was eliminated, the entire program suffered.

Although it was difficult, given the father's new job, Neil's parents began making the extra effort to do regular daily floor time, and fairly quickly Neil responded. His warmth and intimacy and gestural communication returned within weeks, and as the family kept up its rigorous routine he surged ahead. Six months after they had resumed regular floor time he was imitating their vocalizations, carrying on reciprocal, babbled conversations, and moving into pretend play.

The integrated-therapy approach based on the floor-time model is demanding. It requires a lot of time and energy from the child's parents and is unforgiving in terms of the other stresses and demands of life. Seeing progress, however, often helps parents sustain the effort. Many children who begin therapy with aimless, uncommunicative behavior become intimate with their parents and start opening and closing gestural circles of communication within six months. Within a year they begin to express their thoughts and feelings through pretend play and simple words and are comfortable with their peers. Many then work on logic skills, increasing the length of reality-based conversations and reducing their need to withdraw into fantasy when stressed. Although children progress at different rates and to different levels, most children tend to become warm, spontaneous, and loving. (See Appendix C for a discussion of different patterns observed in intervention programs.)

GUIDELINES FOR AN OVERALL
INTERVENTION APPROACH

We have discussed how different interventions may work together within the context of our floor-time philosophy. Now it is time to discuss the specifics of an optimal intervention program.

For children who have severe disorders of relating and communicating—often diagnosed with pervasive developmental disorder, autism, autistic spectrum disorder, or multisystem developmental disorder—a comprehensive, intensive intervention program is needed. For children with very severe language disturbances or motor difficulties, similar programs are also indicated. (See Chapter 15 on special-needs syndromes.)

A comprehensive approach comprises many elements, but the cornerstone is the home floor-time program described in Part 2 of this book. For the more severe and challenging problems, eight to ten 20-to-30-minute floor-time sessions every day is optimal. Following this program often means determining how much each parent can do and how much help is needed. Help can include siblings; other family members; a graduate student in speech pathology, occupational therapy, or education; high school students; neighbors; or volunteers. Individuals working with the child on floor time need a natural ability to relate and interact and a capacity, with experience, to master the guidelines described earlier. Parents or therapists typically need to train other helpers.

There are many hours in the day. If the child spends too large a portion of his day involved in self-absorbed activities, self-stimulation, or one-way communication, such as watching TV, he won't have the practice he needs to learn essential skills. The child's progress is generally proportional to the amount of energy and time spent in the trenches, with someone wooing and pulling him into floor-time interactions.

As the child becomes more verbal and capable of building bridges between ideas, it's important to add reality-based problem-solving discussions to the daily routine. This type of dialogue may be about school, friends, favorite foods, toys. The child also needs help in anticipating challenges that may emerge later in the day or the next day. The techniques for promoting logical thinking and problem solving were discussed in Chapter 12. As the child becomes more logical, six steps—involving floor time, problem-solving time, empathy for the child's perspective,˙ breaking challenges into small component parts, setting limits, and doing extra floor time when there's a need for extra limits—should become a part of the daily routine (see Chapter 14).

It is also important to tackle the problems that the newly logical child has graduated into, such as pulling toys away from friends, wanting his own way all the time, being clingy or demanding, and so forth, by providing extra practice in the situations that bring up the problematic behavior. Parents may want to avoid certain situations, such as those requiring sharing, because their child has trouble with appropriate behavior. The child then continues to misbehave in school or in play dates because those are the settings in which the situation he can't handle arises. By creating similar, controlled situations at home under their guidance, parents can provide extra practice, for example, in learning to share or not to crowd others and get into their body space. When parents are helping their child, they can use problem-solving strategies, such as talking it through, rehearsing, and practice, and they can provide structure, limits, and encouragement. The key is gradually to practice the skills that need to be mastered in the comfort and security of the home, rather than avoid situations or expect the child somehow, magically, to master the skills on his own.

Children with special needs, in order to learn to relate, communicate, and think, often require extra practice, as described in the preceding chapters. As they graduate into the arena of more subtle problems, such as controlling aggression, competitiveness, or jealousy or learning to respect others, the same principle of extra practice applies. Sometimes, rather than seeing these new challenges as relatively little ones in comparison to the bigger challenges of relating, communicating, and thinking, parents and educators become discouraged when the child who is now talking and relating does not operate as the perfect, well-mannered child. Helping children use their new thinking and communicating skills to master these more advanced challenges will give them a lifelong capacity to cope and learn.

Once they are capable of long, interactive sequences (complex gestural communication) and the beginning levels of pretend play or using words purposefully, it is critical for children to have lots of opportunities to practice their skills, not only with adults, but also with peers. Children benefit from three to four play dates a week with a child of the same age, plus or minus a year or two (as long as the playmate can communicate at or above the child's level). Beginning peer play early, often mediated or facilitated by a parent or other adult, helps children practice their new skills in a variety of contexts and become used to peers. Participating in and enjoying peer relationships will help children later on fine-tune and further develop their interactive and intellectual skills.

Siblings can also be part of the home-based program (see Chapter 17). Parents may need to help. For example, if a three-year-old with special needs isn't yet talking and his five-year-old sibling is doing complicated pretend play and talking up a storm, parents may need to pull in the nonverbal three-year-old, perhaps helping him move his truck or doll or hiding with him in the hide-and-seek game. When the nonverbal three-year-old is the leader, parents can help the older sibling set up a road block or other hazard for the three-year-old to negotiate.

In addition to home floor time and peer play, another cornerstone of a comprehensive program is the team of therapists who work on the different component parts of the child's mind that are contributing to the difficulties. This team may include a speech pathologist to help with receptive and expressive language. An optimal program may involve speech therapy in individual sessions one-half to one hour long three or more times per week. An occupational therapist trained in sensory integration may be needed to work on sensory modulation, sensory processing, and motor planning in one-half to one hour sessions two or more times per week. Children with significant motor problems may work with a physical therapist several times per week. Meanwhile parents need to incorporate language, sensory-modulation, sensory-processing, and motor-planning activities into their spontaneous floor time (see Part 2).

Finally, many children benefit from being in an educational program (see Chapter 19). The optimal educational program, in addition to providing services for children with special needs, also provides access to other children who are very interactive and have spontaneous communicative skills. Thus as the child with special needs begins to interact and communicate, he has peers who can interact and communicate back. When children with the same problem are grouped together in one program the problem is sometimes compounded because as one child becomes ready to interact, the other children are not available to harness that interaction and respond in return. Integrated programs that enable children with special needs to interact with children who don't have special needs or who have medical or learning problems that do not limit communication and interaction are very important.

A cautionary note should be inserted here. A program that does not have adequate staffing but uses the concept of integration as a way to reduce costs by placing 20 children with two teachers generally does not work and is not truly an integrated program. A successful integrated program should have a small number of children, perhaps three children with special needs, in a class with agemates without special needs. Special educators should be in the classroom, and speech and occupational therapists should be available either in the class or on a consulting basis. In some situations, early-childhood educators may be appropriate staff, with a special educator available in a consulting or part-time role.

Depending on family patterns and family stress and on the parents' comfort and skill in implementing floor-time approaches, it may be helpful for a developmentally based therapist to consult with the family on facilitating floor-time interactions in the home-based program. This therapist or another with knowledge and experience in assisting families and couples in their relationships may also help a family or a couple work through their challenges. It may be beneficial for a developmentally based floor-time therapist to work directly with the child one to four times a week, in addition to consulting and observing different family members engaged in floor-time interactions. With some families, these two pieces are integrated; the floor-time therapist works directly with the child while the parents are there, and then the parents work with the child while the therapist provides consultation and guidance.

Many children benefit from devices that enhance communication, such as learning signs, pictures or picture-exchange systems, and various types of talkers. These tools should be used as part of spontaneous communication and floor-time activities, for example, to help the child create a make-believe story or negotiate her needs.

A comprehensive program as described appears to require a great deal of time, energy, and, if the services are not covered by insurance or are not available through the school system, financial expenditure. Parents need to work collectively to make these services available through health-insurance and educational programs supported by the school system. There is a systematic tendency in health coverage and managed care to be biased against children with special needs. For example, certain therapies to correct hypotonia or severe, biologically based auditory-processing problems are often not covered by health-insurance plans or managed care, whereas other medical illnesses, such as congenital heart disease, are covered in most health-insurance plans.

In many communities, the educational system does not provide sufficient individual speech therapy or occupational therapy to remediate adequately the processing challenges of many children. In the long run, collective efforts by parents are needed to initiate change. In the meantime, parents can create and structure their own intervention team and, with appropriate knowledge, serve as its quarterback. The heart of the program, again, is the home-based floor-time component. Although it does require a lot of time and effort, this piece can be implemented with a relatively small financial expenditure if, for example, students are hired to help or, even better, volunteers, relatives, or extended-family members work with the child.

Families who are unable financially to provide intensive speech or occupational therapy and for whom services are not available may hire therapists on a consultant basis, perhaps considering speech and occupational therapists who work within the school system as consultants for a home-based program. In this way, in addition to the floor-time exercises, parents can undertake a certain amount of speech-therapy exercises and occupational-therapy exercises each day or every few days.

Even when optimal intensive services are available through the community or through independent arrangements, it is still incumbent on parents to develop an intensive, comprehensive program in which their child, for many hours a day, has an opportunity to practice his new skills and build strong foundations for further development.

ADDITIONAL THERAPEUTIC OPTIONS

Many children may benefit from additional therapies that can enhance auditory processing, attention, thinking abilities, or the regulation of behavior and mood. These involve new training techniques as well as medication. Although in this chapter we cannot go into the details of these additional strategies and techniques, it's important to note that in the fields of rehabilitation, special education, and speech, occupational, and physical therapies, there is a tradition of augmentative devices that can enhance language, cognitive, sensory, and motor capacities.

These new technologies are most helpful when used as part of intentional, two-way communication. For example, a child can use pictures to tell a story or to negotiate needs. She can use hand signs to indicate a desire for juice or for "more," or as part of an ongoing, back-and-forth conversation about how much juice, which kind, and who will get it. Similarly, when a child presses a picture on a portable computer box that can create words for him, his symbols can serve in a rote way to label objects or, more usefully, to negotiate needs as part of a back-and-forth dialogue.

Relatively new techniques, some still evolving, can enhance auditory processing, language, and communication. Among these are two types of *auditory integration training*.[6] One is based on the work of Dr. Alfred A. Tomatis; the other is a shorter form of this approach, based on the work of one of Tomatis's students, Dr. Guy Berard. Although there have not yet been sufficient systematic studies of this training to determine the percentage and degree to which it helps children, many parents report significant progress.

According to parental reports and clinical observations, auditory integration training appears to work best for children who have clear difficulties with sensory modulation, such as overreactivity to sound, as well as significant auditory-processing challenges. Some parents report temporary irritability and, in rare cases, continuing difficulties with this method. Some professionals have expressed concern about potential harm to hearing because of the sound frequencies used in this interevention.

Another technique to enhance auditory processing, originally called the Hailo Approach and now called Fast ForWord, was recently developed by a group at Rutgers University.[7] Slowed-down speech provides cues for doing various activities on the computer; the speech is gradually speeded up to expectable levels. Some researchers studying this method have reported that mastering the computer games by processing the sounds and words was less relevant than the amount of time the child worked at the games, suggesting that practice, rather than the slowing down of speech, may be the operative ingredient. Although this approach has been studied mainly in children with limited language disorders, it is widely used with children with a range of special needs. More systematic study is needed, but many parents report that this method appears to be helpful.

The following story is an example of an integrated program that combines floor time, behavioral approaches, and some dietary changes.

That Jenny did not talk or even vocalize very much and hardly cried did not become a concern until she was almost two years old. Other children in her family had also been late talkers. Her play expanded to arranging toys in different ways. When she turned two she began to notice herself in the mirror and she took great interest in her own image. There followed a period of playfulness with hats; Jenny would put a cap on her head and then look at her Barney doll, who also wore a cap. As their concern grew, Jenny's parents, Sandy and Michael closely observed her more and realized that she almost always turned away when they spoke to her, although she was certainly watchful of them from a distance. She did not respond to her name or to sounds in the environment. They were unsure whether she heard the music on the videotapes she watched, but when they tried using an audiotape without the visual images, Jenny did not attend to it. Jenny had multiple ear infections through her second year of life, but no hearing loss was detected.

Sandy and Michael sought consultation and were encouraged to immerse Jenny in an interactive intervention program immediately. They preferred a private program that included the services they wanted. Jenny started speech therapy twice a week, occupational therapy twice a week, and interactive play therapy once a week. She was enrolled in a local preschool a few days a week, with a one-to-one aide, so that she could be around other children. Both parents attended therapy sessions to learn ways to get Jenny to be more interactive through playful obstruction and other sensory-motor games.

Jenny was quick to notice when her mother took the toy she was holding and asked to play with it or her father covered something she was holding with his hand and initiated a peekaboo game, but after looking she usually moved away and found something else. She did not become angry, but simply switched her attention—her response was to move away—thus rarely closing more than one circle. Her parents persisted, however, and Jenny finally began to let more interaction occur. When Sandy and Michael followed her lead—offering coins to put into the Barney bank, Silly Putty to anchor a figure on a horse, and farm animals to roll down the "hills" one by one—Jenny began to accept their help. But it was clear that she was in control of how long she would stay engaged.

Jenny enjoyed movement a great deal and loved to swing and climb, and she would smile and appear delighted while doing so. This desire created more opportunities for interaction.

Auditory processing was the channel most blocked. Following a series of auditory-training sessions, Jenny became more active, more affectionate, and perhaps more aware of sound, as she responded more to music. Vitamin supplements seemed to boost her level of organization by increasing alertness and activity. At this time new information was emerging about the benefits of gluten- and casein-free diets, and Jenny's parents decided to see whether a change in diet would spur her development. Each additional effort seemed to contribute to her overall organization, relatedness, and affection, but Jenny was still not speaking or even sharing.

In speech therapy Jenny was cooperative, but not yet able to produce more than the simplest sounds. Augmentation using signs was not fruitful and did not go beyond signing for more. Jenny could not imitate the gestures (motions), though she had complex gestures of her own to let others know what she wanted. Nor was she able to imitate any verbal sounds, although she showed some receptive gains. At this point it was recommended that she try a behavioral program in collaboration with a floor time play-interaction program, to help her learn to imitate more readily, possibly leading to more language. The behavioral strategies would be used for a short period of time to help her to learn to better imitate sounds and gestures. Jenny reacted with some not-too-serious protest. At first she was confused when instructed in imitating gestures—she might touch her nose instead of her head, or she might stamp her feet instead of clapping her hands—but she quickly began to understand the commands, and she had little difficulty imitating the visual ones. She enjoyed many of the tasks and was given opportunities to select drills as she progressed.

In her floor time play sessions she was given the freedom to initiate what she would like to do and also had access to any of the materials used in training in order to make them her own. Her intelligence was evident based on the speed with which she was able to use the visual materials—to match form categories, show concept groupings, and build anything presented to her. Verbal imitation came more slowly, but it did come. Jenny moved from imitating sounds to imitating words, although, in contrast to her continued initiation of other visual or visual-motor activities, she always needed prompting. Her symbolic representations also became more complex. When someone insisted on playing with her, Jenny was much more animated and able to open and close multiple circles of communication, although she did so mostly in protest or while correcting someone else as she insisted on preserving her own ideas. Her play continued to be characterized by arrangements of figures. These were quite complex, as if Jenny had a vision of a scene from a video or a book that she was reproducing. She often used Disney movie characters, and she knew who belonged where and never confused any of the figures or the sides they represented. But these scenes remained static.

As Jenny's language developed, she did not label the names of objects, but labeled their functions. She might say "to ride" rather than "car" or "to climb" rather than "steps." Her perceptions of how the world worked were reflected in her drawings. She started spontaneously to draw pictures in which a tiny figure of a person, perhaps herself, sat behind the steering wheel of a car with enormous wheels. She then started to draw other scenes of her life, such as a child going down a slide or someone eating. She went through phases of drawing many similar types of pictures, and then she would move on to a new scene. Later, she started to draw more complex scenes on one piece of paper, so that different parts of the paper represented different aspects of an experience, such as all the things she did on the playground. Next she began to sequence a series of drawings to tell a story. Her drawings always reflected her real-life experiences and observations of the world around her.

While Jenny's language lagged and continued to need prompting, her remarkable gift for drawing allowed her to show her thoughts, her perception of experiences, and her complex cognitive understanding. In school, her classmates were drawn to her remarkable abilities. She was able to play more structured games with them when her aide brought in some of the drills and games she had been doing at home; now she could do these cooperatively with others.

When Jenny was about to turn five an IQ assessment was done for school placement. Jenny did amazingly well, achieving a performance score of 115 in the bright–average range. She was able to do all the verbal items that provided visual support, such as the beginning items on abstract thinking, vocabulary, and even information. She thoroughly enjoyed her own productivity and was able to work on the lengthy assessment as long as she was given the breaks she needed to swing, jump, or move about.

Although Jenny was becoming adept at memorizing social scripts when prompted and cued with pictures, her parents were still concerned about her slow progress with spontaneous speech and sought further consultation to see if any other factor might free up her ability to communicate verbally. They increased the amount of sponteous playful interactions and tried to reduce more structured types of interactions. In addition, medication was used to foster her ability to be flexible, calm, and focused. After an evaluation, Jenny showed a fairly quick spurt in her affect and relatedness. Her symbolic play took a huge leap forward; she now described what she wanted her scenes to look like and spontaneously negotiated verbally for the changes she wanted.

Everyone was overjoyed with Jenny's excitement in relating and interacting with others. In an instant, she would start a three-way game of putting crowns on heads and initiating birthday parties, or she would take another child's hand and pull him over to her toys. She took her visiting therapist on a special tour of her home. Although unable to say how happy she was, she beamed with delight, making it very clear that she knew this was a special relationship to which she wanted to respond.

MEDICATION

For many years, medication has been considered to play a role for some children with special needs. Before considering medication, we recommend a complete evaluation and assessment, including the creation of a profile that takes into account the child's individual differences and development, as described earlier. An intervention program should then be designed that combines home-based floor-time components, technical therapeutic components, and educational components. After a reasonable period of time, often at least six to eight months, the child's learning curve should be observed with an eye to particular types of challenges that may be interfering with optimal learning. In this context, medication may be considered. For example, if a child who is working on auditory-processing and motor-planning problems is still extremely distractible, would medication help her focus and attend? Or, what about the child who has been wooed into an intimate relationship and can be soothed when upset and overloaded, yet, despite parental efforts to try a variety of strategies to assist him in developing more effective ways of coping and self-calming, still experiences extreme variations of mood and is unable to regulate and control his behavior? Even in such cases as these, it is often useful to explore a child's nutritional status before trying biomedical interventions (see Appendix B).

In considering medications, it is critical to consult with a physician (child psychiatrist, developmental or behavioral pediatrician, or pediatric neurologist) who has experience with the condition and age group of the child.[8] It is also critical for parents to be aware of the issues involved. Some of the medications that have been used for children with special needs include the stimulant drugs Ritalin and Dexedrine, which foster focusing and attention. Antidepressant medications, especially those that influence serotonin levels, such as Prozac, Paxil, and Zoloft, may help to reduce repetitive or compulsive behaviors and anxiety and, according to some reports, facilitate auditory processing and language development. Medications such as clonidine have been used to reduce hypersensitivity, reactivity, and anxiety. Anticonvulsants and steroids have been used for children with certain brain-wave (EEG) patterns.[9] Major tranquilizers, such as Mellaril and risperidone, have been used for severe behavioral problems or disturbances of thought.

All of these medications can have serious side effects and can undermine, as well as enhance, cognitive, emotional, and social functioning. It is therefore essential to have a profile of the child's various abilities from a baseline period of observation at school, at home, and in other settings so that the medication can be assessed in terms of how it affects the child in many different areas of functioning in different contexts. For example, some children experience only benefits from Ritalin or Dexedrine, but others experience improved attention and focus at school (there are rave reviews from teachers) but reduced emotional range, subtlety, spontaneity, flexibility, and interactive capacities and, therefore, their ability to learn advanced cognitive skills and abstract patterns of thought is diminished. Some children also experience irritability and sleeping problems with these medications.

Similarly, a number of children given Prozac, which is increasingly popular, become irritable, impulsive, or disinhibited, but at the same time they may have some improvement in language capacities and the capacity to focus and attend. Such a pattern presents a dilemma, because there are both gains and problems. We have found, however, that some children can experience benefits from medications such as Prozac if the doses are kept very, very low. Often one to three milligrams will be tolerated by a child, whereas five, six, or seven milligrams—a small dose according to the adult standards—is associated with an agitated state. Prozac should be introduced in very low doses, beginning with one milligram or less (one-quarter of a cubic centimeter in the liquid form), and increased very gradually under careful observation. It is often best to stop at the point of some therapeutic gain without trying for an optimal therapeutic gain. The therapeutic window for some children is very narrow, and in aiming for the optimal gain children often become more agitated.

Some clinicians have reported beneficial effects from anticonvulsive medications, such as Depakote and Tegretol, especially when the child's EEG results are abnormal. More recently, steroids, such as Prednisone, have been used for children who have a particular clinical syndrome, known as Landau-Kleffner.[10] This pattern includes the presence of some language capacities that are lost after 18 months of age, as well as subtle brain-wave patterns that may require a 24-hour EEG to detect. A favorable response to steroids, however, isn't entirely limited to the group that fits this pattern; some children who do not have the abnormal EEG respond favorably as well. Clinicians are trying different patterns of administering the steroids—from daily over a number of months to once a week at higher doses—to determine their most effective use.

The use of major tranquilizers, such as Risperidone, for children is also increasing. Some children given these medications lose a sense of themselves (sometimes called depersonalization) and seem to show less range and subtlety in their emotional expression and creativity, and some children become more fragmented in their thinking.[11]

A worrisome pattern often occurs with the use of medications for children with special needs. Sometimes the first medication tried seems to help, but produces an unwanted effect, such as agitation or overexcitement. In some cases, rather than reduce the dose or switch to a different medication, another medication is added to reduce the anxiety or agitation. If the child then becomes too depressed, a third medication is given. We have seen a number of children on three or more medications. In several cases, gradual removal of the medications resulted in significantly better functioning. Each medication appeared to be compounding the negative effects of the others: the first medicine produced agitation, the second produced a reduction of cognitive capacities in its attempt to reduce the agitation, and the third led to fragmentation in thinking.

Because multiple medications can sometimes confuse a picture and create multiple types of side effects that obscure a child's capabilities, it is important to proceed cautiously when considering medication. If possible, it is best to consider only one medication at a time. If a second medication is added, it should be added conservatively, and the child should be observed in all areas of functioning to make sure that there are substantial gains without significant losses. The areas of functioning that are most often not observed sufficiently in evaluating the effectiveness of a medication are the more subtle areas, such as the quality of a child's intimacy, the subtlety of his emotional expressiveness, the rapidity with which he can process emotional cuing, and his creativity or symbolic capacities as evidenced in his pretend play, sense of humor, and range and choice of words. These subtle capacities need to be observed along with the child's attention, ability to control aggression, depression, or agitation, which are often the targets of the medication.

In making decisions about medication, it is important to keep in mind the child's sensitivity to relationships with family, at school, with friends, and with the broader environment. Scared or angry feelings, noise overload, unpredictability, insecurity, loneliness, lack of structure, or too much control can trigger extreme emotional reactions that are best dealt with through working on the pattern that is causing the problems. It is important to consider the child's emotional environment in relation to her unique sensitivities and profile. It can be tempting to use medication to help the child adapt to family or educational patterns or environments that may not be the best for her, rather than trying to change these. Yet medications are not as selective as we would wish; they influence more than just the target symptoms. It's best to try to optimize the child's relationships and environment to mobilize growth.

These comments on medications are not intended to be a full discussion of the subject, but to highlight some guidelines for their implementation. Parents should become familiar with any medications that are being considered, not only discussing them with the treating physician, but also reading the literature on side effects and risks as well as potential benefits. Parents need to be frontline observers in evaluating benefits and risk.

NOTES

1. For more information, see Stanley Greenspan, "Intelligence and Adaptation: An Integration of Psychoanalytic and Piagetian Developmental Psychology," *Psychological Issues* 12 (3/4): Monograph 47/48 (New York: International Universities Press, 1979); "Psychopathology and Adaptation in Infancy and Early Childhood: Principles of Clinical Diagnosis and Preventive Intervention," *Clinical Infant Reports*, no. 1 (New York: International Universities Press, 1981); "Infant Developmental Morbidity and Multiple Risk Factor Families: Clinical Impressions and an Approach to Services," *Public Health Reports* (Bethesda, Md.: Department of Health and Human Services, Public Health Service, January 1982); *Infancy and Early Childhood: The Practice of Clinical Assessment and Intervention with Emotional and Developmental Challenges* (Madison, Conn.: International Universities Press, 1992); *The Growth of the Mind and the Endangered Origins of Intelligence* (Reading, Mass.: Addison-Wesley, 1997); *Developmentally Based Psychotherapy* (Madison, Conn.: International Universities Press, 1997); Stanley Greenspan et al., "Infants in Multirisk Families: Case Studies in Preventive Intervention," *Clinical Infant Reports*, no. 3 (New York: International Universities Press, 1987); Serena Wieder, "Integrated Treatment Approaches for Young Children with Multisystem Developmental Disorder," *Infants and Young Children* 8:3 (January 1996).

2. A variety of strategies can be implemented. For an intensive floor-time interactive approach see Stanley Greenspan, *Infancy and Early Childhood: The Practice of Clinical Assessment and Intervention with Emotional and Developmental Challenges* (Madison, Conn.: International Universities Press, 1992); and *The Growth of the Mind and the Endangered Origins of Intelligence* (Reading, Mass.: Addison-Wesley, 1997). For peer models see S. L. Odom and P. S. Strain, "A Comparison of Peer-Initiation and Teacher-Antecedent Interventions for Promoting Reciprocal Social Interaction of Autistic Preschoolers," *Journal of Applied Behavior Analysis* 19:59–71 (1986); and P. S. Strain, R. E. Shores, and M. Timm, "Effects of Peer Social Initiations on the Behavior of Withdrawn Preschool Children," *Journal of Applied Behavior Analysis* 10:289–298 (1977). For intensive behavioral approaches see O. I. Lovaas, "Behavioral Training with Young Autistic Children," *Critical Issues in Educating Autistic Children and Youth*, ed. B. Wilcox and A. Thompson (U.S. Department of Education, Office of Special Education, 1980), 220–233; and "Behavioral Treatment and Normal Educational and Intellectual Functioning in Young Autistic Children," *Journal of Consulting and Clinical Psychology* 55:3–9 (1987). In addition, these technical strategies may include work in related areas. For approaches that include work with family patterns, see P. A. Barber et al., "A Family Systems Perspective on Early Childhood Special Education," in *Early Intervention for Infants and Children with Handicaps: An Empirical Base*, ed. S. L. Odom and M. B. Karnes (Baltimore: Paul H. Brookes, 1988), 179–198; U. Bronfenbrenner, "Ecology of the Family as Context for Human Development Research Perspectives," *Developmental Psychology* 22:723–742 (1986); C. J. Dunst and C. M. Trivette, "A Family Systems Model of Early Intervention with Handicapped and Developmentally At-Risk Children," in *Parent Education as Early Childhood Intervention: Emerging Directions in Theory, Research, and Practice*, ed. D. Powell (New York: Ablex, 1988), 131–180; T. H. Powell, A. Hecimovic, and L. Christensen, "Meeting the Unique Needs of Families," in *Autism: Identification, Education, and Treatment*, ed. D. E. Berkell (Hillsdale, N.J.: Lawrence Erlbaum Associates, 1992); F. R. Robbins, G. Dunlap, and A. J. Plienis, "Family Characteristics, Family Training, and the Progress of Young Children with Autism," *Journal of Early Intervention* 15:173–184 (1991); and A. P. Turnbull and H. R. Turnbull, with J. A. Summers, M. J. Brotherson, and H. A. Benson, *Families, Professionals, and Exceptionality: A Special Partnership* (Columbus, Ohio: Merrill, 1986). For those that include interactive dynamics, see Stanley Greenspan, *Infancy and Early Childhood: The Practice of Clinical Assessment and Intervention with Emotional and Developmental Challenges* (Madison, Conn.: International Universities Press, 1992). For approaches that address behavioral patterns, see V. M. Durand, D. Berotti, and J. S. Weiner, "Functional Communication Training: Factors Affecting Effectiveness, Generalization, and Maintenance," in *Communicative Alternatives to Challenging Behavior: Integrating Functional Assessment and Intervention Strategies*, ed. J. Reichle and D. P. Wacker (Baltimore: P.H. Brookes, 1993), 317–340; T. G. Haring and L. Lovinger, "Promoting Social Interaction through Teaching Generalized Play Initiation Responses to Preschool Children with Autism," *Journal of the Association for Persons with Severe Handicaps* 14:255–262 (1989); and S. L. Odom and T. G. Haring, "Contextualism and Applied Behavior Analysis: Implications for

Early Childhood Education for Children with Disabilities," in *Behavior Analysis in Education: Focus on Measurably Superior Instruction*, ed. R. Gardner et al. (Pacific Grove, Calif.: Brookes/Cole, 1993). For strategies including work with the social milieu see M. M. Ostrosky, A. P. Kaiser, and S. L. Odom, "Facilitating Children's Social-Communicative Interactions through the Use of Peer-Mediated Interventions," in *Enhancing Children's Communication: Research Foundations for Intervention*, ed. A. P. Kaiser and D. B. Gray (Baltimore: Paul H. Brookes, 1993), 2:159–185; and P. J. Wolfberg, and A. L. Schuler, "Integrated Play Groups: A Model for Promoting the Social and Cognitive Dimensions of Play in Children with Autism," *Journal of Autism and Developmental Disorders* 23:467–489 (1993). For educational approaches see D. B. Bailey and M. Wolery, "Normalizing Early Intervention," *Topics in Early Childhood Special Education* 10:33–47 (1992). For therapies that include cognitive and language approaches, see B. M. Prizant and A. M. Wetherby, "Providing Services to Children with Autism (Ages 0 to 2 Years) and Their Families," *Topics in Language Disorders* 9:1–23 (1988); and for sensory and motor-processing approaches see D. Bricker, "Then, Now, and the Path Between: A Brief History of Language Intervention" in *Enhancing Children's Communication: Research Foundations for Intervention*, ed. A. P. Kaiser and D. B. Gray (1993), 2:11–13.

3. Greenspan, *Infancy and Early Childhood*.

4. Greenspan, "Intelligence and Adaptation"; *The Development of the Ego* (Madison, Conn.: International Universities Press, 1989); *Infancy and Early Childhood; The Growth of the Mind;* and *Developmentally Based Psychotherapy*.

5. Lovaas, "Behavioral treatment"; P. S. Strain and M. Hoyson, "Follow-up of Children in LEAP" (paper presented at the meeting of the Autism Society of America, New Orleans, 1988); P. S. Strain, M. Hoyson, and B. Jamison, "Normally Developing Preschoolers as Intervention Agents for Autistic-like Children: Effects on Class, Department, and Social Interaction, *Journal of the Division of Early Childhood* 9:105–119 (1983); S. J. Rogers and H. Lewis, "An Effective Day Treatment Model for Young Children with Pervasive Developmental Disorders," *Journal of the American Academy of Child and Adolescent Psychiatry* 28:207–214 (1989); A. Miller and E. Miller, *A New Way with Autistic and Other Children with Pervasive Developmental Disorder*, monograph, (Boston Language and Cognitive Center, Inc., 1992); and A. S. Bondy and S. Peterson, "The Point Is Not to Point: Picture Exchange Communication System with Young Students with Autism" (paper presented at the Association for Behavior Analysis Convention, Nashville, Tenn., 1990).

6. A. A. Tomatis, *The Conscious Ear: My Life of Transformation through Listening* (Barrytown, N.Y.: Station Hill Press, 1991).

The Society for Auditory Integration Training, 1040 Commercial Street, SE, Suite 306, Salem, Oregon 97302. Website at: http://www.teleport.com/~sait/

7. P. Tallal, S. L. Miller, G. Bedi, G. Byma, X. Wang, S. S. Nagarajan, C. Schreiner, W. M. Jenkins, and M. M. Merzenich. "Language Comprehension in Language-learning Impaired Children Improved with Acoustically Modified Speech," *Science* 5:27(15245):81–84 (1996).

8. C. J. McDougle, L. H. Price, and F. Volkmar, "Recent Advances in the Pharmacotherapy of Autism and Related Conditions," *Psychoses and Pervasive Developmental Disorders*. Child and Adolescent Psychiatric Clinics of North America 3(1):71–87 (January 1994).

9. W. J. Streit, and C. A. Kincaid-Celton, "The Brain's Immune System," *Scientific American* 273:54–61 (1995); and A. W. Zimmerman, V. H. Frye, and N. T. Potter, "Immunological Aspects of Autism," *Int Pediatrics* 8(2):199–204 (1993).

10. S. E. Mouridsen, "The Landau-Kleffner Syndrome: A Review," *Eur Child Adolesc Psychiatry* 4(4):223–228 (October 1995).

Beulow, J. M., Aydelott, P., Pierz, D. M., and Heck, B. "Multiple Subpial Transection for Landau-Kleffner Syndrome." *AORN J* 63(4):727–729, 732–735, 737–739 (April 1996).

11. For further background on the use of medications, see R. F. Tuchman and I. Rapin, "Regression in Pervasive Development Disorders: Seizures and Epileptiform Electroencephalogram Correlates," *Pediatrics* 99(4): 560–566 (April 1997).

A. W. Zimmerman, "Autism: A Neurological Disorder." Talk given at the Infancy and Early Childhood Training Course, Rosslyn, Virginia, May 1997. (Tape 2 in a set of 4.)

19

School and Other Children

Your child's school will play a role in his intervention program, so finding the right one is important. As soon as your child is old enough to be in preschool you may want to take advantage of the opportunity to have him socialize with other children. If he is already related and interactive with you and able to open and close many circles of communication in a row, he may be ready. His interactive ability is more important than his verbal ability in deciding if he is ready to expand to peers. In school he will have the advantage of being with the same children in a familiar setting, with teachers who will get to know him well. Learning to interact and relate with other children in a group setting is the goal for all children and should be provided to your child as soon as he is interactive with you or others on a one-to-one basis. He may learn these skills gradually, first perhaps with one other child with you or a teacher helping. Over time during the preschool years, he may learn about how other children think and feel, how to negotiate and how to share ideas, how to begin and end social interactions, and how to make a friend. A long-term goal is to have him interact warmly, spontaneously, and confidently with others, and he needs practice to make that happen. School or preschool is a perfect place to practice, providing it is a supportive, developmentally oriented setting.

CHOOSING THE RIGHT SCHOOL

There are several important issues to consider in choosing a school.

• How rigid is the setting? To what degree are the children directed to activities rather than allowed to explore and follow their own initiative? What proportion of the time is allowed for free play?

• How individualized is the approach? Do teachers consider the unique ways each child learns? Do they mediate children's ability to learn in different modes (visual-gestural, auditory-verbal, tactile, and kinesthetic)? Is every child offered ways to learn successfully?

• Are the children's regulatory capacities taken into account? As noted earlier, children vary greatly in their abilities to regulate their attention and behavior. They may be sensitive to their environment, including the degree to which it is loud, bright, active, crowded, or visually stimulating. The same environment may be supportive to one child but overwhelming to another. Is mediation provided, and are accommodations made to help each child adapt?

• Does the mix of children assure appropriate attention, engagement, and interaction? Is there sufficient staff?

• What is the nature of the school's curriculum? Is it a play-based, developmentally oriented program guided by the developmental levels of the children? Does it focus on rote skills or thinking skills? Do teachers encourage emotional thinking? Do they understand the relationship between emotions, cognition, and communication?

• Do the teachers get down on the floor to play with the children and mediate interaction among them?

Although most schools try to create a supportive, developmental environment, not all succeed. There are some common problems. Many school programs are not sufficiently individualized. They expect the child to adapt to the program, rather than the program to adapt to the child. The child with special needs does not necessarily have the flexibility to adapt because she hasn't yet developed the skills to do so. When the school fails to take the child's individual differences into account and to meet her at her developmental level, it risks reinforcing the very behavior it hopes to change. When children cannot adapt, they become rigid, anxious, aggressive, or otherwise overwhelmed by demands they cannot yet meet and an environment that overloads them.

Schools vary considerably in their expectations of children's behavior. One school's philosophy may be to allow the child whatever time he needs to become comfortable in a new situation, with the numerous transitions involved; teachers observe and support the child's efforts as they get to know him and help him succeed. Another school's philosophy may be to insist that the child learn the routines and rules as quickly as possible.

Some schools are highly structured. They may require all the children in a class to do the same thing and provide no individual-oriented experiences for the child who has unique developmental patterns. The classic example is circle time, when the child who can't yet relate to *one* person is told to sit in a circle with a group and expected to be quiet and attentive while doing so. The child may cope with this stress by flapping her arms, making noise, covering her ears, pushing another child, or running away; she may learn to tune out the overwhelming experience by becoming more self-absorbed; or she may participate in the group in a rote, fixed way.

Proponents of circle time argue that every child needs to learn to sit in a group and pay attention—these are skills children will need in school. Yet every task has its developmental sequence. A child cannot relate to a group of six until he's learned to relate one-on-one, and then to a group of three. To ask him to do so is like asking him to read without first teaching him the letters.

In some developmentally sensitive preschools, circle time is very brief for younger children and expands in relation to their increasing capacities to attend, learn, and participate in a group. Some of these programs are very flexible with children who benefit more from one-on-one interactive experiences. Some special-education settings, however, insist on longer circle-time sessions, even with children who are not ready for learning in this way. Sometimes they use seat belts, or a teacher sits behind the child to make sure the child stays seated. The hope is that if the child is made to attend some of the content will get through. Unfortunately, the relevance of the content to the child and the child's way of learning may not be taken into account.

Some classes may include children who are very anxious or aggressive, with poor self-control. When these children are grouped with children who are easily frightened or withdrawn, the more passive children are easily overwhelmed. Rather than blossom and learn to communicate, they may withdraw out of self-protection. Furthermore, teachers may have their hands full with the more demanding students, so the withdrawn children may be left to themselves, rather than wooed into interaction.

Perhaps the greatest problem with class makeup is that students are often grouped with peers who have similar special needs, so, for example, it is common to have eight noncommunicative, withdrawn, and intermittently aimless children in one class. Naturally, there will be little interaction among them, so if one spurts ahead in gestural communication, he will receive little feedback from his peers. With lack of feedback, the student's precarious new ability may be jeopardized. Without being immersed in a communicative world with children who reach out, interact, engage in pretend play, and speak, the child will not have adequate opportunities to learn his critical early lessons—to relate, communicate, and think.

Today there are more opportunities for inclusion of children with special needs in general-education classes—classes in which special- and general-education teachers collaborate to integrate the child as well as to meet her individual educational needs. An appropriate educational program will have the following features.

> • *A developmental and individual-difference approach or philosophy that encourages a developmental progression in each child, beginning with mutual attention, engagement, and interactive reciprocity.* It is crucial for teachers to establish these fundamental capacities to lay the foundation for gestural and verbal communication and symbolic play. It is also essential to profile each child's processing capacities so that teachers can work with the way each child deals with sounds, sights, touch, and movement and plans actions.

> • *An approach that incorporates the general principles of floor time as described in this book.* Whatever it is called, the program should follow the child's lead, using her emotions and interests and opening and closing circles of communication. This approach makes the child's learning meaningful; it also encourages the child's initiative and purposefulness and strengthens her ability to learn from day-to-day experiences.

> • *Teachers who know how to facilitate relationships with children with significant developmental delays.* Each child needs to be wooed into interaction.

> • *Teachers who are sensitive to each child's individual differences and who respect each child's strategies for calming himself down.* The child may be permitted to swing before class, to keep his teddy bear or coat with him, or to rock and jump, if that's what he needs.

> • *Small groups led by adults.* Children with developmental challenges need, above all, interaction with teachers and with their

peers. In a large group they may simply withdraw. One teacher working frequently with two or three children at a time ensures safety and fosters interaction among the children. Teachers also need to get down on the floor and play with the children.

• *An environment that provides or permits aides to work one-on-one with the children.* Aides play a dual role: they help children master the class content or academic work that's appropriate for them *while* working on developmental stages and milestones. They use every activity as an opportunity for interaction and negotiating the milestones.

Aides also help children get ready for the next activity by helping them get organized and find the things they need. They work with children on *how* to learn in class. An aide does not simply sit behind the child and prompt him on schoolwork; rather, the aide turns the schoolwork into an opportunity for interaction so that the child learns two skills at once.

With younger children, aides (along with teachers) should help mediate interaction with other students. They may help the child attend and engage with other children in sensory-motor play, or join other children on the swings, playing ball, blowing bubbles, building and knocking down blocks, or playing chase or hide-and-seek. With slightly older children, the aide should mediate beginning symbolic play, following the child's lead as he feeds the animals, constructs a road, pretends to be a firefighter, or plays doctor. Gradually, as the child climbs the developmental ladder, the aide will help him share more complex and elaborate ideas. If the classroom has organized learning centers, the aide should help the child work with the other students to complete the available tasks. With the aide's help, the child will learn to attend to other children's moves and to solve problems as well as to share the pleasure of completing tasks with friends.

Finally, with older children, aides help tailor the work to the child's developmental abilities. For example, if the child is doing addition, the aide might help her visualize the quantities by showing her cards with dots. The aide might also help the child do assignments cooperatively with other students to build her interaction skills.

• *A policy that encourages parental involvement.* Schools often try to foster independence in children before they are ready; they separate children from their parents before they have fully learned to connect. A school should permit parents to participate in the classroom, even if it is not a stated school policy. If the child's challenges make parental involvement desirable, their involvement in the classroom will both strengthen the relationship between child and parents and help the child learn.

• *Openness to parents' suggestions.* With school, as with therapists, parents need to be proactive. Parents should tell school personnel what their child needs. Teachers may not be familiar with the milestones, but they may know how important it is for the child to interact rather than work or play independently. Parents need to show teachers how they work with their child at home and encourage the teachers to do the same. As their child moves up the grades, parents should encourage the school to make every subject interactive. For example, when their child is just learning to read, they may discuss how the school will help him with auditory processing if he needs it; they may stress that adequate time should be spent helping their child process what he is reading. Asking "Where did the boy go? Why did he go there? What happened next?" not only engages the child in interaction, but also encourages him to interpret what he reads, to sequence the information, to reason about it and recall it—all vital skills that many children with developmental disorders fail to achieve simply because they initially relied on sight reading, memorizing the letter configurations. When their child is learning math, parents should encourage the school to do verbal problem solving, using blocks or visual representations of quantities, and to interact with their child on verbal problem solving that requires creative thinking. Both parents and school need to create emotionally compelling situations to help the child learn, such as negotiating for a half or a quarter of a pizza or figuring out why the boy in the story might have been mad at his daddy by asking, "Why would you be mad at your daddy?" If the child practices these skills, he is more likely to develop into an abstract and flexible thinker. If he is allowed to go through school in a rote, noninteractive way, he may never develop the creative thinking skills he needs.

• *An inclusion setting, mixing children with and without special needs.* Many schools now offer inclusion programs, with regular teachers and special-education inclusion specialists working together in the same classroom. Smaller schools may be willing to include a child with special needs if they are provided with consultation or an aide. A consultant can help parents assess whether a particular school would be a good setting for their child and would be able to provide the ongoing support and meetings they and their child will need throughout the year. If an inclusion option is not available, the program should provide a setting in which children with special needs can function at a variety of levels; the program should also include a mainstream component. A non-special-needs program, with an aide who can help the child interact, is another option. The child should be in a situation that allows her to benefit from the responses of her peers. Parents should discuss with the school system the type of inclusion program that would most benefit their child. For example, physical education, music, and art classes don't always provide the best opportunities for interaction. Placement should be guided by the child's individual strengths and the parents' sense of what would afford their child the best opportunity to participate. In some communities, inclusion classrooms are set up to save money and may place 20 children with only a few adults; in others, classroom-inclusion or special-needs programs are poorly organized. Such programs should be avoided.

FLOOR TIME IN THE CLASSROOM

All the floor-time principles you use at home can—and should—be used in the early classroom. Your child will spend many hours in school. Those hours need to foster interaction and help your child master the milestones, not reinforce rote, mechanical behavior. Additionally, the more academic skills are coordinated with the milestones, the more solid your child's learning will be. Work with your child's preschool and kindergarten teachers; explain the floor-time principles so that your child's teachers can incorporate those principles into their work with your child. Even in the later grades, when your child is learning math and reading, the floor-time philosophy of interactive learning is essential.

The most critical point to emphasize to your child's teachers is the importance of spontaneous rather than rote learning. At every step his teachers should be interacting with your child, opening and closing circles of communication so that he learns by doing, not merely by memorization. Your child's learning should be tied to real, interactive experiences—real objects, real activities, pretend play—not to pictures or flash cards. For example, the teacher can mediate the process through which your child learns about cats by letting him observe a real cat, ask questions about it, compare it to other animals, and identify its attributes. Then, as your child masters several letters, he should see that C-A-T spells cat. Immediately he should look at pictures of cats, play with a cat, or pretend to be a cat with a teacher or aide. As your child learns math, she should learn to add and subtract visually, using her fingers or other objects. She should concentrate on the *concept* of numbers under 5, rather than on counting to 20 by rote. She first needs to be able to recognize quantities from 1 to 5 without counting, and then, as you add or take some away, she should be able to recognize the resulting quantity and tell you the number. All learning should be in terms of information that has concrete meaning for her in her life, that can be experienced through day-to-day observation and interaction. If your child's teachers can help her develop her logical interactive thinking while they are working on her mastery of numbers, letters, and words, they will be helping her build a solid conceptual foundation for future academic tasks.

Here are some suggestions you can give your child's teachers to strengthen his school program:

> • *In any interaction with the child, first join him at what he is doing, engage him, and then work up to his highest developmental level.* For example, if your child is touching and smelling a toy stethoscope, tuned out to others around him, the teacher should approach him by joining his activity. "May I touch that, too? Oh, that smells good." The intent is to get interaction going around his interest in the stethoscope. If he doesn't readily interact, the teacher can playfully obstruct him—by putting one ear next to his head so they can both listen—to encourage interaction. The teacher can try bringing in other senses or other parts of the body: "Does it make noise if we shake it?" "How does it feel on your skin?" "Can you wrap it around your leg?" The teacher should also introduce new ideas to create an interactive dialogue with simple gestures.
>
> Once your child is engaged, the teacher should add an element of pretend. "Ernie wants to hear, too!" They should see if your child can listen to Ernie's heart. Then maybe Ernie will need a Band-Aid or other item from the doctor's kit. Bit by bit, the teacher can make the play more complex, then gradually bring in words. In this way the teacher can slowly work your child up to his highest developmental level.
>
> • *Take into account the child's individual differences.* It may take time for your child's teachers to get to know your child's

individual challenges and strengths. If your child is underreactive, show her teachers how a lot of animation and energy pulls her in. Suggest they start each day with jumping, bouncing on a ball, or running exercises to rev her up. If she's overreactive, show them how soothing talk and rhythmic movements and songs help her calm down. Explain to them what works for your child at home so that they can do the same at school. A busy teacher may be able to engage in these interactions part of the time. An aide or volunteer or parent can help.

• *Try not to ignore the child, let him play too much by himself, or engage in parallel play with other children.* He needs to be inter-acting almost all the time.

• *Don't overdirect the child.* In response to directives she may learn to be obedient, but following directives will not help her grow. She needs to be asserting her own initiative and figuring out what to do next. The teacher can model an activity and see if it captures her interest; the goal is to encourage her to imitate spontaneously, rather than force her to do something. The teacher needs to create compelling situations in which your child will want to engage in the activities that are useful for her. Of course in many situations, such as going from one room to another or getting ready for lunch, it will be important to tell her what to do, but she should be challenged and inspired as much as possible.

• *Avoid rote questioning ("What color is this?").* Questions can be part of an interactive game. To get your child to say a number, the teacher can ask how many blocks he wants by offering a choice of one, two, or three, so that these numbers have meaning. Then teacher and child can count out the blocks together. The teacher can take one away and say, "Now I have one. How many do you have?" If they are working on word recognition, rather than ask your child to read flash cards, the teacher can show him pictures and words and the words alone for choices (such as milk or juice, ball or blocks) and ask him to point to the choice he wants. This way, his learning will not be rote, but will derive from his motivation.

• *Let the child do things by herself.* If the teacher wants your child to do something, the teacher should inspire her to do it, rather than move her body for her. The teacher might move your child's body once or twice, just to show her how something is done, or use hand-over-hand actions to help your child if she has severe motor-planning difficulties; these actions can help your child learn new actions or sequences. But after that the teacher should cajole and encourage her to do the action or activity herself.

• *Don't assume that the child understands.* Make him close the circle; make him respond in words or behavior to show that he understood what the teacher asked or said. If your child moves away or shows the teacher something else, the teacher needs to repeat the question. If your child can express what he wants to say better than he can understand what you say or has difficulty with word retrieval, he may take a long time to respond and may offer the wrong word in place of the one he really means. The teacher should not get distracted by his incorrect response, but try to be patient with his response lag.

• *Avoid rote interactions.* Even in structured games, the teacher can encourage your child to play in new ways, by putting obstacles in her path or asking her questions that take the game in a new direction. The teacher must always choose innovation over repetition in order to encourage your child's spontaneity and flexibility.

THE IDEAL CLASSROOM

For mastering the basic skills of engaging, communicating, and thinking, classrooms need to offer a variety of features. Although few classrooms are ideal, children benefit most from those that provide many of these features.

Mini–learning environments inherently promote hands-on, spontaneous learning. Each environment should include a range of toys and learning materials that children and teachers can explore together, at a variety of levels, to practice developmental, cognitive, social, language, and motor skills. Because many children with special needs have constricted their world, they need a great deal of exposure to new experiences. The classroom should be a miniworld that invites curiosity and exploration in small steps. Shelves should be open and full of materials to prompt exploration and initiative.

One area might be the pretend corner, filled with dolls, dress-up clothes, hats, and props that lend themselves to pretend play. In addition to encouraging children to use their imaginations and develop and express ideas, teachers can engage children in gestural and verbal dialogues about their play, just as you do at home.

A math area can contain big and little objects, fast- and slow-moving items, light and heavy objects and scales for comparing them, containers holding a lot and containers holding a little, and other materials that have to do with size, quantity, and sequence. Working with teachers, children can use these materials for counting and number recognition and for learning quantities, sizes, sequencing, and other simple mathematical concepts, all related to real objects that the children can feel, hold, and enjoy.

A third area may involve spatial concepts. This area can be filled with objects to climb on, over, and under, places to hide inside, tall and short structures, balance beams of different sizes, boards with cut-out spaces to navigate, and other materials to help children explore space with their bodies. As they interact with each other and with teachers, children can develop gross-motor skills, engage in playful communication, and master spatial concepts.

A listening and reading corner can provide a place for children to listen to sounds and match them to objects and to play with sound and alphabet blocks, first recognizing the letters, then stringing them together to make words. This area should have small toys with names that are easy to spell so that when a child learns C-A-R, for example, he can play with the toy car, tying the cognitive knowledge to an emotional base. "What does the car do?" the teacher can ask. "Go!" the child might answer, and the teacher can then show him the blocks that spell *go*, again encouraging reading comprehension as the child recognizes his first word. As in the other areas, interaction, pretend, and cognitive skills come together in hands-on learning.

Another area may be devoted to the sensory environment and musical and arts materials. This area should be full of materials to smell, touch, listen to, and see. Rough, smooth, hot, cold, squooshy, firm, noisy, and quiet items should all be available, as should water, ice, and sand tables. Children can sit in large boxes filled with beans and corn to search for hidden objects. An arts and crafts center can serve as a fine-motor center, encouraging children to develop finger dexterity as they glue, paint, and sew with their textured treasures. This area should also have drums, keyboards, and instruments children can blow into so they can experiment with rhythm and sound.

An area near a sink can be reserved for oral-motor activities. Musical instruments, party-favor blowers, bubbles, vibrating toys, and foods with different textures can help children improve their oral muscle tone, and playing with these materials strengthens their skills for eating and helps them form sounds and words.

One area can focus on motor planning and gross-motor and vestibular (balance) functioning. This area may have mini–obstacle courses, in which a child goes under something, into something, and over something to get his desired toy. Hiding games can take place here as well—the child is given clues to help him figure out where his toy is hidden—enhancing sequencing abilities. Playing on swings, mattresses, and small floor-model trampolines fosters balance and movement planning.

As the teachers work with children in these areas, they apply all the floor-time principles you use at home: following the child's lead, joining him in his activity to promote interaction, then gradually drawing him up to his highest developmental level. Some children may require one-on-one attention initially, but as they become more interactive, the teacher/student ratio can be increased.

Each mini-environment enables children to work at their own functional developmental and cognitive level. A child with motor-planning problems who is operating at the 14-month-old level, closing 5 or 6 gestural circles in a row, might play with a teacher in the spatial-motor area, climbing over cushions or crawling into tunnels, strengthening her motor-planning skills while closing 7 to 10 circles in a row. A three-year-old in the spatial-motor area might work with a teacher arranging blocks in patterns, closing 30 or 40 gestural circles in a row. As they play, they can also work on ideas, discussing whether a blue block should go here or there, or if a small block should go on top of a large one. Like the toddler, this child would be doing spatial and motor sequencing and two-way communication, but at a higher developmental level.

In the sensory area, a child who is just developing sensory awareness might play in a box of different textures. The teacher can help him touch the various textures to his skin (by covering him with cloths he chooses or by wrapping toys in swatches of different fabrics) while engaging him with a warm voice and eye contact. Nearby two children might be working on sensory discrimination. As they play a variety of musical instruments the teacher might ask, "Which sound do you like better, the little horn or the big horn? The high pitch or the low pitch? The fast sound or the slow sound?" Depending on the child's level, the teacher can ask questions with words or through facial and bodily gestures, helping the child master the skill of complex two-way communication.

In the math area a three-year-old might work with concepts of quantity by putting two piles of shiny coins into a piggy bank. One pile is big, the other small, and the teacher might ask her to point to the pile she wants. Although the teacher says, "Want big pile?" or "Want more?" the child doesn't need to repeat the words; at this point she needs only a sensory experience of big and little. Later, when she is closing 50 gestural circles in a row and has had a lot of hands-on experience with those concepts, she can be encouraged to label her experience.

The interaction in the classroom need not be exclusively one-on-one; a teacher can work with three or four children at a time if they are at the same developmental level. The group can include children with and without special needs. Therefore, the ratio of teachers to students need not be a lot higher than it is in traditional special-education classrooms. However, the teachers are employed differently. Instead of one teacher cleaning up while a second observes for safety and a third works with a group of 12 to 15 children, all three teachers work interactively with the children at all times. All children receive individual or small-group attention. The child who is withdrawn will be pulled in; the child who needs help closing circles will be encouraged to respond; the child who is making the transition to the world of ideas will have his imagination sparked; the child who is escaping into fantasy will get a lot of reality-based conversation with an emphasis on opening and closing circles of symbolic communication. Include children in housekeeping chores as much as possible.

A classroom set up in this way is able to meet the needs of all children—those with special needs and those without. It is able to offer a traditional educational curriculum that includes both preacademic and academic skills in a way that is matched to the various developmental needs of its students.

Your child's school may already function in a way that is similar to this model. Many schools for young children have areas such as these; it may be that only a little bit of tweaking is necessary to make it more developmentally suitable. If your school is not organized in mini-environments, try talking to the teachers and administrators about gradually introducing some of these elements. If they are unwilling, you might look for a school that can more flexibly meet your child at his current and growing developmental level.

THE IDEAL SCHOOL

Children with challenges should be in an integrated setting that mixes children with and without special needs. This environment permits youngsters with delays to learn from the spontaneous interactions of their peers and affords their peers without special needs an opportunity to learn to be empathetic, helpful, and caring. All children benefit from smaller classes and lower student/teacher ratios, and emerging evidence shows that children without special needs do well in these settings. Today, placing a child in a regular or mainstreamed setting often means giving up the therapeutic help or small-group academic instruction that exists in special classes. This is unfortunate. We would like to see our schools restructured in such a way that children with and without special needs can work together in truly integrated settings with the full range of support services always available. Not every school needs to function that way, but by designating selected schools as integrated settings we would provide valuable services to both populations.

These integrated settings would meet the educational objectives of our traditional curriculum, but their physical and social environments would meet the needs of children with special needs as well. Each classroom would have a few children with special needs along with children who are developing without special needs. A speech pathologist, occupational therapist, and special educator would be on-site so that everyone, even the children without special needs, could take advantage of their expertise.

How realistic is this proposal? We think it is realizable. Certainly creating such integrated settings would be expensive, but no more expensive than the special settings we have now. By restructuring our existing schools, we could redeploy existing resources, including making greater use of parents and volunteers. Meeting the developmental needs of children has varying price tags. Skilled teachers and sophisticated computers for certain developmental challenges may be expensive; helping children learn to engage and communicate with gestures and simple words may not be. Parents and professionals need to work together to create these integrated settings. Some school systems have already started this.

IMPROVING SPECIAL EDUCATION

Families are not always happy with the special-education services they receive, especially if they fail to see adequate progress. Programs are often too homogeneous, failing to meet children's individual needs. Many don't include the child's family as an important part of the intervention program. Many offer adequate, but not optimal, services, which undermine the family's desire for an education that will fulfill their child's potential. Many won't identify additional needs or alternative services and approaches, lest they be compelled to offer them. As a result, there is an atmosphere of conflict and suspicion between parents and school systems, and this conflict has stymied the kind of collaboration that is needed to enhance each and every child's development.

Concrete steps can be taken to break this impasse, and parents, by working with their school administrators, can help make these changes happen.

1. *Parents can lobby for more flexible classrooms and less restrictive programs,* such as the one just described, which can be tailored to children's individual needs rather than to diagnostic labels. The law provides the opportunity to create such programs by requiring individual family service plans (IFSPs) and individual education programs (IEPs).

2. *Parents can encourage their school administrators to include them as a vital and integral part of their child's educational, therapeutic program.* This means more than simply sharing information. It means asking schools to change how they view the child's educational milieu in order to see the vital role that parents play. And it means creating a true partnership with parents in which the school supports the family at home and the family supports the work of the school. To make this partnership functional, schools must change. They must train and support educators in working with parents so that educators can become familiar with family concerns. They must help educators recognize the patterns in the family that support or undermine educational goals, as well as signs of family dysfunction. They also must train parents to support the school's educational efforts in the home. Regular meetings between each family and the school (beyond those required for IEPs and IFSPs) must be scheduled at times convenient for working parents, for these are a critical component of the partnership.

3. *Parents can encourage therapists and educators to change the way they evaluate children.* Many current evaluations rely too much on standardized tests, which often do not give accurate representations of a child's abilities. Many children with special needs cannot cooperate with formal testing, and as a result receive inaccurate, narrow assessments. These invalid assessments are then used to establish eligibility criteria or for comparison purposes. Not surprisingly, they are often the first sign to parents that they and their child are not understood and that the system as a whole can't be trusted. Some educators respond to parents' complaints defensively, with claims that the parents are denying their child's true problems. They may hand the parents a booklet to read, and immediately an adversarial relationship develops.

   Instead of relying on standardized tests, children should be assessed through multisession observations conducted by educators and parents together. The observations should begin only after the child is comfortable in the setting. The child should be observed during free interactions with the educator and with the parents, as well as doing a variety of educational tasks. From these observations, educators and parents should describe the child's strengths as well as his challenges and should pinpoint his developmental level in different areas. When educators and parents disagree, further observations should be made to clarify the confusion. In this way, all observers have a chance to see the child operate at his best, in natural situations, rather than under the artificial and stressful conditions of a test. Standardized tests can be used, if needed, as a second level of evaluation.

4. *Parents can encourage school administrators to create truly integrated classrooms* containing two or three children with special needs and seven or eight children without special needs. An aide should be available for every one or two children with special needs to facilitate their interaction and learning.

5. *Parents can encourage school administrators to create programs of optimal rather than adequate quality.* Such programs should include the types of changes described earlier, as well as the proper ratio of staff to children and continuing in-service training for teachers. Outside advisory groups made up of parents and professionals can help monitor school programs and make suggestions for their improvement.

Obviously, parents can't create these changes on their own. Schools must be willing to rethink their traditional approach to children with special needs. Although money will be an issue, we believe that many of the changes suggested here can be implemented without a great deal of additional expense. Many of these changes can be implemented by redeploying existing resources, rather than bringing in new ones. We hope that the coming years will see more collaboration between schools and parents, so that together we can work toward creating educational programs that will maximize every child's intellectual and emotional growth.

AN EDUCATIONAL PHILOSOPHY: BUILDING A SPECIAL-NEEDS PROGRAM AROUND FUNCTIONAL EMOTIONAL INTERACTIONS

Even after they've done extremely well, many children with special needs evidence difficulties with learning math or interpreting what they read. Because children with special needs often have problems with sequencing information, they can become lost in a sea of numbers or new words and thereby become somewhat frozen. They are then unable to use their abstracting ability to try to understand the critical concepts with which they are working.

Often, in trying to teach children specific concepts or words, we may overlook the different pieces of the foundation that have to be in place. Many behavioral programs, including applied behavioral analysis (ABA), and many educational programs do not pay sufficient attention to the child's capacity for

- rapid, back-and-forth affect-gestural interactions (as described in Chapter 10);

- complex, multiple circles of communication, social problem solving, initially involving simple motor or gestural sequences, but then advancing to two- and three-step motor and gestural problem solving (finding the doll in the house, which is hidden in the box);

- spontaneous, self-generated, interactive pretend play and imagination, beginning with simple sequences such as kissing a doll or putting a doll in the car for a ride and moving to more complex pretend, such as good guys fighting bad guys; and

- generating ideas from desire or emotion as opposed to repeating ideas (from simple ideas, such as asking for juice when he is thirsty, to complex ideas, such as making up a word to get someone to laugh as he hams it up with big smiles at his first joke).

These four capacities, which are part of the developmental stages outlined earlier, must be included in the hierarchy of goals, regardless of the methods used to reach these goals. Any goals that compete with these goals should be carefully reviewed for their potential positive and negative impacts. For example, rote learning of words rather than meaningful interactive learning of words may undermine using words and ideas appropriately and meaningfully. Therefore, when possible, new words and concepts should be taught in situations of natural motivation (for example, if the child wants to open the door to get out we can help her repeat "open" in order to get the door open). By creating learning opportunities in which a child needs and wants to use a word or concept or an earlier skill, such as solving a nonverbal, one-step problem, we are helping the child learn a skill in real life. She is learning and generalizing at the same time, rather than learning something rote and trying to generalize it later. Children ordinarily learn the most important concepts in this one-step fashion. Children with special needs need to learn in the same way. These children often require more practice and higher states of natural motivation, and our job is to help create both these vital conditions for optimal learning.

Teaching Math

Consider a child who "can't learn math." There are many such supposedly poor learners, yet as soon as you start negotiating how many pieces of pizza they're going to get and how many you're going to get you realize that you've met your match in the facile use of numbers.

Most children can look at a pizza and say they want three pieces rather than two. When asked how many they would have if they had their three and someone else's two, they can quickly count from one to five using their fingers or the pizza. When asked what will happen after they eat four of the pieces (how many will they have left), they quickly answer, "One." Even when the problem is made more complex and a six-piece pizza has to be divided among three people, they are able to say that each person will get two pieces. Or, when they have to figure out how many pieces they will need to give three people two pieces each, they quickly multiply or add and get six. They can even tell how many pieces are in half the pie, and when told that half is the same as 50 percent, they quickly understand this concept as well.

Many children who "can't learn math" and even at age ten are not doing simple addition and subtraction quickly become skilled at mathematical calculations that have to do with pieces of pizza. The key appears to be working with the child on the concept at hand, addition or subtraction, with relatively small numbers in an emotionally compelling situation. When we work with children with small numbers, their sequencing difficulties do not get as much in the way of their learning the concepts as they do when the children are trying to work with higher numbers and memorize addition or multiplication facts.

We recommend sticking with small numbers and working on the different related concepts—addition, subtraction, multiplication, division, and even fractions and decimals—with the small numbers. Each of these operations helps clarify the others and fosters understanding. What you take away, you can add; what you divide, you can multiply. You can substitute adding for multiplying if you want to do it the long way, and so forth.

By working with zero to six in an emotionally vibrant manner with objects that have meaning for the child, the child is helped to master the basic concepts of quantity. The concepts are not mastered until the child can close his eyes and picture the pizza or the apples or his fingers in his mind and carry out the operations without the actual objects. At that point, it makes sense to move up to ten and then to keep moving up to higher numbers as the child masters the interrelated mathematical concepts.

With this approach, the child's difficulties with sequencing and, at times, with visualizing do not undermine her ability to learn the core concepts. By keeping the numbers small and emotionally meaningful, we create a context in which the child is relating to the items, be it pizza or apples, in a manageable, emotionally vibrant manner. The items have meanings that become part of the child's emerging new concepts as she discovers she can do interesting mathematical things with these meaningful and manageable objects of her desire.

Teaching Words and Concepts

Children with special needs sometimes have a tendency to learn words and concepts in a rote or concrete manner, because they don't connect affect or meaning to the words and concepts. This difficulty undermines their ability to learn to abstract because abstraction involves attaching multiple meanings to words and concepts, for example, understanding the multiple meanings of "justice" or "love."

Ordinarily, multiple emotional experiences provide the meanings that children use to form abstractions; for instance, experiences with being treated justly or unjustly form part of the concept of justice. Because children with special needs often lack the rich quality of experiences that others have (in part because their processing difficulties may prevent full participation in or full digestion of experiences), they may rely on more rote ways of learning. Their processing difficulties may also make it hard for them to integrate different types of experiences, such as experiences that come through the different senses or in different contexts.

In helping children learn new words and concepts, it is critical to create a vibrant emotional context for such learning. A practice that seems to work well is to have parents, educators, and therapists identify, every few days, a handful of words and concepts that are likely to be used by the child in mastering his world. These words are culture and family dependent; a child in the tropics might learn "snake" and "watch out" early on, whereas a child in a suburban community might learn "juice" and "open" earlier. Words and concepts that most children master early may include "open," "up," "out," "more," "juice," "cookie," "now," "before," "go," "stop," "give," "yes," "no," "happy," "angry," "want." We recommend identifying such new words and concepts based on their utility in the child's life and on the emotional saliency of the words and concepts; that is, consider how important and how meaningful a word—"more," "going," "out," "the door"—is to the particular child. The more useful and emotionally meaningful, the more likely the child will need to try to use that word and concept in an emotionally meaningful way many times a day. By helping the child master words and concepts based on their emotional meaning and utility, we can build up the child's conceptual and verbal vocabulary in a highly meaningful way rather than an arbitrary or rote way. The child wants and needs to use these words and concepts. She therefore not only remembers them more, but understands them better as well.

Children are typically taught words and concepts based on lists that have little relevance to their daily life and their tendency to use words and concepts in this way. Vocabulary building can be particularly impersonal. If words do not apply to the child's life, they won't be well learned, retained, or finely understood; the concepts won't be learned unless they are functional and emotional, which means culturally relevant to the child's daily life.

A parent was working with her three-year-old on understanding the concept of beside (one object being *beside* another object). The child was making good progress, but had a history of moderate language difficulties. Although pleased that the mother was working on a concept that would be useful in the child's life, for example, to identify a toy that was beside another toy, the therapist wondered why she had chosen beside as a concept to work on rather than another concept, such as more/less or a lot/a little, which might be more readily used in the child's daily functioning. The mother explained that she was working on beside because she had seen that word on a development chart as something a three-to-four-year-old should be able to master. She was unaware that the developmental timetable she was using did not list concepts or words in a developmentally meaningful manner, but listed certain illustrative abilities chosen of children at different ages. Therefore, her choice of beside was not based on a developmental model in which the concept of beside followed the concept of more/less, but she had taken an illustrative word and concept and was treating it as a foundation-building one.

The therapist offered an alternative way of helping the child learn new words and concepts. His parents, educators, and therapists would come up with two or three words or concepts every day for a few days based on how often they were likely to be used in the child's ordinary daily activities and also based on the emotional relevance they had for the child, that is, how invested he would be in using the word. For example, if he often looked for his ball, they might tell him, "The ball is *beside* the front door," "The ball is *beside* the chair," and so on.

After the discussion, the mother said, "It's unfair that they provide this information to parents because we think that's what we are supposed to teach our children."

It would most likely be useful, both for children without special needs and for those with special needs, if teachers and parents used this approach in teaching all new concepts.

Because the child with special needs often requires extra practice to master new words and concepts, we create circumstances in the environment in which he will need to use these words many, many times over. For example, if we put his favorite ball outside the door so that he has to open the door to get the ball, especially if he needs help to open the door, he will want to use the concept and word for open.

As therapists, educators, and parents work together on these core words and concepts, a type of synergy occurs that can result in rapid learning. For example, the speech pathologist may be helping the child, through imitative learning, make the sounds that go along with some of the selected words and concepts; educators and parents are creating opportunities to use those words and concepts; and the occupational therapist may be working on the motor-planning and sensory-modulation skills that will enable the child to actually implement the actions associated with the concept (for example, reaching "up high" for the special toy).

Parents and educators can look for opportunities during floor time to use these newly learned concepts in a completely spontaneous manner. For example, the bear might hide the apple "behind" the shelf or "up high" on the shelf.

There is a hierarchy of skills that children with special needs need to master. Beginning with attention and engagement, they need to learn to be intentional, to string together many intentional interactions, to solve preverbal problems, to imitate, to use imagination, and to build and interact with a vocabulary of meaningful words and concepts. Each of these tasks can be approached in both semistructured and unstructured spontaneous floor-time activities. With the semistructured approach, we create situations in which the child is highly motivated to use the skill we are trying to teach. For example, moving the child's car away from his line of cars may spark a protest and a deliberate, purposeful movement of the car back to its original position; initiating the child's favorite tickle game is more likely to succeed in getting the child to imitate and tickle back than is another action, such as touching his nose, in which he is less interested. Similarly, feeding, hugging, or kissing themes, familiar to and enjoyable for the child, are likely to lead to beginning imagination. With this semistructured approach, as the child progresses up the developmental ladder and becomes ready to master words and concepts, she will master the most emotionally relevant and useful words and concepts in an abstract and meaningful way.

For the child who is unable to create the sounds to make intelligible words, his own babble language or use of signs, pictures, or any other symbolic device is an excellent starting point for this same conceptual and verbal exercise. For example, children have been helped to use pictures and even recognition of words on the pictures to communicate their wants and desires long before they could speak. The key is to use the child's available symbolic capacities in an emotionally meaningful and useful manner. This entire approach is based on the concept that the child's own intent and related emotions organize and provide the meaning for her conceptual and verbal world.

Creating lists of functional concepts and words allows parents, therapists, and educators to work even more closely together as a team and provides the type of cohesive, meaningful, emotionally fueled experience that enables children to learn even when faced with considerable challenges.

Children with special needs often require extra help with being sequential, that is, doing things in a logical progression, as well as with being organized and attentive. They may have difficulty following directions and reading complex social cues. Helping children master these challenges in an educational setting means following the same principle used to teach math and language concepts. We need to create practice opportunities that are useful and emotionally meaningful. For example, the child can be given simple, and gradually more complex, directions on how to find his favorite cookie or video game. He can work up to homework assignments later. There can be obstacles or detective games that require creating a prop, such as finding a desired object, to solve a problem. Games should include lots of social interaction; the child should have to read the other person's facial expressions or body posture to win, to get to the next level, or to find the hidden cookie or game. The key is to create ingenious practice opportunities when the child is in a state of high, natural motivation; smiles, frowns, "go away" looks, and "come here" looks are the clues.

HOW AN AIDE CAN HELP YOUR
CHILD GET THE MOST OUT
OF HIS CLASSROOM EXPERIENCE

The following guidelines can be tailored to fit your child's individual biological challenges.

Muscle Tone

If your child's muscle tone is low, first thing in the morning, and whenever needed, the aide can engage him: bounce on the ball, jump, swing in a blanket, play tug of war, and so on. This activity can take place in the classroom or in an occupational therapy room, if available. Other children should be included if possible. This time can be used to work on concepts such as high and low, slow and fast, under and over, up and down.

Responsive Interaction

If your child still uses avoidant patterns—turning away, keeping her back to you, burying herself in a book, and so on—the aide can gently but directly encourage more eye contact and better listening, using such prompts as, "Ben, get ready," "I need to tell you something," "This is important," "Look what I have." These prompts can be varied, and the aide can joke around and be playful. As soon as possible the aide should reduce the verbal prompts to vocal-gestural cues, for instance, clearing the throat, saying, "Wow!" or "Uh-oh," or tapping your child on the shoulder.

The aide can encourage your child's responsiveness with tickles; a gesture, such as tousling his hair; a surprise reward, such as a marble or a baseball card; or, simply and most important, a gleam in the eye. The means of encouragement should vary so that your child anticipates a surprise—a reward for responding well—but does not know what it will be.

The aide can help your child practice new or challenging situations, such as going in the hallway, listening to the teacher's voice, and staying close on a trip, ahead of time by practicing the general skill.

Closure and Transitions

Children need to learn to indicate when they are done rather than simply to walk away. The aide can encourage your child to say that she is done when she wants to change activities or places; or, when possible, the aide can help her stick with a task. By offering a choice of the next activity the aide can help your child gain a feeling of control. When possible, the aide should encourage other children to get involved: "Okay, Jessica, what's next? Come, Maria, let's see what Jessica will choose now." If your child chooses a higher-level activity, all the better. If your child appears aimless, the aide can treat what she is doing as purposeful: "Let's explore the jungle!" if she's wandering aimlessly near a box of toy animals. The aide can help your child learn social cues with peers, such as saying "good-bye" to the other children at her table or with whom she is playing, and encourage the other children to do the same with your child.

The aide can prepare your child for transitions, such as moving from free play to circle time. Before story time the aide can read the story aloud and ask the same types of questions the teacher will ask. Props related to the story will build your child's interest and prepare him for hearing it with the class. Because coming to the end of a familiar story is often hard, the aide can help your child plan what he'll do next.

Social Games

Follow the leader is a good game for learning to take turns. The aide can be your child's partner to coach him through the steps. The aide can provide support by inviting other children to join in, making it exciting, taking your child by the hand, and adding lots of gestures. Other good games are Simon says; hot potato–cold potato; Punchinello, funny fellow; and May I? These games encourage imitation so that your child must attend to what the other players are doing. Teachers may include these games during circle time.

During outdoor play, the aide can help your child turn time on the swings and slides into imaginative adventures: flying to the moon, skiing down the mountain, finding the jungle animals, and so on. More structured games such as red light–green light; freeze; dodgeball; giant steps; Mother, may I; tag; and chasing balloons will bring your child into closer involvement with other children.

Sharing Time

At sharing time, the aide can ask the other children to pass their items so your child can touch them and get involved with them as well as pass them along. If your child sits in the middle of the group most of the time, he can practice watching others and waiting his turn (although he will need to be first sometimes). The aide can vary your child's position so that he is sometimes near his friends but also sits next to different children at times.

Work Time

The various tabletop activities set up by the teachers during work time may or may not be appropriate for your child. The aide can record in a log how your child uses each one so that you can monitor her progress. The aide can encourage interaction. Once your child understands how an activity works, another child (or two others at the most) can do it with her. (Keeping the group small means your child will have more opportunities to respond and won't wait too long for her turn.)

The aide can encourage activities. If your child loves to go to the bead table for the sensory stimulation, this motivation can be used to help her learn concepts, language, and additional uses for the beads. The aide can suggest some of the following activities:

• Trading beads with other children, giving them the beads they ask for and asking them for specific beads.

• Sorting beads by color or size.

• Playing imaginatively with the beads, using them as rain or pebbles or other items in a pretend scenario.

• Pouring the beads into different-size containers using funnels, burying them in sand or Play-Doh, or stringing them into snakes.

The aide can encourage your child to start playing with the materials he can handle successfully, such as pegs, puzzles, bristle blocks, and Tinkertoys. Tasks such as sponging off the tables, wiping off crayon marks, and cleaning up spills can enhance his abilities to do more complex tasks later.

When the class is working on cognitive activities (matching, identifying what's different, numbers, colors, letters, etc.), a child with processing difficulties might benefit from working with the concepts in several different forms, for example, using both the real objects and pictures of the objects.

Organizational Skills

The aide can encourage your child to rotate through the different activities and identify specific goals he is to master, including the organizational aspects. The aide can show pictures of the work he did, then next time the pictures can be used to help your child choose activities. There will be many opportunities for your child to work on organizational skills. For example, he can help with snack time by identifying what is needed and where to put it, making sure everybody has the same thing, categorizing items by what is to eat and what to drink, and so on. He can make choices about where to sit and with whom. If your child has motor-planning difficulties these sequences will not come easily and automatically; they will require lots of practice. Cues and pictures, rather than direct instructions, may be needed to guide him to what's next.

Role-playing

During free play, the aide can take your child to the dress-up corner and encourage her to pretend to be different characters and animals. Your child can play charades with the other children, using simple ideas such as animals. It will be good for her to guess what the other children are doing as well as to act out her own role. The game can start with the children acting out pictures they've pulled from a hat, and then graduate to them deciding what to act out on their own. Some children will enjoy the verbal version of this game: "I'm thinking of something that has four feet and barks."

HELPING YOUR CHILD PLAY WITH ANOTHER CHILD

As soon as your child can open and close circles of communication most of the time, it is important to facilitate interaction between him and other children, starting with one other child. He will then be more ready to enter a group (see later in this chapter). At home you can begin arranging play dates. At preschool, even though there may be many other children present, your child will still need to interact initially with just one other.

1. *Use floor-time principles to follow the children's lead, looking for opportunities to encourage interaction between the two.* As the children play, comment on what they are doing, joining in whenever you can. As soon as you see an opportunity, try to bring one child into the game of the other. For example, if your child is playing with toy cars, hand the other child one of the cars. If this doesn't get an interaction going, try to draw your child into the activity of the other child. Eventually they'll find a way to play together, even if only for two or three circles of communication. From these you can gradually build more.

2. *Use your voice to help each child pay attention to what the other child is doing.* Say things like, "Look! Did you see that? Wow!" The more drama you put into your voice, the easier it will be for both children to attend. And don't limit yourself to positive emotions; include negative emotions, too, such as anger, frustration, and jealousy.

3. *Get both children involved in problem solving.* Plead, play dumb, exaggerate, or do whatever is necessary to make your voice compelling enough to draw both children into the problem-solving activity. "Oh no! The car is missing a wheel! What should we do?" "Help! Help! The door to the house is stuck! The soldier is locked in! How can we help him?"

4. *Help both children become aware of each other's feelings.* Put a lot of drama into your voice and gestures, don't be afraid to shed pretend tears or make angry or jealous faces, and always use the name of the child you're describing. "Oh, poor Seth! He looks so sad!" Or, making an angry face and gesture, "Wow, Jason looks really mad right now!" Your child may be surprised at first, since he's not used to noticing other children's feelings. But if you do this regularly, he will become more comfortable and tuned in to his friends' emotions.

5. *Help the children engage with each other.* The children may tend to do parallel play at first—playing side by side but not interacting. Try to draw them into interactive play by calling each one's attention to what the other is doing. It may take many play dates, but if you do this repeatedly, interaction will begin to occur.

6. *Try to hold each child's attention for as long as possible in order to delay her moving away.* If you sense one of the children is getting ready to leave, create some suspense or excitement to try to lure her to stay. Try using extra emotion in your voice and gestures, adding a twist to the drama, or bringing out something you know the retreating child especially likes. If those efforts fail, try asking, "Why are you leaving? What's the hurry?" Or, "Is Maria yelling too much? Does it hurt your ears?" Or, "Was that a scary idea?" You may not get the child to stay a whole lot longer, but any amount of time provides that much more practice interacting.

7. *Help both children understand the other's behavior by translating that behavior into simple words.* Both children may become confused at times by the other's behavior. You can help them by explaining what the other child is doing. "Sarah screams when she hears someone cry; it hurts her ears." "David looks mad. He's throwing the tea set down so no one will have tea." "Uh-oh! Mary is stuck. She doesn't know what to do next."

8. *Help the children interact by using shared interests.* When one child starts doing something you know the other child likes to do, call the other's attention to it. Hold out a second car, fire truck, or doll and encourage him to join in. Or take all the toys yourself and distribute them equally to the children. This may lead to a shared activity, such as playing school, racing cars, or opening a restaurant for lunch.

9. *Help the children stick with their play by helping them bypass tangential ideas.* Once the children have a play theme going (for example, taking a family of dolls to the park), take on a role yourself in order to help them keep it going. If another theme surfaces (an alligator comes by who has escaped from the zoo), either ignore it and return to the original theme ("When are we going to get to the park?") or incorporate the new theme into the original ("Let's take the alligator with us to the park!").

10. *Help each child notice the feelings and actions of the other by reiterating what each one said or did.* Children often miss the actions or reactions of other children because those actions may be quiet or

subtle. To help them notice, point out what each child has done or said. You might even ask the child to repeat what he just said or did ("Evan, did you really say that?").

11. *Help the children share symbolic ideas.* Encourage playing around themes that you know both children can handle symbolically (perhaps you've already played pirate or doctor with each of them). If you remind them of these experiences, then they can elaborate on them together. Chances are, they will want to be on the same side and mobilize against you, especially if they are into good guy–bad guy themes. That's fine; it will strengthen their alliance with each other. If one child is at a lower symbolic level, then find a way for her to join. You might suggest a victory feast or building a fortress. Although these activities are more concrete, they will bring the children together around a symbolic theme.

12. *Pick up on highly emotional issues (such as separation, fears, body damage, and aggression), and help the children play these issues out symbolically.* These highly emotional themes are shared by all children because they are part of a developmental progression. As children grapple with them, they define their sense of self and reality. Symbolic play that addresses these issues will be of great interest to the children. They may react actively or anxiously (by becoming overreactive, or passive and avoidant).

13. *Identify each child's coping strategies and solutions, and offer symbolic solutions to difficult situations.* Perhaps you notice that every time pirates approach looking for gold, one child falls asleep. You might say, "Jesse goes to sleep every time the pirates come. Jesse, if you go to sleep now you won't be scared. But maybe you'd also like to use a magic sword?" By offering Jesse a symbolic solution to his fear, you might help him find another way of grappling with it.

14. *Help the children resolve conflicts together.* If one child disrupts the play, ask both children to help resolve the problem. For instance, one child might get scared while listening to a story and begin yelling or hitting, or one child might be losing a game and decide to run away. If this happens, explain that it is important for each child to understand how the other one feels, then help them come to a solution to the problem.

15. *Create opportunities for the children to work together.* For example, if you are the bad doggy that is trying to mess up their house, they might need to build barriers together to keep you out. Or they might have to tickle you to see if they can make you laugh.

HELPING YOUR CHILD ENTER A GROUP

Children who have had communication difficulties have not had the multiple social exchanges needed to learn social-entry skills. During the preschool years children practice the skills needed to join others, ask for a turn, and so on: "Can I play too?" "How about if my truck brings the bricks for the building?" "Look at my baby's new dress!" are the kinds of social-entry questions and statements that children learn to phrase. As they gain in skills and develop interests in playing with other children, your mediation (and that of other adults) can be very helpful.

1. *Helping your child with getting in.* When your child approaches a group, encourage her to ask if she can join in. Suggest that she say what she would like to do or contribute an idea about what they are doing. Tell her to use a louder voice if necessary.

Join the group yourself to help them notice. Say, "Hey guys, look who just came over!" then encourage the children to ask your child to play ("Johnny, see if Daniel can help you with that puzzle"). Encourage a discussion of what the children can do together ("Guys, are you building a road to the airport or the zoo?" "Pete wants to build the control tower; Johnny wants to build a faster road; and Daniel wants to build a bridge. How can you fit in all those things?")

2. *Build interactive skills.* When you first start to play with your child, follow his lead. If he's playing at something he's chosen he'll know what he wants and he'll be better able to express his ideas to others. After a little while call one or two other children over and involve them in the play. Try to get them to notice your child and him to notice them. If necessary, turn the activity into follow the leader (still sticking to the chosen theme), making your child the leader much of the time. Then help him follow the others. Use a lot of expression in your voice and gestures to help him bridge to the others.

3. *Become a playmate-mediator.* If you support your child now in learning to play with others, her relationships will develop more quickly. When you get down on the floor to play with her, other children will be drawn to what you are doing. Call out to them, "This plane is going to Disney World. Any more passengers? Fasten your seat belts." The other children will soon also take roles and begin to play. As the children gravitate toward you, they will naturally want to monopolize your attention. Convey to them that you are there to play with your child, but that they may join you.

If your child does not respond to another child, ask the child to repeat the question or comment. If your child still doesn't answer, ask him if he heard what the other child said. If he still doesn't answer, answer the question yourself to encourage the other child to stick around. Your child's responses may be slow, since he is not quick at processing incoming information, but given enough time, he probably will respond. Do not consider his responses (or lack of responses) rejections; don't consider his protests indications to stop. Most important, try not to let him get away with not responding, even if it is to say, "No, I don't want to!" Insist on a response in words or gestures.

4. *Support motor activities.* If your child has poor motor planning abilities, she tends to use toys that are easier to manipulate. Moving wheeled vehicles and pouring at the water table, for example, are easier for her than is building complex structures. Help her practice the more challenging fine-motor activities by giving her hand-over-hand support and by rehearsing these skills before she has to do them in the group. This preparation is especially useful for gestural songs; you can have a tape at home and your child can practice the hand motions with you or her siblings.

5. *Encourage partnerships with others.* Whenever possible, have your child work with another child in order to have more opportunities to interact and build friendships. Hang papers vertically on the easel so that he and another child can work together and talk about their paintings. Give him and another child a big piece of play clay and ask them to divide it. Ask them to make a big dinner with clay, discussing what each one will make. Have another child work with your child on a puzzle. Give each child a group of random pieces and let them figure out how to put their two groups together. You may have to help them at first. As you begin to encourage these partnerships, start with the children who show the most interest in your child and gradually bring in other children as well. Be sure to reward their joint efforts.

6. *Always encourage interaction.* Whatever your child is doing, make sure it is interactive, whether with you or with another child. It's tempting to reward a child for completing a task by herself; however, it is even more important to reward her efforts at interaction. That's the only way she'll master two-way communication.

7. *Create opportunities that motivate children to work together.* For example, set up a game in which the children have to band together to defeat you or see who can build a higher tower. They might even work together to hide your shoes and socks.

20

What Can We Expect?

What can you reasonably expect your child to achieve? Will she be able to live independently? To read and write? To hold a job? To get married? There is no way to predict how high your child's learning curve will go. Her diagnostic group is not an indication, because even within a diagnosis children vary widely. Her test scores and assessments are misleading because they tell you only where she was—on the items the tests measured—when the tests were administered. Comparing her performance with that of her peers is not helpful because it tells you where she is now, but not where she is going. Any static measure—anything that measures a child's performance at one moment in time—is unhelpful as an indicator of potential because it assumes that the child's learning curve will remain the same for the rest of her life. And that assumption is unproved.

The best indicator of your child's potential is the shape of his learning curve once he is in an optimal therapy program. If he is working rigorously with a team of therapists and is doing floor time with you, his learning curve will be indicative of his ability to progress. And as long as that curve is going up, your child will continue to grow. How long will learning continue? Where will your child end up? That we cannot predict. But we know that the steeper the curve, the faster the learning, the more optimistic we can be.

It makes most sense to look at the learning curve after your child has been in therapy for 12 to 24 months and true interactive learning has begun. As no child can learn in isolation, it is best to wait until he is engaging and interacting before making a judgment about his rate of progress. If it takes a while to pull your child into relationships and get him opening and closing circles, wait for that to happen, because while the first circles may take many months to close, subsequent circles will go faster. Your child's learning curve will rise.

The time to be especially concerned about your child's progress is when the learning curve levels off. Typically a child will move ahead, then plateau, and then pick up again. If the plateau lasts for two months we begin to worry, especially about the therapeutic program. When the child plateaus it is often because his needs have stopped being met in some important way.

What can go wrong? Any number of things can cause a slowdown—a regression—in learning.

• *Tension in the family.* If parents are not getting along, if another child is requiring all the parents' attention, if the family has moved and is busy painting and unpacking—all these things can cause a reduction in the amount of floor time and nurturing attention the child receives. In addition, instead of picking up messages of patience and understanding and getting needed problem-solving practice, he'll sense and react to the family's stress. This combination of factors can take a toll on learning.

If your family is under stress, look for ways to increase the stability and security of your child. Unpack fewer boxes each day; try to take time off from work; increase floor time. Replenish the nurturing and interaction.

• *Overload.* Too much of *anything* can derail the learning curve. Too many people in the house, too much noise, too much excitement over a birthday or holiday—any of these things, even when positive, can upset your child's balance and cause learning to falter.

• *Changes in the social world.* Perhaps your child's best friend has moved away, her favorite teacher or therapist has left, or a bully at school is terrorizing her. These kinds of events are frightening to a child who is highly vulnerable to outside experience, and can easily disrupt learning.

• *Changes in the physical world.* Changes in diet can affect your child's learning, as can environmental toxins such as pesticides, perfumes, paint fumes, or other chemicals to which he may be sensitive. Allergies and illness can also depress learning. Medications for physical illness may have side effects that can undermine learning. Sometimes, the ingredients with which a medicine is prepared are the culprit (for instance, a liquid antibiotic may be a syrupy, sugary liquid with dyes and food coloring). Special pharmacies can provide a pure form of these medicines.

• *The therapy program.* Perhaps your child has changed therapists. Or perhaps one therapist was good at helping her get to a certain point but has little experience with the next level. Talk to the therapists; see how they're doing. Consider whether a change might boost your child's learning.

• *A developmental growth spurt.* Sometimes a move up the developmental ladder triggers a temporary slowdown in learning. As your child opens up and becomes more aware of the world, his new perspective may be overwhelming. To protect himself he may withdraw. But with time and extra security and soothing interactions, he may incorporate the new information into his personality, and learning will resume.

As your child progresses in therapy you should anticipate slowdowns, and you should expect some temporary regression. Regression is very frightening when your child has special needs, in part because you fear the ground will never be regained, and in part because children with special needs have a broad regressive range. Whereas a child without special needs may become moody or defiant under stress, a child with special needs may go from talking to tuning out or from cooperating to kicking, biting, and screaming. But just as your child can regress quickly, so can she return to her highest level of development. You need to provide the stability, the soothing, and the interactions that helped her attain that level in the first place.

If you examine your child's world and can find nothing that needs improvement, continue working. It's entirely possible that after a hiatus, his learning curve will pick up. If a flat curve continues for a considerable time, with an ongoing optimal therapy program, it is time for a comprehensive reevaluation.

Concentrate on mastering the current milestone. If your child masters the current milestone, he'll probably master the next. And if he masters that one, he'll probably master the one after. Your efforts toward mastery today hold the key to tomorrow. Don't compare your child with other children; compare him with himself, with where he was before. If earlier he was closing one circle and now he's closing five, he's made a 500 percent improvement. When you find yourself burning out or losing hope, look at where he is right now. Count the circles he is closing. Count the seconds he can sustain eye contact. Measure the time it takes for him to calm down after a tantrum. Use every small gain to motivate yourself to continue. Raising and helping a child with special needs is an endeavor of inches, not 50-yard touchdowns, but every inch of improvement lays a foundation for further growth.

Some people, clinicians as well as parents, are concerned about the age at which a child learns basic skills. Some believe that if, at age one and a half or two, the child functions at 50 percent of his age level, he will always function at that level. Others believe that when a child learns a skill four or five years behind schedule, he will be permanently delayed. This may be true for some children, but it is certainly not true for all. The track record of the children with whom we have worked suggests that when given an optimal therapy program, many children can make rapid progress. Far more important than *when* a child learns basic skills is the *quality* of that learning.

If you think of your child's learning as the building of a skyscraper, you can picture the emotional milestones as the building's foundation. They must support 80 stories—80 years of living in the world. They must be very strong, for if those basic skills are shaky, the entire building will be at risk. It is far better to have a solid foundation developed late, than a shaky foundation developed on schedule. Ideally, all children would function at age level in every area, and some children with special needs with whom we have worked have achieved this level of functioning. But quality of learning must never be sacrificed to the desire to move ahead. If building a solid foundation and strengthening the milestones means temporarily taking *more* time, we encourage that, because without that foundation your child will never be able competently to move on to more complex areas.

Maintaining this philosophy is difficult in a world that places a premium on learning certain skills at certain times. Most children learn to read and write at age 6 or 7. They learn to write in script at age 8. They learn fractions at 9 or 10. Certainly these skills are important, but take a longer view for a moment. When a person is 35, what difference does it make if he learned to write at age 7 or at age 9? In either case, he can write letters to friends and take notes in school. What difference does it make if a person learned to answer a why question at 3 or at 4½? If the quality of the answer is good at age 7—if the child can give three or four answers, all of them logical—the child has a solid foundation for abstract thinking for the rest of her life. There is still plenty of time to fine-tune that skill over the next 30 or 40 years. The emphasis on *when* a child learns skills is misplaced. Far more crucial is how well she learns them.

Unfortunately, our therapeutic and educational systems don't always embrace this way of thinking. Sometimes a child's opportunities are limited at the elementary-school level because he has been grouped with other children who also have difficulty learning. Most often, when a child becomes a teenager and is several years behind his peers, we stop offering interactive therapies (which might build the basic skills) and instead emphasize practical splinter and community-based skills, such as making things and handling money. As a result, the child's cognitive education is halted and he never advances to more abstract levels of thinking and behaving. But why assume that because a child has not learned to think abstractly by age 15 he never will? Our brains continue to develop until our mid-50s. Why not assume that if we continue to work with children in optimal programs, they can move up the ladder of milestones and become—at 20, 30, or even 40— flexible, logical, abstract thinkers?

An example of this approach is the response of the group home to the 19-year-old couple who became chronically late for work after moving into a single room (see Chapter 12). Rather than help them reason out a solution to the problem, the home's counselors sent them back to separate rooms. Inadvertently, they denied the teens a chance to practice abstract-thinking skills.

If we start working with a 12-year-old boy who behaves like a 4-year-old and keep going for as long as his learning curve is going up, by the time he is 16 he may function like a 6-year-old. He'll have made significant progress! If by the time he's 22 he behaves like a 10-year-old, he'll be able to live semi-independently rather than in an institution. If by the time he's 30 he can function like a 15-year-old, he'll be able to go to a two-year college, have a girlfriend, get a job, live a good life. Is this possible? We don't know. The experiment is yet to be done. But we do know that the brain and the nervous system are much more elastic than formerly thought, and we are now seeing large numbers of children who develop skills at later ages than once thought possible. So in fairness to these children, why not continue to offer them the opportunity to learn as long as their learning curves are rising? If we do otherwise, we risk creating a self-fulfilling prophecy; we risk unconsciously limiting a child's potential by limiting the experiences we provide.

Some clinicians argue that to maintain hope for a child's potential when the potential is unknown is to encourage parents falsely. "Parents must be realistic," the argument goes. "They must prepare for the child's future based on what he is likely to achieve."

We don't yet have enough experience with optimal intervention to say what a child is likely to achieve. Moreover, each child is unique. Therefore the only way we can predict a child's future achievement is by watching her learning curve. As long as the curve is rising, the child will continue to grow.

To make predictions any other way is to run a risk far greater than false encouragement. It is to provide false *dis*couragement and thereby limit a child's ability to grow as fully as possible. The child's biology, environment (including family, therapists, and educators), and interactive experiences are all a part of her developmental journey. Only the journey itself, however, can determine the destination.

Floor-Time Strategies: A Quick Reference

We've presented a lot of material in this book—more than most parents will be able to remember. To help you as you work with your child we've added these crib sheets—lists of the key points. Feel free to photocopy them and put them up on your refrigerator or give them to friends or to your child's teachers and therapists.

FLOOR-TIME STRATEGIES FOR HELPING YOUR CHILD TUNE IN TO YOU AND TO THE WORLD, AND BUILD TWO-WAY COMMUNICATION

• Follow your child's lead and join him. It doesn't matter what you do together as long as he initiates the move.

• Persist in your pursuit.

• Treat everything your child does as intentional and purposeful. Give her seemingly random actions new meanings by responding to them as if they were purposeful.

• Help your child do what he wants to do.

• Position yourself in front of your child.

• Invest in whatever your child initiates or imitates.

• Join your child's perseverative play.

• Do not treat avoidance or "no" as rejection.

• Expand, expand, expand; play dumb, make the wrong move, do what your child tells you to do, interfere with what she's doing. Do whatever it takes to keep the interaction going.

• Do not interrupt or change the subject as long as your child is interacting.

• Insist on a response.

• Use sensory-motor play—bouncing, tickling, swinging, and so on—to elicit pleasure.

• Use sensory toys in cause-and-effect ways: hide a toy, then make it "magically" reappear; drop a belled toy so that your child will hear the jingle; bring a "tickle feather" closer, closer, closer until finally you tickle your child with it.

• Play infant games, such as peekaboo, "I'm going to get you," and patty-cake.

• Pursue pleasure over other behaviors and do not interrupt any pleasurable experience.

• Use gestures, tone of voice, and body language to accentuate the emotion in what you say and do.

• Try to be as accepting of your child's anger and protests as you are of his more positive emotions.

• Help your child deal with anxiety (separation, getting hurt, aggression, loss, fear, and so on) by using gestures and problem solving.

FLOOR-TIME STRATEGIES FOR HELPING
YOUR CHILD BUILD A SYMBOLIC WORLD

• Identify real-life experiences your child knows and enjoys and have toys and props available to play out those experiences.

• Respond to your child's real desires through pretend actions:

> • Allow your child to discover what is real and what is a toy, e.g., if he tries to go down a toy slide, encourage him to go on; if she tries to put on doll's clothes, do not tell her it doesn't fit; if he puts foot in pretend pool, ask if it's cold.

> • If your child is thirsty, offer him an empty cup or invite him to a tea party.

> • If he is hungry, open your cardboard-box refrigerator and offer him some food, pretend to cook, or ask if he'll go to pretend market with you to get things.

> • If she wants to leave, give her pretend keys or a toy car.

> • If she lies down on the floor or couch, get a blanket or pillow, turn off the lights, and sing a lullaby.

• Encourage role playing with dress-up props, use puppets—child may prefer to be the actor before he or she uses symbolic figures.

• Use a specific set of figures/dolls to represent family members and identify other figures with familiar names.

• Give symbolic meaning to objects as you play:

> • When your child climbs to the top of the sofa, pretend he is climbing a tall mountain.

> • When she slides down the slide at the playground, pretend she is sliding into the ocean and watch out for the fish.

• Substitute one object for another when props are needed. Pretend that the ball is a cake or the spoon is a birthday candle.

• Return to use of gestures for props.

• As you play, help your child elaborate on his intentions. Ask who is driving the car, where the car is going, whether he has enough money, did he remember the keys, why is he going there, why not somewhere else, and so on. Expand as long as you can.

• Make use of breakdowns. When a problem crops up during play, create symbolic solutions. Get the doctor kit when the doll falls so your child can help the hurt doll, get the tool kit for broken car, etc. Acknowledge your child's disappointment and encourage empathy.

• Get involved in the drama. Be a player and take on a role with your own figure. Talk directly to the dolls rather than questioning your child about what is happening or narrating.

• Both help your child and be your own player. Talk as an ally (perhaps whispering), but also have your figure oppose or challenge your child's ideas.

• Insert obstacles into the play. For example, make your bus block the road. Then, speaking as a character, challenge your child to respond. If necessary, get increasingly urgent (whispering to child to encourage him to deal with the problem, offering help if needed by becoming an ally).

• Use symbolic figures your child already knows and loves, such as Disney or Sesame Street characters, to generate symbolic play. Reenact familiar scenes or songs, create new ideas, and notice characters and themes your child may be avoiding or afraid of.

• Use play to help your child understand and master ideas/themes which may have frightened him. Work on fantasy and reality.

• Let your child be the director. Her play need not be realistic (she may still be a magical thinker) but encourage logical thinking.

• Focus on process as you play: which character to be, what props are needed, when ideas have changed, what the problem is, when to end the idea, etc. Identify the beginning, middle, and end.

• As you play, match your tone of voice to the situation. Pretend to cry when your character is hurt, cheer loudly when your character is happy, speak in rough or spooky tones when you're playing the bad guy. Remember: drama, drama, drama to give your child affect cues.

• Reflect on the ideas and feelings in the story, both while playing and later on, as you would with other real-life experiences.

• Discuss your child's abstract themes such as good guy/bad guy, separation/ loss, and various emotions such as closeness, fear, jealousy, anger, bossiness, competition, etc. Remember symbolic play and conversation is the safe way to practice, reenact, understand, and master the full range of emotional ideas and experiences.

FLOOR-TIME STRATEGIES TO ADDRESS
PROCESSING DIFFICULTIES

Child's Actions	Parent's Solutions
Avoids, moves away	Persist in your pursuit Treat as intentional Provide visual cues Playfully obstruct Attract with "magic" Insist on a response
Stays stuck, does not know what to do next	Provide destination Return object of interest Use object in some way Expand, expand Give new meanings Use ritualized cues to start ("Ready, set, go!")
Uses scripts	Join in Offer alternative script Change
Perseverates	Ask for turn Join, imitate, help Make interactive Ask "how many" more times Set up "special" time
Protests	Act sorry, play dumb, restore, blame figure
Rejects, refuses	Provide more things for him to say "no" to Expand Give other choices or time
Says something unrelated	Insist on a response Notice change Bring closure
Becomes anxious or fearful	Reassure Problem solve Use symbolic solutions
Acts out, pushes, hits	Provide affective cue ("Uh, uh, oh"; "No, no, no") to encourage self-regulation Set limits Reward for absence of negative behaviors

APPENDIX B

Food Sensitivities and Chemical Exposures

When a special-needs child is evaluated, it is worthwhile to consider (along with family stresses and individual biological differences, such as tactile and auditory sensitivities) sensitivity to certain foods and exposure to substances such as petrochemicals, formaldehyde, or paint fumes.

Research on these sensitivities and exposures is not conclusive. The subject of food sensitivities, whether to dairy products, sugar, additives, preservatives, gluten, wheat, or other products, is quite controversial, in part related to the claims of the well-known Feingold approach. Both believers in sensitivities and those who believe that such sensitivities are primarily a function of people's imaginations report their findings with great emotion. Interestingly, the research literature is more balanced than one might anticipate.

Some studies support the notion that food influences behavior[1] and that eliminating certain food groups can help reduce such symptoms as migraines and overactivity.[2] Other studies suggest either no influence of food on behavior, clinically insignificant influence, or only selective influence on very sensitive individuals.[3]

Note: This chapter is adapted from Stanley I. Greenspan's book *Infancy and Early Childhood: The Practice of Clinical Assessment and Intervention with Emotional and Developmental Challenges* (Madison, Conn.: International Universities Press, 1992).

For example, very few studies eliminate sugar or chemicals from the diet for two weeks before a challenge phase (chronic exposure may obscure a response). Also, studies vary on the amount of a substance or food to which a child is exposed and what constitutes a clinically significant response.

The research design can reflect a bias as well, especially because the area is so controversial and emotional (e.g., no elimination phase prior to exposure, low level of food or substance, insensitive measurement tools, or high degree of disturbance required for result to be clinically significant or vice versa).

There is very little research on elements in the environment, such as paint fumes, formaldehyde, petrochemical-based solvents, and cleaning fluids, and their effects on behavior. For example, many people report headaches, sinus problems, irritability, distractibility, and hazy thinking when they are in the presence of paint fumes for a long period of time. Indoor pollution has received a lot of attention in the media, but it is an area that needs more systematic study.

Because the research is not conclusive and because even the most skeptical investigators report extreme reaction in rare sensitive individuals and trends below a level of clinical significance in others, parents and professionals need to pay attention to the possibility that the child may be that rare individual or may have a variety of disability that makes even a subclinical level of impact significant (e.g., a child with sensory reactivity and regulatory differences). Furthermore, because the research is not conclusive and sensitivities to foods and chemicals could be greater than is now known and because some clinical populations, such as children with severe disabilities, have not been adequately studied, easy answers are unlikely.

One way to determine if there is a food or chemical sensitivity in an infant or young child is to set up an elimination diet, such as would be implemented if the child had a rash. The suspected food group is avoided completely for ten days to two weeks. The food group is then reintroduced for one to three days or until negative symptoms appear. Negative symptoms include a change in attention, activity level, irritability, impulse control, frustration tolerance, sleep habits, eating patterns, elimination patterns, or mood or any behavior, feelings, or thoughts that deviate from the child's usual pattern. One doesn't necessarily look for improvement when the child is off the suspected food group. Instead, one looks for worsening when the child is challenged with a lot of the food. Some foods or chemicals, when introduced, lead to negative behaviors even at low levels. Others require high levels for a day or two before having an effect.

The point of such a diet is first to determine whether a sensitivity is present and then, depending on the degree of sensitivity, to determine how much of and how often the food can be eaten. For example, the child may do fine on certain foods once every three or four days, but have to avoid other foods entirely.

One doesn't look for immediate improvement in the elimination phase because many factors may affect negative behavior; other foods, chemicals, and interpersonal and family dynamics can all inhibit improvement. But worsening after challenges with the suspected food group points to the food that was reintroduced into the diet. To be sure, the process can be repeated. Since this is not blinded research, there is the possibility of a false positive result. One should therefore look for marked changes in the challenge phase and repeat the procedure if in doubt.

There are many ways to divide foods into groups to set up an elimination diet. There are also many different foods and chemicals to check out. One way to go about the process is described next.

First, one may want to test pure sugars, chocolate, other foods containing caffeine, and chemicals (additives, preservatives, food colorings, dyes) as a single group. If the child shows a sensitivity, the chemicals and the sugars can be separated to see which group has the greater impact. To test an infant who is breast-feeding, the mother follows the elimination diet, because the foods reach the child through the breast milk.

A second group to test includes foods that contain natural salicylates. Most fruits, including tomatoes, fall into this group. Fruits that do not contain salicylates are bananas, melons, exotic fruits, such as papayas and mangoes, grapefruit, and canned pineapples. Some children are sensitive to natural salicylates. In addition, some pediatricians believe there may be some benefit to taking children off salicylates when they have chronic middle-ear infections.

Next, one may want to test for sensitivity to dairy products—cheeses and milk. Some people who are sensitive to dairy products can tolerate yogurt. Parents and professionals report that some children do better off foods with gluten, which includes most wheat products. It is also helpful to test for nuts, especially cashews and peanut butter, and for yeast if it is suspect. Other food groups may be tested, depending on the child's family history and observations of the child's natural responses to different foods.

A good beginning is to have the family take on the role of food and environmental detectives, noting good days and bad days and keeping track of what the child eats and what fumes may have been in his environment. When parents make remarks such as, "After a birthday party, he goes haywire," or "I noticed on days when I clean house, he doesn't do as well," more systematic study is warranted.

With environmental chemicals—cleaning solvents, pesticides, paint fumes, natural gas (look for leaks), volatile organic compounds (as in new carpets), polyurethane, and other petrochemical-based products—a controlled off/on study is not possible. Parents need to notice patterns in the household routine and not assume that bad days are just bad days. For example, if the child is behaving badly every Monday, and Monday is the regular housecleaning day when a lot of ammonia-based solvents are used, some other cleaning material or only water could be used for a few cleaning days to see if the child does better. If the child suddenly exhibits poor behavior when the house is being painted, parents need to look for a pattern and to make sure that the child's room is well ventilated. Parents need to be alert to many substances, such as lead, that may have a long-term negative impact on the child's development. An overview of household chemicals is available.[4]

Children who exhibit sleeping problems or irritability that continue beyond the first few months of life, as well as children with difficulties with modulating attention, activity, thinking, mood, or behavior, may benefit from exploration of dietary and environmental factors. There is a great need for more research, especially on children who have language and motor problems. Children with behavioral problems and children with overreactivity to touch and sensation or uneven development should be investigated for environmental or food sensitivities.

Even if sensitivities to foods, chemicals, and other facets of the environment are identified, they should not be assumed to be an allergy, although allergies may be present. Factors that can influence behavior may be "sensitivities" in the same way that adults may respond differently to coffee or to a newly painted house. The "detective approach" to observing (i.e., looking for good and bad days) and conducting elimination diets is, therefore, a useful way to identify such sensitivities if they are present.

NOTES

1. See R. J. Prinz, W. Roberts, and E. Huntaranj, "Dietary Correlates of Hyperactive Behavior in Children," *Journal of Clinical and Consulting Psychology* 40:760–769 (1980); M. Virkkunen and M. D. Huttunen, "Evidence for Abnormal Glucose Tolerance Test among Violent Offenders," *Neuropsychobiology* 8:30–34 (1982); M. Virkkunen, "Insulin Secretion during the Glucose Tolerance Test in Antisocial Personality," *British Journal of Psychiatry* 142:598–604 (1983); and "Reactive Hypoglycemic Tendency among Arsonists," *Acta Psychiatrica Scandinavica* 69:445–452

(1984); R. Bolton, "The Hypoglycemia-Aggression Hypothesis: Debate vs. Research," *Currents in Anthropology* 25:1–53 (1984); and M. J. P. Kruesi, M. Linnoila, and J. L. Rapoport, "Carbohydrate Craving, Conduct Disorder, and Low 5-HIAA," *Psychiatric Research* 16:83–86 (1985).

2. See J. Egger et al., "Is Migraine Food Allergy? *Lancet* 2:865–869 (1983); and J. Egger et al., "Controlled Trial of Oligo Antigenic Treatment in the Hyperkinetic Syndrome," *Lancet* 1:540–544 (1985).

3. See M. D. Gross, "Effect of Sucrose on Hyperkinetic Children," *Pediatrics* 74:876–878 (1984); D. Behar, J. L. Rapoport, and A. J. Adams, "Sugar Challenge Testing with Children Considered Behaviorally 'Sugar Reactive,'" *Nutrition and Behavior* 1:277–288 (1984); M. Wolraich, R. Milich, and P. Stumbo, "Effects of Sucrose Ingestion on the Behavior of Hyperactive Boys," *Journal of Pediatrics* 106:675–682 (1985); R. Milich and W. E. Pelham, "Effects of Sugar Ingestion on the Classroom and Playgroup Behavior of Attention Deficit Disorder Boys," *Journal of Consulting and Clinical Psychology* 54:714–718 (1986); and H. B. Ferguson, C. Stoddart, and J. G. Simeon, "Double Blind Challenge Studies of Behavioral and Cognitive Effects of Sucrose-Aspartame Ingestion in Normal Children," *Nutrition Review* 44(suppl.): 144–150 (1986).

4. See N. T. Greenspan, "Infants, Toddlers, and Indoor Air Pollution," *Zero to Three* (Bulletin of the National Center for Clinical Infant Programs) 11 (5):14–21 (1991).

Developmental Patterns and Outcomes in Infants and Children with Disorders in Relating and Communicating: A Chart Review of 200 Cases of Children with Autistic Spectrum Diagnoses

Early diagnosis and intervention for children with disorders of communicating and relating has been difficult to achieve. There is often uncertainty about whether a developmental dysfunction is simply a normal variation, a mild, self-correcting difficulty, or a severe problem, such as an autistic spectrum disorder. Furthermore, if there is a severe disorder, is treatment likely to be helpful or should parents adapt to chronic limitations?

As a consequence of the uncertainty regarding early signs and intervention efficacy, and in order not to alarm parents, there has understandably been a wait-and-see attitude. There are often pessimistic assumptions, however, which underlie the wait-and-see view.

1. There are no reliable early markers for severe disorders of communicating and relating, and, therefore, only time and the full disorder expressing itself will reveal the nature of the communication and relationship disorder.

Note: This material is condensed from an article by Stanley I. Greenspan and Serena Wieder that appeared in *Journal of Developmental and Learning Disorders* 1:87–141 (1997).

2. Interventions, while partially helpful for some areas of functioning such as language, are unlikely to significantly alter the course of the disorder. Therefore, there is no reason to expedite the evaluation and intervention program. In contrast, it is more important to allay parents' anxieties and wait and see in the hope that the child does not have the disorder.

3. The primary impairments in severe disorders of relating and communicating are pervasive, involving the very ability to relate to and communicate with others. While intervention will help some children improve more than others, all children with these disorders will continue to have significant impairments in the way they relate to others, think, and communicate. Therefore, parents have to learn to accept their children's limitations.

4. Children with these disorders are more similar than different. It is, therefore, difficult or unnecessary to individualize the program or treatment and educational programs.

To explore these assumptions, we reviewed the charts of 200 children we saw for consultation or treatment over an 8-year period. While there are limitations to a chart review approach, it can identify patterns, generate potentially useful hypotheses, and offer directions for further inquiry. A chart review may be especially helpful when there is in-depth information available on a large number of cases with a very complex, poorly understood disorder undergoing an intensive intervention program and repeated evaluation. A prospective clinical trial, however, is necessary for the definitive study of outcomes.

All the children had severe problems in relating and communicating and were diagnosed, between 22 months and 4 years of age, as having autistic spectrum disorders (i.e., *DSM-IV* diagnoses of autism or pervasive developmental disorder, not otherwise specified [PDD-NOS]). We found that the majority of these families had asked their primary health care providers about developmental problems three or more months prior to the evaluation and usually it took an additional three or more months for intervention to start. Furthermore, from an analysis of developmental patterns, we found that months before the parents expressed concerns, there were reliable early markers of the communication and relationship dysfunctions in the vast majority of cases. Contrary to textbook descriptions of autistic spectrum disorders, which often describe the majority of children as having an early onset, more than two-thirds of the children showed relatively better development in the first year of life with a clear regression in the second year of life. All 200 cases evidenced auditory-processing, motor-planning, and sensory-modulation dysfunction. There were, however, quite striking differences in the way different children processed information and planned and carried out motor patterns.

After a minimum of 2 years of a comprehensive, relationship- and developmentally based intervention program, 58 percent evidenced very good outcomes. These children became trusting and intimately related to parents, showed joyful and pleasurable affect, and, most impressively, had the capacity for learning abstract thinking and interactive, spontaneous communication at a preverbal and verbal level.

These observations suggest new ways of conceptualizing severe disorders of relating and communicating. Autistic spectrum symptoms may not always be as chronic as originally thought. Rather than constituting primary dysfunctions, the symptoms that characterize autistic spectrum disorder may usefully be viewed as a final, common pathway for a variety of underlying central nervous system processing dysfunctions, the most critical of which may be a neurophysiologic dysfunction in the connection between affect (or intent) and the sequencing of motor patterns and verbal symbols.

BACKGROUND

Severe disorders of relating and communicating appear to be increasing. Estimates have increased from 4/10,000 to 11–21/10,000 (Gillberg, 1990; Wing & Gould, 1979). Many practitioners from different parts of the United States informally report seeing more cases of children who fit the criteria for autism and pervasive developmental disorder not otherwise specified, PDD-NOS (*DSM-III-R*, APA, 1980; *DSM-IV*, APA, 1994), multisystem developmental disorder, MSDD (DC-1 0–3, 1994), and a variety of atypical patterns in communicating and relating.

The criteria for autism described by Kanner (1943) have gradually been broadened in the changing definitions of the *Diagnostic and Statistical Manual of Mental Disorders* published by the American Psychiatric Association. Kanner's original criteria for this disorder involved an infant's completely shutting out the external world from the beginning, especially the interpersonal world. The most recent APA descriptions (e.g., *DSM-III-R* and *DSM-IV*), however, involve *relative* degrees of dysfunction in reciprocal interaction, relating, and symbolic communication, which may emerge at various times in the first 3 years of life.

Research into underlying biological mechanisms for autistic spectrum disorders still appear to lack specificity (Cafiero, 1995; Courchesne et al., 1994; Gillberg, 1990; Rimland, 1964; Schopler & Mesibov, 1987; Courchesne, Yeung-Courchesne, Press, Hesserinck, & Jennigan, 1983). There are a variety of intervention approaches which have promising findings, including behavioral (Lovaas, 1987); pharmacological (Campbell et al., 1989; Gelle, Ritvo, Freeman, & Yuwiler, 1982; Gillberg, 1989; Handen, 1993; Markowitz, 1990; Panskepp, Lensing, Leboyer, & Bouvard, 1991; Ratey, Sorrer, Mikkelsen, & Chmielinski, 1989; Schopler & Mesibov, 1987); educational (Harris, 1975; Koegel et al., 1989; Olley, Robbins, & Morelli-Robbins, 1993; Stokes & Osnes, 1988); language based (Prizant & Wetherby, 1990); and interpersonal (Carew, 1980; Carr & Darcy, 1990; Feuerstein et al., 1979; Feuerstein et al., 1981; Harris, Handleman, Kristoff, Bass, & Cordon, 1990; Odom & Strain, 1986). There are also a number of important outcome studies (Bondy & Peterson, 1990; Lovaas, 1987; Miller & Miller, 1992; Rogers, Herbison, Lewis, Pantone, & Reis, 1988; Rogers & Lewis, 1989; Schopler, 1987; Strain & Hoyson, 1988; Strain, Hoyson, & Jamison, 1983). The question of intervention efficacy, however, is surrounded by controversy, making it still difficult to draw definitive conclusions (Campbell, Schopler, & Hallin, 1996). In addition, there is a tendency to use specific intervention models, such as certain educational or behavioral models for large numbers of children, rather than piecing together a program based on each child's individual differences and developmental patterns. This leaves unclear how different kinds of children respond to different intervention efforts.

Therefore, there are a number of critical questions about these disorders. What is the range of characteristic symptoms that should be included in the definition? What are the early developmental patterns, as well as underlying biological and psychological mechanisms of autistic spectrum disorders? What types of interventions are most likely to be helpful for whom? Are these disorders almost always associated with dire prognoses, where the majority of children are expected to have significant emotional, social, and cognitive impairments, and need ongoing care? Alternatively, can any intervention program enable large numbers of children with these disorders to develop healthy emotional relationships, creative, spontaneous patterns of communication and thinking, and a range of developmentally appropriate abilities?

PROCEDURE AND METHODS

We reviewed the clinical records of 200 children we had evaluated who met the criteria of autism or pervasive developmental disorder not otherwise specified (PDD-NOS) as described in *DSM-III-R* and *DSM-IV*, who scored in the autism range on the Childhood Autism Rating Scale (Western Psychology Services, 1988), with scores ranging from 30 to 52, and who participated in evaluations and interventions for two or more years. Upon entry, each child had a comprehensive diagnostic workup and received recommendations for an intervention program based on the child's individual differences and developmental capacities. Periodic reevaluations followed every 2 to 6 months. Each child has been followed for at least 2 years, some up to 8 years, with the last contact considered the outcome. The children ranged in age from 22 months to 4 years with the majority between 2½ and 3½ years at the initial evaluation.

The clinical work was conducted in a private-practice setting with college-educated families. About half the population was from out of state and half from the local area.

The charts were reviewed for the following information: presenting symptoms and problems, prior developmental history, the child's maturational and constitutional patterns (individual differences), observations of the infant/child and infant/child-parent interaction patterns (including videotapes of these and, where possible, family videotapes of early developmental patterns), family history, and family functioning. In addition, the Childhood Autism Rating Scale (CARS) (Western Psychology Services, 1988), which rates the severity of autistic symptoms, was implemented for the initial presenting symptoms and developmental patterns and at the last follow-up visit.

Information from follow-up visits included parental reports of changes since the last evaluation, including symptoms or difficulties, adaptive and developmental patterns, observations of parent-child interactions, often with videotapes, and reevaluation reports by occupational therapists, speech pathologists, and educators or special educators. The Functional Emotional Assessment Scale (FEAS) (Greenspan, 1992a; Greenspan & DeGangi, 1997), which indicates the functional developmental levels of emotional, social, cognitive, and language functioning, was used clinically at the initial evaluation and at each follow-up visit. For a sample of children who had done exceedingly well, we administered a Vineland Adaptive Behavior Scale on their most recent follow-up and had videotaped interactions with their parents (which were analyzed using the FEAS). Videos on similar-aged children with no diagnosed disorders and a group of children with continuing autistic patterns were included and raters were blind to the children's status.

The intervention program is based on the floor-time model. This is a comprehensive, relationship-based approach tailored to the child's and family's individual differences and the child's developmental level. It includes a home component as well as work with different therapists, such as occupational or physical therapy, speech and language therapy, interactive intensive floor-time work, and early education or special education services (Greenspan, 1992a). The degree to which the family was able to collaborate in and implement all the elements in the program was also rated.

This is a descriptive chart study elucidating patterns from the clinical workups. To remain close to the clinical descriptive data, we summarized patterns and used percentages to describe observed trends. We deliberately avoided statistical analysis, even for some of the data for which drawing statistical conclusions may have been appropriate, to maintain a clinical descriptive focus and respect the limitations of information from medical records. In subsequent analyses, we will use analytic techniques to look, for example, at the degree to which certain antecedent developmental patterns and course of progress may predict certain outcomes. The current study will report on presenting symptoms and problems, early developmental patterns, such as the lack of complex gestures as an early marker, and developmental patterns associated with the intervention program and outcome, including the sequence of improvement and underlying mechanisms associated with autistic spectrum patterns. It will also discuss the limitations in assessment procedures and delays in implementing evaluation and treatment.

PRESENTING SYMPTOMS AND PROBLEMS

All the children met the criteria for *DSM-IV* pervasive developmental disorder, including autism (75 percent) and PDD-NOS (25 percent). All had severe impairments in engaging in reciprocal interactions at both the preverbal and verbal levels, in maintaining consistent pleasurable, affective contact (having various degrees of avoidance or self-absorption), and in entering into states of shared attention, where they would focus with a social partner on objects of interest with long interactive sequences, and with evidencing a range of interactive, subtle, nonverbal cues, such as affects and gestures (the back-and-forth smiles, smirks, head nods and the like).

In addition, all the children evidenced severe difficulties with forming and using symbolic communication. Some of the children had islands of symbolic communication such as using a few words descriptively or functionally, but none could enter into sequences of symbolic give-and-take at an age-appropriate level. The children also all evidenced some degree (from intermittent to most of the time) of self-stimulation and/or perseveration, including rocking, looking at objects through the corner of their eyes, and lining up toys.

There were also differences in presenting symptoms. Some children were completely self-absorbed or avoidant, evidencing only the most fleeting recognition of others or objects, and had no islands of symbolic communication. Other children were self-absorbed and avoidant but could intermittently attend and relate, show islands of warm, pleasurable affect, and occasionally employ sequences of reciprocal communication, and islands of symbolic activity (e.g., they used a few words functionally coupled with echolalia). Each child's expected functional capacities were explored to systematically document symptoms (see Table 1). The patterns were as follows:

Affective Engagement

Self Absorption. Five percent of the children were extremely self-absorbed, evidencing almost no affective engagement or pleasure, reciprocal interaction, or symbolic elaboration. Ninety-five percent, in contrast, evidenced some abilities for emotional relating. This is consistent with studies of attachment and emotional expression in this population (Ricks & Wing, 1976; Sigman & Ungerer, 1984), which suggests that children with autistic patterns have attachments and emotional experiences but demonstrate them in their own idiosyncratic manner. Within this group, however, there was a big range in degree of relatedness and the other capacities. The 95 percent of children with partial abilities for relating divided into the following groups.

Intermittent Engagement. Thirty-one percent evidenced some infrequent, intermittent capacity for engagement, including, on a need-fulfillment basis, seeking a parent out when hungry and using some very basic social gestures, such as looking at the parent briefly, or purposeful types of avoidance (deliberately walking away from or turning away from a parent's approach). These children did not evidence either long sequences of reciprocal interaction or meaningful symbolic activity and were often aimless or self-absorbed in self-stimulating or repetitive behaviors.

Intermittent Reciprocity. Forty percent of the population evidenced intermittent capacities for attending, engaging, using simple, reciprocal gestures, such as looking, turning toward or away from a parent, and organizing complex gestures, such as taking a parent by the hand and walking him to the door to go outside or to the refrigerator to find some food. These children also could intermittently evidence some very basic imitative patterns, such as imitating a simple sound or motor

TABLE 1: Functional Developmental Levels

Mutual Attention—All ages	Child's ability to regulate his or her attention and behavior while being interested in the full range of sensations (sounds, sights, smells, movement).
Mutual Engagement— Observable between 3 and 6 months	Child's ability to engage in relationships, including the depth and range of pleasure and warmth, as well as related feelings, such as assertiveness, sadness, anger, etc. that can be incorporated into the quality of engagement and stability of engagement (even under stress).
Interactive Intentionality and Reciprocity— Observable between 6 and 8 months	Two-way, purposeful communication, both initiating and responding. This may be thought of as opening and closing circles of communication, e.g., child looks at or points to a toy, parent follows lead and gives it to him, child closes circle by reaching and smiling. Gestures become more complex as child strings together many circles of communication showing understanding of what to do to get something or somewhere (e.g., gets coat or keys and takes father by the hand to the door, pointing to the car).
Representational/Affective Communication—> 18 months	Child's ability to create mental representations (emotional symbols) observed in child's ability to do pretend play or use words, phrases or sentences to convey some emotional intention (e.g., "Want that," "Mad," "Happy," "More").
Representational Elaboration—> 30 months	Ability to elaborate in both make-believe and word connections between two or more emotional ideas, e.g., "I'm mad because you took my toy." The ideas need not be related or logically connected but deal with such complex intentions or feelings as closeness, separation, exploration, anger, aggression, self-pride, showing off, etc.
Representational Differentiation—> 36 months	Capacity to deal with complex intentions, wishes, and feelings in pretend play and symbolic communication (conversations), which involves logic and reality testing, modulating impulses and mood, and learning how to concentrate and plan.

gesture (e.g., bang a toy). These children, however, were also self-absorbed or avoidant, depending on the setting and the degree of parental support. Children in this group evidenced complex gestures as much as 30 or 40 percent of the time or as little as 10 percent of the time.

Presenting Patterns: Engagement

No affective engagement	5%
Partial engagement	95%
Of the 95% of children with partial engagement and relatedness:	
Only intermittent engagement. No reciprocity	31%
Intermittent engaging and reciprocal interaction, but no symbols	40%
Intermittent engaging and reciprocal interaction	
Also evidenced islands of symbolic capacity	24%

Islands of Symbolic Activity.   Twenty-four percent of the population intermittently evidenced all the capacities just described—engagement, attention, simple and complex reciprocal gestures, and also employed islands of symbolic capacity. Members of this group could, for example, either use complex imitations and simple pretend sequences (such as copying a doll eating and spontaneously putting a finger in the dolly's mouth when the mother would say, "Dolly hungry"). They might use single words, such as *juice* or *out* to express a need. This group of children, however, frequently also simply repeated words in a nonintentional manner, would enter into self-absorbed and avoidant patterns, and engage in self-stimulatory and perseverative behaviors. In spite of some of their skills, none in this group evidenced age-appropriate reciprocal or symbolic capacities. The degree of perseveration, self-stimulation, and echolalia was not generally related to the developmental level of the child (i.e., whether the child had symbolic or reciprocal capacities).

Language Abilities

Receptive language abilities were more or less advanced than expressive, but generally followed a similar pattern. No obvious understanding of even simple verbal communication was evidenced by 55 percent of the children, 41 percent had intermittent ability to understand single words and follow simple directions, and 4 percent could understand two-sequence commands, but somewhat inconsistently and not in all areas. For example, they might understand a command to get a plate and bring it to the table (especially if those words, and the pattern they were part of, were familiar).

Presenting Patterns: Receptive Language

No receptive language understanding	55%
Intermittent with some words and phrases	41%
To sequence instructions some of the time	4%

Visual-Spatial Abilities

The majority of children were stronger in visual-spatial abilities than auditory processing abilities. A small group of children were precocious in their visual-spatial ability, significantly ahead of age level. They were, for example, able to recognize and discriminate visual patterns or figure out how toys worked. Most of the children had some degree of visual-spatial impairment, although not as great as the auditory-processing dysfunction.

Childhood Autism Rating Scale

The Childhood Autism Rating scale (Western Psychology Services, 1988) rates the degree of autistic symptoms on a scale of 15 to 60. A score below 30 is considered nonautistic, while scores of 30 to 60 reflect mild to the most severely autistic. Thirty-six percent of the population scored between 40 and 60. The highest score was 52 (a considerable degree of dysfunction), with 39 percent scoring between 35 and 40, a moderate degree of dysfunction, and 25 percent scoring between 30 and 35, a mild degree of autistic dysfunction.

Presenting Patterns: CARS

RATING SCALE	SCORE	POPULATION, %
Severe	40–60	36
Moderate	35–40	39
Mild	30–35	25

Individual Differences in Motor Tone and Planning, Sensory Processing, and Sensory Reactivity

The children's presenting developmental patterns were also reviewed with regard to their individual differences in regulatory capacities, which include sensory reactivity, sensory processing, motor planning, and muscle tone (Greenspan, 1992a).

Differences in sensitivity to sensation were quite variable, with 39 percent underreactive to sensation (e.g., were underresponsive to sensations like touch, movement, or sound); 28 percent self-absorbed (some of the self-absorbed children also had low muscle tone, suggesting that whether an underreactive child seeks out sensations or becomes self-absorbed may, in part, depend on motor patterns); and 11 percent active and craving, seeking out extra sensation.

Hypersensitivity to sensations such as touch and sound was evidenced by 19 percent, with 36 percent showing mixed patterns (where they might be oversensitive to touch and undersensitive to sound or, even within a domain such as sound, be oversensitive to certain frequencies and undersensitive to other frequencies), and 6 percent not evidencing sensory modality difficulties.

All the children evidenced dysfunctions in auditory processing (receptive language). All the children showed some difficulties with motor planning (sequencing motor acts, such as copying shapes, manipulating an object in a planned sequence rather than repetitively, e.g., taking a car, putting it in a play house, taking it out, and crashing it into another car rather than just rolling a car back and forth or pushing a train on a track).

Severe difficulties in motor planning were evidenced by 48 percent (i.e., they could not implement a two-step pattern). Some would only do the simplest, dropping and dumping objects, while others repeated simple actions over and over again, such as pushing a car back and forth, using a pop-up toy, knocking down blocks. Significant low muscle tone was evidenced by 17 percent, with associated difficulties such as learning to crawl, walk, or oral motor activities, stamina, and postural control.

Presenting Patterns: Sensory Processing and Motor Planning

Underreactive	39%
Self-absorbed 28%	
Craving sensation 11%	
Oversensitive	19%
Mixed (over and under) reactivity	36%
Auditory-processing dysfunction	100%
Motor-planning dysfunction	100%
Severe motor-planning dysfunction 48%	
Marked low muscle tone 17%	

EARLY DEVELOPMENTAL PATTERNS

Observation of the early developmental patterns suggests that many children evidence a second- or third-year regression. The majority of these children did not have neurophysiologic characteristics consistent with Landau-Kleffner syndrome (Mouridsen, 1995). These symptoms were typical for the autistic spectrum disorders. In addition, exploration of the early developmental patterns suggests that the primary impairment appears to involve reciprocal gesturing rather than relating or engaging. The lack of complex gestures may be a useful early marker.

Early Onset vs. Later Regression

In Kanner's (1943) classic description of autism, children were thought to have severe difficulties "from the beginning" where they completely shut out the external world.

In order to clarify the characteristic patterns associated with autistic spectrum disorders, we looked at the children's developmental patterns preceding their evaluation. In some instances, we had access to home videotapes (the results of those will be reported in a separate communication) and, in general, they supported the parents' descriptions.

We found a number of patterns, which will be presented in more detail later. Some children indeed from the beginning had significant compromises in their ability to engage and relate. They were hard to engage into a pattern of intimacy and pleasure with back-and-forth smiles, gesturing, or other affect cuing. Many of these children had low muscle tone and were passive and quite self-absorbed. Some of them, however, were able to gradually become more engaged even though between ages 18 months and 2½ years they met the criteria for an autistic spectrum disorder.

Many children in the first year had some partial compromises in their ability to engage, relate, and enter into reciprocal interactions. Then they further lost these abilities in the latter part of the second year or early part of the third year of life.

Other children in the first year of life were viewed by their parents as relatively "typical," not too different from siblings, and were described by parents as having been cuddly and warm, enjoying physical contact, showing pleasure (e.g, smiles and laughter), interacting, and using gestures. Many used some words between 11 and 15 months of age. Then, between approximately 18 and 30 months, they lost these verbal abilities and a great deal of their ability for engaging and participating in reciprocal interactions. They gradually became more self-absorbed, avoidant, perseverative, and self-stimulatory. Contrary to the description of the type of late-onset autistic specific disorder labeled disintegrative disorder (*DSM-IV*), many of these children, as will be described later, were quite responsive to intervention. In addition, most did not have the EEG abnormalities associated with the Landau-Kleffner syndrome (Mouridsen, 1995), another type of late-onset disorder with autistic features.

Onset of Symptoms: Early Onset vs. Later Regression

Second- and third-year regression	69%
Gradual onset in the first year	31%

Early Developmental Patterns: Ability to Relate

Completely lacking in engagement	5%
Completely lacking long chains of reciprocal interaction	100%

Many of those children who were warm and even "cuddly" in the first year and described by their parents as first evidencing their disorder around age 2, on closer history taking, however, were found to have compromises in the complex pattern of problem solving, gesturing characteristic of the beginning to middle of the second year of life. For example, these difficulties involved problems with being able to take mother or father to the refrigerator to get food or to the toy shelf for a favorite toy, or other tasks that involve a complex, multiple-circle, nonverbal communication and problem solving. This pattern, as will be described in subsequent sections, may provide a reliable early marker for these disorders.

In reviewing the charts of the 200 children, 69 percent of the population evidenced this second- and third-year regression (i.e., late onset of symptoms of avoidance, self-absorption, perseveration, and self-stimulation somewhere between 18 months and 3 years of age). A gradual onset, beginning in the first year of life, was evidenced by 31 percent. The pattern of early onset of severe problems in relating in the first year described by Kanner, therefore, occurs with relatively low frequency in this sample. While late onset has been described for a portion of the children by many clinicians, the number of children with relatively late onset may be greater than thought. There appears to be a variety of early developmental patterns associated with later autistic patterns.

Primary Impairment in Engagement or Gestural Communication
We also looked at the children's ability for mastering the functional developmental capacities (Greenspan, 1992a) of shared attention, engagement, simple gestures,

complex gestures, use of symbols and nonverbal, symbolic problem solving (see Table 1). The impairment in complex problem-solving, gestural interaction was quite specific for autistic spectrum disorders. The ability to engage in and experience warmth and pleasure in relationships was less specific to this disorder.

Many parents reported that their children might not look at them or signal to them either nonverbally or verbally, but would be warm and cuddly and could enjoy comfort. They enjoyed intimacy not only when they were distressed, but at other times as well. After the "regression" in the second or third year of life, many parents described increasing avoidance and self-absorption, but still some remaining intimacy. Only 10 children (5 percent) of the study sample completely lacked the capacity for some warm or pleasurable engagement. In contrast, all 200 of the children had significant difficulties in generating long chains of reciprocal interchange. This finding is quite different from Kanner's original description of autism, which put the primary impairment in the ability to form a relationship in the first year.

The Lack of Purposeful, Complex Gestures as an Earlier Marker
To determine if the lack of complex gesturing could serve as an early marker, we also looked at the degree to which children diagnosed with autistic spectrum disorders evidenced, by age 2, the presence of complex nonverbal patterns of communication (complex gestures involving long chains of reciprocal interactions used to negotiate a goal such as a toddler taking a caregiver to the door, motioning to go outside). We used age 2, even though this pattern typically emerges between 12 and 16 months of age, so that the delay would be quite significant. One hundred thirty-six children out of 200 (68 percent) did not evidence this normative, expectable pattern prior to age 2. If we used a 16-month cut off, our clinical impression is that, in all likelihood, many more would not have evidenced complex gestures when expected.

To see if the ability for complex, nonverbal, sequential interaction patterns are characteristic only of autistic spectrum problems or also characteristic of children with language delays and motor problems, we looked at 110 children who did not have autistic features, but who, however, had auditory-processing problems, were overreactive to touch or sound, and evidenced motor-planning difficulties. These children are often described as having specific language and motor disorders, regulatory disorders, or sensory integration disorders. Their difficulties did not derail their overall development as with autistic disorders. Ninety-six percent of these children were able to enter into complex interactive, gestural, communication, and social problem-solving strategies prior to age 2. Only 4 percent evidenced difficulties in learning complex, purposeful gesturing. The lack of development of this capacity in the second year of life, therefore, may be a useful early marker for children with autistic spectrum or pervasive developmental–type difficulties. This finding is consistent with other studies which have identified a number of the components that go into the ability for complex gestural interaction and problem solving as lacking in children who develop autistic patterns (Attwood, Frith, & Hermelin, 1988; Baron-Cohen, 1994; Baron-Cohen et al., 1996).

The ability for complex gestures can be elicited with an easy question that could routinely be used in well-baby care. "How does Johnny or Susie let you know what he or she wants?" If a description of some facet of taking a parent by the hand and walking over or pointing or showing comes up, then the child is capable of complex social, problem-solving gesturing. On the other hand, if it involves just looking in a direction or having tantrums or simply some repetitive actions, like pulling at the parent without showing the parent what he or she wants to do, it does not involve this pattern of complex gesturing.

The characteristic pattern of children who evidence autistic spectrum disorders, then, is of children who do not develop complex chains of problem-solving reciprocal interactions in the second year even though many can engage with caregivers, use simple gestures, and might have a few words. They often regress in the second or third year with greater self-absorption, avoidance, self-stimulation, and perseveration. Some lose and some retain partial symbolic capacities.

Lack of Purposeful, Complex Gesturing as an Early Marker

Autistic spectrum	68% did not evidence complex gestures prior to 2 years of age
Nonautistic language, motor, and sensory dysfunction	4% did not evidence complex gestures prior to 2 years of age

DEVELOPMENTAL PROGRESS ASSOCIATED WITH RELATIONSHIP-BASED INDIVIDUAL DIFFERENCE, INTERACTIVE-INTERVENTION MODEL

All children received an intervention approach where all contacts (interactions) with the child throughout the day (at all times, using the "floor-time" model) included an emphasis on: (1) affects and relationships; (2) the child's developmental level; and (3) individual differences in motor, sensory, affective, cognitive, and language functioning. All children received a comprehensive range of services (e.g., including speech therapy, occupational therapy, general and/or special education, and floor-time consultation), and intense floor-time interaction sessions at home, ranging from 2 to 5 hours a day (Greenspan, 1992a, 1992b). Therapeutic and education services utilized a relationship, individual difference, interactive approach. Also, family patterns, feelings, and coping efforts were addressed continuously (Greenspan, 1992a). The use of the words *floor time* includes the comprehensive model of intervention described above and is identical with developmentally based interactive approaches and relationship-, affect-based interventions used at other times.

This approach organizes the intervention around the child's affects and relationships in the context of the child's current developmental level, challenges, and individual differences. For example, with a child who is self-absorbed and not relating to others, the first emphasis would be on pulling the child into a greater degree of pleasure in relating rather than focusing on language or symbolic capacities. For a child who is only able to signal, on a need basis, with repetitive pulling or banging, rather than with a variety of nonverbal signals, the first goal would be to expand these simple gestures into a pattern of more complex reciprocal, affective gestures. For example, to expand a child's perseverative fascination with an object (i.e., tapping it), one might put the object on one's head and challenge the child to take it. With the child who is rubbing a spot on the floor, the clinician or parent might put a hand on the floor covering the spot, inspiring a cat-and-mouse game as the child tries to pick up the hand to get back to his favorite spot. Alternatively, a child who is wandering aimlessly around the room might find his mother or father wandering with him but beating him to his favorite spot. To solve this problem, the child might have to constantly try to hurry up to get there first or to go around his mother or father (generating interaction in place of random or seemingly aimless activity). For the child who is already able to sequence gestures and is beginning to use words, to facilitate the child's elaboration of imaginative ideas, if the child picks up a doll, one might talk for the doll, pretending to be hungry or needing a kiss. In all these examples, the principle is to create circumstances where the child is "wooed" into a developmental trajectory where he or she can master the expectable stages of emotional growth and the related cognitive and language capacities. In this model, one must pull the child into the developmental sequence at the child's current level of functioning and not skip levels to work on splinter skills.

The child's motor, sensory, cognitive, and language profile is taken into account. The underreactive child, for example, is approached with extra energy and wooing, often with more playful obstructive activity than the child who is oversensitive, where the approach is more soothing, gentle, and gradual. At home, parents are asked to spend 6 to 10 20- to 30-minute sessions per day working on the child's ability for affective based interactions, using the child's individual differences and developmental level as a starting point. The different therapies also use this individual difference–developmental-level model (i.e., floor-time model).

The unique features separating this intervention model from other models, such as the behavioral approaches (Lovaas, 1987) or the TEACCH program (Schopler, Mesibov, & Hearsey, 1995), is its focus on relationships and affect, developmental level, individual differences, and comprehensiveness. The theoretical rationale for this intervention (Greenspan, 1992a) is that the child's symptoms are often secondary to underlying biologically based processing difficulties, including auditory, motor-planning, and sensory-modulation and processing difficulties. Relationships and affective interactions become derailed secondarily. These secondary disturbances, however, have a large range of possible configurations and are often more rapidly responsive to intervention than the underlying processing dysfunctions. Therefore, the first goal of the intervention is to help the child try to work around the processing difficulties to reestablish affective contact with primary caregivers and begin the process of mastering the presymbolic stages that serve as a basis for language and other higher-level symbolic capacities. Specific processing difficulties continue to be treated through speech therapy, occupational therapy, special and early childhood education, and other therapies.

Relationship-, affect-based interventions that are used on the child's developmental level and individual differences (in sensory and motor processing) and family patterns should not be confused with play therapy or psychotherapy, which has historically not proved especially helpful for the majority of children with autistic patterns. Traditional psychotherapeutic efforts tend to engage the child in a type of parallel play where he feels the clinician's warmth and support but is not mobilized into types of interaction likely to lead to growth in the critical areas of development (Greenspan, 1992a). The floor-time model, in contrast, mobilizes the child's emerging developmental capacities and is based on the thesis that affective interaction can harness cognitive and emotional growth (Carew, 1980; Feuerstein et al., 1979, 1981; Greenspan, 1979, 1981, 1996a; Klein, Wieder, & Greenspan, 1987).

OUTCOME PATTERNS

The children's patterns and clinical course was based on an experienced clinician's observations and detailed notes organized according to the categories in the Functional Emotional Assessment Scale (Greenspan, 1992a; Greenspan & DeGangi, 1997). To describe outcomes, we divided the children's functioning into three broad groups. A "good to outstanding" outcome group included children who, after two or more years of intervention, evidenced joyful relating, simple preverbal gestures with a variety of affect cues (appropriate, reciprocal smiling, frowns, looks of surprise, annoyance, glee, happiness, and the like). They were able to engage in purposeful, organized, and long, problem-solving interactive sequences (e.g., 50+ circles of spontaneous verbal communication), states of shared social attention on various social, cognitive, or motor-based tasks. They had the capacity for creative and imaginative use of symbols (e.g., create and participate in pretend play), and the ability to construct bridges between their symbols (i.e., hold a logical, two-way conversation, separate fantasy from reality, and anticipate consequences). Most important, in this group, the children's symbolic activity was related to underlying intent and affect, rather than memorized or rote sequences. These children mastered basic ego functions including reality testing, impulse control, organization of thoughts and affects, a differentiated sense of self, and an ability to experience a range of affects, thoughts, ideas, and concerns. They no longer evidenced self-absorption, avoidance, self-stimulation, or perseveration. On the CARS autism rating scale, all the children in this group shifted into the nonautistic range.

Some children in the "good to outstanding" group became precocious in their academic abilities, reading or doing math two or three grade levels above their ages (some perhaps developed their visual-spatial abilities early when auditory processing lagged). Some, even though they had intact basic ego functions, still evidenced auditory or visual-spatial difficulties that were improving. Most of the children in the "good to outstanding" group, even ones with precocious reading or math skills, had some degree of motor-planning challenges (e.g., evidenced in fine-motor control relating to penmanship or drawing or in complex, gross-motor challenges).

A second group made significant gains in their ability to relate and communicate with gestures. They became related to their parents, often seeking them out in a joyful, zestful, and pleasurable manner. Parents commented, "I've discovered a little person inside my child." They could enter into long sequences of purposeful reciprocal affective cuing and interactions (e.g., 30 or more circles of communication). They could also enter into states of shared attention with social, cognitive, and motor problem solving. In this group, however, the children were still having significant challenges in developing their symbolic capacities. Some had some partial ability to use symbols in pretend play and language, but significantly below age levels. For example, in this group many children could engage in concrete pretend-play sequences, such as driving a car or feeding a doll, and use words for some simple negotiations of their desires ("I want to go outside" or "I want juice"), but were not yet able to construct long, creative, interactive symbolic sequences (i.e., couldn't have a give-and-take conversation or elaborate in a play sequence an experience they had). This group, therefore, had relatively good mastery of early developmental levels but were only beginning their symbolic capacities. This group, like the first group, no longer evidenced self-absorption, avoidance of relating, self-stimulation, or perseveration.

A third group continued to have significant difficulties in both the presymbolic and the symbolic realms. They had significant impairments in their ability to attend, enter into simple and complex sequences of gesturing, and, if they were using some concrete symbols in pretend play when props were available or language when they wanted something, it was coupled with a significant degree of self-absorption, avoidance, self-stimulation, and perseveration. In this group, those who had some symbolic capacity (e.g., to sing songs or do puzzles) were unable to imitate and use these abilities in an interactive, communicative manner. Many in this group were making slow progress in their basic ability to relate with warmth to others, but some evidenced vacillation between gaining and losing capacities.

Outcome Findings
The outcomes for the children were addressed in two ways: (1) overall, and (2) relative to the severity that they presented at entry. Each will be described below.

One hundred sixteen of the 200 children (58 percent) were in the "good to outstanding" outcome group, 50 (25 percent) were in the "medium" outcome group, and 34 (17 percent) continued to have significant difficulties. Some of the group with significant continuing difficulties were making very slow progress while a subgroup of those with significant difficulties, 8 (4 percent) of the children, were vacillating or losing capacities.

Floor-Time Intervention Outcomes

Good to outstanding	58%
Medium	24%
Ongoing difficulties	17%

Intervention Outcomes: Severity of Presenting Symptoms
To explore the factors other than the intervention program that might have been associated with outcomes, we looked at the distribution of outcomes and initial ratings on the Childhood Autism Rating Scale (CARS). In the "good to outstanding" group, 20 percent had 40 or more on the CARS, representing a significant degree of autistic difficulty; 43 percent had 35 to 40 on the CARS scores, indicating a moderate

degree of impairment; 37 percent had 30 to 35, indicating a mild degree of autistic impairment. In contrast, in the group who continued to have significant difficulties, 70 percent had scores suggesting a significant degree of impairment, 20 percent had scores in the moderate range, and 10 percent had scores in the mild range. The medium outcome group showed distributions between these two, with 45 percent having scores of 40 and above (significant impairment), 38 percent with 35 to 40, in the moderate range, and 17 percent in the mild range.

The distribution of the CARS scores suggests that the children with poor outcomes had a more extreme degree of autistic symptomatology and impairment than the group with the good to outstanding outcomes. The group with the medium outcomes was in between the two on the CARS. It appears that the severity of the presenting symptomatology is a factor in the developmental patterns associated with the intervention. In all the outcome groups, however, there was a distribution on the autism rating scale scores. In the good to outstanding outcome group, there were children with mild, moderate, and severe dysfunctions as well as in the other two groups. The single largest group of presenting patterns is in the CARS 35 to 40 in the moderate range. In addition, children who have presented with all different degrees of severity have made good to outstanding progress and medium progress, and have continued to have severe difficulties. The degree of impairment in itself, therefore, is not an overriding factor, although likely an important one.

Intervention Outcomes: Comparisons of Children with Floor-Time, Comprehensive, Developmentally Based, Interactive Approaches and Traditional Approaches

We had the opportunity to examine the charts of a group of children we saw who had been receiving other interventions and had not yet implemented our recommendations. In order to compare the developmental patterns of children in a comprehensive, developmental, individual-difference, affect-based model of intervention with traditional approaches, therefore, we studied the charts of these 53 additional children whose parents came seeking additional ideas or second opinions regarding their child's intervention programs or diagnosis. They had been diagnosed with pervasive developmental disorder or autism, and for two or more years they had been receiving speech therapy, occupational therapy, and special education approaches or behavioral therapy. These children presented between ages 4 and 10, the same age range we assessed outcomes in the floor-time intervention model. Their parents were also college-educated and were a self-selected group seeking further evaluation and recommendations. Even though these children had similar diagnoses and comparable family characteristics, the patterns we could see in a comparison with the intensive floor-time intervention group should be viewed as very explorative. The lack of comparative intervention studies for autistic spectrum disorders, however, makes such explorations potentially useful.

Thirty-one of the 53 children (58 percent) evidenced self-absorption, avoidance, and lack of ability to enter into chains of reciprocal interaction. While this subgroup intermittently evidenced some degree of pleasure in their relationships, they were not able to sustain pleasurable interactions. Some, intermittently, had fragmented use of ideation.

Twenty-one of the 53 children (40 percent) had some symbolic capacities, but with severe limitations. They generally could not use their islands of symbolic activity in a consistently creative and logical manner. For example, there were some concrete abilities to use words for needs, such as getting juice or getting the door open (words like *juice* or *out, open, door*). There were also some beginning elements of pretend play, such as feeding the dolly or putting the dolly in the car. However, there was no elaboration on these actions. Occasionally they could respond to multiple-choice questions. Often, however, they would be preoccupied with their own play, babble to themselves, or use ideas in a fragmented manner. They continued to be self-absorbed, self-stimulatory, and perseverative. This subgroup, therefore, tended to operate at a concrete, fragmented level of ideation, rather than an elaborative, creative, and logical one and was not yet consistently engaged.

Floor-Time and Traditional Interventions Comparison Groups

	FLOOR TIME, %	TRADITIONAL SERVICES, %
Good to outstanding	58	2
Medium	24	40
Continuing significant difficulties	17	58

One of the 53 children (2 percent) evidenced intact ego or personality functions consistent with the description of the good to outstanding floor-time intervention group.

On the CARS, 43 percent of the traditional services group were in the severe range, 15 percent in the moderate range, 40 percent were in the mild range, and 2 percent no longer qualified for the diagnosis of autism.

Many children, even with years of intervention, are unable to function beyond the level of fragmented, concrete use of ideation and have significant difficulties in presymbolic relating and gestural interactions (e.g., Gillberg & Steffenburg, 1987; Kanner, 1971; Mesibov, Schopler, & Schaffer, 1989; Piven, Harper, Palmer, & Arndt, 1996; Rumsey et al., 1985; Rutter et al., 1967; Szatmari, Barolucci, Bremmer, Bond, & Rich, 1989). The comparison group provides a picture of how some children with autistic spectrum diagnoses progress in typical programs. The comparison group, as indicated earlier, may be a self-selected group of children who were not making significant progress. Our impression, however, is that they were similar to children in many programs. Programs that can do significantly better than the above description of children receiving traditional services should be carefully studied to learn more about children's potential for growth and what types of interventions may be most helpful.

A number of the comparison children had been in intensive (over 30 hours per week) behaviorally based programs. While some of these children tended to have some use of ideation and some academic abilities, they generally remained at the level of the fragmented and concrete use of ideation and were self-absorbed when not engaged in structured tasks.

In-Depth Study of 20 Children: A Comparison with Children without Developmental Problems

Among the children in the good to outstanding group, we studied 20 of the children who had made the most progress. These children were studied in greater depth to understand the types of changes and potential of some children with autistic spectrum diagnoses in an intensive relationship-based intervention program. The Vineland Adaptive Behavior Scales (Sparrow, Dalla, & Cicchetti, 1984) and the Functional Emotional Assessment Scale (Greenspan, 1992a; Greenspan & DeGangi, 1997) were applied to 200 cases that had made exceptional progress from the good to outstanding outcome group representing children between 5 and 10 years old (5–5 to 10–7). These twenty children were also compared to a group of similar-aged children without any history of developmental problems. The intervention subgroup was selected to include a range of ages: five 5-year-olds, six 6-year-olds, four 7-year-olds, three 8-year-olds, and two 10-year-old boys. These children had all started intervention between 2 and 4 years of age and had received between 2 and 8 years of intervention and/or follow-up consultation. At the time of outcome, all were attending regular schools, enjoyed relationships with friends, and participated in community activities. Many had been assessed for cognitive abilities using standardized tests and were functioning in the superior range.

The Vineland summarizes adaptive behavior in the following three domains: communication (receptive, expressive, and written); daily living (personal domestic and community); and socialization (interpersonal, play and leisure, and coping). All the children were higher than age level in the communication domain with 60 percent scoring 1 to 2 years higher than chronological age level. The highest scores were obtained in the socialization domain, where 95 percent were higher than age levels in socialization, with 25 percent more than one year, 40 percent more than 2 years, and 25 percent more than 3 years ahead of chronological age. The adaptive behavior composite scores which average all the domains reported above were all above age level except for one case, a child who had significant motor difficulties. Again, 60 percent of the children scored 2 or more years above age, and 30 percent between 1 and 2 years beyond age level. None of the children presented maladaptive behavior patterns. Even though the Vineland Adaptive Behavior Scales are limited to the practical and functional aspects of daily living, these findings support the good outcomes found clinically.

Further analysis of this data with regard to outcome age, age at onset of treatment, and initial severity (FEAS and CARS) is under way. Meanwhile, several additional observations are noteworthy. Overall, the longer the child was in treatment and the older the child, the higher his scores relative to his age, suggesting that children continued to function progressively better as they grew older. This was especially true for socialization, where 90 percent of the children received scores 2 to 3 years ahead of age level. Furthermore, of the three domains, socialization was higher than communication and daily living 90 percent of the time. Typically, children with autistic spectrum diagnoses continue to evidence significant social impairments even when there is some progress in language and cognition. The social skills of the children may reflect the impact of an interactive affect-driven model of intervention where social-emotional goals received emphasis and supported the development of interpersonal, play, and coping skills measured by the Vineland. Also, expressive language abilities were better than receptive abilities in *all* the cases. Daily living was lower than communication 60 percent of the time, suggesting motor-planning difficulties, which would affect daily living. Self-care skills are often more challenging for this population and improved somewhat less relative to the communication and socialization domains.

We also rated the same 20 children on a series of relationship and emotional dimensions using videotaped interactions with caregivers. We compared the intervention group of children with a group of children who had no history of language or emotional challenges and who were functioning both emotionally and intellectually at or above age level. In addition, we compared both the intervention group and the normal comparison group with a group of children who continued to have chronic problems in relating and communicating.

In order to make these comparisons, we used the Functional Emotional Assessment Scale (FEAS) (Greenspan, 1992a; Greenspan & DeGangi, 1997). The FEAS is a clinical rating scale that can be applied to videotaped interactions between infants or children and caregivers. The child is rated on the following dimensions: attention and regulation, engagement, affective reciprocity, complex purposeful interaction chains of behavior, functional, creative, and imaginative use of ideas, emotional and thematic range, and logical thinking and problem solving. Raters have been trained to high levels of reliability for each dimension of the scale. The caretaker reliability ranges from .89 to .91 and the child reliability from .90 to .97 (Greenspan & DeGangi, 1997).

There were 20 children in the intervention group, 14 children in the normal comparison group, and 12 children in the continuing difficulties group within the same age range. Each child in each of the groups was videotaped interacting with a caregiver for 15 or more minutes. A reliable judge blind to the identity of the children used the FEAS to score all the videotapes.

The results were as follows. The floor-time intervention group was indistinguishable from the normal control group. Both groups were significantly different from the group with continuing difficulties. Specifically, in the floor-time intervention group, 13 of the 20 children scored 76, the top of the scale. The seven who did not score 76 were all between 70 and 75 (i.e., 73, 73, 74, 75, 70, 71, 72). The mean for the group was 74.8. In the normal comparison group, 12 of the 14 scored 76 at the top of the scale. The two others were 73 and 65. The mean for the group was 74.9. In contrast, of the 13 children in the group with continuing difficulties, seven scored below 20 and six scored below 40, with a mean of 23.7.

In addition, the judge attempted to use subtle observations of the children's affect, voice quality, pattern of articulation, and motor functioning to make an additional clinical judgment and figure out which group the children came from. The judge classified six of the floor-time intervention group as normal comparison group members, while classifying all the continuing difficulty group members correctly.

FEAS Outcomes

	NUMBER OF CHILDREN	MEAN FEAS (76 IS OPTIMAL %)	RANGE
Floor-time intervention group	20	74.8	70–76
Normal comparison group	14	74.9	65–76
Continuing significant difficulties	12	23.7	<20–40

The findings on the FEAS are consistent with the findings on the Vineland ratings. The FEAS clinical ratings are especially important, however, because they reliably rate such subtle features of personality functioning as quality of intimacy, affect expressiveness and reciprocity, creativity and imagination, and abstract, flexible thinking, as well as problem solving and reality testing. All these high-level personality functions are expected to be relatively permanently impaired even in children with pervasive developmental disorders who make considerable progress in their language and cognitive abilities. A subgroup of children who did exceedingly well in the floor-time intervention program were, therefore, able to obtain interpersonal, communicative, coping, and logical capacities quite similar to peers.

We chose to compare the children who had done very well as a subsample with a normal comparison group to also see if objective measures would validate the capacities these children appear to have mastered. If the children who had done extremely well were comparable to peers without developmental disorders, it would suggest, at a minimum, that some of the children who had an autistic spectrum diagnosis (suggesting chronic, severe impairment) could grow into patterns of healthy emotional, social, and adaptive behavior and that the adaptive behavior could be sustained.

UNDERLYING MECHANISMS ASSOCIATED WITH AUTISTIC SPECTRUM PATTERNS

While a variety of mechanisms have been suggested, there is no consensus about underlying psychological and biological patterns associated with autistic spectrum dysfunction. To further understand underlying "processing" difficulties, we looked at the processing challenges of the children who did very well and the children who continued to have significant difficulties.

All the children diagnosed with autistic spectrum problems evidenced auditory-processing, motor-planning, and sensory-modulation difficulties. Many of the children also had visual-spatial processing challenges, but some of the children showed relative strength in this area. These and other underlying psychological and cognitive mechanisms have been postulated to underlie autistic symptoms (Baron-Cohen, 1994; Cook, George, Gurman & Weigel, 1993; Durand, 1990; Frith, 1993; Guess & Carr, 1991; Koegel, Dyer, & Bell, 1987; Kohen-Raz, Volkmar, & Cohen, 1992; Prizant, 1983; Prizant & Wetherby, 1990; Rutter, 1983).

We explored differences between the good to outstanding group and the group that continued to have severe difficulties in the areas of muscle tone, motor planning, and reactivity to sensation.

There were more children with low muscle tone and motor planning difficulties in the group with poor outcomes and more severe difficulties. Also this group generally had a greater degree of underreactivity to sensation, including both greater craving and greater self-absorption. They also were less hyperreactive to sensation and generally showed less mixed reactivity to sensation as well.

The outcome group that did very well tended to have more overreactivity and mixed reactivity and less severe motor-planning problems and less low muscle tone. However, as pointed out earlier, there was still significant individual variation. Some children with low tone and severe motor-planning problems made outstanding progress and some who were oversensitive, with less severe motor-planning problems, continued to have great difficulties.

These patterns suggest that there are different degrees and types of processing difficulties contributing to autistic spectrum disorders.

TABLE 2. Muscle Tone, Motor-Planning, and Sensory-Reactivity Problems

	OUTCOME GROUP GOOD TO OUTSTANDING, %	OUTCOME GROUP POOR, %
Low Muscle Tone	12.5	23.5
Significant Motor-Planning Problems	18	78
Underreactive to Sensation with Patterns of:	30	48
Craving/Stimulus Seeking	7	15
Self-Absorption	23	33
Hyperreactive to Sensation	25	15
Mixed Patterns of Reactivity to Sensation (hyper in some areas like sound and hypo in other areas like pain or touch)	45	37

The nature of these difficulties may have some role in the presentation and the severity of symptoms as well as in the outcomes. Motor-planning and sensory-modulation problems appear to be especially significant contributions to the disorder in addition to the auditory-processing and language problems present in the entire group of children.

LIMITATIONS IN THE ASSESSMENT PROCEDURES USED TO DIAGNOSE AUTISTIC SPECTRUM DISORDERS

In reviewing parents' experiences with evaluation in a variety of different locations in the United States and Canada, we observed two significant problems in the service system. Often, the evaluation did not include observation of infants or children and parents interacting. In addition, there were often delays of over 3 months from the onset of symptoms to the evaluation and another 3 months before interventions were initiated.

Since many of the children were seen in other settings for evaluations before coming to see us, we asked how these were done. There was an enormous range in the way evaluations were implemented to diagnose autistic spectrum–type disorders. In some settings, for example, children were separated from parents and given a battery of tests. In other settings, parents and children came in together, but the children were only observed with caregivers while the parents were giving the clinician a history. The child might then be tested with the parent present or not present. Standardized tests were often scored even though processing difficulties impeded the child's ability to take the test. Often, the child's relationship with the parents and interactions with the parents were only observed incidentally while interviewing the parent or while the parent was letting the child sit on his or her lap during the testing procedures. Only very rarely were children directly observed interacting with parents for any period of time. Only 2.3 percent of the evaluations involved observation of caregiver (parent)-child interaction for 15 minutes or more during a free play session.

Many parents, when asked, were quite concerned that their child's relationship capacity was being diagnosed without being observed. Many lamented that they felt their children related to them more warmly at home or in an informal play situation than in a high-stress situation of being tested or while being distracted during an interview in a new setting. Because their ability to interact with their children was not observed, many felt distrustful of the eventual diagnosis. In some of the evaluations, the examiner attempted to spontaneously interact with the child, often around structured developmental tasks and sometimes in play-type activities.

The evaluation settings varied. They included private practice, clinics or centers, and hospitals. They also included different professional disciplines, developmental pediatrics, child psychiatry, clinical and developmental psychology, pediatric neurology, and special education, speech pathology, and physical and occupational therapy. In general, speech pathologists and occupational therapists, as well as early childhood and special educators, tended to base more of their opinions on extended interaction with the child himself. Here too, however, there was a tendency not to observe the parent interacting with the child.

The ability to distinguish pervasive developmental disorder, autistic spectrum disorder, or autism from a circumscribed language or motor disorder will often depend on the clinician's assessment of the degree of warmth, pleasure, and spontaneous affect the child shows in relationship to a trusted caregiver rather than on such symptoms as perseveration and self-stimulation, which are also seen in other conditions. Children with uneven development and sensory-modulation difficulties are often easily overloaded or underreactive and self-absorbed and may evidence varying degrees of perseveration and/or self-stimulation. We have also found that children's capacities to relate with emotional warmth and range and the degree of their perseverative and avoidant behavior often depend on how comfortable and secure they feel and, conversely, their degree of stress. New situations, new people, and demanding tasks are often stressful. Children, therefore, require in-depth observation of interactions with a trusted and known caregiver with whom they can share their best gestural, communication and complex interactive capacities. Without such observation, a proper diagnosis cannot be made and treatment may be compromised because the child's strengths and vulnerabilities are not known. The fact that this was missing from over 97 percent of the cases presents an important challenge to the field.

DELAYS IN IMPLEMENTING EVALUATION AND TREATMENT

We also looked at how long families waited from the first concern to a formal evaluation. Ninety-six percent of the families waited more than 3 months from the first expressed concern, usually to a family health care provider. In many instances they were told to wait and see—it might simply be delayed language, especially if it's "a boy."

Ninety-seven percent also waited over the 3 months for an intervention program to begin. This often involved typical administrative and bureaucratic time for doing additional evaluations and scheduling a program.

In general, therefore, there were unnecessary delays in helping families obtain an evaluation, if indicated, and begin an intervention program.

DISCUSSION

There are limitations to a chart review approach for identifying developmental patterns and outcomes in children with severe relationship and communication problems. A chart review can identify patterns, generate testable hypotheses, and offer suggestions for further study. A prospective clinical trial is necessary for the definitive study of outcomes. In addition, as will be discussed later, most intervention studies to date have not been with representative samples of children with autistic spectrum diagnoses. This chart review, as indicated, was also of a selective sample of children with autistic spectrum disorders. Therefore, the reported percentages cannot be applied to other populations. While this study suggests that many children can make enormous progress, and describes developmental patterns and an intervention program that may contribute to a child's progress, additional research will be necessary to further study these observed patterns. It is important to emphasize, however, that this chart review does suggest that some children with autistic spectrum diagnoses can not only make significant progress, but can progress in areas of development such as empathy, creative and spontaneous thinking, intimacy, and emotional reciprocity that are often thought to be out of the reach of children with this diagnosis.

Service System Limitation

No observation of caregiver-child interaction	97.7%
More than 3 months from onset of symptoms to evaluation	96.0%
More than 3 months from evaluation to intervention	97.0%

It should also be noted that the information in the charts was based on an experienced clinician's notes and observations, rather than the judgments of a group of clinicians who had achieved reliability in performing clinical ratings. Many of the observations in the charts, however, require a low level of inference; for example, the age at which children developed symptoms. In addition, the reported clinical phenomena involved behaviors such as self-absorption or perseveration, which are readily observed. A chart review of a large number of cases can provide important direction for future studies when looking at complex questions in an understudied problem.

One of the more important implications of looking at developmental patterns and outcome is to more clearly elucidate the developmental patterns of those children who are likely to make different kinds of progress. We observed that the children most capable of learning to relate and interact symbolically in a spontaneous and creative manner tended to have a specific early profile. They had at least some ability for complex gestural interaction with warm and pleasurable affect. They often had some emerging ability for using islands of symbolic functioning (pretend play or functional use of language). As indicated earlier, many of these children were also very perseverative, echolalic, and self-stimulatory. The degree of these typical autistic behaviors was less critical for their later progress than the presence or absence of some gestural and emerging complex imitative and symbolic capacities.

An exception to this pattern, however, was children with low muscle tone and sensory underreactivity who were quite self-absorbed. Some of these children evidenced little gestural or symbolic capacity and yet, once the intervention program started, begin showing rapid gains in these areas. Therefore, it appears that it is important to study both the child's preexisting developmental pattern and the child's early response to the intervention program.

A number of intensive intervention programs are reporting similar patterns of "good" outcomes (Bondy & Peterson, 1990; Lovaas, 1987; Miller & Miller, 1992; Rogers et al., 1988; Rogers & Lewis, 1989; Strain et al., 1983; Strain & Hoyson, 1988). Lovaas, for example, reported 47 percent of good outcomes in an intensive behavioral program. Strain and Rogers, in quite different programs, reported similar trends. While the outcomes from these interventions are quite encouraging, it should be pointed out that none of the intervention studies, including this one, worked with truly representative populations. In this study, the population was limited to parents who were motivated to seek additional help, and, as indicated earlier, most of the families were quite well educated. The children did, however, present with a range of autistic spectrum symptomatology. In Lovaas's well-known and well-documented study, his exclusion criteria left him with children who evidenced functional capacities in the 11-to-18-month-old range (many children with autistic spectrum diagnoses present with functional abilities in the 6-to-8-month range). Lovaas's population was also characterized by relatively motivated and organized parents. Even though the intensive interventions that have been associated with very promising outcomes have not been with truly representative samples, the reported findings of enormous progress in children who met the criteria for pervasive developmental disorder (autism) is extremely encouraging. While reported percentages must be interpreted in the context of the population studied, they nevertheless suggest that a significant number of children can do quite well with very intensive intervention programs.

Also of interest is that in both our program and Lovaas's program, children who did best tended to learn complex imitations rather quickly. Children who quickly learn complex imitation are often strong in motor planning and visual-spatial capacities, capable of making quick progress into symbolic realms.

Many investigators believe that IQ (e.g., below 50) and lack of language discriminates the children that are unlikely to respond significantly to intervention from those who are likely to make significant gains (Rutter, 1996). Often, however, before children are helped to engage and interact purposefully (i.e., open and close many problem-solving circles of communication in a row), it is difficult to determine their IQ levels, including their nonverbal IQ. It is also difficult for such children to develop language abilities without first having a strong foundation in preverbal communication. A number of children in our chart review started out either unable to be tested or with exceedingly low IQ scores. These children also had little or no verbal language. We found that the best indicator of their likely response to intervention was a trial of the intervention program rather than any one cross-sectional testing or observation. As indicated earlier, motor planning was probably the most important single factor that influenced the rate of early progress.

As discussed above, a number of intensive intervention programs appear helpful. It is important, however, to determine which interventions are likely to be most helpful for which types of children and problems. A model characterizing the underlying difficulties in autistic-specific dysfunctions may further this determination.

Model for Underlying Dysfunctions

A number of the observations described earlier suggest a model to understand the underlying dysfunction in children with severe disorders of relating and communicating. The majority of children showed a pattern of regression, after having had a period of relatively better relating earlier in their lives. In addition, the majority of children did not evidence complex behavioral or gestural patterns prior to age 2. As indicated earlier, in the majority of cases, progress was first indicated by improvements in the children's ability to engage and use affect as part of relationships, and then in their use of affects for reciprocal interactions. Furthermore, progress was greater when emerging language and cognitive abilities were directed by internal affect cues rather than external prompts or scripts—the child saying, "I'm hungry," "I want to eat," or "Leave me alone," as opposed to repeating something from a TV show or reciting scripts from a book that are unrelated to the needs and affects of the moment.

Taken together, these observations suggest that a core underlying difficulty may be an inability to connect affect or intent to the sequencing of behaviors or symbols. The children demonstrate an initial inability to go from simple patterns of engagement and gesturing (which many of the children with autistic spectrum diagnoses appear to have mastered) to complex, interactive, purposeful (i.e., involving intent or affect) chains of nonverbal communication. For example, initially most of the children were able to engage in simple give and take of a block, but were unable to take a parent by the hand, walk him to the refrigerator, and show him what they wanted. Taking a caregiver by the hand to the toy chest or refrigerator appears to involve connecting affect or intent to a sequence of complex motor patterns. Later on, the same intent or affect has to be connected to symbols and the sequencing of symbols to give meaning and purpose to symbols. Connecting affect to symbols enables language to become meaningful, organized, and logical.

The affect signaling system (i.e., the intent or desire), in part, tells the motor system what it needs to do. It's hard for a child to get beyond simple motor patterns if the child doesn't have a sense of direction or purpose mediated by affect or intent. If, in the second year of life, the ability to connect affect and intent to complex motor patterns is not forming or is disrupted, the capacity for complex social and motor patterns may be undermined. Simple patterns played out repetitively might well occur in place of the complex goal-directed patterns. As we created high states of motivation to help children learn to affectively cue and connect with others, we saw their motor planning improve. Under states of high motivation, a child who was capable of only repetition could embark on a two-step sequence. For example, a child obviously wanted to go out the door and was vacillating between touching it repetitively and aimless spinning around near it. When the caregiver appeared dumb and pointed to the handle of the door motioning to open and close it or pointed to the window as an alternate exit (thereby providing a destination for their intent), the child was able to quickly begin gesturing toward the doorknob, as if to say, "Hey, dummy, open the door." When his affect was intense enough, he would go from a repetitive touching pattern to a more purposeful, two-step touch and gesture to the doorknob. If the affect got too intense, however, a tantrum might ensue.

In addition to the problem in connecting affect to sequencing, the sequencing ability itself, along with auditory processing and sensory modulating difficulties, was dysfunctional in all the children with autistic spectrum diagnoses. Muscle tone and sequencing was more impaired in the severely affected group with very slow progress than the other groups. They couldn't create a sequence of motor or behavioral patterns and instead repeated patterns. Therefore, it was doubly hard for them to enter into complex social interactions (i.e., they didn't have the behavioral or motor sequencing ability to piece together four- or five-step social gestures—e.g., open and close many circles of communication in a row), and they could not connect intent or direction to their actions to provide purpose or a goal.

The apparent greater difficulty with motor planning in the autistic spectrum disorder and the difficulty this group has in improving in this and other capacities may, in part, be due to the proposed primary difficulty in connecting intent or affect to the capacity for sequencing. It is difficult to engage in or practice a sequence of behavior without intent or affect directing it.

While motor planning, auditory processing, and sensory modulation difficulties are also present in many children with a variety of learning, language, sensory integration, and cognitive disorders, it is being suggested that the inability to connect affect (intent) to sequencing capacities is unique to autistic spectrum disorders and, in part, explains why this disorder is characterized by more pervasive problems and greater treatment challenges.

This proposed mechanism, where affect connects motor to (gestural) sequences, also suggests an explanation for the way autistic patterns emerge during early development. Earlier we described the regressions that occur in many of the children around 18 to 30 months of age. Ordinarily at this age, the children develop symbolic capacities, including complex imitations, pretend play, imagination, and more functional use of language. What would happen, however, if different facets of the central nervous system were developing, but the components of the nervous system that connect affect to complex motor sequencing were not forming? It might be a bit like a machine that's becoming more complex but trying to operate without a guidance system. Without affect or intent, motor capacities and islands of symbols may become idiosyncratic and repetitive, as opposed to sequential, purposeful, and goal-directed (e.g., like an athlete who loses his sense of purpose, but has muscles that keep exercising themselves). Relationships may also become more difficult, as one cannot connect behavior or communication with underlying needs, desires, or affects. Ironically, as the nervous system becomes more complex, it is more and more difficult for it to operate without a guidance system that uses affect and desire.

Particular types of self-stimulatory patterns, such as looking out of the corner of one's eyes (i.e., using peripheral vision rather than central vision—"visual stimming"), are also revealing. The anatomy of the visual system has images from peripheral visual fields (i.e., the far left or right) represented in one or the other hemisphere. Images directly in front of the eyes are represented in both hemispheres. Therefore, to look out of the periphery, one needs only intact functioning in one or the other hemisphere. In order to coordinate the images that emerge from focusing directly in front of oneself, one needs to have both hemispheres connected. Having both hemispheres connected may also be required to fully integrate affect with sequencing capacities (i.e., sequencing tends to be more of a left-sided function and affect more related to right-sided functions). If the difficulty with connecting affect to motor sequencing is related to limitations or deficits with interhemispheric connections, this same difficulty might also affect the ability to focus on visual images directly in front of the eyes.

During the first year of life, we have seen that many infants who later evidenced autistic patterns could focus on objects, experience some affection and warmth, and even enter into simple reciprocal interactions. Perhaps they are able to perform these tasks because these basic patterns can be carried out by either side of the brain alone (Benson & Zaidel, 1985; Courchesne et al., 1994; Dawson, Warrenburg, & Fuller, 1982; Greenspan, 1996b; Sperry, 1985; Wetherby, Koegel, & Mendel, 1981). But to engage in complex, goal-directed, reciprocal patterns in the second year, affects or intents need a direct connection to motor and behavioral sequencing and emerging verbal and spatial symbols.

Perhaps deficits in the parts of the central nervous system that permit affect and intent to connect to sequencing capacities explain why, in many children with autistic pattern, component parts of the nervous system that increase motor, sensory, visual-spatial, and language capacities often keep growing without the synthesizing direction of affects or intent. While children vary in their capacities in each component part (i.e., some children remember in a rote fashion what they hear or see; some are quick to do puzzles, while others clearly have severe limitations in different components), they appear to have a common difficulty connecting intent or affect to these component parts. Many of these children's symptoms, remarkable abilities, and unusual behaviors may, in part, be explained, as these component parts, at various levels of capacity, function without the direction of affects or intent. Interestingly, this model may also explain why some children make rapid progress and even evidence precocious capacities once their affect connects to other capacities. Perhaps their component parts are developing quite well but lack the direction and coordination of affect or intent. Other children may have greater deficits in their component parts. For them, connecting affect to the component parts is only a first step that begins a slower pattern of progress. In all likelihood, the central nervous system pathways that connect affect or intent to sequencing capacities—involving motor behavior, verbal symbols, and visual-spatial capacities—involve many different tracks in different parts of the central nervous system. This would be consistent, in part, with the different areas that have been implicated in autistic patterns (e.g., sequencing and/or planning areas, motor coordination areas, sensory areas).

This suggested mechanism should be contrasted with hypotheses that propose a primary deficit in autism is the child's inability to understand or imagine another person's state of mind (i.e., empathize with the feelings of others) (Baron-Cohen, Frith, & Leslie, 1988; Baron-Cohen, Tager-Flusberg, & Cohen, 1993; Frith, 1999). The lack of ability for empathy may very well be a product of a more primary difficulty in connecting affect to complex behavior and motor patterns and symbols. In our population, the children who made very good progress developed the ability to empathize with and understand the feelings and perspective of others. They learned to empathize gradually as they became more affectively involved in other people's lives. The children who were unable to become affectively involved with others and develop complex, affectively based communication patterns and who instead relied on scripts or prompts did not develop the ability to appreciate the emotions of others.

These observations suggest direction for further study of the biological mechanisms associated with this syndrome. Can the difficulties with connecting affect to sequencing capacities be accounted for by certain critical central nervous system pathways? The role of right hemisphere dominance has been suggested. What biological systems and pathways are forming in the second year of life that are concerned with connecting intent or affect to sequencing capacities as well as the modulation of sensory experience?

Implications for Intervention
There may be a group of children who are capable of doing well with a variety of intensive programs, but who may do relatively better with programs that from the outset foster engagement, affective interchanges, and spontaneous ways of relating, as well as creative and abstract thinking. A core difficulty of children with autistic

spectrum problems is their inability to make generalizations and construct patterns of abstract thinking. Therefore, it may be critical to involve children in dynamic, emotionally based, problem-solving interactions that are likely to foster abstract thinking and the *very ability to generalize itself.*

Some children who had been in intense behavioral programs, we found, could sometimes master rote academic skills and even do well on IQ tests. However, they lacked the ability for spontaneous, creative affective interchanges with adults or peers and could not generalize or engage in abstract thinking (e.g., they might match words to pictures or categories or read, but be unable to fully explain in a nonrote manner why they wanted to go outside or debate the merits of staying up or going to sleep). When we began a dynamic, problem-solving approach that challenged the children to be more intentional and to reason and elaborate on thoughts and feelings, these children began acquiring abstract-thinking skills.

Ironically, we also found that children who were making very slow progress and having a difficult time learning to imitate and symbolize (the ones who did less well in the behavioral programs) were the ones who we found often required a combined behavioral and dynamic floor-time approach. The behavioral approach would help them to master motor and behavioral sequences (e.g., imitation) and the dynamic approach would help them make these sequences their own (as opposed to under the control of external prompts). For example, after learning to repeat the word *cup,* two dolls might use cups in a tea party and keep asking each other for "one more cup." The irony is that children who needed the behavioral approach were the same types of children who found it difficult to imitate purposeful actions and learn to imitate motor and vocal patterns. The children who tend to do best in intensive behavioral programs are those who learn to imitate and become verbal quickly. These are the children who may progress most optimally in an affect- and relationship-based, individual difference–oriented approach (floor time).

It is also important to emphasize, however, that many of the children with relatively more modest outcomes in this review nonetheless were able to make substantial gains. Some of these children, for example, improved their ability to attend and engage with warmth and pleasure. They, however, had a much longer road to travel. While modest from the point of view of the goal of creative, two-way verbal conversation, their gains were not modest from the point of view of degree of improvement. Only a small group of children showed fluctuations or no progress. Therefore, even children with very severe difficulties benefit from an intensive intervention program. It should also be pointed out that this type of an intervention program requires time and effort but need not be enormously costly. Family members, helpers, and students can be important members of the intervention team.

Regardless of the merits of particular intervention philosophies and programs, the results of this chart review suggest that there are a number of underlying patterns associated with autistic spectrum problems. It is, therefore, important to tailor the intervention program to the child's unique profile rather than have the child adapt to a particular program philosophy.

The patterns of improvement described in this chart review and in other intensive intervention programs are quite different from the traditional descriptions of autistic spectrum disorders. Autism has been viewed as a chronic disorder manifesting symptoms into adulthood (e.g., Gillberg & Steffenburg, 1987; Kanner, 1971; Szatmari et al., 1989). Some studies have suggested that selected areas of autistic behavior (Mesibov et al., 1989; Rumsey, Rapoport, & Sceery, 1985; Rutter, Greenfield, & Lockyer, 1967), such as language and social behavior, tend to show more improvement than ritualistic-repetitive behaviors. A recent study (Piven et al., 1996) documents changes from their profiles at age 5 among a group of adolescents and adults. They showed relatively greater improvements in social and language domains than in repetitive-ritualistic behavior. In these studies, however, the vast majority of individuals continued to have significant autistic impairments. Even a small number of individuals who no longer had severe enough symptoms to continue to qualify for a diagnosis of autism retained many autistic traits. These studies suggest that autism is a disorder with chronic features, where limited improvement is possible in certain areas (i.e., communication and social behavior) and less possible in others (i.e., ritualist-repetitive behavior).

In contrast, the present study of 200 children diagnosed with autistic spectrum disorders suggests that many children are capable of significant overall improvement. In fact, the children in the good to outstanding group ceased evidencing ritualistic behavior and became spontaneous and creative in their communication and relationship patterns. Motor planning, i.e., the ability to sequence behavior, did, however, improve more slowly than language and relationship capacities. It is possible that ritualistic behavior is related to motor planning and sequencing deficits and is intensified when children are under stress because they are unable to use reciprocal affective interactions to regulate and master social relationships as well as physiologic and affective states. The ritualistic behavior itself may be an attempt at regulation.

REFERENCES

Note: For a more extensive literature review and discussion of the different studies relating to autistic spectrum disorders, see Tsakiris, E., Treatment effectiveness for preschool autism: A look at affective variables. Dissertation in progress.

American Psychiatric Association. (1980). *Diagnostic and statistical manual of mental disorders* (3rd ed.). Washington, DC: Author.

American Psychiatric Association. (1994). *Diagnostic and statistical manual of mental disorders* (4th ed. rev.). Washington, DC: Author.

Attwood, A. H., Frith, U., & Hermelin, B. (1988). The understanding and use of interpersonal gestures by autistic and Down's syndrome children. *Journal of Autism and Developmental Disorders, 18,* 241–257.

Baron-Cohen, S. (1994). *Mindblindness: An essay on autism and theories of mind.* Cambridge, MA: MIT Press.

Baron-Cohen, S., Cox, A., Baird, G., Swettenham, J., Nightingale, N., Morgan, K., Drew, A., & Charman, T. (1996). Psychological markers in the detection of autism in infancy in a large population. *British Journal of Psychiatry, 168,* 158–163.

Baron-Cohen, S., Frith, U., & Leslie. (1988). Autistic children's understanding of seeing, knowing, and believing. *British Journal of Developmental Psychology, 4*, 315–324.

Baron-Cohen, S., Tager-Flusberg, H., & Cohen, D. (1993). *Understanding other minds: Perspectives from autism.* London: Oxford University Press.

Benson, F., & Zaidel, E. (1985). *The dual brain.* New York: Guilford.

Bondy, A. S., & Peterson, S. (1990). *The point is not to point: Picture exchange communication system with young students with autism.* Paper presented at the Association for Behavior Analysis Convention, Nashville, TN.

Cafiero, J. (1995). *Teaching parents of children with autism picture communication symbols as a natural language to decrease levels of family stress.* Unpublished doctoral dissertation, University of Toledo, OH.

Campbell, M., Overall, J. E., Small, M., Sokol, M., Spinon, E., Adams, P., Foltz, R. L., Monti, K., Perry, R., Nobler, M., & Roberts, E. (1989). Naltrexone in autistic children: An acute open dose range tolerance trial. *Journal of the American Academy of Child and Adolescent Psychiatry, 28*, 200–206.

Campbell, M., Schopler, E., & Hallin, A. (1996). The treatment of autistic disorder. *Journal of the American Academy of Child and Adolescent Psychiatry, 35*, 134–141.

Carew, J. V. (1980). Experience and the development of intelligence in young children at home and in day care. Monograph. *Social Research on Child Development, 45*, 1–115.

Carr, E., & Darcy, M. (1990). Setting generality of peer modeling in children with autism. *Journal of Applied Behavior Analysis, 20*, 45–59.

Cook, E., George, K., Gurman, H., & Weigel, J. (1993). *Pervasive developmental disorders (not otherwise specified) and the autistic spectrum disorders.* Short course presented at the American Speech and Language and Hearing Association National Convention, Anaheim, CA.

Courchesne, E., Akshoomoff, N., Egaas, B., Lincoln, A. J., Saitoh, O., Schreibman, L., Townsend, J., & Yeung-Courchesne, R. (1994). *Role of cerebellar and parietal dysfunction in the social and cognitive deficits in patients with infantile autism.* Paper presented at the Autism Society of America Annual Conference, Las Vegas, NV.

Courchesne, E., Yeung-Courchesne, R., Press, G., Hesserinck, J., and Jennigan, T. (1983). Hypoplasia of cerebellar vermal lobulen and in autism. *New England Journal of Medicine* 318 (21).

Dawson, G., Warrenburg, S., & Fuller, P. (1982). Cerebral lateralization in individuals diagnosed as autistic in early childhood. *Brain and Language, 15*, 353–368.

DC-0-3, Diagnostic Classification Task Force, Stanley Greenspan, M.D., Chair. (1994). *Diagnostic Classification: 0-3: Diagnostic Classification of Mental Health and Developmental Disorders of Infancy and Early Childhood.* Arlington, VA: ZERO TO THREE/ National Center for Clinical Infant Programs.

Durand, V. M. (1990). *Severe behavior problems: A functional communication training approach.* New York: Guilford.

Feuerstein, R., Miller, R., Hoffman, M., Rand, Y., Mintsker, Y., Morgens, R., & Jensen, M. R. (1981). Cognitive modifiability in adolescence: Cognitive structure and the effects of intervention. *Journal of Special Education, 150*, 269–287.

Feuerstein, R., Rand, Y., Hoffman, M., & Miller, R. (1979). Cognitive modifiability in retarded adolescents: Effects of instrumental enrichment. *American Journal of Mental Deficiency, 83*, 539–550.

Gelle, E., Ritvo, E. R., Freeman, B. J., & Yuwiler, A. (1982). Preliminary observations on the effects of fenfluramine in blood serotonin and symptoms in three autistic boys. *New England Journal of Medicine, 307*, 165–169.

Gillberg, C. (1989). The role of endogenous opioids in autism and possible relationships to clinical features. In L. Wing (Ed.), *Aspects of autism: Biological research* (pp. 31–37). Washington, DC: American Psychiatric Press.

Gillberg, C. (1990). Autism and pervasive developmental disorder. *Journal of Child Psychiatry, 31*, 99–119.

Gillberg, C., & Steffenburg, S. (1987). Outcome and prognostic factors in infantile autism and similar conditions: A population-based study of 46 cases followed through puberty. *Journal of Autism and Developmental Disorders 17*, 273–287.

Greenspan, S. I. (1979). Intelligence and adaptation: An integration of psychoanalytic and Piagetian developmental psychology. *Psychological Issues*, Monograph 47/48. New York: International Universities Press.

Greenspan, S. I. (1981). Psychopathology and adaptation in infancy and early childhood: Principles of clinical diagnosis and preventive intervention. *Clinical Infant Reports*, No. 1. New York: International Universities Press.

Greenspan, S. I. (1992a). *Infancy and early childhood: The practice of clinical assessment and intervention with emotional and developmental challenges.* Madison, CT: International Universities Press.

Greenspan, S. I. (1992b). Reconsidering the diagnosis and treatment of very young children with autistic spectrum or pervasive developmental disorder. *ZERO TO THREE, 13* (2), 1–9.

Greenspan, S. I. (1996a). *Developmentally based psychotherapy.* Madison, CT: International Universities Press.

Greenspan, S. I. (1996b). *The growth of the mind and the endangered origins of intelligence.* Reading, MA: Addison-Wesley.

Greenspan, S. I., & DeGangi, G. (1997). *The Functional Emotional Assessment Scale: Revised version and reliability studies.* Unpublished study.

Guess, D., & Carr, E. (1991). Emergence and maintenance of stereotypy and self-injury. *American Journal of Mental Retardation, 96*, 299–319.

Handen, B. (1993). Pharmacotherapy in mental retardation and autism. *School Psychology Review, 22*, 162–183.

Harris, S. L. (1975). Teaching language to non-verbal children with an emphasis on problems of generalization. *Psychological Bulletin, 82*, 565–580.

Harris, S. L., Handleman, J. S., Kristoff, B., Bass, L., & Cordon, R. (1990). Changes in language development among autistic and peer children in segregated and integrated preschool settings. *Journal of Autism and Developmental Disorders, 20*, 23–31.

Kanner, L. (1943). Autistic disturbances of affective contact. *Nervous Child, 2*, 217–250.

Kanner, L. (1971). Follow-up of eleven autistic children originally reported in 1943. *Journal of Autism and Child Schizophrenia, 1*, 119–145.

Klein, P. S., Wieder, S., & Greenspan, S. I. (1987). A theoretical overview and empirical study of mediated learning experience: Prediction of preschool performance from mother-infant interaction patterns. *Infant Mental Health Journal, 8*, 110–129.

Koegel, R. L., Dyer, K., & Bell, L. K. (1987). The influence of child-preferred activities on autistic children's social behavior. *Journal of Applied Behavior Analysis, 20*, 243–252.

Koegel, R. L., Koegel, L. K., & O'Neill, R. (1989). Generalization in the treatment of autism. In L. V. McReynolds & J. E. Spradlin (Eds.), *Generalization strategies in the treatment of communication disorders* (pp. 116–131). Toronto: B. C. Decker.

Kohen-Raz, R., Volkmar, F., & Cohen, D. J. (1992). Postural control in children with autism. *Brain Dysfunction, 4*, 419–429.

Lovaas, O. I. (1987). Behavioral treatment and normal educational and intellectual function-
ing in young autistic children. *Journal of Consulting and Clinical Psychology, 55*, 3–9.
Markowitz, P. I. (1990). Fluoxetine treatment of self-injurious behavior in mentally retarded
patients. *Journal of Clinical Psychopharmacology, 12*, 21–31.
Mesibov, G. B., Schopler, E., Schaffer, B. (1989). Use of the Childhood Autism Rating Scale
with autistic adolescents and adults. *Journal of the American Academy of Child and
Adolescent Psychiatry, 28*, 538–541.
Miller, A., & Miller, E. (1992). *A new way with autistic and other children with pervasive
developmental disorder.* Monograph. Boston: Language and Cognitive Center, Inc.
Mouridsen, S. E. (1995). The Landau-Kleffner syndrome: A review. *European Child and
Adolescent Psychiatry, 4*, 223–228.
Odom, S. L., & Strain, P. (1986). A comparison of peer-interactions and teacher-antecedent
intervention for promoting reciprocal social interactions of autistic preschoolers.
Journal of Applied Behavior Analysis, 19, 59–71.
Olley, J., Robbins, F., & Morelli-Robbins, M. (1993). Current practices in early intervention for
children with autism. In E. Schopler, M. Bourgondien, & M. Bristol (Eds.), *Preschool
issues in autism* (pp. 223–245). New York and London: Plenum.
Panskepp, J., Lensing, P., Leboyer, M., & Bouvard, M. (1991). Naltrexone and other potential
pharmacological treatments for autism. *Brain Dysfunction, 4*, 281–300.
Piven, J., Harper, J., Palmer, P., & Arndt, S. (1996). Course of behavioral change in autism: A
retrospective study of high-IQ adolescents and adults. *Journal of the American Academy
of Child and Adolescent Psychiatry, 35*, 523–529.
Prizant, B. (1983). Language acquisition and communicative behavior in autism: Towards an
understanding of the "whole" of it. *Journal of Speech and Hearing Disorders, 48*,
296–307.
Prizant, B., & Wetherby, A. (1990). Toward an integrated view of early language and
communication development and socio-emotional development. *Topics in Language
Disorders, 10*, 1–16.
Ratey, J. J., Sorrer, R., Mikkelsen, E., & Chmielinski, H. E. (1989). Buspirone therapy for
maladaptive behavior and anxiety in developmentally disabled persons. *Journal of
Clinical Psychiatry, 50*, 382–384.
Ricks, D. M., & Wing, L. (1976). Language, communication, and the use of symbols in normal
and autistic children. In J. K. Wing (Ed.), *Early childhood autism: Clinical, social and
educational aspects.* Oxford: Pergamon.
Rimland, B. (1964). *Infantile autism.* New York: Appleton-Century-Crofts.
Rogers, S. J., Herbison, J. M., Lewis, H., Pantone, J., & Reis, K. (1988). An approach for
enhancing symbolic, communicative, and interpersonal functioning of young children
with autism and severe emotional handicaps. *Journal of the Division of Early Childhood,
10*, 135–145.
Rogers, S. J., & Lewis, H. (1989). An effective day treatment model for young children with
pervasive developmental disorders. *Journal of the American Academy of Child and
Adolescent Psychiatry, 28*, 207–214.
Rumsey, J. M., Rapoport, J. L., & Sceery, W. R. (1985). Autistic children as adults: Psychiatric,
social and behavioral outcomes. *Journal of the American Academy of Child Psychiatry,
24*, 465–473.
Rutter, M. (1983). Cognitive deficits in the pathogenesis of autism. *Journal of Child Psychology
and Psychiatry, 24*, 513–531.
Rutter, M. (1996). Autism research: Prospects and priorities. *Journal of Autism and Developmental Disorders 26* (2), 257–275.

Rutter, M., Greenfield, D., & Lockyer, L. (1967). A five to fifteen year follow-up study of infantile psychosis: II. Social and beavioural outcome. *British Journal of Psychiatry, 112,* 1183–1199.

Schopler, E. (1987). Specific and non-specific factors in the effectiveness of a treatment system. *American Psychologist, 42,* 262–267.

Schopler, E., & Mesibov, G. (Eds.). (1967). *Neurobiological issues in autism.* New York: Plenum.

Schopler, E., Mesibov, G., & Hearsey, K. (1995). Structured teaching in the TEACCH system. In E. Schopler & G. Mesibov (Eds.), *Learning and cognition in autism.* New York: Plenum.

Sigman, M., & Ungerer, J. A. (1984). Attachment behaviors in autistic children. *Journal of Autism and Developmental Disorders, 14,* 231–244.

Sparrow, S. S., Balla, D. A., & Cicchetti, D. V. (1984). Vineland Adaptive Behavior Scales. American Guidance Service.

Sperry, R. W. (1985). Consciousness, personal identity, and the divided brain. In F. Benson & E. Zaidel (Eds.), *The dual brain* (pp. 11–27). New York: Guilford.

Stokes, T. F., & Osnes, P. G. (1988). The developing applied technology of generalization and maintenance. In R. Horner, G. Dunlap, & R. L. Koegel (Eds.), *Generalization and maintenance* (pp. 5–19). Baltimore: Paul H. Brookes.

Strain, P. S., & Hoyson, M. (1988). *Follow-up of children in LEAP.* Paper presented at the meeting of the Autism Society of America, New Orleans, LA.

Strain, P. S., Hoyson, M., & Jamison, B. (1983). Normally developing preschoolers as intervention agents for autistic-like children: Effects on class, department, and social interaction. *Journal of the Division of Early Childhood, 9,* 105–119.

Szatmari, P., Barolucci G., Bremmer, R., Bond S., & Rich, S. (1989). A follow-up study of high-functioning autistic children. *Journal of Autism and Developmental Disorders, 19,* 213–225.

Western Psychology Services. (1988). Childhood Autism Rating Scale (CARS). Los Angeles.

Wetherby, A., Koegel, R. L., & Mendel, M. (1981). Central auditory nervous system dysfunction in echolalic autistic individuals. *Journal of Speech and Hearing Research, 24,* 420–429.

Wing, L., & Gould, J. (1979). Severe impairments of social interaction and associated abnormalities in children: Epidemiology and classification. *Journal of Autism and Developmental Disorders, 9,* 129–137.

Index

About the Authors

STANLEY I. GREENSPAN, M.D., is Clinical Professor of Psychiatry, Behavioral Science, and Pediatrics at the George Washington University Medical School and a practicing child psychiatrist. He is also a supervising child psychoanalyst at the Washington Psychoanalytic Institute in Washington, D.C. He was previously chief of the Mental Health Study Center and director of the Clinical Infant Development Program at the National Institute of Mental Health.

A founder and former president of ZERO TO THREE, National Center for Infants, Toddlers, and Families, Dr. Greenspan has received numerous prestigious awards for his work, including the American Psychiatric Association Ittleson Award for Outstanding Contributions to Child Psychiatry Research, the Heinz Hartmann Prize in Psychoanalysis, and the Edward A. Strecker Award for Outstanding Contributions to American Psychiatry.

Dr. Greenspan is the author of more than one hundred scholarly articles and chapters and the author or editor of twenty-seven books. These include *The Growth of the Mind, Infancy and Early Childhood, Developmentally Based Psychotherapy, Intelligence and Adaptation: An Integration of Psychoanalytic and Piagetian Developmental Psychology, First Feelings* (with Nancy Thorndike Greenspan), and *Playground Politics* and *The Challenging Child* (both with Jacqueline Salmon).

SERENA WIEDER, PH.D., is a clinical psychologist in private practice in Silver Spring, Maryland, specializing in the diagnosis and treatment of infants and young children. She is on the faculty of the Infant Mental Health Program at the Washington, D.C., School of Psychiatry and is a consultant, program director, and board member of ZERO TO THREE, National Center for Infants, Toddlers, and Families. She has published widely in professional

495

journals, contributed numerous chapters to professional books, and conducted over thirty major training workshops, nationally and internationally,
in the diagnosis and treatment of complex developmental problems.

ROBIN SIMONS is the author or coauthor of seven books, including *After
the Tears: Parents Talk about Raising a Child with a Disability* and *The Couples
Who Became Each Other: Tales of Healing and Transformation* (coauthored
with David Calouf). She has worked at the Boston and Denver Children's
Museums and as a consultant to the National Endowment for the Arts.